SAUL L. GEFFNER

Formerly Chairman, Department of Physical Sciences
Forest Hills High School, New York City

Science Editor, Amsco School Publications, Inc.

Fundamental Concepts

of Modern Chemistry

Dedicated to serving

AMSCO

our nation's youth

When ordering this book, please specify:

either **N 303 P**

or FUNDAMENTAL CONCEPTS OF MODERN CHEMISTRY, PAPERBACK EDITION

AMSCO SCHOOL PUBLICATIONS, INC.
315 Hudson Street, New York, N.Y. 10013

PRINTED IN THE UNITED STATES OF AMERICA

PREFACE

Chemistry courses at all levels of instruction are undergoing considerable change in philosophy, in organization, and in content. Influenced by the national curriculum studies, present-day courses in chemistry have become almost completely conceptual, with heavy emphasis on laboratory work.

FUNDAMENTAL CONCEPTS OF MODERN CHEMISTRY presents an introductory course in chemistry from a conceptual and from an experimental view. The content focuses on three basic questions:

1. What drives a chemical reaction?
2. What determines the rate of a reaction?
3. What determines how far a reaction proceeds before equilibrium is attained?

The answers to these questions involve a consideration of the energy relationships in chemical systems. To help answer these questions, models are used throughout the book, enabling the student to relate new concepts to well understood and familiar systems.

The national curriculum studies in chemistry also seek the answers to these questions, utilizing approaches that are creative and stimulating —but completely divorced from tradition. Similarly, the organization and content of this book reflect a considerable departure from the traditional chemistry course. At the same time, however, the author is convinced that certain time-tested traditional approaches are more sensitive to the needs of the majority of students in an introductory chemistry class.

For example, the language of chemistry, stressed throughout this book, is never taken for granted. In addition, the author has provided constant drill and review—perhaps a traditional approach—both in the text and at the end of each chapter. Approximately 1500 questions appear in this book. They include short-answer questions of different types, problems involving calculations, and questions requiring sustained thinking. These questions vary in difficulty to meet the needs of students of all abilities.

Many teachers feel that it is pedagogically unsound to present conceptual material too rapidly. However, most introductory chemistry texts generally present atomic theory and bonding in their entirety in early chapters. Most students do not yet possess the necessary experimental background to interpret and understand this information. As a result,

they often encounter insurmountable difficulties which term.
confusion and discouragement. The difficulties are further compou.
by the limited use of this highly conceptual material until the later ch.
ters. Such organization fails to recognize the *introductory* nature of
first course in chemistry.

The organization of content in FUNDAMENTAL CONCEPTS OF
MODERN CHEMISTRY recognizes the difficulties that a highly conceptual course of study may present to students of average ability. Thus,
the two most highly conceptualized areas in a high school chemistry
course—atomic theory and bonding—are each introduced in two stages.
Chapters 3 and 4 present a simple atomic model and an introduction to
bonding in a somewhat traditional manner. The next 14 chapters, dealing with energy, rates, and equilibrium, utilize this elementary model.
Chapters 19 and 20 bring the student back to atomic theory, presenting
the modern orbital (wave-mechanical) model and bonding. By this time,
the students have had much of the year's work and are better able to ap-
preciate and understand these difficult concepts. It is interesting to note
that, historically, this is how our present atomic model evolved. In the
remaining nine chapters of the book, families and rows of the Periodic
Table are studied, utilizing the orbital model of the atom.

The students and the teacher are thus presented with a framework of
content that is logical and convincing. Each concept builds on what has
been previously learned, so that new material relates to what has pre-
ceded it and what will follow. Experience in the classroom has shown
that such an organization is pedagogically sound.

FUNDAMENTAL CONCEPTS OF MODERN CHEMISTRY may
be used as a text or as a supplement to a text, depending upon local
needs. For highly selected students in upgraded courses, the book may be
used as a supplement. For the broad spectrum of students in these courses,
the book provides both direction and content to be useful as a primary
text.

Thanks are due to Gerard A. Kass who prepared an early draft of
several chapters. The author would like to express his appreciation to
Dr. Morris B. Abramson who read the manuscript, prepared the questions at the end of each chapter, and wrote the answer key.

—S.L.G.

CONTENTS

Chapter 1

MATTER AND ENERGY

1.1 Introduction

When man began to observe his environment and use reason to explain what he observed, he became a scientist. As he rejected his superstitions, he learned two of the most important requirements of science: observation under carefully controlled conditions and logical interpretation. Observation and interpretation are the foundation of practically all experimentation. On them rests a vast storehouse of scientific knowledge.

All experimentation involves measurement. It is important to understand that the results of repeated measurements of the same quantities will not exactly agree. The causes of these deviations will be considered in Chapter 2. Despite this limitation, all science must rely on experimentation, imperfect as it is.

Science constantly corrects itself. Even when new experiments verify long-accepted facts, interpretations based on these facts continue to change and advance man toward a better understanding of his environment.

1.2 The scope of chemistry

Historically, chemistry has been defined as the branch of science that studies matter and the changes that matter undergoes. As we move further in the Atomic Age, we are finding that this definition is restrictive and even misleading. For example, the chemistry of the atomic nucleus reveals relationships between matter and energy that necessitate a considerably broader definition.

"Chemistry is what the chemist does" is one of the broadest definitions that have been suggested. Although admittedly circular, this definition permits an understanding of the tremendous changes that have occurred and are still occurring in chemical experimentation. What does the chemist do? Although he is still essentially concerned with the composition of matter, he is equally concerned with the relationships between the properties of matter and its structure. It is these relationships that enable the chemist to understand how and why different kinds of matter interact.

In the earliest period of his development, man discovered that different kinds of matter behave differently, and he utilized this information in adapting himself to his environment. However, the understanding of chemical phenomena did not begin until the 18th century. Principles and generalizations began to evolve which indicated that nature is not as diverse as it appears to be. Instead, a basic unity seems to govern all that we observe. Modern chemistry—indeed all modern science—seeks to unveil this unity. Thus in our study, we will be concerned with the unifying themes and concepts that relate to the composition of matter and to its interactions.

1.3 What is matter?

Matter is the stuff, or substance, of the universe. It occupies space (has volume) and possesses mass. *Mass is the amount of matter contained in a body.* When a scientist uses the word *body*, he means a single object of any kind. For example, a body may be an atom, a speck of dust, a rock, a book, or a cloud.

The following table lists some common units of volume and mass in the English and metric systems.

	ENGLISH SYSTEM	METRIC SYSTEM
VOLUME	cubic inch (in^3) cubic foot (ft^3)	cubic centimeter (cc or cm^3) liter (l)
MASS	ounce (oz) pound (lb)	gram (g) kilogram (kg)

Although the same units may be used for mass and weight, mass and weight are not the same. Mass may be determined by measuring the inertia of a body—its resistance to change in its motion. The inertia of a body—and hence its mass—remains the same wherever the body may be located.

Weight is a measure of the force with which gravity pulls an object toward the center of the earth. The attractive force varies inversely with the square of the distance between the body and the center of the earth. This means that the weight of a body decreases as its distance from the center of the earth increases. Thus objects weigh a little more at the poles than at the equator, since the earth is somewhat flattened. An object that weighs 1 pound on the earth's surface, a distance of 4000 miles from the center, would weigh $\frac{1}{3600}$ pound at a point 240,000 miles from the center of the earth. (Since the distance has increased by a factor of 60, the attractive force has decreased by the square of $\frac{1}{60}$, or $\frac{1}{3600}$.) However, the object would have the same mass (amount of matter) in both places.

1.4 States and phases of matter

Matter exists in three states: gas, liquid, and solid. Air and carbon dioxide are examples of gases; water and alcohol are examples of liquids; iron and sulfur are examples of solids.

Gases do not have specific volumes but expand or contract to fill their containers. Liquids have specific volumes and take the shapes of their containers. Solids are rigid bodies whose shapes may be altered only by the application of a force.

Within each sample of matter, some portion may have uniform properties and be separated from the rest of the sample by physical boundaries. Such a portion, or region, is called a *phase*. A phase is made up of all the regions that have the same composition and properties. For example, the dust suspended in air may be described as a solid phase present in air. The many pieces of dust suspended in air do not constitute many phases but only one phase, the solid. A mixture of oil and water consists of two sharply defined, uniform regions. This mixture is an example of a liquid state with two phases: an oil phase and a water phase.

1.5 Identifying matter

Matter may also be described by the characteristics it possesses. These characteristics, commonly called *properties*, enable us to recognize different kinds of matter. Frequently, properties suggest how matter may be used. Properties are classified as either physical or chemical.

1.6 Physical properties of matter

Physical properties may describe the appearance of matter, for example, its state (gas, liquid, or solid), its color, and its odor. Physical properties do not describe the composition of matter. Some physical properties, such as solubility and boiling and freezing points, describe the behavior of matter. These properties are known as *physical constants*.

Because physical constants may be measured experimentally, they are frequently used to identify matter. Pure water, for example, may be described as a colorless and odorless liquid. Since many liquids are colorless and odorless, we can use the physical constants of water to identify it. We may identify a colorless and odorless liquid as water if it boils at 100° C and freezes at 0° C at sea level.

1.7 Chemical properties of matter

Chemical properties describe changes in the composition of matter. For example, a colorless and odorless liquid that may be decomposed to form hydrogen and oxygen is probably water. A yellow solid that burns to form a gas with the characteristic odor of sulfur dioxide is probably sulfur. Chemists frequently face the problem of identifying unknown samples of matter. The task increases in difficulty as the matter becomes more complex.

1.8 Pure and impure matter

Some matter is uniform throughout. All samples of such matter have the same characteristics and are called *homogeneous*, or pure, matter. Examples of homogeneous matter are sugar, salt, and water.

Homogeneous matter consists of only one phase and has a fixed composition. Thus all samples of sugar are composed of the same kinds of matter. So, too, are all samples of salt or water.

Most naturally occurring matter—for example, rocks and minerals—is nonuniform throughout. Samples of a piece of rock or mineral may have varying colors or textures, suggesting that the samples are made up of varying amounts of more than one kind of matter. These samples are said to consist of *heterogeneous*, or impure, matter.

Heterogeneous matter consists of more than one phase and has a variable composition. Thus a sample of rock may have more quartz or more mica than another sample. Chemists have devised specialized techniques to separate the different species in heterogeneous matter. You will study some of these techniques in the laboratory.

1.9 Laws and hypotheses

All matter when burned behaves in the same general manner. This observation describes a uniform or regular behavior of matter. Such behavior is commonly called a regularity, or a law, of nature. The Law of Conservation of Matter, stated in section 1.12, illustrates one uniform behavior of matter.

Before the chemist can establish a law, he must obtain experimental evidence. The results of experimentation may suggest a logical interpretation or logical principle that can be utilized to explain a specific behavior of matter. A tentative explanation of a specific behavior of matter is called a *hypothesis*.

1.10 Theories and models

Chemists continue to test hypotheses with more experiments. If a hypothesis continues to be consistent with additional observations, it may be called a *theory*.

Theories are often based on mental pictures that the scientist proposes in order to explain the phenomena being investigated. Each mental picture, called a *model*, represents a well-understood system. A model may take many forms — for example, an analogy, a drawing, or a three-dimensional structure.

One theory used to explain the properties of a gas proposes a model in which the particles of a fixed volume of the gas behave in the same manner as do a number of moving billiard balls (see Figure 1-1). The behavior of the billiard balls is well understood and can be applied to the motions of the particles in the gas.

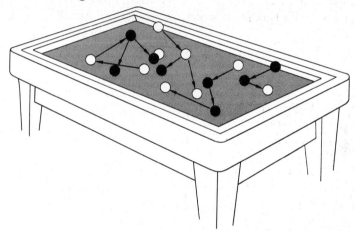

Fig. 1-1   Billiard balls in motion

1.11 The value of models

Models are powerful tools of the chemist because they not only provide a plausible explanation for a given set of observations, but they may also have considerable predictive value.

Occasionally, in the light of new discoveries, a model may have to be amended or even discarded. In Chapters 3 and 4, you will see how an actual model is developed and used. Then, in later chapters, you will see how this model is extended to meet problems created by new discoveries.

1.12 The Law of Conservation of Matter

The weight relationships that are associated with changes in matter were first studied by chemists during the 17th and 18th centuries. In a series of brilliant experiments, the French chemist Antoine Lavoisier established that when matter burns, oxygen in the atmosphere is consumed. Furthermore, he proved that in a closed system—one in which none of the products of change is lost—the total mass (measured by its weight) of matter remains constant. Thus when a sample of matter burns, the total weight of the products equals the weight of the sample plus the weight of oxygen consumed.

Suppose that 4.0 grams of mercury are heated in air until all the mercury is used up. It can be shown that 4.0 grams of mercury always combine with 0.3 gram of oxygen present in the air to form 4.3 grams of new matter, called mercuric oxide. From this experiment and many similar ones, scientists have formulated the *Law of Conservation of Matter: Matter may neither be created nor destroyed in a chemical change.*

1.13 Kinds of matter

We have learned that matter may be classified according to its state, its physical and chemical properties, or its degree of purity. Now we will see how matter may also be classified according to its composition, that is, whether it is an element, a compound, or a mixture.

1.14 Elements

Carbon, oxygen, and mercury are examples of elements. Chemists recognize at least 103 elements, 88 of which are naturally occurring; the rest are man-made. All the matter of the universe, whether simple or complex, is made up of these elements. *An element is the simplest kind of homogeneous matter and cannot be·decomposed by chemical means.* At a specific temperature and pressure, an element has specific physical constants, such as density and boiling point. For example, hydrogen has a density of 0.000089 g/cm^3 at 0° C and 1 atmosphere pressure; it boils at −252.8° C and 1 atmosphere.

Under normal conditions, one element cannot be converted into another. In Chapter 18, you will learn how some elements may be converted into other elements by nuclear changes, such as radioactivity.

1.15 Compounds

Water, hydrogen peroxide, and salt are examples of compounds. Each has a fixed weight composition as shown by the following table.

COMPOUND	PERCENTAGES OF ELEMENTS BY WEIGHT	
water (hydrogen oxide)	hydrogen, 11.1	oxygen, 88.9
hydrogen peroxide	hydrogen, 5.9	oxygen, 94.1
salt (sodium chloride)	sodium, 39.4	chlorine, 60.6

A compound is a sample of homogeneous matter consisting of at least two different elements in fixed proportions by weight. At a specific temperature and pressure, a compound, like an element, has specific physical constants. For example, water has a density of 1 g/cm^3 at 4° C and 1 atmosphere; it boils at 100° C and 1 atmosphere. Note that both water and hydrogen peroxide contain the same elements. However, they are different compounds because the percentages of elements in each compound are different.

1.16 Mixtures

Unlike a compound, which has a single set of properties, a mixture retains the properties of each of its components. Thus a mixture of powdered sulfur and powdered iron has a yellow color like sulfur when the percent of sulfur is high; and portions of the mixture are attracted to a magnet just as pure iron is. Such a mixture is an example of heterogeneous matter.

A mixture is a sample of matter consisting of two or more different substances in varying proportions. The properties of a given mixture depend on the proportion of substances in the mixture. For example, the proper hardness in a cement mixture is obtained by varying the proportion of limestone to clay.

Solutions, such as salt dissolved in water or sugar dissolved in water, are examples of homogeneous mixtures. Volumes of the same sample have the same properties, such as taste, density, and boiling and freezing points.

1.17 Compound or mixture?

Although distinctions exist between elements and compounds, the distinction between compounds and mixtures is not always clear. An alloy, such as brass, may exhibit some of the specific properties of compounds; another alloy, such as steel, may exhibit the variable properties of mixtures.

Compounds always have a fixed composition. Two substances, however, may form an infinite number of mixtures. Thus salt and water each has an unvarying composition, but an infinite number of different solutions can be made by mixing these substances in different proportions.

1.18 The Law of Definite Proportions

Observations dating back to the 18th century reveal an important regularity in all compounds. Since only specific weights of elements are present in compounds, every compound must have a definite and constant composition. From this regularity, scientists have formulated the *Law of Definite Proportions: Elements unite to form compounds in definite proportions by weight.*

Experimentally, the Law of Definite Proportions may be verified as follows: Suppose compound AD is to be prepared from the reaction between compound AC and compound BD. The letters A, B, C, and D represent different elements. The following statement, called an equation, summarizes the reaction. (The arrow in the expression below designates the direction of a chemical change and stands for the word *forms* or *yields*.)

$$AC + BD \rightarrow AD + BC$$

We may vary the amounts of AC and BD at will. The amounts that react, however, always produce compounds AD and BC. Compound AD always has the same composition, and so does compound BC. This relationship is also termed the *Law of Constant Composition.*

From the table in section 1.15, it can be seen that any sample of water always contains 11.1% of hydrogen and 88.9% of oxygen by weight. The composition of water and other compounds suggests a regularity of nature that is intimately related to the structure of matter. We will return to this relationship in Chapter 3.

1.19 What is energy?

Energy is the capacity for doing work, that is, for moving a force through a distance. Two kinds of energy frequently encountered are: potential and kinetic. The compressed air that can operate a pneumatic drill and the stored water that can drive a turbine possess potential energy.

Potential energy is the energy a body possesses because of its condition or position with respect to some other body. As the potential energy of a body decreases, its stability increases. A stone resting on the ground is more stable (has less potential energy) than the same stone perched on a mountaintop. Furthermore, a body may undergo a change spontaneously if the change brings the body to a lower energy level, or lower energy condition. The stone falls down spontaneously but will not move upward unless it is pushed by another object.

Potential energy is stored energy and, if properly harnessed, can do useful work. Consider the pneumatic drill and the turbine. For work to be done by the pneumatic drill, the air in the compressor must be allowed to escape and strike the shaft of the drill. For work to be done by the turbine, the stored water, as in a dam, must flow out and push the blades of the turbine. In both instances, matter is permitted to move; that is, the potential energy is converted into energy of motion, called kinetic energy. *Kinetic energy* is the energy a body possesses because of its motion.

It can be shown experimentally that potential energy can be transformed into kinetic energy without loss. This observation is an illustration of the *Law of Conservation of Energy: The total amount of energy in a system is constant.* Broadly viewed, this law states that under ordinary conditions, energy can neither be created nor destroyed but may be converted from one form to another.

1.20 Changing one form of energy into another

You have already learned that energy may exist in a variety of forms: mechanical, heat, electrical, light, sound, and chemical. In accordance with the Law of Conservation of Energy, one form of energy may be converted into another without loss. A paddle wheel rotating in a sample of water raises the temperature of the water. The kinetic energy of the rotating wheel is transformed into heat energy. Also, the energy in the chemicals of a dry cell (chemical energy) is transformed into electrical energy.

In a practical sense, some losses accompany energy transformations. Such energy losses occur because of inefficient operation of the devices in which the transformations occur, resulting in the conversion of some energy into heat. This is why a light bulb is an inefficient source of light since much of the electrical energy is converted into heat. However, the total amount of energy in the system remains constant.

1.21 How are matter and energy related?

Albert Einstein, in 1905, was the first scientist to suggest that matter and energy are related. Originally a theoretical supposition, this relationship was verified by the British scientists John D. Cockroft and Ernest T. S. Walton in 1932. They observed that when lithium is converted into helium, the lithium undergoes a small mass loss, and energy is evolved in the change. The quantity of energy was measured and corresponded to the mass-energy conversion predicted by Einstein. The mass-energy relationship was later demonstrated on a vast scale with the explosion of the first atomic bomb (1945).

As we came to understand that mass and energy are interconvertible, the fundamental laws of mass and energy were combined into the *Law of Conservation of Mass-Energy: The total quantity of mass and energy in the universe is constant.*

Einstein developed the relationship $E = mc^2$ to calculate the energy that can be derived from a given quantity of matter. The quantity E represents energy expressed in units called ergs; m represents the mass, or quantity, of matter that is converted expressed in grams; and c represents the velocity of light expressed in centimeters/second (3×10^{10} cm/sec).

We can qualitatively describe the relationship $E = mc^2$ in this manner: A small amount of mass multiplied by the very large number $(3 \times 10^{10})^2$, or 9×10^{20}, results in the formation of an enormous amount of energy. A mass of 1 gram may be converted into 9×10^{20} ergs of energy, which is equivalent to about 20 billion kilocalories of heat—sufficient to raise the temperature of 200,000 tons of water from $0°$ C to boiling ($100°$ C).

1.22 Physical and chemical changes

One type of change which matter undergoes is a change in size, shape, or state. For example, a crystal of salt may be pulverized (ground into a powder), or it may be melted. Such changes involving only the form of matter and not its composition are described as *physical changes*. Changes in state, or phase changes, are also generally described as physical changes.

Matter may also undergo a change in composition. For example, a graphite (carbon) rod may be burned to form carbon dioxide, or a quantity of water may be decomposed to yield hydrogen and oxygen. These changes involve the formation of new kinds of matter and are described as *chemical changes*.

The distinction between physical and chemical changes is not always sharply defined. Consider what happens when a solid dissolves in water. The same matter is present in the solution except that the dissolved particles are now too small to be visible.

At first this change appears to be purely physical. More careful study reveals that water may do more than merely change the size of the solid as it dissolves. A solid such as copper sulfate, which is a white powder, undergoes a change in composition during solution in water. Careful evaporation of the water reveals the presence of new matter, a blue, crystalline solid (a compound formed between the copper sulfate and the water).

Another type of change involves the nuclei of atoms and is called a *nuclear change*. Since 1945, elements have been changed into other elements by bombardment of atomic nuclei, a process called *transmutation*.

1.23 Changes require energy

The tendency of matter to resist change, unless the change leads to a more stable condition, seems to be a universal law of nature. It is important to understand that all such changes require some energy input or energy release. Thus mechanical energy is required to alter the size or shape of a sample of matter, and heat energy is evolved when coal burns. Why does one kind of matter change more slowly than another? What are the forces that drive matter to change? The answers to these questions will be considered later.

1.24 Energy involved in some common changes

Heat is the form of energy most frequently associated with the tendency of matter to undergo change. Since energy may be converted from one form into another, we will use the unit of heat, the calorie, to represent the quantity of energy associated with physical and chemical changes. *A calorie is the quantity of heat required to raise the temperature of 1 gram of water 1 C° (usually from 14.5° C to 15.5° C).*

Temperature is a measure of the degree of hotness and indicates the average kinetic energy of the particles composing a body. The table that follows compares the amounts of energy involved in some common changes. (Note: 1000 calories is called a *kilocalorie*, abbreviated kcal)

CHANGE	KIND OF CHANGE	ENERGY CHANGE
converting 1 gram of water at 20° C to steam at 100° C	change of state	absorbs 620 calories (includes the 540 calories required to change 1 gram of boiling water into steam at 100° C)
converting 1 gram of water at 20° C to ice at 0° C	change of state	liberates 100 calories (includes the 80 calories required to change 1 gram of water at 0° C to ice)
burning 1 gram of coal	chemical	liberates 7858 calories, or 7.858 kilocalories
burning 1 gram of hydrogen to form liquid water	chemical	liberates 34,160 calories, or 34.160 kilocalories
fissioning of 1 gram of uranium	nuclear	liberates 20 million kilocalories

The table clearly shows that much higher energies are associated with chemical changes than are associated with changes of state. Note, too, that nuclear changes (fissioning) involve energies that are millions of times greater than the energies involved in changes of state or chemical changes, such as burning.

An interesting observation may be made in the laboratory during an experiment involving changes of state. Suppose we heat a solid at a constant rate until it melts. We continue heating the melted solid until it begins to vaporize. Temperatures are recorded at specific time intervals and the results are summarized in a graph, such as the one shown in Figure 1–2.

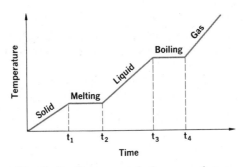

Fig. 1–2   Energy and changes of state

Note the plateaus (flat portions) in the graph. During these time intervals ($t_1 t_2$ and $t_3 t_4$), increased heating does not raise the temperature. Instead, the heat is utilized to effect the change in state. This is another example of a regular behavior of matter.

In succeeding chapters, we will uncover answers to many of the problems posed in this chapter. For example:

1. Why is energy needed to effect changes in matter?

2. Why is less energy generally required to initiate a physical change than to initiate a chemical change?

3. Why do some chemical changes absorb energy, while others release energy?

4. Why do nuclear changes involve tremendous energies?

Multiple-Choice Questions

Write the number preceding the correct answer.

1. When chemical energy is transformed into electrical energy (1) some matter is lost (2) the amount of electrical energy produced is greater than the amount of chemical energy used (3) some heat is produced (4) the resulting chemical products are less stable than the starting materials

2. Compressed air possesses energy because compressed air (1) can be used for burning (2) is hotter than normal air (3) is used to produce energy in the human body (4) can exert a force on an object, causing it to move

3. If different samples of the same substance show slightly different properties under the same conditions, then the substance (1) must contain two elements (2) has a nonuniform composition (3) is a compound (4) is not very stable

4. A liquid which is colorless and odorless (1) is probably water (2) is probably water if it is also tasteless (3) is probably water if it is a compound (4) cannot be identified as water without finding additional properties

5. When 40 g of mercury are heated with oxygen, the mercury unites with 3 g of oxygen to form 43 g of mercuric oxide. This reaction illustrates (1) the fact that elements always combine (2) a nuclear transformation (3) the Law of Conservation of Matter (4) the formation of mixtures

6. An example of a physical change produced by the addition of energy is the (1) condensation of steam (2) melting of ice (3) burning of oil (4) lighting of a match

7. A student observes that when a solid is heated in contact with air and remains hot, a liquid is formed. He may reasonably conclude that (1) a chemical change took place (2) a physical change took place (3) both physical and chemical changes took place (4) no decision can be made concerning the change that occurred from this single observation

8. Potential energy is possessed by (1) a book on a high shelf (2) a bullet in motion (3) a hot wire (4) an electric generator

9. The change from one element to another element involves a (1) nuclear change (2) chemical change (3) physical change (4) combination of chemical and physical changes

10. The burning of hydrogen is a chemical change because (1) a gas changes to a liquid (2) heat is produced (3) a change in volume occurs (4) a new substance with different properties forms
11. Which statement does *not* apply to an element? (1) It cannot be decomposed. (2) It is homogeneous. (3) It has a variable composition. (4) It may exist in three states.
12. Volume is measured in (1) liters (2) pounds (3) ounces (4) kilograms
13. Which statement is correct for water? (1) It is not an element because it can exist in three states. (2) It is a compound because all samples of water are alike. (3) It is not a compound because its properties are different from the properties of the elements it contains. (4) It is not a mixture because it has a definite composition.
14. The correct sequence in the development of scientific knowledge is (1) law, observation, theory, hypothesis (2) observation, law, hypothesis, theory (3) observation, theory, hypothesis, law (4) none of these because there is no definite sequence
15. When we push an object, we obtain some information concerning its (1) inertia (2) composition (3) volume (4) chemical properties
16. Chemistry is the study of (1) electrons and protons (2) explosives (3) the production of new substances (4) the properties, structure, and changes of matter
17. The temperature of an object measures (1) the number of calories of heat present (2) the average kinetic energy of the particles in the object (3) the amount of electricity it can produce (4) the potential energy of the object

Completion Questions

Write the word or expression that correctly completes the statement.

1. Cement is an example of a heterogeneous mixture, while _____ is an example of a homogeneous mixture.
2. Two different compounds formed from hydrogen and oxygen are _____ and _____.
3. A chemical property of sulfur involves burning to form _____.
4. The _____ is a unit of volume in the English system, while the _____ is a unit of volume in the metric system.
5. A stretched rubber band possesses _____ (*more, less*) energy and is _____ (*more, less*) stable than a rubber band that is not stretched.
6. An exploded firecracker possesses _____ (*more, less*) energy and is _____ (*more, less*) stable than it was before it was exploded.

7. A new flashlight battery possesses _____ (*more, less*) energy and is _____ (*more, less*) stable than a used flashlight battery.

8. The Law of Conservation of Energy states that energy may be neither _____ nor _____.

9. The Law of Definite Proportions states that all compounds have a definite _____.

10. The two basic properties common to all matter are that it occupies _____ and possesses _____.

Exercises for Review

1. The density of hydrogen at 0° C is 0.000089 g/cm³ (or g/cc). Find the mass of 200 cm³ of this gas.

2. Use the table on page 11 to answer *a* through *e*.

  a. Find the amount of heat, in kilocalories, needed to change 300 g of water at 20° C to ice at 0° C.

  b. Find the weight of coal that must be burned to obtain 785.8 kcal of heat.

  c. Find .the number of grams of water at 20° C that can be changed to steam at 100° C by the heat supplied from the burning of 1 g of coal.

  d. Find the number of grams of hydrogen that must be burned to produce as much heat as is obtained from burning 20 g of coal.

  e. How many times greater is the heat supplied by the fission of 1 g of uranium than the heat supplied by the burning of 1 g of coal?

3. Calculate the amount of heat, in calories and in kilocalories, needed to change (*a*) 2500 g of water from 14.5° C to 15.5° C (*b*) 80 g of water from 20° C to 80° C

4. From the following substances, select those that are (*a*) compounds (*b*) heterogeneous mixtures (*c*) homogeneous mixtures

  (1) red ink   (5) muddy water
  (2) water   (6) clear air
  (3) raisin cake   (7) concrete
  (4) sugar solution   (8) salt

5. *a.* Give three examples of different types of energy transformations.

  b. What form of energy is always produced along with other transformations?

6. What are the three states of matter? Explain the differences among them in terms of their energy content.

7. *a.* List the states of matter in order of increasing stability.

b. Explain why one state is more stable than the others.

8. What is a hypothesis? Does it come before or after experimentation? Explain.

9. *a.* Explain the difference between a fact in science and an inference based upon a fact.

b. Which is subject to change? Why?

Exercises for Further Study

1. Sodium chloride contains 39.4% sodium and 60.6% chlorine by weight. If 100 g of sodium combine with chlorine, what weight of sodium chloride forms?

2. Using data in the table on page 11, calculate (*a*) the number of calories of heat needed to change 40 g of water at 100° C to steam at 100° C (*b*) the number of calories of heat that must be removed from 120 g of steam at 100° C to change the steam to ice at 0° C

3. Calculate the amount of energy, in ergs, that results when uranium undergoes fission and the resulting products have a mass 10 g less than the original mass of uranium.

4. An elevator is raised to the top of a building by an electric motor receiving power from a plant that utilizes coal as a fuel. List all the changes in energy that take place beginning with the use of the coal.

5. *a.* Which of the three types of change (chemical, physical, nuclear) produces the smallest change in the nature of the matter involved?

b. Which type of change produces the greatest change in the nature of the matter involved? Give reasons for your answers.

6. Explain why physical changes may also involve chemical changes. Cite an example.

7. Describe the experiments you would perform to determine whether a liquid is a compound or a solution containing two compounds.

8. Explain the relationships between the Law of Conservation of Matter, the Law of Conservation of Energy, and the Law of Conservation of Mass-Energy.

9. Which of the following characteristics of matter (volume, mass, density) is a physical constant? Explain.

10. *a.* Using the percentage by weight of elements listed in the table on page 7, find the amount of oxygen in 200 g of water and the amount of oxygen in 200 g of hydrogen peroxide.

b. Is it possible to calculate the amount of hydrogen in 2 l of hydrogen peroxide? Explain.

Chapter 2

THE ROLE OF MEASUREMENT

2.1 Introduction

In the preceding chapter, we discussed matter and its properties. Then we considered forms of energy and their interconvertibility. Our approach was largely *qualitative*; that is, we were concerned with quality, or kind, rather than with amount. Finally, we noted the interconvertibility of matter and energy. Here our approach was *quantitative*; that is, the stress was on the quantities of matter and energy involved in the interconversion.

2.2 Importance of measurement

Chemistry deals with both qualitative and quantitative concepts. The chemist, however, tries to use numbers as often as possible when expressing his observations. The quantitative approach provides him with greater insight and permits him to formulate generalizations that may have important predictive value.

The Law of Definite Proportions (discussed in Chapter 1) states that elements unite in definite proportions by weight. This is a statement of quantitative relationships (proportions) based on quantitative measurements. Let us cite two specific compounds to show how their weight compositions conform to the law.

Under certain conditions, 2 grams of hydrogen always combine with 16 grams of oxygen to form 18 grams of water. The proportion by weight of hydrogen to oxygen in water, therefore, is 1 : 8.

Under different conditions, 2 grams of hydrogen always combine with 32 grams of oxygen to form 34 grams of hydrogen peroxide. The proportion by weight of hydrogen to oxygen in hydrogen peroxide, therefore, is 1 : 16.

2.3 English and metric systems

There are two common systems of measurement: English and metric. Units of measure in the English system include inches, feet, miles, ounces, pounds, and tons. Because these units are difficult to interchange, the English system is cumbersome and is seldom used by chemists. The metric system is a decimal system of weights and measures based on the gram as the unit of mass, the meter as the unit of length, and the second as the unit of time. These metric units can be conveniently interchanged by using prefixes, as shown in the following table.

PREFIX	MEANING	EXAMPLE
deci	one-tenth	1 decigram = 0.1 gram
centi	one-hundredth	1 centigram = 0.01 gram
milli	one-thousandth	1 milligram = 0.001 gram
micro	one-millionth	1 microgram = 0.000001 gram, or 10^{-6} gram
kilo	one thousand times	1 kilogram = 1000 grams

Note that all of the units in the table are related by factors of ten. This decimal relationship makes for considerable ease in calculations.

Units in the English system can be converted into corresponding metric units. The following table lists some common conversion factors.

> 1 inch = 2.54 centimeters
>
> 39.4 inches = 1 meter
>
> 1 pound = 454 grams
>
> 1.06 quarts = 1 liter
>
> (1 milliliter = 1.000027 cubic centimeters, or approximately 1 cm^3)

2.4 Fundamental and derived quantities

Progress in chemistry, indeed in all experimental sciences, has resulted largely from the scientist's ability to communicate the results of his experiments in terms of the measurements he makes. The chemist is generally concerned with two kinds of quantities: *fundamental* (primary) and *derived* (secondary).

Fundamental quantities include length, mass, and time. Derived quantities are calculated from fundamental quantities and include area, volume, and density. Each fundamental and derived quantity is expressed by a number and a unit of measurement.

Derived quantities result from some arithmetic calculation based on fundamental quantities. For example, the area A of a rectangle equals the product of the lengths of any two adjacent sides. Where l is the length of one side and w is the length of an adjacent side,

$$A = l \times w, \text{ or } A = lw$$

If the length of one side of a rectangle is 2 millimeters and the length of an adjacent side is 4 millimeters, the area of the rectangle equals 8 square millimeters, or $A = 8$ mm^2. Thus area is a derived quantity based on the fundamental quantity length.

In the example, note that both the numbers and the units of measurement are multiplied: $2 \times 4 = 8$ and millimeters $\times$ millimeters = square millimeters.

Volume, another derived quantity, can be calculated in a similar manner. The volume V of a cube with a side l can be expressed algebraically as

$$V = l^3$$

If the side of a cube equals 2 millimeters, the volume of the cube equals $2^3 \times$ millimeters^3, or 8 cubic millimeters (mm^3). Again note that both the number and the unit of measurement are multiplied: $2 \times 2 \times 2 = 8$, and millimeters $\times$ millimeters $\times$ millimeters = cubic millimeters.

Density, also a derived quantity, is the mass of a unit volume of a substance. It is calculated by dividing the mass m of the substance by its volume V. Expressed algebraically,

$$D = \frac{m}{V}$$

If a substance has a mass of 8 grams and a volume of 2 cubic centimeters, its density equals 4 grams per cubic centimeter, or $D = 4$ g/cm^3. As in the previous examples, both numbers and units are included in the arithmetic calculation.

You will have many opportunities in the laboratory to use fundamental and derived quantities. Continued practice will give you competence in handling numbers and units.

2.5 Uncertainty in measurement

A student weighs a block of metal on three different centigram balances and obtains the following weights: 14.61 grams, 14.62 grams, and 14.63 grams. What is the weight of the block? In each of the weighings, only the first three digits have been reproduced. This is the same as saying that in each weighing the last digit is doubtful. The weight of the block can therefore be described as lying between 14.61 grams and 14.63 grams. The block could be weighed on any number of centigram balances and the weights would agree only in the first three digits. This experiment and many similar ones that could be performed suggest that it is impossible to reproduce a series of measurements without error.

The limitation of measurement caused by errors is called *uncertainty*. It results from shortcomings of the experimenter or of the equipment used. Consequently, our experimental observations, which we call facts, are uncertain to some degree. The experimenter, by developing his powers of observation and by refining his equipment, cannot eliminate uncertainty but can only reduce it. Thus scientists continue to refine the values of such important quantities as the Avogadro constant, the charge on the electron, and the velocity of light.

2.6 Expressing uncertainty with significant figures

The weight of the metal block in the previous section was described as lying between 14.61 grams and 14.63 grams. To express the proper uncertainty, we can describe the weight as 14.62 grams $\pm$ 0.01 gram. The symbol $\pm$ (plus or minus) expresses the uncertainty range.

The measurement 14.62 grams contains three certain digits (1, 4, and 6) and one doubtful digit (2). We can summarize this information by stating that 14.62 grams contains four significant figures. The numbers that express a measurement (including the last digit, which is doubtful) are called *significant figures.*

The number of significant figures obtained in a measurement is determined by the calibration of the measuring instrument. Centigram balances are calibrated to the nearest 0.01 gram. Hence, measurements obtained from such balances are expressed to at least two decimal places—indicating that the doubtful digit is in the hundredths place, the second figure to the right of the decimal point. In expressing the result of a measurement, use the proper number of significant figures. Where possible, also indicate the $\pm$ range.

2.7 Rules for working with significant figures

The interpretation and use of significant figures require the understanding of some fundamental rules:

1. Zeros that appear before other digits or zeros that show only the position of a decimal point are not considered significant figures. The measurement 0.0043 gram has two significant figures, 4 and 3.

2. Zeros that appear between other digits are significant figures. The measurement 4.003 grams has four significant figures, 4, 0, 0, and 3.

3. Zeros that appear after other digits may or may not be significant, depending on the precision of the measuring instrument. Consider the measurement 14.2 grams. Can it also be expressed as 14.20 grams? If a balance that measures weight to the nearest centigram is used, the measurement must be expressed as 14.20 grams. If a decigram balance is used, the measurement must be expressed as 14.2 grams.

4. In an arithmetic operation involving addition or subtraction, the result of the operation should contain only the number of decimal places of the quantity with the fewest decimal places. Suppose we are required to add 1.46 centimeters and 2.1 centimeters. If we write the sum as 3.56 centimeters, we are assuming that 2.1 centimeters has three significant figures, that it is really 2.10 centimeters. However, 2.1 centimeters has only two significant figures. The correct sum is 3.6 centimeters, obtained by rounding off 3.56 centimeters to two significant figures. Subtraction is performed in a similar manner.

   Rounding off a number means decreasing the number of significant figures. If the new number is to have one less significant figure, follow these rules for rounding off:

   a. If the digit to be discarded is greater than 5, increase the last certain digit by 1. Thus 15.66 becomes 15.7.

   b. If the digit to be discarded is less than 5, retain all the certain digits. Thus 15.63 becomes 15.6.

   c. If the digit to be discarded is 5, the number preceding this digit becomes the nearest *even* number. Thus 15.25 becomes 15.2, and 15.35 becomes 15.4.

5. Multiplying or dividing a measurement by a *number* does not alter the number of significant figures. For example, 2 times the weight of an object weighing 4.131 grams is 8.262 grams.

   If 4.130 grams (four significant figures) is multiplied by 200,000, the answer (826,000) appears to have six significant figures but actually has four. To clearly show that 826,000 has four significant figures, we use exponential notation and write 8.260×10^5. Exponential notation is explained more fully later in this chapter in sections 2.13 and 2.14.

6. In multiplication and division of *measurements*, the result can contain no more significant figures than are contained in the least certain measurement.

   The product obtained from multiplying 4.12 inches by 2.1 inches can contain only two significant figures. The product (8.652) must be rounded off to contain the proper number of significant figures. Thus 4.12 inches $\times$ 2.1 inches equals 8.7 square inches. (Note that the procedure for rounding off 8.652 to two significant figures is the same as the procedure outlined earlier in this section.)

2.8 Precision and accuracy

The *precision* of a measurement shows how closely it can be reproduced. Consider the weighings of the block of metal obtained by the student in section 2.5: 14.61 grams, 14.62 grams, and 14.63 grams. The first three digits (1, 4, and 6) were reproduced in all the measurements. The difference, or deviation, in the results appears only in the last digit. Intuitively, this consistency seems to suggest excellent precision. Let us check this assumption.

Precision is expressed in percentage deviation, or uncertainty. It is calculated by dividing the average deviation by the average measurement and multiplying the quotient by 100%.

MEASUREMENT	DEVIATION FROM AVERAGE MEASUREMENT OF 14.62 GRAMS
14.61 grams	0.01 gram
14.62 grams	0.00 gram
14.63 grams	0.01 gram
43.86 grams	0.02 gram

$$\text{average measurement} = \frac{43.86}{3} \text{ grams} = 14.62 \text{ grams}$$

$$\text{average deviation} = \frac{0.02}{3} \text{ gram} = 0.0067 \text{ gram}$$

$$\text{precision} = \frac{0.0067 \text{ gram}}{14.62 \text{ grams}} \times 100\% = 0.04\%$$

Note that this extremely low percentage deviation expresses extremely high precision, supporting our assumption.

As the percentage of uncertainty for a series of measurements decreases, the likelihood of reproducibility increases. This is the same as saying that the precision of a measurement is determined by the percentage of uncertainty. Errors that affect precision can be traced to carelessness of the experimenter and poor equipment.

The *accuracy* of a measurement describes how close it is to its accepted value. It tells us how correct a measurement is, that is, whether the error in the measurement is large or small.

A student obtains the following values for the boiling point of water at sea level: 102.63° C, 102.64° C, and 102.62° C. These values show high reproducibility and are precise; the uncertainty is about 1 part in 10,000, or about 0.01%. However, the accepted value is 100.00° C. Here the deviation is about 260 parts in 10,000 or about 2.6%. Clearly these measurements are inaccurate, yet they are precise!

What happened? One possible explanation of the poor accuracy is that the thermometer was incorrectly calibrated. By using the incorrectly calibrated thermometer properly, the student could obtain good precision because the error was reproduced with each measurement.

The precision of a measurement may be revealed by the number of significant figures. For example, the atomic weight of sodium may be represented in different charts as 22.9, 22.99, and 22.990. The most precise representation is 22.990 because it contains five significant figures.

Suppose three measurements representing the weights of three separate objects — 5.123 grams, 51.23 grams, and 512.3 grams — have the same accuracy. Which measurement is the most precise? Since 5.123 grams states the weight to the nearest milligram, it is the most precise measurement.

2.9 Measuring mass

Newton's First Law of Motion states that a body at rest tends to remain at rest, and a body in motion tends to remain in motion unless acted on by some outside force. This property of matter, called *inertia*, is proportional to the amount of matter, or mass, that is present in a body. As we have already indicated, the mass of a body remains unchanged anywhere in the universe.

Mass cannot be measured directly. Instead, we measure the gravitational force acting on the mass of the body; that is, we measure the weight of the body. The weight of the body, however, depends on the distance of the body from the center of the earth or from some other object in space, such as the sun.

The weight of a body is proportional to its mass. This means that equal masses have equal weights at equal distances from the center of the earth. Therefore, we can compare masses of objects by weighing them. With this understanding, *we will use mass and weight interchangeably in this book.*

2.10 Laboratory balances

Two widely used balances in the student laboratory are the platform balance and the triple-beam balance.

The platform balance, shown in Figure 2–1, has a beam which supports a pan, or platform, at each end. The beam is centered on an agate knife-edge. The object to be weighed is placed on the left-hand pan, and the weights necessary to balance the object are placed on the right-hand pan. For objects weighing less than 10 grams, the rider (which slides along the beam) may be employed. Balance is indicated by the position of the pointer on the scale. The calibrations on the beam determine how accurately the weighing can be made. If the beam is calibrated in tenths of a gram, weighings can be made to the nearest 0.1 gram.

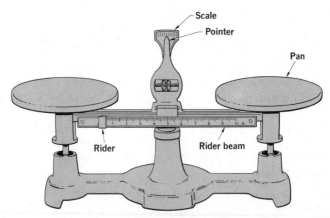

Fig. 2–1 The platform balance

The triple-beam balance, shown in Figure 2–2, has a single pan and three separate beams. The maximum capacity of the three beams is generally 111 grams (100 g + 10 g + 1 g). The 1-gram beam may be calibrated in tenths or hundredths of a gram.

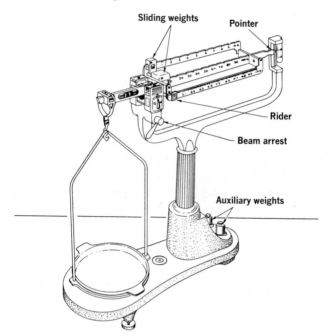

Fig. 2–2   The triple-beam balance

For more precise work, chemists use analytical balances accurate to 0.0001 gram and microbalances accurate to 10^{-7} (0.0000001) gram. Automatic balances of varying accuracies are used where very fast measurements are desired.

2.11   Measuring heat energy

We have indicated previously that chemical changes are accompanied by the evolution or absorption of heat, measured in calories or kilocalories (1000 calories). We will learn later how the quantity of heat associated with a chemical change provides considerable insight into the nature of the change.

Heat is conveniently measured by transferring it to a liquid, usually water. The mass and temperature of the water are known. Since 1 calorie is required to raise the temperature of 1 gram of water 1 C°, the quantity of heat that is transferred may be easily calculated. The heat transfer is usually carried out in a calorimeter (see Figure 2–3), which is a thermally insulated container filled with water and equipped with a thermometer and stirrer.

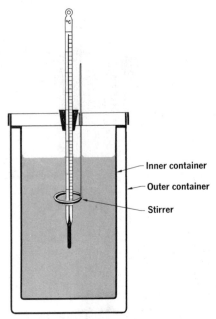

— Inner container

— Outer container

— Stirrer

Fig. 2–3   A calorimeter

The reaction vessel—the vessel in which the chemical change takes place —is immersed in the water in the calorimeter (inner container). Much of the uncertainty in this measurement is due to the loss of heat to the surroundings. This results in incomplete heat transfer from the reaction vessel to the water in the calorimeter.

Ignoring this loss, suppose the calorimeter contains 464.14 grams of water at an initial temperature of 21.2° C. As the reaction proceeds, the water reaches a maximum temperature of 28.4° C. This means the heat given off by the reaction caused 464.14 grams of water to undergo a temperature change of 7.2 C°. Since 1 calorie is required to raise the temperature of 1 gram of water 1 C°, the quantity of heat transferred is

$$464.14 \text{ grams} \times \frac{1 \text{ calorie}}{\text{gram-C}^\circ} \times 7.2 \text{ C}^\circ = 3342 \text{ calories}$$

Rounded off to two significant figures, 3342 calories is 3300 calories or 3.3 kcal.

2.12 Expressing temperatures

Heat cannot be measured directly. Instead, it is measured by the temperature effect that it produces. Temperatures may be expressed with the aid of one of the following scales: *Fahrenheit, Celsius* (or *centigrade*), or *Kelvin*. The relationships between the scales are revealed in the following table.

°F	°C	°K
$\left.\begin{array}{r}212 \\ 32\end{array}\right\}$ 180 F°	$\left.\begin{array}{r}100 \\ 0\end{array}\right\}$ 100 C°	373 273
-40	-40	233
-460	-273	0

Note that °F (degree Fahrenheit) or °C or °K represents a specific temperature *point*. On the other hand, a F° (Fahrenheit degree) or a C° or a K° represents a temperature *interval*.

The table reveals that:

$$\text{degrees K} = \text{degrees C} + 273 \text{ degrees}$$

$$180 \text{ F degrees} = 100 \text{ C degrees}$$

$$1 \text{ F degree} = \frac{5}{9} \text{ C degree}$$

To convert temperatures from one scale into another, use the relationships

$$°K = °C + 273°$$

and

$$°F - 32° = \frac{9}{5} C°$$

Example: Convert $303°$ K to $°$F.

$$°C = °K - 273° = 303° - 273° = 30°$$

$$°F = \frac{9}{5} C° + 32° = \frac{9}{5}(30°) + 32° = 54° + 32° = 86°$$

Thus $303°$ K $= 86°$ F.

The chemist prefers to work with the Celsius scale because this scale is most closely related to the metric system. In section 8.9, we will learn more about the relationships between the Celsius and Kelvin scales.

2.13   Using exponential notation

It is burdensome to use zeros to express very small or very large numbers. For example, using powers of 10, 1 microgram (0.000001 gram) can be expressed as 10^{-6} gram. Similarly 2,000,000,000 pounds (one megaton) may be written more conveniently as 2×10^9 pounds.

The use of exponential notation can serve to emphasize the number of significant figures in a measurement. For example, when 0.0072 gram is written as 7.2×10^{-3} gram, two significant figures (7 and 2) are indicated. The measurement 1000 feet may have one, two, three, or four significant figures. If one significant figure is intended, the quantity is written as 1×10^3 feet. If four significant figures are intended, the quantity is written as 1.000×10^3 feet.

2.14   Rules for working with exponential numbers

1. Numbers written in exponential form (powers of 10) cannot be added or subtracted unless the exponents are the same.

$$5.21 \times 10^4 + 2.61 \times 10^2 = 521 \times 10^2 + 2.61 \times 10^2$$
$$= 523.61 \times 10^2$$
$$= 524 \times 10^2 = 5.24 \times 10^4$$

2. When powers of 10 are multiplied, the exponents are added algebraically.

$$(2 \times 10^4) \times (3 \times 10^2) = 6 \times 10^6$$

3. When powers of 10 are divided, the exponents are subtracted algebraically.

$$\frac{1.8 \times 10^{-8}}{0.3 \times 10^4} = 6.0 \times 10^{-12}$$

4. When a root of a power of 10 is taken, the exponent is divided by the root.

$$\sqrt{4 \times 10^8} = 2 \times 10^4; \quad \sqrt[5]{32 \times 10^{10}} = 2 \times 10^2; \quad \sqrt[3]{64 \times 10^9} = 4 \times 10^3$$

Multiple-Choice Questions

1. A unit of density is (1) g/cm^3 (or g/cc) (2) lb/in (3) ft^3/lb (4) g/cm

2. Two units of measurement that are almost equal are the (1) liter and the quart (2) pound and the gram (3) ton and the kilogram (4) meter and the foot

3. The product of 25×10^2 and 6.0×10^3 is (1) 1.5×10^3 (2) 1.5×10^6 (3) 1.5×10^1 (4) 1.5×10^7

4. The sum of 7.21×10^3 and 2.31×10^2 is (1) 9.52×10^5 (2) 74.4×10^2 (3) 30.3×10^3 (4) 74.4×10^3

5. The amount of heat absorbed or emitted by a substance is measured by a (1) thermometer (2) thermostat (3) heat balance (4) calorimeter

6. A difference between mass and weight is that (1) the weight of an object does not depend on the amount of material present (2) weight units are different (3) the mass of an object is different on different planets (4) the mass of an object is fixed although its weight may vary with the gravitational force acting on it

7. Which of the following expressions uses numerical data incorrectly? (1) 2.31 g + 16.87 g = 19.18 g (2) 22.38 g + 216.8 g = 239.18 g (3) 0.021 g + 0.322 g = 0.343 g (4) 432 g + 14.1 g = 446 g

8. The number with five significant figures is (1) 0.00530 g (2) 0.04290 g (3) 49.370 g (4) 52,970.4 g

9. Two prefixes used for units which differ by a factor of 100 are (1) deci and milli (2) centi and micro (3) kilo and milli (4) micro and kilo

10. The correct arrangement of prefixes in order of *increasing* value is (1) milli, centi, kilo, deci (2) micro, milli, centi, kilo (3) centi, milli, kilo, deci (4) kilo, milli, centi, micro

11. Three examples of fundamental quantities are (1) mass, weight, volume (2) volume, length, density (3) mass, length, time (4) time, cost, color

12. Water and hydrogen peroxide are different substances because (1) they contain different elements (2) they are different mixtures (3) one has two elements; the other has three elements (4) the proportions by weight of the elements differ in the two substances

Completion Questions

1. When a scientist measures the weights of substances in a chemical change, he is determining a _____ (*qualitative, quantitative*) relationship.
2. The measure of volume is a _____ (*fundamental, derived*) quantity which can be calculated from measurements of length, which are _____ (*fundamental, derived*) quantities.
3. Three fundamental units of measurement in the metric system are _____ for length, _____ for mass, and _____ for time.
4. The inability of a scientist to exactly reproduce a set of measurements is due to the characteristic of measurement called _____.
5. To multiply numbers raised to powers of 10, _____ the coefficients and _____ the powers (exponents) of 10.
6. To take the square root of a number multiplied by a power of 10, _____ the coefficient and _____ the power of 10 by _____.
7. A triple-beam balance is sensitive to 0.01 g, and the divisions on the rider beam are 0.1 g. When used properly, the balance can determine the weight of a 12 g object to _____ significant figures.
8. There are _____ ml in 0.25 l.
9. When a number with four significant figures is multiplied by the whole number 2, the proper number of significant figures in the answer is _____.
10. Scientists prefer the use of the metric system over the English system for measurements because _____.
11. Precision is defined as _____, while accuracy is defined as _____.

Exercises for Review

1. Convert (*a*) 20 kg to pounds (*b*) $\frac{1}{4}$ ton to kilograms (*c*) 5 oz to grams
2. Convert (*a*) 2 ft to centimeters (*b*) 3 m to inches (*c*) 200 cm to feet
3. Find the density, in g/cm^3, for a metal block which has the dimensions 6 cm × 8 cm × 20 cm and a mass of 5.50 kg.
4. Find the density, in g/cm^3, of 4.00 l of a liquid which has a mass of 3050 g.
5. State the number of significant figures in (*a*) 0.00936 g (*b*) 89.20 ft (*c*) 68,000 cal (*d*) 68 kcal
6. Add the following, and express the answer in the proper number of significant figures:

$$82.4, \ 75.52, \ 140.8, \ 4.078, \ 10.39$$

7. Solve the following, and express the answer in the proper number of significant figures:

$$\frac{4.33 \times 30.783}{22.14}$$

8. Change to a number expressed as an exponent of 10 (*a*) 100,000 (*b*) 0.0001 (*c*) 243,000 (*d*) 0.00146

9. Find the volume of a block of wood $\frac{1}{4}$ meter long, 10 centimeters wide, and 8 millimeters thick.

10. Convert (*a*) 65° F to Celsius (*b*) −32° C to Fahrenheit (*c*) 180° F to Kelvin (*d*) 0° K to Fahrenheit

Exercises for Further Study

1. Convert (*a*) 4500 cm³ to cubic feet (*b*) $\frac{1}{2}$ quart to milliliters

2. *a*. A student measures the length of a yardstick with a centimeter rule and obtains these values: 91.2 cm, 91.0 cm, 91.1 cm. Express these results showing the uncertainty of the measurement.

   b. The length of the yardstick is known to be 91.44 cm. Compare the precision and the accuracy of these measurements. Explain the difference.

3. Add the following and express the answer in the proper number of significant figures:

   a. $3.21 \times 10^3 + 4.69 \times 10^2 + 0.069 \times 10^3$

   b. $0.00293 + 4.99 \times 10^{-3} + 57.9 \times 10^{-4}$

4. Solve the following and express each answer in the proper number of significant figures:

   a. $\dfrac{2.3 \times 10^{-5} \times 60.1 \times 10^2}{121.9 \times 10^3}$

   b. $\dfrac{(4.3 \times 10^2) \times \sqrt{9.0 \times 10^4}}{0.00323}$

5. If the density of gasoline is 0.68 g/cm³, what is the weight of 10 gallons of gasoline?

Chapter 3

USING A MODEL: INTRODUCTION TO ATOMIC THEORY

3.1 Introduction

The chemist often has to develop a *theory*—a tentative set of explanations—to help him interpret what he observes in the laboratory (see sections 1.10 and 1.11). The theory may employ a mental picture, called a *model*, to fit his observations. Frequently, theories and models are used interchangeably.

If newly discovered facts do not fit the model, the chemist cannot alter the facts. Instead, he amends or perhaps even discards the model, establishing a new one in its place. The history of chemistry is filled with examples of scientific models that have been developed, modified, and in some instances abandoned.

3.2 The phlogiston theory

During the 17th century, chemists attempted to explain the nature of burning. They wondered why certain substances apparently lose weight on burning, whereas other substances gain weight. It was suggested that burning matter expels an invisible substance, called *phlogiston.*

Phlogiston, according to the many who believed in it, accounted for weight being lost during combustion. To explain an increase in weight, they suggested that phlogiston could also have a negative weight; its expulsion would make the burning matter heavier.

The phlogiston theory, almost the reverse of our modern concept of burning, persisted for about a century. Then during the latter part of the 18th century, Lavoisier's experiments disproved the phlogiston theory and suggested oxygen as the necessary substance for burning. Subsequent discoveries have amended this concept only slightly. It is interesting that the oxygen model retained an important part of the phlogiston theory. Both stated that combustion involves a transfer between two bodies: the fuel and phlogiston in one instance, and the fuel and air in the other.

In the next chapter, we will develop a model of the atom based on elementary observations on the structure of matter. This model is admittedly limited in scope. Yet it served chemists quite well and contributed much to the progress of science during the early part of the 20th century.

3.3 Matter consists of particles

A group of early Greek philosophers, the Atomists, believed that the continued subdivision of matter would ultimately yield a particle that was indivisible. This concept remained controversial for many centuries because it was not based upon observation and could not be tested.

In 1803, the English scientist John Dalton, basing his thinking on quantitative evidence gathered during the 18th century, boldly expanded the ancient Atomist concept of matter.

The Dalton model proposed:

1. All matter consists of simple bodies (elements) and compound bodies (compounds). The smallest part of a simple body is the atom; the smallest part of a compound body is the compound atom, later termed the molecule.
2. All atoms of the same element have the same properties, such as shape, size, and weight; atoms of different elements have different properties.
3. When matter undergoes chemical change, atoms of different elements either combine or separate from each other.
4. Atoms are indestructible even during chemical change.

3.4 The Laws of Chemical Combination

The success of a model depends on how well it explains experimental observations. Today we know that Dalton's model was limited and in some ways incorrect. His model was accepted, however, because it did explain many of the experimental observations of his time, including the Law of Conservation of Matter and the Law of Definite Proportions. Dalton's model also predicted the Law of Multiple Proportions. These three laws are called the *Laws of Chemical Combination*.

3.5 The Law of Conservation of Matter

In Chapter 1, we discussed how Lavoisier's experiments led to the Law of Conservation of Matter: Matter may neither be created nor destroyed in a chemical change. Now we can see how Dalton's model explained this law.

Assume that 100 atoms of element A (x atoms) combine with 100 atoms of element B (y atoms) to form compound AB. According to Dalton, all matter consists of indestructible atoms. Therefore, during the chemical change, atoms are conserved: 100 atoms of A and 100 atoms of B ($x + y$ atoms) must be present in the product of the change. In the laboratory, we can demonstrate that the combined weight of the atoms of each element equals the total weight of the atoms in the compound (see Figure 3–1). Since no weight change occurs, all of the atoms are conserved.

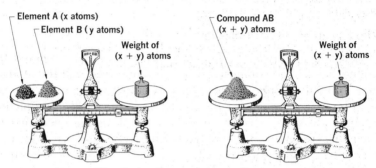

Fig. 3–1   Conservation of matter

Note that the physical state of an atom does not alter its weight. The 100 atoms of element A may be present as a solid, liquid, or gas, depending on the temperature. In all three states, however, the 100 atoms of element A weigh the same.

3.6 The Law of Definite Proportions

In discussing the properties of compounds in Chapter 1, we noted an important regularity: A compound consists of at least two elements united in definite proportions by weight. This regularity, known as the Law of Definite Proportions, suggests that compounds have a constant composition. Let us see how the Dalton model of the atom explains constant composition.

Experiment shows that 23 parts of sodium by weight always combine completely with 35.5 parts of chlorine by weight to form 58.5 parts of sodium chloride by weight.

According to Dalton, there are a specific number of sodium atoms in 23 weight units of sodium and a specific number of chlorine atoms in

35.5 weight units of chlorine. Assume that one atom of sodium combines with one atom of chlorine. This means that sodium chloride consists of a specific number of sodium atoms and the same number of chlorine atoms. Since sodium atoms and chlorine atoms each have a characteristic fixed weight, the composition of the compound must be constant.

As a further verification of the Law of Definite Proportions, suppose we tried to combine 40 parts of sodium by weight with 35.5 parts of chlorine by weight. We would find that 17 parts of sodium by weight remained uncombined because there were insufficient chlorine atoms to combine with all the sodium atoms.

3.7 The Law of Multiple Proportions

In discussing the Laws of Chemical Combination, we observed that a compound has a fixed composition. We also observed that the atoms that combine to form a compound are conserved; that is, the same number of atoms present at the outset of the change is present at the completion of the change. In our discussion, however, we tacitly assumed that when two elements combine, they form only one compound. Now let us consider what happens when two elements form more than one compound.

From the table in section 1.15 we may calculate that 2 grams of hydrogen will combine with 16 grams of oxygen to form 18 grams of water, and that 2 grams of hydrogen will also combine with 32 grams of oxygen to form 34 grams of hydrogen peroxide.

Assume that in forming water, 2 atoms of hydrogen always combine with 1 atom of oxygen to form a molecule containing 3 atoms (see Figure 3-2). Let x equal the number of atoms in 1 gram of hydrogen. Then 2 grams of hydrogen contain $2x$ atoms of hydrogen, and 16 grams of oxygen contain x atoms of oxygen. Therefore, water contains $2x$ atoms of hydrogen combined with x atoms of oxygen. Note that atoms have been conserved and that the composition of the compound water is fixed.

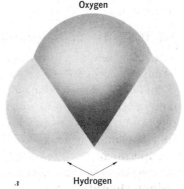

Oxygen

Hydrogen

Fig. 3-2 Model of a water molecule

To form both water and hydrogen peroxide, we chose 2 grams of hydrogen to combine with oxygen. We then observed that 2 grams of hydrogen required 16 grams of oxygen to form water and 32 grams of oxygen to form hydrogen peroxide. The weight ratio of oxygen in the two compounds is 16 : 32, or 1 : 2. This is a mathematical way of stating that the same weight of hydrogen requires twice as much oxygen by weight to form hydrogen peroxide as it requires to form water.

Since we assumed x atoms of oxygen to be present in 16 grams of oxygen, $2x$ atoms of oxygen are present in 32 grams of oxygen. The ratio $x : 2x$, or 1 : 2, which compares the number of oxygen atoms in the two compounds, can be expressed only in small whole numbers. This illustrates, as Dalton suggested, that reactions between elements are essentially reactions between small discrete entities, or atoms. The *Law of Multiple Proportions states: When elements combine to form more than a single compound, the ratios of the weights of the combining elements can be expressed by small whole numbers.*

3.8 Relative atomic weights: the oxygen-16 standard

The Dalton model stimulated scientists to determine atomic weights experimentally. The problem was complex because atoms are too small to be weighed. It soon became apparent that chemists would have to be satisfied with a set of relative, rather than actual, atomic weights. A *relative weight* shows how the weight of one substance compares with the weight of another substance which is selected as the standard.

After many trials with various standards of reference for a relative weight system, it was decided to use the value, oxygen = 16. Oxygen was selected because many different elements combine with it. The value 16 was selected to avoid having an atomic weight of less than 1 for the lightest element, hydrogen, which is almost 16 times lighter than oxygen. Also, the value 16 for oxygen permitted many atomic weights to be whole numbers.

To determine relative atomic weights, it was first necessary to find the weight composition of a compound. For example, an oxide of sodium was found to contain 74.2% sodium and 25.8% oxygen. In this compound, therefore, the sodium atoms contribute $\frac{74.2}{25.8}$, or 2.88, times more weight than do the oxygen atoms.

The next problem was to determine the number of sodium atoms relative to the number of oxygen atoms in the oxide. Assigning a value of 16 to oxygen gives the sodium atom a weight of 16×2.88, or about

46, provided the number of sodium atoms equals the number of oxygen atoms. If the ratio is 1 atom of sodium to 1 atom of oxygen, then 1 sodium atom is $\frac{46}{16}$ times heavier than 1 oxygen atom. If the ratio is 2 sodium atoms to 1 oxygen atom, then one sodium atom is $\frac{23}{16}$ times heavier than 1 oxygen atom. How is the correct ratio determined?

3.9 Using specific heats to determine relative atomic weights

One of the methods that helped to solve the problem of determining the number of combining atoms in a compound used the relationship between the relative atomic weight of an element and its specific heat. This relationship, established by Pierre Dulong and Alexis Petit in 1819, states that the product of the relative atomic weight of a solid element and its specific heat is approximately 6.3.

$$\text{atomic weight} \times \text{specific heat} = 6.3$$

$$\text{atomic weight} = \frac{6.3}{\text{specific heat}}$$

The specific heat of an element equals the number of calories required to raise the temperature of 1 gram of the element 1 C°.

The specific heat of an element may be determined readily in the laboratory by measuring the heat transferred by a specific mass of the element to a specific mass of water at a known temperature. For solids that react with water, such as sodium, other liquids are used. The specific heat of solid sodium at room temperature is 0.295 cal/g-C° (calories per gram per Celsius degree). Thus the *approximate* relative atomic weight of sodium is

$$\frac{6.3}{0.295} = 21$$

Therefore, a sodium atom is approximately $\frac{21}{16}$ times heavier than an oxygen atom.

From the percentage composition of the oxide of sodium, it was assumed that if the ratio of sodium atoms to oxygen atoms is 2 : 1, one sodium atom would be $\frac{23}{16}$ times heavier than one oxygen atom. The value $\frac{23}{16}$ is much closer to the experimentally determined value of $\frac{21}{16}$ than is $\frac{46}{16}$, suggested earlier.

We may infer that in sodium oxide the sodium atoms have an approximate weight of 46. Thus two sodium atoms are present in the compound. Using such methods, chemists determined atomic weights for some 35 elements by the middle of the 19th century.

Although Dalton's ideas contributed to a better understanding of atoms and atomic weights, the concept of a molecule and the concept of molecular weights remained unclear. For the present, we shall consider a molecule as the smallest separate entity of matter consisting of two or more atoms united in a definite manner. Thus the smallest quantity of carbon dioxide is a molecule consisting of one carbon atom and two oxygen atoms (see Figure 3–3).

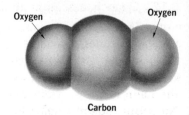

Fig. 3–3   Model of a carbon dioxide molecule

3.10 The new standard: carbon-12

The standard O = 16 assumed the presence of only one kind of oxygen atom, conforming to Dalton's definition of an atom. This assumption was later found to be in error. Three varieties (*isotopes*) of oxygen are now known to exist. This discovery led to many complications in the use of oxygen as the standard for relative atomic weights.

In 1961, chemists abandoned oxygen as the standard for relative atomic weights. In its place, they devised a scale in which $\frac{1}{12}$ the weight (or mass) of the most abundant isotope of carbon is called 1 atomic weight unit, or 1 atomic mass unit (1 awu or 1 amu). The new scale automatically assigns to this form of carbon, called *carbon-12*, a relative atomic weight (see section 3.8) exactly equal to 12. On this scale, the atomic weight of sodium is 22.989 awu and the atomic weight of oxygen is 15.999 awu. These values, it must be remembered, are relative weights only. Chemists would find it extremely cumbersome to use absolute, or actual, weights of atoms.

3.11   How many atoms in a gram-atomic weight?

The actual weight of 1 awu has been calculated as approximately 1.67×10^{-24} g. Since sodium has a relative atomic weight of 22.9, the actual weight in grams of a single sodium atom is $22.9 \times 1.67 \times 10^{-24}$ g, or 3.82×10^{-23} g. How many atoms of sodium are contained in 23 grams of sodium (1 gram-atomic weight)? The number of atoms in 1 gram-atomic weight of sodium is $23 \div 3.82 \times 10^{-23}$, or 6.02×10^{23}. Similar calculations show that the number of atoms in the gram-atomic weight of any element is 6.02×10^{23}. For example, the number of atoms in 12 grams of carbon having a relative atomic weight of 12 is 6.02×10^{23}. This extremely large number is called *Avogadro's number*, after the Italian scientist Amadeo Avogadro (1776–1856).

3.12 Symbols and gram-atomic weights

The chemist uses an abbreviation, called a *symbol*, to designate a particular element. The symbol is usually the first letter or the first letter and another letter of the English name of the element. For example, H is the symbol for hydrogen, and Cl is the symbol for chlorine. In some cases, the Latin names of elements are used in deriving symbols. For example, Na (from the Latin *natrium*) is the symbol for sodium, and K (from the Latin *kalium*) is the symbol for potassium.

The symbol of an element also represents a definite quantity of the element, the *gram-atomic weight*—that is, the relative atomic weight expressed in grams. This quantity is also called a *gram-atom* or a *mole*.

One gram-atom of all elements contains the same number of atoms. This number is Avogadro's number, 6.02×10^{23}, discussed in the previous section. Thus 1 Na represents 1 mole (6.02×10^{23} atoms) of sodium or 1 gram-atom of sodium, which weighs 23 grams. The table that follows lists the symbols and approximate atomic weights for some common elements.

ELEMENT	SYMBOL	ATOMIC WEIGHT (*rounded off*)
hydrogen	H	1
helium	He	4
lithium	Li	7
carbon	C	12
nitrogen	N	14
oxygen	O	16
fluorine	F	19
sodium	Na	23
magnesium	Mg	24
aluminum	Al	27
phosphorus	P	31
sulfur	S	32
chlorine	Cl	35.5
potassium	K	39
calcium	Ca	40
copper	Cu	63.5

3.13 Formulas and gram-molecular weights

When the number of atoms in a molecule is known, the symbols may be combined to designate the molecule. Molecules generally consist of a minimum of two atoms of the same element or a minimum of two atoms of different elements. The composition of a molecule is described by its formula. A *formula* lists the elements and the amounts of each element present in a molecule. A formula also represents 1 gram-molecular weight.

The formula for hydrogen is H_2, and its gram-molecular weight is 2 grams. The formula for water is H_2O, and its gram-molecular weight is 18 grams. The formula for sodium chloride is $NaCl$, and its gram-molecular weight is 58.5 grams. Note that subscripts (lowered numbers that appear to the right of the symbols) are used to denote the number of atoms.

Just as a mole of atoms represents the number of atoms in a gram-atom, a mole of molecules represents the number of molecules in a *gram-mole* (gram-molecular weight). In O_2, we have 2 moles of oxygen atoms, or 1 mole of oxygen molecules.

The table that follows lists the formulas and molecular weights for some common compounds.

COMPOUND	FORMULA	MOLECULAR WEIGHT
hydrogen peroxide	H_2O_2	34
calcium fluoride	CaF_2	78
copper oxide	CuO	79.5
sodium oxide	Na_2O	62
aluminum chloride	$AlCl_3$	133.5

Experimental work during the first half of the 19th century helped to establish the formulas of many compounds. The Dalton model, however, did not explain the differences in the combining powers of atoms. For example, why should the formula for water be H_2O rather than HO, as Dalton himself had supposed? Although the Dalton model explains the laws of chemical combination, the model failed to answer the fundamental question: Why do atoms combine as they do?

Multiple-Choice Questions

1. The atomic weight of Mg is 24, and the atomic weight of Cl is 35.5. One mole of $MgCl_2$ (1) represents 95 molecules of the compound (2) represents 95 grams of the compound (3) contains 35.5 molecules of chlorine (4) contains 2 moles of chlorine molecules

2. Avogadro's number, 6.02×10^{23}, indicates (1) the amount of charge on an electron (2) the number of particles in a mole of particles (3) a comparison of the mass of the proton and the electron (4) the weight of 1 awu

3. The specific heat of a substance is the (1) amount of heat it releases on combustion (2) difference between its boiling point and its melting point (3) number of calories needed to raise 1 g of the substance 1 C° (4) highest temperature it can reach

4. As the specific heats of different elements increase (1) their atomic masses decrease (2) their atomic masses increase (3) there is no change in atomic mass (4) their atomic masses first increase, then decrease

5. A solid element has a specific heat of approximately 0.22 cal/g-C°. The most probable atomic weight of the element is (1) 14 (2) 27 (3) 1.4 (4) 38

Completion Questions

1. *a.* A (An) _____ is a chemical abbreviation for the name of an element.
   b. This term also indicates a definite quantity of the element. The quantity is called the _____ of the element.

2. The modern scale of atomic weights is based on the relative weights of atoms compared with the _____ atom, which is assigned a weight equal to _____.

3. Elements that form more than one compound obey the Law of _____.

4. Three varieties of oxygen atoms, called _____, occur in nature.

5. To interpret what he observes in the laboratory, the chemist often develops a (an) _____, which may make use of a mental construct called a (an) _____.

6. The former standard of relative atomic weights was _____.

7. In our modern concept of burning, _____ is analogous to phlogiston.

8. According to Dalton, matter is _____ (*continuous, discontinuous*).

9. The discovery of isotopes indicates that all atoms of the same element do not have the same _____.

10. The compounds KCl and $KClO_3$ obey the Law of _____ Proportions.

Exercises for Review

1. Distinguish between gram-atomic weight and gram-molecular weight.

2. Why was it necessary to revise Dalton's atomic theory during the present century?

3. Show how the Law of Constant Composition is merely a restatement of the Law of Definite Proportions.
4. How does the Law of Multiple Proportions support the Dalton model of the atom?
5. Distinguish between *relative* and *actual* atomic weights.
6. It is determined that 1.20 grams of a metal form 1.68 grams of oxide. The specific heat of the metal is 0.13 cal/g-C°. What is the atomic weight of the metal?
7. Assume that a mole of H_2O contains 2 gram-atoms of hydrogen and 1 gram-atom of oxygen. Calculate the percentages, by weight, of hydrogen and oxygen in water.
8. Distinguish between an awu and an amu.
9. Distinguish between an atom and a molecule.
10. Calculate the gram-molecular weight for each of the following formulas:

    a. H_2S *b.* CCl_4 *c.* P_4O_{10} *d.* AlN *e.* CuF_2

Exercises for Further Study

1. If 1 gram-atom of lithium weighs 6.94 g, calculate the approximate weight of a single lithium atom.
2. Why was carbon-12 developed as a new standard for relative atomic weights?
3. Why was the phlogiston theory finally abandoned?
4. *a.* Why do chemists employ models in their thinking?
   b. Devise a problem and suggest a model that might be developed to solve this problem.
5. *a.* Why did Dalton suggest HO as the formula for water?
   b. What problems arose as a result of this assumption?
6. It has been shown recently that certain compounds do not appear to follow the Law of Definite Proportions. What might you infer from these observations?
7. Moles of different gases have different weights. State two conclusions that might be made from this observation.
8. On the $C^{12} = 12$ scale, the atomic weight of carbon is stated as 12.01115. Explain.

Chapter 4

INSIDE THE ATOM: A NUCLEAR MODEL

4.1 Introduction

Experimental observation represents the foundation of all our modern science. Yet what path should the scientist follow in the solution of a problem where previous experimentation has been meager or even nonexistent? For example, Dalton suggested that the formula for water was HO, based upon what he termed the *rule of greatest simplicity.*

Not knowing of the existence of hydrogen peroxide, Dalton assumed that if two elements such as H and O formed only a single compound such as water, the atoms of each element would combine in the simplest ratio, that is, 1:1.

This assumption could not be reconciled with the later findings of Gay-Lussac and Avogadro (see section 8.16). However, it did lead to later experimental work which established correct molecular formulas. Dalton's work proved that an intelligent guess—even a faulty one—can contribute to the progress of science.

Discoveries during the latter part of the 19th century and the early part of the 20th century made it necessary to reexamine the Dalton model. One of Dalton's most important concepts did not change: The atom continued to be the smallest particle of an element that still exhibits the properties of the element. However, experiments showed that the atom consists of smaller particles. The arrangement of the smaller particles could account for some of the properties of the atom.

In the next section, we will outline a simple nuclear model of the atom. Later, in Chapter 19, we will extend the simple nuclear model and review the experimental evidence that led to its adoption. Although the simple nuclear model has considerable limitations, it is useful at an elementary level in understanding some of the changes that matter undergoes.

4.2 The nuclear model of the atom

The essential ideas contained in the nuclear model are:

1. An atom is composed of three fundamental particles: electrons, protons, and neutrons. The characteristics of these particles are summarized in the table on the following page.

PARTICLE	CHARACTERISTIC
electron	unit negative electric charge; mass equals $\frac{1}{1837}$ the mass of a proton
proton	unit positive electric charge; mass almost exactly equals the mass of a hydrogen atom
neutron	electrically neutral particle with mass slightly greater than that of a proton

2. Since atoms are electrically neutral, they contain an equal number of electrons and protons. The number of electrons or the number of protons is called the *atomic number*.

3. Since electrons have a very small mass, the neutrons and protons are responsible for almost the entire mass of the atom. The total number (sum) of the neutrons and protons in an atom is called the *mass number*.

4. The neutrons and protons (also called *nucleons*) are located in the center of the atom, in the region called the *nucleus*.

5. The electrons are located outside the nucleus. Each atom has a specific arrangement of electrons.

6. The electrons are arranged in shells which are identified by the numbers 1, 2, 3, and so on, or by the letters *K, L, M*, and so on. Shell 1, the *K*-shell, is the innermost shell.

7. As the atomic numbers of atoms increase, electrons fill the shells in a prescribed fashion. The first shell, the one nearest the nucleus, is filled when it holds two electrons. The second shell can hold a maximum of eight electrons. The third shell can hold a maximum of 18 electrons but in some cases appears to hold only eight. We will discuss the reasons for this variation later.

8. The reactivity of an atom is associated with the number of electrons in its outermost shell.

4.3 Structures of atoms

Our simple atomic model enables us to describe the differences between atoms in terms of their electron arrangements. Using the atomic numbers and the mass numbers of elements, we can show the structures for elements with atomic numbers 1 to 21.

ELEMENT	SYM-BOL	ATOMIC NUMBER	MASS NUMBER	COMPOSITION OF NUCLEUS (p = proton) (n = neutron)	ELECTRON ARRANGEMENT (number of electrons in shells) K L M N			
hydrogen	H	1	1	$1\,p$	1			
helium	He	2	4	$2\,p + 2\,n$	2			
lithium	Li	3	7	$3\,p + 4\,n$	2	1		
beryllium	Be	4	9	$4\,p + 5\,n$	2	2		
boron	B	5	11	$5\,p + 6\,n$	2	3		
carbon	C	6	12	$6\,p + 6\,n$	2	4		
nitrogen	N	7	14	$7\,p + 7\,n$	2	5		
oxygen	O	8	16	$8\,p + 8\,n$	2	6		
fluorine	F	9	19	$9\,p + 10\,n$	2	7		
neon	Ne	10	20	$10\,p + 10\,n$	2	8		
sodium	Na	11	23	$11\,p + 12\,n$	2	8	1	
magnesium	Mg	12	24	$12\,p + 12\,n$	2	8	2	
aluminum	Al	13	27	$13\,p + 14\,n$	2	8	3	
silicon	Si	14	28	$14\,p + 14\,n$	2	8	4	
phosphorus	P	15	31	$15\,p + 16\,n$	2	8	5	
sulfur	S	16	32	$16\,p + 16\,n$	2	8	6	
chlorine	Cl	17	35	$17\,p + 18\,n$	2	8	7	
argon	Ar	18	40	$18\,p + 22\,n$	2	8	8	
potassium	K	19	39	$19\,p + 20\,n$	2	8	8	1
calcium	Ca	20	40	$20\,p + 20\,n$	2	8	8	2
scandium	Sc	21	45	$21\,p + 24\,n$	2	8	9	2

As the atomic numbers increase, note that electrons tend to complete successive shells, beginning with two electrons in the K-shell, eight electrons in the L-shell, and eight electrons in the M-shell. Electrons do not usually enter a new shell until the preceding shell is filled. Under certain conditions some atoms, such as scandium, atomic number 21, tend to fill their next-to-the-outermost shell until the shell is complete with 18 electrons. This deviation represents one important limitation of our simple nuclear model. Other limitations will become apparent as you continue your study of chemistry.

4.4 Chemical reactivity

The table in the preceding section reveals that atoms of helium, neon, and argon have completely filled outermost electron shells. Experimental evidence shows that these elements, belonging to a group called *noble gases*, exhibit unusual stability. This means that the noble gases show very little tendency to enter into chemical changes. Hence, compounds of these elements are uncommon. We may assume that when elements combine to form compounds, their atoms tend to attain a more stable electron arrangement, as is found in the noble gases. Thus when elements combine, their atoms tend to acquire a complete outermost electron shell.

You will see later that many atoms, such as iron, combine chemically without completing their outermost shells. However, a sufficient number of atoms, on combining, do attain the electron configuration of the noble gases to make our limited model useful.

4.5 Electron transfer

Atoms may complete their outermost electron shells if they lose or gain electrons. For example, lithium metal may combine with chlorine gas to form the compound lithium chloride.

	lithium	+	chlorine	→	lithium chloride	
SHELLS	$K\ L$		$K\ L\ M$		K	$K\ L\ M$
ELECTRONS	(2–1)		(2–8–7)		(2)	(2–8–8)

Refer to the table in section 4.3, and note that in lithium chloride, lithium has attained the electron arrangement of helium (2), while chlorine has attained the argon structure (2–8–8). Only one lithium atom and one chlorine atom are required to form lithium chloride. The reaction (chemical change) involves the transfer of one electron from the lithium atom to the chlorine atom.

Consider calcium, Ca, reacting with fluorine, F, to form calcium fluoride, CaF_2. In this reaction, a calcium atom can attain the argon, Ar, structure by losing two electrons. (Argon is the noble gas closest to calcium.) A single fluorine atom can attain the neon, Ne, structure by gaining only one electron. (Neon is the noble gas closest to fluorine.) Two fluorine atoms are required to accept the two electrons from the single calcium atom.

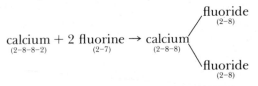

calcium + 2 fluorine → calcium
(2–8–8–2)   (2–7)

fluoride
(2–8)

fluoride
(2–8)

calcium
(2–8–8)

If we use dots to represent the electrons in the outermost shell, the reaction between calcium and fluorine can be represented as

$$\text{Ca} : + \; 2 : \overset{\bullet\bullet}{\underset{\bullet\bullet}{\text{F}}} \bullet \; \longrightarrow \; : \overset{\bullet\bullet}{\underset{\bullet\bullet}{\text{F}}} : \text{Ca} : \overset{\bullet\bullet}{\underset{\bullet\bullet}{\text{F}}} :$$

Formulas employing dots to represent electrons are called *electron-dot formulas.*

4.6 Electron sharing

Atoms may also acquire a stable electron structure by sharing electrons. For example, two chlorine atoms may combine to form a single chlorine molecule by sharing a pair of electrons: Each chlorine atom supplies one electron to form the pair. A molecule of chlorine, therefore, is more stable than two individual chlorine atoms. The change may be represented as

$$: \overset{\bullet\bullet}{\underset{\bullet\bullet}{\text{Cl}}} \bullet \; + \; \bullet \overset{\bullet\bullet}{\underset{\bullet\bullet}{\text{Cl}}} : \; \longrightarrow \; : \overset{\bullet\bullet}{\underset{\bullet\bullet}{\text{Cl}}} : \overset{\bullet\bullet}{\underset{\bullet\bullet}{\text{Cl}}} :$$

Each chlorine atom now has the argon structure.

We previously represented two fluorine atoms as

$$2 : \overset{\bullet\bullet}{\underset{\bullet\bullet}{\text{F}}} \bullet$$

We may now rewrite this notation as

$$: \overset{\bullet\bullet}{\underset{\bullet\bullet}{\text{F}}} : \overset{\bullet\bullet}{\underset{\bullet\bullet}{\text{F}}} :$$

Each fluorine atom now has the neon structure. The first notation represents two isolated fluorine atoms (2 F), whereas the second represents one fluorine molecule (F_2).

Elements that lose electrons readily are said to be *metallic*; elements that gain electrons readily are said to be *nonmetallic*.

We have made no reference to the role of the atomic nucleus in determining the reactivity of elements. You will remember from section 4.2 that the nucleus of an atom contains protons. Consequently, the nucleus possesses a positive charge which exerts a force of attraction on electrons. The atomic number, which represents the number of electrons or protons, also represents the nuclear charge. The tendency to lose, gain, or share electrons is closely related, among other factors, to the magnitude of this charge. The relationship between protons, electrons, and reactivity will be explored fully in subsequent chapters.

4.7 Stability of atoms and molecules

A fundamental problem facing chemists is to determine why and how chemical changes occur. The problem is intricate, and the answer is not completely known. From experimental observations, however, we can state: A chemical change (or any change, for that matter) will occur spontaneously if the products of the change are more stable (are at a lower energy level) than the starting materials. This observation suggests that chemical changes proceed in the direction that liberates energy.

For example, a spring tends to remain unstretched unless a force is applied to it. The stretched spring has more potential energy than the loose spring and is consequently less stable than the loose spring. After the spring unstretches and comes to rest, it possesses minimum potential energy and maximum stability.

Atoms also possess potential or stored energy. When atoms combine, the products possess less potential energy and consequently have greater stability. The loss in potential energy is frequently observed as an evolution of heat. In the example in section 4.5, solid lithium chloride, LiCl, possesses less potential energy (less heat) than the sum of the potential energies of uncombined lithium metal and chlorine gas (see Figure 4–1).

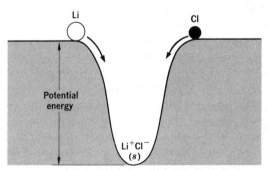

Fig. 4–1   Energy approach to the formation of solid lithium chloride

The formation of solid lithium chloride from its elements, therefore, is accompanied by the release of energy, most often in the form of heat. However, the tendency to attain greater stability is only one of the factors that contributes to the reactions between atoms. The problem is more complex than one first imagines and will require further study.

4.8 Bond formation by transfer of electrons

Consider the reaction between lithium and fluorine. A neutral lithium atom, symbolized as Li^0, contains three protons, four neutrons, and three electrons. All neutral atoms may be symbolized with a superscript zero. For example, an atom of neutral element Z is often written Z^0. A neutral fluorine atom, F^0, contains nine protons, ten neutrons, and nine electrons.

During the formation of lithium fluoride, a lithium atom transfers an electron to a fluorine atom. The lithium in lithium fluoride, having lost an electron, now contains two electrons and has a charge of $+1$, symbolized as Li^+. The fluorine in lithium fluoride, having gained an electron, now contains ten electrons and has a charge of -1, symbolized as F^-.

In forming lithium fluoride, neutral lithium atoms and neutral fluorine atoms have become charged particles called ions. *An ion is an atom or group of atoms with either a positive or negative electric charge.*

The charge on an ion results from the transfer of electrons between two electrically neutral particles. The loss of electrons produces an ion with a positive charge, whereas the gain of electrons produces an ion with a negative charge. The attraction between the oppositely charged ions constitutes a force called a *bond.*

The formation of lithium fluoride may be represented as follows. Note the symbol e^- for electron.

$$Li^0 - e^- \rightarrow Li^+$$

(In subsequent reactions, we will indicate electron loss by using the symbolism $+ e^-$ on the *right* side of the reaction. Thus: $Li^0 \rightarrow Li^+ + e^-$.)

$$F^0 + e^- \rightarrow F^-$$

The combined reaction is

$$Li^0 + F^0 \rightarrow Li^+F^-$$

4.9 Monatomic and polyatomic elements

For the present introduction to chemical bonding, we are using the notation F to represent fluorine. This element actually occurs in the form of diatomic molecules, F_2, as do the following common elements: hydrogen, H_2; oxygen, O_2; nitrogen, N_2; chlorine, Cl_2; bromine, Br_2; iodine, I_2. Under normal temperature and pressure conditions, phosphorus is tetratomic, P_4, and sulfur is octatomic, S_8. The other elements (Na, Ca, and so on) are monatomic.

4.10 Interpreting the reaction of lithium with fluorine

The reaction of lithium with fluorine is more realistically written:

1. $\qquad Li^0 \rightarrow Li^+ + e^-$

2. $\dfrac{1}{2} F_2^0 + e^- \rightarrow F^-$

$$Li^0 + \dfrac{1}{2} F_2^0 \rightarrow Li^+F^-$$

The equations are read:

1. 1 mole of neutral lithium atoms forms 1 mole of lithium +1 ions with the loss of 1 mole of electrons.
2. $\frac{1}{2}$ mole of neutral fluorine molecules, with the gain of 1 mole of electrons, forms 1 mole of fluoride −1 ions.

In its simplest form, the reaction of lithium with fluorine involves the union of two atoms to form a compound. As explained in section 4.7, the molecular structure represented by Li^+F^- is more stable than the Li^0 and F^0 atoms. The increase in stability occurs because both Li^0 and F^0, in forming Li^+F^-, have attained noble gas structures.

Now we will account for the increase in stability in a new and more important way. Since Li^+ and F^- are oppositely charged, an electrostatic force binds the ions together. This force results from the attraction of the oppositely charged ions. When two atoms combine by a transfer of electrons, the force that holds the atoms together is called an *ionic bond*.

Li^+F^-, an ionically bonded species (distinct kind of matter), may also be written as $Li^+ \dashrightarrow F^-$. The arrow represents a single bond, resulting from the transfer of an electron from a lithium atom to a fluorine atom.

4.11 The reaction of calcium and fluorine

Let us consider some additional reactions that lead to the formation of ionic bonds. The reaction between calcium atoms and fluorine atoms, discussed previously, involves the transfer of 2 electrons from 1 atom of calcium to 2 fluorine atoms.

$$\underset{(2-8-8-2)}{Ca^0} \rightarrow \underset{(2-8-8)}{Ca^{+2}} + 2\ e^-$$

$$\underset{(2-7)}{F_2^0} + 2\ e^- \rightarrow \underset{(2-8)}{2\ F^-}$$

$$Ca^0 + F_2^0 \rightarrow Ca^{+2}F_2^-$$

The species $Ca^{+2}F_2{}^-$ contains 3 ions: 1 Ca^{+2} ion and 2 F^- ions. If we represent the formula as $F^- \xleftarrow{\hspace{1cm}} \overset{+2}{Ca} \xrightarrow{\hspace{1cm}} F^-$, we show the presence of 2 bonds. We may represent the formation of sodium oxide from its elements in the same manner.

$$2\ \underset{(2-8-1)}{Na^0} \rightarrow 2\ \underset{(2-8)}{Na^+} + 2\ e^-$$

$$\frac{1}{2}\ \underset{(2-6)}{O_2{}^0} + 2\ e^- \rightarrow \underset{(2-8)}{O^{-2}}$$

$$\overline{2\ Na^0 + \frac{1}{2}\ O_2{}^0 \rightarrow Na_2{}^+O^{-2}}$$

Since an oxygen atom can gain 2 electrons and a sodium atom can lose only 1 electron, 2 sodium atoms will react with 1 atom of oxygen. The species Na_2O contains 3 ions: 2 Na^+ ions and 1 O^{-2} ion. We can represent this formula as $Na^+ \xrightarrow{\hspace{1cm}} \overset{-2}{O} \xleftarrow{\hspace{1cm}} Na^+$.

4.12 Characteristics of ionic bonds

Let us review some of the principles that govern the formation of ionic bonds.

1. An ionic bond results from the transfer of electrons from an atom of a metallic element that can attain a noble gas structure by easily losing electrons to an atom of another element that can attain a noble gas structure by gaining these electrons.
2. The number of ionic bonds formed depends on the number of moles of electrons transferred.
3. Atoms and electrons are conserved during the transfer: The number of moles of ions formed generally equals the number of moles of atoms used, and the number of moles of electrons lost equals the number of moles of electrons gained.

Under what conditions do atoms unite by the transfer of electrons? This is the same as asking, what conditions determine the formation of ionic bonds? We shall discuss this question more fully in Chapter 20. For the present, however, we will make two assumptions:

1. Atoms possessing one or two electrons in their outermost shells (that is, active metals) show a tendency to lose electrons.
2. Atoms possessing six or seven electrons in their outermost shells (that is, active nonmetals) show a tendency to gain electrons.

4.13   Bond formation by sharing of electrons

In the previous discussion, we designated the formula of fluorine as F and the formula of oxygen as O. However, monatomic fluorine and monatomic oxygen are highly unstable. Instead, as we noted, the diatomic species F_2 and O_2 occur most frequently. Similar diatomic species exist for other elemental gases such as nitrogen and chlorine. What type of bonding occurs in molecules of elemental gases?

The electron arrangement in a fluorine atom is K, 2, and L, 7. To attain greater stability, a fluorine atom can gain one electron to attain the structure of neon, a noble gas. A sample of fluorine gas contains large numbers of fluorine atoms, all of which have the same tendency to gain electrons. How can these atoms attain greater stability? Suppose a pair of electrons, constantly moving, spends an equal amount of time between the nuclei of two fluorine atoms. Using dots to represent electrons in the outermost shell of one fluorine atom and x's to represent the electrons in the outermost shell of a second fluorine atom, we can picture the situation as

$$:\overset{\bullet\bullet}{\underset{\bullet\bullet}{F}}\overset{xx}{\underset{xx}{}}F\overset{x}{\underset{x}{}}$$

(2–7)(2–7)

Note that each fluorine atom has its proper number of electrons (7) in the outermost shell. However, the electron pair designated as $\dot{x}$ "feels" the simultaneous attraction of the nuclei of both fluorine atoms. At any given instant, each fluorine atom is associated with eight electrons and has attained the structure of the noble gas neon. In other words, both fluorine atoms are sharing a pair of electrons, using them to complete their outer shells. The sharing of the same electrons by both atoms holds the atoms together. A chemical bond formed by the sharing of electrons is called a *covalent bond*.

We can represent the formation of Cl_2 and O_2 in the same fashion.

$$:\overset{\bullet\bullet}{\underset{\bullet\bullet}{Cl}}\bullet \; + \; _x\overset{xx}{\underset{xx}{Cl}}{}^x_x \longrightarrow :\overset{\bullet\bullet}{\underset{\bullet\bullet}{Cl}}\overset{xx}{\underset{xx}{}}{}^x_x Cl{}^x_x$$

(2–7)   (2–7)   one pair of
shared electrons

$$:\overset{\bullet\bullet}{O}: \; + \; _x^x\overset{xx}{O}{}^x_x \longrightarrow :\overset{\bullet\bullet}{O}{}^x_x\overset{xx}{}O{}^x_x$$

(2–6)   (2–6)   two pairs of
shared electrons

Note that the electron arrangement in the outermost shell of an oxygen atom requires two covalent bonds to form one molecule of oxygen. However, other evidence indicates that the two atoms in a molecule of O_2 share only one pair of electrons. This leaves each atom with one unpaired electron.

$$\overset{..}{\underset{\circ}{:}O\overset{x}{\underset{x}{:}}O\overset{x}{\underset{x}{}}$$

Thus far, we have restricted our discussion of covalent bonds to the union of like atoms. Different atoms may also combine by sharing electron pairs to form covalent bonds. For example, hydrogen can unite with fluorine to form hydrogen fluoride.

$$H^{\bullet} + _{x}\overset{xx}{\underset{xx}{F}}\overset{x}{\underset{x}{}} \longrightarrow H\overset{xx}{\underset{xx}{:}}\overset{x}{\underset{x}{F}}$$
$$(2\text{-}7)$$

Nitrogen can unite with hydrogen to form ammonia.

$$\overset{..}{\underset{\bullet}{\cdot}}N\cdot + 3\,H^{x} \longrightarrow H\overset{..}{\underset{\bullet\,x}{:}}N\overset{x}{:}H$$
$$(2\text{-}5)(1)H$$

4.14 Bond types in molecules

When two atoms combine, what determines whether an ionic or a covalent bond will form? Before this question can be answered, it should be emphasized that ionic bonds and covalent bonds represent two extremes in bond formation. In nature there are no pure ionic bonds or pure covalent bonds; there are only covalent bonds with a greater or lesser degree of ionic character.

The ionic character of a bond depends on the relative attractions which the bonded atoms have for electrons. In the molecule F_2, the two bonded atoms are identical and each has the same attraction for electrons. Since there is no difference in the attraction for the electron pair between the two atoms, the bond possesses minimum ionic character. This is the same as saying that the electrons are shared equally, and there is no marked tendency for one atom to lose an electron or for the other atom to gain an electron.

In a molecule of HF, the fluorine atom, which has the higher nuclear charge, has a considerably greater attraction for electrons than does the hydrogen atom. As a result, the shared electrons spend more time nearer the nucleus of the fluorine atom than to the nucleus of the hydrogen atom. The fluorine atom attains a relatively negative charge, and the hydrogen atom attains a relatively positive charge. The bond formed, therefore, has significant ionic character. (The charge that a nucleus possesses is not the only factor that determines its ability to attract electrons. Other factors, such as atomic size, will be discussed later.)

In lithium chloride, the difference in the electron attracting abilities of lithium and chlorine is sufficiently great to produce an almost complete electron transfer. Positive lithium ions (deficiency of electrons) and negative chlorine ions (excess of electrons) are formed; the compound is said to be ionic.

To summarize: The difference in the ability of atomic nuclei to attract electrons determines the nature of the bond when atoms combine.

4.15 Polar bonds

What is the bonding between the oxygen atom and the hydrogen atoms in a molecule of water? Since oxygen has the greater attraction for electrons, the shared electrons are displaced toward the oxygen and away from the hydrogen. Thus the two O—H bonds in the molecule H—O—H possess ionic character. Bonds with ionic character are also called *polar bonds*, or *polar covalent bonds*. The bonding in an HF molecule or in an H_2O molecule is an example of polar covalent bonding; the bonding in the F_2 molecule is an example of *nonpolar covalent bonding*.

4.16 Polarity and the shapes of molecules

If a bond with ionic character is present, and the entire molecule has a shape that allows one end to be relatively positive and the other end to be relatively negative, then the entire molecule is said to be *polar*, or a *dipole*. As shown in the two diagrams below, hydrogen fluoride and water are polar molecules.

$$H^+ \quad :\overset{\displaystyle \cdot\cdot}{\underset{\displaystyle \cdot\cdot}{F}}:^- \qquad\qquad :\overset{\displaystyle \cdot\cdot}{\underset{\displaystyle \cdot\cdot}{O}}:^-$$
$$H^+ \quad H^+$$

A molecule may contain bonds with ionic character (polar bonds), but the molecule as a whole may be nonpolar because of its shape. In a molecule of CO_2, the carbon-oxygen bonds have some ionic character due to the greater electron-attracting ability of the oxygen atoms. The linear (straight-line) shape of the molecule, however, cancels the polarities, and the molecule is not a dipole.

$$\ddot{O} :: \quad C \quad :: \ddot{O}$$

4.17 Stability and potential energy

When bond formation takes place, the products of the change are more stable than the starting materials. As we have discussed, stability is associated with a net decrease in the total potential energy of a system. In terms of bond formation, the potential energy of the products is less than the potential energy of the reactants; that is to say, energy is released during bond formation. Later we will investigate how energy is absorbed when bonds are broken.

The present discussion of bonding is a short introduction to the subject and is limited by our simplified nuclear model of the atom. The concepts we have discussed, however, provide a firm basis for understanding some elementary chemical changes. To a great extent, chemical reactivity involves the breaking of old bonds and the making of new bonds. The properties of different bonds and the energy involved in both their formation and rupture will be discussed more fully in subsequent chapters.

4.18 Oxidation-reduction: introduction

Historically, oxidation was considered to be a reaction in which an element united with oxygen to form an oxide. Thus rusting of iron is an example of oxidation. If heat and light accompanied the oxidation, the process was usually termed burning, or combustion. For example, calcium burns in oxygen to form an oxide of calcium, and carbon burns in oxygen to form an oxide of carbon. Both processes are accompanied by heat and light.

Thus 1 gram-atomic weight of calcium reacts with 1 gram-atomic weight of oxygen ($\frac{1}{2}$ gram-molecular weight) to form 1 gram-molecular weight of calcium oxide.

$$Ca + \frac{1}{2} O_2 \rightarrow CaO$$

Similarly, 1 gram-atomic weight of carbon reacts with 2 gram-atomic weights of oxygen (1 gram-molecular weight) to form 1 gram-molecular weight of carbon dioxide.

$$C + O_2 \rightarrow CO_2$$

In each reaction, both elements undergo a chemical change. The change of calcium to calcium oxide—that is, the addition of oxygen—was called oxidation. The change of oxygen to calcium oxide—that is, the removal of oxygen—was called reduction. This meant that in any reaction involving oxidation, there was a corresponding reduction. The same reasoning was applied to the conversion of carbon to carbon dioxide.

It should be mentioned that the addition or removal of calcium, in the formation of calcium oxide, and the addition or removal of carbon, in the formation of carbon dioxide, could also be used as a basis for describing the nature of the chemical changes.

4.19 Oxidation-reduction: according to the nuclear model

The nuclear model of the atom casts considerably more light on the reactions just described. For example, when calcium reacts with oxygen, 2 electrons are transferred from a calcium atom to an oxygen atom.

$$\underset{(2-8-8-2)}{Ca} + \frac{1}{2} \underset{(2-6)}{O_2} \rightarrow Ca^{+2}O^{-2}$$

This reaction, in which a calcium atom has lost 2 electrons while an oxygen atom has gained 2 electrons, can also be shown as

$$\underset{(2-8-8-2)}{Ca} \rightarrow \underset{(2-8-8)}{Ca^{+2}} + 2\ e^-$$

$$\frac{1}{2} \underset{(2-6)}{O_2} + 2\ e^- \rightarrow \underset{(2-8)}{O^{-2}}$$

On the basis of electron transfer, it is now possible to look upon oxidation and reduction in a more generalized manner: *Oxidation is any reaction in which a particle (atom or ion) loses electrons. Reduction is any reaction in which a particle gains electrons.*

Electron transfer involves the loss of electrons by one particle and the gain of electrons by another; therefore, *every* oxidation must be accompanied by a corresponding reduction.

Since calcium atoms lost electrons to oxygen atoms, calcium atoms were oxidized. Since oxygen atoms gained electrons lost by calcium atoms, oxygen atoms were reduced. In this reaction, calcium is called the reducing agent, and oxygen is called the oxidizing agent.

4.20 Oxidation-reduction: summary and limitations

Let us summarize the oxidation-reduction relationship as far as we have developed it:

1. Oxidation is any reaction in which a particle loses electrons.
2. Reduction is any reaction in which a particle gains electrons.
3. The oxidizing agent is always reduced while the reducing agent is always oxidized.
4. In any oxidation-reduction reaction, electrons are conserved; that is, the number of electrons lost equals the number of electrons gained.

Applying these ideas to the oxidation of carbon to form carbon dioxide, CO_2, we may represent the changes that occur as follows: (The numbers above the symbols represent the deficiency or excess of electrons resulting from the transfer or the sharing of electrons.)

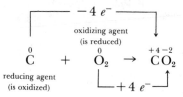

We have assumed in this reaction that electrons are transferred from carbon atoms to oxygen atoms. This is merely a convenient way to show that oxidation-reduction has occurred. Actually, CO_2 is a covalently bonded molecule in which a single carbon atom shares two electron pairs with each of two oxygen atoms.

In a later chapter, we will reconsider the whole concept of oxidation-reduction from the point of view of oxidation state or oxidation number. However, at present, one very important thought must be stressed: The oxidation-reduction model consists of ideas devised by chemists to interpret certain chemical changes. Oxidation-reduction is an explanation, not an experimental observation. Therefore, in some cases, the ideas of oxidation-reduction may have considerable limitation or imperfection.

Multiple-Choice Questions

1. If two atoms exert equal attractions for electrons, they form (1) a nonpolar covalent bond (2) an ionic bond (3) a polar covalent bond (4) no bond

2. An element has the following numbers of electrons in its shells: 2–8–8–2. The element (1) is a nonmetal (2) forms an ion with a charge of +2 (3) can accept two electrons (4) forms a negative ion

3. The number of bonds formed by an atom is most closely associated with (1) its atomic weight (2) the number of electrons in the atom (3) the number of electron shells (4) the number of electrons in the outer shell

4. When Mg unites with Br, there is a transfer of two electrons from each Mg atom to each of two Br atoms. From this, we reason that (1) the Br atom has seven electrons in its outer shell (2) two covalent bonds form (3) the Mg atom is larger than the Br atom (4) two ions form

5. The equation $Mg^0 + Cl_2{}^0 \rightarrow Mg^{+2}Cl_2{}^-$ indicates that (1) Mg receives two electrons from Cl (2) Mg and Cl form covalent bonds (3) Mg is reduced (4) a species forms that contains three ions

6. All chemical changes involve (1) decreased stability (2) electron sharing (3) formation of ions (4) breaking bonds and forming bonds

7. The bond formed by two atoms of the same element is (1) ionic (2) polar covalent (3) impossible to predict (4) nonpolar covalent

8. The equation $Na^0 + Cl^0 \rightarrow Na^+Cl^-$ represents (1) the change taking place when an electron is transferred from Na to Cl (2) the sharing of electrons by Na and Cl (3) the transfer of a proton from Cl to Na (4) the transfer of an electron from Cl to Na

9. When atoms unite (1) electrons are transferred from one atom to another atom (2) a metal and nonmetal combine (3) the product is more stable than the separate atoms (4) heat is absorbed

10. Which statement indicates the difference between the two diagrams for element X?

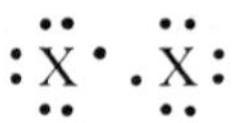

$$:\overset{..}{X}{}^{\cdot}.\overset{..}{\underset{..}{X}}:\qquad\qquad:\overset{..}{\underset{..}{X}}:\overset{..}{\underset{..}{X}}:$$

Figure 1 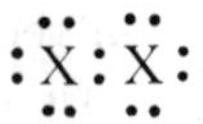   Figure 2

(1) Figure 1 has a larger number of electrons than Figure 2. (2) The two atoms in Figure 2 are united by a pair of shared electrons. (3) Figure 2 shows the formation of ions. (4) The atoms are more stable in Figure 1.

11. The mass number of an element is the number of (1) protons and neutrons in the nucleus (2) free protons in the nucleus (3) electrons and protons in the nucleus (4) electrons in all the shells

12. A characteristic of the noble gases is that they all (1) have eight electrons in the outer shell (2) have low stability (3) form many compounds (4) have stable outer electron shells

13. As the atomic numbers of elements increase, the numbers of electrons in the outer shells (1) decrease (2) increase (3) do not change (4) cannot be determined without additional information

14. The letters *K, L, M, N* in the structures of atoms represent (1) electron shells (2) the symbols for the elements (3) the arrangement of neutrons (4) the number of electrons in the outer shell

15. A characteristic of the nucleus of an atom is that (1) its mass is small compared to the mass of the atom (2) it contains all the electrons of the atom (3) it has a positive charge equal to the atomic number (4) the electrons and the protons balance each other

16. Mass number refers to the number of (1) electrons in an atoms (2) electrons and protons in an atom (3) neutrons and protons in the nucleus (4) atoms in a mole

17. Which of the following is a characteristic of an atom? (1) An atom is the smallest particle of matter. (2) All atoms are alike. (3) All atoms have the same weight, which equals 1 awu. (4) An atom is the smallest particle of an element with the properties of the element.

18. Which of the following is *not* a polar molecule? (1) hydrogen fluoride (2) water (3) hydrogen (4) ammonia (NH_3)

Completion Questions

1. *a.* Molecules such as Cl_2, which contain two atoms per molecule, are called _____ molecules.

   b. The two atoms are held together by a bond consisting of two shared _____.

   c. This type of chemical bond is called a (an) _____ bond.

   d. The energy of the resulting molecule is _____ (*greater, less*) than the energy of the two separate atoms.

2. *a.* The chemical activity of a metal involves the transfer of _____ to a nonmetal.

   b. The metal becomes an ion with a (an) _____ charge, and the nonmetal acquires a (an) _____ charge.

3. The reaction $Fe^0 + \frac{1}{2} O_2^0 \rightarrow Fe^{+2} O^{-2}$ represents oxidation-reduction because an atom of Fe has _____ (*gained, lost*) two electrons, which represents _____; while an atom of oxygen has _____ two electrons, which represents _____.

4. *a.* One calcium atom unites with two atoms of fluorine because the calcium atom possesses _____ electrons in its outer shell which are transferred to the fluorine atom.

   b. Each fluorine atom possesses _____ electrons in its outer shell.

5. *a.* Two major differences between the proton and the electron are the difference in their charge and the difference in their _____.

   b. The charge of the electron is _____, while the charge of the proton is _____.

   c. The _____ of the proton is about 1837 times greater than that of the electron.

6. *a.* The chief difference between a proton and a neutron is that the proton _____, while the neutron _____.

   b. A similarity between the proton and neutron is that they both _____.

7. The table of atomic weights shows that _____ is an element having atoms with a mass approximately twice as great as the mass of oxygen atoms.

8. Some important rules relating the chemical properties of elements and the number of electrons in their outer shells are:

   a. If the outer shell contains _____, the element is a noble gas.

   b. If the outer shell contains _____, the element is a metal.

   c. If the outer shell contains _____, the element is a nonmetal.

Exercises for Review

1. The reaction between barium and chlorine involves the following electron changes:

$$Ba^0 \rightarrow Ba^{+2} + 2\ e^-$$

$$Cl_2^0 + 2\ e^- \rightarrow 2\ Cl^-$$

   a. Write an equation for the total reaction.

   b. How many moles are indicated by the equation for each species involved in the reaction?

2. *a.* Explain the difference between metals and nonmetals in terms of their electron structures.

   b. Do metals show a tendency to unite with each other? Explain.

3. *a.* Draw diagrams showing the particles in the nucleus and the electron arrangement for the three elements X, Y, and Z.

ELEMENT	ATOMIC NUMBER	MASS NUMBER
X	11	23
Y	16	32
Z	10	20

b. Which of these elements will unite?

c. What is the formula of the compound formed?

d. What type of bond(s) form(s)? Why?

4. Suggest a reason to account for the fact that electrons, rather than protons, are transferred during chemical change.

5. Write electron-dot formulas for (*a*) neon (*b*) hydrogen chloride (*c*) carbon dioxide (*d*) magnesium chloride (*e*) carbon tetrafluoride

6. *a.* Does the simple nuclear model of the atom explain the polarity of bonds? Explain.

 b. Does the simple nuclear model of the atom explain the polarity of molecules? Explain.

7. Suggest a simple model that can help to explain why systems tend to become more stable.

8. What is the relationship between the amount of energy liberated during bond-making as compared to the amount of energy absorbed during bond-breaking? Explain.

9. Can the same atom form positive as well as negative ions? Explain, citing examples.

10. Given the reaction $2 A + B_2 \rightarrow 2 AB$.

 a. Which particle is the oxidizing agent?

 b. Which particle is the reducing agent?

 c. Which particle is oxidized?

 d. Which particle is reduced?

 Justify all your answers.

Exercises for Further Study

1. *a.* Explain the difference between oxidation and reduction, both in terms of electrons and in terms of the older concepts.

 b. Which interpretation is more general? Why?

2. Why can it be said that when we describe a chemical change, we describe the manner in which chemical bonds are broken and new bonds are formed?

3. What energy changes take place when elements X and Y unite to form the very stable compound XY? Explain.

4. Why do atoms of the same element or very similar elements unite only by covalent bonding?

5. The bonds in Cl_2 and LiCl represent two extreme bond types. Why do the bonds formed by the various elements represent a gradual variation between these extremes?

6. Indicate some of the limitations of the simple nuclear model of the atom.
7. Explain why the noble gases form monatomic molecules, whereas gases such as chlorine and fluorine form diatomic molecules.
8. Why is it unlikely for a chemical reaction to proceed without an energy accompaniment?
9. Why must charge be conserved in oxidation-reduction reactions?
10. Explain why oxidation-reduction is considered to be merely an explanation of a phenomenon, not an observation of the phenomenon.

Chapter 5

FORMULAS AND EQUATIONS: THE MOLE CONCEPT

5.1 Introduction

We have learned that atoms may combine to form molecules by the transfer of electrons or by the sharing of pairs of electrons. Chapter 3 described how the chemist utilizes an abbreviation, called a symbol, to designate specific atoms. We learned that he uses a combination of these symbols with proper subscripts, called a formula, to designate specific molecules. The electron structures of the combining atoms determine the numbers of atoms that unite, giving us the subscripts used in the formulas of molecules. In this chapter, we will learn how to write formulas and then how to use these formulas in writing equations. We will use a common chemical change—burning—to illustrate these ideas.

5.2 Burning and oxidation

The process of burning has been presented as a special type of oxidation in which (1) the element that burns loses electrons; and (2) the element oxygen, which supports burning, gains electrons. Let us assume that element E unites with oxygen, O, to form the oxide E_aO_b. In the formula E_aO_b, a represents the number of atoms of E, and b represents the number of atoms of O. We can describe the oxidation of E as

$$a\,E + b\,O \rightarrow E_aO_b$$

For example, magnesium, Mg, burns in oxygen, O, to form magnesium oxide. Magnesium, atomic number 12, tends to lose two electrons to attain the structure of the noble gas neon. Oxygen, atomic number 8, tends to gain two electrons to attain the structure of neon. Therefore, one atom of magnesium will unite with one atom of oxygen to form one molecule of magnesium oxide. Note that the total number of electrons lost equals the total number of electrons gained. Thus electric charge has been conserved during the transfer of electrons. The reaction may be represented as

$$Mg + O \rightarrow MgO$$

Remember that we are temporarily using the symbol O to represent oxygen gas. As noted earlier, oxygen gas exists as the molecule O_2. The equation for the burning of magnesium may be written

$$Mg + \frac{1}{2} O_2 \rightarrow MgO$$

5.3 Combining capacities of atoms: valence numbers

Consider again the burning of magnesium. In losing two electrons, magnesium becomes an ion with a charge of +2; oxygen, in gaining two electrons, becomes an ion with a charge of −2. The number of electrons an atom loses or gains in forming a molecule of a compound represents the *combining capacity*, or *valence number*, of the atom.

The atom that loses electrons has a positive combining capacity, or positive valence number. The atom that gains electrons has a negative combining capacity, or negative valence number. For example, the valence number of Mg is +2, and the valence number of O is −2. When magnesium burns to form magnesium oxide, the formula E_aO_b becomes MgO. The subscript a, denoting the number of atoms of E, is 1; and the subscript b, denoting the number of atoms of O, is also 1.

When aluminum combines with oxygen, each aluminum atom tends to lose 3 electrons, whereas each oxygen atom can gain only 2 electrons. The valence number of aluminum is +3, and the valence number of oxygen is −2. To conserve charge, 2 atoms of aluminum, Al, combine with 3 atoms of oxygen to form the molecule Al_2O_3. During the change, 2 atoms of Al lose 6 electrons, and 3 atoms of O gain 6 electrons.

$$2\ Al + 3\ O \rightarrow Al_2O_3$$

or

$$2\ Al + \frac{3}{2} O_2 \rightarrow Al_2O_3$$

The combining capacity of an atom—the number of electrons it can gain or lose—may be predicted from its electron structure. Up to this point, we have used the term *valence number* to denote the number of electrons that represents the combining capacity of an atom through electron transfer. Atoms may also combine by electron sharing.

5.4 Valence number includes sharing of electrons

By sharing two pairs of electrons, a chlorine molecule (atomic number 17) can unite with an oxygen atom to form an oxide of chlorine. Using dots to represent the electrons in the outermost shell of chlorine and x's to represent the electrons in the outermost shell of oxygen, we may illustrate the change as

$$2 \, \overset{..}{:} \overset{.}{\underset{..}{Cl}} \cdot \; + \; \underset{xx}{\overset{xx}{_x O _x}} \longrightarrow \; \overset{..}{:} \underset{..}{Cl} \overset{xx}{\underset{xx}{_x^x O _x^x}} \overset{..}{Cl} \overset{..}{:}$$

chlorine   oxygen   dichlorine monoxide

Note that chlorine has a combining capacity of 1, and oxygen has a combining capacity of 2. Similarly, hydrogen, atomic number 1, may combine with chlorine by sharing a pair of electrons to form hydrogen chloride.

$$H^{\, x} \; + \; . \overset{..}{\underset{..}{Cl}} : \; \longrightarrow \; H \overset{..}{\underset{..}{_x^{} Cl}} :$$

We have now extended the concept of valence number to include the sharing of electrons.

In summary, the term *valence number* represents the number of electrons an atom can donate, receive, or share during a reaction. Electron transfer describes both the donating and the receiving of electrons since both processes occur simultaneously. Electron transfer results in the formation of oppositely charged ions. Electron sharing results in the formation of covalently bonded molecules of varying polarity.

The table that follows lists elements that combine to form compounds by electron transfer or electron sharing.

ELEMENT	SYMBOL	VALENCE NUMBER
lithium	Li	+1
sodium	Na	+1
potassium	K	+1
calcium	Ca	+2
magnesium	Mg	+2
aluminum	Al	+3
fluorine	F	−1
chlorine	Cl	−1
oxygen	O	−2
sulfur	S	−2

5.5 Writing formulas for binary compounds

A *binary compound* consists of only two elements. The formula of a molecule of a binary compound may be written if the valence numbers of the combining atoms are known. The following steps are helpful:

1. Write the symbols for the atoms of the elements that are combining. It is customary for the symbol of the element that has the positive valence number to precede the symbol of the element that has the negative valence number. Suppose we want to write the formula for aluminum sulfide. The symbols for the elements in this compound are written

$$\text{Al S}$$

2. Write the valence number above each symbol as a superscript.

$$\text{Al}^{+3}\text{S}^{-2}$$

3. Crisscross the valence numbers and omit the charge signs. Write the resulting numbers below the symbols as subscripts.

$$\text{Al}_2\text{S}_3$$

Note that crisscrossing the valence numbers conserves charge. Thus the sum of the valence numbers of 2 Al^{+3} atoms is +6; the sum of 3 S^{-2} atoms is −6. The algebraic sum (+6 − 6) is zero. *The algebraic sum of the valence numbers of the atoms in a compound is zero.*

4. When each element has the same valence number, these numbers are dropped, and the formula is correct as written in step 1.

$\text{K}^{+1}\text{Cl}^{-1}$ represents K_1Cl_1, written KCl.

$\text{Mg}^{+2}\text{O}^{-2}$ represents Mg_2O_2, written MgO.

The procedure that we have suggested is useful but tentative. As we continue our study, the concept of valence number will be modified.

We can now represent the formulas of compounds formed by the burning of some specific elements.

1. Burning of lithium

$$2\ \underset{(2\text{-}1)}{\text{Li}} + \frac{1}{2}\ \underset{(2\text{-}6)}{\text{O}_2} \rightarrow \underset{\substack{\text{lithium} \\ \text{oxide}}}{\text{Li}_2\text{O}}$$

2. Burning of calcium

$$\underset{(2\text{-}8\text{-}8\text{-}2)}{\text{Ca}} + \frac{1}{2}\ \underset{(2\text{-}6)}{\text{O}_2} \rightarrow \underset{\substack{\text{calcium} \\ \text{oxide}}}{\text{CaO}}$$

3. Burning of aluminum

$$2\ \underset{(2\text{-}8\text{-}3)}{\text{Al}} + \frac{3}{2}\ \underset{(2\text{-}6)}{\text{O}_2} \rightarrow \underset{\substack{\text{aluminum} \\ \text{oxide}}}{\text{Al}_2\text{O}_3}$$

5.6 Writing formulas for compounds containing more than two elements

Most common compounds generally contain two or three elements. Compounds that contain three elements are called *ternary compounds*. Such compounds are usually held together by both ionic and covalent bonds. For example, sodium hydroxide is a ternary compound containing Na, O, and H. Using a dot to represent the electron in the outermost shell of Na, z's to represent the electrons in the outermost shell of O, and x to represent the electron in the outermost shell of H, we can write the electron formula for sodium hydroxide, NaOH, as

$$\left[\text{Na}\right]^{+} \left[\overset{zz}{\underset{zz}{:}} \overset{}{\underset{}{O}} \overset{x}{\underset{}{:}} H\right]^{-}$$

We see that the single electron in the outermost shell of Na is transferred to OH, forming Na^+ ions and OH^- ions that are held together by ionic bonds. Note also that O and H share a pair of electrons, forming a covalent bond. A combination of atoms that is covalently bonded and possesses a charge is called a *polyatomic ion*, or *radical*. Examples of some polyatomic ions and their valence numbers appear in the table that follows.

POLYATOMIC ION	FORMULA	VALENCE NUMBER
hydroxide	OH	-1
chlorate	ClO_3	-1
nitrate	NO_3	-1
carbonate	CO_3	-2
sulfate	SO_4	-2
phosphate	PO_4	-3

Using the procedure in section 5.5 for writing the formulas of binary compounds, we can write the formulas for some ternary compounds. If we consider the polyatomic ion to behave as a single unit, we can follow the procedure for writing the formulas of binary compounds.

Sodium hydroxide contains sodium ions and hydroxide ions, which we can write as Na^+ $(OH)^-$. Parentheses around the polyatomic ion indicate that it is treated as a single unit. Crisscrossing the valence numbers and dropping the signs produce the formula $Na_1(OH)_1$, which is written conventionally as NaOH.

Similarly, the formula for calcium nitrate is $Ca(NO_3)_2$. The subscript 2 appears outside the parentheses and signifies the presence of 2 NO_3^- ions. This means we have a total of 9 atoms (1 Ca + 2 N + 6 O) and 3 ions (1 Ca^{+2} and 2 NO_3^-) in the formula. In the same manner, the formula for aluminum sulfate becomes $Al_2(SO_4)_3$ for a total of 17 atoms (2 Al + 3 S + 12 O) and 5 ions (2 Al^{+3} and 3 SO_4^{-2}).

5.7 Calculating an unknown valence number in a binary compound

We have already noted that the algebraic sum of all the valence numbers in a compound is zero. For example, the formula for aluminum oxide is Al_2O_3. The table on page 65 shows that Al has a valence number of $+3$. Two Al ions have a total valence number of 2 × ($+3$), or $+6$. Three O ions have a total valence number of 3 × (-2), or -6. The algebraic sum of all the valence numbers is zero ($+6 - 6$).

Suppose we have an oxide with the formula N_2O_4. What is the valence number of N? The same table shows that O has a valence number of -2. Since four O atoms have a total valence number of -8, the total valence number of N is $+8$. The formula N_2O_4 reveals the presence of two N atoms; each N atom therefore has a valence number of $+4$. In this way, the algebraic sum of all the valence numbers is zero ($+8 - 8$).

5.8 Calculating an unknown valence number in a ternary compound

We may find the valence number of an atom in a ternary compound by using the method outlined in section 5.7. Consider the formula $KMnO_4$ (potassium permanganate). What is the valence number of Mn? The table on page 65 shows that K has a valence number of $+1$. O has a valence number of -2, and four O atoms have a total valence number of -8. The valence number of Mn is that number which, when added to the algebraic sum of $+1$ and -8, produces a total algebraic sum of zero. Since $+1$ added to -8 equals -7, Mn has a valence number of $+7$. If Mn in $KMnO_4$ has a valence number of $+7$, the valence number of the MnO_4^- ion (permanganate ion) must be ($+7 - 8$), or -1. Similarly, the valence number of each Cr (chromium) atom in $K_2Cr_2O_7$ (potassium dichromate) is $+6$ $\left[\overset{+2}{K_2} \overset{+12}{Cr_2} \overset{-14}{O_7} \right]$.

Atoms of certain elements, such as copper, form ions with different charges. The atoms of such elements have electron structures that permit more than one valence number. For example, copper has the valence numbers $+1$ and $+2$, forming Cu^+ and Cu^{+2} ions. Iron has the valence numbers $+2$ and $+3$, forming Fe^{+2} and Fe^{+3} ions. At this time we need not concern ourselves with the reasons for this behavior, but we should recognize that it exists.

5.9 Types of formulas

From the table of valence numbers (see page 65), we determine that the formula for sodium chloride is NaCl. How can we be sure that the formula is NaCl and not Na_2Cl_2 or Na_3Cl_3 or Na_xCl_x? In other words, how do we know the exact number of atoms present? Valence numbers permit us to write only the simplest formula of a compound, called the empirical formula. *The empirical formula reveals the relative number of atoms or the percentage by weight of each element in a compound.*

To fix the total number of atoms in a molecule, we have to know the molecular weight of the compound. For example, if the molecular weight of sodium chloride is 58.5 (Na = 23 and Cl = 35.5), the formula must be Na_1Cl_1, or NaCl. Any other formula would indicate an incorrect molecular weight. Thus the molecular weight helps us to write the molecular formula. *The molecular formula denotes the composition of a molecule and the exact number of atoms that are present.*

Nitrogen and oxygen form two compounds that have the same empirical formula, nitrogen dioxide and dinitrogen tetroxide. What is the molecular formula of dinitrogen tetroxide? Since the molecular weight of dinitrogen tetroxide is 92, the molecular formula for dinitrogen tetroxide is N_2O_4, not NO_2 (molecular weight = 46).

5.10 Chemical nomenclature

In this book, we will study for the most part binary and ternary compounds. Chemists have devised a system for naming these compounds, one that facilitates our understanding of chemistry. The following rules will be helpful in using this system:

1. All binary compounds have names that end in *-ide*.

   calcium chloride, $CaCl_2$ hydrogen fluoride, HF
   magnesium nitride, Mg_3N_2 lithium sulfide, Li_2S

2. The valence number of a metallic element with more than one valence number is written in Roman numerals in parentheses following the name of the element.

   copper(I) chloride, CuCl   iron(II) sulfate, $FeSO_4$
   copper (II) chloride, $CuCl_2$ iron(III) sulfate, $Fe_2(SO_4)_3$

   Such compounds may also be described by an older system of nomenclature that uses the suffix *-ous* to represent the element in its lower valence number and the suffix *-ic* to represent the element in its higher valence number.

   cuprous chloride, CuCl   ferrous sulfate, $FeSO_4$
   cupric chloride, $CuCl_2$ ferric sulfate, $Fe_2(SO_4)_3$

Note that the Roman numeral in parentheses gives the actual valence number. On the other hand, the identifying suffix merely indicates the lower or higher valence number.

3. Ternary compounds containing covalently bonded oxygen may have names that end with the suffix *-ate* or with the suffix *-ite*. The *-ite* compound generally contains one less atom of oxygen than the *-ate* compound.

> lithium nitrite, $LiNO_2$ sodium sulfite, Na_2SO_3
> lithium nitrate, $LiNO_3$ sodium sulfate, Na_2SO_4

The existence of an *-ate* compound does not mean that a corresponding *-ite* compound must also exist. For example, although sodium carbonate, Na_2CO_3, exists, no corresponding *-ite* compound is known.

4. In naming compounds, prefixes such as *mon(o)-, di-, tri-, tetr(a)-, pent(a)-,* and *dec(a)-* are employed to designate a specific number of atoms, 1, 2, 3, 4, 5, and 10, respectively.

> mononitrogen oxide, NO carbon monoxide, CO
> dinitrogen oxide, N_2O carbon dioxide, CO_2
> dinitrogen trioxide, N_2O_3 sulfur trioxide, SO_3
> dinitrogen pentoxide, N_2O_5
> tetraphosphorus decoxide, P_4O_{10}

5.11 Using the mole concept

We have said that the symbol of an element represents 1 atomic weight of the element. We then extended this idea to define the gram-atomic weight of an element as a quantity equal to the atomic weight of the element expressed in grams. For example, when we say the atomic weight of sodium is 23, it is the same as saying that 23 grams represent 1 gram-atomic weight of sodium. Similarly, the molecular formula of a substance represents 1 gram-molecular weight of the substance. The formula $NaCl$ represents 58.5 grams of sodium chloride.

The chemist uses the term *mole* to represent different quantities, such as:
The gram-atomic weight of a monatomic element; for example, Li.
The gram-molecular weight of a polyatomic element; for example, Cl_2.
The gram-molecular weight of a compound; for example, $LiCl$.
The gram-ionic weight of an ion; for example, NO_3^-.

Thus the symbol O represents 1 mole of oxygen atoms, weighing 16 grams. The formula O_2 represents 2 moles of oxygen atoms, weighing 32 grams, or 1 mole of oxygen molecules, weighing 32 grams.

The weight of 2 moles of CO_2 (carbon dioxide) is

$$2 \text{ moles} \times \frac{(12 + 32) \text{ grams}}{\text{mole}} = 88 \text{ grams}$$

The weight of 0.1 mole of $CaSO_4$ (calcium sulfate) is

$$0.1 \text{ mole} \times \frac{(40 + 32 + 64) \text{ grams}}{\text{mole}} = 13.6 \text{ grams}$$

5.12 Using Avogadro's number

Broadly speaking, a mole represents a specific number of particles. This number, which we first studied in section 3.11, is Avogadro's number; it equals 6.02×10^{23} particles. Because it is inconvenient to work with so large a number, chemists prefer to use the weight that corresponds to this quantity of particles.

Since atoms are the fundamental particles in elements, a mole of Na represents Avogadro's number of Na atoms. The weight of this number of atoms is the gram-atomic weight of Na; 6.02×10^{23} atoms of Na weigh 23 grams. A mole of O_2 represents Avogadro's number of oxygen molecules. A mole of CO_2 represents Avogadro's number of carbon dioxide molecules. In both instances, the weight of the mole of molecules equals the gram-molecular weight.

The equation $Cl_2 + 2\ e^- \rightarrow 2\ Cl^-$ now reads: 1 mole of chlorine molecules + 2 moles of electrons form 2 moles of chloride ions.

We have seen that a mole of particles is the weight of Avogadro's number of the particles. Thus moles may refer to Avogadro's number of atoms, molecules, electrons, or any other particles. Although it is impossible to conceive the magnitude of the Avogadro number, the mole concept is one of the most widely used tools of the chemist.

5.13 What is a chemical equation?

Consider the burning of magnesium.

$$Mg + \frac{1}{2} O_2 \rightarrow MgO$$

The expression $Mg + \frac{1}{2} O_2 \rightarrow MgO$ is called a chemical equation. A *chemical equation* is the proper combination of symbols and formulas of the reactants and products involved in a chemical change. Note that the reactants appear on the left side of the equation, and the products appear on the right side. The arrow, as noted previously, means yields or forms.

The root *equa-* in the word *equation* suggests that a chemical equation involves equalities between specific quantities of reactants and products. A chemical equation is indeed a quantitative statement. The number of atoms appearing in the reactants must equal the number of atoms appearing in the products (conservation of atoms). Since the symbols for atoms represent gram-atomic weights, we can state: In an equation, the sum of all the gram-atomic weights in the reactants equals the sum of all the gram-atomic weights in the products.

5.14 Conserving atoms and energy in a chemical equation

Consider the reaction:

$$A + B_2 \rightarrow AB$$

Note that atoms of A and atoms of B have combined to form molecules of AB. In addition, energy may be absorbed or liberated. In the equation that described this reaction, we must conserve both atoms and energy.

To conserve atoms, it is usually necessary to balance the reaction by using numerical coefficients written before the symbols and formulas. The balanced reaction becomes

$$2\,A + B_2 \rightarrow 2\,AB$$

To conserve energy, let us consider the energy present in the reactants and the energy present in the product. We will assume that the energy contained in each is different. Furthermore, let us express the energy contained in the reactants and in the product as heat energy.

$$\underbrace{2\,A + B_2}_{\substack{3000 \\ \text{calories}}} \rightarrow \underbrace{2\,AB}_{\substack{2000 \\ \text{calories}}}$$

To conserve energy, the balanced reaction must show the proper energy term, that is, whether energy is absorbed or liberated. The balanced reaction now becomes

$$2\,A + B_2 \rightarrow 2\,AB + \text{heat}$$

If we knew the energy (heat) content of the reactants and product, we could show the magnitude of the energy term. Thus:

$$2\,A + B_2 \rightarrow 2\,AB + 1000 \text{ calories}$$

The states of the reactants and products also contribute to the magnitude of the energy term. For example, energy is absorbed in going from solid to liquid to gas; energy is liberated in going from gas to liquid to solid. This means that we must indicate the state of each reactant and each product in a reaction. We shall do this by writing (s) for solid, (l) for liquid, and (g) for gas after each substance in an equation.

Let us return to the reaction for the burning of magnesium to see how atoms and energy are conserved. We have mentioned previously that naturally occurring oxygen is diatomic. Let us rewrite the equation for the burning of magnesium, using O_2 as the proper formula for the gas and using whole-number coefficients.

$$2 \text{ Mg }(s) + O_2\ (g) \rightarrow 2 \text{ MgO }(s) + \text{heat}$$

The equation now reads that 2 atomic weights of solid Mg react with 2 atomic weights (1 molecular weight) of gaseous O to form 2 molecular weights of solid MgO (2 atomic weights of Mg + 2 atomic weights of O). Note that magnesium and oxygen atoms have been conserved and the reaction liberates energy. Applying the mole concept to the equation, we can say that 2 moles of Mg react with 1 mole of O_2 to form 2 moles of MgO.

5.15 Oxidation and reduction half-reactions

In a chemical equation, charge must be conserved as well as atoms. Let us reexamine the equation for the burning of magnesium from an electron point of view.

A magnesium atom loses 2 electrons to form a magnesium ion.

$$\underset{(2\text{-}8\text{-}2)}{Mg^0} \rightarrow \underset{(2\text{-}8)}{Mg^{+2}} + 2\ e^-$$

This reaction is only the part of the total reaction in which electrons are lost; it is called the *oxidation partial reaction*, or the *oxidation half-reaction.*

A molecule of oxygen gains 4 electrons (each atom gains 2 electrons) to become 2 oxygen ions.

$$\underset{(2\text{-}6)}{O_2{}^0} + 4\ e^- \rightarrow \underset{(2\text{-}8)}{2\ O^{-2}}$$

This part of the reaction, in which electrons are gained, is called the *reduction partial reaction*, or the *reduction half-reaction.*

The algebraic sum of the number of electrons involved in the oxidation half-reaction and the number of electrons involved in the reduction half-reaction equals zero. This is the same as saying: In a chemical equation, the number of electrons lost equals the number of electrons gained; that is, charge is conserved.

The half-reactions can now be rewritten as

OXIDATION $\qquad$ $2\ Mg^0 \rightarrow 2\ Mg^{+2} + 4\ e^-$

REDUCTION $\qquad$ $O_2{}^0 + 4\ e^- \rightarrow 2\ O^{-2}$

When we add both sides of each equation and indicate the proper physical states, the net equation becomes

$$2\ Mg^0\ (s) + O_2{}^0\ (g) \rightarrow 2\ Mg^{+2}O^{-2}\ (s)$$

5.16 Using the mole concept in an equation

The burning of magnesium may also be expressed by the equation

$$\overset{0}{Mg} + \frac{1}{2}\overset{0}{O_2} \rightarrow \overset{+2\ -2}{MgO}$$

with $-2\ e^-$ transferred to O_2 and $+2\ e^-$ returned.

This equation states that 1 mole of Mg reacts with $\frac{1}{2}$ mole of O_2 to form 1 mole of MgO. Equations showing half moles of reactants are frequently used to indicate the energy change associated with the formation of 1 mole of product. Note that the coefficients enable us to conserve atoms and to conserve charge. Generally speaking, however, the coefficients in an equation are the smallest whole numbers that can conserve atoms and charge.

Since all reactions that involve burning produce heat, the complete equation showing that energy is conserved may be written as

$$Mg\ (s) + \frac{1}{2}\ O_2\ (g) \rightarrow MgO\ (s) + heat$$

5.17 Solving problems involving moles

The mole concept expresses the relationship between the weight and the number of particles in a chemical equation. (We shall see later that this concept also applies to the volume relationships of reactions between gases.) At this time, let us consider some simple problems involving the weights of reactants and the weights of products in a chemical change.

Suppose 1 mole of aluminum is completely burned in oxygen. How many moles of oxygen are consumed and how many moles of aluminum oxide are formed?

The symbols and formulas that express the reactants and products in the change are

$$Al\ (s) + O_2\ (g) \rightarrow Al_2O_3\ (s)$$

When the proper coefficients are introduced to conserve atoms and to conserve charge, the equation becomes

$$2 \text{ Al } (s) + \frac{3}{2} O_2 \ (g) \rightarrow Al_2O_3 \ (s)$$

The complete equation with the proper energy term is

$$2 \text{ Al } (s) + \frac{3}{2} O_2 \ (g) \rightarrow Al_2O_3 \ (s) + \text{heat}$$

The equation tells us that 2 moles of Al react with 1.5 moles of O_2 to form 1 mole of Al_2O_3, and heat is liberated. If instead of 2 moles of Al, 1 mole of Al were completely burned, 0.75 mole of O_2 would be consumed, and 0.5 mole of Al_2O_3 would be formed.

The fractional coefficient may be eliminated by multiplying each coefficient by 2 and rewriting the equation as

$$4 \text{ Al } (s) + 3 \ O_2 \ (g) \rightarrow 2 \ Al_2O_3 \ (s) + \text{heat}$$

Now let us reword the problem. How many grams of aluminum oxide are formed when 1 mole of aluminum is completely burned? From the solution to the previous problem, we note that 0.5 mole of Al_2O_3 is formed. We are now required to find the weight, in grams, of 0.5 mole of Al_2O_3. The table of atomic weights (see page 39) reveals that 1 mole of Al_2O_3 (2 Al + 3 O) weighs 102 grams.

$$0.5 \text{ mole } Al_2O_3 = 102 \ \frac{\text{grams}}{\text{mole}} \times 0.5 \text{ mole} = 51 \text{ grams}$$

Thus when 1 mole of Al is burned, 51 grams of Al_2O_3 are formed. What is the weight of the aluminum?

$$1 \text{ mole of Al} = 27 \text{ grams}$$

The equation also shows that $\frac{1}{2}$ of $\frac{3}{2}$ of a mole, or $\frac{3}{4}$ of a mole, of oxygen is used up when 1 mole of Al is burned. What is the weight of the oxygen?

$$\frac{3}{4} \text{ mole of } O_2 = 32 \ \frac{\text{grams}}{\text{mole}} \times \frac{3}{4} \text{ mole} = 24 \text{ grams}$$

The solutions to the problems reveal that 27 grams of aluminum (1 mole) react with 24 grams of oxygen ($\frac{3}{4}$ of a mole) to form 51 grams of aluminum oxide ($\frac{1}{2}$ of a mole). Since we have conserved mass (atoms), we can be reasonably certain that the solutions are correct. In a balanced reaction, it is not necessary to conserve moles of molecules. Why?

Consider the equation for the burning of phosphorus in oxygen.

$$P_4 \ (s) + 5 \ O_2 \ (g) \rightarrow P_4O_{10} \ (s) + \text{heat}$$

Calculate the weights, in grams, of phosphorus and oxygen that will be required to form 0.1 mole of P_4O_{10}.

The equation tells us that 1 mole of P_4 reacts with 5 moles of O_2 to form 1 mole of P_4O_{10}, and heat is liberated. This means that 0.1 mole of P_4O_{10} requires 0.1 mole of P_4 and 0.5 mole of O_2.

$$\text{The weight of 0.1 mole of } P_4 = 124 \ \frac{\text{grams}}{\text{mole}} \times 0.1 \text{ mole}$$
$$= 12.4 \text{ grams}$$

$$\text{The weight of 0.5 mole of } O_2 = 32 \ \frac{\text{grams}}{\text{mole}} \times 0.5 \text{ mole}$$
$$= 16 \text{ grams}$$

$$\text{The weight of 0.1 mole of } P_4O_{10} = 284 \ \frac{\text{grams}}{\text{mole}} \times 0.1 \text{ mole}$$
$$= 28.4 \text{ grams}$$

Our analysis shows that 12.4 grams of P_4 react with 16 grams of O_2 to form 28.4 grams of P_4O_{10}. Since mass has been conserved, we may assume the solution to the problem is correct.

5.18 Classifying chemical reactions

We have already discussed reactions involving electron transfer, called oxidation-reduction. These reactions consist of an oxidation half-reaction and a reduction half-reaction. At this point we can suggest an elementary classification of reactions that involve oxidation-reduction, as follows:

1. Reactions involving the combination of element A with element B to form compound AB. In its simplest form, a reaction of this type can be represented by the equation

$$\overset{0}{A} + \overset{0}{B} \rightarrow \overset{+1 \ -1}{AB}$$

Example:

$$2 \overset{0}{Al} + 3 \overset{0}{S} \rightarrow \overset{+3 \ -2}{Al_2S_3}$$

2. Reactions involving the decomposition of compound AB. In its simplest form, a reaction of this type can be represented by the equation

$$\overset{+1\,-1}{AB} \rightarrow \overset{0}{A} + \overset{0}{B}$$

with $-e^-$ transferred above and $+e^-$ below.

Example:

$$\overset{+3\,-2}{Al_2S_3} \rightarrow 2\,\overset{0}{Al} + 3\,\overset{0}{S}$$

with $-6\,e^-$ transferred above and $+6\,e^-$ below.

Note that reaction 1, commonly called *synthesis*, or *direct combination*, is the opposite of reaction 2, commonly called *analysis*, or *decomposition*.

3. Reactions involving the replacement of element B in compound BC by element A. In its simplest form, a reaction of this type can be represented by the equation

$$\overset{0}{A} + \overset{+1\,-1}{BC} \rightarrow \overset{+1\,-1}{AC} + \overset{0}{B}$$

with $-e^-$ transferred above and $+e^-$ below.

Example:

$$\overset{0}{Zn} + \overset{+2\,-1}{CuCl_2} \rightarrow \overset{+2\,-1}{ZnCl_2} + \overset{0}{Cu}$$

with $-2\,e^-$ transferred above and $+2\,e^-$ below.

Reaction 3 is called *single replacement*.

Chemical reactions 1, 2, and 3 all involve oxidation-reduction. Do oxidation and reduction occur in all chemical reactions? Let us consider the reaction that occurs when a solution of sodium chloride (Na^+ and Cl^- ions) is mixed with a solution of silver nitrate (Ag^+ and NO_3^- ions).

$$Na^+ + Cl^- + Ag^+ + NO_3^- \rightarrow AgCl\,(s) + Na^+ + NO_3^-$$

Solid AgCl settles to the bottom of the solution, and Na^+ and NO_3^- ions are left in solution. During the reaction, a rearrangement of ions takes place without any oxidation-reduction. This type of reaction is called *double replacement*.

Multiple-Choice Questions

1. In the reaction $X^0 + Y^+Z^- \rightarrow X^+Z^- + Y^0$ (1) the particle oxidized is X^0 (2) the particle reduced is Z^- (3) Y^+ loses a proton (4) Y^+ is a reducing agent

2. Which statement is *not* correct for the following reactions?

$$XY \rightarrow X + Y \qquad \text{and} \qquad X + Y \rightarrow XY$$

(1) Both reactions involve oxidation and reduction. (2) One reaction involves a gain of electrons, and the other involves a loss of electrons. (3) Charge is conserved in both reactions. (4) The number of moles of atoms is the same on the right side of the arrows in both reactions.

3. The equation $N_2\,(g) + 3\,H_2\,(g) \rightarrow 2\,NH_3\,(g) + \text{heat}$ shows a change in (1) state (2) the number of atoms (3) the number of moles of atoms (4) the number of moles of molecules

4. The atomic weight of Cl is 35.5 and Avogadro's number is 6.02×10^{23}. Therefore (1) 71.0 g of Cl_2 contain 6.02×10^{23} molecules (2) 71.0 g of Cl contain 6.02×10^{23} atoms (3) 1 mole of Cl_2 contains 12.04×10^{23} molecules (4) 1 mole of chlorine can combine with 1 mole of any metal

5. The name iron(III) sulfate indicates (1) three atoms of iron in the compound (2) the valence number of sulfate is -3 (3) the valence number of iron is $+3$ (4) iron has three different valence numbers

6. In the compound K_2SO_4, the valence number of (1) K is $+2$ (2) S is $+6$ (3) O is $+2$ (4) S is -6

7. The formula $Ba(ClO_3)_2$ represents (1) a molecule consisting of three ions (2) a molecule consisting of five atoms (3) ionic bonds between three different elements (4) a polyatomic ion with a valence number of -2

8. An example of a polyatomic ion is (1) Cl^- (2) NH_3 (3) Ca^{+2} (4) SO_4^{-2}

9. A molecule of a binary compound must (1) consist of two atoms (2) contain a metal and a nonmetal (3) result from electron transfer (4) contain only two elements

10. The formula X_2Y_3 indicates that (1) X is a nonmetal with a valence number of 2 (2) Y has a valence number of -3 (3) X has a valence number of $+3$ (4) the two elements are united by two covalent bonds

Completion Questions

1. The valence number of Cl in NaOCl is _____, and the valence number of Cl in $NaClO_3$ is _____.
2. One molecule of $Ca_3(PO_4)_2$ (calcium phosphate) contains a total of _____ atoms, and a total of _____ ions.
3. The compound NaOH contains _____ elements.
4. If the formula for titanium oxide is TiO_2, then the formula for titanium chloride is _____.
5. To distinguish between Cu_2O and CuO, the first compound is called _____ and the second is called _____.
6. In the formula Bi_2O_3, the valence number of Bi is _____.
7. *a.* CuS is known as a binary compound because it contains _____.
   b. $CuSO_4$ is known as a (an) _____ compound.
8. When magnesium unites with oxygen, magnesium loses two electrons. Sodium loses one electron when combining with oxygen. In both cases, the ions formed have the same electron structure as the element _____.
9. *a.* An abbreviation used to represent an atom of an element is called a (an) _____.
   b. The abbreviation for a molecule is called a (an) _____.
10. From the names of the compounds sodium sulfide and sodium sulfate, we can tell that the first compound does not contain the element _____, which is present in the second compound.

True-False Questions

In some of the following statements, the italicized term makes the statement incorrect. For each incorrect statement, write the term that must be substituted for the italicized term to make the statement correct. For each correct statement, write the word *true*.

1. An equation that represents the loss of electrons by a particle is *a reduction* half-reaction.
2. The reaction H_2 (g) + Cl_2 (g) → 2 HCl (g) does not involve a change of *state*.

3. In the chemical equation $2\ Na + Cl_2 \rightarrow 2\ NaCl$, the numbers of *molecules* on both sides of the arrow are equal.
4. There is one atom of oxygen *less* in calcium chlorite than in calcium chlorate.
5. Binary compounds have names ending in -*ate*.
6. The simplest formula that gives the relative numbers of the different atoms in a compound is its *molecular* formula.
7. In the compound Fe_2S_3, the valence number of Fe is $+2$.
8. In a polyvalent ion, the algebraic sum of the valence numbers *is not* zero.
9. A molecule of $Al(NO_3)_3$ contains *four* atoms.
10. The *sulfide* ion is a very common polyvalent ion.

Exercises for Review

1. Write formulas for:
   a. magnesium chloride
   b. aluminum sulfide
   c. sodium fluoride
   d. hydrogen oxide
   e. calcium bromide
   f. calcium carbonate
   g. magnesium hydroxide
   h. sodium sulfate
   i. aluminum nitrate
   j. potassium phosphate
   k. lithium chlorate
2. Write formulas for:
   a. sulfur dioxide
   b. dinitrogen tetroxide
   c. tetraphosphorus hexoxide
   d. chlorine dioxide
   e. phosphorus pentachloride
   f. iron(II) chloride
   g. copper(II) nitrate
   h. calcium nitrite
   i. sodium sulfite
   j. copper(I) oxide
   k. iron(III) hydroxide
3. What are the chemical names for the following compounds?
   a. $Ca(NO_3)_2$
   b. N_2O
   c. $Fe_2(SO_4)_3$
   d. Cl_2O
   e. $Cu(NO_3)_2$
   f. K_3PO_4
   g. $LiClO_3$
   h. $Al(OH)_3$
   i. MgF_2
   j. SO_3
4. Write equations for the following chemical changes:
   a. copper + oxygen → copper(II) oxide
   b. iron + sulfur → iron(III) sulfide
   c. water → hydrogen + oxygen
   d. sulfur + oxygen → sulfur dioxide
   e. silver oxide → silver + oxygen
   f. hydrogen + chlorine → hydrogen chloride

5. Name each of the compounds in the pairs of compounds. Explain the reasons for the names.

   a. Hg_2S and HgS

   b. KNO_2 and KNO_3

   c. Na_2S and Na_2SO_4

6. Write an equation for each of the following reactions. Include all available information in the equation.

   a. Heating solid calcium carbonate forms gaseous carbon dioxide and solid calcium oxide.

   b. Magnesium metal combines with chlorine gas to form solid magnesium chloride, releasing heat.

   c. Solid mercury(II) oxide, when heated, forms liquid mercury and oxygen gas.

   d. Solid phosphorus unites with oxygen to form solid tetraphosphorus decoxide, releasing heat.

7. For each of the following reactions, write a separate oxidation half-reaction and reduction half-reaction, showing the electron transfer in each:

   a. $2\ Na + Cl_2 \rightarrow 2\ NaCl$

   b. $Ca + Br_2 \rightarrow CaBr_2$

   c. $2\ Al_2O_3 \rightarrow 4\ Al + 3\ O_2$

   d. $Mg + FeCl_2 \rightarrow MgCl_2 + Fe$

   e. $2\ Al + Fe_2O_3 \rightarrow 2\ Fe + Al_2O_3$

8. Complete the following equations, giving the number of electrons either gained $(+e^-)$ or released $(-e^-)$. State whether each reaction represents oxidation or reduction.

   a. $Ca^0 \rule{2cm}{0.4pt} \rightarrow Ca^{+2}$

   b. $2\ O^{-2} \rule{2cm}{0.4pt} \rightarrow O_2{}^0$

   c. $Cl_2{}^0 \rule{2cm}{0.4pt} \rightarrow 2\ Cl^-$

   d. $Cu^{+1} \rule{2cm}{0.4pt} \rightarrow Cu^{+2}$

   e. $Al^{+3} \rule{2cm}{0.4pt} \rightarrow Al^0$

9. The empirical formula of a compound is found to be NH_2. Its molecular weight is 32.

   a. What is the molecular formula?

   b. Knowing that the valence number of N is -3, explain how the atoms are arranged in the molecule.

10. Calculate the number of grams in 1 mole of each of the following compounds:

   a. CuO *d.* $Al(OH)_3$

   b. $CaCl_2$ *e.* $Fe_2(CO_3)_3$

   c. $MgSO_4$ *f.* Na_3PO_4

11. Calculate the number of grams in:

    a. 2 moles NaOH   *d.* 0.02 mole HCl

    b. 0.25 mole $CaCO_3$ *e.* 1.25 moles $Mg(NO_3)_2$

    c. 4.5 moles $CuSO_4$

12. Find the number of moles present in:

    a. 117 g NaCl   *d.* 10 g $CaCO_3$

    b. 6.4 g O_2 *e.* 19.6 g H_2SO_4

    c. 180 g H_2O

13. From the equation $2 K + Cl_2 \rightarrow 2 KCl$, find:

    a. how many moles of K unite with 5 moles of Cl_2

    b. what weight of K unites with 5 moles of Cl_2

    c. what weight of Cl_2 unites with 78.2 g of K

14. When 320 g of copper are heated with an abundant supply of sulfur, copper(II) sulfide forms.

    a. Write the chemical equation.

    b. Calculate the number of moles of Cu that are used and the number of moles of CuS that are formed.

    c. Find the weight of the CuS.

15. When 72 g of magnesium metal are placed in a solution of copper chloride, the magnesium disintegrates completely. Metallic copper and magnesium chloride form.

    a. Write the equation for the reaction.

    b. How many moles of magnesium were used?

    c. How many moles of copper were formed?

    d. What is the weight of the copper?

16. During an experiment, 480 g of carbon burn to form carbon dioxide.

    a. Find the number of moles of carbon that are used, and the number of moles of carbon dioxide that are formed.

    b. What is the weight of the carbon dioxide?

Exercises for Further Study

1. What bonds are broken and what bonds are formed when chlorine and oxygen unite in the reaction

$$2 Cl_2 (g) + O_2 (g) \rightarrow 2 Cl_2O (g)$$

2. When water is electrolyzed to form 2.016 g of hydrogen, how many electrons are supplied to hydrogen atoms?

3. *a.* How many atoms are present in 64 g of oxygen?

    b. When 64 g of oxygen unite with hydrogen, how many O—O bonds are broken?

    c. How many H—H bonds are broken?

4. The formula for mercury(I) chloride is Hg_2Cl_2, not $HgCl$. What is the difference between the information conveyed by the two formulas concerning:

    a. the molecular weight of the compound

    b. the number of atoms per molecule

    c. the number of ions per molecule

    d. the bonds in the molecule

5. Explain why the algebraic sum of the valence numbers of all the atoms in a molecule must be zero.

6. Calculate the valence number of P in KH_2PO_2.

7. Compare the formulas $Ca(OCl)_2$ and $Ca(ClO_2)_2$. For each compound give:

    a. the number of atoms per molecule

    b. the valence numbers of Cl

    c. the types of bonds between the atoms

8. When a ternary compound consists of one metal and two nonmetals, what types of bonds are present in the compound? Explain.

Chapter 6

USING FORMULAS AND EQUATIONS

6.1 Introduction

In the preceding chapters, we studied some of the properties of elements and compounds. Following that discussion, we studied a few of the fundamental concepts that govern the reactions between elements to form compounds. Then we concluded with equations to describe these reactions. In the present chapter, we will continue to explore the fundamental concepts of preceding chapters, using as frames of reference two very abundant and useful compounds — water and salt. Our strategy will be to study the compound and then to study the individual elements that make up the compound. Although we will concentrate on each specific compound and its component elements, we will also be concerned with the principles and generalizations that can be applied to related compounds and their component elements.

6.2 Occurrence of water

Water, in the form of rivers, lakes, seas, and oceans, covers about 75% of the surface of the earth. In the atmosphere, water is present in varying amounts as water vapor. Under proper conditions, water vapor is precipitated as rain, dew, snow, hail, or frost. Water accounts for more than half the weight of the human body; it is abundant in all animal and vegetable matter.

6.3 Properties of water

The physical properties of water may be summarized as follows:

1. At a pressure of 1 atmosphere, water boils at 100° C, or 212° F. At the same pressure, water freezes at 0° C, or 32° F.
2. The density of liquid water at 4° C is 1 g/cm³.
3. The density of ice at 0° C is 0.917 g/cm³.
4. The heat of vaporization of water at 100° C is 539.1 cal/g, or 9.72 kcal/mole. *Heat of vaporization is the quantity of heat required to vaporize 1 g or 1 mole of a liquid at its boiling point.*
5. The heat of fusion of water is 79.2 cal/g, or 1.43 kcal/mole. *Heat of fusion is the quantity of heat required to melt 1 g or 1 mole of a solid at its melting (or freezing) point.*

Water is employed to define a number of physical standards, including volume and heat.

Volume. 1 cm³ is the volume of 1 g of water at 4°C.

Heat. 1 cal is the amount of heat required to raise the temperature of 1 g of water 1 C° (from 14.5°C to 15.5°C).

Water is the most extensively used solvent. Under proper conditions, few substances will fail to dissolve in water at least to some extent. Many chemical reactions occur only in *aqueous* (water) medium, suggesting that water plays an important role in chemical change.

We pointed out previously that water is a polar molecule – the hydrogen ends of the molecule are positive, and the oxygen end is negative. When an ionic species is mixed with water, the positive and negative ions released from the ionic species are surrounded by water molecules. The ions are said to become aquated (or hydrated). They are represented by the term (*aqueous*), or (*aq*), following the formulas of the ions. For example, when salt dissolves in water, the species Na^+ (*aq*) and Cl^- (*aq*) are formed. Aquated ions do not have the same structure as the same ions present in the crystalline solid or the gas phase. The aquation process is treated in Chapter 10.

Although water is a common liquid, it exhibits many unusual properties. For example, at 4°C, water expands if it is heated or if it is cooled. Most liquids expand when heated but contract when cooled. Water may act as an oxidizing or reducing agent, depending on the nature of the substance with which it is reacting. It may also act as an acid or as a base. We shall discuss the properties of water in considerable detail later.

6.4 Composition of water

We have already pointed out that a water molecule consists of two hydrogen atoms covalently bonded to a single oxygen atom.

$$H \overset{\cdot\cdot}{\underset{\cdot\underset{\textstyle H}{\times}}{\overset{x}{O}}} :$$

During bond formation, energy is released. The formation of a mole of liquid water from its elements liberates 68.3 kcal of heat.

$$H_2 \ (g) + \frac{1}{2}O_2 \ (g) \rightarrow H_2O \ (l) + 68.3 \, \text{kcal}$$

The reverse reaction, that is, the decomposition of water, requires breaking the bonds produced during the formation of water. This means that energy is consumed when water is decomposed.

$$H_2O \ (l) + \text{energy} \rightarrow H_2 \ (g) + \frac{1}{2}O_2 \ (g)$$

In water, note that hydrogen atoms have a valence number of $+1$, and oxygen atoms have a valence number of -2. The formation of water and the decomposition of water both involve electron transfer, or oxidation-reduction. The reactions can be summarized as follows:

$$\text{FORMATION} \quad \overset{0}{H_2} + \frac{1}{2}\overset{0}{O_2} \rightarrow \overset{+1\ -2}{H_2O} \qquad\qquad \text{DECOMPOSITION} \quad \overset{+1\ -2}{H_2O} \rightarrow \overset{0}{H_2} + \frac{1}{2}\overset{0}{O_2}$$

The composition of the compound water may be determined either by combining its elements to form the compound (synthesis) or by decomposing the compound into its elements (analysis).

6.5 Synthesis of water

Water may be synthesized in the gas-measuring tube shown in Figure 6–1. Note that the tube has two sealed-in electrodes to permit the passage of an electric spark. If a mixture of 20 ml of hydrogen and 20 ml of oxygen is exploded by the spark, the water in the tube rises to the 10 ml mark in the gas-measuring tube, indicating that 10 ml of gas remain uncombined. By chemical test, it can be shown that the uncombined gas is oxygen. It can be shown that 20 ml of gaseous water form, which condense to form an extremely small quantity of liquid water. This volume of water has practically no effect upon the volume of water that rises in the eudiometer to take the place of the combining gases.

From the preceding experiment, we can see that 20 ml of hydrogen combine with 10 ml of oxygen, a relationship that can be expressed more generally by stating that water is composed of 2 volumes of hydrogen and 1 volume of oxygen.

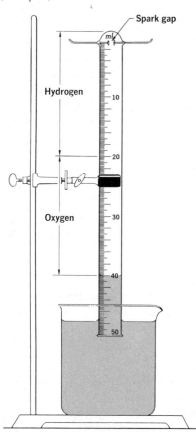

Fig. 6–1   Synthesis of water

6.6 Analysis of water

The volume composition of water may be confirmed by decomposition. Since decomposition requires the breaking of bonds, energy must be added. At room temperature, the decomposition of water proceeds spontaneously only to a slight extent and then too slowly to be useful. Water may be decomposed conveniently and rapidly by using electricity. *The decomposition of a compound by an electric current is called electrolysis.*

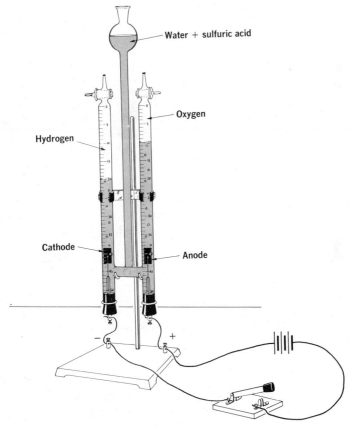

Fig. 6–2   Analysis of water

The apparatus shown in Figure 6–2 consists of an H-tube filled with water. Some sulfuric acid is added to make the water a better conductor of electricity. As in the synthesis of water, a transfer of electrons (oxidation-reduction) occurs. Thus two essential half-reactions accompany electrolysis: oxidation at the anode and reduction at the cathode. Negative ions migrate to the anode, where they undergo oxidation; positive ions migrate to the cathode, where they undergo reduction. (In some special situations, molecules may also undergo oxidation-reduction.) These reactions may be written as

ANODE
$$O^{-2} \ (aq) \rightarrow \frac{1}{2} O_2{}^0 \ (g) + 2 \ e^-$$

CATHODE
$$2 \ H^+ \ (aq) + 2 \ e^- \rightarrow H_2{}^0 \ (g)$$

The above equations are convenient but oversimplified. In reality, water molecules are oxidized and reduced.

ANODE
$$H_2O \rightarrow \frac{1}{2} O_2 \ (g) + 2 \ H^+ \ (aq) + 2 \ e^-$$

CATHODE
$$2 \ H_2O + 2 \ e^- \rightarrow H_2 \ (g) + 2 \ OH^-$$

When the reaction is completed, the volume of hydrogen at the cathode is approximately twice the volume of oxygen at the anode. This $2:1$ relationship confirms the determination of the volume composition of water by synthesis.

If we know the densities of hydrogen and oxygen, we can determine the weight ratio of hydrogen to oxygen in water. The weight composition of water is one part hydrogen to eight parts oxygen. The composition of water by volume and by weight is summarized below.

COMPOSITION OF H_2O	PARTS H	PARTS O
by volume	2	1
by weight	1	8

6.7 Preparation of hydrogen

Large quantities of hydrogen are used in the manufacture of ammonia and in converting unsaturated compounds into more useful saturated compounds (hydrogenation). For example, cottonseed oil or coconut oil — unsaturated compounds — can be hydrogenated to produce margarine. Since free hydrogen does not occur in nature, except in minute quantities, it must be extracted from its compounds.

The electronic structure of hydrogen, atomic number 1, reveals that it can form binary compounds. These compounds may be represented by the general formula H_nX, in which n is the number of hydrogen atoms and

X represents the other element. The valence number commonly exhibited by hydrogen in its compounds is $+1$. To extract hydrogen from these compounds, we must utilize the reaction $2\ H^+ + 2\ e^- \rightarrow H_2\ (g)$. The preparation of hydrogen, therefore, involves the reduction of H^+. (In this discussion, we will not concern ourselves with the extraction of hydrogen from hydride compounds, in which hydrogen has a valence number of -1.)

6.8 Hydronium ion and acids

We are using H^+ as the symbol of combined hydrogen, possessing a valence number of $+1$. Since a neutral H atom possesses only a single electron associated with a single proton, H^+ more accurately represents a free proton. There is considerable experimental evidence to show that the species H^+ (a free proton) exists in the gas phase only. Thus the symbol H^+ represents a gaseous particle that is an atom of hydrogen minus its one electron.

In aqueous medium, the very small H^+ ion is attracted to the polar water molecule to form *hydronium ion*: $H^+(H_2O)$ or H_3O^+ or H^+ (*aq*). The extraction of hydrogen from H^+ compounds in aqueous medium involves the reduction of hydronium ions.

Aqueous solutions of compounds containing H^+ are called *acids*. The formulas of such compounds always include the term (*aqueous*). (The acid concept will be broadened and redefined in Chapter 16.) The table that follows lists the names and formulas of some representative binary and ternary acids.

BINARY ACID	TERNARY ACID
hydrochloric acid HCl (*aqueous*) hydrofluoric acid HF (*aqueous*) hydrobromic acid HBr (*aqueous*)	nitric acid HNO_3 (*aqueous*) sulfuric acid H_2SO_4 (*aqueous*) phosphoric acid (ortho) H_3PO_4 (*aqueous*)

6.9 Reduction of H⁺ (*aq*)

What kind of substance will liberate hydrogen from acids? H^+ (*aq*) must be changed into H, and therefore we require an electron donor. From our study of oxidation-reduction, we know that reducing agents contain particles that tend to donate electrons. According to our table of electron structures (see page 45), elements having small numbers of electrons in their outermost shells should behave as reducing agents. This means that metals should react with acids to form hydrogen, according to the simplest generalized equation

$$\overset{0}{M}\ (s) + \overset{+1}{H}\ (aq) \rightarrow \overset{+1}{M}\ (aq) + \frac{1}{2}\ H_2\ (g)$$

in which $\overset{0}{M}\ (s)$ represents a metal in its solid state.

Whether this reaction will actually occur in the laboratory depends on two conditions:

1. M must be a metal, like zinc, which has a greater tendency to lose electrons than does hydrogen. Copper, silver, gold, and platinum, which do not have this greater tendency, will not generally react with acids to form hydrogen.

2. In addition to H^+ (aq), the acid must *not* contain a particle that can be reduced more easily than H^+ (aq). HCl may be used because Cl^- ion, with a complete outer (M) shell, cannot be reduced (cannot have electrons added to it). However, HNO_3 cannot be used since NO_3^- ion is more easily reduced (is a better oxidizing agent) than H^+ (aq).

6.10 Reactions between metals and acids

Equations for typical reactions between metals and acids that produce hydrogen appear below. Each reaction is divided into the oxidation and reduction half-reactions.

$$Zn\ (s) + 2\ HCl\ (aq) \rightarrow ZnCl_2\ (aq) + H_2\ (g)$$

OXIDATION HALF-REACTION $\qquad Zn\ (s) \rightarrow Zn^{+2}\ (aq) + 2\ e^-$

REDUCTION HALF-REACTION $\qquad 2\ H^+\ (aq) + 2\ e^- \rightarrow H_2\ (g)$

$$2\ Al\ (s) + 6\ HCl\ (aq) \rightarrow 2\ AlCl_3\ (aq) + 3\ H_2\ (g)$$

OXIDATION HALF-REACTION $\qquad 2\ Al\ (s) \rightarrow 2\ Al^{+3}\ (aq) + 6\ e^-$

REDUCTION HALF-REACTION $\qquad 6\ H^+\ (aq) + 6\ e^- \rightarrow 3\ H_2\ (g)$

$$Mg\ (s) + H_2SO_4\ (aq) \rightarrow MgSO_4\ (aq) + H_2\ (g)$$

OXIDATION HALF-REACTION $\qquad Mg\ (s) \rightarrow Mg^{+2}\ (aq) + 2\ e^-$

REDUCTION HALF-REACTION $\quad 2\ H^+\ (aq) + 2\ e^- \rightarrow H_2\ (g)$

6.11 Reactions between metals and water

Water contains hydronium ions, but in much smaller concentration than in acids. For simplicity, we often assume that metals reduce the hydronium ions in water to form hydrogen gas; but in reality, the water molecules are reduced.

The production of hydrogen from water is increased considerably by using those metals that lose electrons most readily. If M represents the symbol of such a reactive metal, the simplest generalized reaction between M and water is

$$\overset{0}{M}\ (s) + \overset{+1}{H}\ (aq) + OH^-\ (aq) \rightarrow \overset{+1}{M}\ (aq) + OH^-\ (aq) + \frac{1}{2} H_2\ (g)$$

with $-e^-$ transferred above and $+e^-$ below.

Another way of writing this reaction is

$$M\ (s) + H_2O \rightarrow M^+\ (aq) + OH^-\ (aq) + \frac{1}{2} H_2\ (g)$$

We have used HOH to represent the formula of water, treating water as a ternary compound that ionizes into $H^+\ (aq)$ and $OH^-\ (aq)$. By using this convenient representation, we clarify both the reduction reaction and the presence of OH^- on the right side of the equation.

Let us now write some specific equations for typical reactions between metals and water.

$$Li\ (s) + HOH \rightarrow LiOH\ (aq) + \frac{1}{2} H_2\ (g)$$

OXIDATION HALF-REACTION $\qquad Li\ (s) \rightarrow Li^+\ (aq) + e^-$

REDUCTION HALF-REACTION
$$\begin{cases} H^+\ (aq) + e^- \rightarrow \dfrac{1}{2} H_2\ (g) \\[2mm] H_2O + e^- \rightarrow \dfrac{1}{2} H_2\ (g) + OH^- \end{cases}$$

$$Ca\ (s) + 2\ HOH \rightarrow Ca(OH)_2\ (aq) + H_2\ (g)$$

OXIDATION HALF-REACTION $\qquad Ca\ (s) \rightarrow Ca^{+2}\ (aq) + 2\ e^-$

REDUCTION HALF-REACTION $\begin{cases} 2\ H^+\ (aq) + 2\ e^- \rightarrow H_2\ (g) \\ \quad 2\ H_2O + 2\ e^- \rightarrow H_2\ (g) + 2\ OH^- \end{cases}$

At higher temperatures, some metals react with hot water or steam to form the metal oxide and hydrogen.

$$Mg\ (s) + H_2O \rightarrow MgO\ (s) + H_2\ (g)$$

$$3\ Fe\ (s) + 4\ H_2O\ (g) \rightarrow Fe_3O_4\ (s) + 4\ H_2\ (g)$$

6.12 Decomposition of hydrogen compounds

We have already noted that hydrogen is formed during the electrolytic decomposition of water. Although the hydrogen in the water is reduced to form hydrogen gas, no actual reducing agent is required. Remember that water is a polar molecule in which the shared pairs of electrons are held closer to the oxygen atom than to the hydrogen atoms. As a result, the hydrogen ends of the molecule are positive and the oxygen end is negative.

During the electrolytic decomposition of water, the bonds between the atoms are broken. An electron is returned to each hydrogen atom, and hydrogen gas is formed. This leaves oxygen atoms, which combine in pairs, to form molecules of oxygen gas. Since the hydrogen portions of the water molecule are positive, we may conclude that reduction occurred during the formation of hydrogen gas.

Hydrogen may also be prepared from the thermal decomposition of hydrocarbons (compounds of carbon and hydrogen).

$$\overset{-4\ e^-}{\overbrace{}}$$
$$\overset{-4+4}{C}\overset{}{H_4} \rightarrow \overset{0}{C} + 2\ \overset{0}{H_2}\ (g)$$
$$\underset{+4\ e^-}{\underbrace{}}$$

Thus during electrolytic or thermal decomposition of certain hydrogen compounds, the bonds that hold the atoms together may be broken. Reduction takes place as electrons are returned to hydrogen particles to form hydrogen gas.

6.13 Preparation of free elements

Elements may occur in nature either free (uncombined) or combined in compounds. Because free, uncombined hydrogen does not occur abundantly in nature, we prepare hydrogen by reduction from its compounds. The free oxygen content of the atmosphere, however, is about 21% by volume and is an abundant source of commercial oxygen. Oxygen is also prepared in the laboratory from its compounds.

Unlike hydrogen, which has a valence number of $+1$ in most of its compounds, oxygen, atomic number 8, most frequently has a valence number of -2 in its compounds. Such compounds may be binary oxide compounds or ternary oxygen compounds. Less frequently, in peroxide compounds such as H_2O_2, oxygen exhibits a valence number of -1.

We have learned that elements possessing positive valence numbers in compounds may be extracted by reduction. Since oxygen almost always has a negative valence number in compounds, it is extracted by oxidation. These relationships can be expressed as follows:

Reduction *restores* electrons to particles possessing positive valence numbers to form the free element (valence number = 0).

Oxidation *removes* electrons from particles possessing negative valence numbers to form the free element (valence number = 0).

6.14 Preparation of oxygen from oxygen compounds

Just as hydrogen was prepared by the decomposition of hydrogen compounds, oxygen may be prepared by the decomposition of oxides, peroxides, and ternary oxygen compounds. An analysis of these reactions reveals that O^{-2} ions and O_2^{-2} ions, shown below, in oxygen compounds lose electrons (are oxidized) to form oxygen gas. As might be expected, these changes require bond breaking and the making of new bonds.

$$\overset{\cdot\cdot\ \ \cdot\cdot}{\underset{\cdot\cdot\ \ \cdot\cdot}{:O:O:}} \qquad \overset{\cdot\cdot}{\underset{\cdot\cdot}{:O:}}$$

peroxide (O_2^{-2}) ion   oxide (O^{-2}) ion

Considerable oxygen is obtained from the electrolysis of water, as described in section 6.6. The following equations represent the preparation of oxygen by thermal decomposition of other typical oxygen compounds:

1. From an oxide, O^{-2}

$$2\ HgO\ (s) \rightarrow 2\ Hg\ (l) + O_2\ (g)$$

OXIDATION HALF-REACTION $2\ O^{-2} \rightarrow O_2\ (g) + 4\ e^-$

REDUCTION HALF-REACTION $2\ Hg^{+2} + 4\ e^- \rightarrow 2\ Hg\ (l)$

2. From a ternary oxygen (*-ate*) compound, ClO_3^-

$$2 \; KClO_3 \; (s) \rightarrow 2 \; KCl \; (s) + 3 \; O_2 \; (g)$$

$$\underset{\text{chlorate}}{\text{potassium}} \qquad\qquad \underset{\text{chloride}}{\text{potassium}}$$

OXIDATION HALF-REACTION $\qquad 6 \; O^{-2} \rightarrow 3 \; O_2{}^0 \; (g) + 12 \; e^-$

REDUCTION HALF-REACTION $\quad 2 \; Cl^{+5} + 12 \; e^- \rightarrow 2 \; Cl^{-1}$

3. From a peroxide, $O_2{}^{-2}$

$$2 \; H_2O_2 \rightarrow 2 \; H_2O + O_2 \; (g)$$

OXIDATION HALF-REACTION $\qquad O_2{}^{-2} \rightarrow O_2 \; (g) + 2 \; e^-$

REDUCTION HALF-REACTION $\quad O_2{}^{-2} + 2 \; e^- \rightarrow 2 \; O^{-2}$

6.15 Occurrence of salt

Now let us turn our attention to another important compound, sodium chloride, commonly called salt. Sodium chloride occurs naturally in sea-water, in brine wells, and in mineral deposits as rock salt. The salt is extracted from these sources as follows:

1. In warm climates, the sun's rays are used to evaporate seawater, leaving the dissolved salt behind.
2. In cold climates, seawater is allowed to freeze in large containers. The ice which forms on top of the water is removed, and the concentrated salt solution is evaporated using artificial heat.
3. Rock salt is mined in the same manner as coal.

6.16 Properties of salt

Salt is a white, crystalline, ionic solid that is almost equally soluble in hot and in cold water. It melts at the relatively high temperature of 801° C. Salt is the source of metallic sodium, gaseous chlorine, and most synthetic sodium and chlorine compounds. Salt is indispensable to the normal diet, although its specific function is not completely understood.

6.17 Composition of salt

Although sodium chloride is abundant in nature and need not be commercially synthesized, it may be synthesized in the laboratory by the combination of its elements. When sodium metal reacts with chlorine gas, each sodium atom transfers one electron to each chlorine atom to form an ionic solid, sodium chloride.

$$\text{Na } (s) + \frac{1}{2} \text{ Cl}_2 \ (g) \rightarrow \overset{+1 \ -1}{\text{NaCl}} \ (s) + 98.23 \text{ kcal}$$

with electron transfer: $-e^-$ from Na to Cl (top), $+e^-$ (bottom)

The evolution of 98.23 kilocalories of heat during the formation of a mole of NaCl indicates the unusual stability of the crystalline solid.

The reverse reaction, the decomposition of sodium chloride, requires breaking the ionic bonds produced during the formation of sodium chloride. Energy is therefore consumed when sodium chloride is decomposed. (Some energy is used to melt the salt before it is decomposed.)

$$\text{NaCl } (s) + \text{energy} \rightarrow \text{Na } (l) + \frac{1}{2} \text{ Cl}_2 \ (g)$$

It can be shown experimentally that 1 mole of sodium chloride may be decomposed completely to yield 1 mole of sodium atoms and 0.5 mole of chlorine molecules (1 mole of chlorine atoms). This analysis suggests that the atomic ratio in salt is 1 Na : 1 Cl.

6.18 Electrolysis of fused salt

The extreme stability of sodium chloride suggests that, like water, it may be more conveniently decomposed by electrolysis than by heat. Since only liquids undergo electrolysis, apparently salt must be either dissolved in water or melted (fused). However, sodium metal, like lithium, cannot be formed in any aqueous medium (see section 6.11). Sodium is an extremely active metal and reacts with water to form hydrogen and sodium hydroxide. This is the same as saying that less energy is required to reduce water molecules than to reduce sodium ions. Thus sodium metal is liberated only during the electrolysis of fused sodium chloride where water is not present.

Since Na^+ ion has a valence number of $+1$ (like hydrogen in its compounds), an electron must be restored when the free metal is formed. Na^+ ion must therefore be reduced. During electrolysis, the reduction occurs at the cathode.

$$Na^+ + e^- \rightarrow \text{Na } (l)$$

At the same time, Cl^- ions are oxidized at the anode to form chlorine gas.

$$Cl^- \rightarrow \frac{1}{2} \text{ Cl}_2 \ (g) + e^-$$

6.19 Preparation of metallic sodium

The extraction of sodium from its compounds involves the reduction of Na^+ ions, accomplished by electrolysis of the fused compound.

Another method of extracting sodium from its compounds may be inferred from the method of extracting hydrogen from its compounds. This method involves the use of a reducing agent, that is, the use of an element that loses electrons more readily than hydrogen. Suppose metal X, which loses electrons more readily than Na, reacts with NaCl. The equation could be represented as

$$\overset{\displaystyle \overset{-e^-}{\longrightarrow}}{X\ (l) + \overset{+1\ -1}{NaCl}\ (l) \rightarrow \overset{+1\ -1}{XCl}\ (l) + Na\ (l)}$$
$$\underset{+e^-}{\longleftarrow}$$

In the table of electron structures on page 45, note that potassium, like sodium, also has one electron in its outermost shell. This electron is farther from the nucleus than is the one electron in the outermost shell of sodium. Consequently, potassium atoms lose electrons more readily than sodium atoms, and potassium can thus reduce sodium ions.

However, the use of potassium to extract sodium from compounds has a number of serious practical limitations. The extraction depends on the availability of metallic potassium, which is as difficult to isolate as metallic sodium. Since both metals react with water, the reduction can be carried out in the absence of water, generally in the fused state. This process is both cumbersome and expensive. Thus electrolysis of molten compounds remains the only feasible method of extracting reactive metals.

6.20 Preparation of chlorine

The liberation of chlorine from its binary compounds parallels the liberation of oxygen from its binary compounds. Both processes involve oxidation.

$$2\ O^{-2} \rightarrow O_2{}^0\ (g) + 4\ e^-$$

$$2\ Cl^- \rightarrow Cl_2{}^0\ (g) + 2\ e^-$$

6.21 Electrolysis of hydrochloric acid

Oxygen may be prepared by anodic oxidation during the electrolysis of water. Similarly, chlorine may be prepared by anodic oxidation during the electrolysis of hydrochloric acid, HCl (*aq*). The reaction occurs in water solution and involves the oxidation of aquated Cl^- ions. Figure 6–3 shows a U-tube containing concentrated HCl. Graphite electrodes are used in each arm of the tube and are connected to the power source. The reactions that occur are

ANODE REACTION $\qquad 2\ Cl^-\ (aq) \rightarrow Cl_2\ (g) + 2\ e^-$

CATHODE REACTION $\quad 2\ H^+\ (aq) + 2\ e^- \rightarrow H_2\ (g)$

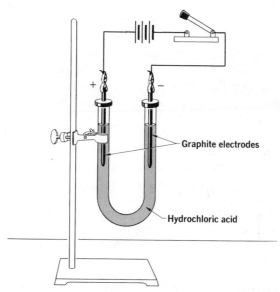

Fig. 6–3   Electrolysis of hydrochloric acid

6.22 Oxidation of chloride ion

Chloride ion is also oxidized by suitable oxidizing agents. Substances containing particles that tend to gain electrons may behave as oxidizing agents. Some common examples of oxidizing agents are the elements containing six or seven electrons in their outermost shells, such as oxygen, sulfur, fluorine, chlorine, bromine, and iodine. In addition, Mn, in MnO_2 and $KMnO_4$, has a high positive valence number, suggesting that these compounds will behave as oxidizing agents. Chlorine may be prepared from binary chlorine compounds as follows:

$$\text{(1)} \quad 2\ \overset{+1\ -1}{\text{NaCl}}\ (aq) + \text{F}_2\ (g) \rightarrow 2\ \overset{+1\ -1}{\text{NaF}}\ (aq) + \overset{0}{\text{Cl}_2}\ (g)$$

with $-2\ e^-$ transferred from NaCl and $+2\ e^-$ to F$_2$

The extreme reactivity of F_2, however, makes this reaction too difficult to control. MnO_2 is a more convenient oxidizing agent.

$$\text{(2)} \quad 4\ \overset{+1\ -1}{\text{HCl}}\ (aq) + \overset{+4\ -2}{\text{MnO}_2}\ (s) \rightarrow \overset{+2\ -1}{\text{MnCl}_2}\ (aq) + \overset{0}{\text{Cl}_2}\ (g) + 2\ \text{H}_2\text{O}$$

with $-2\ e^-$ and $+2\ e^-$ transfer

Note that 2 Cl^- remain unchanged.

The alert student will wonder if MnO_2 will oxidize Cl^- ions in NaCl or in any other metallic chloride. Experiment reveals that MnO_2 does not oxidize metallic chlorides. Why? We have indicated the reduction half-reaction in equation 2 as

$$Mn^{+4} + 2\ e^- \rightarrow Mn^{+2}$$

which should be written as

$$MnO_2 + 4\ H^+\ (aq) + 2\ e^- \rightarrow Mn^{+2}\ (aq) + 2\ H_2O$$

This means that MnO_2 requires H^+ (an acid solution) to behave as an oxidizing agent. Since a metallic chloride contains no H^+ ions, oxidation by MnO_2 does not occur. If H_2SO_4 is added to a mixture of NaCl and MnO_2, Cl_2 gas forms.

$$2\ \overset{+1\ -1}{\text{NaCl}}\ (aq) + 2\ \overset{+1\ -2}{\text{H}_2\text{SO}_4}\ (aq) + \overset{+4\ -2}{\text{MnO}_2}\ (s) \rightarrow \overset{0}{\text{Cl}_2}\ (g) + \overset{+2\ -2}{\text{MnSO}_4}\ (aq) + \overset{+1\ -2}{\text{Na}_2\text{SO}_4}\ (aq) + 2\ \text{H}_2\text{O}$$

with $-2\ e^-$ and $+2\ e^-$ transfer

6.23 Summary of principles of extraction

The following principles are utilized in the extraction of metals and non-metals from compounds:

1. Metals may be extracted by reduction of the corresponding metallic ion.
2. Nonmetals may be extracted by oxidation of the corresponding nonmetallic ion.

3. If a reducing agent is employed, the reducing particle must lose electrons more readily than the particle to be reduced.
4. If an oxidizing agent is employed, the oxidizing particle must gain electrons more readily than the particle to be oxidized.

We have discussed many reactions in the previous pages and have written many equations for these reactions. Bear in mind that the equation is a convenient summary of what has been observed experimentally. At times, the equation is a prediction of what might occur. Simply writing the equation in no way confirms the likelihood of the reaction. Furthermore, the equation tells us nothing about the rate of the reaction or how the reaction occurs—its mechanism. The answers to these questions lie in another domain, to be explored in Chapter 13.

Multiple-Choice Questions

1. When 1 g of water changes to 1 g of ice (1) heat is absorbed (2) a change in mass occurs (3) a decrease in volume occurs (4) a decrease in density occurs
2. Water is an important substance because it (1) is highly ionized (2) has a low boiling point and a low freezing point (3) is a universal solvent (4) has a different percentage composition in the liquid and solid forms
3. The reaction $2 H^+ (aq) + 2 e^- \rightarrow H_2 (g)$ can be classed as (1) hydrogenation (2) oxidation (3) reduction (4) synthesis
4. In the reaction $2 M^0 (s) + 2 H^+ (aq) \rightarrow H_2 (g) + 2 M^+ (aq)$, the metal M is probably *not* (1) silver (2) aluminum (3) magnesium (4) zinc
5. In the reaction $2 M^0 (s) + 2 H_2O \rightarrow 2 M^+ (aq) + 2 OH^- (aq) + H_2 (g)$, the metal M is probably (1) zinc (2) aluminum (3) lithium (4) copper
6. Oxygen has a valence number of -1 in (1) Na_2O_2 (2) $KClO_3$ (3) H_2O (4) $NaOH$
7. The reaction $Zn^0 (s) + Cu^{+2} (aq) \rightarrow Zn^{+2} (aq) + Cu^0 (s)$ shows that (1) electrons are transferred from $Zn^0 (s)$ to $Cu^{+2} (aq)$ (2) $Cu^0 (s)$ is a stronger reducing agent than $Zn^0 (s)$ (3) $Zn^0 (s)$ receives positive charges from $Cu^{+2} (aq)$ (4) $Cu^{+2} (aq)$ is oxidized by $Zn^0 (s)$
8. The composition of water by volume is $H : O = 2 : 1$, but by weight it is $H : O = 1 : 8$. This shows that (1) more oxygen atoms are present than hydrogen atoms (2) more atoms are present in a mole of oxygen than in a mole of hydrogen (3) the density of oxygen is 16 times greater than the density of hydrogen (4) more molecules of oxygen than hydrogen are present in water

9. The type of bond between hydrogen atoms and oxygen atoms in a molecule of water is (1) a hydrogen bond (2) an ionic bond (3) a non-polar ionic bond (4) a polar covalent bond

10. When 40 ml of hydrogen are mixed with 40 ml of oxygen (1) water forms (2) 20 ml of hydrogen remain (3) a mixture of two gases is present (4) 20 ml of oxygen remain

11. The reaction between sodium and chlorine results in the formation of (1) ions (2) molecules (3) atoms (4) ions and molecules

Completion Questions

1. The process by which a compound is formed from its elements is called _____ .

2. When H^+ combines with a molecule of water, it forms a particle called _____ ion.

3. *a.* During electrolysis, chemical bonds between atoms are broken by the application of _____ energy.

   b. During thermal decomposition, chemical bonds between atoms are broken by the application of _____ energy.

4. During electrolysis, oxidation always takes place at the _____ (*anode, cathode*).

5. Sodium chloride has a high melting point because a large amount of energy must be supplied to break the bonds between the _____ in the crystal.

6. The commercial production of chlorine and chlorine compounds utilizes the compound _____ as a raw material.

7. The equation $Na^+Cl^- + H_2O \rightarrow Na^+$ (*aq*) $+ Cl^-$ (*aq*) indicates that the ions released by NaCl, on dissolving, combine with molecules of _____ .

True-False Questions

1. The decomposition of 1 mole of water requires 68.3 kcal, whereas the change of 1 mole of water to steam requires 9.7 kcal. Therefore, *more* energy is required to separate the atoms in water than the molecules in water.

2. The electrolysis of *aqueous* sodium chloride produces metallic sodium.

3. *Oxidizing* agents readily accept electrons from other substances.

4. Water expands when warmed above 4° C and also expands when cooled below 4° C. Thus the density of water at 4° C is *lower than* at other temperatures.

5. The reaction $2 H_2O \rightarrow H_2 (g) + 2 OH^- (aq)$ takes place when two electrons are *added to* two molecules of water.
6. Ten g of hydrogen can combine with sufficient oxygen to form *90* g of water.
7. Both hydrogen and oxygen are abundant in our surroundings and can be obtained by decomposition of *the atmosphere.*
8. Electrolysis is frequently employed to decompose compounds made up of atoms united by *weak* chemical bonds.
9. Chlorine is *more* soluble in cold water than in hot water.
10. The formula HBr (aq) is that of a *ternary* acid.

Equations

1. Aluminum reacts with sulfuric acid to liberate hydrogen.
   a. Write the complete equation for the reaction.
   b. Write the half-reactions.
2. Write the equation for the thermal decomposition of the hydrocarbon ethane, C_2H_6.
3. *a.* Write the equation for the electrolysis of molten potassium chloride.
   b. Write the half-reactions.
4. Hydrogen peroxide decomposes slowly on standing. Write the equation for the chemical change involved.
5. Write the equation for the thermal decomposition of sodium chlorate.
6. *a.* Write the equation for the reaction of Mg with HCl (aq).
   b. Which particles react?
   c. Which particles do not change?
7. Write the half-reactions for the union of hydrogen with chlorine to form hydrogen chloride.
8. *a.* Write the equation for the combination of aluminum with chlorine.
   b. Write the half-reactions.
9. *a.* Write the equation for the reaction of MnO_2 with aqueous HBr, forming $MnBr_2$, Br_2, and H_2O.
   b. Write the half-reactions.

Exercises for Review

1. In a laboratory experiment, 100 g of zinc are added to dilute sulfuric acid to prepare hydrogen.
   a. Write the equation for the reaction.
   b. How many moles of zinc are used?
   c. What is the number of moles and the weight of the zinc sulfate formed?

2. A bottle contains 600 g of a 3%-by-weight solution of hydrogen peroxide in water. After standing for a long time, the bottle contains only water.

   a. What weight of hydrogen peroxide was present originally?

   b. How many moles of oxygen were released?

   c. What is the weight of the liquid left in the bottle?

3. A sample of sodium weighing 0.46 g is added to a bottle containing chlorine gas. Write the equation for the reaction.

4. *a.* A student prepares oxygen by heating 4 g of potassium chlorate. Another student prepares oxygen by heating 4 g of mercury(II) oxide. Write equations for both reactions.

   b. How many moles of starting substance are present in each experiment?

   c. How many moles of oxygen are produced in each experiment?

5. *a.* Electric current is passed through water containing dilute sulfuric acid. The experimenter finds that 3.6 g of water have decomposed. Write the equation for the reaction.

   b. What fraction of a mole of water was used?

   c. What is the weight of each of the products?

6. *a.* A student adds 0.1 g of calcium to one beaker of water and adds 0.1 g of potassium to a second beaker of water. Write equations for both reactions.

   b. How many moles of metallic elements are used in each experiment?

   c. How many moles of hydrogen form in each experiment?

7. *a.* A sample of magnesium weighing 0.480 g is added to an abundant quantity of hydrochloric acid. Write an equation for the reaction.

   b. Calculate the number of moles of magnesium used and the number of moles of hydrogen formed.

   c. What is the weight of the hydrogen?

   d. Would this weight be different if sulfuric acid were used in place of hydrochloric acid? Explain.

8. *a.* A chemist adds 0.46 g of sodium metal to a liter of water. Write an equation for the reaction.

   b. How many moles of sodium are used?

   c. How many moles of each product form?

   d. What is the weight of sodium hydroxide in the resulting solution?

9. *a.* A mixture of 0.4 g of hydrogen and 6.0 g of oxygen is ignited. Write an equation for the reaction.

   b. What is the total number of moles of reactants?

   c. How many moles of product form?

10. *a.* In a laboratory experiment, 0.25 g of hydrogen are mixed with 0.80 g of oxygen. After the mixture is ignited, what gas remains uncombined?

   b. What is the weight of the uncombined gas?

   c. What is the weight of the water that forms?

11. *a.* When 20 ml of hydrogen are mixed with 8 ml of oxygen and then ignited, which gas remains uncombined?

   b. What is its volume?

12. *a.* When 30 ml of hydrogen and 30 ml of oxygen are mixed and ignited, which gas remains uncombined?

   b. What is its volume?

Exercises for Further Study

1. *a.* Why is it necessary either to dissolve NaCl in water or to melt it before electrolysis can take place?

   b. Do dissolved NaCl and molten NaCl have any particles in common? Explain.

2. Electrolyzing molten $CuCl_2$ and electrolyzing an aqueous solution of $CuCl_2$ yield the same products. Will the same amount of electrical energy be required for each process? Explain.

3. What are the differences between the particles H^+ and H_3O^+?

4. In the half-reaction $2\,H^+ (aq) + 2\,e^- \rightarrow H_2 (g)$, what changes take place in the chemical bonds involving hydrogen?

5. Describe some of the important functions of water in the human body.

6. What do underground salt deposits suggest concerning the geologic history of a region?

7. Explain why $KMnO_4$ can act as an oxidizing agent, but $MnSO_4$ cannot.

8. Describe the changes that take place in the average distance between neighboring water molecules when water is heated from $1°\,C$ to $4°\,C$ and then from $4°\,C$ to $99°\,C$.

Chapter 7

CHEMICAL FAMILIES

7.1 Introduction

The 103 different elements that have been identified in nature or created by man exhibit a wide variety of physical and chemical properties. It is difficult, indeed impractical, to study each element separately. Chemists, therefore, arrange elements according to their common properties. In this chapter, we will begin to classify some of the elements previously studied. We will do this by analyzing their properties and by noting similarities and trends in these properties. Finally, we will introduce the Periodic Table to summarize our findings.

7.2 Reactions between atoms

Thus far, we know that all elements consist of atoms which, in turn, consist of protons, electrons, and neutrons. When atoms undergo chemical change and become parts of molecules, the particles in the molecules tend to become more stable; that is, they attain the electron structure of a noble gas. We are not concerned at this time with the reasons why noble gases exhibit unusual stability. Suffice it to say: When atoms unite to form a molecule, each atom in the molecule generally attains the electron structure of a noble gas by the transfer or sharing of electrons.

The number of electrons involved in such changes may provide a partial measure of the reactivity of the atoms in the element. Therefore, it may be possible to categorize elements in terms of the number of electrons required to enable the atom to attain a noble gas structure.

7.3 Comparison of hydrogen and sodium

The extraction of hydrogen gas from compounds in which hydrogen has a valence number of $+1$ involves the restoration of an electron to H^+. The extraction of sodium from its compounds also involves the restoration of a single electron to Na^+.

$$H^+ + e^- \rightarrow H^0$$
$$H^0 + H^0 \rightarrow H_2{}^0 \ (g)$$
$$Na^+ + e^- \rightarrow Na \ (s)$$

This common property suggests that hydrogen and sodium may be related. Let us test this possibility by examining some of the properties of each of these elements.

PROPERTY	HYDROGEN	SODIUM
atomic number	1	11
electrons in outermost shell	1	1
state at room conditions	gas	solid
density (g/cm^3)	0.000089	0.97
melting point $(^\circ C)$	-257.3	97.8
boiling point $(^\circ C)$	-252.8	883

An analysis of the properties reveals that hydrogen and sodium have little in common except the single electron in the outermost (valence) shells. Hydrogen is a gas at room conditions, whereas sodium is a solid. Hydrogen must be cooled considerably to form a liquid that boils at a low temperature. Further cooling forms a solid that melts at an even lower temperature. Sodium, on the other hand, is a metallic solid at room conditions and melts at a considerably higher temperature than hydrogen to form a liquid that boils at an even higher temperature. Let us now examine the properties of hydrogen compounds and the properties of sodium compounds to further ascertain whether similarities or differences predominate.

7.4 Properties of hydrogen compounds

Consider the structure of an atom of hydrogen in terms of our nuclear model (see section 4.2). Hydrogen has a single electron in its K-shell. This shell has a maximum electron occupancy of two electrons.

Hydrogen can gain greater stability by either losing, gaining, or sharing an electron. If it loses its lone electron, it forms the H^+ species, which is, in reality, a free proton. A hydrogen atom may be stripped of its lone electron when subjected to high-voltage discharge in a gas discharge tube. If an atom of hydrogen gains an electron, it forms the H^- ion.

Consider the H^+ species in compound HZ, in which H and Z share a pair of electrons. We have already indicated that, in aqueous solution, this species reacts with water molecules to form the $H^+(H_2O)_n$ ion, usually designated as H_3O^+ or $H^+(aq)$.

$$HZ + H_2O \rightarrow H_3O^+ + Z^-$$

Typical hydrogen compounds containing H_3O^+ ions are shown in the following table.

COMPOUND	COMPOSITION		COMMON NAME
hydrogen chloride (*aq*)	H_3O^+	Cl^- (*aq*)	hydrochloric acid
hydrogen nitrate (*aq*)	H_3O^+	NO_3^- (*aq*)	nitric acid
hydrogen sulfate (*aq*)	$2\ H_3O^+$	SO_4^{-2} (*aq*)	sulfuric acid
hydrogen acetate (*aq*)	H_3O^+	CH_3COO^- (*aq*)	acetic acid

Hydrogen compounds that contain H_3O^+ ions are called *acids*. These compounds were introduced in section 6.8 and will be discussed further in Chapter 16. Hydrogen compounds that contain H^- ions are ionic solids, called *hydrides*, for example, lithium hydride, LiH, and calcium hydride, CaH_2.

The chemistry of hydrogen appears to differ somewhat from the chemistry of other elements. This unique behavior of hydrogen may be ascribed to its relatively small size. Since hydrogen possesses one electron in the K-shell and one proton in the nucleus, the removal of the electron liberates the proton. In water solution, the proton becomes aquated, forming H_3O^+. More frequently, however, hydrogen forms covalent bonds with many nonmetals, such as nitrogen and sulfur.

7.5 Properties of sodium compounds

Let us now consider the electron structure of an atom of sodium. Sodium has completed K- and L-shells and has a single electron in its M-shell, which has a maximum occupancy of eight electrons. The presence of three electron shells means that the sodium atom is larger than the hydrogen atom.

A sodium atom can attain the noble gas structure of neon by losing the electron in its M-shell, forming the Na^+ ion. Consequently, all sodium compounds are ionic, containing the Na^+ ion. This ion exists in sodium compounds in the solid state; it is also produced in gas discharge tubes containing vaporized sodium metal. High voltage is utilized in the gas discharge tube to strip the M-shell electron from a sodium atom. In aqueous solution, the Na^+ ion combines with water molecules to form Na^+ (*aq*) ions. The table that follows lists some typical sodium compounds in water solution.

COMPOUND	COMPOSITION OF WATER SOLUTION	
sodium chloride	Na^+ (*aq*)	Cl^- (*aq*)
sodium nitrate	Na^+ (*aq*)	NO_3^- (*aq*)
sodium sulfate	$2\ Na^+$ (*aq*)	SO_4^{-2} (*aq*)

7.6 How do hydrogen and sodium differ?

Hydrogen atoms differ from sodium atoms in electron structure. Their chemistry, therefore, is quite different. Hydrogen compounds, containing hydrogen with a valence number of $+1$, are covalently bonded. Sodium compounds, on the other hand, are ionic solids and show no tendency to form covalent bonds. In aqueous solution, hydrogen compounds form H^+ (*aq*), and sodium compounds form Na^+ (*aq*). Both of these aquated ions react very differently. We may conclude from our analysis of their properties that hydrogen and sodium bear only a slight resemblance to one another.

7.7 Properties of the alkali metals

Let us continue our search for elements that have a closer relationship to sodium than hydrogen. Perhaps other elements containing one electron in their outermost shells might be related to sodium. Lithium, potassium, rubidium, cesium, copper, silver, and gold also contain one electron in their outermost shells. (We will omit francium, a radioactive element, from this discussion.)

Copper, silver, and gold, unlike sodium, have 18 electrons rather than eight in the next-to-the-outermost shell. Thus in terms of their electron configurations, only lithium, potassium, rubidium, and cesium appear to resemble sodium. These elements are called the *alkali metals*.

The following table lists some of the properties of alkali metals.

PROPERTY	LITHIUM	SODIUM	POTASSIUM	RUBIDIUM	CESIUM
atomic number	3	11	19	37	55
atomic size [radius in Å $(10^{-8}$ cm)]	1.23	1.57	2.02	2.16	2.35
electrons in outermost shell	1	1	1	1	1
number of electron shells	2	3	4	5	6
state at room conditions	solid	solid	solid	solid	solid
density (g/cm³ at 0° C and 760 mm)	0.53	0.97	0.86	1.53	1.90
melting point (° C)	186	97.8	62.7	39.0	28.4
boiling point (° C)	1336	883	776	700	670

Analysis of the table reveals similarities among the alkali metals. Despite differences in atomic size, density, and melting and boiling points, a measurable trend appears in each of these properties. Note the regular increase in atomic sizes and densities and the regular decrease in melting and boiling points. The data suggests that the alkali metals are closely related. The relationship between their properties depends on the number of electron shells and the size of the atoms.

In Chapter 6, we learned that lithium reacts with water to form hydrogen gas and lithium hydroxide. Sodium, potassium, rubidium, and cesium react in the same manner. If M represents an alkali metal, the following equation represents the reaction between an alkali metal and water:

$$M \ (s) + H_2O \rightarrow MOH \ (aq) + \frac{1}{2} H_2 \ (g)$$

The alkali metals also react with halogens (fluorine, chlorine, bromine, and iodine) and with oxygen.

$$M \ (s) + \underset{\text{halogen}}{\frac{1}{2} Z_2} \ (g) \rightarrow MZ \ (s)$$

$$2 \ M \ (s) + \frac{1}{2} O_2 \ (g) \rightarrow M_2O \ (s)$$

From these relationships, we conclude that lithium, sodium, potassium, rubidium, and cesium represent a chemical family, or group. Bear in mind that the members of a family do not have identical properties. Instead, their properties are similar, exhibiting a regular trend as one goes up or down a column of elements arranged in the order of their atomic numbers. Certain members of a family, usually the elements with the lowest and highest atomic numbers, frequently exhibit atypical properties. These deviations will be discussed in a later chapter.

7.8 Comparison of oxygen and chlorine

The extraction of oxygen from its compounds and the extraction of chlorine from its compounds both involve the removal of electrons.

$$2 \underset{\substack{\text{oxide} \\ \text{ion}}}{O^{-2}} \rightarrow O_2 \ (g) + 4 \ e^-$$

$$\underset{\substack{\text{peroxide} \\ \text{ion}}}{O_2^{-2}} \rightarrow O_2 \ (g) + 2 \ e^-$$

$$2 \ Cl^- \rightarrow Cl_2 \ (g) + 2 \ e^-$$

This common property suggests that oxygen and chlorine may be related. Let us test this possibility by examining some of the characteristics of each of these elements.

PROPERTY	OXYGEN	CHLORINE
atomic number	8	17
atomic size (radius in Å)	0.74	0.99
electrons in outermost shell	6	7
number of electron shells	2	3
state at room conditions	gas	gas
density (g/cm³) at 0° C and 760 mm)	0.00143	0.00321
melting point (° C)	−218.9	−102.4
boiling point (° C)	−183.0	−34.0

An analysis of the properties reveals some similarities and some differences. Although both elements are gases, marked differences appear in their densities and melting and boiling points. The outstanding difference between oxygen and chlorine seems to be in their electron structures and in the properties related to these structures. Most commonly, an atom of oxygen requires two electrons to attain the noble gas structure, whereas an atom of chlorine requires a single electron. Let us examine the properties of oxygen compounds and the properties of chlorine compounds to ascertain possible similarities.

7.9 Properties of oxygen compounds

Consider the electron structure of an atom of oxygen (see section 4.3). Oxygen has a completed K-shell and six electrons in its L-shell. Oxygen can attain the noble gas structure of neon by acquiring two electrons. These electrons may be obtained by transfer, in which case an ionic solid containing O^{-2} ions is formed. The table that follows lists some typical oxide compounds containing O^{-2} ions.

COMPOUND	COMPOSITION	
lithium oxide	$2 \, Li^+$	O^{-2}
calcium oxide	Ca^{+2}	O^{-2}
aluminum oxide	$2 \, Al^{+3}$	$3 \, O^{-2}$

Oxygen also forms many compounds in which oxygen atoms are bonded to other atoms by sharing electron pairs (covalent bonds). We have already mentioned H_2O and $KClO_3$ as examples of compounds containing covalently bonded oxygen. The versatility of the oxygen atom makes its chemistry fairly complex.

7.10 Properties of chlorine compounds

Our nuclear model indicates that an atom of chlorine has completed K- and L-shells and has seven electrons in its M-shell. A chlorine atom can attain the noble gas structure of argon by acquiring one electron to form the Cl^- ion. Most metallic chlorides are ionic solids; typical examples are shown below.

COMPOUND	COMPOSITION	
cesium chloride	Cs^+	Cl^-
calcium chloride	Ca^{+2}	$2 \, Cl^-$
zinc chloride	Zn^{+2}	$2 \, Cl^-$

In addition to forming ionic compounds, chlorine exhibits a valence number of -1 in a variety of compounds in which it is covalently bonded to other atoms. For example: hydrogen chloride, HCl; carbon tetrachloride, CCl_4; and phosphorus trichloride, PCl_3. Chlorine also exhibits many positive valence numbers in compounds such as dichlorine monoxide, Cl_2O; potassium chlorite, $KClO_2$; and potassium chlorate, $KClO_3$. Thus like the chemistry of oxygen, the chemistry of chlorine is complex.

In summary, oxygen and chlorine resemble one another closely except in the number of electrons required to give each the corresponding noble gas structure. Let us further examine the electron structures of oxygen and chlorine. We shall relate—separately—oxygen and chlorine to other elements that tend to acquire the same number of electrons to attain the noble gas structure.

7.11 The oxygen family

Examination of the table of properties reveals that in addition to oxygen, the elements sulfur, selenium, and tellurium possess six electrons in their outermost shells. (We will omit polonium, a radioactive element, from this discussion.) Each of these elements tends to gain two electrons to acquire the corresponding noble gas structure. The table that follows lists some of the characteristics of these elements.

PROPERTY	OXYGEN	SULFUR	SELENIUM	TELLURIUM
atomic number	8	16	34	52
atomic size (radius in Å)	0.74	1.04	1.17	1.37
electrons in outermost shell	6	6	6	6
number of electron shells	2	3	4	5
state at room conditions	gas	solid	solid	solid
density (g/cm³ at 0° C and 760 mm)	0.00143	2.06	5.82	6.25
melting point (°C)	−218.9	119.0	220.2	452
boiling point (°C)	−183.0	444.6	688	1390

Analysis of the table reveals some specific trends. The sizes, densities, and melting and boiling points increase with increasing atomic number. The greatest similarity among these elements is in the analogous compounds that they form with hydrogen, oxygen, and metals—for example, H_2O, H_2S, H_2Se and H_2Te; SO_2, SeO_2, and TeO_2; and Na_2O, Na_2S, Na_2Se, and Na_2Te.

7.12 Halogens: the chlorine family

Examination of the table that follows reveals that in addition to chlorine, the elements fluorine, bromine, and iodine possess seven electrons in their outermost shells. (As before, we will omit a radioactive element, astatine, from this discussion.) These elements are called the *halogens* (salt-formers). The table that follows lists some of the characteristics of the halogens.

PROPERTY	FLUORINE	CHLORINE	BROMINE	IODINE
atomic number	9	17	35	53
atomic size (radius in Å)	0.72	0.99	1.14	1.33
electrons in outermost shell	7	7	7	7
number of electron shells	2	3	4	5
state at room conditions	gas	gas	liquid	solid
density (g/cm³ at 0° C and 760 mm)	0.0011	0.00321	3.14	4.9
melting point (°C)	−223	−102.4	−7.3	113.7
boiling point (°C)	−187.9	−34.0	58.8	184.5

The properties of the halogens exhibit specific trends based on increasing atomic number. Note the transition from gas to solid and the regular increases in densities and melting and boiling points. Similar trends are evident when the hydrogen compounds of the halogens are studied. Again we must emphasize the relationship of properties in a chemical family. The properties of the members of a chemical family are not identical but show a regular variation as a function of atomic number. Some deviations from regular behavior are observed among the members of all chemical families.

All the halogens form binary ionic compounds corresponding to the general formula MZ, where M represents the symbol of a metal and Z represents the symbol of a halogen. In addition, all the halogens form binary hydrogen compounds, covalently bonded; for example, HCl and HBr.

7.13 Summary of the relationships in a chemical family

We can summarize the relationships among the elements in a chemical family as follows:

1. Each element in the family possesses the same number of electrons in its outermost shell and, generally, the same number of electrons in its next-to-the-outermost shell.
2. Members of a chemical family possess similar, rather than identical, chemical properties.
3. The properties of each element vary regularly as a function of atomic number.
4. Elements that begin and end a chemical family may have some atypical properties.

7.14 Early attempts to classify the properties of elements

Scientists have always searched for relationships among elements. At least three important attempts were made during the past 150 years to determine such relationships—by the English physician William Prout, the German chemist Johann Döbereiner, and the English chemist John Newlands.

PROUT'S HYPOTHESIS

Using the Dalton model of the atom, Prout, in 1815, suggested that hydrogen was the fundamental element from which all of the other elements were constructed. His conclusion was based on the observation that the weights of atoms were whole-number multiples of the atomic weight of hydrogen. This idea appeared revolutionary early in the 19th century. Now we know that Prout may have been close to the truth. Modern experimental evidence, gathered during nuclear transformations, indicates that all elements may be derived from helium.

DÖBEREINER'S TRIADS

Also using the Dalton model of the atom, Döbereiner, in 1817, observed that certain groups of three elements had related properties. If these groups of elements, called *triads*, are arranged in order of increasing atomic weight, the atomic weight of the middle member is the average of the atomic weights of the other elements. For example, chlorine (atomic weight 35), bromine (atomic weight 80), and iodine (atomic weight 127), behave as a triad. Note that the atomic weight of the middle member of the triad—bromine—is close to the arithmetic average of the atomic weights of chlorine and iodine.

Furthermore, the properties of the middle element are approximately midway between the other elements. Thus bromine is less reactive than chlorine but more reactive than iodine.

NEWLANDS' LAW OF OCTAVES

Again using the Dalton model of the atom, Newlands, in 1865, suggested that if the elements are arranged in order of increasing atomic weight, the first and eighth members will have related properties.

Suppose we arrange, in columns of seven, the first 14 elements known at that time in order of increasing atomic weight (omitting hydrogen).

lithium	sodium
beryllium	magnesium
boron	aluminum
carbon	silicon
nitrogen	phosphorus
oxygen	sulfur
fluorine	chlorine

Just as the first note in an octave of the musical scale resembles the eighth note, so the first element — lithium — resembles the eighth element — sodium; the second element resembles the ninth; and so on. This relationship, because of its resemblance to the musical scale, was termed the *Law of Octaves*.

The ideas of Prout, Döbereiner, and Newlands were met with considerable skepticism and, in some instances, with scorn. Yet these ideas proved to be forerunners of the most important single correlation in all chemistry — the periodic classification.

7.15 The periodic classification of the elements

In 1869, Dmitri Mendeléef, a Russian chemist, stated that the properties of the elements are periodic functions of their atomic weights. His conclusion was based on a study of the observed chemical properties of the elements known then. At about the same time, Lothar Meyer, a German chemist, came to the same conclusion from a study of some of the physical properties of the same elements. The observation by both chemists was termed the *Periodic Law*. This law states that if the elements are arranged in order of increasing atomic weight, the physical and chemical properties will repeat themselves regularly. (Actually, these properties are periodic functions of atomic numbers, as will be shown later.)

A portion of the original Mendeléef-Meyer table is reproduced below.

SERIES	GROUPS						
	I	II	III	IV	V	VI	VII
1	H						
2	Li	Be	B	C	N	O	F
3	Na	Mg	Al	Si	P	S	Cl
4	K Cu	Ca Zn	□ □	□ Ti	As V	Se Cr	Br Mn
5	Rb Ag	Sr Cd	In Y	Sn Zr	Sb Nb	Te Mo	I □

□ represents an element that was predicted
but undiscovered.

Chemical families are represented by the elements in each group (vertical column). The properties of an element in any group are closely related to the properties of the elements directly above and below it.

Observe that each group has a corresponding sub-group written to the right of the elements in the main group. Elements in a sub-group, such as Cu and Ag in Sub-group I, are more closely related to one another than to the elements in a main group such as Li and Na in Main Group I. These predictions were borne out in our previous discussions.

7.16 Evaluation of the Mendeléef-Meyer table

The Mendeléef-Meyer table reflected all the insufficiencies of the Dalton model of the atom, on which it was based. The reasons for the periodicity of properties were not apparent. The presence of sub-groups within main groups could not be explained. Finally, if the positions of certain pairs of elements follow in order of increasing atomic weight, the pairs — such as argon and potassium, cobalt and nickel, and tellurium and iodine — would have to be reversed.

Despite these limitations, the table successfully predicted the presence of many undiscovered elements, indicated by the symbol □ in the table on page 115. The table that follows lists the prediction of some of the properties of the element directly below silicon. Next to these predictions are the observed properties of the element germanium, discovered in 1886.

PROPERTY	PREDICTION FOR ELEMENT BELOW SILICON	OBSERVED PROPERTY OF GERMANIUM
atomic weight	72	72.32
specific heat	0.073	0.076
specific gravity	5.5	5.47
formula of oxide	XO_2	GeO_2

The Mendeléef-Meyer table encouraged chemists to classify the elements properly and to discover missing elements. This stimulus and the discoveries it fostered led to the development of the modern Periodic Table.

7.17 The modern Periodic Table

Research during the latter half of the 19th century necessitated a restatement of the *Periodic Law: The properties of the elements are periodic functions of their atomic numbers.*

Atomic numbers represent the number of protons and also the number of electrons in a neutral atom. The electron structures of atoms, therefore, provide an important basis for the regular repetition of the properties of elements. The modern table (which we shall discuss in considerable detail beginning with section 19.22) arranges the elements in order of increasing atomic number, resulting in the vertical and horizontal arrangements shown on pages 620-621.

As in the earlier table, the elements in the vertical columns represent the chemical families. This arrangement is based on the electron structure of the atom in its outermost and next-to-the-outermost shells. For example, the alkali metals are in Group IA (Main Group I) because they all have a single electron in their outermost shells and eight electrons in their next-to-the-outermost shells. (Lithium is an exception.) The metals in Group IB (Sub-group I) also have one electron in their outermost shell but have 18 electrons in their next-to-the-outermost shells. In the same manner, electron structures provide a basis for classifying the members of all the families, such as the oxygen family (Group VIA) and the halogens (Group VIIA).

7.18 Trends within a given family (column)

A given family of elements tends to form compounds by the transfer of the same number of electrons or by the sharing of the same number of pairs of electrons. Each of the elements in the compounds thus attains the electron structure of a noble gas. For example, the elements in the lithium column (alkali metals) react with hydrogen to form metallic hydrides. If M represents the symbol for any member of that family the generalized reaction becomes

$$2 \text{ M } (s) + \text{H}_2 \ (g) \rightarrow 2 \text{ MH } (s)$$

Electronically, the reaction can be represented as

$$2 \text{ M} \cdot + 2 \text{ H} \cdot \longrightarrow 2 \text{ M}^+ + 2 \left[\text{H} \colon \right]^-$$

Note that metal M has become a positive ion, having attained the electron structure of the noble gas just preceding it in the Periodic Table. Similarly, H has become a negative ion, having attained the electron structure of helium.

The tendency to lose electrons is a function of nuclear charge and the size of the atom. It would appear that as the nuclear charges of members of a family increase, the tendency to lose electrons would decrease because of greater attractive force. However, the number of energy levels (shells) increases as the atomic numbers increase. As the atoms become larger, the distances between their nuclei and their outermost electrons also increase; thus valence electrons can be lost more readily. For example, cesium — a larger atom than sodium — loses electrons more readily than sodium.

In a given family, the tendency to gain electrons increases with decreasing atomic number. Therefore, fluorine — a smaller atom than iodine — gains electrons more readily than iodine.

7.19 Trends within a given series (row)

The atoms in a given series generally have the same number of electron shells. Thus as atomic numbers increase, changes in atomic size are not as great in a given series as they are in a given family. It might appear, therefore, that all atoms in a given series should transfer electrons equally well. But the tendency to transfer electrons also depends mainly on nuclear charge. As the tendency to lose electrons decreases, the tendency to gain electrons increases. In row 2, lithium loses electrons more readily than beryllium. Fluorine, which shows only a slight tendency to lose electrons, gains electrons more readily than oxygen.

Since the tendency to lose electrons is an important property of metals, the trend in a given series, such as row 2, is to proceed from more metallic to less metallic elements. For example, in this row, lithium is the most metallic element, whereas fluorine is the least metallic (most nonmetallic) element.

We have now completed our introduction to the study of some typical elements and their compounds. Although our discussions centered on specific examples, we have emphasized some of the broad principles governing chemical reactions. In succeeding chapters, we will probe more deeply into the organization of matter and the forces that drive specific reactions. Finally, we will consider the nature of chemical change in terms of modern atomic theory.

Multiple-Choice Questions

1. Hydrogen and sodium have the same (1) states at room temperature (2) boiling points when liquid (3) densities (4) numbers of valence electrons

2. As we proceed from left to right in a series of elements in the Periodic Table, we note an increase in the (1) atomic radius (2) number of electron shells (3) tendency to gain electrons (4) tendency to lose electrons

3. Which of the following statements is true? (1) elements in Sub-group B have eight electrons in the shell below the valence shell (2) elements in Sub-group B have 18 electrons in the shell below the valence shell (3) Sub-group B contains more elements than Sub-group A (4) Subgroup B contains only the newly discovered elements

4. When elements are grouped in triads, it is observed that (1) the atomic weights of the three elements are almost equal (2) the chemical activity of the middle element is greatest (3) the properties of the second element are intermediate between the first and last (4) the last element resembles the first element in the next triad

5. A chemical family of elements contains elements with (1) identical chemical properties (2) the same nuclear charge (3) the same physical properties (4) related chemical and physical properties

6. One important difference between the original and the modern Periodic Table is that the modern table (1) begins with hydrogen, while the original table began with helium (2) does not have Subgroups (3) has no place for the noble gases (4) is based on the atomic numbers of the elements, not their atomic weights

7. The Periodic Law points out that (1) eight related elements always have similar properties (2) the properties of elements vary in a periodic manner with increasing atomic weight (3) all elements are composed of hydrogen (4) the valence numbers of elements increase with their atomic weights

8. As the atomic numbers of the halogen elements increase (1) the number of atoms in the molecule increases (2) their valence numbers in binary compounds with hydrogen decrease (3) their states change from gas to solid (4) their atomic radii decrease

9. The alkali metals have very similar properties because they all (1) possess the same number of valence electrons (2) have the same atomic radius (3) react with water to form oxygen (4) readily form positive ions

10. In a given series (row) of the Periodic Table, a property that shows the smallest variation is (1) atomic radius (2) density (3) melting point (4) specific heat

Completion Questions

1. The most active nonmetal in the Periodic Table is _____.

2. The Periodic Table is arranged so that the _____ (*columns, rows*) represent families of elements, while the _____ (*columns, rows*) represent a series of different families.

3. The elements of Group VIA, including oxygen and sulfur, combine with metals to form ions that have a charge of _____.

4. A common characteristic of aqueous solutions of hydrogen chloride, hydrogen nitrate, and hydrogen sulfate is that they all contain the hydrated H^+ ion, which has the formula _____.

5. The alkali metals readily lose one electron as shown by the equation $X \rightarrow X^+ + e^-$. In the equation, X^+ represents a (an) _____ of element X.

6. Iodine is the least active halogen because it exhibits the greatest tendency to _____ electrons.

7. The properties of gallium (Ga) were predicted before its discovery. Since it belongs in column IIIA, the formula for its oxide is _____.

8. The Group VIIA elements are called halogens, which means _____.

9. In the original Periodic Table, the element manganese was placed in a sub-group in column VII because it forms some compounds that resemble compounds containing elements of the _____ family.

10. The properties of germanium were predicted by a study of the properties of the element above it in the Periodic Table. This element is _____.

Decreases, Increases, Remains the Same

Write the term (*decreases, increases, remains the same*) that, when inserted in the blank, will make the statement true.

1. From left to right in a row of elements in the Periodic Table, the number of shells of electrons _____.
2. In a series of elements, as the tendency to gain electrons increases, the metallic nature of the elements _____.
3. In a family of elements, as the number of shells of electrons increases, the tendency to gain electrons in the valence shell _____.
4. In the halogen family, as the atomic weights of the elements increase, the tendency to gain an electron _____.
5. From the top to the bottom of any column in the Periodic Table, the number of electron shells in the atoms _____.
6. From the top of the alkali metal column to the bottom, the melting point of each successive element _____, while the density _____.
7. In the series of compounds H_2O, H_2S, H_2Se, H_2Te, the covalent character of the bonds in a molecule _____ from H_2O to H_2Te.
8. In the series of compounds $NaClO$, $NaClO_2$, $NaClO_3$, the valence number of chlorine _____ from left to right.
9. As the atomic weights of the alkali metals increase, the number of electrons in the valence shell _____.
10. As the atomic numbers of the alkali metals increase, the temperature at which each element melts _____.

Exercises for Review

1. The alkali metals combine with hydrogen. Write equations for the combination of (*a*) lithium with hydrogen (*b*) sodium with hydrogen (*c*) potassium with hydrogen
2. Write equations for the reaction of (*a*) sulfur with oxygen (*b*) selenium with oxygen (*c*) tellurium with oxygen
3. Using lithium as a typical alkali metal, write an equation for (*a*) lithium combining with bromine (*b*) lithium combining with oxygen
4. Write an equation for the reaction of (*a*) HBr with water (*b*) HNO_3 with water (*c*) H_2SO_4 with water
5. Write an equation to show the electron change when Ca^{+2} is reduced to Ca.
6. How does the Periodic Table show that the atomic numbers of elements are more important than their atomic weights in determining the properties of elements?

7. In the modern Periodic Table, hydrogen appears both in the alkali metal column and in the hydrogen column. Why?

8. Suggest a reason why hydrogen forms covalently bonded binary compounds, while the alkali metals form ionic binary compounds.

9. Why are the alkali metal halides very stable compounds?

10. Why is the periodic classification the most important single correlation in all chemistry?

Exercises for Further Study

1. Explain why the elements in Sub-group B first appear in the row of elements beginning with potassium and not in the preceding rows.

2. Sulfur and oxygen, members of the same family, unite to form SO_2.
   a. Do members of the alkali metal family similarly unite?
   b. Explain in terms of the atomic structures of the alkali metals.

3. Suggest a possible explanation for the variation in the melting points and boiling points of the alkali metals from lithium to cesium.

4. The metals copper, silver, and gold are not listed with the alkali metals, although they also possess one valence electron.
   a. What are some important differences in the properties of these metals and the properties of the alkali metals?
   b. What difference in atomic structure is responsible for these differences in properties?

5. a. What properties of hydrogen are considered to be unique?
   b. How can the unique properties of hydrogen be explained in terms of atomic structure?

6. From an inspection of the melting points and boiling points for hydrogen and for sodium, what conclusion can you reach concerning the relative strengths of the forces binding the particles in the two elements?

7. Explain how Mendeléef was able to predict the existence of several elements which were later discovered.

8. When chemists sought to discover some of the missing elements predicted by the Periodic Table, why did they carefully analyze the minerals containing known elements in the same periodic column?

9. When chemists discovered the elements which belonged in the unoccupied spaces in the Periodic Table, how were they able to determine the valence numbers of the elements?

10. The noble gases were not known at the time of Mendeléef. As they were discovered, they could be added to the Periodic Table without disrupting the table. Why was this possible?

Chapter 8

GASES

8.1 Introduction

Dalton reasoned that the process of subdividing matter must ultimately yield a particle, the atom, incapable of further subdivision. He developed the atomic theory and later predicted the Law of Multiple Proportions. Studies of the combining weights (equivalent weights) of atoms confirmed Dalton's ideas (see section 11.14). The concept that matter cannot be subdivided indefinitely (matter is discontinuous at some level) receives additional support from a study of the properties of gases.

8.2 Properties of gases

The following properties are common to all gases:

1. Gases do not possess a specific shape or a specific volume. Instead, a gas takes the shape and volume of its container. For example, a quantity of gas has a volume of 1 liter in a 1-liter flask. In a larger container, the same quantity of gas has the larger volume.

2. Gases expand and contract with relative ease; that is, gases are compressible. For example, at different altitudes, the volume of a toy balloon will vary because the outside pressure varies. As the balloon rises, the pressure of the atmosphere decreases. The air in the balloon continues to expand until the balloon bursts.

3. Gases at the same temperature exert pressures that are proportional to their concentrations. For example, the pressure in a tire increases as more molecules of air (a greater concentration of gas) are pumped into the tire.

4. The density of a gas is considerably less than the density of the same matter in the solid or liquid state. The volume of a given weight of gas is approximately 1000 times greater than the volume of the same substance in the solid or liquid state. For example, the volume of 28 g of gaseous nitrogen at $0°$ C and 1 atm pressure is approximately 22,400 ml; the volume of the same weight of solid nitrogen is about 27.2 ml.

8.3 The kinetic-molecular model

To explain the observed properties of gases, chemists have adopted the *kinetic-molecular model*, which is based upon the following assumptions:

1. All gases consist of extremely small particles, called molecules. Gas molecules may be monatomic, as with helium, He, and argon, Ar; or polyatomic, as with oxygen, O_2, and ozone, O_3.

2. The total space between the molecules of a gas is very large compared to the space occupied by the molecules themselves. At normal pressures, a volume of gas is largely empty space, suggesting that gases can be readily compressed and that the molecules of one gas can readily intermingle with the molecules of other gases in the same container.

3. Gas molecules are in constant random motion (see Figure 8–1). This explains why gases have no definite shape but can expand to fill the volume of any container.

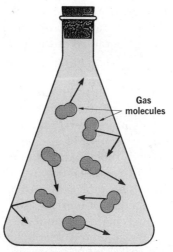

Gas molecules

Fig. 8–1   Random motion of gas molecules

4. Because gas molecules are in motion, they collide with one another. These collisions are assumed to be *elastic*; that is, the gas molecules rebound after collision with no loss in energy. Gas molecules also collide with the walls of their container. The collisions of gas molecules against the walls of the container constitute the pressure of the gas. This pressure is proportional to the number of collisions per unit time and to the force of each collision. As the number of gas molecules in a given volume (concentration) increases, the number of collisions increases and the pressure increases.

5. The molecules of a gas move very rapidly, which explains why gases diffuse. At ordinary temperatures, the speeds of gas mole-

cules may exceed one thousand miles per hour. Such high speeds explain why gases, despite relatively small masses, may exert high pressures.

Gas molecules are in random motion, colliding with each other in different directions. Thus it is unlikely that, at a given temperature, all the molecules will possess the same speed. Some molecules will attain increased speeds as a result of the collisions.

We have indicated previously that particles in motion possess kinetic energy. Since, at any given temperature, all gas molecules in a container do not possess the same speed, we may infer the following condition: All gas molecules in a container do not possess identical kinetic energies.

At a given temperature, we cannot describe the kinetic energy of any single molecule of a gas. Instead, we describe the average kinetic energy of all the molecules. The average kinetic energy of the molecules of a gas is proportional to the temperature of the gas.

8.4 Gas pressure

Pressure is defined as the force exerted by a body on some unit of area. The pressure exerted by the atmosphere may be demonstrated by the operation of a *barometer.* A narrow-bore glass tube, closed at one end and more than 76 centimeters long, is filled with mercury. The tube is inverted with the open end in a dish of mercury (see Figure 8–2). The mercury falls until the weight of the mercury column can be held up by the pressure of the surrounding air.

The space above the mercury is a partial vacuum, named torricellian vacuum after the Italian scientist Evangelista Torricelli, who devised the first barometer in the 17th century. Since the pressure of the atmosphere at different altitudes varies, the height of the column of mercury it supports varies accordingly. By agreement, the standard for atmospheric pressure at sea level is taken as 76 centimeters, or 760 millimeters, of mercury. The pressure of a gas is measured with a barometer.

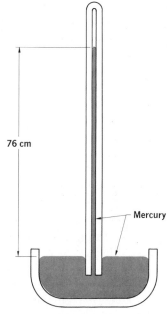

76 cm

Mercury

Fig. 8–2
The barometer tube

8.5 The gas laws

In section 8.3, we utilized the kinetic-molecular model to explain the properties of gases. Now we will discuss these properties in terms of some unifying concepts, called the gas laws. Finally, we will show how the gas laws can be correlated with the kinetic-molecular model.

8.6 Boyle's Law

The English scientist Robert Boyle, in 1660, was the first to determine how the volume of a gas at constant temperature varies with changes in pressure. His findings are summarized in the law that bears his name.

Boyle's Law: At constant temperature, the volume of a gas varies inversely with its pressure. This relationship can be expressed mathematically as

$$V \text{ (at constant temperature)} = \frac{K}{P} \quad \text{or} \quad PV = K$$

where V = volume, P = pressure, and K = some constant number.

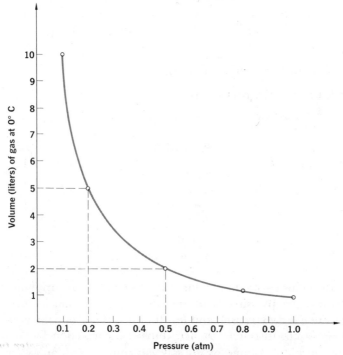

Fig. 8–3 Boyle's Law

The equation $PV = K$ tells us that, using the proper units, the product of the pressure and volume of a fixed weight of gas has a fixed value. Note, in Figure 8–3 on the preceding page, if we multiply any value of P by the corresponding value of V, the product is always the same. This means that P and V are *inversely* related (at constant temperature).

8.7 Does the kinetic-molecular model explain Boyle's Law?

The kinetic-molecular model readily accounts for Boyle's Law. Pressure in a gas equals the force exerted by the gas molecules on a unit area. The force depends on the number of collisions between the gas molecules and the walls of the container and on the force of each collision. Reducing the volume by one-half doubles the number of molecules in each unit of volume; thus it doubles the number of collisions between the gas molecules and the walls of the container. In effect, the pressure of the gas on the container is doubled. The pressure of the container on the gas is also doubled. Why?

8.8 Solving a problem involving Boyle's Law

The pressure on 1.20 liters of a gas at constant temperature is increased from 760 mm to 780 mm. What is the new volume of the gas? At constant temperature,

$PV = K$ (under original conditions)

$P_1V_1 = K$ (under new conditions)

The expressions PV and P_1V_1 equal the same constant and therefore equal each other.

$$PV = P_1V_1$$

This can be rewritten as

$$V_1 = V \times \frac{P}{P_1}$$

new   original correction
volume volume   factor

Substituting,

$$V_1 = 1.20 \text{ liters} \times \frac{760 \text{ mm}}{780 \text{ mm}} = 1.17 \text{ liters}$$

The Boyle's Law correction factor is always equal to the original pressure divided by the new pressure. This quotient is greater than 1 if the original volume of the gas is expanded and less than 1 if the original volume of the gas is compressed. In our example, we used a correction factor of $\frac{760 \text{ mm}}{780 \text{ mm}}$ because the original volume of the gas was compressed, and we required a quotient less than 1.

8.9 Charles' Law

The French scientist Jacques Charles, in 1787, studied how the volume of a gas at constant pressure varies with a change in temperature. By experiment, he found that when a gas is heated at constant pressure, its volume increases by $\frac{1}{273}$ of its original volume at 0° C for every 1 C° rise in temperature. Conversely, when a gas is cooled at constant pressure, its volume decreases by $\frac{1}{273}$ of its original volume at 0° C for every 1 C° drop in temperature.

Suppose Z liters of a gas at 0° C and constant pressure are heated to 273° C. The new volume equals the original volume plus the increase in volume, or

$$Z \text{ liters} + \frac{273}{273}Z \text{ liters} = 2Z \text{ liters}$$

Suppose X liters of a gas at 0° C and constant pressure are cooled to −273° C. The new volume equals

$$X \text{ liters} - \frac{273}{273}X \text{ liters} = 0 \text{ liters}$$

According to the equation, a gas possesses no volume at −273° C, also called 0° Kelvin (see Figure 8–4 on the following page). However, all gases liquefy and solidify before they reach −273° C. The equation, therefore, can be applied only to the gaseous state.

The temperature −273° C has special significance and is called *absolute zero*. It is the lowest temperature on the absolute scale of temperature (the Kelvin scale) and the lowest temperature that can exist. Absolute temperature in degrees Kelvin (° K) equals Celsius (or centigrade) temperature plus 273°.

$$° K = ° C + 273°$$

We can now state Charles' Law in terms of absolute temperature.

Charles' Law: The volume of a gas at constant pressure varies directly with its absolute temperature (° C + 273°). This relationship can be expressed mathematically as

$$V \text{ (at constant pressure)} = KT \quad \text{or} \quad \frac{V}{T} = K$$

where V = volume, K = a constant, and T = absolute temperature.

If the absolute temperature of a gas at constant pressure is doubled, the equation tells us that the volume is also doubled (see Figure 8–4 on the following page).

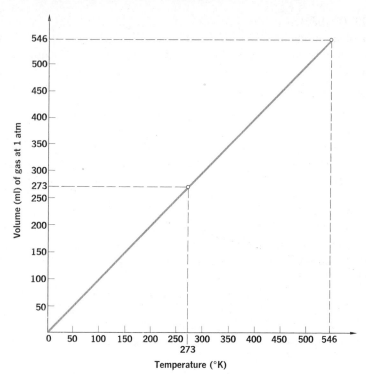

Fig. 8–4   Charles' Law

8.10 The relationship between temperature and pressure

Charles also studied the effect of temperature changes on the pressure of a gas at constant volume. He found that if a gas at constant volume is heated, its pressure increases $\frac{1}{273}$ of its pressure at 0° C for each 1 C° rise in temperature.

Suppose a fixed volume of a gas at 0° C and a pressure of P atmospheres is heated to 273° C. The new pressure equals the original pressure plus the increase in pressure.

$$P \text{ atm} + \frac{273}{273}P \text{ atm} = 2P \text{ atm}$$

Suppose a fixed volume of a gas at 0° C and a pressure of Z atmospheres is cooled to −273° C. The new pressure equals

$$Z \text{ atm} - \frac{273}{273}Z \text{ atm} = 0 \text{ atm}$$

At $-273°$ C, therefore, the pressure of a gas would be zero; that is, the motion of its molecules would cease. As mentioned previously, however, all gases liquefy and solidify before this temperature (absolute zero) is reached.

8.11 Does the kinetic-molecular model explain Charles' Law?

According to the kinetic-molecular model, the average kinetic energy of the molecules of a gas is proportional to the temperature of the gas. If it were possible to reduce the temperature of a gas to $-273°$ C (absolute zero), the gas would cease to have volume and would no longer possess kinetic energy. Therefore, it is more accurate to say: The average kinetic energy of the molecules of a gas is directly proportional to the absolute temperature of the gas.

If the absolute temperature of a gas is doubled, the average kinetic energy of its molecules is also doubled. If the volume is kept constant and the absolute temperature is doubled, the pressure is doubled because of the increased number of collisions and the force of each collision. If the pressure is kept constant and the absolute temperature is doubled, the volume doubles to maintain the same pressure. These examples, based on the kinetic-molecular model, support Charles' Law.

For convenience, we have assumed that, at absolute zero, the volume of a gas equals zero. Actually the gas would have a small volume. As the temperature drops and molecular motion decreases, the average distance between the molecules decreases. If the gas could be cooled to absolute zero, the spaces between the molecules would be zero. The volume of the gas, therefore, would not be zero but would equal the volume of the motionless molecules.

8.12 Solving a problem involving Charles' Law

Suppose we increase the temperature of 150 ml of a gas at constant pressure from 20° C to 40° C. What is the new volume of the gas? At constant pressure,

$$\frac{V}{T} = K \text{ (under original conditions)}$$

$$\frac{V_1}{T_1} = K \text{ (under new conditions)}$$

Thus $\dfrac{V}{T} = \dfrac{V_1}{T_1}$, or $V_1 = V \times \dfrac{T_1}{T}$.

$$\underset{\substack{\text{new} \\ \text{volume}}}{V_1} = \underset{\substack{\text{original} \\ \text{volume}}}{V} \times \underset{\substack{\text{correction} \\ \text{factor}}}{\frac{T_1}{T}}$$

Substituting, $V_1 = 150 \text{ ml} \times \dfrac{313° \text{ K}}{293° \text{ K}} = 160 \text{ ml.}$

Since the temperature of the gas was increased at constant pressure, the volume of the gas was also increased, according to Charles' Law. The correction factor that would produce an increased volume might appear to be $\dfrac{40° \text{ C}}{20° \text{ C}}$. However, the volume change is proportional to the change in absolute temperature, so that the correction factor is $\dfrac{40° \text{ C} + 273°}{20° \text{ C} + 273°}$, or $\dfrac{313° \text{ K}}{293° \text{ K}}$. Doubling the Celsius temperature of a gas at constant pressure, therefore, does not double the volume.

8.13 Further verification of Boyle's Law and Charles' Law

We may approach the laws of Boyle and Charles by another line of reasoning. Consider the pressure exerted by the gas molecules on one side of the box shown in Figure 8–5. As previously stated, the pressure of a gas is proportional to the number of collisions per unit time (for example, collisions per second) and to the force of each collision. We will analyze each of these factors separately and then combine them.

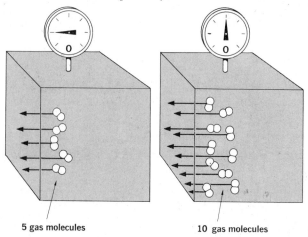

5 gas molecules   10 gas molecules

Fig. 8–5   Collisions of gas molecules and pressure

If more gas molecules are placed in the box (at constant temperature), the pressure will increase due to an increase in the number of collisions per unit time. Conversely, the pressure will decrease if some gas molecules escape from the box. Therefore, the number of collisions per unit time is proportional to the concentration of the gas molecules. It is also proportional to the velocity of the gas molecules, since higher velocities will produce more collisions than lower velocities. We can combine these relationships in the expression

$$\text{pressure is proportional to } \frac{Nv}{V}$$

where N = the number of molecules, v = the average velocity of the molecules, V = the volume of the gas, and $\frac{N}{V}$ = the concentration of the gas.

We also stated that pressure is proportional to the force of each collision. The force, or change in momentum, of each collision of a gas molecule is related to the product of the mass (M) of the molecule and its velocity (v). This relationship can be expressed as F is proportional to Mv. Combining both expressions, we obtain

$$\text{pressure is proportional to } \frac{NMv^2}{V}$$

Note that Mv^2 is related to the average kinetic energy of the gas molecules, since $KE = \frac{1}{2} Mv^2$. The average kinetic energy, in turn, depends on the temperature of the gas.

The expression pressure is proportional to $\frac{NMv^2}{V}$ therefore reveals:

1. At constant temperature, NMv^2 is constant because N remains unchanged and Mv^2 depends on temperature. Thus pressure $= \dfrac{K}{\text{volume}}$ or the pressure and volume of a gas are inversely related, $PV = K$ (Boyle's Law).

2. At constant pressure, increasing the temperature increases the Mv^2 term in the numerator. This means that the term V (volume) in the denominator must also increase to maintain the constant value of the pressure. Thus $K = \dfrac{T}{V}$ or the temperature and volume of a gas are directly proportional (Charles' Law).

8.14 Graham's Law of Diffusion

We have already indicated that the continuous, random motion of the molecules of a gas causes the gas to diffuse in all directions. The rate at which gas molecules diffuse depends on the mass of the molecules and their temperature. Under the same conditions of temperature and pressure, therefore, light molecules diffuse more rapidly than heavy molecules. This relationship was investigated by the Scottish scientist Thomas Graham in 1833.

Graham's Law: At constant temperature and pressure, the rates of diffusion of gases are inversely proportional to the square root of their molecular weights. Expressed mathematically,

$$\frac{R_1}{R_2} = \sqrt{\frac{M_2}{M_1}}$$

where R_1 is the rate of diffusion of a gas with molecular weight M_1, and R_2 is the rate of diffusion of a second gas with molecular weight M_2.

If M_1 represents the molecular weight of hydrogen gas (2) that diffuses at rate R_1, and M_2 represents the molecular weight of oxygen gas (32) that diffuses at rate R_2,

$$\frac{R_1}{R_2} = \sqrt{\frac{32}{2}} = \sqrt{16} = 4$$

Therefore, the rate of diffusion of hydrogen molecules is four times the rate of diffusion of oxygen molecules.

8.15 Dalton's Law of Partial Pressures

Suppose we mix 1 liter of gas X and 1 liter of gas Z in a container that has a volume of 1 liter. Assume that the gases do not react chemically with one another. How do the pressures of the individual gases before mixing compare with the total pressure of the mixture of gases?

The pressure of a gas is proportional to its concentration, so that the pressure of the mixture of gases is twice the pressure of each gas. This means that, in a mixture of gases that do not react, each gas exerts the same pressure as if it were in the given volume alone. In 1805, Dalton expressed these observations as follows:

Law of Partial Pressures: At constant temperature, the pressure of a mixture of gases that do not react equals the sum of the partial pressures of the gases in the mixture. Expressed mathematically,

$$P = p_1 + p_2 + p_3 + \ldots$$

where P = total pressure, and $p_1, p_2, p_3, \ldots$ = partial pressures.

8.16 Gay-Lussac's Law of Combining Volumes of Gases

In Chapter 6, we observed that 2 volumes of hydrogen gas at a given temperature and pressure combine with 1 volume of oxygen gas at the same temperature and pressure to form 2 volumes of gaseous water, still at the same temperature and pressure.

$$2 \text{ H}_2 \text{ } (g) + \text{O}_2 \text{ } (g) \rightarrow 2 \text{ H}_2\text{O} \text{ } (g)$$

2 volumes   1 volume   2 volumes

When water is decomposed by electrolysis, 2 volumes of hydrogen gas and 1 volume of oxygen gas are formed. As another example, suppose we combine hydrogen gas with chlorine gas, and measure all gases at the same conditions of temperature and pressure.

$$H_2 \ (g) + Cl_2 \ (g) \rightarrow 2 \ HCl \ (g)$$

1 volume   1 volume   2 volumes

The French chemist Joseph Louis Gay-Lussac investigated these and similar reactions. In 1808, he summarized his observations in the following law:

Law of Combining Volumes of Gases: The volumes of reacting gases and gaseous products in a chemical change may be expressed in simple volume ratios of small integers.

This relationship puzzled Dalton, who held that hydrogen and oxygen were monatomic. Indeed, he assigned the formula HO to water. According to the Dalton model of the atom, Gay-Lussac's findings were unacceptable.

A new problem now arose: Was there any relationship between the number of molecules contained in equal volumes of different gases at the same temperature and pressure? It remained for Avogadro to answer this question. In doing so, he reconciled the findings of Dalton and Gay-Lussac.

8.17 Avogadro's Law

To explain Gay-Lussac's findings, Avogadro proposed, in 1811, the law that bears his name.

Avogadro's Law: Equal volumes of all gases at the same temperature and pressure contain the same number of molecules.

This number, known as Avogadro's number, was discussed in sections 3.11 and 5.12.

We can deduce Avogadro's Law easily from the kinetic-molecular model.

We indicated that the pressure P of a gas is proportional to $\dfrac{NMv^2}{V}$. Consider equal volumes of two gases at the same temperature and pressure. Let subscript *1* represent one gas and subscript *2* represent the second gas. Since the pressures of both gases are the same,

$$\frac{N_1 M_1 v_1^2}{V_1} = \frac{N_2 M_2 v_2^2}{V_2}$$

Since the temperatures are the same, $M_1v_1^2 = M_2v_2^2$, and since we are dealing with equal volumes of gases, $V_1 = V_2$. Thus $N_1 = N_2$; that is, equal volumes of gases at the same temperature and pressure contain the same number of molecules.

Let us reexamine the reaction for forming gaseous water in terms of Avogadro's Law.

$$\text{hydrogen } (g) + \text{oxygen } (g) \rightarrow \text{water } (g)$$

2 volumes   1 volume   2 volumes

Applying Avogadro's Law to the reaction, we realize that the number of water molecules must equal the number of hydrogen molecules because the volumes of water and hydrogen are equal. Let $2N$ represent this number of molecules. The volume of oxygen is half the volume of hydrogen; therefore, the number of molecules of oxygen is half that of hydrogen, or N.

Each water molecule that forms must contain at least one atom of oxygen. Since the number of water molecules that are formed equals $2N$, the number of oxygen atoms contained in the water also equals $2N$. The oxygen atoms contained in the water all came from N molecules of oxygen. The $N : 2N$, or $1 : 2$, relationship leads us to the conclusion that each molecule of oxygen contains two atoms. Similar reasoning shows that hydrogen, nitrogen, chlorine, and other elemental gases are also composed of diatomic molecules.

8.18 Deviations from the gas laws

Thus far, we have assumed that the gas laws are valid at all pressures and at all temperatures. When we stated, for example, that collisions between gas molecules result in no energy loss on rebound, we assumed that gas molecules do not attract one another. Furthermore, we assumed that the space occupied by the molecules themselves is insignificant when compared to the sum of the spaces separating the molecules, that is, the total volume of gas. We must now reconsider these assumptions.

As the pressure of a gas increases or its temperature decreases, or as both changes occur, the molecules are brought closer together. Because of their closeness, the molecules exert a greater attractive force on each other. The attractive force acts as a restraint, so that after collision, the molecules rebound with lower energy, reducing the actual pressure of the gas below the value calculated by the gas laws.

If the volume of a gas is reduced greatly, the volume of the molecules themselves will become a significant part of the total volume of the gas.

At reduced volumes, therefore, the volume of a gas calculated from the gas laws will be different from the actual volume.

Thus calculations of the volumes of gases at very high pressures and very low temperatures yield values that do not conform exactly to Boyle's Law and Charles' Law. The term *real gases* is used to distinguish actual gases, such as H_2 and O_2, from *ideal gases*, which do not exist but which are assumed to obey the gas laws perfectly.

8.19 Relationship between the weight and the volume of a gas

According to Avogadro, at equal temperatures and pressures, moles of different gases have the same number of molecules and the same volumes. For example, at 0° C and 1 atmosphere, called *standard temperature and pressure* (*STP*), the following relationships exist between 1 mole (1 gram-molecular weight) of a gas and its volume:

2 grams of hydrogen have a volume of 22.4 liters.

32 grams of oxygen have a volume of 22.4 liters.

44 grams of carbon dioxide have a volume of 22.4 liters.

From these and similar relationships, we can state an important law that correlates the weight of a gas with the volume the gas occupies: *1 mole of any gas at STP occupies 22.4 liters.*

The value 22.4 liters is called the *gram-molar volume*. Note that the gram-molar volume concept applies to ideal gases. The behavior of real gases differs slightly from that of ideal gases, so that calculations based on the gram-molar volume, 22.4 liters, yield answers that are approximate.

To determine the molecular weight of a gas, we could collect 22.4 liters of the gas at STP and then weigh the gas. But handling such a large volume of gas is cumbersome. Instead, we weigh a measurable volume of the gas at known laboratory conditions and then correct this volume to the volume at STP. If the gas occupies Z liters, then

$$\frac{\text{weight of } Z \text{ liters}}{Z \text{ liters of gas at STP}} = \frac{\text{gram-molecular weight of gas}}{22.4 \text{ liters}}$$

The molecular weight of a gas may also be determined by a slightly different method. As stated previously, the gram-molar volumes of all gases contain the same number of molecules. The weights of equal volumes of gases at the same conditions are therefore in the same ratio as their gram-molecular weights. If the gram-molecular weight of oxygen (32 grams) is taken as the standard reference for molecular weights of gases, we now have another convenient method for determining molecular

weights of gases in the laboratory. For example, at 0° C and 1 atm, 224 ml
of gas X weigh 0.64 g, and the same volume of oxygen weighs 0.32 g.

$$\text{molecular weight of gas X} = \frac{0.64 \text{ g}}{0.32 \text{ g}} \times 32 \text{ g/mole} = 64 \text{ g/mole}$$

8.20 Working with gases in the laboratory

Determining the molecular weight of a gas in the laboratory frequently
requires measuring a weight of some specific volume of the gas at laboratory temperatures and pressures.

Assume that we have collected 48 ml of oxygen by displacement over
water, as shown in Figure 8–6. The temperature of the gas is assumed
to be the temperature of the water. Note that the water level in the gas-
collecting tube (eudiometer) is higher than the water level in the pan.
This means that the gas pressure inside the eudiometer is less than atmospheric pressure.

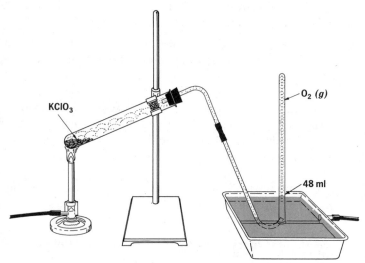

Fig. 8–6   Gas collection by water displacement

To bring the gas to atmospheric pressure, the height of the tube must be
adjusted until the inside and outside water levels are the same (see Figure
8–7 on the next page). At this point, the volume can be read directly from
the water level in the eudiometer. This reading is the volume of gas at the
temperature of the water and at atmospheric pressure.

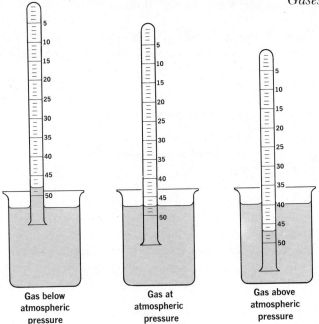

Gas below
atmospheric
pressure

Gas at
atmospheric
pressure

Gas above
atmospheric
pressure

Fig. 8-7   Equalizing gas pressures

When gases are collected over water, the evaporation of the water produces water vapor that contributes partly to the total pressure of the gas.
After equalization of levels, the pressure of a given volume of oxygen
equals the atmospheric pressure. Suppose, according to the barometer,
this pressure is 761.4 mm. The pressure of the oxygen gas plus the pressure of the water vapor retained by the gas together equal the total gas
pressure, 761.4 mm.

$$p_{\text{oxygen}} + p_{\text{water vapor}} = P_{\text{total}}\quad\text{(Dalton's Law)}$$

The determination of the molecular weight of a gas, such as oxygen,
requires the pressure exerted by the oxygen alone.

$$p_{\text{oxygen}} = P_{\text{total}} - p_{\text{water vapor}}$$

The total gas pressure is obtained from a barometer after equalization
of water levels. The pressure of water vapor is a function of temperature
and may be obtained from a table of vapor pressures (see the table on
page 152).

8.21 Solving a molecular weight problem

In the laboratory, the following data were gathered to determine the molecular weight of gas M collected over water:

weight of gas M = 0.08 g

volume of gas after equalization = 112 ml
(adjusted to atmospheric pressure)

barometer reading = 759.2 mm

temperature of the water = 21° C

At 21° C, the vapor pressure of water = 18.7 mm.

The pressure exerted by gas M alone = 759.2 mm − 18.7 mm = 740.5 mm.

The volume of gas M at STP (0° C and 760 mm)

$$= 112 \text{ ml} \times \frac{\text{pressure correction}}{\text{factor (Boyle's Law)}} \times \frac{\text{temperature correction}}{\text{factor (Charles' Law)}}$$

Since the pressure increases from 740.5 mm to 760 mm, the volume of the gas must be decreased, and the pressure correction factor $= \frac{740.5 \text{ mm}}{760 \text{ mm}}$.
Since the temperature decreases from 21° C (294° K) to 0° C (273° K), the volume of the gas must again be decreased, and the temperature correction factor $= \frac{273° \text{ K}}{294° \text{ K}}$.

The volume of gas M at STP

$$= 112 \text{ ml} \times \frac{740.5 \text{ mm}}{760 \text{ mm}} \times \frac{273° \text{ K}}{294° \text{ K}} = 101 \text{ ml}$$

$$\frac{\text{gram-molecular weight of gas M}}{22.4 \text{ liters}} = \frac{\text{weight of gas M}}{\text{volume of gas M in liters at STP}}$$

$$\text{gram-molecular weight of gas M} = \frac{0.08 \text{ g} \times 22.4 \text{ liters}}{0.101 \text{ liter}}$$

$$= 17.7 \text{ g}$$

molecular weight = 18

Multiple-Choice Questions

1. All gases (1) are compressible (2) are invisible (3) are more reactive than solids or liquids (4) possess less potential energy than solids or liquids

2. Gases diffuse readily because (1) gas molecules are much smaller than the molecules of liquids or solids (2) gases generally possess more molecules per unit of volume than do liquids or solids (3) large spaces are present between the molecules of a gas (4) strong attractive forces are present between the gas molecules

3. At a given temperature, the molecules present in a gas always possess different (1) kinetic energies (2) chemical properties (3) densities (4) rates of diffusion

4. The pressure of an enclosed gas depends on (1) the number of molecules in a unit volume and their average kinetic energy (2) its chemical composition (3) the altitude above sea level (4) the number of atoms per molecule

5. The pressure of a given quantity of gas must increase if (1) the temperature and the volume increase (2) the temperature and the volume decrease (3) the temperature increases and the volume decreases (4) the temperature decreases and the volume increases

6. All gases (1) decompose at absolute zero (2) cease to possess molecular motion at $0°$ C (3) at constant pressure show the same increase in volume when warmed from $0°$ C to $1°$ C (4) at a given temperature possess molecules that have a fixed velocity

7. One liter of hydrogen and one liter of oxygen (1) contain the same number of molecules (2) react completely with each other (3) possess the same total amount of energy (4) will combine to form one liter of water

8. All gases (1) condense at the same temperature (2) have the same density at equal temperatures and pressures (3) possess volumes that are proportional to the temperature above $0°$ C (4) possess a volume of 22.4 l/mole at $0°$ C and atmospheric pressure

9. Standard temperature and pressure refers to (1) absolute zero and 1 atmosphere pressure (2) $100°$ C and zero pressure (3) $0°$ C and a pressure of 76 cm of mercury (4) $0°$ C and zero pressure

10. When oxygen is collected by the displacement of water (1) the pressure of the oxygen is the observed pressure less the pressure of the water vapor (2) some oxygen combines with water (3) the oxygen dissociates into atoms (4) the oxygen from the water increases the amount of oxygen collected

Completion Questions

1. Hydrogen gas diffuses more rapidly than any other gas at the same temperature and pressure because hydrogen has the lowest _____.
2. For a reaction that involves gases and solids only, Gay-Lussac's Law can be applied to the substances that are present in the _____ state.
3. Avogadro's Law states that equal _____ of all gases at the same temperature and pressure contain equal numbers of molecules.
4. The collisions of gas molecules with the walls of the container are described as the _____ of the gas.
5. The relationship between the volume of a gas and its _____ is given by Charles' Law.
6. The distances that molecules can travel between collisions is greatest in the _____ state.
7. The molar volume of all gases is 22.4 l, measured at a temperature of _____° C and a pressure of _____ cm of mercury.
8. Gases are more compressible than liquids because in a gas there are large spaces between the _____ of the gas.
9. In a gas that has been collected by the displacement of water, part of the observed pressure is due to the _____ of the water.
10. The relationship $\frac{Mv^2}{2}$ describes the _____ of a particle.

True-False Questions

1. At $0°C$, a gas is thought to possess zero volume.
2. The ability of gases to *diffuse* into each other results from the motions of the molecules and the spaces between them.
3. When a solid changes to a *liquid*, the volume increases approximately 1000 times.
4. Normal atmospheric pressure supports a column of *water* 76 cm tall.
5. Gases that follow Boyle's Law and Charles' Law without deviation are said to be *real* gases.
6. Heating a gas from $0°C$ to $273°C$ causes its volume to double.

7. Equal volumes of gases at the same temperature and pressure contain equal numbers of *atoms.*

8. At STP, 8 g of gas X occupy a volume of 44.8 l. Therefore, the molecular weight of X is *8.*

Decreases, Increases, Remains the Same

1. The density of water _____ as water changes from liquid to steam.

2. As the molecular weights of gases increase, the numbers of molecules in one liter, measured at the same temperature and pressure, _____.

3. In a mixture of gases at constant total pressure, if the concentration of one gas is increased, its partial pressure _____.

4. *a.* As the temperature increases, the rate of diffusion of a gas _____.
   b. At constant temperature, as the molecular weights of gases increase, the rates of diffusion _____.

5. At constant volume, if the temperature of a gas is decreased, its pressure _____.

6. When the volume of a gas is decreased at constant temperature, the number of collisions between the molecules of the gas and each square centimeter of the walls of the container _____.

7. If the pressure applied to a sample of gas is increased while the temperature remains constant, the volume of the gas _____.

8. As the number of collisions between the molecules of a gas and the walls of its container increases, the pressure of the gas _____.

9. If the volume of a gas at constant temperature and pressure is increased, the total number of molecules present _____.

10. When the temperature of water is raised, the partial pressure of water vapor in a gas collected over the water _____.

Exercises for Review

1. A cylinder contains 80 cc of air at normal atmospheric pressure. The volume of the air is reduced to 15 cc without changing the temperature. What is the pressure of the air in the cylinder?

2. A tank of compressed air has a volume of 10 cu ft. What volume of air at normal atmospheric pressure must be forced into the tank so that the pressure of the air in the tank equals 12 atmospheres? (Assume that the temperature of the air does not change in the process.)

3. At 20° C, a rubber balloon contains 800 ml of air at normal atmospheric pressure. If the temperature of the air increases to 35° C, and the pressure remains unchanged, what will be the volume of the balloon?

4. A student collects a gas at 76 cm pressure and finds the volume to be 320 ml when the temperature of the gas is 47° C. What will the volume of the gas be when it cools to 27° C at the same pressure?

5. A steel cylinder holds 1.2 cu ft of air at atmospheric pressure and a temperature of 17° C. What is the pressure of the air if the cylinder is placed in an oven at 447° C?

6. A sample of gas has a volume of 120 cc at 20° C and atmospheric pressure. After the gas is warmed, its volume becomes 360 cc at the same pressure. What is the final temperature of the gas?

7. If a mole of gas has a volume of 22.4 l at STP, what is its volume at 100° C and a pressure of 80 cm of mercury?

8. Carbon dioxide gas is heated to 800° C in a 1-liter sealed container which bursts when the pressure reaches 3.5 atmospheres. What volume does the carbon dioxide occupy after it is cooled to 27° C at normal atmospheric pressure?

9. A compressor takes 0.5 cu ft of a gas at 33° C and normal pressure and compresses it to 0.1 cu ft, cooling it to −50° C at the same time. What is the pressure of the gas at these conditions?

10. *a.* The temperature of a gas is 80° C. At what temperature will its kinetic energy be doubled?

    b. To what temperature must a gas be brought so that its kinetic energy is 25% of its kinetic energy at 50° C?

11. A gas originally fills a 500-ml container at a pressure of 1000 mm of mercury and a temperature of 473° C. After expanding into a 2-liter container, the gas has a temperature of 223° C. What is the new pressure of the gas?

12. A bottle of oxygen is collected over water at normal pressure and a temperature of 30° C. What is the partial pressure of the oxygen in the bottle?

13. A 500-ml flask is filled with hydrogen which was collected by water displacement at a temperature of 26° C. The gas is brought to atmospheric pressure which, at the time, is 75.5 cm of mercury. What is the volume of dry hydrogen at STP?

14. What fraction of a mole of hydrogen is present in a liter flask filled with hydrogen at 17° C and a pressure of 79 cm of mercury?

15. What fraction of a mole of oxygen is present in 400 ml of oxygen at 0° C and normal atmospheric pressure?

16. What is the ratio of the rates of diffusion of oxygen and hydrogen at the same temperature and pressure?

17. A tank holds a mixture of methane gas and propane gas. The molecular weight of methane is 16 and that of propane is 44. What is the ratio of the rates by which the two gases will escape through small leaks in the tank?

18. If air contains 79% nitrogen by volume, what is the partial pressure of the nitrogen in air at normal atmospheric pressure?

19. The decomposition of a compound produces 1 mole of X gas and 3 moles of Y gas. If the two gases are collected together in a container at a pressure of 80 cm of mercury, what is the partial pressure of each gas?

20. *a.* Knowing that Avogadro's number is 6.02×10^{23} particles per mole, calculate the number of particles in (1) 4 moles of helium (2) $\frac{1}{1000}$ mole of oxygen

   b. Calculate the number of atoms in 0.01 mole of H_2O.

21. Calculate the volume of the following gases at STP:

   a. 1.7 g of ammonia, NH_3

   b. 560 g of carbon monoxide, CO

   c. 12.8 g of sulfur dioxide, SO_2

22. What volume does 90 g of steam occupy at 227° C and a pressure of 5 atmospheres?

23. Calculate the molecular weights of the following gases from their densities at 0° C and 76 cm pressure:

   a. gas A density: 1.64 g/l

   b. gas B density: 1.25 g/l

24. The molecular weight of CH_3Cl is 50.5. Calculate its density at STP.

25. A 500-ml sample of a gas is collected dry at 27° C and 740 mm pressure. Its mass is found to be 1.40 g. Find its molecular weight.

Exercises for Further Study

1. Why can we state only the average kinetic energy for all the molecules of a gas rather than the kinetic energy of a single gas molecule?

2. If the collisions between the molecules of a gas were not essentially elastic, explain what would happen to the volume of a gas on standing.

3. *a.* An equal mixture of the two isotopes of hydrogen, H_2 and D_2, is placed in a container, and the container is closed with a porous plug. What will happen to the contents of the container on standing?

   b. If a mixture of the two isotopes of chlorine, Cl^{35} and Cl^{37}, is placed in a similar container, will the change be as great as it was with hydrogen?

4. *a.* Explain why gases do not follow Boyle's and Charles' Laws at high pressures and low temperatures.

   b. Why does helium follow these laws better than carbon dioxide?

5. In an experiment verifying Charles' Law, the gas decomposed to form two molecules for each original molecule. How would this decomposition affect the results of the experiment?

6. Explain why Avogadro's Law cannot be applied to liquids and to solids.

7. *a.* Show how Gay-Lussac's Law applies to the reaction

$$N_2 \ (g) + 3 \ H_2 \ (g) \rightarrow 2 \ NH_3 \ (g)$$

   b. For the reaction $CO_2 \ (g) + C(s) \rightarrow 2 \ CO \ (g)$, to which substances can Gay-Lussac's Law be applied? Why not to all? Explain.

8. Assuming that the density of liquid water at 100° C and atmospheric pressure is 1.00 g/ml, what is the volume of 1 mole of liquid water at these conditions?

9. In one experiment, 0.1 g of oxygen is collected by the displacement of water; and in another experiment, 0.1 g of oxygen is collected by the displacement of mercury. Will the volumes of the two gases be the same at the same temperature and pressure? Explain.

10. A technician mixes 1 l of gas A at atmospheric pressure with 1 l of gas B at the same pressure. The mixture of two gases has a volume of 1 l and a pressure of 1.9 atmospheres. There has been no change in temperature.

    a. Theoretically, what should be the final pressure?

    b. Explain the difference between the observed pressure and the theoretical pressure.

Chapter 9

LIQUIDS AND SOLIDS

9.1 Introduction

Gases have been described in Chapter 8 as consisting of molecules which are in constant, random motion. Thus a given mass of a gas can fill any container; that is, a gas can adjust its volume by changes in temperature or pressure according to Boyle's Law or Charles' Law. For example, when 1 liter of a gas at a fixed temperature is allowed to completely fill a 2-liter flask, the pressure of the gas is reduced to half of its original pressure (see Figure 9–1).

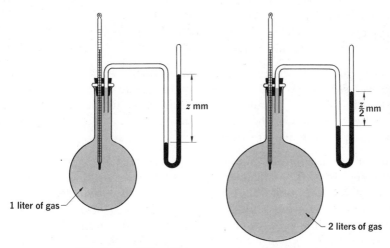

Fig. 9–1   PV = K (at constant temperature)

For 1 liter of a gas at a given pressure to completely fill a 2-liter flask at the same temperature, the absolute temperature of the gas must double. These observations suggest that the attractive forces in gases are weak. In this chapter, we will study the effects of increasing the attractive forces between gas molecules.

9.2 Liquefaction of gases

Suppose we compress a given mass of gaseous ammonia while keeping the temperature constant at 20° C. As the pressure increases, the volume of the gas decreases according to Boyle's Law. At a certain pressure, the volume shrinks considerably more than this law predicts, and droplets of liquid ammonia appear. Attempting to increase the pressure beyond this point causes more ammonia gas to condense, increasing the volume of the liquid. When all of the gas has condensed, further compression has very little effect upon the volume of the liquid.

A similar set of observations accompanies the cooling of a gas at constant pressure. All gases may therefore be liquefied by compression and cooling. Why don't the molecules of a liquid separate to fill their container as do the molecules of a gas?

9.3 Attractive forces

According to our model, the molecules of a gas possess a certain average kinetic energy at a given temperature, and the motion of the molecules is sufficient to separate them. It can be shown experimentally that all bodies exert an attractive force on one another. In a gas, however, the kinetic energy of the molecules overcomes the attractive forces between the molecules, and they remain separated.

When gases are liquefied, the average kinetic energy of the molecules is lowered sufficiently so that the intermolecular attractive forces hold them together in the more organized liquid state. Compression and cooling of a gas decrease the spaces between the molecules and permit the attractive forces to operate more effectively.

Compression alone will not liquefy a gas. Liquefaction requires that the kinetic energy of the molecules of a gas be lowered sufficiently to enable the attractive forces between the molecules to predominate. To achieve liquefaction by compression, gases must be cooled below a certain fixed temperature—different for each gas—called the critical temperature. *The critical temperature of a gas is that temperature above which a gas cannot be liquefied no matter what pressure is applied. The critical pressure of a gas is that pressure which must be applied to liquefy the gas at its critical temperature.*

For some easily liquefied gases, such as ammonia and sulfur dioxide, the critical temperature is above room temperature. These gases may be liquefied by compression alone, since no further cooling is required.

9.4 Properties of liquids

The general properties of liquids may be summarized as follows:

1. Liquids have clearly defined boundaries and take the shape of their containers. Therefore, a liquid of given volume, unlike a gas, cannot fill every container.
2. Liquids, like gases, are able to flow; both are called *fluids.*
3. Increasing the pressure upon a liquid does not appreciably affect its volume. Thus liquids are virtually incompressible.
4. Increasing the temperature of a liquid produces only small increases in its volume. All liquids do not expand at the same rate for the same increase in temperature. (Because mercury expands uniformly on heating and contracts uniformly on cooling, it is useful in thermometry.)
5. Liquids exhibit resistance to flow in varying degrees, a property called *viscosity.* This property depends on the sizes and shapes of the molecules and on the attractive forces between them. Where the attractive forces are small and the molecules are small, the viscosity is low. Liquids with low viscosity flow easily, as in the case of alcohol and ether. Where the attractive forces are large and the molecules are large and complex, the viscosity is high. Liquids with high viscosity flow with difficulty, as in the case of glycerine and heavy oils. As the temperature rises, the increasing kinetic energy of the liquid molecules weakens the attractive forces, and the resistance to flow decreases in most liquids.
6. The surface of a liquid behaves like a stretched membrane upon which objects denser than the liquid may float. This property, called *surface tension*, results from the unequal distribution of attractive forces at the surface of the liquid (see Figure 9-2).

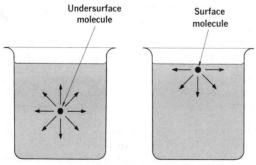

Fig. 9–2   Surface tension

The surface molecules are attracted by other molecules of the liquid in all directions except from the top. The net effect of this nonuniform distribution of forces is to pull the surface molecules together. Surface tension accounts for the spherical shape of liquid drops. It also explains why liquids rise in narrow tubes (capillary action), apparently against the force of gravity. With increasing temperature, the attractive forces between the molecules of a liquid tend to weaken, and surface tension decreases.

7. Liquids evaporate spontaneously; that is, they change into vapor at any temperature.

9.5 Evaporation of liquids

We have indicated previously that all the molecules of a gas at any given temperature do not possess identical kinetic energies. Hence, we say that gas molecules at a given temperature possess an average kinetic energy. Similarly, all the molecules of a liquid do not possess the same kinetic energy at any given temperature. Those molecules of liquid that possess higher kinetic energies move more rapidly and may escape from the surface of the liquid in the form of vapor. This phenomenon, called *evaporation* or *vaporization*, may occur at any temperature. As the temperature increases, a larger number of molecules gain greater kinetic energy, and more of them escape to form vapor. During evaporation, the molecules that escape possess higher kinetic energies. The remaining liquid is left with molecules that possess lower kinetic energies.

The temperature of a liquid drops during evaporation, an observation that may be made experimentally. To maintain the evaporating liquid at the same temperature, heat from some outside source must be supplied. Ether evaporating on the hand cools the hand because heat is withdrawn from the hand in order to maintain the temperature of the ether that is evaporating.

9.6 Liquid-vapor equilibrium

Consider a stoppered flask, half-filled with water (see Figure 9–3 on the next page). The level of liquid in the vessel appears unchanged indefinitely. How do we account for this observation in view of the fact that a liquid continues to evaporate at a fixed rate depending on the temperature?

It can be shown experimentally that the evaporation of a liquid is accompanied by an opposite change in which the molecules of vapor continue to collide at the surface of the liquid to re-form molecules of liquid. The change of state from a vapor, or gas, to a liquid is called *condensation*.

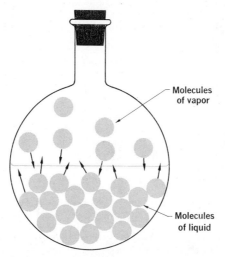

Fig. 9-3   Liquid-vapor equilibrium

When a liquid is placed in a sealed vessel, at first only evaporation occurs, but soon molecules of vapor condense. In time, the rates of these opposing changes—evaporation and condensation—become equal. At this point, we say that an *equilibrium* exists. No visible changes seem to be occurring. However, at the molecular level, a balance exists between evaporation and condensation—both continue to occur at the same rate.

If a drop of liquid is introduced into a barometer tube, the liquid rises to the mercury surface and evaporates, causing the level of the mercury to be depressed. The mercury will be depressed different amounts for different liquids (see Figure 9-4 on the next page).

The barometer experiment demonstrates that once a liquid has evaporated, the resultant vapor exerts pressure, called *vapor pressure*. Which has greater vapor pressure—warm water or boiling water? The answer can be generalized for all liquids. The vapor pressure of a liquid is a function of temperature. Increasing the temperature increases the vapor pressure. Decreasing the temperature decreases the vapor pressure.

We can postulate, with reason, that the attractive forces between liquid molecules (which are different for each liquid) influence the vapor pressure. Strong attractive forces permit relatively few molecules to escape into the vapor phase. Liquids with strong attractive forces, therefore, have low vapor pressures and are *nonvolatile*. Conversely, weak attractive forces permit many molecules to escape. Liquids with weak attractive forces, therefore, have high vapor pressures and are *volatile*. Our model also

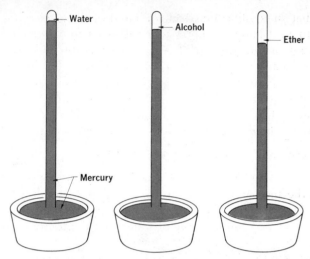

Fig. 9–4   Liquids have different vapor pressures

explains why increasing the temperature of a liquid increases its vapor pressure: the greater kinetic energy permits more molecules to overcome attractive forces and to escape into the vapor phase.

9.7 Subjecting an equilibrium to stress

At equilibrium—where the rate of evaporation equals the rate of condensation—the vapor pressure of a liquid remains constant and is called the *equilibrium vapor pressure*. Since evaporation and condensation involve the addition or the removal of heat, these changes may be summarized in the following equilibrium equation:

$$\text{liquid} \underset{-\text{ heat}}{\overset{+\text{ heat}}{\rightleftharpoons}} \text{vapor}$$

Note that we use a double arrow to indicate a reaction that proceeds in opposite directions.

We will encounter equilibrium systems frequently in chemistry. What happens when the conditions of these systems, such as temperature and pressure, are changed? The effect of changing the conditions of a system in equilibrium was predicted by the French chemist Henri Le Chatelier in the 19th century.

Le Chatelier's Principle: If a system at equilibrium is subjected to a stress (change), the system reacts to partially remove the stress.

Assume that an equilibrium system of liquid water-water vapor is heated. According to Le Chatelier, the system will react to remove (absorb) the heat. The equilibrium equation shows that heat is absorbed during evaporation. This means that heating a sample of water in a sealed flask — **Dangerous!** — increases the rate of evaporation of the water. Equilibrium is reestablished when the rate of the reverse reaction — condensation — increases and equals the rate of evaporation. A new set of equilibrium concentrations is now established at the higher temperature.

9.8 Evaporation and boiling

Let us return to the flask, half-filled with water, and remove the stopper. We insert a thermometer and carefully heat the flask until the water begins to boil (see Figure 9–5). The temperature is approximately 100° C. Continued boiling reduces the volume of water, but the temperature remains unchanged.

Quickly we seal the flask with a one-hole rubber stopper containing another thermometer. The water has stopped boiling. *Very carefully* we place the flask under running cold water (see Figure 9–5). The water in the flask resumes boiling, but the temperature is much below 100° C. How do we explain these observations?

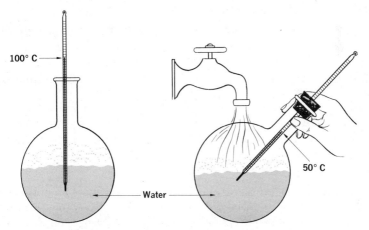

100° C

50° C

Water

Fig. 9–5 Boiling under reduced pressure

As the temperature of the water was raised, its vapor pressure increased. The table on the following page shows the change in the vapor pressure of water with changing temperature.

TEMPERATURE (° C)	VAPOR PRESSURE (mm of Hg)	TEMPERATURE (° C)	VAPOR PRESSURE (mm of Hg)
0	4.6	50	92.5
5	6.5	60	148.9
10	9.2	70	233.3
20	17.5	80	354.9
30	31.5	90	525.5
40	54.9	100	760.0

When water reaches a temperature of 100° C, its vapor pressure equals 760.0 mm of mercury, the pressure of the atmosphere at sea level. In the open flask, water boiled at 100° C, the temperature at which the vapor pressure of the water equals the pressure of the atmosphere acting upon it. In the sealed flask, water boiled at a lower temperature; consequently, the vapor pressure of the water was lower than atmospheric pressure.

The cooling of the flask caused increased condensation of the water vapor (Le Chatelier's Principle). This means that the concentration of vapor molecules was decreased, resulting in a decrease in the pressure of the gas above the water. In time, the reduced vapor pressure of the water became equal to the pressure of the gas acting upon the water, and boiling resumed. Thus a liquid will boil at any temperature at which its vapor pressure equals the pressure of the gas acting upon it.

This phenomenon explains why the boiling point of a liquid at high altitudes (reduced air pressure) is lower than the boiling point of the same liquid at sea level. During the purification of sugar, water is removed from sugar solutions by evaporation under reduced pressure. Thus boiling takes place at a lower temperature, avoiding the decomposition of the sugar that would occur if the solution were heated hot enough to boil at atmospheric pressure. Similarly, increasing the pressure acting upon the surface of a liquid increases the boiling point of the liquid. Thus it is possible to raise the temperature of boiling water above 100° C. Pressure cookers, for example, make use of this principle.

9.9 Solidification (freezing) of liquids

The average kinetic energy of the molecules of a gas is sufficiently great to overcome the attractive forces between the molecules. As a gas is cooled, the average kinetic energy of its molecules is decreased until it is no longer sufficient to overcome the attractive forces between the molecules. As a result, liquefaction occurs. Continued cooling of the liquid further decreases the kinetic energy of the molecules until solidification occurs.

How do solids differ from liquids and gases? The kinetic energy of the molecules is greatest in the gaseous state. Since the molecules are widely spaced, the potential energy (energy of position) of the molecules is also greatest. This is true because work was done and energy was consumed in order to separate the molecules. In liquids, the kinetic energy of the molecules is lower because heat is evolved in the cooling process. A decrease in kinetic energy also results in a decrease in potential energy because the molecules have come closer to one another.

You will recall from section 1.19 that as a stone is raised above the ground, the potential energy of the stone increases, and the stability of the stone decreases. At ground level, the potential energy of the stone is minimal, and its stability is greatest. Solids possess the least potential energy because energy has been released in all the changes from the gaseous to the solid state. In a solid, the particles are arranged in the least random (most ordered) fashion.

A study of the heat required to melt and boil some common solids reveals that more energy is required to go from the liquid state to the gas state (vaporization) than from the solid state to the liquid state (melting). For example, 9.72 kilocalories are required to vaporize 1 mole of liquid water at its boiling point at sea level, but only 1.4 kilocalories are required to melt 1 mole of solid water (ice). Similarly, 73 kilocalories are required to vaporize 1 mole of copper, but only 3 kilocalories are required to melt 1 mole of copper. From these observations, we may again conclude that solids are generally more stable (possess less energy) than the corresponding liquids, and liquids are generally more stable than the corresponding gases.

9.10 Attractive forces in solids

The melting points of solids may be taken as a fair measure of the magnitude of the attractive forces within them. The table that follows reveals a wide range in melting points of solids.

SOLID	MELTING POINT ($^\circ$ C)
oxygen	−218.4
water	0
potassium	62.3
sodium chloride	801
iron	1535

The boiling points of liquids differ markedly but generally do not exhibit as wide a range of values as do solids (see the following table). This means that solids may exhibit a wider range in properties due to a wider range in structures.

LIQUID	BOILING POINT ($^\circ$C)
oxygen	−183.0
carbon tetrachloride	76.8
ethyl alcohol	78.3
glycerine	290
mercury	356.6

9.11 Types of solids

The differences in the magnitudes and types of attractive forces in solids provide a convenient means for classifying solids. X-ray analysis reveals that the internal structure of a solid consists of particles arranged in a regular (ordered) fashion called a *lattice*. These particles—molecules, atoms, or ions—occupy fixed points on the lattice. The smallest grouping of these particles in the lattice is called a *unit cell*, which is repeated in three dimensions (see Figure 9–6). When the unit cell is repeated a great many times, the solid becomes sufficiently large to be viewed and is called a *crystal*. Let us now describe solids according to the different types of attractive forces.

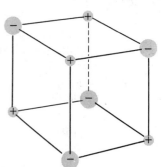

Fig. 9–6   Unit cell (crystal)

9.12 Molecular solids

The unit cell in a molecular solid consists of regularly spaced molecules. Molecular solids are crystalline and are characterized by low melting temperatures, generally below room temperature. Low melting temperatures suggest weak attractive forces, called van der Waals forces, which, in turn, signify relative instability of the solid structure.

Many common gases can be cooled sufficiently to form molecular solids. Solid carbon dioxide (dry ice), for example, consists of a repeated arrangement of CO_2 molecules bonded together by weak van der Waals forces. At room temperature, solid CO_2 vaporizes to form gaseous molecules of

CO_2. A molecule of CO_2 does not break up into atoms at room temperature. The molecule consists of two atoms of oxygen strongly bonded to one atom of carbon. (These bonds, called *covalent bonds*, have been described briefly in section 4.13 and will be treated in detail in Chapter 20.) Molecular solids, such as gases that have been solidified, are thus made up of relatively loosely held molecules which, in turn, are made up of atoms that are more tightly held by covalent bonds.

Sugars such as glucose, $C_6H_{12}O_6$, and sucrose, $C_{12}H_{22}O_{11}$, are also examples of molecular solids. These substances form crystals that consist of weakly bonded sugar molecules.

9.13 Macromolecular (network) solids

The unit cell in a *macromolecular solid* is an interlocking array of atoms. The attractive forces, or bonds, between the atoms in the crystal are very strong, as characterized by the hardness (resistance to scratching) of macromolecular solids and by their very high melting points.

For example, diamond is a crystal consisting of a regularly repeated arrangement of carbon atoms covalently bonded. This arrangement, typical of carbon atoms, can extend indefinitely into three-dimensional space; therefore, no simple carbon molecule exists. Instead, the structure forms a giant molecule called a *macromolecule*. Diamond is the hardest naturally occurring substance and is extremely difficult to melt.

In some instances, all the atoms in a network solid may not be the same. For example, silicon carbide, SiC (also called carborundum), resembles diamond structurally, but half the atoms are silicon and the other half are carbon atoms. Like diamond, silicon carbide is a very hard crystalline material and is very difficult to melt.

9.14 Metallic solids

The unit cell in a metallic solid consists of regularly spaced atoms arranged so that they make up a regular geometric solid, such as a cubical or a hexagonal solid. In many metals, the atoms are arranged in the smallest possible volume. This crowding together of the atoms in a solid is called *closest-packing* (see Figure 9-7).

As we have learned, atoms of metals readily lose their outermost (valence) electrons. In a given sample of a metallic crystal, the outermost electrons of the atoms of the metal are

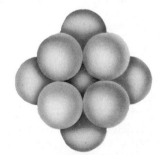

Fig. 9-7   *Closest-packing of spheres*

not always associated with a specific atom but act as part of the total crystal. Therefore, the particles in a metal are really positive ions surrounded by *mobile electrons*, which can drift from one atom to another.

The strong bonds between the atoms of metals result from the attraction of all the positive ions for the electrons surrounding them. Strong bonding accounts for the generally high melting points of metals. The mobile electrons account for the luster of metals and their ability to conduct heat and electricity. The absence of mobile electrons renders network solids nonconducting.

Why are most metals malleable and ductile? The positive ions in a metal are continuously attracted to the surrounding electrons. Consequently, when a positive ion is forced out of its position, it does not easily break away from its neighbors.

9.15 Ionic solids

Ionic solids, like metals, are also strongly bonded, as shown by their high melting points. For example, copper sulfate melts at 200° C, lithium nitrate melts at 255° C, and sodium chloride melts at 801° C. An ionic solid is made up of an ordered lattice of alternate positive and negative ions. The attraction between the oppositely charged ions provides a strong force that holds the ions in fixed positions in the crystal (see Figure 9–8).

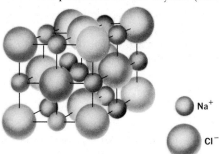

Na^+

Cl^-

Fig. 9–8   Ionic crystal

Unlike metals, however, ionic solids are nonconducting. And unlike network solids, water solutions of ionic solids or fused (melted) ionic solids conduct electricity. This property suggests the presence of charged particles in the ionic solid. When dissolved in water or fused, the charged particles become mobile, permitting electrical conductivity.

The electrolysis of water solutions of ionic solids or fused ionic solids produces electrically neutral species at each electrode. Oxidation of the negative ion occurs at the anode, and corresponding reduction of the positive ion occurs at the cathode (see section 6.18).

9.16 Glasses

Glasses are noncrystalline solids. The particles in glasses are not regularly arranged as they are in crystalline solids. Unlike crystalline solids, which have a fixed composition, glasses have a variable composition. As a result, glasses do not possess a sharp melting point. Tar, glue, asphalt, and glass are examples of glassy solids.

9.17 Properties of solids

As with the properties of gases and liquids, the properties of solids are related to their internal structures. The general properties of solids may be summarized as follows:

1. Solids have a specific volume (unlike gases) and a definite shape (unlike gases and liquids).
2. Solids do not flow. Instead, they are rigid bodies, ranging from very brittle to mechanically tough.
3. Solids are considerably denser than gases but in most cases are only slightly denser than liquids.
4. Increasing the pressure upon a solid has very little effect on its volume. Thus solids are virtually incompressible.

Multiple-Choice Questions

1. When the pressure of ammonia gas is increased at constant temperature (1) the energy of the molecules increases (2) the spaces between the molecules increase (3) the bonds between the atoms are broken (4) liquid ammonia forms
2. Gases can be liquefied if they (1) dissolve in water (2) expand above the critical temperature (3) are compressed at a temperature below the critical temperature (4) are compressed at a temperature above the critical temperature
3. The surface tension of a liquid results from (1) a film that forms on the surface of the liquid (2) unequal forces that act on the molecules of the liquid at the surface (3) the inability of the molecules of the liquid to flow easily (4) unequal kinetic energies of the molecules of the liquid
4. In a closed bottle partly filled with a liquid (1) the number of molecules in the gaseous state increases as the liquid continues to evaporate (2) the space above the liquid is a partial vacuum (3) the number of molecules that evaporate in one second equals the number that condense in the same second (4) all the liquid eventually changes to gas

5. Two properties of liquids that decrease in magnitude with increasing temperature are (1) volume and pressure (2) viscosity and surface tension (3) density and volume (4) molecular motion and viscosity

6. Two factors that might account for the high vapor pressure of a liquid are (1) strong forces between the molecules and low molecular kinetic energy (2) strong forces between the molecules and high molecular kinetic energy (3) weak forces between the molecules and high molecular kinetic energy (4) weak forces between the molecules and low molecular kinetic energy

7. When a liquid in equilibrium with its vapor is heated (1) the rate of the reaction, vapor → liquid, is increased (2) the same equilibrium mixture is re-established (3) a new equilibrium mixture with a higher vapor pressure is established (4) a new equilibrium mixture is established in which the rate of evaporation is greater than the rate of condensation

8. Water in a pressure cooker boils above 100° C because (1) the molecules of water form heavier units at high pressure (2) the vapor molecules cannot move rapidly at high pressure (3) a higher temperature is needed to produce a vapor pressure equal to the pressure in the cooker (4) heat is needed for the decomposition of water

9. The heat needed to vaporize 1 mole of a solid is usually greater than the heat needed to melt 1 mole of the same solid because (1) more energy is required to separate the molecules than to disrupt the solid structure (2) molecules in the solid state possess higher potential energies and require less additional energy for melting (3) melting takes place at a lower temperature than vaporization, and all changes at the lower temperature require less energy (4) the closest-packing of molecules in the solid state allows the molecules to absorb heat more efficiently

10. Particles that are weakly bonded to one another are probably (1) ions (2) atoms (3) molecules (4) free electrons

11. Ionic solids (1) are soft and have low melting points (2) melt to form liquids that conduct electricity (3) are malleable (4) conduct electricity

12. Solid sodium metal and molten sodium chloride conduct electricity because both contain (1) mobile electrons (2) active metals which are good conductors (3) mobile charge carriers (4) mobile ions

13. Two differences between a solid such as sodium chloride and a glass are that (1) sodium chloride is not transparent and does not melt, while a glass is transparent and melts (2) sodium chloride is crystalline and has a definite melting point, while a glass is noncrystalline and does not have a melting point (3) sodium chloride does not conduct electricity

and is not crystalline, while a glass conducts electricity and is crystalline (4) sodium chloride is made up of molecules and has a crystalline structure, while a glass contains ions and is not crystalline

Completion Questions

1. An example of a solid that does not have a crystalline structure is _____.
2. Liquids and gases are classed as fluids because they can _____.
3. The ability of liquids to rise into narrow tubes depends on the property called _____.
4. A liquid is in equilibrium with its vapor when the rate of _____ of the liquid equals the rate of condensation.
5. _____ Principle may be used to predict the effect of increasing the temperature on the equilibrium system   liquid + heat ⇌ vapor.
6. A regular geometric arrangement of the particles of a substance is a characteristic of the _____ state of matter.
7. Low melting points characterize solids bonded by _____ forces.
8. The metallic lattice is composed of positive ions and mobile _____.
9. Marked differences in the melting points of solids indicate that they have a wider range of _____ than liquids or gases.
10. Mercury is an excellent liquid for use in thermometers because _____.

True-False Questions

1. When a gas is compressed at constant temperature and its volume decreases more than the amount predicted by *Charles' Law*, liquefaction may take place.
2. *Viscosity* is the resistance of a fluid to flow.
3. The vapor pressure of a liquid is the pressure exerted by molecules of the *liquid* when the liquid is in equilibrium with its vapor.
4. Removing heat from the equilibrium   liquid + heat ⇌ vapor   will increase the rate of the *forward* reaction.
5. Water in a sealed flask is observed to boil at 80° C. From the table on page 152, we see that the pressure in the flask must be *35.49 cm* of mercury.
6. The most random arrangement of molecules exists in the *solid* state.
7. A high *melting point* indicates relatively strong forces between the particles in a solid.
8. Weak van der Waals forces are present in a crystalline solid composed of *ions*.

9. In ice, *stronger* bonds exist between the molecules of H_2O than between the H and O atoms in the individual molecules of H_2O.
10. Malleability and ductility are characteristic properties of *ionic* solids.

Decreases, Increases, Remains the Same

1. As the temperature of a gas increases, the attractive forces between its molecules _____.
2. As the critical temperatures in a series of gases increase, the ease of liquefying the gases _____.
3. As the pressure applied to a liquid at constant temperature is decreased, its volume _____.
4. Raising the temperature of a liquid _____ its viscosity and _____ its surface tension.
5. As the rate of evaporation of a liquid is increased, the temperature of the remaining liquid _____.
6. At a given temperature, decreasing the attractive forces between the molecules of a liquid _____ the vapor pressure of the liquid.
7. With increasing temperature, the vapor pressure of all liquids _____.
8. As heat is supplied to a liquid boiling at atmospheric pressure, the temperature of the liquid _____.
9. As the altitude increases, the boiling point of a liquid in an open vessel _____.
10. When a substance changes from gas to liquid to solid, the potential energy of its molecules _____.

Exercises for Review

1. The heat of fusion (melting) of ice is 1.4 kcal/mole. Calculate the heat needed to melt 1 kg of ice.
2. A vessel is partly filled with water and is sealed at $50°C$. It is then cooled to $10°C$. By how much does the pressure in the vessel change?
3. *a.* A vessel contains oxygen in contact with water. What is the vapor pressure of the water if the temperature is $60°C$?
   b. If the total pressure in the vessel is 762 mm of Hg, what is the partial pressure of the oxygen?
4. *a.* The heat of vaporization of water is 9.72 kcal/mole. How much heat is required to vaporize 1 kg of water?
   b. The heat of vaporization of copper is 73 kcal/mole. How much heat is needed to vaporize 1 kg of copper?
5. *a.* Write equations for the evaporation of water and for the condensation of water. Include the heat terms.
   b. Write the equilibrium equation for these changes.

6. *a.* Write the equilibrium equation for the vaporization and condensation of methanol, CH_3OH.

  b. By changing the length of the appropriate arrow, show how an increase in temperature affects these changes.

7. *a.* Write equations for the melting of ice and the freezing of water. Include the heat terms.

  b. Write the equilibrium equation for these changes.

8. Write separate oxidation and reduction equations for the reactions at the two electrodes when molten $MgCl_2$ is electrolyzed.

Exercises for Further Study

1. *a.* Draw a graph of the vapor pressure data given on page 152, using the horizontal axis to represent temperature.

  b. Is the increase in vapor pressure uniform with increasing temperature? Explain.

2. When ordinary glass breaks, the surfaces formed are often curved. Does this indicate a crystalline or noncrystalline structure? Explain.

3. *a.* Select a row of eight elements in the Periodic Table. Beginning with the element on the left, list the name, the number of valence electrons, and the type of structure shown by the element in the solid state.

  b. Explain the different types of structures in terms of the number of valence electrons.

4. Using the atomic structures of carbon and silicon, explain why silicon carbide (SiC) has a network structure similar to the diamond structure.

5. Why is the term *molecule* not applied to solid sodium chloride?

6. Explain why molecular solids and network solids are insulators, but metallic solids are conductors.

7. Draw a triangle, and label its three points *gas*, *liquid*, and *solid*.

  a. Connect the three points with reversible arrows, and label each arrow with the name of the process it represents.

  b. Draw arrows to show the direction for increasing potential energy.

  c. Draw arrows to show the direction of increasing randomness.

8. Sublimation is the change from the solid to the gaseous state without liquefying. If you could measure the heat of sublimation and the heat of fusion for a substance, how would you calculate the heat of vaporization?

9. Different liquids rise to different heights in open capillary tubes of the same bore at the same atmospheric pressure. Explain.

10. Explain why free-falling liquids form spherical droplets.

Chapter 10

SOLUTION AND IONIZATION

10.1 Introduction

In Chapter 6, we referred briefly to the role of water in the solution process. Water is termed the universal solvent because, given sufficient time, it will dissolve at least small amounts of almost every kind of matter.

Water solutions have considerable practical importance. The digestion of foods is hastened by the solvent action of water. The transfer of nutrients to living cells and the removal of waste materials from cells depend on the solvent action of water. The extraction of salt from mineral deposits in the earth is made possible by the dissolving action of water. We will study many chemical reactions that can occur in water solution only.

Although water is the most common solvent, there are many other important solvents. For example, alcohol solutions—called *tinctures*—are widely used medicinally. Many industrial chemical processes utilize solutions of substances in ether or in acetone. No matter what solvent is used, all solution processes involve the same or related principles.

10.2 What is a solution?

A *solution* is a homogeneous mixture consisting of a *solvent* (that which does the dissolving) and a *solute* (that which is dissolved). Under some conditions, especially when one liquid dissolves in another, it is difficult to distinguish the solvent from the solute. This distinction, however, is unimportant.

We have stated previously that a homogeneous system consists of a single phase; that is, it is a system that is uniform in all respects. Because solutions are uniform systems, we may consider them homogeneous. For example, a water solution of salt consists of the solvent (water) and the solute (salt). Since equal volumes of salt solution have the same quantities of solvent and solute, the salt solution is homogeneous.

Solutions contain one distinguishable phase, which suggests that one kind of matter is present. This is true only macroscopically. At the molecular level, solutions contain two kinds of matter: solute and solvent particles. Systems that contain more than one distinguishable phase are called *mixtures*. Consider a mixture such as salt and sugar. However finely ground, the mixture still reveals the presence of two macroscopic phases: a salt phase and a sugar phase. Specific boundaries separate the components of a mixture. However, no boundaries can be detected in a solution. We can state, therefore, that solutions are homogeneous down to the molecular level.

10.3 Types of solutions

Solids dissolved in liquids represent the most common type of solution. Other types of solutions include:

1. Solutions of gases in liquids. For example, carbon dioxide dissolved in water (forming carbonated water).
2. Solutions of liquids in liquids. For example, alcohol dissolved in water.
3. Solutions of gases in gases. For example, nitrogen and oxygen dissolved in each other in air.
4. Solutions of gases in solids. For example, air dissolved in ice.
5. Solutions of solids in solids. For example, copper dissolved in zinc (in such alloys as brass).
6. Solutions of solids in gases or solutions of liquids in gases. For example, iodine vapor (finely divided particles of solid iodine) dissolved in air or carbon tetrachloride vapor (finely divided particles of liquid carbon tetrachloride) dissolved. in air. Both types of solution are generally considered solutions of gases (or vapors) in gases.

10.4 Expressing the concentration of a solution

To distinguish between different solutions of the same solvent and the same solute, it is necessary to describe the concentration of the solution, that is, its quantitative composition.

Concentration denotes the quantity of dissolved matter contained in a unit of volume or weight of solvent or solution. Several methods are used to express the concentration of a solution.

An approximate measure of the concentration of a solution is indicated by the terms *dilute* and *concentrated*. These terms do not have precise meanings, but the following descriptions are useful. A dilute solution contains a much larger proportion of solvent than solute. A concentrated solution contains somewhat less solute than the maximum that can be dissolved. In the sections that follow, we will describe more precise methods of expressing the concentration of a solution: percentage, molarity, molality, and normality.

10.5 Percentage concentration

Most commonly, the percentage concentration of a solution expresses the parts by weight of solute per 100 parts by weight of total solution. A 10% salt solution by weight contains 10 g of salt dissolved in 90 g of water, that is, in 100 g of solution.

Mole percentage equals the moles of solute per moles of solvent plus solute, all multiplied by 100%. Mole percentage may be calculated from weight percentage. The mole percentage of a 10% salt solution

$$= \frac{\text{moles of salt in 10 g of salt}}{\text{moles of water in 90 g of water} + \text{moles of salt in 10 g of salt}} \times 100\%$$

$$= \frac{\dfrac{10 \text{ g}}{58.5 \text{ g/mole}}}{\dfrac{90 \text{ g}}{18 \text{ g/mole}} + \dfrac{10 \text{ g}}{58.5 \text{ g/mole}}} \times 100\%$$

$$= \frac{0.17 \text{ mole}}{5 \text{ moles} + 0.17 \text{ mole}} \times 100\%$$

$$= 3.4\%$$

The weight of solute in a given weight of solution may be computed from the percentage concentration of the solution. For example, how many grams of salt are present in 50 g of a 5% salt solution?

$$\text{weight of solute} = \text{weight of solution} \times \text{weight percentage of solution}$$

$$= 50 \text{ g} \times 5\%$$

$$= 2.5 \text{ g of salt}$$

If the density of the salt solution is known, we may calculate the volume of solution that will deliver a given weight of solute. For example, the density of a salt solution is 1.2 g/ml. What volume of a 10% solution will deliver 24 g of salt? A milliliter of the 10% salt solution contains 10% of 1.2 g, or 0.12 g, of salt. To deliver 24 g of salt, we need $\dfrac{24 \text{ g}}{0.12 \text{ g/ml}}$, or 200 ml, of solution.

10.6 Molarity concentration

A 1-molar (1 M) solution contains one mole (gram-molecular weight) of solute dissolved in 1 l of solution. Note that it is the volume of the *solution*, not the volume of the solvent, that is involved in this definition.

A 1 *M* solution also contains 1 millimole (0.001 mole) of solute per milliliter (0.001 liter) of solution. A 1 *M* NaCl solution contains 58.5 g (23 g + 35.5 g) of NaCl/l of solution, or 0.0585 g/ml, or 58.5 mg/ml.

How many grams of NaCl are present in 25 ml of 0.1 *M* NaCl solution? By definition, 0.1 *M* NaCl contains 0.1 millimole of NaCl (0.0058 g) per milliliter of solution. Thus 25 ml of solution contain 0.0058 g/ml × 25 ml, or about 0.14 g.

How would you prepare 25 ml of 0.1 *M* NaCl solution? Dissolve 0.14 g of NaCl (0.0058 g/ml × 25 ml) in sufficient water to reach a final volume of 25 ml. The concentration of this solution is 0.14 g/25 ml, or 0.0058 g/ml, which is the concentration of a 0.1 *M* solution of NaCl.

How would you prepare 2 l of 0.1 *M* Na_2SO_4 solution? A 1 *M* Na_2SO_4 solution contains 142 g of Na_2SO_4/l of solution. This means that a 0.1 *M* solution contains 0.1 mole/l, or 14.2 g of Na_2SO_4/l. To prepare 2 l of solution, dissolve 28.4 g of Na_2SO_4 in sufficient water to reach a final volume of 2 l (2000 ml).

In the laboratory, it may be necessary to dilute a given volume of a solution of fixed molarity to prepare another solution of lesser molarity. For example, how much water must be added to 100 ml of a 0.2 *M* solution to obtain a 0.1 *M* solution? The following steps will solve such dilution problems.

1. Calculate the number of moles in the original solution.

$$\text{moles} = \text{molarity} \times \text{volume of solution}$$

2. Calculate the volume of the dilute solution that contains the same number of moles of solute.

Thus 100 ml of a 0.2 *M* solution contain 0.2 mole/l × 0.1 l, or 0.02 mole. To prepare a 0.1 *M* solution that will contain 0.02 mole, dissolve 0.1 mole of solute in 200 ml of solution (0.1 mole/l × 0.2 l = 0.02 mole). This means we must add 100 ml of water to the original solution. Intuitively, we can see that this answer is correct: by doubling the volume, we halved the molarity.

Another problem typically encountered in the laboratory is: How many milliliters of a 5.0 *M* HCl solution must be used to make 100 ml of a 0.25 *M* solution? The problem may be solved in the following steps:

1. Calculate the number of moles of HCl present in the final solution.

100 ml of 0.25 *M* HCl contain 0.025 mole

2. Calculate the volume of the concentrated solution that contains that number of moles (0.025) of solute.

By definition, 5 M HCl contain 5 moles of HCl/l. Since the solution to be made must contain 0.025 mole of HCl,

$$\frac{5 \text{ moles}}{1000 \text{ ml}} = \frac{0.025 \text{ mole}}{x}$$

$$5x = 25 \text{ ml}$$

$$x = 5 \text{ ml}$$

Thus 5 ml of 5.0 M HCl will deliver $\frac{5}{1000} \times 5$ moles of HCl = 0.025 mole.

10.7 Molality concentration

A 1-*molal* solution (1 m) contains 1 mole of solute dissolved in 1000 g of *solvent*. Since a 1-molar (1 M) solution contains 1 mole of solute dissolved in 1 l of solution, a 1-molar solution contains less solvent than a 1-molal solution. A given volume of a 1-molar solution is a little more concentrated than the same volume of a 1-molal solution of the same solute. Why? A 1-molar solution contains less than 1000 g of solvent. Molal solutions will be utilized later in the chapter when we discuss the boiling points and freezing points of solutions (see section 10.25).

10.8 Normality concentration

A 1-*normal* (1 N) solution contains 1 *gram-equivalent weight* of solute dissolved in 1 l of solution. The gram-equivalent weight of the solute equals the gram-molecular weight of the solute divided by the total positive valence number. (See section 11.14.)

A 1-normal (1 N) solution of calcium chloride contains the gram-molecular weight of $CaCl_2$, 111 g, divided by 2 (total valence number of Ca), or 55.5 g of solute dissolved in sufficient water to reach a volume of 1 l. We will return to normal solutions in Chapter 16.

Each method of expressing the concentration of a solution has its peculiar advantages and limitations. In this book, we will express concentration by the method which contributes most to our understanding of the concept being studied.

10.9 The nature of the solution process

When two elements react to form a compound, the properties of the compound generally differ from the individual properties of the elements. For example, we have observed that the very reactive metal sodium combines with the poisonous gas chlorine to form sodium chloride, an indispensable aid to the diet. Solutions, however, retain some of the properties of the solute and the solvent. For example, a K_2CrO_4 solution is yellow in color like the solute K_2CrO_4 and also exhibits many of the properties of the solvent water.

On the other hand, solutions have boiling points, freezing points, and densities that differ from those of the solute or the solvent. The act of dissolving may also be accompanied by an energy change; that is, during dissolving, heat may be evolved or liberated. The changes that occur during solution suggest that, in some cases, the process of dissolving is merely the mixing of substances. In other cases, interactions between the solute and the solvent occur. What is the nature of these interactions?

10.10 Molecular liquids

We have previously defined a molecular solid as a crystal composed of a lattice of molecules weakly bonded together. On melting, usually at relatively low temperatures, such solids form molecular liquids. Let us consider the composition and structure of each of the following molecular liquids: gasoline, carbon tetrachloride, water, and glycerine.

Gasoline is a mixture of compounds containing hydrogen and carbon, called *hydrocarbons*. Octane, C_8H_{18}, the chief ingredient of gasoline, has the graphic (structural) formula

$$
\begin{array}{c}
\;\;\;\;\text{H}\;\;\;\text{H}\;\;\;\text{H}\;\;\;\text{H}\;\;\;\text{H}\;\;\;\text{H}\;\;\;\text{H}\;\;\;\text{H} \\
\;\;\;\;|\;\;\;\;\;|\;\;\;\;\;|\;\;\;\;\;|\;\;\;\;\;|\;\;\;\;\;|\;\;\;\;\;|\;\;\;\;\;| \\
\text{H}-\text{C}-\text{C}-\text{C}-\text{C}-\text{C}-\text{C}-\text{C}-\text{C}-\text{H} \\
\;\;\;\;|\;\;\;\;\;|\;\;\;\;\;|\;\;\;\;\;|\;\;\;\;\;|\;\;\;\;\;|\;\;\;\;\;|\;\;\;\;\;| \\
\;\;\;\;\text{H}\;\;\;\text{H}\;\;\;\text{H}\;\;\;\text{H}\;\;\;\text{H}\;\;\;\text{H}\;\;\;\text{H}\;\;\;\text{H}
\end{array}
$$

Carbon has a slightly greater attraction for electrons than hydrogen and tends to attract the shared pairs of electrons more strongly, producing a slightly polar bond. However, the shape of the octane molecule (its symmetry) cancels the charge separations, and the result is a nonpolar molecule.

The graphic formula of carbon tetrachloride is

$$
\begin{array}{c}
\;\;\;\;\text{Cl} \\
\;\;\;\;| \\
\text{Cl}-\text{C}-\text{Cl} \\
\;\;\;\;| \\
\;\;\;\;\text{Cl}
\end{array}
$$

Although there is a charge separation due to the greater attraction of chlorine than carbon for electrons, again the symmetry of the molecule cancels the charge. Thus carbon tetrachloride is also a nonpolar liquid.

We have already discussed the structure of a water molecule, thus:

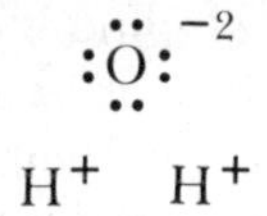

$$:\overset{\cdot\cdot}{\underset{\cdot\cdot}{O}}:^{-2}$$

$$H^+ \quad H^+$$

Since oxygen has a greater attraction for electrons than hydrogen, charge separation occurs and polar bonds form.

The water molecule is bent (angular), making the molecule unsymmetrical. The charge separations do not cancel each other. Water, therefore, is a polar molecule. From the preceding examples, we see that polar bonds alone do not necessarily produce a polar molecule. The shape of the molecule also determines its polarity.

The water molecule possesses a negative charge at the oxygen end and positive charges at the hydrogen ends. In a sample of water, the positive (hydrogen) ends of one molecule of water are attracted to the negative (oxygen) ends of neighboring water molecules by weak bonds called *hydrogen bonds*, as shown in Figure 10–1. Dashed lines represent the hydrogen bonds.

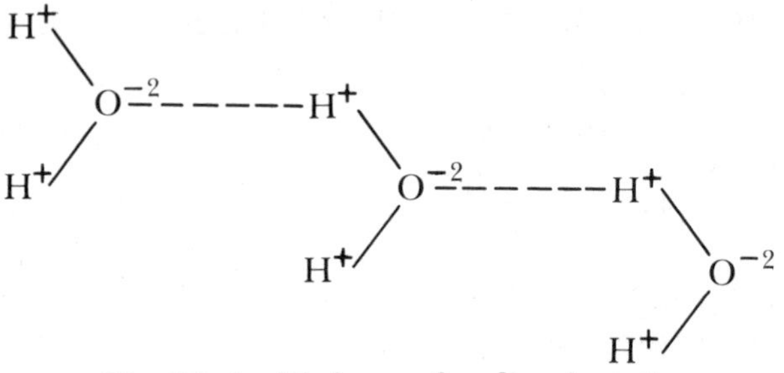

Fig. 10–1   Hydrogen bonding in water

Glycerine is a derivative (a substance that can be made from another substance) of the hydrocarbon propane, C_3H_8.

Note that three OH groups in glycerine have replaced three H atoms in propane. As in water, since the OH groups are polar and the glycerine molecule lacks symmetry, glycerine is therefore a polar molecule. Also, as in water, glycerine molecules form more complex aggregates through hydrogen bonding.

10.11 A solubility model for molecular liquids

Experimentally, we find that gasoline is soluble in carbon tetrachloride, but gasoline is not soluble in water or in glycerine. Glycerine dissolves in water but does not dissolve in gasoline or in carbon tetrachloride. These observations permit us to adopt a model that may be judiciously used to predict the solubilities of molecular liquids. In general, our model predicts: Molecules that are polar will dissolve in polar solvents. Molecules that are nonpolar will dissolve in nonpolar solvents. Polar and nonpolar compounds will not dissolve in each other (see Figure 10–2).

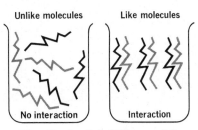

Fig. 10–2   Solubility models

It must be emphasized that our model, like all models, does not fit every situation. Many compounds show varying degrees of polarity, and it is difficult to predict their solubilities without error. For example, carbon tetrachloride, a nonpolar liquid, will dissolve in ethyl alcohol, a polar liquid; but carbon tetrachloride will not dissolve in water, which is more polar than ethyl alcohol. The extent of polarity is frequently a factor in determining whether polar and nonpolar liquids will dissolve in each other.

Using the solubility model for molecular liquids, we can explain why glycerine dissolves in water, whereas octane does not. As we have seen, glycerine contains polar OH groups that can bond to polar water molecules through hydrogen bonds. Octane, however, does not contain any polar groups. This means that the nonpolar octane molecules cannot bond to the hydrogen-bonded water molecules.

On the other hand, octane, a nonpolar liquid, is soluble in hexane, another nonpolar liquid. Since the attractions (bonds) in both liquids are van der Waals forces, interaction between the solute and the solvent occurs, resulting in solubility. (Van der Waals forces are thought to originate from the mutual repulsions of the electrons of two neighboring molecules. These repulsions cause the molecules to behave as temporary polar molecules — dipoles — favoring interaction.)

10.12 The solubility of solids in water

The preceding discussion seems to imply that "like dissolves like." Can we use this generalization to account for other solutions, particularly solids dissolved in water?

In section 9.12, we discussed molecular solids. As we shall see, these substances dissolve in water to form solutions that do not conduct electricity. In section 9.15 we discussed ionic solids such as lithium nitrate, sodium chloride, and copper sulfate. Solutions of these solids are characterized by the presence of ions, electrically charged particles which permit the solutions to conduct electricity. Since pure water is almost nonconducting (from a strictly structural viewpoint), these solids should not dissolve in water. Since they do dissolve, what is the nature of this solution process?

10.13 A solubility model for solids

Studies reveal that polar molecules, such as water, can lessen the attractive forces between the ions in an ionic solid. This permits the ions to break away from each other so that the solid dissolves. The polar water molecules are attracted to the ionic crystal. The positive end of the water molecule is oriented toward the negative ion in the crystal. The negative end of the water molecule is oriented toward the positive ion in the crystal.

As the ions break away from the solid, the water molecules remain attached to the ions. This phenomenon is called *solvation*. When water is the solvent, the process is also called *hydration*, or *aquation*. The particles in a solution of an ionic solid are aquated ions. One or more water particles are attached to each aquated ion. The following aquations are typical of ionic solids.

$$LiNO_3\ (s) + H_2O \rightarrow Li^+\ (aq) + NO_3^-\ (aq)$$

$$NaCl\ (s) + H_2O \rightarrow Na^+\ (aq) + Cl^-\ (aq)$$

$$CuSO_4\ (s) + H_2O \rightarrow Cu^{+2}\ (aq) + SO_4^{-2}\ (aq)$$

The dissolving of an ionic solid and the melting of an ionic solid have much in common. In both, the bonds that maintain the shape of the crystal are weakened sufficiently to permit the ions to become mobile. The dissolving of ionic solids in water, however, involves the additional step in which the mobile ions become aquated.

Each of these processes — destruction of the crystal lattice and aquation — has an energy requirement. The destruction of the crystal lattice requires the addition of energy (is *endothermic*). Aquation evolves energy (is *exothermic*). The net energy effect depends on the magnitude of these energy terms. Since the solution of most ionic solids in water is an endothermic process, the energy liberated during aquation is less than the energy required to break the crystal lattice. When the solution of an ionic solid in water is exothermic, the energy evolved during aquation is larger than the energy required to break the crystal lattice.

The solution of a molecular solid in water, such as glucose (sugar), has much in common with the solution of an ionic solid in water. Glucose is related structurally to the hydrocarbon hexane, as shown by the following graphic formulas:

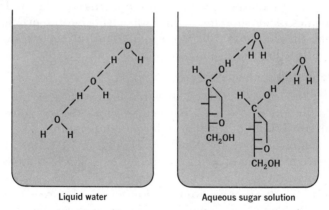

hexane   glucose

The polar water molecules interact with the polar sugar molecules through hydrogen bonding (as shown in Figure 10–3). This process destroys the crystal lattice of the glucose, and solution occurs. Unlike solutions of ionic solids, which consist of aquated ions, the glucose solution consists of aquated glucose molecules.

Liquid water   Aqueous sugar solution

Fig. 10–3   Solution of a molecular solid

10.14 How do energy and randomness influence solubility?

Is the solution of solids in water governed by energy factors alone? We stated previously that chemical changes proceed in the direction that liberates energy. Therefore, the potential energy of the products of a spontaneous change is lower than the potential energy of the reactants. Thus the products are more stable than the reactants. This means that dissolving processes which are exothermic should proceed spontaneously. Conversely, dissolving processes which are endothermic should not proceed spontaneously. Experimentally, however, we observe that exothermic and endothermic processes may occur spontaneously.

We can resolve the conflict between what we think should happen and what actually happens by assuming that energy may not be the only factor that influences solubility. The solution of a solid in water is governed by another factor in addition to the energy factor. This new factor, one of the most important in nature, is called randomness, or entropy. *Randomness* represents the tendency of matter to become as disordered as possible.

As we learned, solids are more ordered than liquids, which in turn are more ordered than gases. When a solid dissolves, however, there is an increase in randomness because the crystal lattice breaks up and the particles become more mobile (more randomly arranged). In an endothermic solution process, despite the higher energy of the solution (lesser stability), the larger randomness factor permits the process of solution to be spontaneous. Since the conditions that govern the magnitude of the randomness factor are difficult to predict, we shall return to a more quantitative study of the randomness factors in the solution process in Chapter 12.

In summary, we must emphasize: No simple rules can be used to predict the solubilities of all substances. Since dissolving represents change, it is safe to say that interaction between solute and solvent will occur if the change satisfies the energy and randomness requirements.

10.15 Saturated solutions

Consider the solubility curves, shown in Figure 10–4 on the next page, for eight different solid solutes. Each curve shows the weight of solid that will dissolve in 100 ml of water at different temperatures.

In the solubility curve for $NaNO_3$, note that at 10° C, 80 g of $NaNO_3$ solid dissolve in 100 ml of water. Suppose 1 g of $NaNO_3$ solid were added to this solution (80 g of $NaNO_3$ in 100 g of water) while maintaining the temperature at 10° C. What would we observe? The excess solid would settle to the bottom of the container. If the solid were separated from the solution by filtering, then dried and weighed, it would weigh 1 g.

At 10° C, 100 ml of water can dissolve only 80 g of $NaNO_3$. At this temperature, the solution is said to be saturated. At 40° C, however, it takes an additional 25 g of $NaNO_3$, or a total of 105 g, to saturate 100 ml of water.

Saturated solutions are not necessarily concentrated. The solubility curve for $KClO_3$ shows that at 10° C, only 6 g of solid dissolve in 100 ml of water. At 10° C, less than 1 milligram of AgCl dissolves in 100 ml of water.

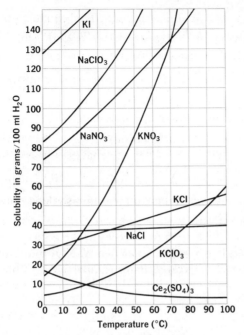

Fig. 10-4 Solubility curves

If a saturated solution is cooled, the excess solute crystallizes. For example, if a saturated solution of $NaNO_3$ is cooled from $30°$ C to $20°$ C, 11 g of solute crystallize out. At $30°$ C, the solubility of $NaNO_3$ is 97 g/100 ml of H_2O, whereas at $20°$ C, the solubility is 86 g/100 ml of H_2O. Under special conditions and with specific solutes (such as sodium acetate), cooling a hot saturated solution does not cause the excess solute to crystallize. Such solutions are called supersaturated.

In summary, a *saturated solution* is a solution containing the maximum solute that will normally dissolve at a given temperature and pressure. An *unsaturated solution* is a solution that can dissolve more solute at a given temperature and pressure. A *supersaturated* solution is a solution containing more than the maximum solute that will normally dissolve at a given temperature and pressure.

On a macroscopic level, it appears as though a saturated solution is a completely static system. Any attempt to increase the solubility of a given solid in its saturated solution by adding more solute results in the settling of solid on the bottom of the container. The equation to represent the formation of a saturated solution of $NaNO_3$ may be written as

$$NaNO_3 \ (s) + H_2O \rightarrow NaNO_3 \ (aq)$$

Since $NaNO_3$ is an ionic solid, the equation is more informative if written as

$$NaNO_3 \ (s) + H_2O \rightarrow Na^+ \ (aq) + NO_3^- \ (aq)$$

The equation may also be further simplified. By convention, water does not always appear in a reaction where it behaves only as a solvent.

$$NaNO_3 \ (s) \rightarrow Na^+ \ (aq) + NO_3^- \ (aq)$$

10.16 Equilibrium between dissolved and undissolved solute

Thus far, we have tacitly assumed that the excess solid added to a saturated solution is the same solid that settles to the bottom. This assumption may be tested by adding 1 g of radioactive $NaNO_3$ to a saturated solution of $NaNO_3$. Radioactive $NaNO_3$ contains radioactive sodium, Na^{24}, a variety of Na having a mass slightly heavier than the more common Na^{23}. Radioactive sodium affects a Geiger counter, a device used to detect radiation.

When 1 g of radioactive $NaNO_3$, containing Na^{24}, is added to a saturated solution of $NaNO_3$, excess solid settles out, as would occur if nonradioactive $NaNO_3$ had been added. On separation from the solution, the solid is dried and weighed. The solid weighs 1 g and affects the Geiger counter.

We also observe that the solution has become radioactive, as it also affects the Geiger counter. The only reasonable explanation for this observation is to assume that some of the radioactive $NaNO_3$, containing Na^{24}, dissolved in the solution while the same amount of solid, containing Na^{23} and Na^{24}, crystallized from the solution.

Our model of a saturated solution suggests that the solution and crystallization processes occur simultaneously. Since the saturated solution does not appear to change, the concentration remains constant. The rate of dissolving must therefore equal the rate of crystallization. As explained previously (see section 9.6), when the rates of two opposing reactions in a system become equal, the system has attained equilibrium.

These ideas may be summarized as follows:

A saturated solution represents an equilibrium between the dissolved and undissolved phases. For molecular solid M, we may represent this change as

$$M \ (s) \rightleftarrows M \ (aq)$$

For ionic solid XZ, we may represent this change as

$$XZ\ (s) \rightleftarrows X^{+n}\ (aq) + Z^{-n}\ (aq)$$

where n is the charge on the ions. The equation to represent a saturated solution of $NaNO_3$ is

$$NaNO_3\ (s) \rightleftarrows Na^+\ (aq) + NO_3^-\ (aq)$$

On the macroscopic level, no changes seem to occur in a saturated solution. On the molecular level, solution and crystallization occur simultaneously in a saturated solution at the same rate.

10.17 Other factors affecting solubility

We learned that the solubility of a solute in a given solvent is determined by the extent of interaction between the solute and the solvent. It can be shown experimentally that temperature and pressure also influence solubility. The magnitude of these effects depends on the physical states of the solute and solvent and can be predicted from the application of Le Chatelier's Principle (see section 9.7) to the equilibrium in a saturated solution.

10.18 Effect of temperature on solubility

Let us again return to the solubility curves, shown in Figure 10–4. At any specific temperature, a curve describes the composition of the saturated solution. For five of the eight solutes shown (KI, $NaClO_3$, $NaNO_3$, KNO_3, and KCl), the curves rise, indicating increased solubilities of the solids in water with an increase in temperature. For NaCl, the curve is almost horizontal, revealing little change in solubility with increasing temperature. For one compound only, $Ce_2(SO_4)_3$, increasing the temperature of the water reduces the solubility of the solid.

It appears from these observations that the dissolving of most solids in water is an endothermic (heat absorbing) process. Why does increasing the temperature generally cause more solid to dissolve? Let us represent the saturated solution equilibrium of solid M as

$$M\ (s) + heat \rightleftarrows M\ (aq)$$

According to Le Chatelier's Principle, when an equilibrium system is subjected to stress, the system reacts to partially relieve the stress. Therefore, when an endothermic equilibrium system is heated, the equilibrium shifts to the right. This means that more product is formed. Thus increasing the temperature causes more solid to dissolve.

We have already mentioned that the solution of a solid in water involves these steps:

1. The crystal lattice of the solid is destroyed, a process that always requires energy.

2. If the solute is ionic, the ions interact with water and become aquated, a process that always liberates heat. If the solute is non-ionic, hydrogen bonds form between the solute molecules and the water molecules.

3. The randomness of the system increases.

In an endothermic solution process, the heat evolved during aquation is generally less than the heat absorbed during the change of state. Similarly, in an exothermic solution process, the heat evolved during aquation generally exceeds the heat absorbed during the change of state.

The solution of a liquid solute in water (alcohol or glycerine, for example), involves only a small energy change. Since such solutions do not require a change of state, the hydration (aquation) effects are generally small. The alcohol and glycerine molecules contain OH groups which form hydrogen bonds with water molecules.

Dissolving concentrated sulfuric acid in water is highly exothermic, due largely to the heat evolved during hydration. Generally speaking, most liquids that dissolve in water have only a minor energy accompaniment; thus the effect of temperature on the solubility of a liquid in water is generally small.

The solution of a gas in water is always an exothermic process. We may assume that gaseous molecules condense to the liquid state when they dissolve in water, giving up energy. Assume that gas X has saturated a volume of water at a fixed temperature. The equilibrium may be represented as

$$X \ (gas) \rightleftarrows X \ (dissolved) + heat$$

According to Le Chatelier's Principle, the application of heat drives the equilibrium to the left. Hence, gases become less soluble in water as the temperature is raised. Drinking water, after standing and attaining room temperature, tastes flat. The dissolved air that gives drinking water its taste leaves the solution as the temperature of the water rises. To increase the solubility of a gas in water at constant pressure, the temperature of the water must be lowered.

10.19 Effect of pressure on solubility

Because liquids and solids are virtually incompressible, a change in pressure has little effect on their solubility.

The solubility of a gas in water at constant temperature is proportional to the pressure of the gas. This means that more gas will dissolve in water as the pressure of the gas is increased. In the manufacture of carbonated beverages, for example, the solubility of carbon dioxide in water is increased greatly by increasing its pressure. We may again apply Le Chatelier's Principle to account for this observation. The stress is an increase in pressure, which tends to lower the volume of the gas. On dissolving, the gas molecules condense to form a liquid that has a much smaller volume. The equilibrium system offsets the stress by shifting toward the side with the smaller volume. The solubility of the gas increases with increasing pressure (at constant temperature).

10.20 Properties of solutions

We will learn in a later chapter that the speed of a chemical reaction is influenced by the ability of the reacting substances to make proper contact with each other. Since reactions generally proceed more rapidly in solution, we must study solutions more carefully to ascertain the changes that occur during dissolving.

10.21 Conductivity

Consider the experimental setup shown in Figure 10–5, called a conductivity apparatus. When the electrodes are in air, the bulb does not light although the switch is closed. Air is a poor conductor of electricity, and the circuit remains incomplete. If a piece of metal, such as a knife-blade (held by an insulated handle), is placed across the electrodes, the bulb glows brightly, indicating that the circuit is complete.

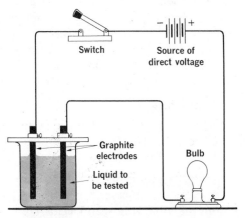

Fig. 10–5 Conductivity apparatus

We discussed the metallic lattice briefly in section 9.14 and ascribed the conductivity of metals to the presence of mobile electrons, which serve as charge carriers. Nonmetals are nonconductors because of the absence of free electrons. If we now test a number of compounds with the conductivity apparatus, we obtain the results summarized in the following table.

DOES NOT CONDUCT ELECTRICITY	CONDUCTS ELECTRICITY
1. water 2. glycerine, carbon tetrachloride, and water solution of glucose 3. solids: sodium chloride, copper(II) nitrate, potassium hydroxide, calcium hydroxide	1. water solutions of acids and water solutions of solids listed under 3 2. molten (fused) solids listed under 3

The conduction of electricity requires the presence of charge carriers, either electrons or mobile ions. Since free electrons are present only in the metallic lattice, all other substances that conduct electricity must contain mobile ions. Compounds that conduct electricity in solution are called *electrolytes*.

Further experimentation with the conductivity apparatus reveals that some electrolytes conduct better than others. For example, solutions of hydrochloric acid, nitric acid, and sulfuric acid each cause the bulb to glow more brightly than equally concentrated solutions of acetic acid or ammonia. This variation in conductivity suggests that some electrolytes are more highly ionized than other electrolytes. Electrolytes that are highly ionized are called *strong electrolytes*, whereas electrolytes that are weakly ionized are called *weak electrolytes*. Compounds, such as glucose, that do not conduct electricity are called *nonelectrolytes*. These compounds are generally molecular solids that do not form ions in water. According to our conductivity setup, water did not conduct electricity. With more sensitive equipment, it can be shown that water is a weak electrolyte.

10.22 Characteristics of ions

In 1887, Svante Arrhenius, a Swedish chemist, attempted to explain why some liquids conduct electricity. His ideas were enlightening but hampered by his limited knowledge of the structure of matter. Let us incorporate some of Arrhenius' ideas into a summary of some important modern ionization concepts:

1. Water solutions of ionic solids and acids contain mobile charge carriers, called *ions*.

2. An ion is an atom or group of atoms that possesses an electrical charge. The magnitude of the charge is related to the valence number of the atom or group of atoms in the compound.

3. In water solutions of electrolytes, the total positive charge equals the total negative charge.

10.23 Dissociation of ionic solids

Consider the ionic solid NaCl, which consists of a crystalline lattice containing Na^+ and Cl^- ions. The presence of strong ionic bonds accounts for the unusual stability of the solid. This is the same as saying that the Na^+ and Cl^- ions occupy relatively fixed positions in the crystal lattice and hence possess limited mobility. Since electrical conductivity requires the presence of mobile ions, the solid cannot conduct electricity. Melting, however, weakens the bonds sufficiently, permitting the ions to become mobile and to serve as charge carriers. Thus when ionic solids are melted (fused), they conduct electricity.

We have noted experimentally that solutions of ionic solids also conduct electricity. How do we account for this behavior? We have already indicated that the dissolving of an ionic solid in water is caused by the interaction of the ionic solid with polar water molecules. This interaction weakens the ionic bonds, so that the ions separate from each other as the solid dissolves. Aquated ions, which act as mobile charge carriers, are formed. Since ions were present in the solid, the aquation process is also called *dissociation*. Following are equations for typical aquation reactions involving ionic solids:

$$NaCl\ (s) \rightarrow Na^+\ (aq) + Cl^-\ (aq)$$

$$Cu(NO_3)_2\ (s) \rightarrow Cu^{+2}\ (aq) + 2\ NO_3^-\ (aq)$$

$$(NH_4)_2SO_4\ (s) \rightarrow 2\ NH_4^+\ (aq) + SO_4^{-2}\ (aq)$$

$$KOH\ (s) \rightarrow K^+\ (aq) + OH^-\ (aq)$$

$$Ca(OH)_2\ (s) \rightarrow Ca^{+2}\ (aq) + 2\ OH^-\ (aq)$$

The properties of water solutions of ionic solids are, in reality, the properties of the aquated ions formed during solution. Thus all solutions of hydroxides, called *bases*, contain OH^- (aq) ions. Bases turn litmus blue and turn phenolphthalein pink. All solutions of ionic copper(II) compounds are colored blue because they contain the blue Cu^{+2} (aq) ion. All ionic chlorides precipitate AgCl (s) on the addition of Ag^+ (aq) ions. The equations for this reaction may be written as

$$\underbrace{Ag^+\ (aq) + NO_3^-\ (aq)}_{AgNO_3\ (s) + H_2O} + \underbrace{Na^+\ (aq) + Cl^-\ (aq)}_{NaCl\ (s) + H_2O} \rightarrow AgCl\ (s) + \underbrace{Na^+\ (aq) + NO_3^-\ (aq)}_{NaNO_3\ (s) + H_2O}$$

The same quantities of Na^+ (aq) and NO_3^- (aq) ions appear on both sides of the equation. This suggests that these ions do not undergo change and may be conveniently omitted from the equation.

$$Ag^+ (aq) + Cl^- (aq) \rightarrow AgCl (s)$$

The ions that interact in an equation are called the *essential ions*, or the *predominant species*. It does not matter whether AgCl precipitates from the reaction between solutions of $AgNO_3$ and NaCl, or from solutions of AgF and KCl, or from solutions of $AgCH_3COO$ (silver acetate) and LiCl. In each case, the equation that shows the predominant species remains the same. The ions that do not react are called *spectator ions*. In the reaction between aqueous $AgNO_3$ and aqueous NaCl previously described, NO_3^- (aq) ions and Na^+ (aq) ions appear on both sides of the equation and behave as spectator ions.

10.24 Ionization of acids

Hydrogen chloride (HCl) is a gas that, on sufficient cooling, forms a liquid that does not conduct electricity. The molecules in the gas and the molecules in the liquid are held together by polar covalent bonds.

$$H \overset{\times}{} + \cdot \overset{\cdot\cdot}{\underset{\cdot\cdot}{Cl}} \colon \longrightarrow H \overset{\times}{\cdot} \overset{\cdot\cdot}{\underset{\cdot\cdot}{Cl}} \colon$$

The water solution of HCl, however, does conduct electricity. Why? Covalent compounds may react with solvents, such as water, to form mobile ions. Since ions were not present in the original species, this phenomenon is called *ionization*. We shall consider ionization reactions in detail in Chapter 16. For the present, we will suggest a generalized equation to represent this change. In the following equation, let HX represent a covalent hydrogen compound:

$$HX + H_2O \rightarrow H_3O^+ + X^- (aq)$$

Let us apply the generalized equation to some specific hydrogen compounds.

$$HCl + H_2O \rightarrow H_3O^+ + Cl^- (aq)$$

$$H_2SO_4 + H_2O \rightarrow H_3O^+ + HSO_4^- (aq)$$

$$HNO_3 + H_2O \rightarrow H_3O^+ + NO_3^- (aq)$$

$$CH_3COOH + H_2O \rightarrow H_3O^+ + CH_3COO^- (aq)$$

10.25 Boiling points and freezing points of water solutions

It may be observed experimentally that water solutions containing a nonvolatile solute boil at temperatures above that of pure water and freeze at temperatures below that of pure water.

We have defined the boiling point as that temperature at which the vapor pressure of a liquid equals the pressure of the gas acting upon it. The presence of dissolved matter in water opposes the tendency of water molecules to leave the surface of the water. This is the same as saying that the vapor pressure of a solution is lower than the vapor pressure of the pure solvent. Consequently, the temperature at which a solution boils is somewhat higher than the temperature at which the pure solvent boils. When a solution boils, its vapor pressure has been increased sufficiently to equal the pressure of the gas acting upon it.

The freezing point of a liquid is that temperature at which the liquid and its solid form have the same vapor pressure. Since the vapor pressure of the solution is lower than the vapor pressure of pure water, it follows that the freezing point of the solution will be somewhat lower than the freezing point of pure water.

The elevation of the boiling point and the depression of the freezing point of water solutions are related to the composition of the solution and its concentration. For nonconducting solutions (nonelectrolytes), the boiling point and the freezing point are proportional to the molal concentration of the solution.

The boiling point elevation per mole of solute is higher for conducting solutions (electrolytes) than it is for nonconducting solutions. For conducting solutions, the boiling point elevation is roughly proportional to the molal concentration of the solute multiplied by the number of moles of ions formed from 1 mole of the solute. Similarly, the freezing point depression is roughly proportional to the molal concentration of the solute multiplied by the number of moles of ions formed from 1 mole of the solute.

For approximate calculations, we can state that each mole of dissolved particles (molecules or ions) will raise the boiling point $0.52 \ C°$ and depress the freezing point $1.86 \ C°$.

A 1-molal sugar solution at atmospheric pressure boils at approximately $100.52° \ C$ and freezes at approximately $-1.86° \ C$. Neglecting some small deviations, we can calculate that a 1-molal NaCl solution boils at $100° \ C + 2(0.52 \ C°)$, or $101.04° \ C$. It freezes at $0° \ C + 2(-1.86 \ C°)$, or $-3.72° \ C$. A 2-molal $CaCl_2$ solution boils at $100° \ C + 6(0.52 \ C°)$, or $103.12° \ C$. It freezes at $0° \ C + 6(-1.86 \ C°)$, or $-11.16° \ C$.

The fairly regular boiling point and freezing point changes of solutions were observed by Arrhenius and utilized by him to support his theory of ionization. We will look further into these properties when we investigate ionic equilibria in Chapter 15. These properties are called *colligative* properties, which means additive properties, and are a function of concentration. The definition tells us that colligative properties—in this instance, boiling and freezing points—depend on the number of solute particles that are in solution. Solutions exhibit other colligative properties which lie beyond the scope of this book.

Multiple-Choice Questions

1. All solutions (1) contain water (2) are liquids (3) contain dissolved solids (4) are homogeneous mixtures
2. A solution differs from a mixture in that the solution (1) contains only one distinguishable phase (2) contains no specific boundaries (3) is uniform (4) has a definite composition
3. The concentration of a solution containing 1 g of solute dissolved in 20 g of water is (1) 1 mole percent (2) 5% by weight (3) 1% by weight (4) 5 mole percent
4. A 1-molar solution of $NaNO_3$ and a 1-molar solution of KCl both (1) contain the same weight of solute in 1 l of solution (2) contain the same volume of solute in 1 l of solution (3) have the same density (4) contain the same numbers of moles of solute particles in 1 l of solution
5. A 1-molal solution contains (1) 1 mole of solute plus 1 mole of solvent (2) 1 mole of solute in 1 l of solution (3) 1 mole of solute in 1000 g of water (4) 1 g of solute in 1 mole of water
6. The molecular weight of H_2SO_4 is 98. A 1-normal solution contains (1) 49 g of H_2SO_4 in 1 l of solution (2) 98 g of H_2SO_4 in 1 l of solution (3) 196 g of H_2SO_4 in 1 l of solution (4) 49 g of H_2SO_4 in 1000 g of water
7. The dissolving of sodium chloride is not a simple physical change because (1) oxidation-reduction takes place (2) sodium hydroxide is formed (3) the sodium reacts with the water to release hydrogen (4) the Na^+ and Cl^- ions unite with water molecules
8. The dissolving of a solid in water may be spontaneous if (1) an increase in the randomness of the system results (2) the energy of the system increases (3) the randomness of the solution is less than the randomness of the solid (4) the randomness of the system increases and the energy of the system decreases

9. Most solids are more soluble in hot water than in cold water because (1) water molecules decompose in hot water (2) the disruption of the crystal structure during dissolving is an endothermic process (3) the increased vapor pressure of the hot water aids dissolving (4) the rate of crystallization increases in hot water

10. Alcohol is very soluble in water because both compounds (1) are liquids (2) are ionic (3) possess molecules that can link by hydrogen bonds (4) are nonpolar

11. The solubility of gases in water (1) increases with increased temperature and increased pressure (2) decreases with increased temperature and decreased pressure (3) decreases with increased temperature and increased pressure (4) increases with decreased pressure and increased temperature

12. A saturated solution (1) is concentrated (2) cannot dissolve more solvent (3) is not affected by temperature change (4) represents an equilibrium system

13. Solutions that conduct electricity (1) are concentrated (2) contain mobile electrons (3) contain either dissolved ionic solids or acids (4) are dilute

14. Melting solid sodium chloride (1) produces ions (2) decomposes the compound (3) releases ions from fixed positions in the solid (4) produces free electrons

15. Solutions of copper(II) chloride, copper(II) nitrate, and copper(II) sulfate have a blue color because (1) molecules of all copper compounds are blue (2) the Cu^{+2} (aq) ion is blue (3) copper is blue in covalent compounds (4) finely divided copper is blue

16. In the reaction between solutions of sodium chloride and silver nitrate (1) oxidation-reduction takes place (2) the number of ions in the solution increases (3) two ions react, and two ions are spectators (4) two new molecules form

17. The reaction between HCl (g) and H_2O involves (1) electron transfer (2) proton transfer (3) oxidation-reduction (4) electron-proton transfer

18. The same boiling point is shown by solutions of (1) 1-molal sugar and 0.5-molal sodium chloride (2) 1-molal sugar and 1-molal sodium chloride (3) 1-molal sugar and 2-molal sodium chloride (4) 2-molal sugar and 1-molal sodium chloride

Completion Questions

1. A solution with a relatively small number of solute molecules compared to the number of solvent molecules is a (an) _____ solution.

2. Two moles of solute molecules are dissolved in 48 moles of solvent molecules. The mole percentage of the resulting solution is _____.
3. Carbon tetrachloride, CCl_4, does not dissolve in a polar solvent because CCl_4 molecules are _____.
4. An ion that has united with one or more molecules of water is called a (an) _____ ion.
5. When sugar, or any other nonionic solid, dissolves in water, the solvent forms _____ bonds with the water molecules.
6. When an equilibrium exists between the dissolved solute and undissolved solute, the solution is _____.
7. Electrolytes are solutions of compounds that _____.
8. Water solutions of potassium chloride, KCl, sodium chloride, NaCl, and hydrogen chloride, HCl, react similarly with a solution of silver nitrate, $AgNO_3$. Carbon tetrachloride, CCl_4, does not because _____.
9. The formula of the positive ion formed when the compound HX reacts with water is _____.
10. The table of solubility curves shows that _____ is a solid, less soluble in hot water than in cold water.

True-False Questions

1. When the dissolving of an ionic solid in water is *exothermic*, the energy released by the hydration of the ions is greater than the energy absorbed in disrupting the crystal structure.
2. Dissolving sulfuric acid in water releases a large amount of heat because the hydration of the ions is *endothermic*.
3. The solubility of gases increases with decreased temperature because the change of state from gas to liquid *releases* heat.
4. Dissolving solid potassium nitrate, KNO_3, in water and *melting* solid potassium nitrate, KNO_3, are related processes because both processes produce a liquid with mobile ions.
5. In the following reaction the Ag^+ (aq) and Br^- (aq) ions are termed *spectator ions*:

$$Na^+ (aq) + Br^- (aq) + Ag^+ (aq) + NO_3^- (aq) \rightarrow AgBr (s) + Na^+ (aq) + NO_3^- (aq)$$

6. A tincture is a solution in which *iodine* is the solvent.
7. In a *solution*, no boundaries exist between the components.
8. Carbonated water is an example of a solution containing a *liquid* solute and a liquid solvent.
9. A 1-molar solution contains 1 mole of solute per liter of *solvent*.
10. *Polar* solutes are more soluble in carbon tetrachloride, CCl_4, than in water.

Decreases, Increases, Remains the Same

1. As the number of solvent molecules per unit volume of solution increases, the concentration of the solution _____.
2. As we continue to stir a saturated solution, the amount of dissolved solute _____.
3. As the symmetry of a series of molecules increases, the polarity of the molecules _____.
4. As the polarity of a series of compounds increases, the tendency of the compounds to dissolve in water _____.
5. As the energy required to break the crystal structure of solids increases, the energy released when the solids dissolve _____.
6. As a crystalline solid dissolves in water, the randomness of the solute particles _____.
7. When the pressure is increased, the solubility of a solid in water at constant temperature _____.
8. When solute is added to a saturated solution, the concentration of the solution _____.
9. When the concentration of a solution is increased, the freezing point of the solution _____.
10. When HCl (g) is dissolved in water, the conductivity of the water _____.

Equations

1. Write equations for the dissociation of the following compounds into ions as they dissolve in water: (*a*) KCl (*b*) LiOH (*c*) $Ba(NO_3)_2$ (*d*) $CaBr_2$ (*e*) Na_2CO_3
2. Write ionic equations to show (*a*) the melting of $MgCl_2$ (*b*) the dissolving of $MgCl_2$ in water
3. Write an equation that expresses the equilibrium in a saturated aqueous solution of the ionic compound $CuSO_4$. Include the heat term in the equation.
4. Write an equation for the equilibrium in a saturated aqueous solution of the molecular solid glucose $(C_6H_{12}O_6)$.
5. *a.* Write a molecular equation showing the formation of insoluble AgBr from the reaction between solutions of KBr and $AgNO_3$.
   b. Rewrite the equation, showing the predominant ionic species present.
6. *a.* Write a molecular equation showing the formation of insoluble $BaSO_4$ from the reaction between solutions of Na_2SO_4 and $BaCl_2$.
   b. Rewrite the equation, showing the predominant ionic species present.

Exercises for Review

1. How much solute and how much solvent must be mixed to obtain the following solutions in water?
   a. 100 g of a 5% sugar solution
   b. 20 g of a 10% alcohol solution
   c. 250 g of a 3% $NaNO_3$ solution
2. a. How much water is used to dissolve 5 g of a compound to produce a 10% solution?
   b. How much water is used to dissolve 100 g of sugar to produce a 2% solution?
3. a. Calculate the number of grams of KNO_3 present in 40 g of a 4% solution.
   b. What is the volume of a 10% alcohol-water solution that contains 24 g of alcohol?
   c. In an experiment, 20 g of a 5% solution of H_2SO_4 are to be replaced by a 2% solution of H_2SO_4. What volume of the 2% solution contains the same amount of H_2SO_4?
4. a. A 58.5-g sample of NaCl is dissolved in 1800 g of water. What is the mole percentage of the solution?
   b. A solution contains 9.8 g of H_2SO_4 in 100 g of water. What is its mole percentage?
5. Find the mole percentage of the following aqueous solutions from their weight percentages: (a) 10% HNO_3 (b) 2% $AgNO_3$ [*Hint:* Consider 100 g of the solution.]
6. A 10% by weight solution of a compound has a density of 1.15 g/ml. What volume of the solution contains 4.5 g of the solute?
7. Calculate the weights of solutes that must be used to make the following solutions:
   a. 1 l of 2.0 *M* KCl   c. 200 ml of 0.40 *M* $NaNO_3$
   b. 500 ml of 3.0 *M* H_2SO_4 d. 4 l of 0.50 *M* $CuSO_4 \cdot 5H_2O$
8. Calculate the amount of solute present in each of the following solutions:
   a. 2 l of 3 *M* HCl   c. 10 ml of 0.50 *M* $AgNO_3$
   b. 300 ml of 0.25 *M* NaOH   d. 40 ml of 0.20 *M* sucrose ($C_{12}H_{22}O_{11}$)
9. How would you dilute the following solutions to obtain the desired concentrations?
   a. 40 ml of 2 *M* H_2SO_4 to 0.5 *M* H_2SO_4
   b. 1 l of 3 *M* NaOH to 1.2 *M* NaOH
   c. 10 ml of 0.8 *M* $CaCl_2$ to 0.25 *M* $CaCl_2$

10. What volume of each of the following solutions should be used to deliver the desired amount of each of the solutes?
    a. 0.2 mole of $ZnCl_2$, using a 1.0-molar solution
    b. 1.5 moles of H_2SO_4, using a 12.0-molar solution
    c. 0.60 mole of KOH, using a 2.0-molar solution
11. a. What volume of 2.0 M KOH contains 10 g of KOH?
    b. What volume of 0.4 M H_2SO_4 contains 0.98 g of H_2SO_4?
12. a. For an experiment, a student requires approximately 100 ml of 2.0-molal LiCl and also 100 ml of 2.0-molal KOH. What quantities of solute and solvent must be used for each solution?
    b. Express the concentration of each solution in terms of weight percentage.
13. Calculate the equivalent weights for (a) $AgNO_3$ (b) $CaCl_2$ (c) Na_2SO_4 (d) $FeCl_3$ (e) $Al_2(SO_4)_3$ (f) $CuSO_4 \cdot 5H_2O$
14. a. Calculate the weight of solute needed to prepare:
    1. 500 ml of 2.0 N $LiNO_3$
    2. 1.5 l of 0.3 N NaOH
    3. 500 ml of 1.0 N $BaCl_2$
    4. 350 ml of 0.25 N H_3PO_4
    5. 2500 ml of 0.3 N $MgSO_4 \cdot 7H_2O$
    b. Calculate the molar concentration of each solution in part a.
15. Using the solubility curves on page 173, determine how many grams of each of the following solutes will dissolve in the quantities of water indicated at the stated temperatures:
    a. KCl in 200 ml of H_2O at 90° C
    b. $NaNO_3$ in 50 ml of H_2O at 40° C
    c. NaCl in 1000 ml of H_2O at 100° C
16. a. A saturated solution of $NaNO_3$ is prepared at 64° C with 50 ml of H_2O. It is then cooled to 10° C. How much solid $NaNO_3$ separates out?
    b. Compare the quantity found in answer to part a with the quantity of NaCl that would separate out of a saturated solution of NaCl prepared at 64° C with 50 ml of H_2O and then cooled to 10° C.
17. A saturated solution of $Ce_2(SO_4)_3$ is prepared at 20° C with 100 ml of H_2O. What change takes place when this solution is heated to 50° C?
18. Calculate the boiling points and the freezing points of the following solutions in water:
    a. 2.0 molal glucose
    b. 0.50 molal glycerol
    c. 3.0 molal ethylene glycol

19. In each of the following solutions, calculate (1) the weight of solute (2) the number of moles of solute (3) the number of equivalents of solute:

    a. 500 ml of 5 N H_2SO_4 *c.* 400 ml of 3 M Na_2CO_3
    b. 1.5 l of 2 M NaOH   *d.* 200 ml of 1.5 M H_3PO_4

Exercises for Further Study

1. *a.* Explain why dissolving many compounds in water involves chemical as well as physical changes.
   b. Will a chemical change occur when carbon tetrachloride, CCl_4, dissolves in octane? Explain.

2. In an experiment, the conductivity of a solution of barium hydroxide, $Ba(OH)_2$, is measured as sulfuric acid, H_2SO_4, is added. The conductivity first decreases, then increases. Knowing that barium sulfate, $BaSO_4$, is insoluble, how do you explain these changes?

3. Assume you have a compound of known molecular weight. Describe an experiment that you could perform to show (*a*) that the compound produces ions in solution (*b*) the number of ions formed per molecule of the compound

4. Why does adding alcohol to the water in an automobile radiator cause the alcohol-water solution to act as an "antifreeze"?

5. Explain why the reaction between silver nitrate, $AgNO_3$, and sodium chloride, NaCl, does not involve oxidation-reduction.

6. Hydrogen chloride, HCl, dissolves in water to form a solution that conducts electricity; but methane, CH_4, does not form a conducting solution. What can you conclude concerning the strength of the bond between hydrogen and the other element in each of the two compounds?

7. The properties of an aqueous sugar solution are the properties of a single dissolved particle. But in an aqueous solution of copper(II) sulfate, the solute exhibits two sets of properties. Why?

8. Knowing that carbon-14 is radioactive, suggest an experiment to determine whether an equilibrium exists between the dissolved and the gaseous carbon dioxide in a stoppered bottle of carbonated water.

9. In pure water, the molecules of water are linked in groups by hydrogen bonding. Alcohol molecules are also linked by hydrogen bonding. What changes take place when alcohol dissolves in water?

10. *a.* In what ways does the dissolving of a solid in water resemble the melting of the solid?
    b. In what ways are the two processes different?

Chapter 11

CHEMICAL CALCULATIONS

11.1 Introduction

We have already noted that chemists prefer to express what they observe in quantitative rather than in qualitative terms. This means that measurement represents an important part of chemical science. In this chapter, we will study the essentials of chemical arithmetic – the application of mathematics to further the description of the properties of matter.

11.2 Percentage by weight of an element in a compound

The Law of Definite Proportions (see section 1.18) states that all compounds have an unvarying composition by weight. To determine the weight composition of any component in a compound, we must know the molecular formula of the compound and the atomic weights of each of the component elements. From this data, we can obtain the percentage by weight of each element.

Method. To find the percentage by weight of an element in a compound:

1. Find the weight of the total number of moles of atoms of the element in the compound. This equals the total number of moles multiplied by the atomic weight of the element.
2. Divide the answer in step 1 by the weight of one mole of molecules (molecular weight) of the compound.
3. Multiply the answer in step 2 by 100%.

Thus the percentage by weight of Z in the compound Z_2Q_3

$$= \frac{\text{weight of 2 moles of Z}}{\text{weight of 1 mole of } Z_2Q_3} = \frac{\text{2 atomic weights of Z}}{\text{1 molecular weight of } Z_2Q_3} \times 100\%$$

11.3 Sample problems involving percentage by weight of an element in a compound

1. Calculate the percentage composition by weight of carbon dioxide (CO_2).

$$\%C = \frac{\text{1 atomic weight of C}}{\text{1 molecular weight of } CO_2} \times 100\%$$

$$\%O = \frac{2 \text{ atomic weights of O}}{1 \text{ molecular weight of CO}_2} \times 100\%$$

molecular weight of $CO_2 = 12 + 2(16) = 44$

$$\%C = \frac{12}{44} \times 100\% = 27.3$$

$$\%O = \frac{2(16)}{44} \times 100\% = 72.7$$

2. Calculate the percentage composition by weight of pitchblende (U_3O_8).

$$\%U = \frac{3 \text{ atomic weights of U}}{1 \text{ molecular weight of U}_3O_8} \times 100\%$$

$$\%O = \frac{8 \text{ atomic weights of O}}{1 \text{ molecular weight of U}_3O_8} \times 100\%$$

molecular weight of $U_3O_8 = 3(238) + 8(16) = 842$

$$\%U = \frac{3(238)}{842} \times 100\% = 84.8$$

$$\%O = \frac{8(16)}{842} \times 100\% = 15.2$$

The percentage by weight of an element in a compound may be utilized to calculate the weight of the element required to produce a given weight of the compound.

3. Find how many grams of phosphorus are required to produce 250 g of H_3PO_4 (phosphoric acid).

The percentage by weight of phosphorus in H_3PO_4

$$= \frac{1 \text{ atomic weight of P}}{1 \text{ molecular weight of H}_3PO_4} \times 100\%$$

$$= \frac{31}{98} \times 100\% = 31.6\%$$

The weight of phosphorus required to produce 250 g of H_3PO_4

$$= \%P \text{ in } H_3PO_4 \times 250 \text{ g}$$

$$= 31.6\% \times 250 \text{ g} = 79 \text{ g}$$

11.4 Percentage of water in hydrates

Hydrates also conform to the Law of Definite Proportions. Therefore, we can calculate the percentage of water in hydrates by the same method as in the preceding sample problems. To calculate the percentage of water in a hydrate, divide the weight of the total number of moles of water (total number of moles multiplied by molecular weight) by the weight of one mole (molecular weight) of the hydrated compound; then multiply by 100%.

Calculate the percentage composition by weight of water in hydrated copper(II) sulfate ($CuSO_4 \cdot 5H_2O$).

$$\% H_2O = \frac{5 \text{ molecular weights of } H_2O}{1 \text{ molecular weight of } CuSO_4 \cdot 5H_2O} \times 100\%$$

molecular weight of $5\ H_2O = 5(2 + 16) = 90$

molecular weight of $CuSO_4 \cdot 5H_2O = 63.5 + 32 + 64 + 5(2 + 16) = 249.5$

$$\% H_2O = \frac{90}{249.5} \times 100\% = 36.1$$

11.5 Determination of a formula

Determining a formula is the reverse of determining percentage composition. The percentage by weight of the elements in a compound enables us to determine the empirical formula of the compound — the relative number of atoms of each element in a compound — as follows. The relative number of atoms of each element in a compound (or the relative number of moles of atoms of each element in a compound) equals the percentage of the element divided by the atomic weight of the element.

To deduce the molecular formula, we must first know the molecular weight.

Method. To determine an empirical formula, divide the percentage of an element by the atomic weight of the element. The quotients are the relative numbers of atoms (or moles of atoms) in a mole of the compound.

11.6 Sample problems involving the determination of a formula

1. A gaseous hydrocarbon has the following composition by weight: carbon 92.3%, hydrogen 7.7%. What is the empirical formula of the gas?

$$\text{relative number of moles of C atoms} = \frac{92.3}{12} = 7.7$$

relative number of moles of H atoms $= \dfrac{7.7}{1} = 7.7$

The proportion of component atoms is $C_{7.7}H_{7.7}$, or C_1H_1. Thus the empirical formula of this compound is C_1H_1. This means that any number of moles of carbon atoms and an equal number of moles of hydrogen atoms will satisfy the stated percentage composition by weight.

Suppose that the density of this hydrocarbon at STP is 1.18 g/l. We learned previously (see section 8.19) that a mole of any gas at STP occupies approximately 22.4 l. At STP, 22.4 l of the hydrocarbon gas weigh 1.18 g/l × 22.4 l, or 26.4 g. This is the weight of a mole of molecules (molecular weight) of the gas.

Knowing the molecular weight, we can now proceed to determine the molecular formula. Since the atomic weight of carbon is 12 and the atomic weight of hydrogen is 1, the molecular weight given by the empirical formula C_1H_1 is $12 + 1$, or 13. However, we have seen that the molecular weight of the gas is approximately 26 g. To obtain a molecular weight of 26, we must multiply the weight given by the empirical formula, 13, by 2. Thus the molecular formula is C_2H_2. Note that this formula is consistent with the $1:1$ carbon-to-hydrogen ratio required by the empirical formula.

2. A gaseous oxide of nitrogen has the following composition by weight: nitrogen 30.4%, oxygen 69.6%. The density of the gas at STP is 4.1 g/l. What is the molecular formula of the gas?

relative number of moles of N atoms $= \dfrac{30.4}{14} = 2.17$

relative number of moles of O atoms $= \dfrac{69.6}{16} = 4.35$

The proportion of component atoms is $N_{2.17}O_{4.35}$, or NO_2. If the density of the gas at STP is 4.1 g/l, the weight of a mole of molecules (molecular weight) equals 22.4 l × 4.1 g/l, or 92 g. Since the atomic weight of nitrogen is 14 and the atomic weight of oxygen is 16, the molecular formula of the gas is N_2O_4 (molecular weight $= 28 + 64 = 92$).

3. We observe that 6.01 g of carbon react with sufficient nitrogen to form 13.1 g of a gaseous carbon-nitrogen compound. The density of the gaseous compound is 2.33 g/l at STP. What is the molecular formula of the gaseous compound?

relative number of moles of C atoms $= \dfrac{6.01}{12} = 0.5$

relative number of moles of N atoms $= \dfrac{7.09}{14} = 0.5$

The proportion of component atoms is $C_{0.5}N_{0.5}$, or C_1N_1.

If the density of the gas is 2.33 g/l at STP, the weight of 1 mole (molecular weight) $= 22.4 \ l \times 2.33$ g/l $= 52.2$ g.

Since the atomic weight of carbon is 12 and the atomic weight of nitrogen is 14, the molecular formula of the gas is C_2N_2 $(24 + 28 = 52)$. The difference between the molecular weights 52.2 and 52 stems from the fact that the molar volumes of actual gases vary slightly from the ideal volume, 22.4 liters.

11.7 A review of the mole concept

In Chapter 5, we introduced the mole concept in terms of the weight relations involved in chemical reactions. We will now see how this concept may be applied to the study of chemical changes. Consider the general reaction

$$2 \ A \ (s) + 3 \ B_2 \ (g) \rightarrow 2 \ AB_3 \ (g)$$

The mole concept suggests two ways to analyze this reaction:

1. Two moles of A (atoms) react completely with 3 moles of B_2 (molecules) to form 2 moles of AB_3 (molecules).
2. Two moles of A (atoms) react completely with 6 moles of B (atoms) to form 2 moles of AB_3 (molecules).

Recall that each mole of atoms represents 6.02×10^{23} atoms (see section 5.12). Therefore, the reaction can be read: 12.04×10^{23} atoms of A react completely with 36.12×10^{23} atoms of B to form 2 moles of molecules of AB_3, which contain $2 \times 6.02 \times 10^{23}$ atoms of A and $6 \times 6.02 \times 10^{23}$ atoms of B. In a balanced reaction, atoms, or moles of atoms, are always conserved.

Let us assume that the reaction involves the following half-reactions:

$$2 \ A^0 \rightarrow 2 \ A^{+3} + 6 \ e^-$$

$$3 \ B_2{}^0 + 6 \ e^- \rightarrow 6 \ B^{-1}$$

For every 2 moles of A atoms or 6 moles of B atoms (3 moles of B_2 molecules), 6 moles of electrons are transferred. Thus the half-reactions show that in a balanced reaction, charge is always conserved.

11.8 Weight relations in chemical reactions

Let us return to the equation

$$2 \text{ A } (s) + 3 \text{ B}_2 \ (g) \to 2 \text{ AB}_3 \ (g)$$

Assume that A represents 127.5 g/mole of atoms. (This is also the atomic weight of A.) Assume that B represents 35.5 g/mole of atoms (atomic weight of B). How many moles of AB_3 molecules are formed when 71 g of gaseous B_2 react completely with sufficient solid A? What will this quantity of AB_3 weigh?

The equation reveals that 2 moles of A atoms react with 3 moles of B_2 molecules to form 2 moles of AB_3 molecules. The 71 g of B represent $\dfrac{71 \text{ g}}{71 \text{ g/mole}}$, or 1 mole of B_2 molecules (2 moles of B atoms). Since 3 moles of B_2 form 2 moles of AB_3, 1 mole of B_2 will form $\frac{2}{3}$ mole of AB_3 ($3:2 = 1: \frac{2}{3}$). Thus $\frac{2}{3}$ of a mole of AB_3 molecules will be formed. The weight of 1 mole of AB_3 molecules is 234.0 g (127.5 + 106.5). The weight of $\frac{2}{3}$ of a mole is $\frac{2}{3}$ mole $\times$ 234 g/mole, or 156 g.

This problem may also be solved by the proportion method. First we note from the equation that 255 g (2 moles) of A react with 213 g (6 moles) of B to form 468 g (2 moles) of AB_3. Then to find how many grams of AB_3 (x) are formed from 71 grams of B_2, we write the quantities above and below the parts of the chemical equation to which they apply.

$$
\begin{array}{c}
71 \text{ g} \qquad x \\
2 \text{ A} + 3 \text{ B}_2 \to 2 \text{ AB}_3 \\
213 \text{ g} \qquad 468 \text{ g}
\end{array}
$$

$$\frac{71 \text{ g}}{213 \text{ g}} = \frac{x}{468 \text{ g}}$$

$$x = \frac{71 \text{ g} \times 468 \text{ g}}{213 \text{ g}} = 156 \text{ g of AB}_3$$

Since 1 mole of AB_3 molecules weighs 234 g, then the number of moles in 156 g is $\dfrac{156 \text{ g}}{234 \text{ g/mole}} = \dfrac{2}{3}$ of a mole of AB_3.

11.9 Sample problems involving moles

1. Given the balanced reaction

$$2 \text{ KClO}_3 \ (s) \to 2 \text{ KCl } (s) + 3 \text{ O}_2 \ (g)$$

how many moles of $KClO_3$ must be decomposed to form 120 grams of O_2?

We must first convert 120 g of O_2 into the corresponding number of moles.

$$\frac{120 \text{ g}}{32 \text{ g/mole}} = 3.75 \text{ moles of } O_2$$

The equation reveals that the decomposition of 2 moles of $KClO_3$ liberates 3 moles of O_2 gas. From the equation, we see that to form 1 mole of O_2, we require $\frac{2}{3}$ of a mole of $KClO_3$. To form 3.75 moles of O_2, we require $\frac{2}{3} \times 3.75 = 2.50$ moles of $KClO_3$.

Using the proportion method, we may solve this problem as follows: The equation reveals that 245.2 g (2 moles) of $KClO_3$ decompose to form 149.2 g (2 moles) of KCl and 96 g (3 moles) of O_2. To find how many grams of $KClO_3$ (x) are formed from 120 g of O_2, we use the proportion

$$\frac{x}{245.2 \text{ g}} = \frac{120 \text{ g}}{96 \text{ g}}$$

$$x = \frac{120 \text{ g} \times 245.2 \text{ g}}{96 \text{ g}} = 306 \text{ g of } KClO_3$$

Since 1 mole of $KClO_3$ weighs 122.6 g, the number of moles in 306 g of $KClO_3$ is $\dfrac{306 \text{ g}}{122.6 \text{ g/mole}} = 2.50$ moles of $KClO_3$.

2. Given the balanced reaction

$$2 \text{ Na } (s) + 2 \text{ H}_2\text{O} \rightarrow 2 \text{ NaOH } (aq) + \text{H}_2 \text{ } (g)$$

how many grams of sodium are required to react with sufficient water to form 0.5 mole of H_2 gas?

The equation reveals that 2 moles of Na react with H_2O to form 1 mole of H_2 gas. This means that 46 g of Na (2 moles $\times$ 23 g/mole) will liberate 1 mole of H_2 gas. To liberate 0.5 mole of H_2, therefore, we require 23 g of Na.

Using the proportion method, we may solve this problem as follows: The equation reveals that 46 g (2 moles) of Na react with 36 g (2 moles) of H_2O to form 80 g (2 moles) of NaOH and 2 g (1 mole) of H_2. To find how many grams of Na are required to react with sufficient H_2O to form 0.5 mole of H_2, we must first find the weight of H_2 in 0.5 mole.

Since 1 mole of H_2 weighs 2 g, 0.5 mole weighs 1 g. Letting x = the required weight of Na, we can now set up the proportion

$$\frac{x}{46 \text{ g}} = \frac{1 \text{ g}}{2 \text{ g}}$$

$$x = \frac{1 \text{ g} \times 46 \text{ g}}{2 \text{ g}} = 23 \text{ g of Na}$$

3. Given the balanced reaction

$$2 \text{ NaCl } (l) \rightarrow 2 \text{ Na } (l) + Cl_2 \ (g)$$

how many grams of fused NaCl must be electrolyzed to yield 300 g of Cl_2 gas?

We must first convert 300 g of Cl_2 into the corresponding number of moles.

$$\frac{300 \text{ g}}{71 \text{ g/mole}} = 4.23 \text{ moles of } Cl_2$$

The equation reveals that 2 moles of NaCl will produce 1 mole of Cl_2 gas. This quantity of Cl_2 will be formed from 8.46 moles of NaCl. We know that 1 mole of NaCl weighs 58.5 g (23 g + 35.5 g). Thus 8.46 moles of NaCl weigh

$$58.5 \text{ g/mole} \times 8.46 \text{ moles} = 495 \text{ g}$$

Using the proportion method, we may solve this problem as follows: The equation reveals that 117 g (2 moles) of NaCl decompose to form 46 g (2 moles) of Na and 71 g (1 mole) of Cl_2 (g). To find how many grams of NaCl (x) will yield 300 g of Cl_2, we use the proportion

$$\frac{x}{117 \text{ g}} = \frac{300 \text{ g}}{71 \text{ g}}$$

$$x = \frac{300 \text{ g} \times 117 \text{ g}}{71 \text{ g}} = 495 \text{ g of NaCl}$$

11.10 Volume relations in chemical reactions

Again, let us return to the equation

$$2 \text{ A } (s) + 3 \text{ B}_2 \ (g) \rightarrow 2 \text{ AB}_3 \ (g)$$

The atomic weight of A equals 127.5, and the atomic weight of B equals 35.5. How many liters of B_2 gas are required to react with sufficient A to form 0.5 mole of AB_3? Assume all gases are at STP.

The equation reveals that 3 moles of B_2 react with sufficient A to form 2 moles of AB_3. This means that 0.75 mole of B_2 is required to form 0.5 mole of AB_3. At STP, 1 mole of any gas occupies 22.4 l. Thus 0.75 mole of B_2 occupies 16.8 l.

Problems involving volume relations may also be solved using the proportion method, as follows: The equation reveals that 2 moles of A react with 67.2 l (3 moles) of B_2 (g) to form 44.8 l (2 moles) of AB_3 (g). All gases are at STP. Since 1 mole of a gas at STP occupies 22.4 l, 0.5 mole occupies 11.2 l. Letting $x =$ the required volume of B_2, we can now set up the proportion

$$\frac{x}{67.2 \text{ l}} = \frac{11.2 \text{ l}}{44.8 \text{ l}}$$

$$x = \frac{11.2 \text{ l} \times 67.2 \text{ l}}{44.8 \text{ l}} = 16.8 \text{ l of } B_2$$

11.11 Sample problems involving volume relations

1. Given the balanced reaction

$$H_2 (g) + Cl_2 (g) \rightarrow 2 \text{ HCl } (g)$$

how many milliliters of HCl gas will be formed at STP when 0.1 mole of H_2 reacts completely?

The equation reveals that 1 mole of H_2 reacts with sufficient Cl_2 to form 2 moles of HCl. This means that 0.1 mole of H_2 will form 0.2 mole of HCl. Since 1 mole of gas at STP occupies 22.4 l, 0.2 mole of HCl (g) will have a volume of 0.2×22.4 l, or 4.48 l (4480 ml).

Using the proportion method, we may solve this problem as follows: The equation reveals that 22.4 l (1 mole) of H_2 (g) react with 22.4 l (1 mole) of Cl_2 (g) to form 44.8 l (2 moles) of HCl (g). At STP, 0.1 mole of H_2 occupies 2.24 l (2240 ml). Letting $x =$ the required volume of HCl , we can now set up the proportion

$$\frac{x}{44,800 \text{ ml}} = \frac{2240 \text{ ml}}{22,400 \text{ ml}}$$

$$x = \frac{2240 \text{ ml} \times 44,800 \text{ ml}}{22,400 \text{ ml}} = 4480 \text{ ml of HCl}$$

2. Given the balanced reaction

$$N_2 (g) + 3 \text{ H}_2 (g) \rightarrow 2 \text{ NH}_3 (g)$$

how many liters of NH_3 (g) will be formed at STP when 0.6 mole of H_2 reacts with sufficient N_2?

The equation reveals that 3 moles of H_2 react with sufficient N_2 to form 2 moles of NH_3. This means that 0.6 mole of H_2 will form 0.4 mole of NH_3. At STP, 1 mole of NH_3 occupies 22.4 l. Thus 0.4 mole of NH_3 has a volume of 0.4 mole $\times$ 22.4 l/mole, or 8.96 l.

Using the proportion method, we may solve this problem as follows: The equation reveals that 22.4 l (1 mole) of N_2 (g) react with 67.2 l (3 moles) of H_2 (g) to form 44.8 l (2 moles) of NH_3 (g). Since 1 mole of H_2 occupies 22.4 l at STP, 0.6 mole occupies 13.4 l. Letting $x =$ the required volume of NH_3, we can now set up the proportion

$$\frac{x}{44.8 \text{ l}} = \frac{13.4 \text{ l}}{67.2 \text{ l}}$$

$$x = \frac{13.4 \text{ l} \times 44.8 \text{ l}}{67.2 \text{ l}} = 8.96 \text{ l of } NH_3$$

3. Given the balanced reaction

$$2 \text{ } H_2S \text{ (g)} + 3 \text{ } O_2 \text{ (g)} \rightarrow 2 \text{ } H_2O \text{ (g)} + 2 \text{ } SO_2 \text{ (g)}$$

how many moles of O_2 are required to burn completely 5.6 l of H_2S at STP?

A mole of any gas occupies 22.4 l at STP. Thus 5.6 l of H_2S is equivalent to $\dfrac{5.6 \text{ l}}{22.4 \text{ l/mole}} = 0.25$ mole.

The equation reveals that 2 moles of H_2S will react completely with 3 moles of O_2 at STP. This means that 0.25 mole of H_2S will require 0.25 mole $\times$ 1.5, or 0.375 mole of O_2. Since 1 mole of O_2 at STP occupies 22.4 l, 0.375 mole of O_2 will occupy 0.375 mole $\times$ 22.4 l/mole, or 8.4 l.

Using the proportion method, we may solve this problem as follows: The equation reveals that 67.2 l (3 moles) of O_2 (g) react completely with 44.8 l (2 moles) of H_2S (g) to form 2 moles of H_2O (g) and 2 moles of SO_2 (g). Letting $x =$ the required volume of O_2, we can now set up the proportion

$$\frac{x}{67.2 \text{ l}} = \frac{5.6 \text{ l}}{44.8 \text{ l}}$$

$$x = \frac{5.6 \text{ l} \times 67.2 \text{ l}}{44.8 \text{ l}} = 8.4 \text{ l of } O_2$$

Since 1 mole of O_2 occupies 22.4 l at STP, the number of moles contained in 8.4 l $= \dfrac{8.4 \text{ l}}{22.4 \text{ l/mole}} = 0.375$ mole of O_2.

11.12 Weight and volume relations in chemical reactions

Once again, consider the reaction

$$2 \text{ A } (s) + 3 \text{ B}_2 \ (g) \rightarrow 2 \text{ AB}_3 \ (g)$$

The atomic weight of A equals 127.5, and the atomic weight of B equals 35.5. How many grams of A will react with sufficient B_2 to form 100.8 l of AB_3 gas at STP?

One mole of AB_3 at STP occupies 22.4 l. Thus 100.8 l of AB_3 will be the volume of AB_3 occupied by $\dfrac{100.8 \text{ l}}{22.4 \text{ l/mole}}$, or 4.5 moles of AB_3.

The equation reveals that 2 moles of A will react with sufficient B_2 to form 2 moles of AB_3 at STP. This means that 4.5 moles of A will be required to form 4.5 moles of AB_3. The weight of 4.5 moles of A

$$= 4.5 \text{ moles} \times 127.5 \ \frac{\text{g}}{\text{mole}} = 574 \text{ g}$$

Using the proportion method, we may solve this problem as follows: The equation reveals that 255 g (2 moles) of A react with sufficient B_2 to form 44.8 l (2 moles) of AB_3 (g). To find how many grams of A (x) will form 100.8 l of AB_3 at STP, we use the proportion

$$\frac{x}{255 \text{ g}} = \frac{100.8 \text{ l}}{44.8 \text{ l}}, \ x = \frac{100.8 \text{ l} \times 255 \text{ g}}{44.8 \text{ l}} = 574 \text{ g of A}$$

11.13 Sample problems involving weight and volume relations

1. Given the balanced reaction

$$2 \text{ NaCl } (s) + 2 \text{ H}_2\text{SO}_4 \ (aq) + \text{MnO}_2 \ (s) \rightarrow$$

$$\text{Na}_2\text{SO}_4 \ (aq) + \text{MnSO}_4 \ (aq) + 2 \text{ H}_2\text{O} + \text{Cl}_2 \ (g)$$

how many liters of Cl_2 (g) at STP will be liberated from the reaction between sufficient H_2SO_4, MnO_2, and 0.1 mole of NaCl?

The equation reveals that 2 moles of NaCl will liberate 1 mole of Cl_2 (g). Thus 0.1 mole of NaCl will yield 0.05 mole of Cl_2. At STP, 0.05 mole of Cl_2 occupies 22.4 l/mole $\times$ 0.05 mole $= 1.12$ l.

To solve this problem by the proportion method, first convert 0.1 mole of NaCl to grams.

$$0.1 \text{ mole} \times \frac{58.5 \text{ g}}{\text{mole}} = 5.85 \text{ g}$$

The equation reveals that 117 g (2 moles) of NaCl liberate 22.4 l (1 mole) of Cl_2. To find how many liters of Cl_2 (x) will be liberated from 5.85 g (0.1 mole) of NaCl, we use the proportion

$$\frac{x}{22.4\ l} = \frac{5.85\ g}{117\ g}$$

$$x = \frac{5.85\ g \times 22.4\ l}{117\ g} = 1.12\ l\ of\ Cl_2$$

2. In the reaction given in problem 1, how many grams of NaCl are required to liberate 0.1 mole of Cl_2 (g) at STP? Since 2 moles of NaCl are required to form 1 mole of Cl_2, 0.2 mole of NaCl is required to liberate 0.1 mole of Cl_2. The weight of 1 mole of NaCl equals 58.5 g (23 g + 35.5 g). The weight of 0.2 mole of NaCl = 58.5 g/mole × 0.2 mole = 11.7 g. Using the molar relations revealed by the equation, we can find how many grams of NaCl (x) are required to liberate 2.24 l (0.1 mole) of Cl_2 at STP by solving the proportion

$$\frac{x}{117\ g} = \frac{2.24\ l}{22.4\ l}$$

$$x = \frac{2.24\ l \times 117\ g}{22.4\ l} = 11.7\ g\ of\ NaCl$$

3. Given the balanced reaction

$$2\ Al\ (s) + 3\ H_2SO_4\ (aq) \rightarrow Al_2(SO_4)_3\ (aq) + 3\ H_2\ (g)$$

how many liters of H_2 (g) at STP will be produced by the reaction between 81 g of Al and sufficient H_2SO_4?

The atomic weight of Al is 27, which means that 81 g of Al are equivalent to 3 moles. The equation reveals that 2 moles of Al will react with sufficient H_2SO_4 to form 3 moles of H_2. This means that 3 moles of Al will liberate 4.5 moles of H_2. At STP, 1 mole of H_2 occupies 22.4 l; thus 4.5 moles of H_2 will occupy 22.4 l/mole × 4.5 moles = 100.8 l.

The equation reveals that 67.2 l (3 moles) of H_2 at STP are formed from the reaction between 54 g (2 moles) of Al and sufficient H_2SO_4. To find the volume of H_2 (x) liberated from the reaction between 81 g of Al and sufficient H_2SO_4, we use the proportion

$$\frac{x}{67.2\ l} = \frac{81\ g}{54\ g}, \quad x = \frac{81\ g \times 67.2\ l}{54\ g} = 100.8\ l\ of\ H_2$$

11.14 The concept of equivalent weight

In the reaction

$$Zn + H_2SO_4 \rightarrow ZnSO_4 + H_2 \ (g)$$

note that 1 mole of zinc is required to liberate 1 mole (2.016 g) of hydrogen gas. Thus 0.5 mole of zinc will liberate 1.008 g of hydrogen.

The *equivalent weight* of an element is the weight of the element that will liberate 1.008 g (0.5 mole) of hydrogen or 35.5 g of chlorine or 8.00 g of oxygen. The equivalent weight of zinc, therefore, is the weight contained in 0.5 mole of zinc, or 32.5 g. This means that 1.008 g of hydrogen, 35.5 g of chlorine, 8.00 g of oxygen, and 32.5 g of zinc are chemically equivalent. These quantities also represent the combining weights of these elements as shown in the following molecular equations:

$$H_2 + Cl_2 \rightarrow 2 \ HCl$$
2.016 g 71 g

$$Zn + Cl_2 \rightarrow ZnCl_2$$
65 g 71 g

$$H_2 + \frac{1}{2} O_2 \rightarrow H_2O$$
2.016 g 16.00 g

$$Zn + \frac{1}{2} O_2 \rightarrow ZnO$$
65 g 16.00 g

These equivalent relationships offer evidence in support of the atomic theory.

The concept of equivalent weight may be stated in another manner. Equivalent weight equals the weight of a mole of element divided by the number of hydrogen equivalents (moles of H atoms). For example, the equivalent weight of zinc

$$= \frac{\text{weight of 1 mole of zinc (atomic weight)}}{\text{moles of hydrogen atoms liberated by 1 mole of zinc (number of H equivalents)}}$$

$$= \frac{65 \text{ g}}{2} = 32.5 \text{ g}$$

It follows that when the number of hydrogen equivalents equals 1, the equivalent weight and the molar weight are identical. For example, in the reaction

$$2 \ Na + 2 \ HCl \rightarrow 2 \ NaCl + H_2 \ (g)$$

2 moles of Na liberate 2.016 g of H, or 1 mole of Na liberates 1.008 g of H. Thus the equivalent weight of Na is 23, the same as the molar weight.

The concept of equivalent weight is also useful in acid-base chemistry, which we will develop in Chapter 16.

11.15 Sample problems involving equivalent weight

1. From the reaction

$$2 \text{ Al } (s) + 3 \text{ H}_2\text{SO}_4 \ (aq) \rightarrow \text{Al}_2(\text{SO}_4)_3 \ (aq) + 3 \text{ H}_2 \ (g)$$

calculate the equivalent weight of Al.

The equation reveals that 2 moles (54 g) of Al liberate 3 moles (6.048 g) of H. Thus $\frac{2}{6}$ of a mole of Al liberates 1.008 g. The equivalent weight of Al is $\frac{2}{6}$ mole $\times \dfrac{27 \text{ g}}{\text{mole}} = 9$ g. We can also calculate the equivalent weight of Al by using the relationship

$$\text{equivalent weight} = \frac{\text{weight of 1 mole}}{\text{number of H equivalents}} = \frac{27 \text{ g}}{3} = 9 \text{ g}$$

2. If 1.0 g of metal X liberates 0.084 g of hydrogen, what is the equivalent weight of X?

The equivalent weight of X liberates 1.008 g of hydrogen. Thus:

$$\frac{\text{equivalent weight of X}}{1.008 \text{ g}} = \frac{1.0 \text{ g}}{0.084 \text{ g}}$$

$$0.084 \text{ X} = 1.008 \text{ g}$$

$$\text{X} = 12 \text{ g}$$

3. If 0.112 g of metal Z liberates 67.2 ml of hydrogen at STP, what is the equivalent weight of Z?

The equivalent weight of metal Z liberates 1.008 g of hydrogen, which occupy 11.2 l, or 11,200 ml, at STP. Therefore:

$$\frac{\text{equivalent weight of Z}}{11,200 \text{ ml}} = \frac{0.112 \text{ g}}{67.2 \text{ ml}}$$

$$67.2 \text{ Z} = 11,200 \times 0.112 \text{ g} = 1254.4 \text{ g}$$

$$\text{Z} = 18.7 \text{ g}$$

Multiple-Choice Questions

1. The formula CO_2 indicates that (1) twice as much oxygen as carbon is present in the compound (2) a molecule of the compound contains one molecule of O_2 (3) 1 mole of the compound contains 1 mole of carbon atoms and 2 moles of oxygen molecules (4) 1 mole of the compound contains 1 mole of carbon atoms and 2 moles of oxygen atoms

2. The percentage by weight of sulfur in SO_2 is (1) 33% (2) 67% (3) 50% (4) 4.25%

3. The weight of 1 mole of $CaSO_4 \cdot 2H_2O$ is (1) 11 g (2) 154 g (3) 172 g (4) 300 g

4. The molecular weight of CO_2 is 44; therefore, at STP (1) 1 l of CO_2 weighs 44 g (2) 11.2 l of CO_2 weigh 22 g (3) the molar volume of CO_2 is 44 l (4) 22.4 g of CO_2 have a volume of 44 l

5. In the reaction $CO\ (g) + 2\ H_2\ (g) \rightarrow CH_3OH\ (l)$ (1) the volumes of CO and CH_3OH are equal (2) the numbers of moles of molecules are conserved (3) the volume of hydrogen is twice the volume of carbon monoxide (4) no change in volume occurs

6. The weight of a mole of a gas divided by 22.4 l equals (1) the density of the gas at STP (2) the volume of the gas (3) the empirical formula of the gas molecule (4) the volume of 6.02×10^{23} molecules of the gas

7. In the reaction $2\ Na\ (s) + 2\ H_2O \rightarrow 2\ NaOH\ (aq) + H_2\ (g)$ (1) the ratio of the volumes of Na to H_2 is 2:1 (2) the ratio of the weights of H_2O and NaOH is equal to the ratio of their molecular weights (3) the volumes of Na and NaOH are equal (4) the numbers of moles of molecules are conserved

8. The reaction $Cu^{+2}\ (aq) + 2\ e^- \rightarrow Cu\ (s)$ (1) involves oxidation (2) can only occur at the anode (3) requires 2 moles of electrons to produce 1 mole of Cu (s) (4) occurs only at a high temperature

9. In the reaction $2\ Cl^-\ (aq) \rightarrow Cl_2\ (g) + 2\ e^-$ (1) 22.4 l of Cl_2 form when 1 mole of electrons is released (2) 1 mole of $Cl_2\ (g)$ forms from 1 mole of $Cl^-\ (aq)$ (3) the release of 6.02×10^{23} electrons forms 22.4 l of $Cl_2\ (g)$ (4) the release of 6.02×10^{23} electrons forms 11.2 l of $Cl_2\ (g)$

10. The compound with the highest percentage by weight of nitrogen is (1) NH_4Cl (2) $(NH_4)_2SO_4$ (3) NH_3 (4) NH_4NO_3

True-False Questions

1. One sample of U_3O_8 contains only the isotope uranium-238. A second sample contains uranium-238 and also some uranium-235. The percentage by weight of U in the first sample is *the same as* the percentage of U in the second sample.

2. Multiplying the density of a gas at STP by 22.4 l provides the weight of one *mole* of the gas.

3. In the reaction $2\ X_2 + 3\ Y_2 \rightarrow 2\ X_2Y_3$, the total number of moles of *molecules* is conserved.

4. In the reaction $H_2\ (g) + Cl_2\ (g) \rightarrow 2\ HCl\ (g)$, the volumes of *$H_2$ and HCl* are equal.

5. The equation C (*s*) + CO$_2$ (*g*) → 2 CO (*g*) shows that the volume of CO is twice the volume of C.
6. In a given reaction, the *weights* of reacting substances differ at different temperatures.
7. In the reaction 2 O^{-2} (*aq*) → O$_2$ (*g*) + 4*e*$^-$, the volume of O$_2$ is proportional to the number of electrons *lost* in the reaction.
8. The percentage by weight of Cu in CuSO$_4$ is *less than* in CuSO$_4$ · 5H$_2$O.
9. One mole of any gas has a volume of 22.4 l at *any temperature and at any pressure.*
10. The equivalent weight of a metallic element is that weight which will liberate *1.008 g* of hydrogen gas.

Exercises for Review

1. Find the weight of
   a. Ag needed to produce 200 g of AgNO$_3$
   b. I needed to produce 40.0 g of CHI$_3$
   c. S needed to form 15 lb of Fe$_2$S$_3$
   d. Cu needed to form 270 g of Cu(NO$_3$)$_2$
2. A compound contains 70.0% by weight of iron and 30.0% by weight of oxygen. Calculate its empirical formula.
3. A compound has the following composition by weight: 56.3% oxygen and 43.7% phosphorus. Calculate its empirical formula.
4. A compound contains 7.69% hydrogen, and the remainder is carbon. If the molecular weight of the compound is 78, what is its molecular formula?
5. Calculate the percentage composition by weight of (*a*) ZnCl$_2$ (*b*) Na$_2$SO$_4$ (*c*) Al(OH)$_3$ (*d*) H$_3$PO$_4$ (*e*) C$_2$H$_5$OH
6. A compound that contains 25% H and 75% C has a density of 0.715 g/l at STP. Find its molecular formula.
7. The percentage composition by weight of a compound is 87.5% N and 12.5% H. If the molecular weight is 32, what is the molecular formula?
8. A compound that contains 36.9% N by weight and 63.1% O by weight has a density of 3.39 g/l at STP. Calculate its molecular formula.
9. Using Avogadro's number (6.02 × 10^{23} particles per mole), indicate the number of atoms in (*a*) 2 moles of H$_2$ (*b*) 1 mole of He (*c*) 0.1 mole P$_4$ (*d*) 3 moles S$_8$ (*e*) 0.5 mole O$_3$
10. Using Avogadro's number, indicate the number of atoms in (*a*) 4 g of oxygen (*b*) 6.35 g of copper (*c*) 27.0 g of aluminum (*d*) 71.0 g of chlorine (*e*) 5.6 g of nitrogen

11. Calculate the number of atoms of each element present in the following samples of compounds. (*a*) 1 mole of Al_2O_3 (*b*) 0.30 mole of KOH (*c*) 2.5 moles of $CaCl_2$ (*d*) 0.25 mole of H_2SO_4

12. For each half-reaction, indicate the number of moles of electrons that must be added or removed to produce 1 mole of the product.

   a. $Ca^{+2} (l) + 2 e^- \rightarrow Ca (s)$ *c.* $Na^+ (l) + e^- \rightarrow Na (l)$

   b. $2 Br^- (aq) \rightarrow Br_2 (l) + 2 e^-$ *d.* $2 O^{-2} \rightarrow O_2 (g) + 4 e^-$

13. A chemist converts 6.4 g of SO_2 to SO_3, according to the equation

$$2 SO_2 (g) + O_2 (g) \rightarrow 2 SO_3 (g)$$

   a. Find the number of moles of SO_3 formed.
   b. Find the weight of SO_3 formed.

14. A sample of aluminum weighing 54 g is used to prepare aluminum oxide according to the following equation:

$$2 Al (s) + \frac{3}{2} O_2 (g) \rightarrow Al_2O_3 (s)$$

   a. Find the number of moles of aluminum oxide formed.
   b. Find the weight of the aluminum oxide in grams.

15. The reaction between magnesium and hydrochloric acid proceeds as follows:

$$Mg (s) + 2 HCl (aq) \rightarrow MgCl_2 (aq) + H_2 (g)$$

   a. If 9.6 g of magnesium are used, how many moles of HCl are needed?
   b. What is the weight of this number of moles of HCl?

16. We note that 13.08 g of zinc react with sulfuric acid to form zinc sulfate and hydrogen.
   a. How many moles of zinc sulfate form?
   b. What is the weight of the zinc sulfate?

17. A solution containing 23.4 g of sodium chloride reacts with an excess quantity of silver nitrate. Calculate the number of moles and the weight of the silver chloride that forms.

18. Hydrogen peroxide decomposes as shown by the equation

$$2 H_2O_2 \rightarrow 2 H_2O + O_2 (g)$$

   a. How many moles of H_2O_2 will produce 0.96 g of oxygen?
   b. What is the weight of the hydrogen peroxide in grams?

19. Heating copper(II) oxide with hydrogen produces metallic copper and water. If 25.4 g of copper were formed by this reaction:
   a. How many moles of copper(II) oxide were used?
   b. What was the weight of this oxide?

20. Sulfur burns to form sulfur dioxide: $S_8 (s) + 8 O_2 (g) \rightarrow 8 SO_2 (g)$
  a. What volume of SO_2 at STP forms when 2.5 moles of sulfur burn?
  b. How many moles of sulfur are needed to produce 10 l of SO_2?

21. Methanol (CH_3OH) can be produced from carbon monoxide and hydrogen.

$$CO (g) + 2 H_2 (g) \rightarrow CH_3OH (l)$$

What volume of CO and what volume of H_2 at STP must be used to produce 10 moles of CH_3OH?

22. The reaction of calcium with water produces calcium hydroxide and hydrogen. How many moles of calcium hydroxide form if the reaction produces 1.0 l of hydrogen at STP?

23. How many grams of mercury(II) oxide must be decomposed to form 4 ml of oxygen at STP?

24. What volume of chlorine at STP must be added to 80 g of calcium oxide to convert it to $CaOCl_2$ by the following reaction?

$$CaO (s) + Cl_2 (g) \rightarrow CaOCl_2 (s)$$

25. Electrolysis of an aqueous solution of NaCl produces hydrogen.

$$2 NaCl (aq) + 2 H_2O \rightarrow 2 NaOH (aq) + Cl_2 (g) + H_2 (g)$$

What is the volume of the hydrogen formed at STP when 5.85 g of NaCl are electrolyzed?

26. Calcium carbonate reacts with hydrochloric acid as shown below.

$$CaCO_3 (s) + 2 HCl (aq) \rightarrow CaCl_2 (aq) + H_2O + CO_2 (g)$$

  a. What is the volume of the CO_2 formed at STP when 20 g of $CaCO_3$ react with excess HCl?
  b. What is the weight of the $CaCl_2$ formed?

27. *a.* In the electrolysis of molten $CaCl_2$, how many moles of electrons must be removed from Cl^- ions to produce a volume of chlorine gas equal to 44.8 l at STP?
  b. What is the weight of the calcium that forms?

28. The electrolysis of molten aluminum oxide by the reaction

$$2 Al_2O_3 (l) \rightarrow 4 Al (l) + 3 O_2 (g)$$

can also be expressed by the following half-reactions:

$$4 Al^{+3} + 12 e^- \rightarrow 4 Al$$

$$6 O^{-2} \rightarrow 3 O_2 (g) + 12 e^-$$

a. How many moles of electrons must be supplied to produce 6.72 l of oxygen at STP?

b. What is the weight of the aluminum formed?

29. Calculate the weight of (*a*) 2 moles of HNO_3 (*b*) 1 mole of K_2SO_4 (*c*) 0.1 mole of $Na_2CO_3 \cdot 10H_2O$ (*d*) 1.5 moles of $(CaSO_4)_2 \cdot H_2O$

30. Hydrogen sulfide burns in air to form sulfur dioxide and water. If the volume percent of oxygen in air is 21%, what volume of air is needed to burn 1.5 moles of H_2S?

Exercises for Further Study

1. When limestone, $CaCO_3$, is heated, it decomposes to form CaO and CO_2. If 2 kg of $CaCO_3$ are heated to 900° C, and the pressure is 760 mm, what is the volume of CO_2 that forms at these conditions?

2. Magnesium reacts with dilute sulfuric acid to form magnesium sulfate and hydrogen. In a laboratory experiment, 200 ml of hydrogen are collected by water displacement at 24° C and 756 mm.

   a. What is the volume of the dry gas at STP?

   b. What weight of magnesium is consumed?

3. Oxygen is produced by heating 20.0 g of $KClO_3$ to 400° C. What is the volume of the oxygen released at that temperature and 760 mm pressure?

4. Water and oxygen form when 90.0 g of a 3% solution by weight of hydrogen peroxide, H_2O_2, decompose in the presence of a catalyst. What is the volume of the oxygen at 25° C and 750 mm pressure?

5. In an experiment on electroplating, 0.200 g of metallic copper forms at the cathode from a solution of $CuSO_4$ (*aq*).

   a. Write an equation for the half-reaction that takes place at the cathode.

   b. What fraction of a mole of copper is formed?

   c. What is the total number of electrons used to deposit the copper?

6. In any given reaction, atoms are conserved but not molecules. Why?

7. Why must charge be conserved in a reaction?

8. To determine the weight or volume relationships in a given reaction, what assumptions must be made?

9. NO_2 and N_2O_4 have the same empirical formulas but different molecular formulas. Explain.

10. How may the density of a gaseous compound be utilized to determine its molecular formula?

Chapter 12

CHEMICAL ENERGY

12.1 Introduction

We have seen that energy is involved in the changes that matter under-goes. For example, consider the following changes:

CHANGE OF STATE H_2O (l) → H_2O (g) 9,720 cal/mole absorbed at 100° C

CHEMICAL CHANGE H_2 $(g) + \frac{1}{2} O_2$ (g) → H_2O (l) 68,300 cal/mole released

SOLUTION PROCESS HCl $(g) + H_2O$ (l) → HCl (aq) 17,960 cal/mole released

What is the source of this energy? Why is heat absorbed sometimes and released at other times? Are energy changes related to the tendency for a given reaction to proceed spontaneously? In this chapter, we will investigate the answers to these questions.

12.2 Enthalpy

All matter possesses a certain amount of energy for each state in which it exists. The different energies and their sources are summarized below.

KIND OF ENERGY	SOURCE
kinetic energy	molecular motions: to-and-fro (gas), rotational (liquid), vibrational (solid); see Figure 12-1 on the next page electron motions
potential energy (chemical binding forces)	attractive forces between molecules (maximum in solids, minimum in gases) repulsive forces between similarly charged particles in atoms attractive forces that bind atoms
nuclear energy	binding energy of particles in the nucleus

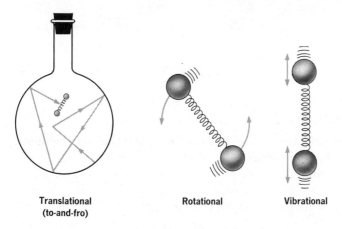

Translational
(to-and-fro)   **Rotational**   **Vibrational**

Fig. 12–1   Molecular motions

Kinetic energy is responsible for the random motions of molecules, especially gases. Potential energy, on the other hand, opposes these motions and makes for greater stability. In this chapter, we will be concerned with potential energy as represented by the chemical binding forces that operate between molecules and between particles in molecules. Chemical bond energy makes up the largest part of the heat content of a molecule.

The terms *heat content* and *enthalpy* are both used to indicate the energy stored in a sample of matter. These terms are measured in calories (or kilocalories) and are denoted by the symbol H.

It will be useful at this point to relate three concepts: potential energy, stability, and enthalpy. Matter always acts to attain a condition of lowest potential energy, which represents maximum stability. As we know, a ball will roll down a smooth hill until it arrives at the lowest point possible – the point of minimum potential energy, or maximum stability. Since the ball continues to roll by itself, its action is said to be spontaneous.

The enthalpy of a substance is so closely related to the potential energy of its particles that, for all practical purposes, we may use enthalpy and potential energy interchangeably. For a chemical system, the natural drive toward maximum stability is the drive toward minimum enthalpy.

12.3 Enthalpy change: the drive toward maximum stability

Figure 12–2, on the following page, describes a general reaction A + B → AB where the heat content (or potential energy or enthalpy) of the product is higher than that of the reactants.

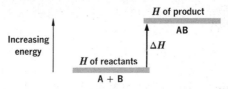

**Fig. 12-2   Energy diagram:
endothermic reaction**

ΔH represents the change in enthalpy. (The Greek letter *delta*, Δ, is used to designate "change in.")

We recognize the reaction between A and B as an endothermic reaction, one in which heat is absorbed. The endothermic nature of the reaction is indicated in the equation by a minus sign before the heat term.

$$A + B \rightarrow AB - \text{heat}$$

An equation that includes a heat term is called a *thermochemical equation*. Since H_{product} is higher than $H_{\text{reactants}}$, the change in enthalpy (ΔH) is positive. This means that *energy must be added* to the system to convert the reactants to product. The reaction is endothermic and involves an enthalpy increase, a direction opposite to that which nature favors. Just as a ball cannot roll uphill by itself, this reaction cannot proceed spontaneously so far as the enthalpy change is concerned.

Now consider the general reaction

$$C + D \rightarrow CD + \text{heat}$$

This is an *exothermic* reaction, one in which heat is released. H_{product} is now lower than $H_{\text{reactants}}$. (See Figure 12-3.)

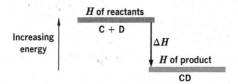

**Fig. 12-3   Energy diagram:
exothermic reaction**

Since the enthalpy of the product is lower than the enthalpy of the reactants, ΔH is negative. The difference represents calories that are released by the reaction as it goes from reactants to product. The reaction follows the direction which nature favors—an enthalpy decrease. This suggests that this reaction can occur spontaneously, like the ball rolling downhill.

12.4 Enthalpy change involved in the formation of carbon dioxide

Consider the burning (or oxidation) of carbon monoxide to form carbon dioxide.

$$CO\ (g) + \frac{1}{2}\ O_2\ (g) \rightarrow CO_2\ (g)$$

The enthalpy values for reactants and products are indicated in Figure 12–4. (The enthalpy value for an element is taken as zero. See section 12.10.)

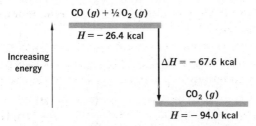

Fig. 12–4 Energy diagram: formation of CO₂

Note that the enthalpy (heat content) of the reactants is −26.4 kcal (the reason for the negative sign is explained in section 12.9). The enthalpy of the product is −94.0 kcal. Thus the energy state (energy content) of CO_2 is lower than that of the system $CO + \frac{1}{2}\ O_2$. The difference in enthalpy between product and reactants is calculated as follows:

$$\text{change in enthalpy} = \underset{\substack{\text{enthalpy} \\ \text{of product}}}{-94.0\ \text{kcal}} - \underset{\substack{\text{enthalpy} \\ \text{of reactants}}}{(-26.4\ \text{kcal})} = -67.6\ \text{kcal}$$

The difference, 67.6 kcal (67,600 calories), represents the heat given off when 1 mole of CO reacts with $\frac{1}{2}$ mole of O_2 to form 1 mole of CO_2. Since the reaction proceeds in the direction of lower enthalpy (it is an exothermic reaction), we can predict that it will proceed spontaneously.

12.5 Enthalpy change involved in the formation of carbon monoxide

Consider the reaction between steam and coke to form carbon monoxide and hydrogen.

$$C\ (s) + H_2O\ (g) \rightarrow CO\ (g) + H_2\ (g) - \text{heat}$$

The energy of the products, CO and H_2, is higher than that of the reactants, C and H_2O. The enthalpy values for reactants and products are indicated in Figure 12–5 on the following page.

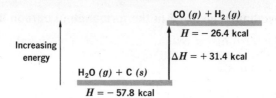

Fig. 12-5   *Energy diagram: reaction
between steam and coke*

The enthalpy change is positive (toward a higher heat content).

$$-26.4 \text{ kcal} - (-57.8 \text{ kcal}) = +31.4 \text{ kcal}$$

This means that the reaction is endothermic, and that 31.4 kcal must be absorbed per mole of products. From what we have learned about enthalpy, we can predict that this reaction should *not* proceed spontaneously.

Earlier, we said that the heat content, H, of a substance in a given state depends primarily on chemical bond energy. Let us now investigate the bond energy of molecules.

12.6 Bond energy

Experimental evidence supports the statement: Energy is released when chemical bonds are formed. Examples of relatively common types of bonds, together with the amount of energy released when these bonds are formed, are listed below. The energy involved in forming a bond may be less than the energy involved in forming a molecule. For example, the water molecule contains two O—H bonds.

BOND	ENERGY RELEASED DURING FORMATION OF BOND (*in kcal per mole of bonds formed at 25° C*)
H—H	104.3
C—C	80
C—H	98.7
C—Cl	81.0
O—H	110
Cl—Cl	57.8
H—Cl	103.2
C—O	85.5
C=O (in CO_2)	192
C=C	145.8
C≡C	199.6

In the preceding table, the symbol — represents a bond formed by one pair of shared electrons. The symbol = represents a bond formed by two pairs of shared electrons. The symbol ≡ represents a bond formed by three pairs of shared electrons.

12.7 Enthalpy of a hydrogen molecule

To be consistent with our previous discussions about energy and stability, the release of energy during bond formation must mean that a system of lower potential energy, or greater stability, has been attained. Why should this be so?

Consider two hydrogen atoms coming together. As they approach each other, new forces of attraction and repulsion come into play. The electron of the first atom now "feels" the attraction of the positive nucleus of the second, and the electron of the second atom "feels" the attraction of the positive nucleus of the first. At the same time, the two electrons repel each other and the two nuclei repel each other. When the attractive forces balance the repulsive forces, a system of lower potential energy, or greater stability, is attained. This situation is shown in Figure 12–6.

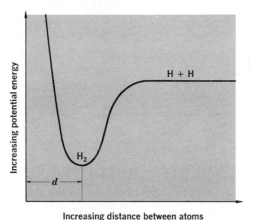

Fig. 12–6   *Potential energy diagram*
for the formation of a hydrogen molecule

Note that d is the distance between the two atoms where the potential energy is lowest. At this position, a stable bond can form between the two atoms. If the atoms come closer than this position of maximum stability, the positive nuclei begin to repel each other strongly, and the electrons also begin to repel each other strongly. A sharp increase in potential energy results, which means that the repulsive forces are prevailing. The interatomic distance corresponding to the lowest potential energy can be represented as the distance between the two nuclei (d) in the hydrogen molecule. (See Figure 12–7.) Since the electrons are in motion, this distance is not fixed, but rather is an average distance corresponding to 0.74 Angstrom. (One Angstrom = 10^{-8} cm.) This bond is extremely strong since 104.3 kcal/mole are required to break it.

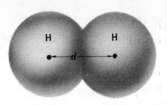

Fig. 12–7   Interatomic distance in a hydrogen molecule (lowest potential energy)

Thus our model indicates that energy is released during bond formation because there is a decrease in potential energy. We may now predict: When a bond is broken, an amount of energy is absorbed equal to the energy released when a bond is formed.

Bond-breaking and bond-forming involve a potential energy change of the same magnitude but of opposite direction. Experiment confirms this. For example, the 104.3 kcal/mole released when a H—H bond is formed must be absorbed again if this bond is to be broken. The same is true of other bonds with their own particular energies. Since bond formation involves a change from higher to lower enthalpy, ΔH will have a negative sign, representing a potential energy *decrease*. Bond-breaking, on the other hand, represents a potential energy *increase*, and the sign of ΔH will be positive.

12.8 Bond-forming vs. bond-breaking

The following example may help to clarify the role of bond energies in chemical reactions. Consider the *substitution reaction* between methane (CH_4) and chlorine, in which an atom of chlorine replaces an atom of hydrogen in CH_4.

$$CH_4 + Cl_2 \rightarrow CH_3Cl + HCl$$

methane   chlorine   monochloro-   hydrogen
methane   chloride

The equation may be rewritten to show the bonds involved. (Remember that the symbol — represents one shared pair of electrons.)

$$
\begin{array}{c}
\text{H} \\
| \\
\text{H—C—H} \\
| \\
\text{H}
\end{array}
+ \text{Cl—Cl} \rightarrow
\begin{array}{c}
\text{H} \\
| \\
\text{H—C—Cl} \\
| \\
\text{H}
\end{array}
+ \text{H—Cl}
$$

If we consider the chemical bonds involved, the equation now reads: One carbon-to-hydrogen bond and one chlorine-to-chlorine bond must first be broken, and then one carbon-to-chlorine bond and one hydrogen-to-chlorine bond must form.

We know that energy is absorbed when bonds are broken and energy is released when bonds are formed. Let us tally the energies involved in the bond-breaking and in the bond-forming that accompany this substitution reaction. (The bond energies are from the table in section 12.6.)

BOND BROKEN	ENERGY ABSORBED	BOND FORMED	ENERGY RELEASED
$1 \times$ C—H $1 \times$ Cl—Cl	98.7 kcal/mole 57.8 kcal/mole	$1 \times$ C—Cl $1 \times$ H—Cl	81.0 kcal/mole 103.2 kcal/mole

total energy
    absorbed $= 156.5$ kcal/mole
        $\Delta H = 156.5$ kcal/mole
		total energy
		    released $=$ 184.2 kcal/mole
		        $\Delta H = -184.2$ kcal/mole	

In this substitution reaction, more calories are released by bond-forming than are absorbed by bond-breaking. Thus the net effect is a release of 27.7 kcal. This means that the products of the reaction are more stable than the reactants, and the reaction proceeds in the direction as written. Stated differently, the overall enthalpy change is favorable for spontaneous reaction. We can rewrite this exothermic reaction in either of two ways:

1. Use the energy (enthalpy) change in the equation as a reaction term.

$$CH_4 + Cl_2 \rightarrow CH_3Cl + HCl + 27.7 \text{ kcal}$$

2. Show the energy (enthalpy) change by a marginal ΔH notation.

$$CH_4 + Cl_2 \rightarrow CH_3Cl + HCl \qquad \Delta H = -27.7 \text{ kcal}$$

Note that for an exothermic reaction, the energy term is positive if used as a reaction term; negative if used as a ΔH notation.

12.9 Heat of formation (enthalpy of formation)

Consider what must happen when a mole of gaseous H_2O is formed from its elements.

$$H_2 \ (g) + \frac{1}{2} O_2 \ (g) \rightarrow H_2O \ (g) + 57.8 \text{ kcal}$$

This equation can be rewritten to show the bonds involved.

$$H—H + \frac{1}{2} O—O \rightarrow \ \overset{\displaystyle H \qquad H}{\underset{\displaystyle O}{\diagdown \diagup}}$$

One mole of H—H bonds must be broken; $\frac{1}{2}$ mole of O—O bonds must be broken; and 2 moles of O—H bonds must be formed. The net energy of the reaction reflects the relationship between the absorbed energy (bond-breaking) and the released energy (bond-forming).

Since 57.8 kcal/mole are released, we can state that in this reaction, more energy is released by bond-forming than is absorbed by bond-breaking.

The product H_2O (g) possesses lower potential energy than the system H_2 (g) and $\frac{1}{2}$ O_2 (g). This difference in energy, called *heat of formation* or *enthalpy of formation*, is an index to the stability of compounds and is very useful to chemists. In the definition that follows, elements are considered to be in their normal state at 25° C and 1 atmosphere.

The *heat of formation of a compound*, symbolized as ΔH_f, is the amount of heat released or absorbed by the reaction which forms 1 mole of the compound from its elements.

Consider the equation

$$2\ Al\ (s) + \frac{3}{2}\ O_2\ (g) \rightarrow Al_2O_3\ (s)$$

which represents the formation of 1 mole of the compound aluminum oxide from its elements. The ΔH for this reaction is -399.09 kcal; the heat of formation, ΔH_f, for Al_2O_3 is -399.09 kcal/mole. Some ΔH_f values for a few common compounds are listed below.

COMPOUND	HEAT OF FORMATION (ΔH_f in kcal/mole at 25° C and 1 atm)
NaCl (s)	−98.2
CO₂ (g)	−94.0
H₂O (l)	−68.3
H₂O (g)	−57.8
CO (g)	−26.4
HgO (s)	−21.7
HI (g)	+5.9
NO (g)	+21.6

The positive ΔH_f's for hydrogen iodide and for nitric oxide indicate that these compounds are relatively unstable.

The heat of formation is the same as the change in heat content (enthalpy) described earlier in this chapter. In addition to revealing the stability of compounds, the heat of formation is also useful for calculating the net enthalpies of chemical reactions.

12.10 Enthalpy of reactions

If the heats of formation of the compounds involved in a reaction are known, the net ΔH for the reaction can be calculated as follows:

net ΔH = (sum of ΔH_f's of products) − (sum of ΔH_f's of reactants)

$$= \Sigma \, \Delta H_f \text{ products} - \Sigma \, \Delta H_f \text{ reactants}$$

where the Greek letter *sigma*, Σ, is used to designate "sum of."

In view of our definition of heat of formation, elements are assigned a ΔH_f value of zero.

Consider again the oxidation of carbon monoxide. The table of heats of formation (see page 216) shows that the ΔH_f of $CO_2 = -94.0$ kcal; the ΔH_f of $CO = -26.4$ kcal. The ΔH_f of elemental oxygen $= 0$.

Writing these values along with the chemical equation, we obtain

$$CO \ (g) \ + \ \frac{1}{2} O_2 \ (g) \ \rightarrow \ CO_2 \ (g)$$

ΔH_f VALUES/MOLE $\quad -26.4$ kcal $\quad\quad$ 0 kcal $\quad\quad -94.0$ kcal

$$\Delta H = \Sigma \, \Delta H_f \text{ products} - \Sigma \, \Delta H_f \text{ reactants}$$

$$= \Delta H_f \ CO_2 \ (g) - \Delta H_f \ CO \ (g)$$

$$= -94.0 \text{ kcal/mole} - (-26.4 \text{ kcal/mole})$$

$$= -67.6 \text{ kcal/mole}$$

Note the importance of designating state (solid, liquid, or gas) in the calculations. For example, the ΔH_f for H_2O $(g) = -57.8$ kcal/mole, but the ΔH_f for H_2O $(l) = -68.3$ kcal/mole. The additional 10.5 kcal are liberated when a mole of liquid water is formed. This heat is liberated in the change of state from gas to liquid and is called the *heat of condensation*.

Let us recalculate the ΔH for the change of state of water, using a step-by-step procedure.

$$H_2O \ (g) \rightarrow H_2O \ (l)$$

From the table of heats of formation, we know that

$$(1) \quad H_2 \ (g) + \frac{1}{2} O_2 \ (g) \rightarrow H_2O \ (g) \qquad \Delta H = -57.8 \text{ kcal}$$

$$(2) \quad H_2 \ (g) + \frac{1}{2} O_2 \ (g) \rightarrow H_2O \ (l) \qquad \Delta H = -68.3 \text{ kcal}$$

If we reverse reaction 1, it becomes

$$(3) \quad H_2O \ (g) \rightarrow H_2 \ (g) + \frac{1}{2} O_2 \ (g) \qquad \Delta H = +57.8 \text{ kcal}$$

If the reaction is exothermic in one direction, it must be endothermic in the other. If the equation is reversed, therefore, the sign of the ΔH must also be reversed.

If we now add reactions 2 and 3, and also add their respective ΔH values, we obtain

$$H_2 \ (g) + \frac{1}{2} O_2 \ (g) + H_2O \ (g) \rightarrow H_2O \ (l) + H_2 \ (g) + \frac{1}{2} O_2 \ (g)$$
$$\Delta H = -68.3 \text{ kcal} + 57.8 \text{ kcal} = -10.5 \text{ kcal}$$

The equation may be simplified by canceling like terms from both sides of the equation.

$$H_2O \ (g) \rightarrow H_2O \ (l) \quad \Delta H = -10.5 \text{ kcal (at } 25° \text{ C and 1 atm)}$$

12.11 Hess's Law

The step-by-step procedure we used in the previous section is an example of the *Law of Additivity of Heats of Reaction,* or *Hess's Law.*

Hess's Law: The heat of reaction of a chemical reaction is the same whether the reaction takes place in one step or in several steps.

Let us consider another example of a step-by-step procedure. In the laboratory, it is difficult to measure the ΔH for the reaction

$$C \ (s) + \frac{1}{2} O_2 \ (g) \rightarrow CO \ (g)$$

because some CO invariably is oxidized to CO_2. However, using Hess's Law, we can determine the ΔH of this reaction from the heat evolved in two related reactions.

$$(1) \quad C \ (s) + O_2 \ (g) \rightarrow CO_2 \ (g) \qquad \Delta H = -94.0 \text{ kcal}$$

$$(2) \quad CO \ (g) + \frac{1}{2} O_2 \ (g) \rightarrow CO_2 \ (g) \qquad \Delta H = -67.6 \text{ kcal}$$

Reversing equation 2, we obtain

$$(3) \quad CO_2 \ (g) \rightarrow CO \ (g) + \frac{1}{2} O_2 \ (g) \quad \Delta H = +67.6 \text{ kcal}$$

Adding equations 1 and 3, we obtain

$$C \ (s) + O_2 \ (g) + CO_2 \ (g) \rightarrow CO_2 \ (g) + CO \ (g) + \frac{1}{2} O_2 \ (g)$$

Canceling like terms from both sides of the equation, we obtain

$$C \ (s) + \frac{1}{2} O_2 \ (g) \rightarrow CO \ (g) \quad \Delta H = -26.4 \text{ kcal}$$

This procedure provides the desired reaction, with a ΔH of -26.4 kcal (-94.0 kcal $+67.6$ kcal). Thus the ΔH of a reaction can be obtained experimentally or read directly from a table of heats of formation or calculated from Hess's Law using related heats of formation.

12.12 Enthalpy of solution

The solution process, discussed in Chapter 10, generally involves the breaking of bonds (accompanied by the absorption of energy) and the formation of new bonds (accompanied by the release of energy). For example, when ionic solids dissolve in water, energy must be absorbed to separate the positive and negative ions held together by electrostatic forces (ionic bonds). Energy is released when the separated positive and negative ions interact with the water molecules to form aquated ions.

Whether the overall solution process is exothermic or endothermic depends on which is greater—the energy that is absorbed or the energy that is released. Typical enthalpies of solution follow:

$$(1) \quad HCl \ (g) + H_2O \rightarrow H_3O^+ + Cl^- \ (aq) \quad \Delta H = -17.96 \text{ kcal}$$

or

$$HCl \ (g) \rightarrow H^+ \ (aq) + Cl^- \ (aq)$$

$$(2) \quad NaCl \ (s) \rightarrow Na^+ \ (aq) + Cl^- \ (aq) \quad \Delta H = +1.02 \text{ kcal}$$

We interpret reaction 1 by saying that the energy liberated by the hydration (aquation) of the hydrogen ions and the chloride ions must exceed the energy needed to break the covalent H—Cl bond. In reaction 2, we postulate that the energy required to break down the crystal lattice of sodium chloride must exceed the energy released when the sodium and chloride ions hydrate.

The dissolving of NaCl in water is an endothermic process. The enthalpy change is positive, which suggests that the change should not occur spontaneously. However, we know from experience and experiment that the dissolving of salt in water does take place spontaneously. Is there a conflict between fact and theory? We have already indicated (see section 10.14) how some endothermic changes may proceed spontaneously. Let us further investigate the factors that influence spontaneity in chemical reactions. At the end of our investigation, in section 12.21, we shall answer the question about the dissolving of salt.

12.13 Entropy

When we speak of the state, or phase, of a substance, we are describing the degree of order of its particles. The converse of the degree of order of a substance may be expressed by the disorder, or *randomness*, of its particles. Substances are most organized in the solid state and least organized in the gaseous state. This is the same as saying that the particles in a solid possess the least degree of randomness, whereas the particles in a gas possess the maximum degree of randomness. The term *entropy* is used to describe randomness and is a function of temperature. Thus a gas has greater entropy than a solid. Entropy is denoted by the symbol S.

12.14 Entropy change: the drive toward maximum randomness

We have already stated that matter will always tend to attain minimum potential energy. Another fundamental property of matter is that it will tend to attain a state of maximum randomness. One of the universal laws in nature is: Matter tends to attain maximum entropy, that is, to assume the least organized (most random) state possible.

Consider a box with a vertical partition, as shown in Figure 12–8 on the following page. One compartment contains gas A, while the other contains gas B. This system represents some degree of order, or organization, because each gas is present in its own compartment.

If we remove the partition, there will be a spontaneous change. Molecules of gas A will soon be found where only B molecules were, and B molecules will be found where only A molecules were. Less order and more randomness are now present in the system.

The opposite type of change, in which A molecules will return to one compartment and B molecules to the other compartment, does not take place spontaneously. Since the gaseous state is the least ordered (most random), it is the state that nature favors. All matter is not gaseous because bonding forces—forces which lead to greater order and to lower energy—tend to counteract the natural drive toward randomness.

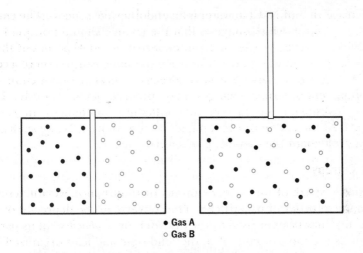

● Gas A
○ Gas B

Fig. 12–8 Drive toward maximum randomness

12.15 Entropy and probability

Because of the natural drive toward randomness, chemists speak of the *probability* that a substance will exist in a specified state. A highly organized state has a low probability of existing, while a random state has a high probability.

Chemists use the term *absolute entropy* (S), also designated as S^0, to denote the probability that a substance will exist in a specified state. Some absolute entropy values can be measured experimentally, but the methods lie beyond the scope of this book.

The unit for expressing entropy is *calories per mole-degree* because entropy is measured by the heat transferred (cal/mole) divided by the absolute temperature. The higher the value of S, the more probable is the specified state.

SUBSTANCE	ABSOLUTE ENTROPY (S) (cal/mole-deg at 1 atm at 298° K)
C (graphite)	1.37
C (diamond)	0.6
H_2O (*l*)	16.73
H_2O (*g*)	45.1

The S values indicate that carbon in the graphite state is more probable than carbon in the diamond state; and water in the gaseous state is more probable than water in the liquid state. We know from crystal studies that carbon in the graphite state is less organized than carbon in the diamond state. We also know that gaseous water is more random than liquid water. Therefore, the S values support our earlier discussion.

12.16 Entropy change in chemical reactions

What role does entropy play in determining the direction of a given chemical change? Just as we have talked of ΔH, we can also talk of ΔS, or change in entropy. A high entropy indicates a high probability of existence. Therefore, a change that leads toward a higher entropy for a system, or a positive ΔS, indicates the direction of the change that nature favors. Summarizing:

Enthalpy. A negative ΔH indicates a favorable driving force.

Entropy. A positive ΔS indicates a favorable driving force.

Let us discuss some examples of entropy drive.

EXAMPLE 1.   Unfavorable entropy drive.

$$CO\ (g) + \frac{1}{2} O_2\ (g) \rightarrow CO_2\ (g) \qquad \Delta S = -41.4 \text{ cal/mole-deg}$$

The kind and number of atoms are the same on both sides of the equation, but their organization is not the same. There is a higher degree of organization on the product side than on the reactant side. The oxygen atoms and the carbon atom are arranged in one molecule in CO_2, but there is less organization when the same atoms are in two different molecules. Thus there is a more random arrangement on the reactant (left) side of the equation, that is, a negative ΔS value and an unfavorable entropy drive.

EXAMPLE 2.   Favorable entropy drive.

$$CaCO_3\ (s) \rightarrow CaO\ (s) + CO_2\ (g) \qquad \Delta S = +38.4 \text{ cal/mole-deg}$$

This entropy drive is the reverse of the entropy drive described in example 1. The single, solid reactant is more ordered than the two products. In addition, the presence of a gas indicates a greater degree of randomness on the right side of the equation. Thus the positive value for ΔS indicates that the entropy drive is favorable.

12.17 Entropy change in the solution of a solid

The drive toward maximum randomness applies to the solution process as well as to other chemical changes. Consider the dissolving of sodium chloride in water.

$$NaCl\ (s) + H_2O \rightarrow Na^+\ (aq) + Cl^-\ (aq)$$

In this case, the particles are *less* organized in the dissolved state than in the undissolved, solid state. On the left is a highly organized ionic lattice; on the right are separated, mobile ions. The entropy drive is favorable to solution. Increasing the temperature increases the state of randomness, which increases the entropy drive even further. Thus solids generally dissolve to a greater extent in heated solvents.

12.18 Entropy change in the solution of a gas

$$O_2\ (g) + H_2O \rightarrow O_2\ (aq)$$

When oxygen dissolves in water, the molecules of O_2 proceed from the less ordered gaseous state to the more ordered dissolved state. Since the entropy change for this system is unfavorable, how do we dissolve a gas in water?

We know from experiments that the solubility in water of gases such as O_2 decreases as the temperature of the water increases. Increasing the temperature of a substance means increasing the kinetic energy of its particles, and this, in turn, means greater randomness. But if a gas dissolves in water, its entropy decreases. This means that the two changes oppose each other. Therefore, heating the water opposes the change that must occur if the gas is to dissolve. This is the same as saying that in order to dissolve a gas in a liquid, the liquid must be cooled. Thus the solubility of a gas in a liquid increases with decreasing temperature and decreases with increasing temperature.

12.19 The combined effect of enthalpy and entropy changes

To predict whether a reaction will occur spontaneously, we must consider both the drive toward minimum enthalpy and the drive toward maximum entropy. It is entirely possible that, in a given reaction, the enthalpy change is negative and thus favorable, but the entropy change is also negative and thus unfavorable. Which factor predominates, enthalpy or entropy? We must consider the relative magnitudes of the terms, that. is, their combined effect. The combined effect of the enthalpy and entropy changes is called the *free energy* change, represented by the symbol ΔG.

12.20 Free energy: the driving force of a reaction

As we saw previously, two driving forces govern the behavior of chemical systems: (1) the tendency toward minimum enthalpy and (2) the tendency toward maximum entropy. Free energy is the function which assesses both of these tendencies simultaneously. The spontaneity of a given reaction is determined by the free energy change, ΔG. As will be shown later, the sign of ΔG has the same meaning as the sign of ΔH.

A negative ΔG signifies a decrease in the free energy of a system and a favorable drive. A positive ΔG signifies an increase in the free energy of a system and an unfavorable drive.

Keeping the meaning of negative and positive ΔG in mind, consider the following data.

REACTION		ΔH (kcal/mole)	ΔG (kcal/mole)
(1)	$2 \, Al \, (s) + \dfrac{3}{2} \, O_2 \, (g) \rightarrow Al_2O_3 \, (s)$	-399.09	-376.77
(2)	$\dfrac{1}{8} \, S_8 \, (s) + O_2 \, (g) \rightarrow SO_2 \, (g)$	-70.96	-71.79

The data show that for reaction 1 the enthalpy change is favorable. However, when we consider the free energy change of the system, the degree of favorableness has been reduced by 22.32 kcal/mole. This reduction must be due to an unfavorable entropy contribution. Indeed, a careful inspection of the equation shows that the change is not favored by the driving force of entropy: the state of randomness is greater for the reactants than it is for the products. In reaction 2, the degree of favorableness has been increased by 0.83 kcal/mole, signifying that both the entropy change and the enthalpy change are favorable.

12.21 Free energy depends on temperature

Change in free energy can be defined in an exact way, as follows:

$$\Delta G = \Delta H - T \Delta S$$

The equation states that the change in free energy equals the change in enthalpy minus the product of the absolute temperature times the entropy change. Note that when ΔS units in cal/mole-deg are multiplied by T in degrees, the unit for the product, $T\Delta S$, is cal/mole, the same as the unit for ΔH and ΔG. Examination of the equation will show that a positive (favorable) ΔS will make ΔG more negative, while a negative (unfavorable) ΔS will make ΔG less negative.

Temperature also has an effect on the free energy change. To clarify this point, let us consider the reaction

$$H_2O\ (l) \rightarrow H_2O\ (g)$$

$\Delta H = 10{,}494$ cal/mole at 1 atm and $298°$ K (unfavorable enthalpy change)

$\Delta S = 28.4$ cal/mole-deg at 1 atm and $298°$ K (favorable entropy change)

There is competition between both changes. The enthalpy change is unfavorable for the vaporization of water, but the entropy change is favorable. The net change depends on temperature because the reaction will proceed to the right if ΔG is negative.

From the relation $\Delta G = \Delta H - T\Delta S$, we know that ΔG can be negative only if $T\Delta S$ is greater than ΔH. Thus T must be greater than $\dfrac{\Delta H}{\Delta S}$ if the reaction is to proceed. Substituting the given values for ΔH and ΔS, we find: T is greater than $\frac{10{,}494}{28.4}$, or T is greater than $373°$ K (approximately).

What is significant about the temperature needed to make the reaction go spontaneously to form $H_2O\ (g)$ at *atmospheric pressure*? It is $373°$ K, or $100°$ C, precisely the temperature which we know to be necessary for the boiling of water at *atmospheric pressure*. At this temperature and pressure, the formation of $H_2O\ (g)$ predominates over the formation of $H_2O\ (l)$ from the condensation of $H_2O\ (g)$. Similarly, we observe that liquid water can evaporate spontaneously at any temperature because the favorable entropy drive results in a net negative free energy change. (To check this observation, we would need ΔH and ΔS values at different conditions.)

In summary, if the enthalpy change and the entropy change for a given reaction are known, then the free energy change, ΔG, can be calculated and used as a reliable index to the spontaneity of the reaction.

We can now answer the question asked in section 12.12 about the dissolving of NaCl (s) in water. The enthalpy change is unfavorable toward solution, yet we know it takes place spontaneously. The driving force is the favorable entropy of the system. If the temperature is sufficiently high, and $T\Delta S$ is greater than ΔH, then the NaCl dissolves.

Multiple-Choice Questions

1. In the reaction $X_2 + Y_2 \rightarrow 2\ XY$ + heat (1) the enthalpy of the system increases (2) the system becomes more stable (3) the bonds between like atoms are more stable than the bonds between unlike atoms (4) the number of moles of molecules decreases

2. The bond energy for C—C is 80 kcal/mole; for C—H it is 98.7 kcal/mole. Therefore (1) the C—C bond is more stable than the C—H bond (2) a greater increase in enthalpy occurs when C—C bonds are broken than when C—H bonds are broken (3) the C—H bond is more stable than the C—C bond (4) the formation of both types of bonds is an endothermic process

3. As two hydrogen atoms approach each other (1) the potential energy of the system decreases continuously (2) the attraction between the atoms increases constantly (3) the atoms repel each other at all distances (4) a distance is reached at which the potential energy of the system is lowest

4. In the reaction $H_2\ (g) + Cl_2\ (g) \rightarrow 2\ HCl\ (g)$ + heat (1) no bonds are broken (2) to form 2 moles of HCl, 1 mole of H—H and 1 mole of Cl—Cl bonds must be broken (3) bonds between molecules must first be broken (4) an increase in potential energy takes place

5. The heat of formation refers to the heat (1) released when elements form (2) required to form 1 g of a compound (3) absorbed in forming bonds (4) change on forming 1 mole of a compound

6. The enthalpy change for a chemical reaction can be found from (1) the heats of formation of products minus the heats of formation of reactants (2) the boiling and freezing points of the reactants and products (3) the number of electrons lost or gained per mole of product (4) the solubilities of reactants and products

7. An endothermic process may take place spontaneously if (1) the system receives an increase in energy (2) the system goes to a lower energy state (3) a sufficient increase in entropy occurs (4) a solid is formed

8. The dissolving of solid sodium nitrate, $NaNO_3$, in water is an endothermic process. This indicates that (1) the energy required to break the bonds between ions is greater than the energy released by hydration of the ions (2) the energy of hydration is greater than the energy of the ionic bonds (3) weak forces are present between ions (4) Na^+ ions do not react with NO_3^- ions

9. The change H_2O $(g) \rightarrow H_2O$ (l) + heat is accompanied by (1) an increase in enthalpy and an increase in entropy (2) a decrease in enthalpy and a decrease in entropy (3) an increase in entropy and a decrease in enthalpy (4) a decrease in entropy and an increase in enthalpy

10. A system will show the greatest tendency to change if the change is accompanied by a (1) large increase in enthalpy (2) large decrease in entropy (3) large decrease in free energy (4) decrease in entropy greater than the increase in enthalpy

Completion Questions

1. The heat content of a substance is also called its _____.
2. When heat is produced by a chemical change, a decrease in the _____ of the system results.
3. In order to break a bond between two atoms, _____ must be added to the system.
4. The additivity of heats of reaction is known as _____ Law.
5. The _____ of a system is defined' as the amount of randomness of the system.
6. Of the three forms of H_2O — ice, water and steam — the form which has the greatest entropy is _____.
7. A chemical reaction will proceed spontaneously if the reaction leads to a decrease in _____ and to an increase in _____.
8. Units of cal/mole-deg are used for the measurement of _____.
9. The combined effect of the enthalpy change and the entropy change that is associated with a chemical reaction is the change in _____.
10. When a chemical change takes place with a decrease in enthalpy, _____ is released by the reaction.

True-False Questions

1. The reaction $NO + \frac{1}{2} O_2 \rightarrow NO_2$ requires that the O—O bond be *broken* before a new bond is formed.
2. A reaction may take place spontaneously if the enthalpy of the products is *greater than* the enthalpy of the reactants.
3. The bond energy for C—H is 98.7 kcal/mole; for C—Cl it is 81.0 kcal/mole. The C—H bond is therefore *more* stable than the C—Cl bond.

4. In forming a stable compound from its elements, the energy absorbed by breaking bonds is *greater than* the energy released by forming bonds.
5. The difference between the heats of formation of CH_3OH (*g*) and CH_3OH (*l*) equals the *heat of vaporization* of CH_3OH.
6. When a liquid is changed to its corresponding *solid*, an increase in the entropy of the system results.
7. A *positive* value for the ΔH of a given chemical change indicates a decrease in enthalpy.
8. The normal distance between the atoms in a molecule of hydrogen is the distance at which the potential energy of the molecule is a *maximum*.
9. Entropy changes are dependent upon *temperature*.
10. The potential energy stored in a molecule is most closely related to its *kinetic* energy.

Decreases, Increases, Remains the Same

1. In an exothermic reaction, the enthalpy of the system _____.
2. When the distance between the nuclei of a diatomic molecule becomes less than the normal interatomic distance, the potential energy of the system _____.
3. As a stable bond is formed between two atoms, the enthalpy of the system _____.
4. When the organization of the particles in a system increases, the entropy of the system _____.
5. When the randomness, or disorder, of a system increases, its probability _____.
6. If the free energy of a system decreases during a chemical change, the tendency for that change to take place _____.
7. If the enthalpy remains unchanged in a chemical reaction, as the entropy increases, the free energy of the system _____.
8. Systems become more stable if the free energy of the system _____.
9. As the temperature increases, the heat of formation of an element _____.
10. As the heats of formation of a series of compounds decrease, the stabilities of the compounds _____.

Exercises for Review

1. Write a thermochemical equation for the formation of sodium chloride, NaCl, from its elements. Use the data for the enthalpy of formation on page 216.

2. The table of heats (enthalpy) of formation lists ΔH_f for nitric oxide, NO (g), as $+21.6$ kcal/mole. Write a thermochemical equation for the formation of this compound from its elements.

3. *a.* Write a thermochemical equation for the formation of hydrogen sulfide, H_2S (g), from its elements.

b. Compare the enthalpies of formation of H_2S (g) and H_2O (g).

c. What do these values mean in terms of the bonds in the two compounds?

4. *a.* From the values given in the table of enthalpy of formation for HF, HCl, HBr, and HI, which compound is the most stable and which is the least stable? Explain.

b. What do the enthalpy values reveal about the energy of the bonds in the four compounds?

5. Using the values for enthalpy of formation for SO_2 (g) and SO_3 (g), calculate the enthalpy change for the following reaction:

$$SO_2\ (g) + \frac{1}{2}\ O_2\ (g) \rightarrow SO_3\ (g)$$

6. From the value for the enthalpy of formation, calculate the heat released when 1 g of H_2O (l) forms from H_2 (g) and O_2 (g).

7. Explain in terms of the enthalpy of formation why it is much easier to obtain oxygen from mercury(II) oxide, HgO (s), than from magnesium oxide, MgO (s).

Exercises for Further Study

1. Using the following equations, draw an energy diagram showing the changes from C to CO to CO_2:

$$C\ (s) + \frac{1}{2}\ O_2\ (g) \rightarrow CO\ (g) \qquad \Delta H = -26.4 \text{ kcal/mole}$$

$$CO\ (g) + \frac{1}{2}\ O_2\ (g) \rightarrow CO_2\ (g) \qquad \Delta H = -67.6 \text{ kcal/mole}$$

2. In this chapter, we discussed the following endothermic reaction:

$$C\ (s) + H_2O\ (g) \rightarrow CO\ (g) + H_2\ (g) \qquad \Delta H = 31.4 \text{ kcal/mole}$$

a. List the bonds broken in the reacting substances and the bonds formed in the product.

b. How do the energy changes for these two processes compare?

3. *a.* Nitric oxide, NO (g), can be formed by direct combination of the two elements. List the bonds that are broken and formed in this reaction.

    b. The enthalpy of formation of NO (g) is +21.6 kcal/mole. What do you conclude concerning the enthalpy changes in breaking bonds and in forming new bonds?

4. The enthalpy of formation of ozone, O_3, is +34.0 kcal/mole. The enthalpy of formation of CO_2 (g) from C (s) + O_2 (g) is −94.0 kcal/mole. What is the enthalpy change for the following reaction?

$$3 \; C \; (s) + 2 \; O_3 \; (g) \rightarrow 3 \; CO_2 \; (g)$$

5. The enthalpy of formation of Al_2O_3 (s) is −399.1 kcal/mole, and that of Fe_2O_3 (s) is −196.5 kcal/mole. Using this data, calculate the enthalpy change for the following reaction:

$$2 \; Al \; (s) + Fe_2O_3 \; (s) \rightarrow 2 \; Fe \; (l) + Al_2O_3 \; (s)$$

6. From the values for the enthalpies of formation, calculate the enthalpy change for the gaseous reaction $H_2S + \frac{1}{2} \; O_2 \rightarrow H_2O + S$.

7. The enthalpy of formation for methane, CH_4 (g), is −17.9 kcal/mole; for CO_2 (g) it is −94.0 kcal/mole; and for H_2O (g) it is −57.8 kcal/mole. Calculate the heat released when 1 mole of CH_4 burns according to the following equation:

$$CH_4 \; (g) + 2 \; O_2 \; (g) \rightarrow CO_2 \; (g) + 2 \; H_2O \; (g)$$

8. The enthalpy of formation for H_2O (l) is −68.3 kcal/mole; and for hydrogen peroxide, H_2O_2 (l), it is −44.8 kcal/mole. What bond is probably responsible for this difference? How stable is this bond?

9. HCl (g) can be formed by the reaction $\frac{1}{2} \; H_2 \; (g) + \frac{1}{2} \; Cl_2 \; (g) \rightarrow HCl \; (g)$. Using the bond energies for the bonds that are broken and formed, calculate the enthalpy of formation for HCl (g).

Chapter 13

RATES OF CHEMICAL REACTIONS:
CHEMICAL KINETICS

13.1 Introduction

In previous chapters, we have seen that much useful information is revealed by a properly balanced reaction. For example, the equation

$$2 \text{ Na } (s) + \text{Cl}_2 (g) \rightarrow 2 \text{ NaCl } (s)$$

describes the nature of the substances involved in the reaction. It also provides quantitative information about the number of moles of each substance. The equation states that 2 moles of solid sodium react with 1 mole of gaseous chlorine to form 2 moles of solid sodium chloride. The equation, however, does not answer some important questions: How does the reaction proceed; that is, does the reaction take place in one step or more than one step? What is the rate at which the reaction takes place; that is, are the 2 moles of NaCl (s) formed instantly or is there a time lapse?

The rate of a reaction is defined as the quantity of product formed in some stated interval of time. More strictly, the rate of a chemical reaction can be defined in terms of the change in concentration of any species in the reaction with respect to time. The study of chemical reaction rates is called *chemical kinetics*.

When solutions of barium chloride and sodium sulfate are mixed, a white precipitate of barium sulfate forms immediately. When a dilute solution of potassium permanganate is added slowly to an acidified solution of sodium sulfite, the characteristic purple color of the permanganate ion disappears. In this instance, however, the observer notes a brief interval between the time the chemicals are mixed and the time the purple color disappears. In the laboratory, it can be shown that the rate of decolorization of potassium permanganate by acidified sodium sulfite varies with different concentrations of the reactants. The rate of the reaction also depends on the temperature at which the reaction proceeds.

When a piece of iron is exposed to the atmosphere, rust (iron oxide) is formed. To change all the iron into rust may take years. The rate of this reaction depends on the state of subdivision of the iron present, on the moisture content and temperature of the air, and on other conditions.

In this chapter, we will investigate the answers to these questions: How do particles react chemically? What are the factors that determine the rate of a reaction? Why do reaction rates differ?

13.2 Collision theory

When gaseous hydrogen and gaseous iodine are mixed, they react slowly to form hydrogen iodide gas. The rate of the reaction could be determined by measuring how fast the product is formed after the reactants are mixed, that is, how many moles of HI are formed per second. The equation

$$H_2 (g) + I_2 (g) \rightarrow 2 \text{ HI } (g)$$

suggests that H—H and I—I bonds must be broken before H—I bonds can be formed. This cannot take place unless the particles involved come into contact with each other, or collide. In addition, the collisions must have sufficient energy and a favorable geometry before chemical change can occur. Favorable geometry means the angle at which the particles collide. For example, a head-on collision between two cars is much more effective (produces more change) than a sideswipe.

13.3 Energy of the collision

If we assume a favorable geometry, then each collision requires a certain minimum energy if it is to be effective. This energy is termed the energy of activation. It depends on the nature of the reacting particles and is different for different reactions. *Energy of activation* is the energy needed to weaken or break bonds before new bonds can form.

Let us consider the reaction

$$NO_2 (g) + CO (g) \rightarrow NO (g) + CO_2 (g)$$

| nitrogen dioxide | carbon monoxide | nitric oxide | carbon dioxide |

which is shown as an energy profile in Figure 13–1 on the following page.

In the figure, note that the reactants possess more energy than the products: A is higher on the energy axis than B. Therefore, the reaction between NO_2 and CO is exothermic. However, the path from A to B is *not* direct. The colliding NO_2 molecules and CO molecules must acquire sufficient energy (C) before the products (NO and CO_2) can be formed. This quantity of energy, represented by the height C, is the minimum energy required for an effective collision. It is the energy of activation, discussed in the first paragraph of this section. In all reactions, we can picture the energy of activation as a potential energy barrier which the reacting particles must overcome before they can unite. Note that the interval D minus C is ΔH, the heat of reaction.

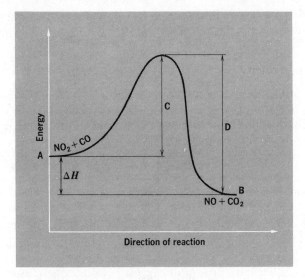

Fig. 13–1   *Energy profile: NO_2 + CO*

For some reactions, the energy of activation (potential energy barrier) is relatively large, as shown in Figure 13–2 (right). For other reactions, it is relatively small, as shown in the same figure (left).

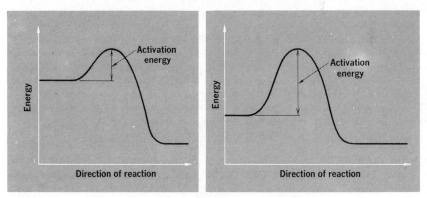

Fig. 13–2   *Energy profiles: different activation energies*

The required energy of activation applies equally to the forward and reverse reactions in a chemical system. In the direction of the exothermic change, the energy of activation is small. It is correspondingly larger for the endothermic reaction in the reverse direction. (See Figure 13–3 on the following page.)

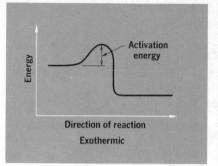
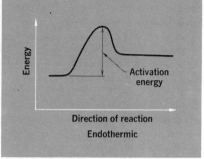

Fig. 13–3   Energy profiles

According to modern kinetic theory, the reactants exist for a very brief period of time in a transitional, or intermediate, state. The reactants partially bond together in this transitional state to form a temporary highly active species called an *activated complex*.

The transitional state is unstable and exists only for the brief period of time that the colliding particles remain together. The position of the activated complex in Figure 13–1 is represented as the top of the crest which forms the potential energy barrier. With sufficient collision energy, the activated complex changes into products ($NO + CO_2$ molecules), but some portion of the complex may also return to the unchanged reactant form. If the collision energy is insufficient, the complex does not form; the reactants repel each other and remain unchanged.

13.4 Collision geometry

We have already discussed the energy of the collision. The collision angle, or favorable geometry, is also a factor in determining the overall effectiveness of a collision. For example, H_2 and I_2 molecules might collide as shown in Figure 13–4 on the following page.

Situation *A* is more favorable for bond-breaking than Situation *B*, and bond-breaking must take place before the complete reaction can occur. If the collision geometry is unfavorable, the potential barrier is raised, so that more than minimum energy must be available if the reaction is to take place.

Recent research indicates that the reaction between H_2 (g) and I_2 (g) may not be bimolecular (a reaction between two molecules). Rather, it may be a reaction of one hydrogen molecule with two iodine atoms.

The activation energy given in tables or shown in diagrams is usually the minimum energy, that is, the energy required for the reaction to proceed with a favorable collision geometry.

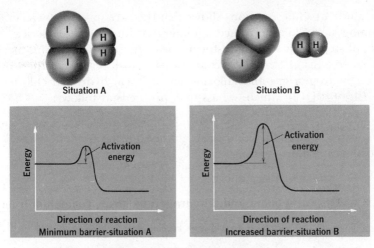

Fig. 13–4 Collision geometry

13.5 Reaction mechanism: the rate-determining step

We have presented a model to describe how reacting particles behave. Such particles are always colliding; under proper conditions, the collisions result in bond-breaking with subsequent chemical change.

The decolorization of potassium permanganate by acidified sodium sulfite, mentioned earlier, can be described by the following equation, which indicates the reacting aqueous ions:

$$5 \ SO_3^{-2} + 2 \ MnO_4^- + 6 \ H^+ \rightarrow 5 \ SO_4^{-2} + 2 \ Mn^{+2} + 3 \ H_2O$$

How likely is an effective simultaneous collision between 5 sulfite ions, 2 permanganate ions, and 6 hydrogen ions? An effective collision between 13 particles is most unlikely. It is much more likely that the reaction takes place in many small steps, each step consisting of a two-particle collision. The net chemical change constitutes the sum of all these steps. The sequence of intermediate steps that makes up a chemical reaction is called the *reaction mechanism*.

Our understanding of reaction mechanisms comes chiefly from experimental evidence on the rates of reactions. Many reactions take place in a series of steps in which the product of the preceding step becomes the reactant of the next step. Suppose a given reaction takes place in six steps. Each of the intermediate steps must have its own rate, and the overall reaction cannot take place faster than the slowest of these steps. For this reason, the slowest in-between step is known as the *rate-determining step*.

The study of some reactions shows that they are initiated by an energy-consuming step, which produces an energetic intermediate species. Then a series of steps occurs which re-forms the energetic species. This mechanism is called a *chain reaction*. An example of a chain reaction is the reaction between hydrogen gas and chlorine gas to form hydrogen chloride gas ($H_2 + Cl_2 \rightarrow 2$ HCl), which, we assume, proceeds as follows:

STEP 1. A molecule of yellow-colored chlorine gas absorbs light energy. This energy ruptures the bond between the chlorine atoms in the molecule and forms two chlorine atoms.

$$Cl_2 + energy \rightarrow Cl + Cl$$

STEP 2. A chlorine atom and a hydrogen molecule collide and react.

$$Cl + H_2 \rightarrow HCl + H$$

STEP 3. The hydrogen atom and a chlorine molecule collide and react.

$$H + Cl_2 \rightarrow HCl + Cl$$

The chlorine atom now proceeds as in step 2. It can be shown experimentally that step 2 is the slowest step. Therefore, step 2 is the rate-determining step.

Some conclusions that can be drawn from this example are:

a. The mechanism for this reaction has a chain character. After step 1 has taken place, the reaction can be self-propagating; that is, it can continue unaided.

b. Collisions resulting in reactions such as

$$Cl + Cl \rightarrow Cl_2 \text{ or } H + H \rightarrow H_2$$

break the sequence of steps and could be chain-terminating. This means that no Cl atoms would be available for step 2, or no H atoms would be available for step 3.

c. Step 1 differs from the other steps because it involves the interaction of light energy with a molecule that is capable of absorbing such energy (usually a molecule of a colored species). Such a reaction is often termed a *photochemical reaction*. In the reaction between hydrogen gas and chlorine gas, the photochemical reaction initiates the chain.

13.6 What are the factors that influence reaction rate?

A discussion of the factors that determine the rate of a reaction raises many questions, among them:

1. What are the nature and concentration of the reactants?
2. What is the strength of the bonds that must be broken?
3. Is the reaction mechanism simple or is it complex; that is, does the reaction take place in one step or in a series of steps?
4. What kind of collision processes occur?

We will consider these questions in the sections that follow.

13.7 Nature of the reactants

In general, reactions in which chemical bonds are broken are slower than reactions in which particles merely undergo rearrangement without bond-breaking. For example, the reaction between H_2 and Cl_2, described in section 13.5, involves rupturing the Cl—Cl bond. In the absence of light, this reaction is relatively slow. On the other hand, the addition of $AgNO_3$ solution to NaCl solution causes the immediate formation of insoluble AgCl (precipitation).

$$AgNO_3 \ (aq) + NaCl \ (aq) \rightarrow AgCl \ (s) + NaNO_3 \ (aq)$$

The reaction is essentially ionic and can be rewritten as

$$Ag^+ \ (aq) + NO_3^- \ (aq) + Na^+ \ (aq) + Cl^- \ (aq) \rightarrow$$
$$AgCl \ (s) + Na^+ \ (aq) + NO_3^- \ (aq)$$

Note that this reaction involves a rearrangement of ions, not the breaking and remaking of bonds.

Reactions in which relatively strong bonds must be broken are generally slower than reactions in which relatively weak bonds must be broken. For example, when $KClO_3$, an ionic solid, is heated, solid KCl and gaseous O_2 are formed. The bond between K^+ and ClO_3^- is a strong ionic bond,

$$O$$

whereas the Cl—O bonds are relatively weak. Thus heating favors the

$$O$$

rupture of the weaker bonds to form O_2 gas. Prolonged heating at very high temperatures is required to break the very stable K—Cl bond.

13.8 Concentration of the reactants

Reactant particles are colliding constantly, but only a few of the collisions result in chemical change. When the concentration of reactants is increased, more reactant particles are present in a given volume. Under these conditions, the number of collisions between reactant particles also increases, producing a larger number of more effective collisions.

At constant temperature, the concentration of a gas is proportional to its pressure. A variation in pressure, therefore, will change the reaction rates of a gaseous system by changing the frequency of collisions.

13.9 Temperature

In Chapter 8, we noted that the temperature of a system reflects the average kinetic energy of the particles in the system. The distribution of kinetic energies for a system at a given temperature can be shown by the curve in Figure 13-5.

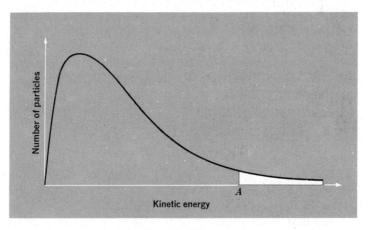

*Fig. 13-5   Distribution of kinetic energies at a
given temperature*

From this curve, known as the Maxwell-Boltzmann energy distribution curve, we note that all the particles do not possess the same kinetic energy. Relatively few particles possess either very low or very high kinetic energy. Most of the particles have moderate kinetic energy.

Suppose that the energy of activation required for an effective collision (the minimum energy required to overcome the potential energy barrier) is at point *A*. The total number of particles with this minimum energy or greater amounts of energy is represented by the white area under the curve from point *A* to the right. These particles equal but a small fraction of all the particles present.

Consider Figure 13–6, in which curve T_1 represents the distribution of energies at temperature T_1. Curve T_2 represents the distribution of energies at the higher temperature, T_2. Point *A*, as before, represents the energy of activation, or the minimum energy required for effective collisions. Compare the areas under each curve at point *A*. Note the number of particles with sufficient energy in system T_2 (hatched and white) as compared with the number of particles in system T_1 (white).

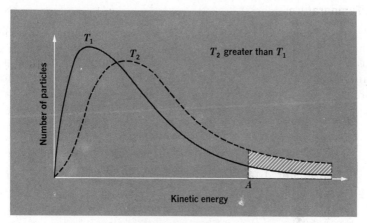

**Fig. 13–6   *Distribution of kinetic energies at
different temperatures***

As the temperature increases, more particles obtain sufficient energy for effective collisions. (It is also true that there will be more collisions per unit time, as in the case of increased concentration; however, the major effect of increased temperature is to provide a number of particles with the necessary kinetic energy sufficient to activate the reaction.) The shape of the Maxwell-Boltzmann curve informs us that a *small* increase in temperature produces a *large* increase in the total number of particles with the necessary activation energy. Thus the effect of small temperature changes on rate is considerable. An approximate rule states that the rate of a reaction is doubled for each 10 C° increase in temperature.

13.10 Catalysis

We have noted that the rusting of iron is a chemical change with a generally slow rate that depends on the environment. For example, experiment shows that the rate of rusting is considerably faster if the environment includes both carbon dioxide and moisture rather than moisture alone. Since rusting is a reaction between Fe and O_2 to form Fe_2O_3, the CO_2 is not essential. Without CO_2, the iron, exposed to moisture and the oxygen of the air, would continue to rust—however, at a slower rate. CO_2 speeds up the reaction; that is, it acts as a catalyst. A *catalyst* is a substance that alters the rate of a reaction without being permanently altered itself.

Whether or not a reaction occurs at all depends on the nature of the reactants, the temperature, and other factors previously described. It does not depend on the presence or absence of a catalyst. Catalysts influence only the *rates* of chemical reactions.

While the details of many catalyzed reactions are still not understood, chemists agree that catalysts influence reaction rates by changing the activation energy requirements of the reaction. Thus a catalyst which speeds up a reaction does so by lowering the potential energy barrier which the reactants must overcome. For the decomposition of hydrogen iodide, the activation energy (potential energy barrier)—symbolized $\Delta H_{act.}$—is approximately 45 kilocalories per mole.

$$2 \text{ HI } (g) \rightarrow H_2 (g) + I_2 (g) \qquad \Delta H_{act.} = 45 \text{ kcal/mole}$$

When this reaction is catalyzed with the metal platinum, the activation energy requirement drops to 25.0 kilocalories per mole. In Figure 13–7 on the following page, the solid line represents the uncatalyzed decomposition of HI; the dashed line shows the energy-lowering effect of the platinum catalyst.

Note that the catalyst does not change the energy of the reactants or the products. Thus the catalyst does not influence the ΔH (change in enthalpy), but it does change the path by which the reaction proceeds.

Certain substances, known as *negative catalysts* or *inhibitors*, retard the rate of a reaction. For example, in the decomposition of HI just discussed, the platinum catalyst has a finely divided surface which *adsorbs* (holds and concentrates) the HI molecules. However, arsenic has a much greater affinity for the platinum surface than does HI. What can we predict, therefore, if arsenic is present in a platinum-catalyzed decomposition of HI? The arsenic will act as a negative catalyst, crowding out the HI molecules. The decomposition of HI will not be able to take the path of lower activation energy, and the reaction rate will be retarded.

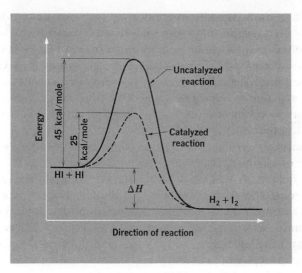

**Fig. 13–7   *Energy profile: catalyzed
reaction***

Let us consider some reasonable explanations of the action of a catalyst.

The catalyst enables the formation of intermediates. Suppose the reaction $A + B \rightarrow AB$ occurs at a very slow rate. In the presence of catalyst C, the rate is increased because the formation of an intermediate product offers a new reaction path that requires lower activation energy.

(1)   SLOW REACTION $A + B \rightarrow AB$

(2*a*)   FAST REACTION $A + C \rightarrow AC$

(2*b*)   FAST REACTION $AC + B \rightarrow AB + C$

Note that catalyst C enters the reaction momentarily at equation 2*a* but is evolved at equation 2*b* unchanged.

The catalyst furnishes a favorable surface for the reaction. The atoms on the surface of a solid catalyst exert forces of attraction for gaseous or liquid reactants. If the catalyst is finely divided, it will have a very large surface area and be capable of adsorbing very large volumes of reactant molecules. For example, it is not unusual for a finely divided metallic catalyst to adsorb several hundred times its own volume of gaseous molecules. The effect of adsorbing, or concentrating, the reactants is to lower the energy required for effective collisions. Thus the catalyst fulfills its role of lowering the activation energy requirement, and the reaction proceeds more rapidly.

13.11 Kinetics and chemical equilibrium

Let us consider the following reaction, shown graphically in Figure 13–8:

$$H_2 \ (g) + I_2 \ (g) \rightarrow 2 \ HI \ (g)$$

Our kinetic model states that as H_2 and I_2 molecules are mixed, they will collide with one another. A certain fraction of all the collisions will favor chemical change. Slowly, more and more HI molecules will form as a result of such favorable collisions.

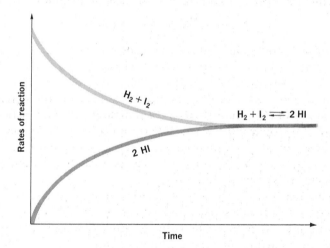

Fig. 13–8   Kinetic profile: reaction of hydrogen and iodine

If the reaction is confined to a closed vessel, the product HI molecules will also collide with one another. The frequency of HI-HI collisions will increase as the concentration of HI increases. Some of the HI-HI collisions will have sufficient energy and the proper geometry to change back to H_2 and I_2. We now have a reaction which is the reverse of the initial one. Soon the rate at which H_2 and I_2 molecules produce HI and the rate at which HI molecules collide to produce H_2 and I_2 become equal. The system has reached a state of equilibrium (see Figure 13–8).

$$H_2 + I_2 \underset{R_2}{\overset{R_1}{\rightleftarrows}} 2 \text{ HI}$$

$$R_1 = \text{forward rate}$$

$$R_2 = \text{reverse rate}$$

$$R_1 = R_2 \text{ at equilibrium}$$

At equilibrium, H_2 and I_2 molecules still collide to form HI, and HI molecules still collide to form H_2 and I_2. However, the rates of the opposing processes are equal ($R_1 = R_2$), which means that no net change in the concentrations of H_2, I_2, or HI occurs. We shall learn more about equilibrium systems in the next chapter.

Multiple-Choice Questions

1. In order for nitrogen and oxygen to react according to the equation

$$N_2 \ (g) + O_2 \ (g) \rightarrow 2 \text{ NO} \ (g)$$

   (1) nitrogen and oxygen particles must first collide (2) the gases must be liquefied (3) a catalyst must be used (4) the product must be dissolved in water

2. When the energy released by the products of a reaction is greater than the energy of activation (1) the reaction stops (2) the reaction is exothermic (3) the product is unstable (4) no collisions take place

3. In a reaction, the activated complex (1) possesses more energy than the reactants or the products (2) acts as a catalyst (3) always forms products (4) is a stable compound

4. A chain reaction (1) consists of a series of steps, each proceeding at a faster rate (2) takes place only in atomic bombs (3) can only be endothermic (4) occurs when the product of one step supplies the energy and starting material for another step

5. In a chain reaction, if the products of the second step unite to form the reactant of the first step (1) an explosion results (2) the chain mechanism is terminated (3) the reaction goes on endlessly (4) a potential energy barrier does not exist

6. Reactions that involve a rearrangement of ions (1) are usually very rapid (2) have high potential energy barriers (3) require the breaking of covalent bonds (4) are always endothermic

7. The rate of a chemical reaction involving liquids only will *not* be influenced by the (1) temperature of the system (2) number of reacting particles per liter (3) stability of the bonds (4) pressure of the system

8. The effect of an increase in temperature on a chemical reaction is to increase the (1) energy of activation (2) concentration of reactants (3) frequency of collisions (4) potential energy barrier

9. One effect of a catalyst is to (1) decrease the energy released in a reaction (2) make a reaction take place when it does not take place without a catalyst (3) decrease the energy of activation for a reaction (4) increase the total energy of the products

10. Surface acting catalysts (contact catalysts) function by (1) attracting reacting particles to the surface (2) increasing the surface of the particles (3) increasing the energy of activation (4) forming precipitates

Completion Questions

1. The study of reaction rates is called chemical _____.

2. According to the collision theory, before substances A and B can react, they must first _____.

3. The minimum amount of energy that must be present before the particles in a chemical system can react is called the _____.

4. If the reaction A + B → AB is exothermic, the reaction AB → A + B must be _____.

5. A photochemical reaction is one that uses energy in the form of _____.

6. If a reaction proceeds in steps, the _____ (*reactant, product*) of the first step is the _____ (*reactant, product*) of the second step.

7. A substance that decreases the rate of a chemical reaction is called a (an) _____.

8. The function of a catalyst is to provide a different reaction path that requires a lower energy of _____.

9. Some catalysts act by forming an intermediate product which reacts by another step to re-form the _____.

True-False Questions

1. The energy of activation of a reaction depends on the energy required to *form* chemical bonds.

2. A temporary, unstable unit that forms when the particles in a chemical reaction collide is called *an activated complex*.

3. At a given temperature, the rate of a reaction with a large energy of activation is *greater than* the rate of a reaction with a small energy of activation.

4. The rates of chemical reactions between *liquids* are greatly influenced by pressure.

5. When the temperature of a gas is increased, the number of molecules with *low* energies decreases.

6. At a specific temperature for a given gas, the number of molecules with very high energies is *greater than* the number of molecules with moderate energies.

7. If the addition of a catalyst lowers the energy of activation for the reaction A + B → AB, then the addition of the catalyst *raises* the energy of activation for the reverse reaction, AB → A + B.

8. Some catalysts function by forming an intermediate product at a *faster* rate than the rate of the uncatalyzed reaction.

Decreases, Increases, Remains the Same

1. If the energy of activation for a reaction is high without a catalyst but is lower with a catalyst, then the addition of a catalyst causes the heat of the reaction to _____.

2. In a chemical reaction, if the amount of substance that changes per unit time increases, the rate of the reaction _____.

3. When the energy of activation of a system increases, the height of the potential energy barrier _____.

4. If the speed of the rate-determining step in a chemical change increases, the rate of the complete reaction _____.

5. When the strength of the bonds in the reacting particles increases, the rate of reaction of the particles _____.

6. When the concentration of reacting particles in a chemical system increases, the number of collisions per second _____.

7. As the temperature of a system increases, the energy of activation for a reaction _____.

8. If a reaction releases energy without the use of a catalyst, the amount of energy released with the addition of a catalyst _____.

9. At equilibrium, if the rate of the reaction in one direction increases, the rate of the reaction in the opposite direction _____.

Exercises for Review

1. Explain why steel wool rusts much more rapidly than an iron nail of the same weight.

2. Using the concept of energy of activation, explain why a flame must be brought to a mixture of hydrogen and oxygen before the mixture explodes.

3. Nitrogen and oxygen can be united when an electric spark passes through a mixture of the two gases. The equation is

$$N_2 \ (g) + O_2 \ (g) \rightarrow 2 \ NO \ (g)$$

Indicate the bonds that must be broken and the bonds that form in this reaction.

4. Draw an energy diagram for the reaction

$$H_2 \ (g) + I_2 \ (g) \rightarrow 2 \ HI \ (g) + 5.9 \ kcal/mole$$

In the diagram, label the energy of activation and the energy changes for the complete reaction.

5. *a.* What is meant by a potential energy barrier?
   b. Explain how it applies to a chemical reaction.

6. *a.* Draw an energy diagram for the reaction $CO \ (g) + \frac{1}{2} \ O_2 \ (g) \rightarrow CO_2 \ (g) +$ heat.
   b. What bond(s) must be broken before the product forms?

7. *a.* Does a catalyst enter into a chemical reaction? Explain.
   b. Is it correct to say that the total mass of a catalyst does not change because of a chemical reaction? Explain.

8. *a.* Does a catalyst have any effect on the enthalpy change of a reaction?
   b. Does a catalyst have any effect on the energy of activation of a reaction?
   c. Explain any differences in the two effects.

Exercises for Further Study

1. *a.* Applying the collision theory to the reaction $H_2 \ (g) + I_2 \ (g) \rightarrow 2 \ HI \ (g)$, what effect would there be on the frequency of collisions if only the concentration of H_2 were doubled?
   b. What effect would there be on the frequency of collisions if the concentrations of both H_2 and I_2 were doubled?

2. In terms of the types of bonds present, explain why the reaction between solutions of hydrochloric acid, HCl, and sodium hydroxide, NaOH, takes place very rapidly, while the reaction for the decomposition of hydrogen peroxide, H_2O_2, takes place slowly.

3. A mixture of hydrogen and chlorine gases can combine explosively. However, if the mixture contains a very large amount of one gas and a much smaller amount of the other gas, there is no explosion although the gases may combine. Explain.

4. Nitrogen dioxide decomposes when heated according to the equation $2 \, NO_2 \, (g) \rightarrow 2 \, NO \, (g) + O_2 \, (g)$.

    a. Draw an energy diagram for the changes that take place.

    b. Write the formula for a possible activated complex that may form.

    c. Name the bonds that are broken and formed during the reaction.

5. *a.* Draw an energy diagram for the reaction $A + B \rightarrow AB$, in which $\Delta H = -Q$ kcal/mole. Show that the energies of activation for the forward and reverse reactions are not equal.

    b. Show that the enthalpy changes for the forward and reverse reactions are the same except that the signs are different.

6. The equation for the formation of ammonia from nitrogen and hydrogen is

$$N_2 \, (g) + 3 \, H_2 \, (g) \rightarrow 2 \, NH_3 \, (g) + heat$$

    a. Is it probable that the reaction takes place in the manner shown by the equation? Explain.

    b. List the bonds that must be broken and formed. Suggest a possible series of steps by which this can occur.

7. A mixture of hydrogen and chlorine gases remains stable in the dark but explodes in the presence of light. Explain.

Chapter 14

EQUILIBRIUM

14.1 Introduction

We have learned that some of the changes that matter undergoes are spontaneous. If the change is exothermic, such as burning, the gaseous products possess minimum energy and maximum randomness. If the change is endothermic and spontaneous, such as the evaporation of a liquid, the increase in randomness of the gas compensates for the increase in energy. These changes may be summarized thus:

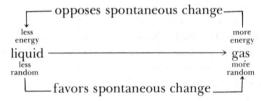

Both exothermic and endothermic changes occur when particles of matter collide with sufficient energy to break old bonds and form new bonds.

14.2 Reversible changes

In this chapter, we will study changes that may occur in opposite directions; that is, the products of the change may re-form the original substances. First the particles of the reactant species attain sufficient energy at the proper temperature to break existing bonds and form another species with a new bonding arrangement. Then, at this same temperature, the particles of the product species also collide effectively and re-form the reactant species. The comparative strengths of the bonds in the reactant species and in the product species determine the extent to which the reaction proceeds in a given direction. The comparative bond strengths, therefore, determine the fraction of the starting materials that are converted to form products.

Consider the reaction in which molecules of A_2 gas react with molecules of B_2 gas to form molecules of AB gas. At a given temperature, the bonds of a definite fraction of the molecules of A_2 and B_2 will break. Then the particles in the new, intermediate species will collide to form AB, which has a more stable bonding arrangement. These changes may occur in three steps.

$$A_2 \rightarrow 2\ A$$

$$B_2 \rightarrow 2\ B$$

$$2\ A + 2\ B \rightarrow 2\ AB$$

The particles of AB, at the same temperature, may also collide; the rupture of their bonds will re-form some A_2 and B_2.

$$2\ AB \rightarrow A_2 + B_2$$

The equation for the complete reaction is written with a double arrow, the arrows pointing in opposite directions.

$$A_2\ (g) + B_2\ (g) \rightleftarrows 2\ AB\ (g)$$

Many changes that take place in matter can occur in opposite directions. We have already studied some of these changes, which are called *reversible reactions*. For example, hydrogen and iodine unite to form hydrogen iodide, which can decompose to re-form hydrogen and iodine. As another example, liquid water evaporates to form gaseous water, which can condense to re-form liquid water.

14.3 Saturated solutions

Now let us look more deeply into a common reversible system — a saturated solution of a solid in water. For example, the solubility curve of NaCl reveals that at 20° C, 100 ml of water will dissolve approximately 35 g of NaCl. This is the composition of the saturated solution at that temperature. If additional solid is placed in the solution, an amount equal to that added drops to the bottom of the container. We have already learned that the solution of an ionic solid in water contains aquated ions.

$$NaCl\ (s) \rightarrow Na^+\ (aq) + Cl^-\ (aq)$$

We have also found that the aquated ions can recombine to form the solid, thus reversing the reaction. Since the total quantity of solid NaCl remains unchanged, we assumed that the rates of the opposing changes — the rate of dissolving and the rate of crystallization — were the same. Consequently, we defined a saturated solution as a solution in which the solid solute is in equilibrium with the dissolved solute, in this case, aquated ions of the solute.

Saturated solutions are, by definition, examples of reversible systems. When the rate of dissolving equals the rate of crystallization, the system has attained equilibrium. Therefore, the rate at which the bonds in the crystal lattice break equals the rate at which the aquated ions combine to re-form the crystalline solid. The composition of the equilibrium mixture (the concentrations of reactants and products) depends on the solubility of the solid. For example, the table of solubilities shows that at $20°$ C

10 g of $KClO_3$ dissolve in 100 ml of water

35 g of NaCl dissolve in 100 ml of water

145 g of KI dissolve in 100 ml of water

If additional solid can dissolve in a solution at a given temperature, the solution is *unsaturated.* Additional solid will continue to dissolve until the solution becomes saturated. Under certain conditions, the concentration of a solution such as sodium acetate may be greater than that required for saturation, and the solution is *supersaturated.* Such solutions are unstable and tend to crystallize until they attain equilibrium, forming a saturated solution.

14.4 Chemical equilibrium

The principles relating to equilibria in saturated solutions also apply to chemical reactions if they take place in a closed system. Matter cannot enter or leave a *closed system,* but energy can enter or leave. A sealed tube represents a closed system because the total matter in the tube cannot be changed but can be made hotter or colder by the application or withdrawal of heat. Matter and energy can enter or leave an *open system.* An open beaker of water represents an open system in which both matter and energy can enter or leave. In a closed system at a fixed temperature, a reaction may be reversible and may reach equilibrium.

Consider the reaction between gaseous hydrogen and bromine vapor in a sealed tube at $1000°$ C.

$$H_2 \ (g) + Br_2 \ (g) \rightleftarrows 2 \ HBr \ (g)$$

Analysis of the mixture present in the tube reveals that at equilibrium the reaction has proceeded largely to the right: 99.5% of the H_2 and Br_2 has combined, and about 0.5% of the reactants has not combined. At $1000°$ C, therefore, the covalent bond that unites H and Br in HBr is much more stable than the covalent bonds that unite the H atoms in the H_2 molecule and the Br atoms in the Br_2 molecule.

Recall from Chapter 13 that the rate of a reaction is influenced by concentration and temperature. By concentration is meant the number of particles (moles) per unit volume; for example, grams (or moles) per liter. If the temperature in the reaction vessel is fixed, the rate of reaction depends on concentration.

An increase in the number of reacting particles increases the likelihood of effective collisions. If the forward reaction proceeds more rapidly than the backward reaction, a larger concentration of product species is obtained. As the concentrations of the reacting species diminish, the forward reaction proceeds more slowly. Because the concentration of the product species has been increased, the backward reaction proceeds more rapidly.

Experiment reveals that if we start with HBr, at 1000° C, about 0.5% of the HBr has decomposed. The concentrations of reactants and product are such as to make the rates of the opposing reactions equal. At this level of concentration, the HBr decomposes as rapidly as it forms. *Visual* examination of the reaction vessel reveals no change in the composition of the reactants and product. Note, however, that both changes occur simultaneously at the same rate. At the molecular level, therefore, the equilibrium state represents a dynamic rather than a static condition in which the forward reaction proceeds at the same rate as the backward reaction. Under the same conditions, the equilibrium state may be approached from either direction without affecting the concentrations of reactants and products.

14.5 The composition of the equilibrium mixture

From the previous section, we can conclude: At a fixed temperature and at fixed initial concentrations of reactants, the composition of an equilibrium mixture is constant. What determines the composition of an equilibrium mixture? At a fixed temperature, how much of the reactant species and how much of the product species that will be present at equilibrium are determined by the initial concentrations of the reactants?

In the reaction $H_2 + Br_2 \rightleftarrows 2$ HBr, assume that we start with 0.1 mole of each reactant in a vessel that has a volume of 1 liter. Equilibrium is attained at a certain temperature after 0.09 mole of HBr has formed. What is the composition of the equilibrium mixture? Set up the problem in the following form:

$$H_2 + Br_2 \rightleftarrows 2 \text{ HBr}$$

	H_2	Br_2	HBr
INITIAL CONCENTRATIONS (moles/l)	0.1	0.1	0
EQUILIBRIUM CONCENTRATIONS (moles/l)	?	?	0.09

The molar relations in the balanced reaction and the initial concentrations of reactants determine the composition of the equilibrium mixture. From the equation, we see that for every mole of HBr formed, 0.5 mole of H_2 and 0.5 mole of Br_2 are required. Thus to form 0.09 mole of HBr, we require 0.045 mole of H_2 and 0.045 mole of Br_2. At equilibrium, the composition of the mixture is

$$H_2 \ \ = 0.1 \text{ mole} - 0.045 \text{ mole} = 0.055 \text{ mole}$$

$$Br_2 \ = 0.1 \text{ mole} - 0.045 \text{ mole} = 0.055 \text{ mole}$$

$$HBr = 0.09 \text{ mole}$$

If more H_2 and Br_2 are used, more HBr will be formed; and more H_2 and Br_2 will remain in the equilibrium mixture. If we start with the same concentrations of H_2 and Br_2, but the temperature is changed, then the amounts of H_2, Br_2, and HBr at equilibrium will be different.

We can calculate the composition of an equilibrium mixture by the following steps:

1. Note the molar relations in the balanced reaction.
2. Note the given equilibrium concentration of any one species in the reaction.
3. From the molar relations, compute the necessary concentrations of the other substances required to form the given equilibrium concentration.
4. By subtraction, determine the composition of the entire equilibrium mixture.

As a further example, consider the generalized reaction

$$2 \text{ A} + 3 \text{ B} \rightleftarrows \text{C} + \text{D}$$

for a 1-liter system at equilibrium. Assume the following data:

	A	B	C	D
INITIAL CONCENTRATIONS (moles/l)	2	1	0	0
EQUILIBRIUM CONCENTRATIONS (moles/l)	?	?	0.2	?

If 0.2 mole of C is formed at equilibrium, the molar relations reveal that 0.2 mole of D is also formed. Twice as much A, or 0.4 mole, and three times as much B, or 0.6 mole, are therefore required. The composition of the equilibrium mixture is shown on the next page.

A = 2 moles − 0.4 mole = 1.6 moles

B = 1 mole − 0.6 mole = 0.4 mole

C = 0.2 mole (given)

D = 0.2 mole (from the molar relations in the equation)

14.6 Factors that control equilibrium

In Chapter 13, we discussed the factors that determine the rate of a reaction: concentration, surface area, temperature, and the presence of a catalyst. Once equilibrium has been attained, only a change in those rate factors that affect the opposing reactions differently will tend to upset the equilibrium. Surface area (involving reactions between two phases only) and the presence of a catalyst affect the rates of the opposing reactions equally. Therefore, these rate factors do not upset an equilibrium. However, changes in the concentrations of reactants (or changes in pressure, if any of the reactants are gaseous) and changes in temperature cause the equilibrium point to change. The composition of the equilibrium mixture adjusts to compensate for these changes.

Do not confuse the factors that determine the *rate* of a reaction with the factors that *drive* a reaction in a particular direction. The rate of a reaction is determined by concentration and temperature. The driving force of a reaction represents the competition between the tendency to reach a state of minimum energy and the tendency to reach a state of maximum randomness.

14.7 Applying Le Chatelier's Principle to an equilibrium

The principle formulated by Le Chatelier, discussed in section 9.7, enables us to predict the effect of concentration changes, pressure changes, and temperature changes on a system in equilibrium. This principle may be stated as follows:

If a system in equilibrium is subjected to a stress (a change in concentration, a change in pressure, or a change in temperature), the system adjusts to partially relieve the stress. This is the same as saying that a change in the concentrations of the reactants (or pressures if the reactants are gaseous) or a change in temperature of the system favors either the forward or the backward reaction. The change produces a system with new equilibrium concentrations.

14.8 How does concentration affect equilibrium?

As the concentrations of reactants increase, the likelihood of effective collisions becomes greater. Thus the rate of reaction also increases. If a system is at equilibrium and the concentrations of the reactant species are increased, the equilibrium shifts toward the right, that is, toward the formation of a larger concentration of the product species. This means that the new equilibrium mixture will contain more product. According to Le Chatelier's Principle: An equilibrium system will offset the stress of an increase in the concentration of reactants by forming more product. Conversely, an equilibrium system will offset the stress of an increase in the concentration of product by forming more reactants.

The commercial preparation of hydrogen chloride gas from salt illustrates an important application of Le Chatelier's Principle. The reaction, which occurs below 500° C, is

$$NaCl + H_2SO_4 \rightleftarrows NaHSO_4 + HCl \ (g)$$

A high concentration of H_2SO_4 drives the reaction to the right, consuming almost all the NaCl. Furthermore, the gaseous product, HCl, is continuously being removed, which acts as another stress. To relieve this stress, the equilibrium shifts to form more HCl.

14.9 How does pressure affect equilibrium?

We noted in sections 9.4 and 9.17 that solids and liquids are virtually incompressible. This means that equilibrium systems involving solids and liquids will not react appreciably to changes in pressure. However, the volume (concentration) of a gas, at constant temperature, is determined by its pressure.

According to Avogadro (see section 8.17), equal volumes of gases at the same temperature and pressure contain the same number of molecules (moles). The volume of a gas, therefore, is proportional to the number of molecules (moles). The equation

$$H_2 \ (g) + Br_2 \ (g) \rightleftarrows 2 \ HBr \ (g)$$

states that 1 mole of H_2 gas reacts with 1 mole of Br_2 gas to form 2 moles of HBr gas. Since the volumes of the gases are proportional to the number of moles, the equation also states that 1 volume of H_2 reacts with 1 volume of Br_2 to form 2 volumes of HBr. Note that the total volume of the reactants equals the volume of the product.

If the pressure on this system is increased, the volume of the reactants and the volume of the product undergo the same change. Thus a change in pressure on such an equilibrium system does not constitute a stress. A change in pressure will have no effect on the composition of this equilibrium mixture.

In the equilibrium

$$PBr_3 \ (g) + Br_2 \ (g) \rightleftarrows PBr_5 \ (g)$$

note that a total of 2 moles of gas (1 mole of phosphorus tribromide and 1 mole of bromine) react to form 1 mole of gas (phosphorus pentabromide). In this system, a change of pressure has a different effect on the volumes of the reactants and on the volume of the product. Thus a change of pressure constitutes a stress on this equilibrium system. To offset the stress, the equilibrium shifts toward the direction which absorbs the stress. An increase in pressure shifts the equilibrium toward the formation of more product because the smaller volume of the product offsets this change in pressure. Similarly, a decrease in pressure favors the production of more reactants because the larger volume of reactants offsets this change.

Summarizing the effect of a change in pressure (at constant temperature) on an equilibrium involving gases:

1. An increase in pressure favors the direction that produces a smaller number of moles (smaller volume).
2. A decrease in pressure favors the direction that produces a larger number of moles (larger volume).
3. A change in pressure has no effect on the equilibrium if the number of moles of products equals the number of moles of reactants.

14.10 How does temperature affect equilibrium?

Consider the generalized equilibrium

$$A \ (g) + B \ (g) \rightleftarrows C \ (g) + heat$$

The positive value of the heat term indicates that the forward reaction is exothermic and the backward reaction is endothermic. To use Le Chatelier's Principle to predict the effect of a change in temperature on an equilibrium system, we must know in which direction the reaction liberates or absorbs heat.

According to Le Chatelier, a change in temperature (stress) is offset in the direction which partially relieves the change. If a system comes to equilibrium with a net release of heat (exothermic), an increase in temperature favors the endothermic reaction. Similarly, if a system comes to equilibrium with a net absorption of heat (endothermic), an increase in temperature again favors the endothermic reaction. Increasing the temperature in the equilibrium system

$$H_2 \ (g) + Br_2 \ (g) \rightleftarrows 2 \ HBr \ (g) + heat$$

drives the system to the left, increasing the concentrations of the reactants in the equilibrium mixture and decreasing the concentration of the product. However, increasing the temperature in the equilibrium system

$$N_2 \ (g) + O_2 \ (g) \rightleftarrows 2 \ NO \ (g) - heat$$

drives the system to the right, since the formation of product requires the absorption of heat. Thus an increase in temperature on an endothermic system causes an increase in the concentration of the product or products in the equilibrium mixture.

14.11 Summary of displacements in gaseous equilibria

The following table summarizes the applications of Le Chatelier's Principle to changes of concentration, pressure, and temperature in gaseous equilibrium systems.

STRESS	DIRECTION OF DISPLACEMENT OF EQUILIBRIUM
$A \ (g) + B \ (g) \rightleftarrows C \ (g) + heat$	
increased concentration of A or B	⟶
increased concentration of C	⟵
increased pressure	⟶
decreased pressure	⟵
increased temperature	⟵
decreased temperature	⟶
$2 \ A \ (g) + B \ (g) \rightleftarrows 2 \ C \ (g) + 2 \ D \ (g) - heat$	
increased concentration of A or B	⟶
increased concentration of C or D	⟵
increased pressure	⟵
decreased pressure	⟶
increased temperature	⟶
decreased temperature	⟵

14.12 A practical application of Le Chatelier's Principle

Ammonia, NH_3, an extremely important raw material in the preparation of nitrates and ammonium compounds, is prepared commercially by the Haber process. The equation is

$$N_2 (g) + 3 H_2 (g) \rightleftarrows 2 NH_3 (g) + 22 \text{ kcal}$$

Note that this system comes to equilibrium with a release of heat. Since all the species in the reaction are gases, an increase in the pressure of the system will tend to increase the concentrations of both reactants and products. However, the number of moles (the volume) of the product is one-half the total number of moles (the volume) of the reactants. An increase in pressure, according to Le Chatelier, is offset by the formation of more product.

To insure conversion of reactants to product in a reasonably short time, the rate of reaction must be increased. This can be done by increasing the temperature. However, how will the temperature increase affect the equilibrium? As stated previously, an increase in the temperature of a system that releases heat favors the endothermic change (formation of reactants). A high temperature, therefore, would drive the reaction to the left.

In actual practice, a catalyst is employed to reach equilibrium rapidly. The reaction proceeds rapidly around 700° C, but the yield of ammonia is low, as predicted by Le Chatelier's Principle. A compromise is achieved between a temperature that increases the rate of reaching equilibrium and a temperature that does not drive the reaction backward too far. The Haber process provides a satisfactory yield of ammonia at temperatures between 450° C and 600° C and pressures between 400 and 600 atmospheres.

14.13 The quantitative aspects of equilibrium

Thus far, we have considered the principles of equilibrium in a qualitative manner; that is, we have merely expressed the proportions of reactant to product in the equilibrium mixture. Chemists, however, seek to convey information in quantitative terms, extending the usefulness of qualitative principles.

The Norwegian scientists Cato Guldberg and Peter Waage investigated the quantitative relationships that determine the rate of a reaction. In 1846, they summarized their findings in the following law:

Law of Mass Action: The rate of a reaction is directly proportional to the product of the molar concentrations of the reacting species.

From the Law of Mass Action, we can develop a quantitative relationship that expresses the concentrations of all the species in an equilibrium.

Consider the generalized equilibrium reaction

$$A + B \rightleftarrows C + D$$

Let R_1 equal the rate of the forward reaction. R_1 depends on the frequency of collisions and is proportional to the product of the molecular (molar) concentrations of A and B. Expressed mathematically,

$$R_1 = k_1 \times [A][B]$$

where k_1 is the proportionality constant, or rate constant, for the forward reaction (discussed in Chapter 13). The brackets [ ] represent the concentration of a species in moles/liter. This notation will be used throughout this book.

For the reverse reaction,

$$R_2 = k_2 \times [C][D]$$

where R_2 is the rate of the reverse reaction, and k_2 is the rate constant of the reverse reaction.

At equilibrium, the forward and reverse reactions proceed at equal rates. Therefore, $R_1 = R_2$, and

$$k_1 \times [A][B] = k_2 \times [C][D]$$

If the generalized reaction is

$$2\,A + 3\,B \rightleftarrows C + 2\,D$$

$$k_1 \times [A][A][B][B][B] = k_2 \times [C][D][D]$$

$$k_1 \times [A]^2[B]^3 = k_2 \times [C][D]^2$$

Further generalizing the reaction, we obtain

$$n\,A + m\,B \rightleftarrows x\,C + y\,D$$

$$k_1 \times [A]^n[B]^m = k_2 \times [C]^x[D]^y$$

Dividing both sides by k_2 and rearranging the terms, we obtain

$$\frac{k_1}{k_2} = \frac{[C]^x[D]^y}{[A]^n[B]^m}$$

Dividing one constant by another yields a quotient that is also constant, and the expression becomes

$$K_C = \frac{[C]^x [D]^y}{[A]^n [B]^m}$$

The constant K_C is called the *equilibrium constant.*

14.14 Significance of the equilibrium constant

In the expression for the equilibrium constant, note that each concentration is raised to a power equal to the number of moles of the species in the balanced reaction. At a given temperature, therefore, the product of the molar concentrations of products divided by the product of the molar concentrations of reactants (all concentrations raised to the proper powers) is a constant. This means that an infinite number of concentrations can satisfy the value of K_C.

What happens to the concentrations of products and the concentrations of reactants when K_C changes? In the three following examples, we will assume we are dealing with the generalized reaction $A + B \rightleftarrows C + D$ in which we start with equal initial concentrations of A and B.

1. K_C *equals* 1. At equilibrium, the concentrations of products *equal* the concentrations of reactants.
2. K_C is *greater* than 1. At equilibrium, the concentrations of products are *greater* than the concentrations of reactants.
3. K_C is *less* than 1. At equilibrium, the concentrations of products are *less* than the concentrations of reactants.

14.15 Calculating K_C from an experiment

K_C may be calculated from an experimental study of an equilibrium system. Solutions of iron(III) compounds react with solutions of thiocyanate (SCN^-) compounds to form an ionic species ($FeSCN^{+2}$) that has a deep red color. From this color, the equilibrium concentration can be measured. Assume the initial concentration of Fe^{+3} (*aq*) is 4×10^{-2} mole/l and SCN^- (*aq*) is 10^{-3} mole/l. The equilibrium concentration of $FeSCN^{+2}$ (*aq*) is 9.2×10^{-4} mole/l.

The equation that represents the equilibrium is

$$Fe^{+3} \ (aq) + SCN^- \ (aq) \rightleftarrows FeSCN^{+2} \ (aq)$$
thiocyano-iron(III)

The remaining equilibrium concentrations may be determined in the manner shown in section 14.5. .

$$[Fe^{+3} \ (aq)]_{equil.} = [Fe^{+3} \ (aq)]_{initial} - [SCN^- \ (aq)]_{equil.}$$

$$= 4.2 \times 10^{-2} - 9.2 \times 10^{-4}$$

$$= 3.9 \times 10^{-2}$$

$$[SCN^- \ (aq)]_{equil.} = [SCN^- \ (aq)]_{initial} - [SCN^- \ (aq)]_{equil.}$$

$$= 10^{-3} - 9.2 \times 10^{-4}$$

$$= 8 \times 10^{-5}$$

$$K_C = \frac{[FeSCN^{+2} \ (aq)]}{[Fe^{+3} \ (aq)][SCN^- \ (aq)]}$$

$$= \frac{9.2 \times 10^{-4}}{3.9 \times 10^{-2} \times 8 \times 10^{-5}} = 290 \ (approximately)$$

If K_C is known, it becomes possible to calculate the equilibrium concentrations of the products and the reactants.

Multiple-Choice Questions

1. In a solution that is unsaturated (1) an unbalanced equilibrium exists (2) the dissolving process occurs at a faster rate than the crystallizing process when more solute is added (3) increasing the temperature has no effect on the rate of solution (4) the concentration of solute is always low

2. For all systems at equilibrium (1) temperature and pressure have equal effects (2) no energy of activation is required (3) no changes occur at a molecular level (4) two opposing changes occur at the same rates

3. Increasing the initial concentrations of reactants (1) has no effect on a reaction (2) increases the energy produced per mole of reactant (3) has no effect on the reverse reaction (4) increases the number of collisions per second

4. When a stress is applied to a system at equilibrium (1) the reaction is driven to the left (2) the equilibrium is altered to relieve the stress (3) a new product forms (4) the reaction is driven to the right

5. For a chemical equilibrium involving gaseous reactants and products, an increase in pressure (1) always displaces the equilibrium to form more of the products (2) displaces the equilibrium in the direction in which the number of moles of molecules decreases (3) always displaces the equilibrium to form more of the reactants (4) has no effect on the equilibrium

6. In the reaction $N_2 (g) + 3 H_2 (g) \rightleftarrows 2 NH_3 (g) + 22$ kcal, maximum formation of NH_3 occurs when (1) the temperature and pressure are increased (2) the temperature and pressure are decreased (3) the temperature is decreased, and the pressure is increased (4) the temperature is increased, and the pressure is decreased

7. The use of a catalyst in a reaction that goes to equilibrium (1) displaces the equilibrium to form more of the product (2) increases the energy released (3) increases the rates of the forward and the reverse reactions (4) decreases the rates of the forward and the reverse reactions

8. The Law of Mass Action describes (1) the relationship between mass and energy in a nuclear change (2) the concentrations of reactants and products at equilibrium (3) the quantity of matter produced in a chemical reaction (4) the rate at which a reaction reaches equilibrium

9. An equilibrium constant will not remain constant (1) if the temperature of the system changes (2) if the concentrations of reactants are changed (3) if the concentrations of products change (4) if a catalyst is used

10. The equation for the equilibrium constant $K_C = \dfrac{[C]^2}{[A] \times [B]^2}$ is correct for the reaction

   (1) $A + 2 B \rightleftarrows 2 C$ (3) $2 C \rightleftarrows A + 2 B$

   (2) $A + B_2 \rightleftarrows C_2$ (4) $2 A + B \rightleftarrows 2 C$

11. In a saturated solution (1) the processes of dissolving and crystallization occur at equal rates (2) energy is always released (3) energy is always absorbed (4) the processes of dissolving and crystallization occur at different rates

Completion Questions

1. A solution with excess solid in which the rate of dissolving exceeds the rate of crystallization is called a (an) _____ solution.

2. When two opposite processes are occurring in a system at equal rates, the system is in a condition of _____.

3. The effect of a stress on the position of equilibrium in a system is described by _____ Principle.

4. A change in pressure will have no effect on the position of equilibrium for the reaction X_2 (g) + Y_2 (g) $\rightleftarrows$ 2 XY (g) because the _____ of reactants and products are equal.

5. For a system in equilibrium, a decrease in temperature will favor the reaction which _____ heat.

6. The Haber process for the manufacture of _____ is an example of an industrial application of the principles of equilibrium.

7. In a solution of a weak acid, an equilibrium exists betweeen the molecules of the acid and the _____ that the acid forms in water.

8. Consider a 0.1 M solution of the weak acid HX in water. If the concentration of X^- ion is 0.01 M, then the concentration of molecular HX in equilibrium is _____ M.

True-False Questions

1. If the rate of crystallization in a solution with excess solid occurs more rapidly than the rate of dissolving, the solution is *saturated.*

2. When two reactants are mixed, the rate of the reaction is *greatest* soon after mixing because then the concentration of reactants is greatest.

3. If a system is at equilibrium and a change is brought about in the system which affects the forward and reverse reactions equally, the equilibrium is *not changed.*

4. In the Haber process, the temperature is kept moderately high because the rate of attaining equilibrium is *fast* at lower temperatures.

5. For the reaction 2 A (g) + B (g) $\rightleftarrows$ A_2B (g), doubling the concentration of A will have *a greater* effect on the rate of the reaction than doubling the concentration of B.

6. In a 0.1 M solution of acetic acid, a weak acid, the concentration of acetate ion is *equal to* 0.1 M.

7. When *molecular* solids dissolve in water, the solution contains aquated ions.

8. After crystallization takes place in a supersaturated solution, the solution formed is *unsaturated.*

9. When additional solute is added to *saturated* solutions, the rate of the dissolving process increases.

10. In a spontaneous endothermic change, the tendency toward maximum randomness is *greater than* the tendency toward minimum energy.

Decreases, Increases, Remains the Same

1. When additional solute is added to a saturated solution, the rate of the dissolving process _____.
2. Consider the reaction A + B ⇄ AB. From the moment that A and B are mixed, the rate of the forward reaction _____, while the rate of the reverse reaction _____.
3. When the concentrations of the reactants are increased in a system at equilibrium, the rate of formation of products _____.
4. Given: the reaction A + B ⇄ C + heat. When the temperature is increased, the rate of the forward reaction _____.
5. In the reaction X (g) + Y (g) ⇄ XY (s), increasing the pressure displaces the equilibrium so that the formation of XY (s) _____.
6. Given: the reaction A + B ⇄ C + D. If the concentration of A is doubled and, at the same time, the concentration of B is reduced by one-half, the rate of the reaction to the right _____.
7. As the ionization of a weak acid increases, the concentration of the molecular form of the acid _____.
8. As a solution of a solid in water becomes more concentrated, the rate of the crystallization process _____.

Exercises for Review

1. Given: a saturated solution of copper(II) sulfate, $CuSO_4$; an unsaturated solution of $CuSO_4$; and a supersaturated solution of $CuSO_4$. A small crystal of $CuSO_4$ is added to each solution. Compare the rate of dissolving with the rate of crystallization in each of the three solutions.
2. Given: the reaction AB ⇄ A + B. We start with 0.1 mole/l of AB; at equilibrium, 20% has decomposed. What are the equilibrium concentrations of AB, A, and B?
3. Explain how it is possible for changes to occur in an equilibrium system without macroscopic changes being in evidence.
4. Consider the reaction X + Y ⇄ XY. We start with 0.1 M X and 0.1 M Y and find that at equilibrium the concentration of XY is 0.04 M. What fraction of X has been changed to XY?
5. Consider the reaction P_2 + Q_2 ⇄ 2 PQ, starting with 0.2 M P_2 and 0.2 M Q_2.
   a. At equilibrium, the concentration of PQ is 0.05 M. What are the equilibrium concentrations of P_2 and Q_2?
   b. What fraction of P_2 has been converted to product?

6. What is meant by a stress applied to a chemical equilibrium?

7. Write the equation for finding the equilibrium constant, K_C, for the reaction $3\,O_2 \rightleftarrows 2\,O_3$.

Exercises for Further Study

1. Crushed ice mixed with water represents an equilibrium system.
   a. Write the equation for the change of state, showing the heat term.
   b. What is the effect of adding small amounts of heat?

2. The reaction $A + B \rightleftarrows C + D$ can be started with A and B or with C and D.
   a. Compare the rates of the reaction to the right and the reaction to the left when A and B are the starting materials or when C and D are the starting materials.
   b. How do the equilibrium concentrations compare in the two cases?

3. Finely crushed copper(II) sulfate crystals are added to a saturated solution of copper(II) sulfate. When the solution is allowed to stand in a closed container for several weeks, larger crystals form. How does this experiment show that an equilibrium exists between the processes of dissolving and crystallizing?

4. When an ionic solid such as sodium nitrate, $NaNO_3$, dissolves in water, it forms aquated ions.
   a. Write the equation for the equilibrium in a saturated solution of $NaNO_3$.
   b. What bonds are broken and formed in the process of dissolving?

5. Consider the reaction $2\,X + Y \rightleftarrows X_2Y$, starting with 2 moles/l of X and 1 mole/l of Y. At equilibrium, 75% of Y has been used up. Find the equilibrium concentrations of X, Y, and X_2Y.

6. Given: the reaction $2\,SO_2\,(g) + O_2\,(g) \rightleftarrows 2\,SO_3\,(g)$ + heat.
   a. How will increasing the pressure affect the amount of product?
   b. How will increasing the temperature affect the amount of product?

7. Write the equation for the equilibrium constant, K_C, for the reaction

$$4\,NH_3\,(g) + 5\,O_2\,(g) \rightleftarrows 4\,NO\,(g) + 6\,H_2O\,(g)$$

8. Why is it likely that most reactions in closed systems will proceed in both directions rather than in one direction?

9. Does a value of 1 for K_C always indicate equal concentrations of reactants and products at equilibrium? Explain.

10. Using Le Chatelier's Principle, explain why ice melts more rapidly with increasing pressure.

Chapter 15

IONIC EQUILIBRIA

15.1 Introduction

We have learned from conductivity experiments that solutions differ in their ability to conduct an electric current. Whether or not a solution is an effective conductor depends on the presence of charge carriers, or mobile ions, in the solution. From a study of the data gathered in conductivity experiments, we may list three classes of solutions:

1. Strong electrolytes are solutions that are good conductors of electricity because of the presence of large numbers of ions. Examples of strong electrolytes are solutions of ionic solids such as $NaCl$, $CaCl_2$, Na_3PO_4, $NaOH$, and $Ca(OH)_2$; and solutions of strong acids such as HCl, H_2SO_4, and HNO_3.
2. Nonelectrolytes are solutions that do not conduct electricity because of the absence of ions. Examples of nonelectrolytes are solutions of covalently bonded compounds such as glucose and glycerine.
3. Weak electrolytes are solutions that conduct electricity poorly because of the presence of only a small number of ions. Examples of weak electrolytes are solutions of some covalently bonded compounds such as acetic acid, CH_3COOH; ammonia, NH_3; and water.

Do solutions of electrolytes and nonelectrolytes represent equilibrium systems? We will deal with this question in later sections of this chapter.

15.2 Boiling and freezing point changes

The boiling point of a water solution depends on the nature of the solute and the concentration of the solution. Generally, the boiling point of water is elevated 0.52 C° for each mole of solute particles in 1000 grams of water (see section 10.25). For non-ionic solutes, the number of moles of solute particles equals the number of gram-molecular weights (moles) of solute. For ionic solutes, the number of moles of solute particles equals the number of moles of ions produced by the dissociation of 1 mole of solute. Since 1 mole of ionic solute produces at least 2 moles of ions, solutions of nonionic solutes have lower boiling points than solutions of ionic solutes of the same concentration.

A solution containing 1 gram-molecular weight of solute dissolved in 1000 grams of water is called a 1-molal solution, abbreviated 1 *m*. Thus 0.52 C° is called the *molal boiling point elevation constant* of water. Similarly, the freezing point of a water solution depends on the *molal freezing point depression constant* of water (−1.86 C°) multiplied by the number of moles of solute particles dissolved in 1000 grams of water. Thus solutions of nonionic solutes have higher freezing points than solutions of ionic solutes of the same concentration.

The following table lists the approximate boiling points and freezing points of some solutions of common substances in water. You can recognize the greater effect from electrolytes, since they produce more than one mole of particles per mole of solute.

SOLUTION	CONCENTRATION	BOILING POINT (°C)	FREEZING POINT (°C)
$C_6H_{12}O_6$ (glucose)	1 *m*	100.52	−1.86
$C_3H_5(OH)_3$ (glycerine)	1 *m*	100.52	−1.86
NaCl	1 *m*	101.04	−3.72
$CaCl_2$	1 *m*	101.56	−5.58
Na_3PO_4	1 *m*	102.08	−7.44

The following equations give the relationships for the observed elevation of the boiling point, ΔT_b, and the lowering of the freezing point, ΔT_f, for solutions of nonelectrolytes in water:

$$\frac{\text{observed } \Delta T_b}{0.52 \text{ C}°} = \frac{\text{weight of solute in g/1000 g H}_2\text{O}}{\text{gram-molecular weight of solute}}$$

$$\frac{\text{observed } \Delta T_f}{-1.86 \text{ C}°} = \frac{\text{weight of solute in g/1000 g H}_2\text{O}}{\text{gram-molecular weight of solute}}$$

For solutions of strong electrolytes (completely ionized), the constants in the two equations, 0.52 C° and −1.86 C°, are multiplied by the number of moles of ions produced by the complete ionization of each mole of the solute.

15.3 Calculations involving boiling and freezing point changes

The molecular weight of a nonelectrolyte can be calculated if we know the boiling or freezing point change it produces in a solvent. For example, assume that a solution containing 18 g of a nonelectrolyte in 100 g of

H_2O boils at $100.52° C$. We know that a solution that boils at $100.52° C$ is 1 molal. Therefore, the weight of solute present in 1000 g of water is $\dfrac{1000 \text{ g } H_2O}{100 \text{ g } H_2O} \times 18 \text{ g} = 180$ g. Since the concentration of the solution is 1 molal, the molecular weight of the solute is 180. We can obtain the same result by substituting the proper values in the relationship

$$\frac{\text{observed } \Delta T_b}{0.52 \text{ C}°} = \frac{\text{weight of solute in g/1000 g } H_2O}{\text{gram-molecular weight of solute}}$$

$$\frac{0.52}{0.52} = \frac{180 \text{ g}}{x} \quad \text{or} \quad x = 180 \text{ g}$$

The observed changes in the boiling and freezing points of solutions of strong electrolytes are somewhat less than the calculated values. These deviations are caused by the attractive forces between ions in the solution (Debye-Hückel forces) and need not concern us in our study.

Solutions of weak electrolytes have almost the same boiling and freezing points as solutions of nonelectrolytes of the same concentration. This near equality suggests that the species present in solutions of weak electrolytes are largely nonionic (the concentration of ions is low).

15.4 Equilibria in solutions

Solutions of strong electrolytes consist almost entirely of ions, as represented by the following equations:

AN IONIC SOLID $M^+Z^- \ (s) + H_2O \rightarrow M^+ \ (aq) + Z^- \ (aq)$

A STRONG ACID $H \text{:} Z \ (g) + H_2O \rightarrow H_3O^+ + Z^- \ (aq)$

These ionization reactions proceed almost completely to the right, suggesting that equilibrium, for all practical purposes, does not exist. All ionic solids exist as ions in the crystalline state. There is little likelihood that the ions, when in solution, will unite to form nonionized molecules. With a strong acid, the H^+ of the acid unites with water more strongly than with Z^-, the negative ion of the acid. Thus in a strong acid, the proton (H^+) rarely transfers from H_3O^+ to Z^-, and the reverse of the ionization reaction is very slight.

From conductivity and boiling and freezing point measurements, we may conclude that solutions of weak acids are essentially nonionic.

A WEAK ACID $H \text{:} X + H_2O \underset{\longleftarrow}{\overset{\longrightarrow}{}} H_3O^+ + X^- \ (aq)$

The directions of the arrows in the generalized reaction indicate that the particles in the solution are largely molecular. (The longer arrow points to the left.) The weakly electrolytic nature of HX may be attributed to the greater strength of the bonds in the molecule. Acetic acid (CH_3COOH) and ammonium hydroxide ($NH_3 + H_2O$) are examples of weak electrolytes. The equilibria in these solutions may be represented by the following equations:

$$CH_3COOH + H_2O \rightleftarrows H_3O^+ + CH_3COO^- \ (aq)$$

$$NH_3 \ (g) + H_2O \rightleftarrows NH_4^+ \ (aq) + OH^- \ (aq)$$

15.5 Common ion effect

Since solutions of weak electrolytes represent equilibrium systems, it is possible to vary the composition of an equilibrium mixture by applying Le Chatelier's Principle.

Suppose we add a few drops of litmus solution to a 0.1 M solution of the weak electrolyte acetic acid. Litmus is an *indicator*, a substance that changes color at a specific hydronium (H_3O^+) ion or hydroxyl (OH^-) ion concentration. In acid solutions, litmus solution is pink. As the hydronium ion concentration is decreased or as the hydroxyl ion concentration is increased, the pink color fades. It changes to blue in basic solutions, that is, solutions which contain more hydroxyl ions than hydronium ions.

We have represented the ionization of acetic acid as

$$CH_3COOH + H_2O \rightleftarrows H_3O^+ + CH_3COO^- \ (aq)$$

As expected, the addition of litmus colors the solution pink. Suppose we add sodium acetate (CH_3COONa) to the solution. Sodium acetate, an ionic solid, dissolves in the water in the solution to form a large concentration of $Na^+ \ (aq)$ and $CH_3COO^- \ (aq)$ ions. The $Na^+ \ (aq)$ ions do not influence the equilibrium and may be neglected. The effect of the $CH_3COO^- \ (aq)$ ions is to increase the concentration of one of the products of the ionization of acetic acid. According to Le Chatelier's Principle, the equilibrium will shift toward the left, that is, toward the formation of more reactants. This change in the composition of the equilibrium mixture uses up H_3O^+ ions. Thus the ionization of the acetic acid has been suppressed (lessened). Experimentally, we note that the color of the litmus solution becomes less pink.

The phenomenon we have just discussed is called the *common ion effect*, which may be summarized as follows:

The addition of a common ion to the solution of a weak electrolyte suppresses the ionization of the weak electrolyte. The common ion must be in large concentration and, therefore, must come from a strong electrolyte.

The ionization of ammonium hydroxide may be suppressed by the addition of an ionic solid such as ammonium acetate. In this instance, litmus solution, which is blue in the solution of ammonium hydroxide, becomes less blue. Phenolphthalein, another indicator, is pink in solutions of strong bases (high hydroxyl ion concentration) and is colorless in acid solutions. The addition of solid ammonium acetate to a solution of ammonium hydroxide containing phenolphthalein will cause the pink color of the solution to lessen. We will return to the study of indicators in the next chapter.

15.6 The ionization constant

Since the solution of a weak electrolyte represents an equilibrium system, it should be possible to apply the Law of Mass Action to the system.

Consider again the ionization of acetic acid.

$$CH_3COOH + H_2O \overset{\rightarrow}{\longleftarrow} H_3O^+ + CH_3COO^- \ (aq)$$

Applying the law (see section 14.13), we obtain

$$K_C = \frac{[H_3O^+]\,[CH_3COO^- \ (aq)]}{[CH_3COOH]\,[H_2O]}$$

In dilute solutions, the concentration of water is approximately 1000 g/l. Since 18 g of water represents 1 mole, 1000 g of water represents

$$\frac{1000 \text{ g}}{18 \text{ g/mole}} = 55.5 \text{ moles}$$

The addition of moderate amounts of solute will not produce much change in the concentration of H_2O, which we may therefore consider to be constant. The concentration of water may be combined with K_C to form a new constant, K_i, called the *ionization constant*. For acetic acid,

$$K_i = \frac{[H_3O^+]\,[CH_3COO^- \ (aq)]}{[CH_3COOH]}$$

At 25° C, K_i for $CH_3COOH = 1.8 \times 10^{-5}$. This low value indicates that reactants are favored in the equilibrium mixture. Why?

15.7 K_i and the common ion effect

The ionization constant can be used to explain the common ion effect. For example, at a given temperature, the ionization constant of CH_3COOH has a fixed value. The addition of CH_3COONa to a solution of CH_3COOH increases the concentration of CH_3COO^- ions. This quantity appears in the numerator of the ionization expression. To maintain the fixed value of K_i, the concentration of H_3O^+ must be decreased or the concentration of CH_3COOH must be increased. Actually both processes occur: the CH_3COO^- combines with H_3O^+ (decreasing its concentration) to form CH_3COOH (increasing its concentration).

15.8 K_i and acid strength

The ionization constant of an acid solution also denotes the strength of the acid. Among the acids listed in the following table of ionization constants, phosphoric acid is the strongest acid and hypochlorous acid is the weakest acid.

ACID	K_i AT $25°$ C
hypochlorous acid (HOCl)	3.5×10^{-8}
carbonic acid (H_2CO_3)	4.3×10^{-7} primary
acetic acid (CH_3COOH)	1.8×10^{-5}
phosphoric acid (H_3PO_4)	7.5×10^{-3} primary

The primary ionization constant refers to the release of the first proton (see section 16.10).

15.9 Calculations involving the ionization constant

The ionization constant of a weak electrolyte may be calculated from the concentration of the solution and from the extent of ionization. For example, at $25°$ C, a 0.1 M solution of acetic acid (CH_3COOH) is 1.35% ionized. What is the K_i of CH_3COOH at $25°$ C?

The ionization of CH_3COOH may be represented (with all ions aquated) as

$$CH_3COOH + H_2O \rightleftarrows H_3O^+ + CH_3COO^-$$

If the solution were 100% ionized, 0.1 M CH_3COOH would produce 0.1 mole of H_3O^+ ion and 0.1 mole of CH_3COO^- ion in one liter of solution.

Since the solution is only 1.35% ionized, $0.1 \times 0.0135 = 0.00135 = 1.35 \times 10^{-3}$ mole of H_3O^+ and 1.35×10^{-3} mole of CH_3COO^- per liter of solution are formed. All the H_3O^+ and CH_3COO^- ions come from CH_3COOH. Therefore, the concentration of CH_3COOH at equilibrium is

0.1 mole/l (original concentration) $-$ 0.00135 mole/l (ions formed) $=$

0.0987 mole/l $= 9.87 \times 10^{-2}$ mole/l

$$K_i = \frac{[H_3O^+][CH_3COO^-]}{[CH_3COOH]} = \frac{1.35 \times 10^{-3} \times 1.35 \times 10^{-3}}{9.87 \times 10^{-2}}$$

$$= 1.84 \times 10^{-5}$$

Now assume that 0.1 mole of sodium acetate (CH_3COONa) is added to a liter of solution of acetic acid. What will be the H_3O^+ ion concentration? From our previous discussion, we know that adding a common ion to acetic acid suppresses the ionization of the acid. This means that $[H_3O^+]$ will be lowered. Let us test this conclusion.

$$K_i = \frac{[H_3O^+][CH_3COO^-]}{[CH_3COOH]}$$

The addition of 0.1 mole of sodium acetate, a strong electrolyte, to the equilibrium mixture has practically the same effect as adding 0.1 mole of acetate ion. From the previous discussion, note that the concentration of acetate ion in acetic acid at equilibrium is 0.00135 mole/l. The new concentration of acetate ion, therefore, becomes approximately 0.1 mole/l $+$ 0.00135 mole/l $=$ 0.10135 mole/l. However, 0.1 and 0.10135 are close in value. We will simplify our calculations by assuming the new concentration of acetate ion to be 0.1 mole/l.

$$1.84 \times 10^{-5} = \frac{[H_3O^+][0.1]}{9.87 \times 10^{-2}}$$

$$[H_3O^+] = \frac{1.84 \times 10^{-5} \times 9.87 \times 10^{-2}}{0.1}$$

$$= 1.82 \times 10^{-5}$$

The addition of CH_3COONa to CH_3COOH has decreased the $[H_3O^+]$ from 1.35×10^{-3} mole/l to 1.82×10^{-5} mole/l, about $\frac{1}{100}$ of its original value.

15.10 The ionization of water

Conductivity experiments reveal that pure water is a weak electrolyte. The ionization of water may be written as

$$2 \ H_2O \rightleftharpoons H_3O^+ + OH^- \ (aq)$$

At 25° C, equilibrium exists in pure water when 2×10^{-7} % of the water has ionized. This means that the equilibrium mixture is chiefly nonionized molecules of water and very small concentrations of hydronium ion and hydroxyl ion. We will investigate the effects produced by the ionization of water in the next chapter.

15.11 Equilibria in saturated solutions of slightly soluble ionic solids

In section 10.16, we defined a saturated solution of an ionic solid as a solution in which the excess undissolved solute (solid) is in equilibrium with the dissolved solute (ions).

$$MZ \ (s) \rightleftharpoons M^+ \ (aq) + Z^- \ (aq)$$

Applying the Law of Mass Action, we obtain

$$K_C = \frac{[M^+ \ (aq)] \ [Z^- \ (aq)]}{[MZ \ (s)]}$$

At a given temperature, the concentration of solid MZ (s) is fixed. This concentration may be combined with K_C into a new constant, K_{SP}, called the *solubility product constant*.

$$K_{SP} = [M^+ \ (aq)] \ [Z^- \ (aq)]$$

If the concentrations of ions are high (above 0.01 mole/l), the ions exert considerable attractive force on each other. As a result, the solubility product relationship varies from its predicted value. A similar variation in the solubility product relationship occurs with ions that are polyvalent (ions that carry more than a single charge). These ions also exert considerable attractive force on each other, altering the predicted concentrations of the equilibrium mixture. We must therefore note the following restrictions on the solubility product constant: The solubility product constant is primarily useful for saturated solutions of slightly soluble ionic solids containing ions that are monovalent (ions that carry a single charge).

Saturated solutions of slightly soluble ionic solids are very dilute, and we may assume that the dissolved solid in the solution is completely ionized. In these solutions, the solubility product relationship is approximately valid and holds for a stated temperature, usually 25° C.

15.12 How are solubilities and solubility product constants related?

In the following table of solubility product constants (K_{SP}), all ions are aquated.

SOLID	ION PRODUCT	SOLUBILITY PRODUCT CONSTANT *(at 25°C)*
Tl I	$[Tl^+][I^-]$	3.7×10^{-8}
AgCl	$[Ag^+][Cl^-]$	1.6×10^{-10}
AgBr	$[Ag^+][Br^-]$	4.8×10^{-13}
AgI	$[Ag^+][I^-]$	8.3×10^{-17}

A high solubility product constant (a low negative exponent) signifies a large concentration of solute ions. This means that the solubility of the solid is correspondingly high. Similarly, a low solubility product constant (a high negative exponent) signifies a small concentration of solute ions and a correspondingly low solubility. For example, the preceding table reveals that Tl I, thallium(I) iodide, although relatively insoluble, is much more soluble than AgI.

Let us calculate the solubilities of Tl I and AgI, using the concepts we have just discussed.

$$Tl\,I\ (s) \rightleftarrows Tl^+\ (aq) + I^-\ (aq)$$

$$K_{SP} = [Tl^+\ (aq)][I^-\ (aq)] = 3.7 \times 10^{-8}$$

The equation reveals that for every 1 mole of Tl I (s) that dissolves, 1 mole of Tl^+ (aq) and 1 mole of I^- (aq) are formed. Let x represent the molar concentration of Tl I in solution. We know that x mole/l of Tl I will yield x mole/l of Tl^+ (aq) ions and x mole/l of I^- (aq) ions.

$$[x][x] = [x]^2 = 3.7 \times 10^{-8}$$

$$[x] = \sqrt{3.7 \times 10^{-8}} = 1.9 \times 10^{-4}\ \text{mole/l}$$

Let y represent the molar concentration of AgI in solution. Following the method of calculation in the previous example, we obtain

$$[y][y] = [y]^2 = 8.3 \times 10^{-17} = 83 \times 10^{-18}$$

$$[y] = \sqrt{83 \times 10^{-18}} = 9.1 \times 10^{-9} \text{ mole/l}$$

The solubility of AgI is 9.1×10^{-9} mole/l, considerably less than the solubility of Tl I (1.9×10^{-4} mole/l).

15.13 Calculating the solubility product constant from solubility data

The solubility of a solid may be determined in the laboratory. From the solubility data, we may then calculate the solubility product constant. For example, the solubility of copper(I) chloride at 25° C is about 6.2 $\times 10^{-2}$ g/l. Since the gram-molecular weight of CuCl is 99, the solubility of CuCl in moles/l

$$= \frac{6.2 \times 10^{-2} \text{ g/l}}{99 \text{ g/mole}}$$

$$= 6.3 \times 10^{-4} \text{ mole/l}$$

To determine the solubility product constant of CuCl, we first write the ionization and K_{SP} equations.

$$CuCl \ (s) \rightleftarrows Cu^+ \ (aq) + Cl^- \ (aq)$$

$$K_{SP} = [Cu^+ \ (aq)][Cl^- \ (aq)]$$

The equation reveals that for every mole of CuCl (s) that dissolves, 1 mole of Cu^+ (aq) and 1 mole of Cl^- (aq) are formed. The solubility of CuCl (s) is 6.3×10^{-4} mole/l. Therefore, 6.3×10^{-4} mole/l of CuCl (aq) furnishes 6.3×10^{-4} mole/l of Cu^+ (aq) ions and 6.3×10^{-4} mole/l of Cl^- (aq) ions.

$$K_{SP} = [6.3 \times 10^{-4}][6.3 \times 10^{-4}] = 40 \times 10^{-8} = 4 \times 10^{-7}$$

15.14 The solubility product constant and precipitation

The solubility product expression permits us to make another important deduction: For a solid to precipitate from solution, the product of the molar concentrations of the solute ions must exceed the solubility product constant.

In a solution of CuCl, for example, suppose the molar concentrations of Cu^+ (aq) ions and Cl^- (aq) ions are each less than 6.3×10^{-4} mole/l. The product of the concentrations will be less than the solubility product constant (4×10^{-7}). There will be insufficient Cu^+ (aq) ions and Cl^- (aq) ions to saturate the solution, and CuCl will not precipitate. Conversely, if the ion concentrations exceed 6.3×10^{-4} mole/l, CuCl will precipitate. If these concentrations are then lowered until their product fails to exceed the solubility product, the precipitate will dissolve.

15.15 Formation of precipitates

Suppose we mix 100 ml of 10^{-6} M $AgNO_3$ with 100 ml of 10^{-6} M NaCl. Each solution furnishes aquated ions.

$$AgNO_3 \ (aq) \rightarrow Ag^+ \ (aq) + NO_3^- \ (aq)$$

$$NaCl \ (aq) \rightarrow Na^+ \ (aq) + Cl^- \ (aq)$$

The only new solids that can form are $NaNO_3$ (s) and AgCl (s). How can we predict which solid will precipitate? The solubility of each solid follows.

$$NaNO_3: \quad 90 \ g/100 \ ml \ at \ 25° \ C$$

$$AgCl: \quad 1.8 \times 10^{-5} \ g/100 \ ml \ at \ 25° C$$

Clearly, AgCl is much less soluble than $NaNO_3$. Will AgCl precipitate when these solutions are mixed?

As indicated previously, a solid will precipitate if the product of the molar concentrations of its ions exceeds the solubility product. At 25° C, the K_{SP} of AgCl $= 1.6 \times 10^{-10}$. The initial concentration of Ag^+ $(aq) = 1 \times 10^{-6}$ mole/l. After the two solutions are mixed, the volume is doubled, and the concentration of Ag^+ (aq) is halved to 0.5×10^{-6}. Similarly, the concentration of Cl^- $(aq) = 0.5 \times 10^{-6}$. To precipitate AgCl (s), $[Ag^+ \ (aq)]$ $[Cl^- \ (aq)]$ must exceed 1.6×10^{-10}. However, in our solution, the product of the molar concentration of the ions is

$$[5 \times 10^{-7}] \ [5 \times 10^{-7}] = 25 \times 10^{-14} = 2.5 \times 10^{-13}$$

The product of the molar concentrations of Ag^+ (aq) and Cl^- (aq) is less than the K_{SP} of AgCl, and AgCl (s) will not precipitate. If the concentrations of the ions are increased to 5×10^{-5} mole/l, the product of the molar concentrations becomes

$$[5 \times 10^{-5}] \ [5 \times 10^{-5}] = 25 \times 10^{-10} = 2.5 \times 10^{-9}$$

This quantity exceeds the K_{SP} of AgCl (1.6×10^{-10}), and AgCl (s) will precipitate.

15.16 Dissolving a precipitate by shifting the equilibrium

We know that exceeding the solubility product constant of a solid of limited solubility causes the solid to precipitate. Extending this idea, we should be able to dissolve such a solid by lowering the concentration of its ions so that their product is lower than the solubility product constant.

In the previous example, we noted that a solution that contains 5×10^{-5} mole/l of Ag^+ (*aq*) ions and 5×10^{-5} mole/l of Cl^- (*aq*) ions precipitates AgCl (*s*). Precipitation occurs because the product of the molar concentrations of the ions exceeds 1.6×10^{-10}, the K_{SP} of AgCl. In a saturated solution of AgCl, we find the equilibrium

$$AgCl \text{ } (s) \rightleftarrows Ag^+ \text{ } (aq) + Cl^- \text{ } (aq)$$

According to Le Chatelier's Principle, if the concentration of Ag^+ (*aq*) ions, Cl^- (*aq*) ions, or both ions is lowered sufficiently, the equilibrium will shift to the right and the solid will dissolve.

The simplest way to shift the equilibrium to the right is to add water and cause the ionic concentrations to decrease. If the solid is not too insoluble, it will dissolve until all of the solid is in solution. However, if this procedure requires too much water, it may be impractical.

15.17 Dissolving a precipitate by forming a complex ion

By experiment, we know that AgCl (*s*) dissolves readily in an aqueous solution of the gas NH_3 (ammonia). Why? If our previous reasoning is correct, the addition of NH_3 must lower the concentration of Ag^+ (*aq*) ions, Cl^- (*aq*) ions, or both below the K_{SP} value required for precipitation. The dissolving of AgCl (*s*) in NH_3 may be explained in the following steps (in which all ions are aquated):

1. NH_3 combines with some of the Ag^+ ions present in the solution to form a *complex ion* (an ion consisting of more than one species), the silver ammonia ion.

$$2 \text{ } NH_3 + Ag^+ \rightleftarrows Ag(NH_3)_2^+$$

The $Ag(NH_3)_2^+$ complex ion is relatively stable, which means that the reverse reaction is slight. The forward reaction removes Ag^+ ions from the solution and, in effect, decreases the concentration of Ag^+.

2. Some AgCl (*s*) dissolves to reestablish the equilibrium.

$$AgCl \ (s) \rightleftarrows Ag^+ + Cl^-$$

because the product of the concentrations of Ag^+ ions and Cl^- ions has become less than the K_{SP} of AgCl.
3. The Ag^+ ions formed in step 2 combine with more NH_3 to form more $Ag(NH_3)_2{}^+$, and AgCl (*s*) continues to dissolve. If sufficient NH_3 is present, all the AgCl (*s*) will dissolve to form a solution of $Ag(NH_3)_2{}^+$ ions and Cl^- ions.

The solution now contains silver ammonia chloride, a stable ionic substance which dissociates in water to form a silver ammonia ion and a chloride ion. Silver ammonia ions are stable and liberate only a minute amount of Ag^+ ions. When this minute amount of Ag^+ ions is expressed in moles/l and multiplied by the molar concentration of Cl^- ions (which remains unchanged), the product is lower than the K_{SP} of AgCl (*s*). This means that AgCl (*s*) cannot re-form and thus remains in solution.

15.18 Reactions involving aqueous ions

Reactions between electrolytes are essentially reactions between aqueous ions. For example, consider the reaction between solutions of the ionic compounds AB and CD (all ions are aquated).

$$A^+ + B^- + C^+ + D^- \rightarrow AD \ (s) + C^+ + B^-$$

When two pairs of ions are mixed, a reaction will take place only if there is a decrease in free energy for the system. If any two ions of opposite charge come together and remain together, the free energy of the system decreases. Under these conditions, the reaction is said to *go to completion.*

A decrease in the free energy of a system results whenever ions unite to form: (1) an insoluble solid (2) a slightly soluble gas (3) a weak electrolyte, such as water or acetic acid. In all such reactions, the number of ions that remains in solution decreases.

Note that C^+ and B^- appear on both sides of the preceding equation in the same amounts. Therefore, they are not involved in the reaction and are *spectator ions.* The ions that are involved in the reaction (those ions that form the new product) are the *predominant species.* Rewriting the equation to show the predominant species, we obtain

$$A^+ + D^- \rightarrow AD \ (s)$$

If AD were a slightly soluble gas, the equation showing the predominant species would be

$$A^+ + D^- \rightarrow AD \ (g)$$

What happens if mixing the four ions does not produce a precipitate, a slightly soluble gas, or a weak electrolyte? No reaction occurs because there is no decrease in free energy when the ions come together. In this case, the ions appear in the same amounts on both sides of the equation.

$$A^+ + B^- + C^+ + D^- \rightarrow A^+ + B^- + C^+ + D^-$$

15.19 Reactions that go to completion

We have stated that reactions between ions that form precipitates or slightly soluble gases or weak electrolytes are said to go to completion. This means that when the reaction reaches equilibrium, the concentrations of the reactant ions that remain unchanged are so small that for all practical purposes, the reaction has proceeded completely to the right. Suppose we mix equal volumes of $0.1 \ M$ $AgNO_3$ and $0.1 \ M$ $NaCl$. The product of the concentrations of Ag^+ ions and Cl^- ions is higher than the K_{SP} of $AgCl$, and precipitation occurs. We may write the equation as follows (all ions are aquated):

$$Ag^+ + NO_3^- + Na^+ + Cl^- \rightarrow AgCl \ (s) + Na^+ + NO_3^-$$

Showing the predominant species only, we may rewrite the equation as

$$Ag^+ + Cl^- \rightarrow AgCl \ (s)$$

This equation, in effect, states that any source of Ag^+ ions (any soluble Ag compound) will combine with any source of Cl^- ions (any soluble chloride compound) to precipitate $AgCl$ (assuming the concentrations have exceeded the K_{SP} of $AgCl$).

Suppose we mix equal volumes of $0.1 \ M$ H_2SO_4 and $0.1 \ M$ Na_2CO_3. This reaction rapidly produces CO_2 gas. The following equation shows all the ions (all ions are aquated):

$$2 \ H^+ + SO_4^{-2} + 2 \ Na^+ + CO_3^{-2} \rightarrow H_2O + CO_2 \ (g) + 2 \ Na^+ + SO_4^{-2}$$

Showing the predominant species only, we may rewrite the equation as

$$2 \ H^+ + CO_3^{-2} \rightarrow H_2O + CO_2 \ (g)$$

The equation now states that the addition of H^+ ions (any acid solution) will react with CO_3^{-2} ions (any carbonate) to form gaseous CO_2.

15.20 Predicting ionic reactions

To predict whether or not an ionic reaction will occur (go to completion), we must be able to identify at least one of the products as either a precipitate, a slightly soluble gas, or a weak electrolyte.

To make the prediction, we need to refer to a table of solubilities, or a table of solubility products, or a table of gas solubilities. (Since the reactions we are studying occur in water, we need to know which gases are soluble in water.)

Let us try to predict whether the following reactions will occur in water. To write a possible equation, we must know the charges of the ions in the ionic compounds (see the table inside the front cover).

EXAMPLE 1. $CuSO_4 + NaOH$

Both substances are ionic solids. In water, they liberate aquated ions with the charges indicated.

$$Cu^{+2} + SO_4^{-2} + Na^+ + OH^-$$

A table of solubilities shows that $Cu(OH)_2$ is only slightly soluble and that Na_2SO_4 is soluble. The reaction can be written as follows (all ions are aquated):

$$Cu^{+2} + SO_4^{-2} + Na^+ + OH^- \rightarrow Cu(OH)_2 \ (s) + Na^+ + SO_4^{-2}$$

Since atoms and charge must be conserved, the equation becomes

$$Cu^{+2} + SO_4^{-2} + 2 \ Na^+ + 2 \ OH^- \rightarrow Cu(OH)_2 \ (s) + 2 \ Na^+ + SO_4^{-2}$$

or, showing the predominant species,

$$Cu^{+2} + 2 \ (OH)^- \rightarrow Cu(OH)_2 \ (s)$$

From the equation, we may predict that any source of Cu^{+2} ions will react with any source of OH^- ions to form $Cu(OH)_2$. In the laboratory, we find that the addition of $CuSO_4$ solution to $NaOH$ solution forms a precipitate of blue $Cu(OH)_2$. Again, we assume we have more than the minimum concentrations of ions sufficient to exceed the K_{SP} of $Cu(OH)_2$.

EXAMPLE 2. $NaCl + KNO_3$

Using the same procedure outlined in example 1, we note that the liberated aquated ions are

$$Na^+ + Cl^- + K^+ + NO_3^-$$

Reference to a table of solubilities and to a table of gases soluble in water indicates no possible precipitate or gas from any combination of these ions. Thus no reaction occurs. If solutions of $NaCl$ and KNO_3 are mixed in the laboratory, there is no visible evidence of the formation of a precipitate or of a gas. When this solution of four ions is evaporated to dryness, a mixture of four solids is collected. The mixture contains all possible combinations of the four ions: KCl, $NaNO_3$, $NaCl$, and KNO_3.

EXAMPLE 3. $K_2SO_3 + HCl$

The liberated aqueous ions are

$$2 K^+ + SO_3^{-2} + H^+ + Cl^-$$

The table of gases soluble in water reveals that SO_2 is only moderately soluble in H_2O, and H_2SO_3 decomposes to form $SO_2 (g) + H_2O$. The reaction may be written as follows (all ions are aquated):

$$2 K^+ + SO_3^{-2} + H^+ + Cl^- \rightarrow H_2O + SO_2 (g) + 2 K^+ + Cl^-$$

Conserving atoms and charge, we balance the reaction and obtain

$$2 K^+ + SO_3^{-2} + 2 H^+ + 2 Cl^- \rightarrow H_2O + SO_2 (g) + 2 K^+ + 2 Cl^-$$

Showing the predominant species only, we may rewrite the equation as

$$SO_3^{-2} (aq) + 2 H^+ (aq) \rightarrow H_2O + SO_2 (g)$$

If any sulfite is added to an acid solution, a saturated solution of SO_2 forms, and bubbles of gaseous SO_2 appear. (The characteristic choking odor of SO_2 also reveals its presence.)

We have deliberately avoided discussing the reaction between acid (H^+) solutions and basic (OH^-) solutions. Such reactions may or may not go to completion and will be considered in detail in Chapter 16.

Multiple-Choice Questions

1. Some solutions can conduct electricity because (1) large numbers of electrons are present (2) mobile ions are present (3) the molecules of the solute are charged (4) the molecules of the solvent are charged
2. Which of the following statements is true? (1) The freezing point of a solution is lower than that of the pure solvent. (2) A solution always conducts electricity. (3) The boiling point of a solution is lower than that of the pure solvent. (4) A solution always contains ions.

3. A 1-molal solution of NaCl has a lower freezing point than a 1-molal solution of glucose ($C_6H_{12}O_6$) because (1) NaCl has greater chemical activity (2) glucose contains oxygen and hydrogen in the same proportion as water (3) NaCl decomposes on freezing (4) each mole of NaCl forms two moles of particles in solution

4. When sodium acetate is added to a solution of acetic acid (1) the ionization of sodium acetate is increased (2) the acetic acid forms a precipitate (3) the concentration of hydronium ion increases (4) the ionization of acetic acid decreases

5. Given K_i for acetic acid $= 1.8 \times 10^{-5}$, and K_i for hypochlorous acid $= 3.5 \times 10^{-8}$. From this data, we may conclude that (1) 0.1 M hypochlorous acid contains more H_3O^+ than 0.1 M acetic acid (2) acetic acid is the stronger electrolyte (3) hypochlorous acid is more soluble than acetic acid (4) hypochlorous acid is the weaker acid

6. If a 0.1 M solution of the weak acid HX is 10% ionized, then (1) the concentration of HX molecules is 10% of 0.1 M (2) the concentration of H_3O^+ is 0.01 M (3) the concentration of X^- ions is 0.09 M (4) no equilibrium can exist between ions and molecules of HX

7. The solubility product constant (1) is a relationship between solvent and solute (2) applies only to nonelectrolytes (3) is a relationship between the ions in a saturated solution of a solid of limited solubility (4) applies to solutions that are not in equilibrium

8. Magnesium hydroxide, $Mg(OH)_2$, is a slightly soluble ionic solid. The expression for its solubility product constant is

   (1) $K_{SP} = [Mg^{+2} (aq)]^2 [2\ OH^- (aq)]$

   (2) $K_{SP} = [Mg^{+2} (aq)] [OH^- (aq)]$

   (3) $K_{SP} = [Mg^{+2} (aq)] [O^{-2} (aq)] [H^+ (aq)]^2$

   (4) $K_{SP} = [Mg^{+2} (aq)] [OH^- (aq)]^2$

9. When NaCl is added to a solution of silver nitrate, $AgNO_3$, a precipitate of AgCl forms when (1) the solution becomes saturated with NaCl (2) the product of the molar concentrations of aqueous Ag^+ and Cl^- ions exceeds the K_{SP} for AgCl (3) the water is removed (4) the concentration of aqueous Na^+ ions is greater than the concentration of aqueous Ag^+ ions

10. A slightly soluble ionic solid can be made to dissolve (1) by stirring vigorously (2) by reducing the concentrations of the ions it forms until the solubility product constant is not exceeded (3) by evaporating the solvent (4) by use of a catalyst

11. In the reaction

$$A^+ (aq) + B^- (aq) + C^+ (aq) + D^- (aq) \rightarrow CB (s) + A^+ (aq) + D^- (aq)$$

(1) $A^+ (aq)$ and $B^- (aq)$ are the spectator ions (2) two new types of molecules form (3) $C^+ (aq)$ and $B^- (aq)$ are the predominant species (4) no ions remain in solution

Completion Questions

1. Solutions of strong electrolytes are very good conductors of electricity because the solute in the solution is present in the form of _____.
2. If 2 moles of a solute are dissolved in 1000 g of water, the concentration of the solution is 2 _____.
3. A solution of a nonelectrolyte is found to have a boiling point of 100.26° C. The concentration of this solution is _____ molal.
4. When a solution of an acid is found to consist mainly of molecules of acid, then the acid is _____ (*weak, strong*).
5. The addition of sodium carbonate to a solution of the weak acid carbonic acid is an example of the _____ effect.
6. In a reaction involving two ionic compounds in which an insoluble substance forms, the two ions that unite are called the predominant species. The two ions that do not change are called the _____ ions.
7. When ions in solution unite to form an insoluble solid or a (an)_____, the free energy of the system decreases.
8. Reactions between two electrolytes which result in a decrease in the number of ions in solution are said to go to _____.

True-False Questions

1. Compounds containing *covalent* bonds are strong electrolytes.
2. A solution that contains 1 mole of solute in 1000 g of water is a 1-*molar* solution.
3. A solution of a 1-molal electrolyte has a freezing point *higher than* $-1.86°$ C.
4. The addition of *NaCl* to a solution of nitrous acid, HNO_2 (a weak acid), will cause a decrease in the ionization of HNO_2.
5. Water is an example of a weak electrolyte because the concentration of the molecular form of water is *much less than* the concentration of its ions.
6. The solubility product constant for silver bromide, AgBr, is 4.8×10^{-13}; for silver chloride, AgCl, it is 1.6×10^{-10}. This indicates that AgCl is *more* soluble than AgBr.

7. A slightly soluble ionic solid, such as barium sulfate, $BaSO_4$, will form a precipitate when the product of the molar concentrations of the ions in solution is *less than* its K_{SP}.

8. Two solutions of electrolytes, such as NaCl and KNO_3, are mixed and no reaction takes place. *Two* different types of ions are left in the solution.

Decreases, Increases, Remains the Same

1. When the concentration of solute in a solution increases, the boiling point of the solution _____.

2. As the ionization of 1-molal solutions of different acids increases, their freezing points _____.

3. As the strength of the bond between H and X increases, the ionization of the acid HX _____.

4. As the ionization of an acid increases, the molar concentration of hydronium ion in the solution _____.

5. If the numerical value for the ionization constant of an acid increases, the concentration of the molecular form of the acid _____.

6. Ammonium acetate is added to a solution of acetic acid. As the concentration of acetate ions increases, the H_3O^+ concentration _____.

7. As more solute is added to a saturated solution of an ionic solid, the solubility product constant _____.

8. Adding NH_3 to a saturated solution of AgCl forms the stable species $Ag(NH_3)_2^+$ (*aq*). As a result, the concentration of Ag^+ (*aq*) ions in solution _____.

9. When two electrolytes are mixed in solution and no insoluble solid, gas, or weak electrolyte forms, the number of ions that remain in solution _____.

10. When two electrolytes are mixed in solution and a reaction goes to completion, the number of different types of ions that remain in solution _____.

Exercises for Review

1. An aqueous solution of a nonelectrolyte boils at 101.04° C. What is the molal concentration of this solution?

2. A solution contains 0.20 mole of a nonelectrolyte dissolved in 200 g of water. What is the freezing point of this solution?

3. Which of the following mixtures of electrolytes illustrate the common ion effect? Explain your choices.
    a. $HCl + NaNO_3$ *c.* $HNO_2 + NaNO_2$
    b. $H_2CO_3 + Na_2CO_3$ *d.* $NH_4OH + NH_4Cl$

4. The ionization constant for hypobromous acid, HOBr, is 2×10^{-9}. Is HOBr a stronger or weaker acid than hypochlorous acid, HOCl? Explain. (Refer to the table on page 270.)

5. Write the mathematical expressions for the solubility product constants for the following slightly soluble ionic solids:

a. AgI   *c.* Al(OH)$_3$
b. PbCl$_2$ *d.* Fe$_2$S$_3$

6. Indicate whether an insoluble (or slightly soluble) solid or a gas forms when the following solutions of electrolytes are mixed. Write the equations showing the predominant species.

a. hydrochloric acid + thallium(I) nitrate
b. calcium sulfide + hydrochloric acid
c. sulfuric acid + sodium sulfite
d. sodium hydroxide + ammonium chloride
e. hydrochloric acid + sodium carbonate

7. When solutions of the following electrolytes are mixed, an insoluble (or slightly soluble) solid forms in some of the mixtures but not in others. Using the table of solubilities of solids on page 622, select the examples in which an insoluble solid forms. Write the equations showing the predominant species.

a. barium chloride + potassium sulfate
b. sodium chloride + calcium nitrate
c. lead(II) nitrate + sodium carbonate
d. zinc chloride + sodium sulfide
e. sodium bromide + silver nitrate

8. Solutions of the following pairs of electrolytes are mixed:

(1) copper(II) sulfate + sodium hydroxide
(2) sodium carbonate + hydrochloric acid
(3) lead(II) nitrate + sodium sulfide
(4) magnesium chloride + potassium sulfate
(5) iron(III) chloride + calcium hydroxide

a. Where a reaction occurs, write an equation showing all the ions present and the nonionic substances that form.
b. Where a reaction occurs, write an equation showing only the predominant species.
c. Where a reaction does not occur, write an ionic equation showing that the reaction is reversible.

9. Solutions of the following pairs of electrolytes are mixed:

> (1) sodium sulfite + hydrochloric acid
> (2) calcium chloride + sulfuric acid (heated)
> (3) copper(II) sulfate + nitric acid
> (4) iron(II) sulfide + sulfuric acid

  a. Where a reaction occurs, write an equation showing all the ions present and the gaseous products that form.
  b. Where a reaction occurs, write an equation showing only the predominant species.
  c. Where a reaction does not occur, write an ionic equation showing that the reaction is reversible.

Exercises for Further Study

1. A solution containing 9.2 g of a nonelectrolyte dissolved in 100 g of water is found to have a freezing point of $-1.86°$ C. What is the molecular weight of the solute?

2. A solution contains 0.10 mole of solute dissolved in 200 g of water. The boiling point of the solution is $100.30°$ C.
  a. Is the solute a nonelectrolyte, a weak electrolyte, or a strong electrolyte? Explain.
  b. At what temperature will this solution freeze? Why?

3. Consider a nonelectrolyte with a molecular weight of 120. How much of this solute must be dissolved in 500 g of water to obtain a solution that freezes at $-3.72°$ C?

4. A nonelectrolyte has an empirical formula of CH_3O. When 6.2 g of this substance are dissolved in 100 g of water, the resulting solution freezes at $-1.86°$ C.
  a. What is the molecular weight of the compound?
  b. What is the molecular formula of the compound?

5. In a system containing different independent particles, such as ions and molecules, the average energy for each particle is the same at a given temperature.
  a. Using this concept, explain why the boiling point of a solution is higher than the boiling point of water.
  b. Explain why the boiling point is even higher for a solution of an electrolyte.

6. When sodium nitrate, $NaNO_3$, is added to a solution of nitric acid, HNO_3, little change in the acid strength of the solution occurs. When sodium lactate is added to a solution of lactic acid, a change is noted in the acidity of the solution.
   a. Would you expect the lactic acid solution to become more or less acidic? Explain.
   b. Why does no change occur in the first case?

7. The ionization constant of acetic acid, CH_3COOH, is 1.8×10^{-5}. A related compound, chloracetic acid, $CH_2ClCOOH$, has an ionization constant of 1.4×10^{-3}.
   a. Which is the stronger acid?
   b. What effect does the presence of the Cl atom have on the strength of the bond between O and H?

8. A 0.05 M solution of butyric acid, C_3H_7COOH, is found to be 1.18% ionized. Calculate the ionization constant of this acid.

9. The ionization constant of hydrocyanic acid, HCN, is 7×10^{-10}. Calculate the H_3O^+ concentration in a 0.1 M solution of HCN.

10. A solution is prepared to have a concentration of 0.05 M propionic acid, C_2H_5COOH, and 0.2 M sodium propionate, C_2H_5COONa. What is the concentration of H_3O^+ in this solution? (The ionization constant for propionic acid equals 1.6×10^{-5}.)

11. Ammonium hydroxide, or aqueous ammonia, NH_4OH, ionizes as a weak base with an ionization constant of 1.8×10^{-5}. Find the OH^- ion concentration in a 0.2 M solution of NH_4OH.

12. The concentration of a saturated solution of calcium sulfate, $CaSO_4$, is 4.8×10^{-3} M. Calculate the solubility product constant for $CaSO_4$.

13. The solubility of lead(II) iodide, PbI_2, is 1.6×10^{-3} mole/l. Calculate the solubility product constant for PbI_2. [*Hint:* Remember that the concentration of I^- is twice the concentration of Pb^{+2} (*aq*).]

14. A saturated solution of calcium carbonate, $CaCO_3$, contains 6.9×10^{-3} g of solute per liter. Calculate the K_{SP} for $CaCO_3$.

15. The solubility product constant for silver bromide, AgBr, is 5.2×10^{-13}. If a solution contains 2×10^{-2} M of Br^- ion, what concentration of Ag^+ (*aq*) ion is needed before precipitation of AgBr begins?

16. The solubility product constant for strontium chromate, $SrCrO_4$, is 3.6×10^{-5}. If a saturated solution of $SrCrO_4$ is prepared in 0.01 M K_2CrO_4, what is the concentration of Sr^{+2} (*aq*) ion in the solution?

Chapter 16

PROTON TRANSFER: ACIDS AND BASES

16.1 Introduction

In the previous chapter, we described some strong and some weak electrolytes, relating their properties to the presence of aquated ions.

$$\text{STRONG ACID} \quad \text{HCl } (g) + \text{H}_2\text{O} \longrightarrow \text{H}_3\text{O}^+ + \text{Cl}^- \ (aq)$$
$$\text{WEAK BASE} \quad \text{NH}_3 \ (g) + \text{H}_2\text{O} \rightleftharpoons \text{NH}_4^+ \ (aq) + \text{OH}^- \ (aq)$$

Some solutions that contain aquated ions interact with substances called *indicators* to produce a characteristic color. For example, litmus (a plant derivative) dissolves in water to form a solution that turns red in the presence of H_3O^+ ions and blue in the presence of aquated OH^- ions. We have already classified solutions that contain excess H_3O^+ ions as *acids* and solutions that contain excess OH^- ions as *bases*.

A water solution of HCl (g) turns litmus red, and a water solution of NH_3 (g) turns litmus blue. Both solutions conduct electricity. However, the liquefied gases HCl (l) and NH_3 (l) do not conduct electricity and have no effect on litmus. It is not surprising that HCl (l) and NH_3 (l) do not conduct electricity, since both substances are covalent compounds and do not contain ions as charge carriers. But why does limus react one way to the liquefied gases and a different way to their water solutions?

In this chapter, we will see that the study of acids and bases is, in large measure, a logical extension of the behavior of ions in aqueous solution.

16.2 Definitions of acid and base

From the observed properties of water solutions of acids, we define an acid as a substance that

1. turns litmus solution red.
2. has a sour taste. (Chemicals should never be tasted unless it is absolutely certain that they are not poisonous.)
3. neutralizes bases. (During neutralization, an acid reacts with a base; the original properties of both substances change.)
4. conducts an electric current.
5. liberates hydrogen on reacting with certain metals such as Al, Mg, or Zn.

From the observed properties of water solutions of bases, we define a base as a substance that

1. turns litmus solution blue.
2. has a bitter taste.
3. neutralizes acids.
4. conducts an electric current.
5. feels slippery to the touch. (Chemicals should never be touched unless it is absolutely certain that they are not corrosive.)

A definition of a class of substances based upon observed behavior is called an *operational* definition. A definition of a class of substances based upon an explanation of observed behavior is called a *conceptual* definition. Conceptual definitions frequently employ models.

It is apparent that acids and bases have related properties. Let us see if we can develop an appropriate model to explain these properties.

16.3 The Arrhenius model of acids and bases

In section 10.22, we introduced the theory, or model, of ionic dissociation promulgated in 1887 by Arrhenius. (Remember that we are using the terms *theory* and *model* interchangeably.) The Arrhenius model accounted for some of the observed properties of acids and bases, such as electrical conductivity. Arrhenius assumed that certain substances in water solution dissociate into charged particles, or ions. He postulated the following:

1. Acids dissociate to produce hydrogen ions.
2. Bases dissociate to produce hydroxyl ions.

The Arrhenius model also explained why some acids and bases are strong, while others are weak. According to the model, strong acids ionize almost completely to yield a maximum quantity of H^+; strong bases ionize almost completely to yield a maximum quantity of OH^-.

$$\text{STRONG ACID} \qquad HCl \rightarrow H^+ + Cl^-$$

$$\text{STRONG BASE} \qquad NaOH \rightarrow Na^+ + OH^-$$

On the other hand, weak acids and bases ionize only partially to yield a small quantity of ions; equilibrium exists between the molecules and the ions. For example, consider the ionization of acetic acid, CH_3COOH (a weak acid), and magnesium hydroxide, $Mg(OH)_2$ (a moderately weak base).

$$\text{WEAK ACID} \qquad CH_3COOH \underset{\longleftarrow}{\overset{\rightarrow}{}} H^+ + CH_3COO^-$$

$$\text{WEAK BASE} \qquad Mg(OH)_2 \underset{\longleftarrow}{\overset{\rightarrow}{}} Mg^{+2} + 2\ OH^-$$

The properties common to acids were considered to be a result of the H^+ ions produced by acids in solution; the properties common to bases were considered to be a result of the OH^- ions produced by bases in solution.

Soon after Arrhenius proposed his theory, it was found that substances such as ammonia, NH_3, and sodium carbonate, Na_2CO_3, could neutralize (react with) acids and affect indicators in the manner of typical bases. However, NH_3 and Na_2CO_3 do not contain hydroxyl ions. Chemists further observed that, in some instances, NH_3 (a weak base) can also act as an acid. The concept of acids and bases had to be broadened to include molecules and ions that exhibited this dual behavior. In addition, the existence of a free hydrogen ion (or proton) in water was most unlikely because of the strong attraction between the positively charged ion and the polar water molecule. The Arrhenius model, apparently in need of modification, was amended and enlarged in 1923 by Johannes Brönsted, a Danish scientist, and Martin Lowry, an English scientist.

16.4 The Brönsted-Lowry model of acids and bases

The Brönsted-Lowry model extends our definition of acids and bases to include particles such as NH_3 and carbonate ion. According to this model, an *acid* is a substance that donates protons. A *base* is a substance that accepts protons. Therefore, a substance cannot function as an acid unless a base is present; and a substance cannot function as a base unless an acid is present. *In all equations involving water in this chapter, all ions are aquated.*

The acidic properties of HCl result from the ability of HCl to donate protons to water or to other substances that can accept protons, such as NH_3.

$$\overset{\frown}{HCl} + H_2O \rightleftarrows H_3O^+ + Cl^-$$
$$\text{acid} \quad \text{base}$$

$$\overset{\frown}{HCl} + NH_3 \rightleftarrows NH_4^+ + Cl^-$$
$$\text{acid} \quad \text{base}$$

The basic properties of NH_3 result from the ability of NH_3 to accept protons from water or from other substances that can donate protons (acids), such as HCl.

$$\overset{\frown}{NH_3} + H_2O \rightleftarrows NH_4^+ + OH^-$$
$$\text{base} \quad \text{acid}$$

$$\overset{\frown}{NH_3} + HCl \rightleftarrows NH_4^+ + Cl^-$$
$$\text{base} \quad \text{acid}$$

16.5 Acid-base conjugate pairs

In the reaction

$$HCl + H_2O \rightarrow H_3O^+ + Cl^-$$

the acid HCl donates a proton to the base H_2O, in accordance with the Brönsted-Lowry definition of acids and bases. However, all chemical reactions are reversible unless driven to completion. The above equation, therefore, can also be read from right to left: The acid H_3O^+ donates a proton to the base Cl^- to re-form HCl and H_2O.

Thus HCl and Cl^- ion are related. Cl^- ion is the base formed when HCl acts as an acid. HCl is the acid formed when Cl^- ion acts as a base. The HCl molecule and the Cl^- ion are called an *acid-base conjugate pair*. Using the same reasoning, we can also identify H_2O as the base and H_3O^+ as the acid, suggesting that in an acid-base reaction, there are two conjugate pairs of acids and bases.

$$\underset{\text{acid}_1}{HCl} + \underset{\text{base}_2}{H_2O} \rightleftarrows \underset{\text{acid}_2}{H_3O^+} + \underset{\text{base}_1}{Cl^-}$$

HCl and Cl^- are identified as conjugate pair 1, and H_2O and H_3O^+ as conjugate pair 2.

If we read from left to right in the reaction

$$\underset{\text{base}_1}{NH_3} + \underset{\text{acid}_2}{H_2O} \rightleftarrows \underset{\text{acid}_1}{NH_4^+} + \underset{\text{base}_2}{OH^-}$$

we see that NH_3 behaves as a base. It accepts protons from H_2O, which, in this case, acts as an acid. In the reverse direction, NH_4^+ ions donate protons to OH^- ions to re-form NH_3 and H_2O. Once again, it is possible to identify two conjugate acid-base pairs. Note that H_2O has a dual role; it can act either as an acid or a base.

The identification of conjugate pairs is useful for judging the strengths of acids and bases and for predicting the direction of acid-base reactions.

16.6 Strengths of acids and bases

In the reaction

$$HCl + H_2O \rightleftarrows H_3O^+ + Cl^-$$

experiment shows that HCl is a strong acid. Because HCl has a strong tendency to donate protons, we can reasonably expect its conjugate base, Cl^- ion, to have a weak tendency to hold or to accept protons. If we look at the same reaction in the opposite direction, we see that the Cl^- ion is a weak proton acceptor; therefore, its conjugate acid (HCl) must be a strong proton donor.

In the reaction

$$CH_3COOH + H_2O \rightleftarrows H_3O^+ + CH_3COO^-$$
$$\text{acid}_1 \qquad \text{base}_2 \qquad \text{acid}_2 \qquad \text{base}_1$$

the CH_3COOH molecule is a relatively weak acid, and its conjugate base (CH_3COO^- ion) is a relatively strong base.

Careful examination of these two equations shows that for an acid to react (donate protons), a base must be present (to accept protons). The extent of the overall reaction depends not only on the proton-donating properties of the acid, but also on the proton-accepting properties of the base.

The strengths of acids can be compared by measuring their ability to donate protons to the same base, usually water. In this comparison, only the proton donor is shown, and the proton acceptor is understood to be water. For example, in the following table, HCl is the strongest acid, and H_2O is the weakest acid. Similarly, Cl^- is the weakest base, and OH^- is the strongest base.

	ACID $\longrightarrow$				CONJUGATE BASE	
	CONJUGATE ACID $\longleftarrow$				BASE	
↑	HCl	$\rightarrow$	H^+	$+$	Cl^-	
	H_2SO_4	$\rightarrow$	H^+	$+$	HSO_4^-	
increasing acid strength	H_3O^+	$\rightarrow$	H^+	$+$	H_2O	increasing base strength
	HSO_4^-	$\rightarrow$	H^+	$+$	SO_4^{-2}	
	CH_3COOH	$\rightarrow$	H^+	$+$	CH_3COO^-	
	H_2CO_3	$\rightarrow$	H^+	$+$	HCO_3^-	
	H_2S	$\rightarrow$	H^+	$+$	HS^-	
	$H_2PO_4^-$	$\rightarrow$	H^+	$+$	HPO_4^{-2}	
	NH_4^+	$\rightarrow$	H^+	$+$	NH_3	
	HCO_3^-	$\rightarrow$	H^+	$+$	CO_3^{-2}	
	HPO_4^{-2}	$\rightarrow$	H^+	$+$	PO_4^{-3}	
	HS^-	$\rightarrow$	H^+	$+$	S^{-2}	
	H_2O	$\rightarrow$	H^+	$+$	OH^-	↓

Note that acids may be either molecules or ions; the same is true for bases. In addition, several species, such as HCO_3^- and H_2O, can behave as either acids or bases, depending on the nature of the other reactants. A species that behaves as an acid under certain conditions and as a base under other conditions is called *amphiprotic*, or *amphoteric*.

For example, the hydrogen carbonate ion (HCO_3^-) is amphiprotic. It behaves as follows:

1. As an acid toward the strong base OH^-.

$$HCO_3^- + OH^- \rightleftarrows H_2O + CO_3^{-2}$$
$$\text{acid}_1 \quad\quad \text{base}_2 \quad\quad \text{acid}_2 \quad\quad \text{base}_1$$

2. As a base toward the strong acid H_3O^+.

$$HCO_3^- + H_3O^+ \rightleftarrows H_2CO_3 + H_2O$$
$$\text{base}_1 \quad\quad \text{acid}_2 \quad\quad \text{acid}_1 \quad\quad \text{base}_2$$

Water has already been shown to have this dual property. Some other species that can behave as either an acid or a base are ammonia, NH_3; hydrogen sulfate ion, HSO_4^-; hydrogen sulfite ion, HSO_3^-; and mono-hydrogen phosphate ion, HPO_4^{-2}.

16.7 Amphiprotic hydroxides

Experiments show that some hydroxides behave either as acids or as bases, depending on their chemical environment. One such compound is the hydroxide of zinc. Experimental evidence indicates that zinc hydroxide is best represented by the formula $Zn(H_2O)_2(OH)_2$. The compound is relatively insoluble in water, but it dissolves in both acidic and basic solutions. This dual behavior is explained as follows:

1. Dissolving in a base (acting as a proton donor).

$$Zn(H_2O)_2(OH)_2 + 2\ OH^- \rightarrow Zn(OH)_4^{-2} + 2\ H_2O$$

2. Dissolving in an acid (acting as a proton acceptor).

$$Zn(H_2O)_2(OH)_2 + 2\ H^+ \rightarrow Zn(H_2O)_4^{+2}$$

Other examples of amphiprotic hydroxides are $Cr(OH)_3$, $Pb(OH)_2$, $Al(OH)_3$, and $Sn(OH)_2$.

16.8 The acid constant: K_A

The table in section 16.6 compares the strengths of acids and bases in a qualitative manner. Now let us compare these strengths quantitatively. Consider the following general equation for the ionization of a weak acid (all ions are aquated):

$$HA \underset{\longleftarrow}{\overset{\longrightarrow}{\rightleftharpoons}} H^+ + A^-$$

In our study of equilibria (see section 14.13), we learned that the equilibrium expression can be written as

$$K_C = \frac{[H^+][A^-]}{[HA]}$$

The equilibrium constant for this reaction has already been defined as the ionization constant (K_i). It is also called the *acid constant* (K_A).

Acid constants provide a quantitative measure of the tendency of HA to donate protons. The higher the constant, the larger the numerator of the equilibrium fraction, and the greater the proton-donating tendency of the acid. Strong acids have high K_A values. The values for K_A for some common acids follow.

ACID				CONJUGATE BASE	K_A
HCl	$\rightarrow$	H^+	$+$	Cl^-	very large
HNO_3	$\rightarrow$	H^+	$+$	NO_3^-	very large
H_2SO_4	$\rightarrow$	H^+	$+$	HSO_4^-	very large
H_3O^+	$\rightarrow$	H^+	$+$	H_2O	1
HSO_4^-	$\rightarrow$	H^+	$+$	SO_4^{-2}	1.3×10^{-2}
H_3PO_4	$\rightarrow$	H^+	$+$	$H_2PO_4^-$	7.1×10^{-3}
HF	$\rightarrow$	H^+	$+$	F^-	6.7×10^{-4}
CH_3COOH	$\rightarrow$	H^+	$+$	CH_3COO^-	1.8×10^{-5}
H_2CO_3	$\rightarrow$	H^+	$+$	HCO_3^-	4.4×10^{-7}
H_2S	$\rightarrow$	H^+	$+$	HS^-	1.0×10^{-7}
$H_2PO_4^-$	$\rightarrow$	H^+	$+$	HPO_4^{-2}	6.3×10^{-8}
HSO_3^-	$\rightarrow$	H^+	$+$	SO_3^{-2}	6.2×10^{-8}
NH_4^+	$\rightarrow$	H^+	$+$	NH_3	5.7×10^{-10}
HCO_3^-	$\rightarrow$	H^+	$+$	CO_3^{-2}	4.7×10^{-11}
HPO_4^{-2}	$\rightarrow$	H^+	$+$	PO_4^{-3}	4.4×10^{-13}
HS^-	$\rightarrow$	H^+	$+$	S^{-2}	1.3×10^{-13}
H_2O	$\rightarrow$	H^+	$+$	OH^-	1.8×10^{-16}

The strongest acid in this list is HCl, and the weakest acid is H_2O. The strongest base is OH^-, and the weakest base is Cl^-. Let us now see how we may use such a list to predict acid-base reactions.

16.9 Predicting acid-base reactions

Suppose you are given two solutions: aqueous potassium hydrogen sulfate, $KHSO_4$, and aqueous sodium hydrogen carbonate, $NaHCO_3$. The problem is to predict (1) what reaction (if any) will take place after the solutions are mixed, and (2) whether reactants or products will be favored after the reaction (if one takes place) has reached equilibrium. The chemical species involved are derived from the ionization reactions

$$KHSO_4 \rightarrow K^+ (aq) + HSO_4^- (aq) \text{ and } NaHCO_3 \rightarrow Na^+ (aq) + HCO_3^- (aq)$$

Potassium and sodium ions do not interact and do not have any acidic or basic properties. Therefore, the problem involves the possible interaction between the HSO_4^- and HCO_3^- ions. Examination of the table on page 293 shows that either of these ions can act as both an acid and a base, but that the HSO_4^- is the stronger acid of the two. Since the stronger acid HSO_4^- will have the greater tendency to donate protons, HCO_3^- will behave as a base and will accept the protons.

$$\underset{\text{acid}_1}{HSO_4^-} + \underset{\text{base}_2}{HCO_3^-} \rightleftarrows \underset{\text{acid}_2}{H_2CO_3} + \underset{\text{base}_1}{SO_4^{-2}}$$

What is the composition of the equilibrium mixture? HSO_4^- is the stronger of the two possible acids, and HCO_3^- is the stronger of the two possible bases. The tendency to donate and accept protons going from left to right is greater than the same tendency in the right-to-left direction. One can reasonably predict that, at equilibrium, the concentration of products (H_2CO_3 and SO_4^{-2}) will be greater than the concentration of reactants (HSO_4^- and HCO_3^-). We assume that the solutions are dilute and that the reaction is carried out in a closed container, so that the decomposition of H_2CO_3 does not occur.

Every chemistry laboratory has bottles of aqueous ammonia, usually labeled NH_4OH. What is the composition of the liquid? Examination of the reaction

$$\underset{\text{base}_1}{NH_3} + \underset{\text{acid}_2}{H_2O} \rightleftarrows \underset{\text{acid}_1}{NH_4^+} + \underset{\text{base}_2}{OH^-}$$

shows that both the stronger acid and the stronger base lie on the right-hand side of the equation, so that reactants are favored at equilibrium. The K_A values support this conclusion. Thus a bottle of ammonia water consists mostly of ammonia gas and water molecules, and, to a lesser degree, ammonium ions and hydroxyl ions.

16.10 Polyprotic acids

In the preceding discussion, each acid liberated only a single proton. How does an acid such as H_2SO_4 behave? Experiment shows that this substance actually donates protons in two steps (all ions are aquated).

(1) $H_2SO_4 \rightarrow H^+ + HSO_4^-$ $K_A =$ very large

(2) $HSO_4^- \rightarrow H^+ + SO_4^{-2}$ $K_A = 1.3 \times 10^{-2}$

Acids which can donate more than one proton are termed *polyprotic acids*. We find that the first proton is donated the most readily; the second, less readily; and the third (if there is one), still less readily. Consider, for example, the ionization of phosphoric acid.

(1) $H_3PO_4 \rightarrow H^+ + H_2PO_4^-$ $K_A = 7.1 \times 10^{-3}$

(2) $H_2PO_4^- \rightarrow H^+ + HPO_4^{-2}$ $K_A = 6.3 \times 10^{-8}$

(3) $HPO_4^{-2} \rightarrow H^+ + PO_4^{-3}$ $K_A = 4.4 \times 10^{-13}$

16.11 What is the role of water in acid-base chemistry?

As we saw, water can behave as an acid or as a base. Summarizing:

$$H_2O + H_2O \rightleftarrows H_3O + OH^-$$

$$\text{acid}_1 \quad \text{base}_2 \quad \text{acid}_2 \quad \text{base}_1$$

This ionization reaction can be shown more simply as

$$H_2O \rightleftarrows H^+ + OH^-$$

The equilibrium constant governing the ionization reaction is

$$K_C = \frac{[H^+][OH^-]}{[H_2O]} = 1.8 \times 10^{-16}$$

We have already shown that in dilute solutions, the concentration of a liter of water is $\dfrac{1000 \text{ g/l}}{18 \text{ g/mole}} = 55.5$ molar. If we substitute 55.5 M for $[H_2O]$ and rearrange the terms, we obtain

$$55.5 \times K_C = [H^+][OH^-] = 55.5 \times 1.8 \times 10^{-16} = 1 \times 10^{-14} \text{ (at } 25° \text{ C)}$$

$$K_W = 1 \times 10^{-14}$$

where K_W is a constant equal to the product of the equilibrium constant and the constant 55.5. K_W is especially useful in the study of acids and bases and is called the *water constant*, or the *ion product of water*.

What is the concentration of H^+ and OH^- in pure water at 25° C? (In this discussion, all ions are aquated.) For every mole of H_2O that ionizes, 1 mole of H^+ and 1 mole of OH^- are formed. The concentration of H^+ ions therefore equals the concentration of OH^- ions.

$$\text{let } x = [H^+] = [OH^-]$$

$$[H^+][OH^-] = 10^{-14}$$

$$x^2 = 10^{-14}$$

$$x = \sqrt{10^{-14}} = 10^{-7} \text{ mole/l}$$

In pure water at 25° C, the concentration of H^+ (*aq*) and OH^- (*aq*) is 10^{-7} molar, or 10^{-7} mole/l, each.

16.12 pH

We have seen that solutions containing more H_3O^+ ions than OH^- ions are acidic. Similarly, solutions that contain more OH^- ions than H_3O^+ ions are basic. Pure water, on the other hand, contains an equal amount of H_3O^+ and OH^- ions and is neutral. Using the ionization product of water, $K_W = 10^{-14}$, we can now express acidity, basicity, and neutrality in mathematical terms:

An *acidic solution* contains more than 10^{-7} mole/l of H_3O^+ ions.

A *basic solution* contains more than 10^{-7} mole/l of OH^- ions.

A *neutral solution* — one that is neither acidic nor basic — contains 10^{-7} mole/l of H_3O^+ ions and 10^{-7} mole/l of OH^- ions.

A logarithmic system has been devised to express the acidity or basicity of a solution. Logarithms permit us to bypass awkward calculations involving negative exponents. In this system, devised by Sören Sörensen in 1909, acidity is expressed as a positive number, though not necessarily a whole number. The number, called the pH of the solution, is the logarithm of the reciprocal of the hydronium ion concentration.

$$pH = \log \frac{1}{[H_3O^+]} \quad \text{or} \quad pH = -\log [H_3O^+]$$

16.13 Calculations involving pH

If a solution has a H_3O^+ ion concentration equal to 10^{-5} mole/l, the pH of the solution is 5.

$$pH = \log \frac{1}{[H_3O^+]} = \log \frac{1}{10^{-5}} = \log 10^5 = 5 \log 10 = 5$$

Suppose the H_3O^+ ion concentration of a solution equals 4×10^{-3} mole/l. What is the pH of the solution?

$$pH = \log \frac{1}{[H_3O^+]}$$

$$= \log \frac{1}{4 \times 10^{-3}} = \log \frac{10^3}{4} = \log 10^3 - \log 4$$

$$= 3 - 0.60 = 2.40$$

Knowing pH, we may compute $[H_3O^+]$. For example, suppose the pH of a solution equals 4. What is $[H_3O^+]$?

$$\log \frac{1}{[H_3O^+]} = pH$$

$$\frac{1}{[H_3O^+]} = 10^{pH}$$

$$[H_3O^+] = 10^{-pH}$$

$$[H_3O^+] = 10^{-4} \text{ mole/l}$$

(As a check, note that $\log \frac{1}{10^{-4}} = \log 10^4 = 4 \log 10 = 4$.)

As we have seen, the pH of a solution need not necessarily be a whole number. Suppose the pH is 3.6. What is the $[H_3O^+]$? By inspection, we note that a pH of 3.6 means that $[H_3O^+]$ must be between 10^{-3} and 10^{-4} mole/l (between 0.001 and 0.0001).

$$\log \frac{1}{[H_3O^+]} = pH$$

$$[H_3O^+] = 10^{-pH}$$

$$= 10^{-3.6}$$

$$= 10^{-4} \times 10^{0.4}$$

$10^{0.4}$ is a number whose logarithm is 0.4. Thus $10^{0.4} = 2.5$, and

$$[H_3O^+] = 2.5 \times 10^{-4} \text{ mole/l}$$

We have seen from the previous examples that decreasing the pH of a solution from 4 to 3.6 increases $[H_3O^+]$ from 10^{-4} to 2.5×10^{-4}. Similarly, increasing the pH decreases $[H_3O^+]$. What happens to the pH when we substantially increase $[H_3O^+]$? Consider a 1-molar solution of HCl in which $[H_3O^+] = 1$ mole/l. What is the pH of this solution?

$$pH = \log \frac{1}{[H_3O^+]}$$

$$= \log \frac{1}{1} = \log 1 = 0$$

The pH of this solution $= 0$. In general, the pH scale is not used for solutions in which $[H_3O^+]$ exceeds 1 mole/l. Such solutions have negative pH values. For example, the pH of a 10 M HCl solution $= \log \frac{1}{10} = -1$.

We may infer, therefore, that the pH scale is generally but not necessarily limited to values between 0 and 14. The concentration of H_3O^+ ion always determines the pH of the solution, but the product $[H_3O^+][OH^-]$ must equal 10^{-14} at 25° C. Thus a solution containing 0.1 mole/l of H_3O^+ ion (10^{-1}) also contains 10^{-13} mole of OH^- ion. The solution has a pH of 1 ($\log \frac{1}{0.1} = \log 10 = 1$).

Solutions with pH values equal to 7 are neutral; solutions with pH values greater than 7 are basic; solutions with pH values less than 7 are acidic.

16.14 pOH

When $[OH^-]$ is to be emphasized, chemists sometimes use the expression pOH to describe the basicity (alkalinity) of a solution. Just as $pH = \log \frac{1}{[H_3O^+]}$, $pOH = \log \frac{1}{[OH^-]}$. A simple relationship exists for these two expressions:

$$pH + pOH = 14$$

Using this relationship, we can compute the pOH from the pH of a solution. For example, consider an acidic solution with a pH of 4. The pOH $= 14 - pH = 10$. Solutions with pOH values greater than 7 are acidic, and solutions with pOH values less than 7 are basic.

16.15 Comparison of acidity and basicity

The relationships between pH, pOH, and the molar concentrations that these expressions represent are summarized in the following table.

	$[H_3O^+]$	$[OH^-]$	pH	pOH	
↑	10^1	10^{-15}	-1	15	
	10^0	10^{-14}	0	14	
	10^{-1}	10^{-13}	1	13	
	10^{-2}	10^{-12}	2	12	
	10^{-3}	10^{-11}	3	11	
increasing acidity	10^{-4}	10^{-10}	4	10	increasing basicity
	10^{-5}	10^{-9}	5	9	
	10^{-6}	10^{-8}	6	8	
	10^{-7}	10^{-7}	7	7	
	10^{-8}	10^{-6}	8	6	
	10^{-9}	10^{-5}	9	5	
	10^{-10}	10^{-4}	10	4	
	10^{-11}	10^{-3}	11	3	
	10^{-12}	10^{-2}	12	2	
	10^{-13}	10^{-1}	13	1	
	10^{-14}	10^0	14	0	↓

16.16 Indicators

A convenient method for determining the pH of a solution is to observe the change in color of indicators—complex molecules that behave as weak acids or weak bases. Indicators change color in a specific pH range. The change of color and the pH range vary with the indicator.

Suppose we represent the formula of an indicator as HIn. As in the case of acetic acid, HIn molecules react with H_2O.

$$HIn + H_2O \rightleftharpoons H_3O^+ + In^-$$

The HIn molecule and the In^- ion have different colors. At equilibrium

$$K_i = \frac{[H_3O^+]\,[In^-]}{[HIn]} \quad \text{or} \quad \frac{K_i}{[H_3O^+]} = \frac{[In^-]}{[HIn]}$$

The ratio $\dfrac{K_i}{[H_3O^+]}$ determines the ratio $\dfrac{[In^-]}{[HIn]}$, which, in turn, determines the color of the indicator in the solution to which the indicator has been added. If we apply Le Chatelier's Principle, we see that increasing the concentration of H_3O^+ drives the equilibrium to the left. This decreases the concentration of In^- and increases the concentration of HIn. The color of HIn will therefore predominate in acid solutions. The addition of OH^- ions (which decreases H_3O^+ concentration) drives the reaction to the right. This increases the concentration of In^- and decreases the concentration of HIn. Thus, in a basic solution, the color of In^- will predominate.

For litmus solution, we may picture the color change as

$$\underset{\text{red}}{HIn} + H_2O \underset{\longleftarrow}{\overset{\longrightarrow}{\rightleftharpoons}} H_3O^+ + \underset{\text{blue}}{In^-}$$

If hydrochloric acid is added to a litmus solution, the equilibrium shifts to produce more HIn, and the solution becomes red.

For phenolphthalein, another common indicator, we may picture the color change as

$$\underset{\text{colorless}}{HIn} + H_2O \underset{\longleftarrow}{\overset{\longrightarrow}{\rightleftharpoons}} H_3O^+ + \underset{\text{pink}}{In^-}$$

If sodium hydroxide is added to water containing phenolphthalein, H_3O^+ ions are removed. The equilibrium shifts to produce more In^-, and the solution becomes pink.

The following table lists the color changes and pH ranges of some common indicators.

INDICATOR	COLOR CHANGE	pH RANGE
Congo red	blue to red	3–5
methyl orange	red to yellow	3.2–4.5
methyl red	red to yellow	4.3–6
litmus	red to blue	4.5–8.2
phenolphthalein	colorless to pink	8.3–10

16.17 Hydrolysis

Experiment shows that a 1-molar solution of sodium carbonate turns phenolphthalein pink, which indicates a pH range between 8.3 and 10. This means that the solution is basic. To understand the pH of a sodium carbonate solution, we must examine the chemical species present in the solution.

$$Na_2CO_3 \rightarrow 2\ Na^+\ (aq) + CO_3^{-2}\ (aq)$$

$$H_2O \rightleftharpoons H^+\ (aq) + OH^-\ (aq) \qquad K_W = 1 \times 10^{-14}$$

The Na^+ ion cannot behave as an acid since it has no protons to donate. It cannot behave as a base since positive ions do not accept protons. Thus no proton exchange between Na^+ ions and H_2O molecules seems possible. The carbonate ion, on the other hand, can behave as a base toward water, as shown by the following reaction, in which all ions are aquated:

$$CO_3^{-2} + H_2O \rightleftharpoons HCO_3^- + OH^-$$
$$\text{base}_1 \qquad \text{acid}_2 \qquad \text{acid}_1 \qquad \text{base}_2$$

Although HCO_3^- is a stronger acid than H_2O (favoring the reaction to the left), sufficient H^+ ions are removed from water to upset the water equilibrium. This means that $[OH^-]$ is greater than $[H^+]$. Thus there is an excess of OH^-, and the solution is basic. The reaction of the CO_3^{-2} ion with water is termed hydrolysis.

Hydrolysis is the reaction of a substance (especially an ion) with water to form either a weak base and excess hydronium ions or a weak acid and excess hydroxyl ions. Thus hydrolysis is essentially an acid-base reaction.

We have used a hydrolysis model to explain why a CO_3^{-2} solution is basic. Now let us use the model to predict whether NH_4Cl will be acidic, basic, or neutral.

As in the previous example, let us note the species in solution.

$$NH_4Cl \rightarrow NH_4^+ \ (aq) + Cl^- \ (aq)$$

$$H_2O \rightleftharpoons H^+ \ (aq) + OH^- \ (aq) \quad K_W = 1 \times 10^{-14}$$

We can regard Cl^- as a spectator ion, as it does not interact appreciably with water. However, the NH_4^+ ion does hydrolyze, acting as an acid, that is, acting as a proton donor.

$$NH_4^+ + H_2O \rightleftharpoons NH_3 + H_3O^+$$
$$\text{acid}_1 \qquad \text{base}_2 \qquad \text{base}_1 \qquad \text{acid}_2$$

Although NH_3 is a stronger base than H_2O, the increased $[H_3O^+]$ disturbs the water equilibrium, resulting in a decreased $[OH^-]$ concentration. Thus H_3O^+ ions are in excess, and the NH_4Cl solution is acidic. We can confirm our reasoning with a few drops of litmus, which will turn the solution red. Is the pH of the solution greater or less than 7?

16.18 Predicting the hydrolysis of a salt

In the previous section, we described the hydrolysis reactions of Na_2CO_3 and NH_4Cl. Now we will generalize our conclusions by describing the hydrolysis of the theoretical compound MX. (Similar treatment can be given to compounds with other general formulas.)

If the positive ion reacts with water, it forms the weak base MOH and excess hydronium ions; the solution is acidic. Thus solutions containing positive ions that react with water are acidic. (This assumes that the negative ion does *not* react with water.)

$$M^+ (aq) + H_2O \rightarrow MOH + H^+ (aq)$$

Examples of such solutions are $HgNO_3$ and $TlNO_3$, thallium(I) nitrate.

If the negative ion reacts with water, it forms the weak acid HX and excess hydroxyl ions; the solution is basic. Thus solutions containing negative ions that react with water are basic. (This assumes that the positive ion does *not* react with water.)

$$X^- (aq) + H_2O \rightarrow HX + OH^- (aq)$$

Examples of such solutions are CH_3COONa (sodium acetate) and NaCN (sodium cyanide).

Where both ions do not react with water, the solution is neutral. Examples of neutral solutions are NaCl and KNO_3. When both ions react with water, the solution may be acidic, basic, or neutral. The pH of the solution depends on the comparative strengths of the acid and the base that form.

The hydrolysis model that we have been developing is useful in predicting whether a salt solution will be acidic, basic, or neutral. The formula MX that we used in the model can be regarded as the general formula for a salt. Thus NaCl, NH_4Cl, $AgNO_3$, and CH_3COONa are classed as salts. *Salts* are compounds formed when one or more hydrogen particles of an acid are replaced by one or more positive ions of a base.

Actually, a salt may be formed by a different process, such as the direct combination of elements. However, it is often convenient to think of a salt as the product of an acid-base reaction for purposes of chemical classification. For example, common salt, NaCl, may be regarded as a compound in which the H of HCl has been replaced by the Na of NaOH. Other examples of salts are $NaHCO_3$, $CaSO_4$, NaCN, $TlNO_3$, and KH_2PO_4.

Summary: To predict if a salt solution will be acidic, basic, or neutral, we must first ascertain whether the positive or negative ions present can react with water. As our discussion has shown, the effect of this reaction on the displacement of the water equilibrium will determine the pH of the solution.

16.19 How the different *K*'s are related

K_C is the fundamental equilibrium constant from which all the other K's are derived. For the general reaction $A + B \rightleftarrows C + D$

$$K_C = \frac{[C][D]}{[A][B]}$$

K_i is the ionization constant referring specifically to ionic equilibria. For the general reaction $MB \rightleftarrows M^+ + B^-$

$$K_i = \frac{[M^+][B^-]}{[MB]}$$

K_A is the ionization constant referring specifically to acid-base equilibria. For the general reaction $HA \rightleftarrows H^+ + A^-$ or $MOH \rightleftarrows M^+ + OH^-$

$$K_A = \frac{[H^+][A^-]}{[HA]} \quad \text{or} \quad \frac{[M^+][OH^-]}{[MOH]}$$

K_W is the ionization product referring specifically to the water equilibrium

$$K_W = [H^+][OH^-]$$

K_{SP} is the equilibrium constant referring specifically to saturated solutions of difficultly soluble solids. For the general reaction $MZ \rightleftarrows M^+ + Z^-$

$$K_{SP} = [M^+][Z^-]$$

16.20 Acidic and basic oxides

The oxides of some metals react with H_2O to form bases and are called *basic anhydrides*. The term *anhydride* is of Greek derivation and means without water. Sodium and calcium oxides are typical basic anhydrides.

$$\text{ANHYDRIDE} \qquad \qquad \text{BASE}$$

$$Na_2O \ + H_2O \rightarrow 2\ NaOH$$

$$CaO \ + H_2O \rightarrow Ca(OH)_2$$

The oxides of some nonmetals react with water to form acids and are called *acid anhydrides*. Some relatively common acid anhydrides and the acids they form are shown in the following reactions:

ANHYDRIDE	ACID

$$SO_2 + H_2O \rightarrow H_2SO_3$$

$$SO_3 + H_2O \rightarrow H_2SO_4$$

$$CO_2 + H_2O \rightarrow H_2CO_3$$

$$P_4O_{10} + 6\ H_2O \rightarrow 4\ H_3PO_4$$

An acid anhydride can react directly with a basic anhydride to form a salt, as in the following reactions:

BASIC ANHYDRIDE		ACID ANHYDRIDE		SALT

$$CaO + CO_2 \rightarrow CaCO_3$$

$$Na_2O + SO_3 \rightarrow Na_2SO_4$$

16.21 The Lewis model of acids and bases

We have considered the Arrhenius and the Brönsted-Lowry models of acids and bases. Now we will consider a third model. This model, proposed by the American chemist Gilbert Lewis, expands our understanding of acids even further because it includes those substances which do not contain hydrogen ions or protons.

A *Lewis acid* is a substance that can accept pairs of electrons, and a *Lewis base* is a substance that can donate pairs of electrons.

It should not be surprising that a proton donor (Brönsted acid) and an electron acceptor (Lewis acid) are closely related. Let us again consider the reaction between HCl and H_2O, using dots to represent the electrons in the valence shells of each atom.

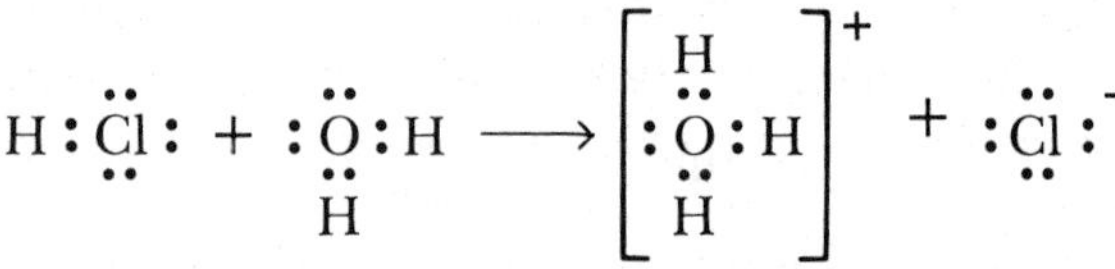

$$H:\overset{..}{\underset{..}{Cl}}: + :\overset{..}{O}:H \longrightarrow \left[:\overset{..}{O}:H \atop H \right]^+ \ + \ :\overset{..}{\underset{..}{Cl}}:^-$$

The proton in HCl accepts a pair of electrons from H_2O in order to bond to H_2O. Thus HCl is an electron acceptor (Lewis acid) or a proton donor (Brönsted acid). In the same manner, water is an electron donor (Lewis base) or a proton acceptor (Brönsted base).

From the Lewis point of view, it is not necessary to restrict acids and bases to the transfer of protons or to substances containing hydrogen. For example, a positive ion such as Cu^{+2} qualifies as a Lewis acid. In the reaction

$$Cu^{+2} + 4 \; NH_3 \rightarrow Cu(NH_3)_4^{+2}$$

a pair of electrons from each of four ammonia molecules is donated to the Cu^{+2} ion, which has an empty N-shell (outermost shell). As shown in the following figure, the Cu now has eight electrons—a stable configuration:

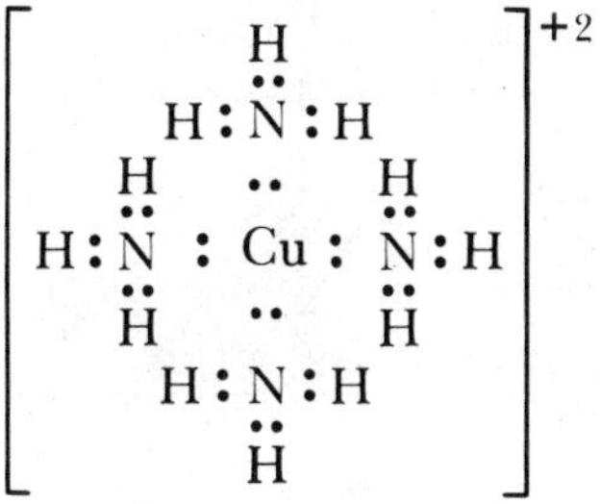

$$\begin{bmatrix} \text{H} \\ \overset{\bullet\bullet}{\text{H}:\text{N}:\text{H}} \\ \text{H} \quad \overset{\bullet\bullet}{\quad} \quad \text{H} \\ \text{H}:\overset{\bullet\bullet}{\text{N}} : \text{Cu} : \overset{\bullet\bullet}{\text{N}}:\text{H} \\ \overset{\bullet\bullet}{\text{H}} \quad \overset{\bullet\bullet}{\quad} \quad \overset{\bullet\bullet}{\text{H}} \\ \text{H}:\overset{\bullet\bullet}{\text{N}}:\text{H} \\ \text{H} \end{bmatrix}^{+2}$$

16.22 Equivalence and normality in acid-base chemistry

Solutions of 1 M HCl and 1 M H_2SO_4 have the same molar concentrations: Each solution contains 1 mole of acid solute per liter. However, the 1 M H_2SO_4 solution contains 2 moles of protons per liter, whereas the 1 M HCl solution contains 1 mole of protons per liter. How do the concentrations of these solutions compare, based on the ability to donate protons?

The H_2SO_4 solution can donate twice as many protons as an equal volume of the HCl solution and is, therefore, twice as concentrated. Similarly, we can compare the concentrations of bases in terms of the ability to accept protons. For example, a 1 M $Ba(OH)_2$ solution is twice as concentrated as an equal volume of a 1 M NaOH solution.

Chemists find it convenient to describe the concentrations of both acids and bases by the ability to donate or accept protons. For this purpose, the weight of the solute is expressed in gram-equivalents. In acid-base chemistry, *1 gram-equivalent* is the weight of solute in grams that can donate or accept 1 mole of protons.

For example, the weight of H_2SO_4 that can donate 1 mole of protons $= 1$ gram-equivalent $= \frac{1}{2}$ mole $= \frac{98 \text{ g}}{2} = 49$ g. In this example, $\frac{1}{2}$ mole of H_2SO_4 equals 1 gram-equivalent of H_2SO_4. However, the relationship between molarity and gram-equivalence depends on the specific acid or base that is being considered, as shown in the following table.

	SOLUTE	NUMBER OF MOLES PER GRAM-EQUIVALENT	NUMBER OF GRAM-EQUIVALENTS PER MOLE
ACID	HCl	1	1
	H_2SO_4	$\frac{1}{2}$	2
	H_3PO_4	$\frac{1}{3}$	3
BASE	NaOH	1	1
	$Ba(OH)_2$	$\frac{1}{2}$	2

We have used the concept of gram-equivalents to express the concentration of a solute such as an acid or a base (see section 10.8). A solution that contains 1 gram-equivalent of solute per liter is termed 1 normal, or 1 *N*. Note that a 1-molar solution contains 1 mole of solute per liter.

For a substance such as HCl, a 1 *M* solution is the same as a 1 *N* solution because 1 mole equals 1 gram-equivalent. However, for a substance such as H_2SO_4, the following relationships apply:

$$1 \text{ } M \text{ solution} = 2 \text{ gram-equivalents/l}$$

$$0.5 \text{ } M \text{ solution} = 1 \text{ } N \text{ solution}$$

$$1 \text{ } M \text{ solution} = 2 \text{ } N \text{ solution}$$

16.23 Acid-base titrations

To determine the unknown concentrations of acids or bases, a method of analysis known as titration is often used. *Titration* is a method of finding the unknown concentration of a solution by allowing the solution to react completely with another solution of known volume and known concentration. Usually an indicator is present which changes color sharply when the reaction is completed.

A specific example of an acid-base reaction will help to clarify titration. Suppose we want to find the unknown concentration of a solution of H_2SO_4. We place a few drops of phenolphthalein indicator in the H_2SO_4 solution. (Phenolphthalein is colorless in acid solutions but turns pink in the presence of a very slight excess of OH^- ions.) We find that 42.0 ml of 0.2 N NaOH solution cause 25.0 ml of H_2SO_4 solution to turn pink. These amounts of base and acid are therefore chemically equivalent. We may ignore the very slight excess of OH^- ions used to turn the indicator pink. The molarity and normality of the H_2SO_4 solution can be conveniently calculated by the mole method or by the method of equivalents.

MOLE METHOD

1. The reaction between sulfuric acid and sodium hydroxide is

$$H_2SO_4 \ (aq) + 2 \ NaOH \ (aq) \rightarrow 2 \ H_2O + Na_2SO_4 \ (aq)$$

2. Moles of NaOH that completely react with the sample of H_2SO_4

$$= 42.0 \ \text{ml} \times \frac{0.2 \ \text{mole}}{1000 \ \text{ml}} = 0.0084 \ \text{mole}$$

3. Since 2 moles of NaOH react with 1 mole of H_2SO_4, there are $\frac{0.0084}{2} = 0.0042$ mole of H_2SO_4 in the 25-ml sample.

4. $\dfrac{0.0042 \ \text{mole}}{25 \ \text{ml}} = 0.0042 \ \text{mole} \times \dfrac{40}{1000 \ \text{ml}} = \dfrac{0.17 \ \text{mole}}{1000 \ \text{ml}}$

5. The unknown concentration of the H_2SO_4 solution

$$= 0.17 \ M = 0.34 \ N$$

METHOD OF EQUIVALENTS

1. At the end of the titration, equivalents of acid = equivalents of base. Expressed mathematically,

$$\underset{\text{(in liters)}}{\text{acid volume}} \times N_{\text{acid}} = \underset{\text{(in liters)}}{\text{base volume}} \times N_{\text{base}}$$

$$\frac{\text{ml}}{1000} \times N_{\text{acid}} = \frac{\text{ml}}{1000} \times N_{\text{base}}$$

$$\frac{25.0 \times N_{\text{acid}}}{1000} = \frac{42.0 \times 0.2}{1000}$$

$$N_{\text{acid}} = 0.34$$

2. The unknown concentration of the H_2SO_4 solution

$$= 0.34 \ N = 0.17 \ M$$

Now let us see what happens when we titrate a weak acid, such as acetic acid. The question that concerns us is: Will the reaction go to completion? First, let us consider the ionization of acetic acid in water (all ions are aquated).

$$CH_3COOH \ \rightleftharpoons \ CH_3COO^- + H^+$$

The ionization constant, K_A, equals 1.8×10^{-5}. At equilibrium, therefore, most of the species present are molecules; very few are ions.

If the CH_3COOH is titrated with a strong base, such as NaOH, the CH_3COO^- ion and the Na^+ ion are spectator ions. The essential reaction that takes place (all ions are aquated) is

$$H^+ + OH^- \rightarrow H_2O$$

According to Le Chatelier's Principle, we find that the equilibrium system $CH_3COOH \ \rightleftharpoons \ CH_3COO^- + H^+$ shifts to the right as H^+ ions combine with (are removed by) OH^- ions. The CH_3COOH, despite its low ionization constant, continues to ionize as more NaOH is added. Eventually, the reaction is driven to completion by the continual removal of H^+, and the titration is valid.

Multiple-Choice Questions

1. A lemon has a sour taste because (1) all fruits are sour (2) it contains a base (3) it contains an acid (4) it does not contain sugar
2. According to the Brönsted-Lowry theory, NH_3 can act as an acid because it (1) can donate a proton (2) forms aquated H^+ ions in water (3) can be liquefied (4) can accept a proton
3. HNO_3 is a stronger acid than HNO_2. Therefore (1) a solution of 1-molar HNO_3 contains fewer particles than a solution of 1-molar HNO_2 (2) NO_2^- ion is a stronger base than NO_3^- ion (3) NO_3^- ion is a better proton acceptor than NO_2^- ion (4) the bond between H^+ and NO_3^- is stronger than the bond between H^+ and NO_2^-
4. An example of an amphiprotic particle is (1) HCO_3^- (2) H_2SO_4 (3) OH^- (4) NH_4^+
5. An example of a polyprotic acid is (1) H_2O (2) CH_3COOH (3) H_3PO_4 (4) HSO_4^-
6. An acid solution (1) reacts with metals (2) has a bitter taste (3) has a pH less than 7 (4) affects all indicators

7. A solution with a pH of 5 (1) has a concentration of H_3O^+ equal to 1×10^{-5} mole/l (2) is more acid than a solution that has a pH of 3 (3) contains no OH^- (*aq*) ions (4) can be made neutral by adding acid

8. A solution of sodium acetate turns litmus paper blue because (1) sodium is an active metal and reacts with water (2) all acetates are acids (3) all solutions of salt affect litmus (4) acetate ion is a base and removes protons from water

9. If the solution of an oxide, XO, is strongly basic, then (1) XO reacts with water, releasing protons (2) X is an active metal (3) XO resembles oxides of nonmetals (4) XO removes OH^- from water

10. The reaction of SO_2 with CaO (1) is a reaction between an acidic anhydride and a basic anhydride (2) cannot occur (3) involves proton transfer (4) involves oxidation-reduction

11. Ammonia is classed as an amphiprotic substance because it (1) is an excellent solvent (2) contains hydrogen (3) is a nonelectrolyte (4) can either accept or donate protons

12. A solution turns red when Congo red indicator is added to it. Another portion of the same solution turns red when methyl red is added to it. The pH of the solution (see table on page 300) may be (1) 3 (2) 8 (3) 6.5 (4) 4.5

Completion Questions

1. In the reaction $HNO_3 + H_2O \rightleftarrows H_3O^+ + NO_3^-$ (*aq*), the conjugate base of HNO_3 is _____.

2. The theory of ionic dissociation was first proposed by the scientist _____.

3. The reaction of a solution of any acid with a solution of any _____ is called neutralization.

4. Water can accept a proton to form H_3O^+ and can also donate a proton to form OH^- (*aq*). Water is therefore classified as a (an) _____ substance.

5. A solution that has a pH of 7 is classed as a (an) _____ solution.

6. Indicators behave as weak acids or as _____ bases.

7. The reaction of CO_3^{-2} ion with water is called _____.

8. The oxides of active metals react with water to form solutions that are _____ (*acidic, basic*).

9. Oxides of nonmetals that react with water to form acids are known as _____.

10. A solution of an acid that contains 1 mole of hydronium ion per liter of solution has a concentration designated as 1 _____.

True-False Questions

1. In the presence of *a base*, an amphiprotic substance acts as an acid.
2. The anhydride of sulfuric acid is SO_2.
3. Sulfur dioxide reacts with water to form a solution having an excess of H_3O^+. Sulfur dioxide is therefore classed as *a basic anhydride*.
4. An indicator can measure the H_3O^+ concentration of a solution because the ionized and nonionized forms of the indicator have different colors.
5. A solution with a *pOH* of 4 is basic.
6. A beverage that has a pH *greater than* 7 probably has a sour taste.
7. An example of a substance that can act only as *an acid* is SO_4^{-2}.
8. A difference between the Arrhenius model of acids and bases and the Brönsted-Lowry model is that according to the *Arrhenius* model, a base must form OH^- ions.
9. In the Brönsted-Lowry model, the particle that is associated with all acid reactions is the *electron*.
10. Metals such as Mg react with *HCl (l)* to produce hydrogen.

Decreases, Increases, Remains the Same

1. As the strength of an acid increases, the fraction of the acid in the molecular form _____.
2. When the strength of a base increases, the strength of its conjugate acid _____.
3. As the value for K_A increases, the strength of the acid _____.
4. When the acid HX releases protons, its ionization constant _____.
5. As the H_3O^+ concentration in water increases, the concentration of OH^- _____.
6. As acid is added to water, the product of the concentration of H_3O^+ ions and the concentration of OH^- ions _____.
7. As acid is added to a solution, the sum of the pH and pOH of the solution _____.
8. When more solid NaCl is added to a solution of NaCl in water, the pH of the solution _____.
9. As the metallic characteristics of elements increase, the acidity of corresponding oxides _____.

Exercises for Review

1. Provide an operational definition and a conceptual definition for each of the following: (*a*) solids (*b*) liquids (*c*) gases

2. Explain why 100% acetic acid is a very poor conductor of electricity and shows little reaction with metals, while moderately dilute acetic acid is a better conductor of electricity and reacts with metals.
3. Hydrocyanic acid, HCN, is a weak acid.
   a. Write an equation showing the reaction of the acid with water.
   b. Label the acids and bases present in the equation.
4. a. Define conjugate acid-base pairs.
   b. Explain why in acid-base reactions, two acid species and two basic species always appear.
5. In accordance with the Brönsted-Lowry model, explain why an acid does not function as an acid unless a base is present.
6. Using equations, show how the HSO_3^- ion is amphiprotic.
7. The ionization constant for HCN is 2×10^{-9}; for HNO_2, it is 4.5×10^{-4}.
   a. Which is the stronger acid? Explain.
   b. Which is the stronger base, CN^- or NO_2^-? Explain.
8. a. What is the concentration of OH^- ions in a solution of which the H_3O^+ concentration is $2.5 \times 10^{-4}\ M$?
   b. What is the concentration of H_3O^+ ions in a solution of which the OH^- concentration is $6.0 \times 10^{-5}\ M$?
9. In tabular form, list the following under the headings of *acid solution*, *basic solution*, and *neutral solution*:
   a. the concentration range of H_3O^+ ions
   b. the concentration range of OH^- ions
   c. the range of pH values
   d. the range of pOH values
10. Would you expect a solution of the following compounds to be neutral, acidic, or basic? Give your reason for each choice.
    a. sodium acetate, CH_3COONa c. ammonium nitrate, NH_4NO_3
    b. potassium sulfate, K_2SO_4 d. sodium borate, $Na_2B_4O_7$
11. Express the concentrations in normality for the following solutions:
    a. 3 M HCl   c. 1.5 M H_2SO_4
    b. 0.6 M $Ca(OH)_2$ d. 0.2 M H_3PO_4
12. How many moles of H_3O^+ ion are present in the following solutions?
    a. 2 l of 3 M HCl   c. 800 ml of 5 N HNO_3
    b. 0.5 l of 2 M H_2SO_4 d. 1.5 l of 2 N H_2SO_4
13. In a titration experiment, it is found that 32.0 ml of 0.100 N HCl are needed to neutralize 40.0 ml of a solution of NaOH. What is the concentration of the NaOH solution?
14. What volume of 2.00 N HNO_3 is needed to neutralize 24.0 ml of 5.00 N NaOH?

15. An experiment shows that 70 ml of 2.0 N KOH are needed to neutralize 45 ml of a solution of H_2SO_4. What is the concentration of the H_2SO_4 in normality and in molarity?

Exercises for Further Study

1. In which of the following reactions are protons transferred?
   a. HSO_4^- (aq) + F^- (aq) or SO_4^{-2} (aq) + HF (aq)
   b. HSO_3^- (aq) + CH_3COO^- (aq) or SO_3^{-2} (aq) + CH_3COOH (aq)

2. The Arrhenius model of acids and bases is a "two-particle model," while the Brönsted-Lowry model is a "one-particle model."
   a. What are the particles in each of the models?
   b. What is the advantage of one model over the other?

3. Show how NH_3 resembles H_2O as an amphiprotic substance.

4. Strong acids such as HCl, HNO_3, and $HClO_4$ are practically completely ionized in dilute solutions.
   a. What is the acid present in these solutions?
   b. Would you expect these solutions to show much difference in their acid strengths?
   c. What is (are) the acid(s) present in a solution of acetic acid?

5. Phosphoric acid, H_3PO_4, releases protons to water in three steps.
   a. Write an equation for each step.
   b. List the different species containing phosphorus and name each.
   c. Show which are acidic, basic, or amphiprotic species.

6. Show why every solution of acid in water contains OH^- ions, and why every solution of base in water contains H_3O^+ ions.

7. The ionization constant of acetic acid is 1.8×10^{-5}. Find the pH of a 0.2 M solution of acetic acid.

8. Some of the fluids of the body have a pH of 7.4. What is the concentration of H_3O^+ ion present?

9. Prove that pH + pOH = 14. (*Hint:* Recall that the product $[H_3O^+]$ $[OH^-]$ must equal 10^{-14}.)

10. According to the Brönsted-Lowry model, explain why the hydrolysis of a salt such as sodium sulfide is an example of an acid-base reaction.

11. Addition of water to an acid solution decreases the $[H_3O^+]$ of the solution and increases the pH value. Will the addition of sufficient water make the solution basic? Explain.

12. Aluminum hydroxide, $Al(OH)_3 \cdot 3H_2O$, is insoluble in water but can dissolve in dilute hydrochloric acid and also in a solution of sodium hydroxide. Write equations to show these reactions with the acid and with the base.

Chapter 17

ELECTRON TRANSFER:
OXIDATION AND REDUCTION

17.1 Introduction

In the previous chapter, we discussed acid-base reactions. Such reactions involve the transfer of protons. In this chapter, we will deal with another large class of reactions, oxidation-reduction (redox) reactions. Such reactions involve the transfer of electrons.

If a coil of copper wire is immersed in a solution of silver nitrate, $AgNO_3$, a deposit of silver soon appears on the coil, and the solution develops a blue color. The reaction may be written to show the predominant species.

$$2 \text{ Ag}^+ (aq) + \text{Cu } (s) \rightarrow \text{Cu}^{+2} (aq) + 2 \text{ Ag } (s)$$

As we saw in section 5.15, reactions involving a transfer of electrons may also be written as two half-reactions.

$$2 \text{ Ag}^+ (aq) + 2 \ e^- \rightarrow 2 \text{ Ag } (s)$$

$$\text{Cu } (s) \rightarrow \text{Cu}^{+2} + 2 \ e^-$$

We have already termed the half-reaction in which electrons are lost the *oxidation half-reaction* and the accompanying half-reaction in which electrons are gained the *reduction half-reaction*.

17.2 Oxidation number (oxidation state)

In section 5.3, we used the term *valence number* to denote combining capacity, which is the number of electrons an atom can donate, receive, or share during a reaction. The donating and receiving of electrons (both processes are called electron transfer) results in the formation of oppositely charged ions. The sharing of electrons results in the formation of covalently bonded molecules of varying polarity.

$$\text{ELECTRON TRANSFER} \qquad \text{Na} \cdot + \ ^\times_{\times}\ddot{\text{Cl}}^\times_\times \longrightarrow \text{Na}^+ + \ ^\times_\times\ddot{\text{Cl}}^\times_\times$$

$$\text{ELECTRON SHARING} \qquad \text{H}^\bullet + \ _\times\text{H} \longrightarrow \text{H} \overset{\times}{\cdot} \text{H}$$

Since many reactions involve oxidation-reduction (or a partial displacement of electrons), we will use the term *oxidation number*, or *oxidation state*, in place of valence number.

Electron transfer and electron sharing occur only when a reaction takes place. Uncombined atoms, therefore, are assigned an oxidation number of zero. Bear in mind that the oxidation number of an ion represents a true charge; however, the oxidation number of a particle in a covalently bonded species is a convenient representation of the extent of electron attraction (electron displacement).

17.3 Determining oxidation numbers

We may indicate the bonding arrangement in hypochlorous acid, HOCl, by the formula

$$\overset{+1}{\text{H}} \overset{-2}{\text{:O:}} \overset{+1}{\text{Cl:}} \quad \text{or} \quad \overset{+1}{\text{H}} \overset{-2}{\text{--O--}} \overset{+1}{\text{Cl}}$$

In this formula, x represents the electron of H, • represents one of the six valence electrons of O, z represents one of the seven valence electrons of Cl, and — represents a pair of shared electrons. O has a stronger attraction for electrons than either H or Cl, and attracts one electron from each of these atoms. The tendency to attract electrons—called *electronegativity* and discussed further in section 20.13—gives O an oxidation number of -2. To preserve electrical neutrality, H and Cl have oxidation numbers of $+1$ each. Note that two ions are present in HOCl: H^+ and OCl^-.

Let us examine the bonding arrangement in another compound of H, Cl, and O: chlorous acid, $HClO_2$.

$$\overset{+1}{\text{H}} \overset{-2}{\text{:O:}} \overset{+3}{\text{Cl:}} \quad \text{or} \quad \overset{+1}{\text{H}} \overset{-2}{\text{--O--}} \overset{+3}{\text{Cl}} \overset{-2}{\text{--O}}$$

Cl has given up three of its valence electrons (z): one has been pulled toward oxygen ⊙ , and two have been pulled toward oxygen ⊝ . In addition, the sole electron possessed by H has been pulled toward oxygen ⊙ . Oxygen atoms ⊙ and ⊝ have oxidation numbers of -2 each, Cl has an oxidation number of $+3$, and H has an oxidation number of $+1$.

Similarly, in chloric acid, $HClO_3$, H has an oxidation number of $+1$; Cl, $+5$; and each O, -2. In perchloric acid, $HClO_4$, H has an oxidation number of $+1$; Cl, $+7$; and each O, -2.

The following table contains some useful guides for determining oxidation numbers. We can utilize this information to write formulas by following the same procedure shown in sections 5.5 and 5.6.

PARTICLE	OXIDATION NUMBER
uncombined atoms	0
oxygen in compounds	-2 exceptions: peroxides, such as hydrogen peroxide (H_2O_2), where the oxidation number equals -1
hydrogen in compounds	$+1$ exception: hydrides, such as calcium hydride (CaH_2), where the oxidation number equals -1
alkali metals (Li, Na, K, Rb, Cs) of Group IA in compounds	$+1$
alkaline earth metals (Be, Mg, Ca, Sr, Ba) of Group IIA in compounds	$+2$
halogens (F, Cl, Br, I) in binary compounds with H or with metals	-1
monatomic ions	equals charge on ion

17.4 Electron transfer: an analogy

In acid-base reactions, both the acid (proton donor) and the base (proton acceptor) must be present before proton transfer can take place. In oxidation-reduction (redox) reactions, both the reducing agent (electron donor) and the oxidizing agent (electron acceptor) must be present before electron transfer can take place.

17.5 Oxidation

Oxidation has been defined as a reaction in which a particle loses electrons. Electron loss results in an increase in oxidation number. Examples of oxidation reactions follow:

EXAMPLE 1. Change from a free element to a positive ion.

$$Cu^0 \rightarrow Cu^{+2} + 2\ e^-$$

EXAMPLE 2. Change from a lower positively charged ion to a higher positively charged ion.

$$\underset{\substack{\text{ferrous} \\ \text{or Fe(II)}}}{Fe^{+2}} \rightarrow \underset{\substack{\text{ferric} \\ \text{or Fe(III)}}}{Fe^{+3}} + e^-$$

EXAMPLE 3. Change from a negatively charged ion to a free element.

$$2\ Cl^- \rightarrow Cl_2 + 2\ e^-$$

EXAMPLE 4. Change in oxidation state involving a polyatomic ion.

$$\overset{+4\ \ -2}{MnO_2} + 2\ H_2O \rightarrow \overset{+7\ \ -2}{MnO_4^-} + 4\ H^+ + 3\ e^-$$

Mn^{+4} is a fictitious charge representing the oxidation state of Mn in MnO_2. On the other hand, MnO_4^- is a specific polyatomic ion with a true charge of -1; it contains Mn with an oxidation state of $+7$.

Keep in mind that these oxidation reactions cannot take place unless a species capable of gaining electrons is also available. Each of the four examples represents only half of the total reaction; each is a half-reaction.

17.6 Reduction

Reduction has been defined as a reaction in which a particle gains electrons, with a resulting decrease in oxidation number. Following are some half-reactions which illustrate reduction:

EXAMPLE 1. Change from a free element to a negative ion.

$$I_2 + 2\ e^- \rightarrow 2\ I^-$$

EXAMPLE 2. Change from a higher positively charged ion to a lower positively charged ion.

$$Fe^{+3} + e^- \rightarrow Fe^{+2}$$

EXAMPLE 3. Change from a positive ion to a free element.

$$Ag^+ + e^- \rightarrow Ag^0$$

EXAMPLE 4. Change in oxidation state involving a polyatomic ion.

$$NO_3^- + 4\ H^+ + 3\ e^- \rightarrow NO + 2\ H_2O$$

In this half-reaction, note that the oxidation state of N changes from $+5$ in NO_3^- ion to $+2$ in NO.

17.7 Oxidizing agents

Since oxidation is a reaction in which a species loses electrons, we can state: An *oxidizing agent* contains a species that can cause the loss of electrons. The oxidizing species is itself reduced; that is, it gains electrons.

Many of the oxidizing agents that a student will encounter in a high school chemistry course may be classified as follows:

1. Positive ions that gain electrons, as shown in the general reaction

$$M^{+n} + n\ e^- \rightarrow M^0$$

where M represents a metal and n represents the charge on the metallic ion.

2. Nonmetallic elements, frequently halogens or oxygen, that gain electrons, as shown in the general reaction

$$X_2 + 2\ e^- \rightarrow 2\ X^-$$

$$Z_2 + 4\ e^- \rightarrow 2\ Z^{-2}$$

where X_2 represents a halogen molecule or where Z_2 represents an oxygen molecule.

3. Negative ions containing oxygen that also contain another atom in a relatively high oxidation state. The atom tends to lower its oxidation state by gaining electrons. These oxidizing agents and typical half-reactions which they undergo are shown in the following examples:

a. The permanganate ion, MnO_4^-.

$$MnO_4^- + 8\ H^+ + 5\ e^- \rightarrow Mn^{+2} + 4\ H_2O$$

Manganese in MnO_4^- gains 5 electrons and changes in oxidation state from $+7$ to $+2$.

b. The nitrate ion, NO_3^-.

$$NO_3^- + 4\ H^+ + 3\ e^- \rightarrow NO + 2\ H_2O$$

Nitrogen in NO_3^- gains 3 electrons and changes in oxidation state from $+5$ to $+2$.

c. The dichromate ion, $Cr_2O_7^{-2}$.

$$Cr_2O_7^{-2} + 14\ H^+ + 6\ e^- \rightarrow 2\ Cr^{+3} + 7\ H_2O$$

Each chromium atom in $Cr_2O_7^{-2}$ gains 3 electrons and changes in oxidation state from +6 to +3.

Note again that the atoms whose oxidation states are being lowered have fictitious charges. These atoms, however, are present in specific ions that do have true charges.

17.8 Reducing agents

Since reduction is a reaction in which a species gains electrons, we can state: A *reducing agent* contains a species that can cause the gain of electrons. The reducing species is itself oxidized; that is, it loses electrons.

Reducing agents can be classified as follows:

1. Active metals, such as Na, K, and Al, which tend to lose electrons readily. A general equation for the behavior of a metal as a reducing agent is

$$M^0 \rightarrow M^{+n} + n\ e^-$$

M represents the metal and n the charge on the metallic ion.

2. Halide ions that undergo the reaction

$$2\ X^- \rightarrow X_2 + 2\ e^-$$

where X^- represents a halide ion, for example, Cl^-.

3. Positive ions that can lose still more electrons to attain a higher oxidation state, for example:

   a. Stannous ion, tin(II), converted to stannic ion, tin(IV).

$$Sn^{+2} \rightarrow Sn^{+4} + 2\ e^-$$

   b. Ferrous ion, iron(II), converted to ferric ion, iron(III).

$$Fe^{+2} \rightarrow Fe^{+3} + e^-$$

17.9 Conjugate pairs in oxidation-reduction

Consider the oxidation half-reaction $K \rightarrow K^+ + e^-$. Because each potassium atom readily loses one electron, potassium is a strong reducing agent. The unipositive K^+ ion, however, does not have a strong tendency to gain electrons (to act as an oxidizing agent).

Consider the reduction half-reaction $\frac{1}{2}\ Cl_2 + e^- \rightarrow Cl^-$. Because the chlorine atom shows a strong tendency to gain an electron, the reaction takes place readily. Thus chlorine is a strong oxidizing agent. Again the converse is true: The Cl^- ion is a poor reducing agent.

We may extend the model of conjugate pairs developed in Chapter 16 for acids and bases to redox chemistry. First, we will restate the conclusions we reached about K and Cl: (1) Because the K atom loses electrons readily, the K^+ ion does not gain electrons readily. (2) Because the Cl^- ion does not lose electrons readily, the Cl atom gains electrons readily. We have experimental evidence that the behavior of K and Cl is typical of a large number of reducing and oxidizing agents. We can, therefore, reasonably expect that conjugate pairs in oxidation-reduction reactions will behave according to the following model: A strong reducing agent has a weak conjugate oxidizing agent. A weak reducing agent has a strong conjugate oxidizing agent.

17.10 Balancing oxidation-reduction reactions

Let us analyze the two half-reactions in an oxidation-reduction (redox) reaction on the basis of electron transfer. In the oxidation half-reaction, the increase in oxidation number is accompanied by a loss of electrons. In the reduction half-reaction, the decrease in oxidation number is accompanied by a gain of electrons. We can readily see that to conserve charge, the number of electrons lost must equal the number of electrons gained.

In the sections that follow, we will balance a redox reaction by two methods: the oxidation number method and the ion-electron method. Once we know the reactants and products, we will select the correct half-reactions. Then by balancing the half-reactions, we will balance the overall reaction. Throughout we will apply the concept that the numbers of electrons lost and gained are equal.

17.11 The oxidation number method of balancing oxidation-reduction reactions

Consider the reaction

$$HCl + KMnO_4 \rightarrow KCl + MnCl_2 + H_2O + Cl_2$$

in which all ions are aquated. As the first step in balancing the reaction, we will determine which particles are undergoing a change in oxidation number. We must, therefore, indicate the oxidation numbers of all the particles in the reaction.

$$H^+ + Cl^- + K^+ + \overset{+7\ -2}{MnO_4^-} \rightarrow K^+ + Cl^- + Mn^{+2} + 2\ Cl^- + \overset{+1\ -2}{H_2O} + \overset{0}{Cl_2}$$

The numbers above the symbols indicate the oxidation numbers. For example, -2 is the oxidation number of oxygen and $+7$ is the oxidation number of Mn in MnO_4^-.

The oxidation half-reaction is

$$2\ Cl^- \rightarrow Cl_2^0 + 2\ e^-$$

Some Cl^- ions are also present on the right side of the equation, indicating that not all Cl^- ions are oxidized to Cl_2^0. Some Cl^- ions, therefore, do not participate in the reaction and remain unchanged.

The reduction half-reaction is

$$Mn^{+7} + 5\ e^- \rightarrow Mn^{+2}$$

Note that Mn^{+7} does not exist as a specific particle. It appears only as part of the MnO_4^- ion.

By balancing the atoms in each half-reaction, we have conserved particles. If we multiply the entire oxidation half-reaction by 5 and the entire reduction half-reaction by 2 and add both reactions, we will also conserve charge; that is, the number of electrons gained will equal the number of electrons lost.

$$10\ Cl^- \rightarrow 5\ Cl_2 + \cancel{10\ e^-}$$
$$\underline{2\ Mn^{+7} + \cancel{10\ e^-} \rightarrow 2\ Mn^{+2}}$$
$$2\ Mn^{+7} + 10\ Cl^- \rightarrow 5\ Cl_2 + 2\ Mn^{+2}$$

We may now balance the overall reaction by using the coefficients obtained when we added the half-reactions. Thus we need $2\ Mn^{+7}$ or 2 moles of $KMnO_4$ to form 2 moles of Mn^{+2}; we need 10 moles of Cl^- or 10 moles of HCl to form 5 moles of Cl_2. Note that 2 moles of $KMnO_4$ also yield 2 moles of KCl and 2 moles of $MnCl_2$, which means that we have to account for 6 additional Cl particles. A total of 16 moles of HCl is required to react with 2 moles of $KMnO_4$ to form 8 moles of H_2O. The balanced overall reaction is

$$2\ KMnO_4 + 16\ HCl \rightarrow 2\ KCl + 2\ MnCl_2 + 5\ Cl_2 + 8\ H_2O$$

The oxidizing agent is $KMnO_4$ and the reducing agent is HCl.

17.12 The ion-electron method of balancing oxidation-reduction reactions

Again, consider the reaction

$$HCl + KMnO_4 \rightarrow KCl + MnCl_2 + H_2O + Cl_2$$

in which all ions are aquated. To balance this reaction by the ion-electron method, we will follow the procedure used in the oxidation number method. However, we will work with the specific ions that are involved in the oxidation and reduction half-reactions.

The oxidation half-reaction in this example remains unchanged.

$$2\ Cl^- \rightarrow Cl_2 + 2\ e^-$$

The reduction half-reaction begins with an ionic change.

$$MnO_4^- \rightarrow Mn^{+2}$$

Before we can conserve charge, we must first conserve particles (atoms). Since the reaction occurs in acid solution (HCl), the O in the MnO_4^- ion is converted by the H^+ ion, in the acid, into H_2O.

$$MnO_4^- + H^+ \rightarrow Mn^{+2} + H_2O$$

To conserve particles, we balance this reaction.

$$MnO_4^- + 8\ H^+ \rightarrow Mn^{+2} + 4\ H_2O$$

To conserve charge, we add 5 electrons to the left side of the reaction.

$$MnO_4^- + 8\ H^+ + 5\ e^- \rightarrow Mn^{+2} + 4\ H_2O$$

To balance the overall reaction, we multiply the entire oxidation half-reaction by 5 and the entire reduction half-reaction by 2, and follow the same procedure as in the oxidation number method. Note that we now have the same coefficients obtained by the previous method.

17.13 Balancing a more difficult reaction: Cu + HNO₃

We will balance the reaction between metallic copper and dilute nitric acid first by the oxidation number method and then by the ion-electron method.

OXIDATION NUMBER METHOD

Before writing the half-reactions, it is necessary to know the reactants and the products, as shown in the following unbalanced reaction (all ions are aquated):

$$Cu + HNO_3 \rightarrow Cu(NO_3)_2 + H_2O + NO$$

The oxidation half-reaction is

$$Cu^0 \rightarrow Cu^{+2} + 2\ e^-$$

The reduction half-reaction is

$$N^{+5} + 3\ e^- \rightarrow N^{+2}$$

Again, it must be emphasized that N^{+5} is fictitious and is present only as part of the NO_3^- ion.

The two half-reactions are balanced for electron loss and gain by multiplying them by the factors that will conserve electrons. Then the half-reactions are added.

$$3 \, [Cu^0 \rightarrow Cu^{+2} + 2 \, e^-]$$
$$\underline{2 \, [N^{+5} + 3 \, e^- \rightarrow N^{+2}]}$$
$$3 \, Cu^0 + 2 \, N^{+5} \rightarrow 3 \, Cu^{+2} + 2 \, N^{+2}$$

The coefficients indicated in the balanced half-reactions are now *tentatively* inserted in the original unbalanced reaction.

$$\overset{?}{3} \, Cu + \overset{?}{2} \, HNO_3 \rightarrow \overset{?}{3} \, Cu(NO_3)_2 + H_2O + \overset{?}{2} \, NO$$

In the reduction half-reaction, note that only 2 N^{+5} undergo reduction. In the unbalanced reaction with tentative coefficients, however, for each mole of Cu that is oxidized, 2 N^{+5}—in $Cu(NO_3)_2$—are present in the product and are not reduced. For 3 moles of Cu, therefore, 6 N^{+5} that are not reduced are needed. Since 2 N^{+5} are reduced and 6 N^{+5} remain unchanged, we need a total of 8 N^{+5} on the left side of the equation. The completely balanced reaction can now be written as

$$3 \, Cu + 8 \, HNO_3 \rightarrow 3 \, Cu(NO_3)_2 + 4 \, H_2O + 2 \, NO$$

ION-ELECTRON METHOD

In the ion-electron method, the oxidation half-reaction ($Cu^0 \rightarrow Cu^{+2} + 2 \, e^-$) is written in the same way as it is for the oxidation number method. However, the reduction half-reaction is based on NO_3^- ion rather than N^{+5}. In the reduction half-reaction, NO_3^- reacts with H^+ to form NO and H_2O.

$$3 \, [Cu^0 \rightarrow Cu^{+2} + 2 \, e^-]$$
$$\underline{2 \, [NO_3^- + 4 \, H^+ + 3 \, e^- \rightarrow NO + 2 \, H_2O]}$$
$$3 \, Cu^0 + 2 \, NO_3^- + 8 \, H^+ \rightarrow 3 \, Cu^{+2} + 2 \, NO + 4 \, H_2O$$

The net redox equation clearly shows that 3 moles of Cu reduce 2 moles of NO_3^-. The complete equation then follows from the oxidation number method previously described. Remember that the 6 NO_3^- ions in 3 $Cu(NO_3)_2$ do not undergo reduction and must be present in the total HNO_3.

For redox reactions that take place in aqueous solution, the ion-electron method of balancing is preferable. It indicates more accurately all the actual particles involved in the transfer of electrons.

17.14 Using chemical reactions to produce electricity: electrochemical cells

Consider Figure 17–1 below. Beaker A contains a strip of metallic zinc immersed in a 1-molar $ZnSO_4$ solution. Beaker B contains a strip of metallic copper immersed in a 1-molar $CuSO_4$ solution. A copper wire connects the two strips of metal through a voltmeter. An inverted U-tube filled with aqueous ammonium nitrate, NH_4NO_3, dips into both beakers (cotton or glass wool plugs keep the NH_4NO_3 solution from flowing out of the U-tube). This tube is called a *salt bridge*, and the entire setup is called an *electrochemical cell.*

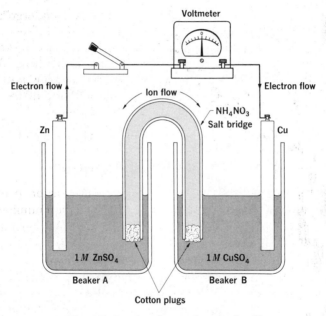

Fig. 17–1   An electrochemical cell

When the switch is closed, completing the circuit, the voltmeter needle is deflected, showing that electrons are flowing through the connecting wire. The zinc and copper strips were weighed before the circuit was completed and were weighed again after the experiment was concluded. The zinc strip lost weight, and the copper strip gained weight.

Let us analyze the preceding information by answering a series of questions. (In the following discussion, all ions are aquated.)

1. What is the direction of the electron flow?

As will be explained later, zinc has a greater tendency than copper to lose electrons (it is a stronger reducing agent). Thus the flow of electrons can be explained in terms of two half-reactions.

OXIDATION AT THE ZINC STRIP $Zn^0 \rightarrow Zn^{+2} + 2\ e^-$

REDUCTION AT THE COPPER STRIP $Cu^{+2} + 2\ e^- \rightarrow Cu^0$

The electrons given off by the zinc flow through the wire to the copper strip, where they are picked up by the Cu^{+2} ions present in the solution surrounding the copper strip. The electrode where oxidation takes place is called the *anode*, and the electrode where reduction takes place is called the *cathode*. The connecting wire offers a path for the flow of electrons from the oxidation half-reaction (zinc strip) to the reduction half-reaction (copper strip).

2. Why does the zinc electrode lose weight and why does the copper electrode gain weight?

As shown in the half-reaction, zinc dissolves to form Zn^{+2} ions, reducing the weight of the zinc. At the copper strip, Cu^{+2} ions are reduced to form metallic copper, which deposits on the copper strip, increasing its weight.

3. What is the function of the salt bridge?

We have already learned that charge must be conserved in chemical reactions. In the zinc half of the electrochemical cell (the half-cell), there is a gradual accumulation of positive charge in the solution as Zn^{+2} ions are formed. In the copper half-cell, there is an accumulation of negative charge in the solution as Cu^{+2} ions are removed. The NH_4NO_3 in the salt bridge supplies positive NH_4^+ ions and negative NO_3^- ions which flow into the two half-cells to keep the total charges neutral. NO_3^- ions flow into the zinc half-cell, and NH_4^+ ions flow into the copper half-cell. If this neutralization of charge did not occur, the reaction in the whole cell would stop, and current would no longer flow through the wire.

Another essential function of the salt bridge is to provide a path for ion flow. Electrical conductivity requires charge carriers, which may be mobile electrons or mobile ions. Without the salt bridge, the electrical circuit would not be complete. The wire provides a path for electron flow, and the salt bridge provides a path for ion flow. Both are needed to complete the circuit.

Note that we have avoided labeling the anode as the positive terminal and the cathode as the negative terminal. From the point of view of electron flow, the electrons produced during the oxidation of zinc at the anode accumulate on the electrode, creating an excess of electrons, or a negatively charged electrode. Thus the anode behaves as the negative terminal in an electrochemical cell. Similarly, the cathode behaves as the positive terminal.

Contrast the situation in terms of the ionic current. Note that negative NO_3^- ions entered the zinc half-cell. The zinc anode, from this point of view, is positive. Similarly, the positive NH_4^+ ions entered the copper half-cell, which means that the cathode in this instance is negative. We will encounter the same situation later in electrolysis reactions.

To avoid confusion, it is best to consider the anode as the terminal where oxidation occurs and the cathode as the terminal where reduction occurs. These definitions remain unchanged whether we are discussing the direction of electron current or the direction of ion current. The actual signs associated with anode and cathode therefore become unimportant.

In the system just described, electricity has been produced by a chemical reaction. Such a system is called an electrochemical cell. It is a combination of two half-cells separated physically but connected by a salt bridge. In one, oxidation occurs and in the other, reduction. Examples of commercial electrochemical cells are the dry cell and the storage battery (see section 17.17).

Two questions concerning the action of an electrochemical cell still need to be answered: Why do the electrons flow from zinc to copper and not in the reverse direction? What is the significance of the voltage reading on the meter?

17.15 E^0: a measure of the strengths of oxidizing and reducing agents

Suppose we want to compare the relative tendencies of different metals to lose electrons in aqueous medium. Remember that these tendencies represent driving forces and tell nothing about the rate of a reaction. It is convenient to compare these tendencies against some standard, using 1 M solutions for each half-cell. One such standard, called a *hydrogen electrode*, utilizes the half-reaction

$$H_2 \ (g) \rightarrow 2 \ H^+ \ (aq) + 2 \ e^-$$

The electrode consists of a strip of platinum on which hydrogen gas has been adsorbed (held on the surface). The platinum strip dips into a 1 M

acid solution. (See Figure 17–2.) When zinc is compared to the standard hydrogen electrode, the voltmeter reads approximately 0.76 volt. To secure meaningful comparisons, it is necessary to maintain these fixed concentrations. A voltmeter permits some electron flow through the half-cells, which changes the ionic concentrations. In actual practice, a *potentiometer* is used in place of the voltmeter. The potentiometer permits no current to flow through the half-cells and thus measures only the potential difference (voltage) between the half-cells at fixed conditions, called *standard states*.

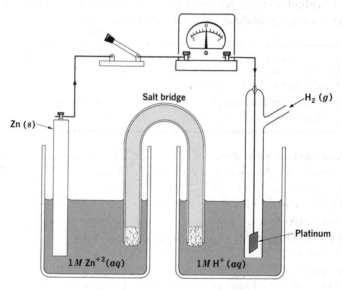

Fig. 17–2   Determining E^0

If we weigh the zinc electrode before the circuit is completed and again at the end of the experiment, we will note that the zinc strip lost weight. The loss of weight suggests that zinc atoms go into solution (are oxidized) when the cell operates.

$$Zn\ (s) \rightarrow Zn^{+2}\ (aq) + 2\ e^-$$

We can assume that electrons are released on the zinc plate. Bubbles of hydrogen appear at the platinum surface, suggesting that H^+ (*aq*) ions are being reduced and electrons are being consumed.

$$2\ H^+\ (aq) + 2\ e^- \rightarrow H_2\ (g)$$

Since electrons flow from the point of excess to the point of deficiency, the electrons flow from Zn → H$^+$.

When copper is tested against hydrogen, the electrons flow from the hydrogen electrode to the copper electrode, and the voltmeter reads approximately 0.34 volt in the opposite direction.

We can conclude that electrons flow from zinc to hydrogen and from hydrogen to copper. This means that zinc is a stronger reducing agent than hydrogen, and hydrogen is a stronger reducing agent than copper. The voltage reading associated with a half-cell reaction in a 1 M aqueous solution is called *E-zero*, symbolized E^0. The following table compares the relative reducing abilities of these elements.

HALF-REACTION	VOLTAGE READING, E^0
Zn (s) → Zn^{+2} (aq) + 2 e^-	0.76 v
H$_2$ (g) → 2 H$^+$ (aq) + 2 e^-	0.00 v
Cu (s) → Cu^{+2} (aq) + 2 e^-	−0.34 v

Note that the reducing ability of hydrogen has been assigned an arbitrary value of zero volts. As long as hydrogen is assigned a value of 0.00 volts, reducing agents stronger than hydrogen must be assigned a positive voltage value, while reducing agents weaker than hydrogen must be assigned a negative voltage value. We may infer from the table that zinc is a stronger reducing agent than hydrogen by 0.76 volt and that copper is a weaker reducing agent than hydrogen by 0.34 volt. Zinc is a stronger reducing agent than copper by 1.1 volts [0.76 v − (−0.34 v)]. This is why electrons flowed from zinc to copper. In time, the voltage reading would drop as [Zn^{+2} (aq)] increases and [Cu^{+2} (aq)] decreases.

E^0 values refer to voltage, a measure of the energy supplied to the electrons as they are transferred through the circuit from one electrode to the other. E^0 values are not influenced by the number of electrons being transferred. Thus E^0 for the oxidation of metallic sodium is +2.71 volts, whether the reaction is written as

$$\text{Na} \rightarrow \text{Na}^+ + e^- \qquad \text{or} \qquad 2\,\text{Na} \rightarrow 2\,\text{Na}^+ + 2\,e^-$$

A table of E^0 values appears on pages 328–329. The half-reactions near the top of the table indicate a greater tendency to lose electrons. Therefore, the stronger reducing agents appear near the top of the table. Similarly, the half-reactions near the bottom of the table indicate a lesser tendency to lose electrons, which means a greater tendency to gain electrons. Therefore, the stronger oxidizing agents appear near the bottom of the table.

In reality, a half-cell reaction represents an equilibrium system. This means that under proper conditions, the reaction can be reversed. The E^0 value for the reverse reaction has the same magnitude as the forward reaction but the *opposite* sign.

TABLE OF E^0 VALUES
(STANDARD OXIDATION POTENTIALS)

IONIC CONCENTRATIONS 1 MOLAR IN WATER AT 25°C
*(All ions are aquated. All gases are at
a partial pressure of 1 atmosphere.)*

HALF-CELL REACTION	E^0 (VOLTS)
$Li \rightleftarrows Li^+ + e^-$	3.05
$Rb \rightleftarrows Rb^+ + e^-$	2.93
$K \rightleftarrows K^+ + e^-$	2.92
$Cs \rightleftarrows Cs^+ + e^-$	2.92
$Ba \rightleftarrows Ba^{+2} + 2\ e^-$	2.90
$Sr \rightleftarrows Sr^{+2} + 2\ e^-$	2.89
$Ca \rightleftarrows Ca^{+2} + 2\ e^-$	2.87
$Na \rightleftarrows Na^+ + e^-$	2.71
$Mg \rightleftarrows Mg^{+2} + 2\ e^-$	2.37
$Be \rightleftarrows Be^{+2} + 2\ e^-$	1.85
$Al \rightleftarrows Al^{+3} + 3\ e^-$	1.66
$Mn \rightleftarrows Mn^{+2} + 2\ e^-$	1.18
$Zn \rightleftarrows Zn^{+2} + 2\ e^-$	0.76
$Cr \rightleftarrows Cr^{+3} + 3\ e^-$	0.74
$S^{-2} \rightleftarrows S + 2\ e^-$	0.48
$Fe \rightleftarrows Fe^{+2} + 2\ e^-$	0.44
$Cd \rightleftarrows Cd^{+2} + 2\ e^-$	0.40
$Co \rightleftarrows Co^{+2} + 2\ e^-$	0.28
$Ni \rightleftarrows Ni^{+2} + 2\ e^-$	0.25
$Sn \rightleftarrows Sn^{+2} + 2\ e^-$	0.14
$Pb \rightleftarrows Pb^{+2} + 2\ e^-$	0.13
$H_2\ (g) \rightleftarrows 2\ H^+ + 2\ e^-$	0.00
$Sn^{+2} \rightleftarrows Sn^{+4} + 2\ e^-$	-0.15
$Cu^+ \rightleftarrows Cu^{+2} + e^-$	-0.15
$Cu \rightleftarrows Cu^{+2} + 2\ e^-$	-0.34

HALF-CELL REACTION	E^0 (VOLTS)
$2\ I^- \rightleftarrows I_2 + 2\ e^-$	-0.53
$Fe^{+2} \rightleftarrows Fe^{+3} + e^-$	-0.77
$2\ Hg \rightleftarrows Hg_2^{+2} + 2\ e^-$	-0.79
$Ag \rightleftarrows Ag^+ + e^-$	-0.80
$Hg_2^{+2} \rightleftarrows 2\ Hg^{+2} + 2\ e^-$	-0.92
$NO\ (g) + 2\ H_2O \rightleftarrows NO_3^- + 4\ H^+ + 3\ e^-$	-0.96
$2\ Br^- \rightleftarrows Br_2\ (l) + 2\ e^-$	-1.06
$2\ H_2O \rightleftarrows O_2\ (g) + 4\ H^+ + 4\ e^-$	-1.23
$2\ Cr^{+3} + 7\ H_2O \rightleftarrows Cr_2O_7^{-2} + 14\ H^+ + 6\ e^-$	-1.33
$2\ Cl^- \rightleftarrows Cl_2\ (g) + 2\ e^-$	-1.36
$Au \rightleftarrows Au^{+3} + 3\ e^-$	-1.50
$Mn^{+2} + 4\ H_2O \rightleftarrows MnO_4^- + 8\ H^+ + 5\ e^-$	-1.51
$2\ F^- \rightleftarrows F_2\ (g) + 2\ e^-$	-2.87

17.16 Predicting oxidation-reduction reactions

The table of E^0 values may be used to predict whether or not a given redox reaction will proceed spontaneously under standard state conditions. As we have seen, an oxidation-reduction reaction consists of two half-reactions. Each half-reaction has its own characteristic E^0 value, which gives information about the tendency of the half-reaction to proceed to the right.

To predict the course of a given redox reaction, we add algebraically the E^0 values of the two correctly written half-reactions. If the net E^0 for the overall reaction is *positive*, the reaction tends to proceed spontaneously as written. If the net E^0 is *negative*, the reaction does not tend to proceed spontaneously as written. Thus the net E^0 provides a measure of the driving force of the reaction.

Let us examine a few reactions and determine whether they will proceed spontaneously. (All ions are aquated.)

1. Will Cl_2 gas react with a solution of KBr in water?

The species which could interact are Cl_2 (g), K^+ (aq), and Br^- (aq). The table of E^0 values shows that both Cl_2 and K^+ are oxidizing agents, and that Cl_2 is by far the stronger one. Br^- is a reducing agent, and so the reaction to consider is

$$Cl_2 + Br^- \rightarrow ?$$

It is reasonable to predict that the products will be Br_2 and Cl^-. The appropriate half-reactions with their individual E^0 values follow:

OXIDATION	$2 Br^- \rightarrow Br_2 + 2e^-$	$E^0 = -1.06$ v
REDUCTION	$Cl_2 + 2e^- \rightarrow 2 Cl^-$	$E^0 = +1.36$ v
NET REACTION	$Cl_2 + 2 Br^- \rightarrow Br_2 + 2 Cl^-$	net $E^0 = +0.30$ v

The E^0 value for the oxidation reaction $2 Br^- \rightarrow Br_2$ appears in the table as written. However, the reduction reaction $Cl_2 \rightarrow 2 Cl^-$ does not appear as written. Instead, the table gives the E^0 value for the reaction $2 Cl^- \rightarrow Cl_2$ as -1.36 v. To obtain E^0 for the reverse reaction, we must change the sign, which means that E^0 for $Cl_2 \rightarrow 2 Cl^-$ is $+1.36$ v. The E^0 value for the net reaction is the algebraic sum of -1.06 v and $+1.36$ v, or 0.30 v. Another way of looking at this reaction is to note that Br^- is above Cl^- in the E^0 table. This means that Br^- ions lose electrons (are oxidized) more readily than Cl^- ions, necessitating reversal of the E^0 half-reaction, $2 Cl^- \rightarrow Cl_2 (g) + 2 e^-$.

The positive value for the net E^0 signifies that the reaction proceeds spontaneously as written, $Cl_2 + 2 Br^- \rightarrow Br_2 + 2 Cl^-$. To test this conclusion, assume that the reverse reaction, $Br_2 + 2 Cl^- \rightarrow 2 Br^- + Cl_2$, might occur.

OXIDATION	$2 Cl^- \rightarrow Cl_2 + 2e^-$	$E^0 = -1.36$ v
REDUCTION	$Br_2 + 2e^- \rightarrow 2 Br^-$	$E^0 = +1.06$ v
NET REACTION	$Br_2 + 2 Cl^- \rightarrow Cl_2 + 2 Br^-$	net $E^0 = -0.30$ v

The net E^0 would be -0.30 v, which means that the reaction cannot occur spontaneously as written. Thus chlorine can oxidize bromide ions, but bromine cannot oxidize chloride ions (under the conditions that the E^0 values were determined).

Recall that another oxidizing agent, K^+, was present in the mixture of KBr and Cl_2. Can K^+ oxidize Br^-? Let us check by using the E^0 values for the half-reactions that would have to occur.

OXIDATION	$2 Br^- \rightarrow Br_2 + 2e^-$	$E^0 = -1.06$ v
REDUCTION	$2 K^+ + 2e^- \rightarrow 2 K$	$E^0 = -2.92$ v
NET REACTION	$2 K^+ + 2 Br^- \rightarrow 2 K + Br_2$	net $E^0 = -3.98$ v

The net E^0 is -3.98 v, the high negative value signifying that the reaction cannot proceed spontaneously as written.

2. Will metallic Na react with water?

Na is a reducing agent, and the table indicates that water can be reduced. The appropriate half-reactions follow:

OXIDATION	$2\ Na \rightarrow 2\ Na^+ + 2e^-$	$E^0 =\quad 2.71$ v
REDUCTION	$2\ H_2O + 2e^- \rightarrow 2\ OH^- + H_2$	$E^0 = -0.83$ v

NET REACTION	$2\ H_2O + 2\ Na \rightarrow 2\ Na^+ + 2\ OH^- + H_2$	net $E^0 = +1.88$ v

The positive net E^0 value indicates that metallic sodium does reduce water spontaneously. This conclusion is borne out experimentally.

3. Will metallic Ag react with an aqueous solution of $CuSO_4$?

The appropriate half-reactions follow:

OXIDATION	$2\ Ag \rightarrow 2\ Ag^+ + 2e^-$	$E^0 = -0.80$ v
REDUCTION	$Cu^{+2} + 2e^- \rightarrow Cu$	$E^0 =\quad 0.34$ v

NET REACTION	$Cu^{+2} + 2\ Ag \rightarrow 2\ Ag^+ + Cu$	net $E^0 = -0.46$ v

The negative net E^0 indicates that this reaction cannot occur spontaneously. It must be driven by putting energy into the system. Will the reverse reaction occur?

Does the presence of SO_4^{-2} in $CuSO_4$ affect the course of the reaction? A more complete E^0 table will show that SO_4^{-2} can be reduced to SO_3^{-2}. However, E^0 for this half-reaction is 0.17 v, less favorable than the E^0 for the reduction of Cu^{+2}. Thus the reaction between Ag and SO_4^{-2} would have a net E^0 of -0.63 v, making the reaction even less likely to occur than the already unlikely reaction between Ag and Cu^{+2}.

17.17 Commercial electrochemical cells

In section 17.14, we described a simple electrochemical cell in which electrons produced by the oxidation of zinc atoms are transferred through an external circuit to aqueous copper ions. This cell, called a *galvanic cell* or a *voltaic cell*, was first demonstrated by Luigi Galvani and Alessandro Volta at the end of the 18th and beginning of the 19th centuries. Since that time, electrochemical cells have been improved considerably and represent an important method of generating electricity.

All commercial electrochemical cells have the same general components: an oxidation half-cell, a reduction half-cell, and a means of separation so that the electrons produced by the oxidation reaction can be supplied through an external circuit into the reduction reaction. Since these cells do not operate under standard state conditions, the cell output is not necessarily equal to the net E^0. The voltage of the cell is the net voltage (potential) of the two half-cell reactions.

THE LECLANCHÉ DRY CELL

This cell consists of a zinc container (the anode) in which a rod of graphite (the cathode) dips into a paste made of water, ammonium chloride, zinc chloride, and manganese dioxide (see Figure 17–3).

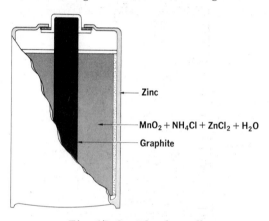

     Zinc

     $MnO_2 + NH_4Cl + ZnCl_2 + H_2O$

     Graphite

Fig. 17–3   The dry cell

The half-cell reactions are as follows. (All ions are aquated.)

ANODE $Zn \; (s) \rightarrow Zn^{+2} + 2 \; e^-$

CATHODE $2 \; NH_4^+ + 2 \; e^- \rightarrow 2 \; NH_3 \; (g) + H_2 \; (g)$

$$2 \; H_2 \; (g) + 3 \; MnO_2 \rightarrow Mn_3O_4 \; (s) + 2 \; H_2O$$

The formation of hydrogen tends to coat the zinc (polarization) and thus interferes with the oxidation of zinc. The presence of manganese dioxide, however, converts the hydrogen into water, permitting the oxidation reaction to continue. Ammonia gas, another deterrent, is removed by the Zn^{+2}, forming a stable complex ion.

$$Zn^{+2} + NH_3 \; (g) \rightarrow Zn \; (NH_3)_4^{+2}$$

As long as the zinc remains intact and the hydrogen and ammonia gases are removed, the cell continues to function. The voltage (net potential) of the dry cell is about 1.5 volts. The reaction in this cell cannot be reversed by any practical method, and the cell cannot be recharged.

THE LEAD STORAGE CELL

This cell consists of a series of lead grids separated by an insulating material. The grids are alternately filled with spongy lead and lead(IV) oxide (lead dioxide). The grids dip into a solution of about 3.7 M H_2SO_4. Figure 17–4 shows a simplified version of this cell consisting, as in the dry cell, of two electrodes and an electrolyte.

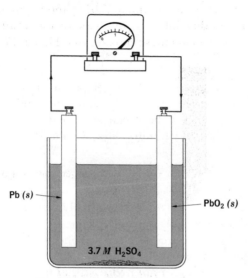

Pb (s)

PbO$_2$ (s)

3.7 M H_2SO_4

Fig. 17–4 The lead storage cell

The half-cell reactions are as follows. (All ions are aquated.)

ANODE $Pb\ (s) + SO_4^{-2} \rightarrow PbSO_4\ (s) + 2\ e^-$

CATHODE $PbO_2\ (s) + 4\ H^+ + SO_4^{-2} + 2\ e^- \rightarrow PbSO_4\ (s) + 2\ H_2O$

As long as the grids remain intact, the cell will deliver about 2 volts. Unlike the reaction in the dry cell, the reaction in the storage cell is reversible. Since the net potential of the forward reaction (discharging) is positive, the reaction is spontaneous in that direction. The net potential of the reverse reaction is negative, and electrons have to be pumped (forced) into the cell (charging) to favor the re-forming of reactants. We may summarize these changes in the overall reaction

$$Pb\ (s) + PbO_2\ (s) + 2\ H_2\ SO_4 \underset{charge}{\overset{discharge}{\rightleftarrows}} 2\ PbSO_4\ (s) + 2\ H_2O$$

During discharge, the cell forms H_2O, which dilutes the H_2SO_4. The density of the acid therefore provides an approximate measure of the extent of chemical change.

THE NICKEL-CADMIUM STORAGE CELL

This cell has a cadmium anode and a nickel(III) oxide cathode. Unlike the lead storage cell, which contains acid, all the components of the nickel-cadmium cell are immersed in an alkaline (basic) solution of potassium hydroxide. The half-cell reactions are as follows. (All ions are aquated.)

ANODE $\quad Cd\ (s) + 2\ OH^- \rightarrow Cd(OH)_2\ (s) + 2\ e^-$

CATHODE $\quad Ni_2O_3 + 3\ H_2O + 2\ e^- \rightarrow 2\ Ni(OH)_2\ (s) + 2\ OH^-$

The concentration of OH^- remains constant. The nickel-cadmium storage cell therefore has a longer life than the lead storage cell and delivers a more constant voltage, although the net potential is lower. Like the reaction in the lead storage cell, the reaction in a nickel-cadmium cell is reversible, and the cell can be recharged. In its earlier form, this cell contained iron in place of cadmium and was known as an Edison cell.

FUEL CELLS

A recent development in electrochemical cell technology is based on converting into electricity the energy obtained by oxidizing certain gaseous fuels. Since this conversion is extremely efficient, fuel cells are expected to become an important source of electrical energy. In a typical hydrogen fuel cell, hydrogen and oxygen are made to react at about 60° C in the presence of concentrated potassium hydroxide. The half-reactions are as follows. (All ions are aquated.)

ANODE $\qquad 2\ H_2\ (g) + 4\ OH^- \rightarrow 4\ H_2O + 4\ e^-$
CATHODE $\quad O_2\ (g) + 2\ H_2O + 4\ e^- \rightarrow 4\ OH^-$

NET REACTION $\qquad 2\ H_2\ (g) + O_2\ (g) \rightarrow 2\ H_2O + 136\ kcal$

17.18 Using electrical energy to produce chemical reactions: electrolysis

We have suggested that the driving force behind the redox reactions described in the previous sections depends on the oxidizing and reducing abilities of the chemical species involved. In these redox reactions, which proceed spontaneously, electrical energy is produced from the chemical energy of the reacting species. This type of electrochemical cell we have called a *galvanic* or *voltaic* cell. Now we shall investigate a group of redox reactions that do not proceed spontaneously but must be driven by an external "electron pump," or battery. This is the reverse of the reaction in a galvanic cell and is called an *electrolytic* cell. The entire process—the input of electrical energy and the resultant redox half-reactions—is called *electrolysis*. Such reactions take place in the liquid state, either in the fused compound or in a solution of the compound, where mobile ions can conduct the electricity.

17.19 Electrolysis of fused salts

When NaCl is melted (fused), the ordered crystals break down, and the Na^+ and Cl^- ions become mobile. Figure 21-1 on page 444 shows how molten NaCl can be electrolyzed commercially in the Downs cell, using a d-c (direct current) source as an electron pump. The mobile ions in the liquid permit conduction, so that the electrical circuit is complete. Carbon, in the form of graphite, is used for the anode because carbon conducts an electric current but does not react easily itself. Similarly, an iron or copper cathode is employed.

The negative Cl^- ions, which are oxidized, are attracted to the anode. The positive Na^+ ions, which are reduced, are attracted to the cathode. Since oxidation occurs at the anode, by definition, the anode is the positive (+) terminal during electrolysis. Similarly, reduction occurs at the cathode, which is the negative (−) terminal. Energy must be supplied to make the reaction proceed; that is, the reaction must be driven.

17.20 Electrolysis of aqueous solutions

Let us now consider the electrolysis of a solution of NaCl in water, all species being aquated. The cathode and anode reactions are complicated by the presence of more than one chemical species at each electrode.

At the cathode, there are Na^+ ions and H_2O molecules. Thus two possible reduction reactions may occur at the cathode.

(1) $\quad Na^+ + e^- \rightarrow Na^0$ $\qquad\qquad E^0 = -2.71$ v

(2) $\quad 2\,H_2O + 2\,e^- \rightarrow H_2 + 2\,OH^-$ $\qquad E^0 = -0.42$ v $(10^{-7}\,M)$

The E^0 values reveal that the reduction of water is more likely to occur since it requires less energy than the reduction of Na^+ ions. We can reasonably predict that hydrogen gas will be liberated at the cathode along with the formation of OH^- ions in solution.

At the anode, there are Cl^- ions and H_2O molecules. Two possible anode reactions may occur.

(1) $\quad 2\,Cl^- \rightarrow Cl_2 + 2\,e^-$ $\qquad\qquad E^0 = -1.36$ v

(2) $\quad 2\,H_2O \rightarrow O_2 + 4\,H^+ + 4\,e^-$ $\qquad E^0 = -0.82$ v $(10^{-7}\,M)$

336   *Fundamental Concepts of Modern Chemistry*

The E^0 values of the two possible anode reactions reveal that the oxidation of water to form O_2 is more likely to occur since it requires less energy than the oxidation of Cl^- ions to form Cl_2. This is indeed the case if the NaCl solution is about 1 molar. If the NaCl solution is made more concentrated, the electrode potential (voltage) values change slightly, and mostly chlorine gas is liberated at the anode. In summary:

If a binary ionic solid is fused and electrolyzed, only one cathode and one anode reaction is possible. If, on the other hand, an aqueous solution of an ionic solid is electrolyzed, we must consider at least two possible reactions at each electrode, one of which involves water.

Note that the net E^0 value for the electrolysis of aqueous NaCl is negative. This means that electrolysis requires energy.

17.21 Electrolysis of water

Since water ionizes only very slightly ($K_W = 1 \times 10^{-14}$), the electrolysis of water can be accelerated by the addition of an electrolyte. The electrolyte must be chosen carefully so that it is not electrolyzed in preference to water. Suppose sodium sulfate is used as an electrolyte. Following are the possible anode and cathode reactions, with the most probable reactions marked by a check. (All species are aquated.)

CATHODE

✔ $2 H_2O + 2 e^- \rightarrow H_2 + 2 OH^-$ $E^0 = -0.42$ v $(10^{-7} M)$

   $Na^+ + e^- \rightarrow Na^0$ $E^0 = -2.71$ v

ANODE

✔ $2 H_2O \rightarrow O_2 + 4 H^+ + 4 e^-$ $E^0 = -0.82$ v $(10^{-7} M)$

   $SO_4^{-2} \rightarrow$ not easily oxidized

Multiplying the cathode reaction by 2 and adding both reactions, we obtain

$$6 H_2O \rightarrow 2 H_2 + O_2 + 4 H^+ + 4 OH^-$$

Since the 4 H^+ ions and the 4 OH^- ions re-form water, the net reaction is

$$2 H_2O \rightarrow 2 H_2 + O_2$$

Sulfuric acid is often used to accelerate the electrolytic decomposition of water. When $0.5\ M$ H_2SO_4 is the electrolyte, the half-reactions are

CATHODE

$$2\ H_2O + 2\ e^- \rightarrow H_2 + 2\ OH^- \qquad\qquad E^0 = -0.83\ \text{v}$$

✔ $\quad 2\ H^+ + 2\ e^- \rightarrow H_2 \qquad\qquad\qquad\quad E^0 = 0.00\ \text{v}$

ANODE

✔ $\quad 2\ H_2O \rightarrow O_2 + 4\ H^+ + 4\ e^- \qquad\qquad E^0 = -1.23\ \text{v}$

$SO_4^{-2} \rightarrow$ not easily oxidized

Note that once again H_2 and O_2 are the products at the cathode and anode; thus H_2SO_4, which is inexpensive, soluble, and readily available, is a useful electrolyte for this reaction.

17.22 Electroplating

Examination of the E^0 table on pages 328–329 reveals that metallic ions below hydrogen can be easily reduced. This means that metals such as copper and silver can be plated easily on the surface of other metals such as iron. Depositing a metal coating on the surface of another metal through the use of an electric current is called *electroplating* (see Figure 17-5).

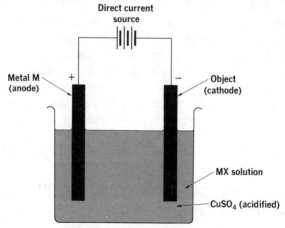

Fig. 17–5   Electroplating

To plate copper or any metal M on an iron or on a steel object, the object to be plated is made the cathode of the cell. Metal M then becomes the anode. The half-reactions that occur are

ANODE $\qquad Cu\ (s) \rightarrow Cu^{+2} + 2\ e^-$

CATHODE $\quad Cu^{+2} + 2\ e^- \rightarrow Cu\ (s)$

The electrolyte is an acidified solution of $CuSO_4$, or for metal M, an acidified solution of MX. As Cu^{+2} ions are plated out, more Cu (s) dissolves to replenish the ions that are used up. Note that electroplating essentially involves electrolysis.

Electroplating is used for decorating metals, for protecting metals, and frequently for both. Thus steel automobile parts that are plated with nickel have a better appearance and offer more resistance to corrosion than un-plated parts. Sometimes a more corrodible metal can be used to protect a less corrodible metal. For example, galvanized iron is made by coating iron with zinc, even though zinc corrodes more readily than iron. Zinc has a more positive E^0 than iron, and the two metals form a cell in which zinc is the anode and iron is the cathode. In an oxidizing atmosphere, zinc offers "sacrificial protection" to the iron and is preferentially oxidized. Moreover, when zinc reacts with oxygen in the presence of carbon dioxide and water, it forms a protective coating of basic zinc carbonate which resists further oxidation. Thus zinc-coated iron rusts more slowly than free iron.

17.23 Preparation of metals by electrolysis of their fused salts

It is difficult to prepare highly active metals such as sodium, potassium, calcium, or magnesium by reduction with chemicals. The E^0 values of these metals are much too high. In nature, metals occur in compounds as positive ions. Extraction of the metal requires reduction of the metallic ions. The safest and most efficient way to reduce an ion to a free element is by electrolysis of a readily available salt. The salt must be electrolyzed in the molten state. As shown previously, electrolysis of a water solution would result in the reduction of H_2O instead of the desired metallic ion. Thus magnesium is extracted by the electrolysis of fused $MgCl_2$ obtained from seawater.

17.24 Preparation of chlorine and sodium hydroxide by electrolysis of brine (NaCl in water)

The electrolysis of a concentrated solution of NaCl (see section 17.20) yields H_2 at the cathode and Cl_2 at the anode. The Na^+ ions are spectator ions, and OH^- ions are formed as a by-product of the cathode reaction.

If the solution remaining after electrolysis is evaporated, solid NaOH is obtained. The electrolysis of brine is an important source for hydrogen as well as chlorine and sodium hydroxide.

17.25 Equivalence in redox chemistry

In redox chemistry, as in acid-base chemistry, it is sometimes useful to know the weight of one gram-equivalent of oxidizing agent or reducing agent and to use normal solutions instead of molar solutions. In section 16.22, a gram-equivalent for acid-base reactions was defined as the amount of acid or base that donates or accepts 1 mole of protons. In oxidation-reduction, a *gram-equivalent* is defined as the amount of reducing agent or oxidizing agent that donates or accepts 1 mole of electrons.

To determine the weight of one equivalent in redox reactions, we must know the exact half-reaction which the oxidizing or reducing agent is undergoing. For example, the nitrate ion can be reduced either to NO_2 or NO.

EXAMPLE 1. Reduction of NO_3^- to NO_2.

$$NO_3^- + 2\ H^+ + e^- \rightarrow NO_2 + H_2O$$

One mole of NO_3^- accepts 1 mole of electrons. One equivalent of NO_3^- = 1 mole.

EXAMPLE 2. Reduction of NO_3^- to NO.

$$NO_3^- + 4\ H^+ + 3\ e^- \rightarrow NO + 2\ H_2O$$

One mole of NO_3^- accepts 3 moles of electrons. One equivalent of NO_3^- = $\frac{1}{3}$ mole.

If the NO_3^- ion is undergoing the change shown in example 1, a 1-normal solution of HNO_3 = a 1-molar solution of HNO_3. If the NO_3^- ion is changing as in example 2, a 1-normal solution = a $\frac{1}{3}$-molar solution.

17.26 The faraday

The English scientist Michael Faraday (1791–1867) discovered that the amount of change occurring during electrolysis depends on the amount of current used. The amount of current is expressed in *coulombs* and is equal to the current in *amperes* multiplied by the time in seconds that the current flows. Expressed mathematically:

1 coulomb = a current of 1 ampere flowing for 1 second

coulombs = amperes × seconds

The amount of current required to change 1 mole of particles at an electrode is 96,489 coulombs, or 1 *faraday*. Expressed mathematically:

96,489 coulombs = 1 mole of electrons = 1 faraday

Thus the half-reaction $Na^+ + e^- \rightarrow Na$ states that 1 mole of Na ions reacts with 1 mole of electrons (1 faraday) to form 1 mole of Na atoms.

How much sodium and how much chlorine are obtained when fused NaCl is electrolyzed for 8 hours at a current of 10 amperes?

The number of seconds in 8 hours is

$$60 \ \frac{\text{seconds}}{\text{minute}} \times 60 \ \frac{\text{minutes}}{\text{hour}} \times 8 \ \text{hours} = 28,800 \ \text{seconds}$$

$$\text{coulombs} = \text{amperes} \times \text{seconds}$$

$$= 10 \ \text{amperes} \times 2.9 \times 10^4 \ \text{seconds}$$

$$= 2.9 \times 10^5 \ \text{coulombs}$$

Let Y represent the number of faradays required.

$$\frac{2.9 \times 10^5 \ \text{coulombs}}{Y} = \frac{9.65 \times 10^4 \ \text{coulombs}}{1 \ \text{faraday}}$$

$$Y = 3 \ \text{faradays (approximately)}$$

The calculations show that a current of 10 amperes for 8 hours transfers 3 faradays, or 3 moles of electrons. According to the half-reactions for the electrolysis of NaCl,

$$Na^+ + e^- \rightarrow Na^0$$

$$Cl^- \rightarrow \frac{1}{2} Cl_2 + e^-$$

the transfer of 1 mole of electrons produces 1 mole of Na and $\frac{1}{2}$ mole of Cl_2. The 3 faradays in the example therefore produce 3 moles of Na and $1\frac{1}{2}$ moles of Cl_2. The 3 moles of Na can be expressed in grams if desired. The $1\frac{1}{2}$ moles of Cl_2 can be expressed either in weight or in volume at a given temperature and pressure.

The relationship between chemical change and the number of electrons involved is further considered in the following problem. When a dilute solution of sulfuric acid is electrolyzed, 1.6 g of oxygen are liberated at the anode. How much hydrogen is liberated at the cathode?

$$\text{moles of } O_2 = \frac{1.6 \ \text{g}}{32 \ \text{g/mole}} = 0.05 \ \text{mole}$$

According to the half-reaction at the anode,

$$2 \ H_2O \rightarrow O_2 + 4 \ H^+ + 4 \ e^-$$

the liberation of 0.05 mole of O_2 requires $4 \times 0.05 = 0.20$ mole of electrons, or 0.20 faraday. The only question which remains is how much H_2 will be liberated by 0.20 faraday? The half-reaction for the liberation of H_2 at the cathode is

$$2 \ H^+ + 2 \ e^- \rightarrow H_2$$

Two moles of electrons are required to produce 1 mole of H_2. Thus 0.20 mole of electrons will produce 0.10 mole of H_2. This amount of H_2 can be expressed in weight units (0.2 g) or in volume units (2.24 l at STP).

Multiple-Choice Questions

1. A reduction reaction always involves the (1) loss of electrons (2) gain of electrons (3) addition of oxygen (4) removal of oxygen
2. The oxidation number of Cl in $KClO_4$ is (1) -1 (2) $+3$ (3) $+7$ (4) $+1$
3. If X is an oxidizing agent that reacts with a reducing agent, Y, then (1) X increases in oxidation number (2) X becomes oxidized (3) Y loses electrons (4) Y gains protons
4. To complete the equation for the half-reaction $N^{-3} \rightarrow N^{+2}$, the term missing on the right side of the equation is (1) $+5 \ e^-$ (2) $+1 \ e^-$ (3) $-5 \ e^-$ (4) $-1 \ e^-$
5. Given the following half-reactions and net reaction:

$$Fe^{+3} + e^- \rightarrow Fe^{+2}$$
$$Sn^{+2} \rightarrow Sn^{+4} + 2 \ e^-$$

NET REACTION $\quad Fe^{+3} + Sn^{+2} \rightarrow Fe^{+2} + Sn^{+4}$

   The first half-reaction is multiplied by 2 because (1) the oxidation number of the reducing agent is 2 (2) both metals have two oxidation numbers (3) the number of electrons gained must equal the number of electrons lost (4) the oxidation number of Fe is $+2$
6. In the half-reaction $SO_4^{-2} \rightarrow S^{-2} + 4 \ H_2O$, atoms and charge can be conserved (balanced) by (1) adding 8 H^+ and 8 e^- to the left side (2) adding 4 O to the right side (3) adding 8 H^+ to the left side and 6 e^- to the right side (4) subtracting 4 O from the left side
7. A salt bridge is used in an electrochemical cell (1) so that electrons may flow from one half-cell to the other (2) so that ions may flow from one half-cell to the other (3) to maintain the proper concentration in each half-cell (4) to supply acid where needed

8. Which of the following statements is correct for all electrochemical cells? (1) H^+ ions are either formed or used up. (2) Oxidation occurs at the positive electrode while reduction occurs at the negative electrode. (3) Oxidation occurs at the anode while reduction occurs at the cathode. (4) The net reaction always involves two metals and their ions.

9. Given: $K (s) \rightarrow K^+ (aq) + e^-$ $E^0 = 2.92$ v
   $Al (s) \rightarrow Al^{+3} (aq) + 3 e^-$ $E^0 = 1.66$ v

   From the preceding two half-reactions, we note that (1) Al is a stronger reducing agent than K (2) the E^0 value for K must be multiplied by 3 before comparing it with Al (3) K is a stronger reducing agent than Al (4) Al is a weaker reducing agent than H_2

10. In the electrolysis of molten NaCl and in the electrolysis of a solution of NaCl (1) metallic Na is formed (2) the same product forms at the anode (3) electrons flow through both liquids (4) chlorine is reduced

11. One gram-equivalent of an oxidizing agent (1) accepts 1 mole of electrons (2) releases 16 g of oxygen (3) contains 1 g of oxidizer (4) reacts with 1 g of oxygen

12. One faraday of charge (96,489 coulombs) is *not* equivalent to (1) 1 mole of electrons (2) one gram-equivalent weight of reducing agent (3) E^0 of hydrogen (4) 1.008 g of hydrogen formed by electrolysis of HCl

Completion Questions

1. The oxidation number of an element describes the number of _____ that this element forms in a compound.

2. The oxidation number of oxygen in its compounds is -2, except in _____, where it is -1.

3. Ca^{+2} ion can act only as a (an) _____ (*oxidizing, reducing*) agent because it can only _____ (*gain, lose*) electrons.

4. In the compounds NaI, $NaIO_3$, and $NaIO_4$, the oxidation number of the element _____ increases.

5. The function of the wires in an electrochemical cell is to provide a pathway for _____ from one half-cell to the other.

6. The ions in solid sodium chloride can become mobile if the solid is dissolved in water or if the solid is _____.

7. In the reaction $Ag^+ + e^- \rightarrow Ag^0$, one gram-equivalent of Ag^+ equals 1 mole. In the reaction $Al \rightarrow Al^{+3} + 3 e^-$, one gram-equivalent of Al^{+3} equals _____ mole(s).

8. The oxidation number of hydrogen in NH_4^+ is _____.

True-False Questions

1. In binary ionic compounds, the oxidation number of an element equals its *ionic charge*.
2. The tendency of *nonmetallic* atoms to lose electrons accounts for their activity as reducing agents.
3. Aluminum is an active reducing agent. Its conjugate oxidizing agent, Al^{+3}, is therefore a *strong* oxidizing agent.
4. In an electrochemical cell, the electrode at which *reduction* takes place is the anode.
5. *Electrolysis* is an oxidation-reduction reaction in which electrical energy is supplied to the system.
6. An active metal can be prepared by electrolysis of a salt, which must first be *dissolved*.
7. The replacement reaction $Fe\ (s) + Cu^{+2}\ (aq) \rightarrow Fe^{+2}\ (aq) + Cu\ (s)$ involves a transfer of electrons from *Fe (s) to Cu^{+2} (aq)*.
8. An electrochemical cell consists of one half-cell containing Mg (s) in $MgSO_4$ (aq) and the other half-cell containing Cu (s) in $CuSO_4$ (aq). SO_4^{-2} ions will move from the *Cu to the Mg* half-cells through the salt bridge.

Decreases, Increases, Remains the Same

1. As the tendency of metals to lose electrons increases, the activity of the metals as reducing agents _____.
2. In the series of compounds $HOCl$, $HClO_2$, $HClO_3$, and $HClO_4$, the oxidation number of O _____.
3. As the strength of an oxidizer increases, the strength of its conjugate reducer _____.
4. In the hydrides HCl, H_2S, NH_3, and CH_4, as the oxidation number of the other element increases, the oxidation number of H _____.
5. As the charge of an ion increases, its oxidation number _____.
6. As the concentration of a solution of NaCl increases, the gram-equivalent of Cl^- _____.
7. When the amount of charge that passes through a solution of $CuSO_4$ increases, the mass of copper that forms at the cathode _____.
8. As the activity of metals increases, the ease with which they can be extracted by electrolysis _____.
9. As the net value for E^0 for two half-reactions becomes more negative, the tendency for the redox reaction to proceed spontaneously _____.
10. As we go from $Cl^-\ (aq) \rightarrow Cl\ (g) + e^-$ to $2\ Cl^-\ (aq) \rightarrow Cl_2\ (g) + 2\ e^-$, the E^0 values for the half-reactions _____.

Exercises for Review

1. *a.* Explain why oxidation cannot take place without corresponding reduction.

   b. Why can an oxidizing agent function only if a reducing agent is present?

2. Give the oxidation numbers of each element in the compounds.

   a. Na_2SO_3

   b. $AlPO_4$

   c. H_2CO_3

   d. Na_2O_2

   e. $NaBiO_3$

3. Complete the following half-reactions:

   a. $I_2 + 2\ e^- \rightarrow$

   b. $Sn^{+4} \rightarrow Sn^{+2}$

   c. $Cu^{+2} + 2\ e^- \rightarrow$

   d. $2\ O^{-2} \rightarrow O_2$

   e. $Cr^{+2} \rightarrow + e^-$

4. The replacement reaction $Zn\ (s) + 2\ Ag^+\ (aq) \rightarrow 2\ Ag\ (s) + Zn^{+2}\ (aq)$ occurs when a piece of zinc is dipped into a solution of $AgNO_3$. The reaction can also take place in an electrochemical cell.

   a. Write the reaction in each half-cell.

   b. Which is the spectator ion?

   c. Into which half-cell will the spectator ion migrate? Why?

5. Complete the following half-reactions by supplying H^+ or H_2O where needed to conserve atoms, or by adding or removing electrons to conserve charge:

   a. $NO_3^- \rightarrow NO$

   b. $ClO_3^- \rightarrow Cl_2$

   c. $SO_4^{-2} \rightarrow S^{-2}$

6. Using the values for E^0 given in the table on pages 328–329, calculate the net E^0 for the following redox reactions in solution:

   a. $Mg\ (s) + 2\ AgNO_3 \rightarrow Mg(NO_3)_2 + 2\ Ag\ (s)$

   b. $Mn\ (s) + FeSO_4 \rightarrow MnSO_4 + Fe\ (s)$

7. For each of the following oxidation-reduction reactions, write the two half-reactions. Where necessary, complete the equation by supplying the correct products. (Assume all ions are aquated.)

   a. $Ni\ (s) + Ag^+ \rightarrow$

   b. $Mg\ (s) + Hg^{+2} \rightarrow$

   c. $2\ Fe^{+3} + Sn^{+2} \rightarrow 2\ Fe^{+2} + Sn^{+4}$

   d. $Zn\ (s) + Cl_2\ (g) \rightarrow Zn^{+2} + 2\ Cl^-$

8. Balance the following reactions by the oxidation number method:
   a. $MnO_2 + HCl \rightarrow MnCl_2 + Cl_2 + H_2O$
   b. $Ag + HNO_3 \rightarrow AgNO_3 + NO_2 + H_2O$
   c. $H_2SO_4 + Cu \rightarrow CuSO_4 + SO_2 + H_2O$
9. Calculate the number of coulombs of charge that passes through an electrolysis cell in each of the following:
   a. 2.0 amperes for 30 seconds
   b. 0.5 ampere for 5 minutes
   c. 0.15 ampere for 2.2 minutes
   d. 5 milliamperes for 1 hour and 15 minutes
10. After Cl_2 (*g*) has been bubbled into 1 *M* KI and equilibrium has been reached, is it possible to detect Cl^- (*aq*) ions and I^- (*aq*) ions? Explain.

Exercises for Further Study

1. *a.* Draw an electron-dot diagram for a molecule of sulfuric acid.
   b. Draw an electron-dot diagram for a molecule of sulfurous acid.
   c. Explain why the oxidation number of S is different in the two compounds.
2. The following are E^0 values for several half-reactions, assuming all ions are aquated:

$$Ba\ (s) \rightarrow Ba^{+2} + 2\ e^- \quad E^0 = \quad 2.90\ v$$
$$Zn\ (s) \rightarrow Zn^{+2} + 2\ e^- \quad E^0 = \quad 0.76\ v$$
$$Ni\ (s) \rightarrow Ni^{+2} + 2\ e^- \quad E^0 = \quad 0.25\ v$$
$$Cu\ (s) \rightarrow Cu^{+2} + 2\ e^- \quad E^0 = -0.34\ v$$
$$Hg\ (l) \rightarrow Hg_2^{+2} + 2\ e^- \quad E^0 = -0.79\ v$$

   a. Select the two half-reactions that will produce the highest voltage in an electrochemical cell.
   b. Which metals can produce H_2 gas when placed in a solution containing 1-molar H^+ (*aq*) ions?
   c. Compare the Ni half-reaction when combined with (1) a cell containing Hg (*l*) and (2) a cell containing Ba (*s*).
3. Calculate the gram-equivalent weights of the following substances when used in the given half-reactions in which all ions are aquated. (*Hint:* Complete and balance each half-reaction.)
   a. H_2SO_4 in $SO_4^{-2} \rightarrow S^{-2}$
   b. HNO_3 in $NO_3^- \rightarrow NH_4^+$
   c. K_2CrO_4 in $CrO_4^{-2} \rightarrow Cr^{+3}$

4. Find the weight of silver deposited at the cathode of an electroplating cell when a current of 0.75 ampere flows for 12 minutes through the silver-plating solution.

5. Using examples, explain why the E^0 of a metal is related to its activity as a reducing agent.

6. *a.* Describe the construction of the two half-cells to measure the net potential (E^0) developed by the reaction

$$Ni\ (s) + Cu^{+2}\ (aq) \rightarrow Ni^{+2}\ (aq) + Cu\ (s)$$

b. Draw a diagram of the apparatus used.

7. Why do the half-reaction equations written by the ion-electron method provide a better indication of the reactions in an electrochemical cell than the half-reaction equations written by the oxidation number method?

8. Balance the following equations using the ion-electron method:
   a. $K_2Cr_2O_7 + HCl \rightarrow CrCl_3 + Cl_2 + KCl + H_2O$
   b. $KMnO_4 + SnSO_4 + H_2SO_4 \rightarrow Sn(SO_4)_2 + MnSO_4 + H_2O + K_2SO_4$
   c. $H_2SO_4 + KI \rightarrow I_2 + H_2S + K_2SO_4 + H_2O$

9. By means of equations, show why $KMnO_4$ and $K_2Cr_2O_7$ require the presence of an acid when acting as oxidizing agents.

10. *a.* Define oxidation number and ionic charge.
    b. Which term includes the other? Explain.

11. A current of 0.4 ampere passes through an electrolysis cell for 5.5 minutes. How many moles of electrons pass through the cell?

12. Convert the following amounts of charge to moles of electrons, using the relationship 1 faraday = 96,489 coulombs:
    a. 9.65×10^3 coulombs
    b. 1.93×10^7 coulombs

13. Does an operating electrochemical cell represent an equilibrium system? Explain.

Chapter 18

NUCLEAR CHEMISTRY

18.1 Introduction

We have indicated that the energy involved in a chemical change is considerably greater than the energy involved in a change of state (see section 1.24). For example, when hydrogen gas burns to form gaseous water, 57.8 kcal of heat are evolved per mole of water. The condensation of 1 mole of gaseous water, on the other hand, liberates only 9.7 kcal of heat. If we consider the combustion to be a typical chemical change and the condensation to be a typical change of state, we observe that the chemical change involves about six times more energy than the change of state. The energies involved in chemical changes may be up to 100 times the energies involved in changes of state.

We have already indicated that *nuclear changes* are also possible. Nuclear changes are accompanied by the conversion of matter into energy. For example, if 1 mole (1.008 g) of hydrogen atoms could be completely converted into energy, about 2.25×10^{10} kcal of heat would be liberated. This energy is about 100 million times the energy involved in chemical changes; it is approximately equivalent to the quantity of energy released by the explosion of some 40,000 tons of TNT.

Chemical changes and changes of state involve the making and breaking of bonds, processes usually associated with the electrons present in atoms. The energy released during mass-energy conversions involves changes in the nuclei of atoms. This chapter will discuss the atomic nucleus and the changes which it may undergo.

18.2 The atomic nucleus

Ernest Rutherford's alpha-scattering experiment, described in section 19.6, is the basis for an atomic model that describes an extremely small nucleus containing most of the mass of the atom. This nucleus is independent of chemical changes such as those previously described in acid-base reactions and redox reactions. The nucleus, however, can undergo change spontaneously, as in natural radioactivity; or artificially, as in transmutation processes. Both processes will be discussed later.

18.3 Nuclear size

The radius of an average atom is on the order of 10^{-8} cm (1 Å), but the radius of an average nucleus is only on the order of 10^{-13} cm (1 fermi). Thus the radius of the whole atom is 100,000 times the radius of the nucleus.

If we consider both the atom and the nucleus as spheres, the ratio of atomic volume to nuclear volume involves the cube of the corresponding radii: $\dfrac{(10^{-8} \text{ cm})^3}{(10^{-13} \text{ cm})^3} = \dfrac{10^{-24} \text{ cm}^3}{10^{-39} \text{ cm}^3}$, or 10^{15}. (The volume of a sphere is proportional to the cube of its radius.) Thus the volume of an atom is approximately one quadrillion (10^{15}) times larger than the volume of its nucleus. Virtually all the mass of an atom is packed into its infinitesimally small nucleus.

18.4 Nuclear particles

The exact makeup of the atomic nucleus is still unknown. In our study of nuclear chemistry, however, we will consider only neutrons and protons. These particles are called *nucleons*. A nucleus containing a specific combination of neutrons and protons is called a *nuclide*. (The nucleus also contains mesons, hyperons, neutrinos, muons, and other particles which we will not discuss.) Some of the properties of neutrons and protons are listed in the table on the following page. Mass is expressed in *amu* (atomic mass units).

$$1 \text{ amu} = 1.67 \times 10^{-24} \text{ g}$$

The subscript to the left of the symbol of each nucleon denotes charge; the superscript to the left denotes mass number.

NUCLEON	CHARGE	MASS	SYMBOL
neutron	0	1.008982 amu	$_0^1 n$
proton	+1	1.008142 amu	$_1^1 p$

18.5 Nuclear forces

Atomic nuclei contain protons packed into a very small volume. Since particles of like charge repel each other, the forces which hold an atomic nucleus together (binding forces) must be strong enough to overcome this repulsion. For an elementary understanding of binding forces, the following concepts are useful:

1. Nuclear binding forces are considered to be very strong because they overcome proton-proton repulsion.
2. Nuclear binding forces are effective only at extremely small distances. These forces operate at nuclear dimensions of approximately 10^{-13} cm, becoming almost totally ineffective at larger distances.
3. Other subnuclear particles, such as mesons, play a major role in the nuclear binding force.
4. No nucleus (with the exception of hydrogen) consists solely of protons. Hence, neutrons and the ratio of neutrons to protons also play a major role in holding the nucleus together.

18.6 Nuclear stability

An interesting and important property of atoms is that the nuclei of certain atoms are stable, while other nuclei are unstable and undergo spontaneous change. Experimental evidence indicates that the stability of a nucleus is related to the ratio of neutrons to protons. A graph based on the neutron/proton ratio of some stable nuclides is shown in Figure 18-1 on the following page.

The curve, indicated by the heavy line, represents the neutron/proton ratio and is termed the stability zone, or the stability belt. The dashed line represents nuclides that contain an equal number of neutrons and protons. For the heavier atoms (high number of protons or high atomic number), nuclides with an equal number of neutrons and protons lie increasingly outside the stability zone. For the lighter atoms (up to calcium-20), many of

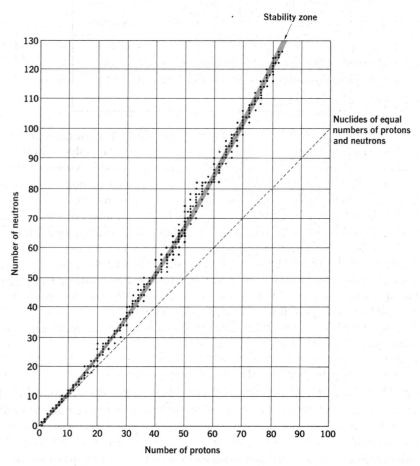

Fig. 18–1   Neutron/proton ratio of some stable nuclides

the stable nuclides (except for H) contain an equal number of protons and neutrons; however, stable nuclides of the heavier atoms contain a greater number of neutrons than protons. Examination of the stable nuclides in the graph reveals the information in the following table.

NUMBER OF PROTONS	NUMBER OF NEUTRONS	NUMBER OF STABLE NUCLIDES
even	even	166
even	odd	53
odd	even	57
odd	odd	8

We note that a nucleus is most likely to be stable if it contains an even number of protons and neutrons. It is least likely to be stable if both the number of neutrons and the number of protons are odd. Nuclides which contain 2, 8, 20, 28, 50, 82, or 126 protons or neutrons or both are especially stable. These numbers are often called "magic numbers."

Because these numbers remind scientists of the numbers of electrons in the energy levels of atoms, the "magic numbers" have encouraged study of a *shell model* for the nucleus. In this model, protons and neutrons lie in quantized (clearly separated) energy levels similar to the energy levels of electrons. Prior to the development of the shell model by Maria Goeppert-Mayer (1948), Niels Bohr had postulated the *liquid drop model* (1936). The nucleons were arranged in random fashion in Bohr's model, exerting an attractive force on each other in the same way that the molecules in a liquid attract each other.

18.7 Nuclear instability

We have just discussed nuclear binding forces and the composition of stable atoms. Now we will examine atoms which do not have nuclear binding forces strong enough to keep their nuclei intact. These atoms lie outside the belt of stability. To attain greater stability, an atom in this group must undergo a rearrangement of nucleons to form a new nucleus with a more favorable neutron/proton ratio.

18.8 Natural radioactivity

In 1896, the French scientist Henri Becquerel discovered that uranium ores emit invisible rays that pass through the dark paper covering of a photographic plate and affect the plate much the same as light rays do. What strange substances emitted these penetrating rays? And what was the nature of the rays? He encouraged the scientists Pierre and Marie Curie to look for the answers. Within a few years, the Curies had discovered that the uranium ore contained two new elements in addition to uranium. Like uranium, these elements, which they named polonium and radium, spontaneously emit invisible rays. When the nuclei of atoms of naturally occurring elements undergo spontaneous change to become more stable, the process is called *natural radioactivity*.

During natural radioactivity, one or more of the following phenomena occur:

Alpha decay, the emission of positively charged particles called alpha particles.

Beta(−) decay, the emission of negatively charged particles called beta(−) particles.

Gamma radiation, the emission of energy in the form of gamma rays, which resemble X rays of short wavelength.

18.9 Alpha decay

We will use a new type of equation, termed a *nuclear equation*, to represent alpha decay and other nuclear changes. Let us examine the symbolism that is used in nuclear equations. In the expression

$$_Z^M E$$

E is the symbol for the atom, z is the atomic number (number of protons), and M is the mass number (the sum of the number of protons and the number of neutrons).

For example, an alpha particle is the nucleus of a helium atom and is symbolized as $_2^4 He$. The number of protons is 2; and the number of neutrons is also 2, which gives a mass number of 4. Alpha particles carry a positive charge of +2 because they do not have the two *K*-shell electrons normally present in helium.

Which atoms exhibit alpha decay? We know that in atoms with an atomic number of 84 or higher, the proton-proton repulsion in the nucleus is quite large. We can therefore predict that many such atoms (for example, uranium-238), exhibit spontaneous alpha decay. In the following nuclear equation, observe that alpha decay reduces both the number of protons and the number of neutrons of the radioactive element.

$$^{238}_{92}\text{U} \rightarrow ^{234}_{90}\text{Th} + ^{4}_{2}\text{He}$$

n/p RATIO $\quad 146/92 = 1.58 \quad 144/90 = 1.60$

In alpha decay, the atomic number always decreases by 2, and the mass number decreases by 4.

Note that the neutron/proton ratio increases during alpha decay. This ratio is not the sole factor in determining nuclear stability. Apparently, in nuclides of high atomic number, the repulsions exerted by the protons are also an important factor. An increase in the neutron/proton ratio tends to overcome the effect of increased proton-proton repulsions.

18.10 Beta(−) decay

If the neutron/proton ratio is too high (left of the stability belt), the spontaneous change favors lowering the number of neutrons and raising the number of protons. This change is achieved when a beta(−) particle is emitted from the nucleus. Experiments show that the beta(−) particle is an electron. Since electrons do not exist in nuclei, it is postulated that, during beta(−) decay, a neutron breaks up into a proton and an electron. (In the equation that follows, recall that the subscript denotes charge, or atomic number, and the superscript denotes mass number.)

$$^{1}_{0}n \rightarrow ^{1}_{1}p + ^{0}_{-1}e$$

The electron is emitted from the nucleus with considerable energy. In the nucleus, a neutron disappears; a new proton is produced; and the n/p (neutron/proton) ratio decreases.

Using the symbolism described for alpha decay, we can write the nuclear equations for the beta(−) decay of an isotope of carbon into nitrogen and for the conversion of an isotope of oxygen into fluorine. The symbol β^-, the Greek letter *beta* with a minus sign superscript, is often used in nuclear equations to represent an electron. Note the decrease in the n/p ratio in both changes that follow. (The original nucleus is designated as the parent nucleus, the new nucleus as the daughter nucleus.)

	PARENT NUCLEUS		DAUGHTER NUCLEUS		EMISSION
	$^{14}_{6}C$	$\rightarrow$	$^{14}_{7}N$	$+$	$^{0}_{-1}e$
	or				
	$^{14}_{6}C$	$\rightarrow$	$^{14}_{7}N$	$+$	β^-

n/p RATIO $\overbrace{8/6 = 1.33}$ $\overbrace{7/7 = 1.00}$

	$^{19}_{8}O$	$\rightarrow$	$^{19}_{9}F$	$+$	$^{0}_{-1}e$
	or				
	$^{19}_{8}O$	$\rightarrow$	$^{19}_{9}F$	$+$	β^-

n/p RATIO $\overbrace{11/8 = 1.38}$ $\overbrace{10/9 = 1.11}$

If we regard these equations as representative, we can state the following principles for nuclear changes involving beta($-$) decay:

1. The atomic number increases by 1.
2. The mass number remains the same.
3. The sum of the subscripts (atomic numbers) on both sides of the equation is equal. (This is also true for alpha decay.)
4. The sum of the superscripts (mass numbers) on both sides of the equation is equal. (This is also true for alpha decay.)
5. The n/p ratio is decreased, or the proton-proton repulsion forces are lowered.

18.11 Gamma radiation

The nuclear emissions we have described consist of alpha particles or beta($-$) particles. Now we come to a new type of nuclear emission — *gamma emission*, or *gamma radiation*, as it is frequently called. Gamma radiation has neither charge nor mass. It consists of high-energy electromagnetic waves. These waves resemble X rays but have a higher frequency and a shorter wavelength. Due to its high energy, gamma radiation has great penetrating power and can seriously damage living tissue. The energy of gamma radiation can be calculated from Planck's formula (see section 19.12).

18.12   The U-238 series

An interesting example of naturally occurring nuclear changes is the gradual decay of uranium-238 to lead-206, as shown in the following table.

Note that radioactive U-238 decays to stable Pb-206 in a series of alpha or beta(−) decays, leading to the formation of more stable atoms.

ELEMENT	ATOMIC NUMBER	MASS NUMBER	PARTICLE EMITTED
uranium	92	238	alpha
thorium	90	234	beta
protactinium	91	234	beta
uranium	92	234	alpha
thorium	90	230	alpha
radium	88	226	alpha
radon	86	222	alpha
polonium	84	218	alpha
lead	82	214	beta
bismuth	83	214	beta
polonium	84	214	alpha
lead	82	210	beta
bismuth	83	210	beta
polonium	84	210	alpha
lead	82	206	

18.13 Artificial radioactivity

Certain nuclei may be rendered artificially radioactive by man-made processes, as described in section 18.29. These unstable nuclei may attain stability by undergoing one or both of the following:

1. Emitting positively charged beta(+) particles.
2. Capturing an electron from the innermost electron shell, called *K*-capture.

18.14 Beta(+) decay and *K*-capture

If the n/p ratio is too low (right of the stability belt), the spontaneous change favors raising the number of neutrons and lowering the number of protons. This change may be achieved in one of two ways:

BETA(+) DECAY

A beta(+) particle, also called a *positron* ($_{+1}^{0}e$), has the mass of an electron but carries a positive charge. When a positron is emitted from a nucleus, it is thought that a proton breaks up into a neutron and positron.

$$_{1}^{1}p \rightarrow {}_{0}^{1}n + {}_{+1}^{0}e$$

Thus when a proton is lost, a neutron is gained; and the n/p ratio is increased. Following is an example of beta(+) decay, or positron decay, involving an isotope of carbon:

$$^{10}_{6}C \quad \rightarrow \quad ^{10}_{5}B \quad + \quad ^{0}_{+1}e$$

n/p RATIO $\quad 4/6 = 0.67 \quad 5/5 = 1.00$

Note that in positron decay the n/p ratio is increased.

K-CAPTURE

In K-capture, an electron close to the nucleus is attracted into the nucleus. The K refers to the K-shell, or first energy level of electrons, that is, the electrons closest to the nucleus. It is postulated that this electron combines with a proton to form a neutron.

$$^{0}_{-1}e + ^{1}_{1}p \rightarrow ^{1}_{0}n$$

As before, when a proton is lost, a neutron is gained; and the n/p ratio is increased. Oxygen-15, for example, exhibits K-capture.

$$^{15}_{8}O \quad + \quad ^{0}_{-1}e \rightarrow \quad ^{15}_{7}N$$

n/p RATIO $\overbrace{7/8 = 0.875} \qquad \overbrace{8/7 = 1.14}$

18.15 Summary of spontaneous nuclear changes

The following table summarizes the emissions from unstable nuclei.

NAME	SYMBOL	CHARGE	MASS	APPROXIMATE RELATIVE PENETRATING POWER
alpha	α or $^{4}_{2}He$	$+2$	$+4$	1
beta($-$)	β^- or $^{0}_{-1}e$	-1	0	100
beta($+$)	β^+ or $^{0}_{+1}e$	$+1$	0	100
gamma	γ	0	0	10,000

18.16 Half-life

Studies of radioactive elements have shown that a definite fraction of a radioactive element undergoes change in a given unit of time. For some elements, an appropriate unit of time may be one year. For elements that decay at a more rapid rate, time may be expressed in hours, minutes, seconds, or in a fraction of these units. As decay proceeds, the amount of radioactive material becomes smaller. However, the fraction that undergoes change per unit of time remains the same. It is possible, therefore, to predict the time required for a given fraction of radioactive material to decay. Because some radioactivity, no matter how slight, always remains, the time required for an entire sample of radioactive material to decay cannot be predicted.

Radioactive decay proceeds at a steady rate and is unaffected by the chemical or physical makeup of the radioactive atom. To study and compare the rates of decay of radioactive atoms, scientists have introduced the concept of half-life. *Half-life* is the time required for one-half of any given mass of radioactive nuclei to decay.

For example, thorium-234 undergoes beta(−) decay with a half-life of 24 days. If we start with 10 g of Th-234, 5 g are left after 24 days; 2.5 g are left after 48 days; 1.25 g are left after 72 days, and so on. These figures are not typical, for the half-lives of different atoms vary enormously. The half-life for the alpha decay of U-238 is 4.5 billion years. In extreme constrast, the half-life for the alpha decay of Po-214 is 1.6×10^{-4} second.

18.17 The radiocarbon clock

The dating of archeological objects is an interesting application of the half-life concept. The "radiocarbon clock" used by archeologists is based on the bombardment of the nitrogen gas in the atmosphere by neutrons resulting from cosmic radiation.

$$^{14}_{7}\text{N} + ^{1}_{0}n \rightarrow ^{14}_{6}\text{C} + ^{1}_{1}\text{H}$$

Since the amount of nitrogen in the atmosphere and the intensity of cosmic radiation are fairly constant, a constant amount of carbon-14 (radiocarbon) finds its way into the life cycle of plants and animals as part of the CO_2 in the air.

Carbon-14 undergoes beta(−) decay with a half-life of 5668 years. It is convenient to measure the radioactivity of a substance by counting the number of emissions per unit time, for example, counts per minute (cpm). At full activity, the decay rate per gram of carbon-14 averages 15.3 cpm.

While a plant or animal is alive, the amount of C-14 in its system is constant because it takes in CO_2 containing some C-14 from the air. After the organism dies, it ceases to ingest C-14. Thus the C-14 that is present at time of death undergoes decay at a steady rate. Consider a wooden carving with an activity of 7.65 cpm/g of C-14, which is half the original activity of 15.3 cpm/g of C-14. One half-life, or 5668 years, must have elapsed since the living wood stopped taking in C-14.

18.18 Isotopes

Isotopes are nuclides of the same element that differ slightly in mass number due to different numbers of neutrons. For elements with atomic numbers 1 through 83 (H through Bi), each of the elements has both stable and unstable isotopes. For example, C-12 and C-13 are stable isotopes of carbon, whereas C-14 is unstable and radioactive.

$$^{14}_{6}C \rightarrow {}^{14}_{7}N + {}^{0}_{-1}e$$

However, the isotopes of elements with atomic numbers 84 through 103 (Po through Lw) are all unstable; that is, they are all radioactive.

$$^{212}_{84}Po \rightarrow {}^{208}_{82}Pb + {}^{4}_{2}He$$

$$^{216}_{84}Po \rightarrow {}^{212}_{82}Pb + {}^{4}_{2}He$$

18.19 Mass-energy interconversion

In Chapter 1, we learned that the great theoretical physicist Albert Einstein related matter and energy in the equation

$$E = mc^2$$

where E represents energy in ergs, m represents mass in grams, and c represents the speed of light in centimeters/second. The speed of light is 3×10^{10} cm/sec, and the speed of light squared is 9×10^{20} cm²/sec². This very large number determines the magnitude of E. It indicates that when matter can be converted into energy, a very small amount of matter will release an enormous amount of energy. For example, the energy equivalent of a mass of 1 gram is 9×10^{20} ergs, or about 2.2×10^{10} kilocalories. What is the source of this energy? For the answer we will look deeper into the atom and examine nuclear binding energy. We will see how nuclear binding energy is related to mass-energy interconversion by the Einstein equation.

18.20 Nuclear binding energy

Consider the formation of a nucleus of O-16 by the union of 8 protons and 8 neutrons. The mass of a proton is 1.008142 amu. The mass of a neutron is 1.008982 amu. The sum of the mass of 8 protons and the mass of 8 neutrons is

$$8(1.008142) + 8(1.008982) = 16.136992 \text{ amu}$$

However, the measured mass of O-16 = 16.000000 amu

$$\text{loss of mass} = 0.136992 \text{ amu}$$

The union of 8 protons and 8 neutrons to form an oxygen nucleus results in a mass loss of 0.136992 amu. This mass is converted to energy according to the $E = mc^2$ relationship (see section 1.21). The resultant energy is called *nuclear binding energy*, which is the energy released when nucleons (protons and neutrons) come together to form a nucleus. It is also the energy absorbed when a nucleus is split into its individual nucleons.

To compare different nuclides (which contain different numbers of nucleons), scientists find it convenient to divide the nuclear binding energy by the number of nucleons. In the previous example, the binding energy per nucleon for oxygen in amu $= \dfrac{0.136992 \text{ amu}}{16} = 0.00855$ amu/ nucleon.

18.21 Expressing nuclear binding energy

Nuclear scientists express binding energy in units of *million electron volts*, abbreviated *Mev*. These units are related to calories by the equation 1 million electron volts (1 Mev) = 3.8×10^{-14} calorie. Using the equation for the interconvertibility of mass and energy, $E = mc^2$, we can also relate Mev to atomic mass units: 931 Mev = 1 amu. The quantity 931 Mev is the amount of energy released when 1 amu is converted to energy.

When we discussed the binding energy of O-16 in the preceding section, we saw that a mass of 0.136992 amu is converted to energy when the nucleus forms (from the union of 8 protons and 8 neutrons). We can convert amu to Mev or to calories by the expressions

$$0.136992 \text{ amu per nucleus formed} \times 931 \frac{\text{Mev}}{\text{amu}}$$
$$= 128 \text{ Mev per nucleus formed}$$

$$128 \text{ Mev per nucleus formed} \times 3.8 \times 10^{-14} \frac{\text{cal}}{\text{Mev}}$$
$$= 4.86 \times 10^{-12} \text{ cal per nucleus formed}$$

Remember that 4.86×10^{-12} cal represents the energy released when only one O-16 nucleus is formed from 8 protons and 8 neutrons. For one mole of O-16, the energy released is

$$4.86 \times 10^{-12} \ \frac{\text{cal}}{\text{nucleus}} \times 6.02 \times 10^{23} \ \frac{\text{nuclei}}{\text{mole}} = 2.93 \times 10^{12} \ \frac{\text{cal}}{\text{mole}}$$

This energy equals almost 3 trillion (3000 billion) calories per 16 grams of oxygen nuclei.

Binding energy may be expressed in Mev/nucleon. For O-16,

$$\text{binding energy} = \frac{128 \ \text{Mev/nucleus}}{16 \ \text{nucleons/nucleus}} = 8 \ \text{Mev/nucleon}$$

18.22 Nuclear binding energy vs. mass number: a graph

If binding energy/nucleon is plotted against mass number (total number of protons and neutrons), the following graph is obtained for various atoms. (See Figure 18–2.)

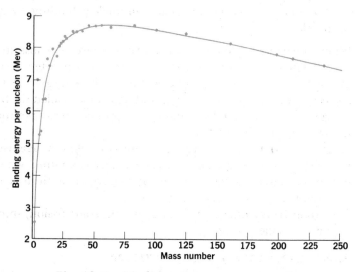

Fig. 18–2   *Binding energy vs. mass number*

Examination of the graph reveals the following:

1. The most stable nuclei lie in the region of mass number 60 (the approximate atomic mass of iron) because the values for binding energy/nucleon are greatest in this region.

2. The very small nuclei and the very large nuclei have low binding energies/nucleon and are less stable than the nuclei in the middle range.

3. With increasing mass number up to about 60, we find an increase in binding energy. We also find an increase in stability accompanied by a release of energy equivalent to the increased binding energies. This release of energy occurs when small nuclei combine to form larger nuclei (atomic fusion).

4. If large nuclei (such as uranium) are split into smaller nuclei, there is an increase in binding energy. A release of energy also occurs during this type of change (atomic fission).

5. The change in binding energy (slope of the curve) is sharper with increasing mass number up to about 60 than with decreasing mass number to the same point. The curve shows that a greater increase in binding energy, and therefore a greater release of energy, may occur in fusion changes than in fission changes.

18.23 Nuclear binding energy: a summary

Some of the observations we have made on nuclear binding energy are summarized below.

1. When nucleons coalesce into a nucleus, there is a loss in mass. The lost mass—known as the *mass defect*—is converted to energy in accord with the relationship $E = mc^2$. The energy released for a specific combination of protons and neutrons is called the binding energy of the nucleus. The higher the binding energy per nucleon, the more stable the nucleus.

2. A graph of binding energy per nucleon plotted against mass number shows that greater nuclear stability is attained when:
   a. Certain light nuclei, such as hydrogen or lithium, combine (fusion) to form a heavier nucleus.
   b. Certain heavy nuclei, such as uranium, split (fission) into more stable, smaller nuclei.

18.24 Detecting radioactivity through ionization

The detection of radioactivity is based on the ability of radiation to ionize atoms and molecules in its path. In other words, alpha particles, beta particles, gamma rays, mesons, and other nuclear emanations possess sufficient energy so that when they collide with atoms or molecules, they remove some electrons. The collision leaves behind positively charged species and free electrons. The detection devices discussed in the sections that follow—the electroscope, the Geiger-Müller counter, the Wilson cloud chamber, and the bubble chamber—all depend on this ionizing property of radiation.

18.25 The electroscope

The electroscope (shown in Figure 18–3) is a container with a glass window, represented by a flask. The container houses two thin strips of gold foil or aluminum foil attached to an insulated metal rod. From this rod, a metal knob projects outside the container. To detect radiation, we start with a charged electroscope. The knob of the electroscope is given a charge which is conducted to the two pieces of foil, causing them to diverge. A sample of radioactive material placed near the knob of the charged electroscope causes the air around the knob to become ionized. The ionized air, in conducting charge away from the knob, causes the leaves to converge.

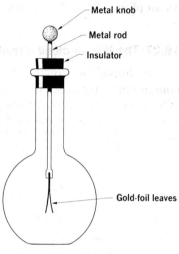

Fig. 18–3   The electroscope

18.26 The Geiger-Müller counter

The Geiger-Müller counter houses a sealed glass tube containing argon gas at low pressure (shown in Figure 18–4). A metallic cylinder serves as the cathode, and a wire running through the center of the cylinder serves as the anode.

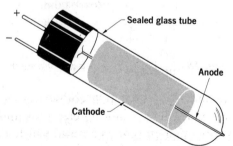

Fig. 18–4   The Geiger-Müller tube

Although a high voltage is maintained between the cathode and anode, current normally does not flow between them. Current flow requires the presence of charged particles, and argon is electrically neutral. In the presence of radiation, however, argon ions and electrons are formed. These charged particles permit the current to flow, or discharge, through an amplifier. Each flow of current is detected as a flash of light or a clicking noise.

18.27 The Wilson cloud chamber

The simple form of the Wilson cloud chamber, shown in Figure 18–5, contains air saturated with water vapor in a cylinder with a movable piston. When the piston moves forward, the air in the chamber is compressed. When the piston is moved backward suddenly, the air in the chamber expands, cools, and becomes supersaturated with water vapor.

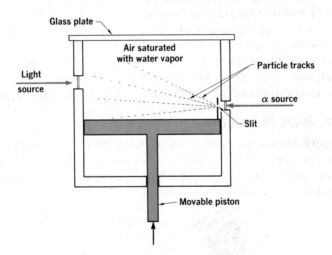

Fig. 18–5   The Wilson cloud chamber

Radiation, such as alpha particles, that enters the chamber through a slit strikes some air molecules, removing electrons and producing ions. The ions serve as condensation centers around which a cloud-like trail of water droplets forms. The various trails of droplets are visible to the eye through the glass plate and may also be photographed for detailed study.

18.28 The bubble chamber

In the bubble chamber, invented by Donald Glaser in 1952, the pressure on a sample of liquid hydrogen is suddenly released. The liquid becomes superheated; that is, its temperature is above the normal boiling point at the reduced pressure. When fast moving radiation enters the chamber, it creates ions along its trail. The ions have high energy given to them by the radiation and cause local boiling which produces small bubbles. The trails of bubbles, like the trails of droplets in the cloud chamber, are visible and may be photographed.

18.29 Artificial transmutation

In 1934, Frederic and Irene Joliot-Curie discovered that a stable nucleus could be made unstable (radioactive) by bombardment with a high-energy particle, or "bullet." The Joliot-Curies bombarded stable boron-10 atoms with alpha particles from naturally radioactive radium, producing artificially radioactive nitrogen-13.

$$\ce{^{10}_{5}B} + \ce{^{4}_{2}He} \rightarrow \ce{^{13}_{7}N} + \ce{^{1}_{0}n}$$

The changing of one element into another represents the kind of artificial transmutation (change) that the early alchemists had sought. Since 1934, a large number of artificial radioactive elements have been produced by nuclear bombardment. In artificial transmutation, as in natural radioactivity, the sum of the superscripts is equal on both sides of the equation, and the sum of the subscripts is equal on both sides of the equation.

The nuclear projectiles, or bullets, are usually positively charged particles such as protons, deuterons ($\ce{^{2}_{1}H}$, the nucleus of the hydrogen isotope deuterium), and alpha particles. To penetrate into the nucleus, such particles must possess very high energies. A particle with low energy cannot overcome the repulsive force of the positively charged nucleus. To obtain nuclear bullets with sufficiently high energy, special machines called *particle accelerators* are used. For many nuclear changes, the neutron serves as the bullet. Because it does not possess a charge, the neutron is not repelled by the nucleus that it approaches. Neutrons, therefore, need not be accelerated to higher energies.

18.30 Accelerating charged particles

The principle behind particle accelerators is that charged particles, such as protons, can be accelerated by electrical fields, magnetic fields, or both.

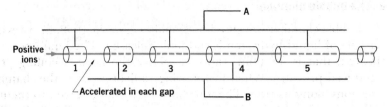

Fig. 18–6   The linear accelerator

For example, in the linear accelerator (see Figure 18–6), positively charged particles are passed through a series of tubes of increasing length. The tubes are wired so that their polarity (positive or negative charge) can be alternated very rapidly. This alternation permits the projectile particle to be simultaneously pushed out of a positive tube and pulled into a negative tube until sufficiently high velocity has been achieved.

In circular accelerators, such as the cyclotron shown in Figure 18–7, the charged particles move in a circular path that increases in radius like a spiral. The cyclotron is a cylindrical chamber in which there is a partial

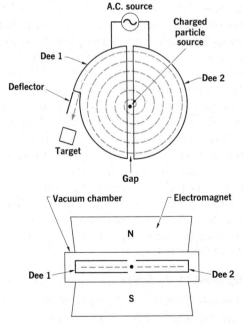

Fig. 18–7   The cyclotron

vacuum. The chamber lies between the poles of a powerful electromagnet. The source of the particles is placed between two hollow D-shaped electrodes called *dees*, which lie inside the chamber. Alternating current, synchronized to the movement of the charged particles, is applied to the dees. At the same time, the strong magnetic field created by the electromagnet acts perpendicularly to the dees. The alternating current and the magnetic field cause the particles to move in a circular path. As the particles acquire greater energy and velocity, the radius of their circular path increases. When the particles reach the outer circumference of the dees, they are deflected into the target.

18.31 The transuranium elements

Since 1940, the elements with atomic numbers 93 through 103 have been produced by artificial transmutation. Because these elements follow uranium in the Periodic Table, they are called *transuranium elements*. Nine of these elements were discovered at the University of California at Berkeley by Glenn T. Seaborg and his co-workers. Professor Seaborg was awarded the 1951 Nobel Prize in chemistry for this work. Some typical reactions which were carried out to produce these man-made elements follow:

EXAMPLE 1. Production of uranium-239 by neutron-bombardment of uranium-238.

$$^{238}_{92}\text{U} + ^{1}_{0}n \rightarrow ^{239}_{92}\text{U}$$

After formation, the uranium-239 undergoes beta-decay to form neptunium. Note that the projectile is the neutron, a particle with a charge of 0.

$$^{239}_{92}\text{U} \rightarrow ^{239}_{93}\text{Np} + ^{0}_{-1}e$$

EXAMPLE 2. Production of curium by alpha bombardment of plutonium-239.

$$^{239}_{94}\text{Pu} + ^{4}_{2}\text{He} \rightarrow ^{240}_{96}\text{Cm} + 3\,^{1}_{0}n$$

Curium resembles another transuranic element, americium-95, which is made by bombarding plutonium-239 with neutrons. All the transuranic elements fall in the transition series of elements, called the actinides, and are discussed in section 23.2.

18.32 Nuclear fission

The binding energy curve on page 360 shows that a heavy nucleus, such as uranium-238, can change into more stable nuclei if it undergoes fission and splits into fragments. A related change occurs during natural radioactivity. For example, uranium-238 spontaneously changes into smaller, more stable atoms until it finally becomes lead-206 (see section 18.12). Energy is released as the more stable atoms form.

An example of artificial transmutation is the neutron bombardment of uranium-235, one of the less common isotopes of uranium. This bombardment splits the uranium-235 into smaller, more stable nuclei and releases an enormous amount of energy.

$$^{235}_{92}U + {}^{1}_{0}n \rightarrow {}^{143}_{56}Ba + {}^{90}_{36}Kr + 3\,{}^{1}_{0}n + 4.6 \times 10^9 \text{ kcal/mole}$$

The three neutrons emitted from this reaction have considerable energy and high velocity. After being slowed down to permit control, they can bombard three more uranium-235 atoms, which split and release more energy and more neutron bullets. The chain reaction which is set up releases a huge reservoir of nuclear energy. The world first learned about this energy of fission — and its tragic potential — in 1945 when atomic bombs fell on the Japanese cities of Hiroshima and Nagasaki.

18.33 The nuclear reactor

To maintain a chain reaction, the fast neutrons produced by fission must be slowed down. On colliding with atoms of uranium-235, the slower neutrons are captured, and the chain reaction fission process is set up.

In 1942, Enrico Fermi and his co-workers discovered how to slow down the fast neutrons produced in fission. They placed the fissionable uranium-235 in blocks of graphite. Substances such as graphite and heavy water, D_2O, that slow down neutrons are called *moderators*. To control the speed of the fission process and to prevent it from becoming explosive, excess neutrons are absorbed by cadmium or boron steel control rods.

The device that controls neutrons and permits utilization of the energy of fission reactions is called a *nuclear reactor*. Since 1943, many nuclear reactors for controlled fission have been built. One of the most promising uses for nuclear reactors is to convert the energy of fission reactions to electricity to supply power for ships, homes, and industrial plants. Nuclear reactors are also making a significant contribution to medicine. Radioisotopes produced in nuclear reactors are valuable for treating and diagnosing malignancies and other disorders. For example, cobalt-60 inhibits the growth of cancerous cells, and iodine-131 helps to detect malfunctioning of the thyroid gland.

18.34 Nuclear fusion

We have described *fission* as the splitting of a heavy nucleus into nuclei of lighter mass. In *fusion* reactions, light nuclei combine to form a heavier nucleus. The binding energy curve indicates that both processes lead to greater stability. In the reaction

$$\,^2_1H + \,^3_1H \rightarrow \,^4_2He + \,^1_0n$$

the energy released is about 4.05×10^8 kcal/mole. Fusion reactions occur in the hydrogen bomb and are thought to occur in our sun and in other stars. At present, much research is being directed toward controlling fusion reactions for peaceful purposes.

Multiple-Choice Questions

1. Three types of changes are illustrated below:

    (a) $CO_2\ (s) \rightarrow CO_2\ (g)$

    (b) $C\ (s) + O_2\ (g) \rightarrow CO_2\ (g)$

    (c) $6\,^1_0n + 6\,^1_1H \rightarrow \,^{12}_6C$

    (1) All three changes represent the formation of chemical bonds. (2) Nuclear changes occur in all.(3) The size of particles increases from change *a* to change *c*. (4) The energy released per mole of carbon increases from change *a* to change *c*.

2. Natural radioactivity occurs in all of the following *except* (1) a change from one nuclide to another (2) conversion of mass to energy (3) a change in chemical bonding (4) a change from a less stable nucleus to a more stable nucleus

3. The most stable nuclides possess (1) fewer neutrons than protons (2) even numbers of neutrons and protons (3) twice as many protons as neutrons (4) an odd number of protons and neutrons

4. When a radioactive element emits a beta($-$) particle (1) the positive charge of the nucleus increases by 1 (2) the number of neutrons in the nucleus increases (3) oxidation takes place (4) the atomic mass of the element increases by 1

5. In the nuclear change $^{239}_{93}\text{Np} \rightarrow {}^{239}_{94}\text{Pu} + X$, the particle X is (1) a positron (2) a neutron (3) an alpha particle (4) an electron

6. When an atom undergoes alpha decay, it is *not* correct to say that (1) the atomic number decreases by 2 (2) the mass of the nucleus decreases by 4 amu (3) fission occurs (4) charge is conserved

7. Carbon-14 dating may be used to (1) determine the age of a specimen (2) measure the life span of a carbon atom (3) find how long it takes for carbon to return to the atmosphere (4) measure the half-life of carbon

8. The mass of a proton is 1.008142 amu; the mass of a neutron is 1.008982 amu; and the atomic mass of helium is 4.0026. Therefore, the value for the mass loss of a nucleus of ^4_2He is closest to (1) zero (2) 0.0899 amu (3) 0.026 amu (4) 0.0026 g

9. In the nuclear transmutation $^{40}_{18}\text{Ar} + {}^4_2\text{He} \rightarrow Y + {}^1_0 n$, the element Y is (1) $^{44}_{19}\text{K}$ (2) $^{43}_{20}\text{Ca}$ (3) $^{44}_{22}\text{Ti}$ (4) $^{43}_{19}\text{K}$

10. Which of the following is *not* characteristic of both atomic fusion and atomic fission? (1) Energy is released. (2) Increased mass defects occur for the nuclides formed. (3) The capture of a neutron is required. (4) Mass is converted to energy.

11. A particle that cannot be accelerated by a cyclotron is (1) a proton (2) a deuteron (3) a neutron (4) an alpha particle

Completion Questions

1. The control rods in a nuclear reactor slow down the fission process by absorbing some of the _____ which are produced during the fission process.

2. A (An) _____ is a device for detecting nuclear particles which form bubbles of gas when radiation passes through it.

3. A nuclide is an atom that shows the property of _____.

4. *K*-capture occurs when the nucleus of an atom acquires a (an) _____ from the *K*-shell.

5. The emission of an electron by a radioactive element is known as _____ decay.

6. Isotopes of elements that are not radioactive represent _____ (*stable, unstable*) nuclides.

7. A spontaneous change that takes place in the nucleus of an unstable atom is called natural _____.

8. Gamma radiation most closely resembles _____.

9. One Mev is _____ (*smaller, larger*) than 1 calorie.

10. The least penetrating particle produced during natural radioactivity is the _____.

Decreases, Increases, Remains the Same

1. From electron to proton to neutron, the masses of the particles
   _____ .

2. When the temperature of a radioactive element is increased, the rate
   of disintegration _____ .

3. When the atomic numbers of elements increase, the ratio of neutrons
   to protons in the stable atoms _____ .

4. When a radioactive element releases a beta(+) particle, the ratio of
   neutrons to protons _____ .

5. When a radioactive element releases an alpha particle, the number of
   neutrons in the nucleus _____ .

6. When a radioactive element emits a beta(−) particle, the atomic mass
   of the nucleus _____ .

7. As the binding energy of a nucleus increases, its stability _____ .

8. As the atomic masses of a series of isotopes of a given element increase, the number of protons in each nucleus _____ .

9. A stream of neutrons is used to bombard different atoms. As the
   atomic numbers of the atoms being bombarded increase, the repulsion exerted by the neutrons _____ .

10. During alpha decay, the neutron/proton ratio _____ .

True-False Questions

1. A nuclear reactor is a device for utilizing the energy produced by the
   fusion of uranium atoms.

2. The half-life of element X is 10 days. If we start with 80 g of X, twenty
   days later *20* g of X will remain.

3. The mass defect per nucleon is *greatest* for elements with atomic
   weights that are not very large or not very small.

4. A characteristic of the elements that have *high* atomic numbers is that
   they may be radioactive.

5. The fact that ^{206}Pb is the end product of the natural disintegration of
   ^{238}U indicates that Pb is *less* stable than the elements between uranium
   and lead.

6. The emission of an electron from the nucleus is accompanied by a
   decrease in the number of *neutrons.*

7. The difference between the three isotopes of hydrogen results from
   the different numbers of *protons* in the nuclei of their atoms.

8. A definite combination of *electrons and protons* is known as a nuclide.

Exercises for Review

1. Briefly describe the important contributions made by the following scientists in the development of nuclear science: (a) Marie Curie (b) Einstein (c) Fermi (d) Lawrence (e) Seaborg
2. State the purpose of each of the following in a nuclear reactor: (a) control rods (b) moderator (c) uranium slugs (d) concrete walls
3. Compare the process of fission with the process of fusion.
   a. Compare the elements used.
   b. How is each process started?
   c. What changes take place in the atoms?
4. Compare the radioactive process in which a beta(−) particle is emitted with the radioactive process in which an alpha particle is emitted.
   a. State the change in atomic number and the change in mass number that takes place in each process.
   b. Explain how each process leads to a more stable nuclide.
5. Calculate the mass defect for the isotope of fluorine $^{19}_{9}F$, which has an atomic mass of 19.0044 amu. (The mass of a proton is 1.008142 amu, and the mass of a neutron is 1.008982 amu.)
6. Complete the following nuclear reactions. Give the symbol of the missing element with its atomic number and mass number.
   a. $^{234}_{90}Th \rightarrow \underline{\hspace{1cm}} + ^{0}_{-1}e$
   b. $\underline{\hspace{1cm}} \rightarrow ^{222}_{86}Rn + ^{4}_{2}He$
   c. $^{4}_{2}He + \underline{\hspace{1cm}} \rightarrow ^{12}_{6}C + ^{1}_{0}n$
   d. $^{1}_{1}H + ^{23}_{11}Na \rightarrow \underline{\hspace{1cm}} + ^{4}_{2}He$
7. Define each of the following terms:
   a. radioactivity   d. K-capture
   b. nucleon   e. particle accelerator
   c. binding energy

Exercises for Further Study

1. After a period of 32 days, only $\frac{1}{16}$ of a radioactive material remains. What is the half-life of this radionuclide?
2. Write the nuclear equations for the following radioactive changes:
   a. alpha decay of $^{208}_{84}Po$ c. beta(+) decay of $^{22}_{11}Na$
   b. beta(−) decay of $^{239}_{93}Np$ d. K-capture of $^{7}_{4}Be$

3. *a.* Why was the discovery of radioactivity important in the development of our ideas concerning the structure of the atom?

 b. What effect did this discovery have on the Dalton model of the atom?

 c. How did Rutherford use radioactivity in his work?

4. If half a sample of thorium disintegrates in 24 days, explain why the entire sample does not disintegrate in 48 days.

5. Calculate the energy released in the formation of 1 mole of ^3_1H by the following transmutation:

$$^2_1H + {}^2_1H \rightarrow {}^3_1H + {}^1_1H$$

$^1_1H = 1.00814$ amu

$^2_1H = 2.01474$ amu

$^3_1H = 3.01699$ amu

6. *a.* What particles are emitted during beta($-$) decay and beta($+$) decay?

 b. Explain how the emitted particles might originate and how a more stable nucleus results from the change.

7. Using the rules for the stability of nuclides, arrange the following atoms in the order of increasing stability. Give your reason for each selection.

$$^{20}_{10}Ne \qquad ^{15}_{8}O \qquad ^{19}_{9}F \qquad ^{12}_{7}N$$

8. Explain why the radioactive properties of radium are the same in its compounds and in the uncombined element.

9. Consider the following changes: melting ice, decomposing water, and changing hydrogen to helium. For each change:

 a. Compare the amounts of energy per mole released or consumed.

 b. Describe the types of bonds involved.

 c. Compare the particles united by these bonds.

10. List as many nuclides as you can which contain the "magic number" of neutrons or protons or both neutrons and protons. Write the symbol of the element, its atomic number, and its mass number.

11. How is the neutron/proton ratio related to the stability of a nucleus?

12. Discuss the likelihood of producing elements beyond atomic number 103.

Chapter 19

MODERN ATOMIC THEORY

19.1 Introduction

In Chapter 4, we utilized a simplified nuclear model of the atom to provide an elementary basis for understanding chemical changes. With this model, we postulated the existence of electrons, protons, and neutrons as the fundamental particles that make up an atom. Let us now return to the study of atomic structure to consider the experimental evidence on which the nuclear model is based. We will extend this model in the light of more recent discoveries concerning the nature and properties of electrons.

19.2 Electrons

As early as the middle of the 19th century, scientists observed that gases under very low pressure conduct electricity. The English physicist William Crookes investigated the conductivity of gases by means of evacuated glass tubes, later called Crookes tubes.

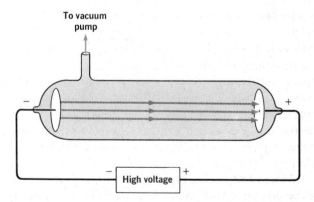

Fig. 19–1   The Crookes tube

The apparatus shown in Figure 19-1 is a Crookes tube containing a gas at very low pressure (0.01 mm Hg). To permit the passage of electricity, electrodes are sealed into each end of the tube. When the electrodes are connected to a source of high voltage, the glass walls of the tube glow (fluoresce) with a green light. This light, it was found, came from the striking of the glass walls by rays emanating from the cathode. The rays appear to emerge from the negative terminal and travel in straight lines to the positive terminal. Thus, if a metal cross is placed in the discharge tube (see Figure 19-2), the glass walls continue to fluoresce except in the region of the shadow cast by the cross.

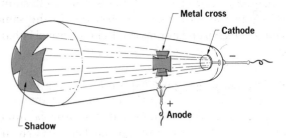

Fig. 19–2   *Cathode rays travel in straight lines*

The rays can be deflected (bent) by a magnet or by charged electrical plates placed above and below the tube as shown in Figure 19-3.

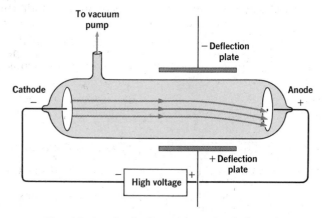

Fig. 19–3   *Cathode rays can be deflected*

From such observations, and from the fact that the rays were attracted to the positive terminal, it was concluded that the rays consisted of *negatively* charged particles, or electrons. Since the rays emanated from the negative terminal, they were called *cathode rays.*

19.3 Protons

Eugen Goldstein, a German physicist who was a contemporary of Crookes, further studied electrical discharges through gases. He discovered the presence of rays issuing from the positive terminal and directed toward the negative terminal. In this experiment, a Crookes tube containing a perforated cathode was used. Although the rays were also deflected by magnetic and electrical fields, the deflections were in a direction opposite to the movement of electrons in the same fields. The rays, called *positive rays*, were later shown to be positively charged particles (positive ions).

19.4 The ratio of charge to mass $\left(\dfrac{e}{m}\right)$

Subatomic particles possess properties that can be used to identify them: amount and type of electric charge, and mass. Early in this century, it was impossible to measure each of these quantities, but Joseph J. Thomson, an English physicist, measured the ratio of electric charge to mass $\left(\dfrac{e}{m}\right)$ for electrons and for positive ions. He utilized the property that electrons can be deflected in magnetic and electrical fields. From his work, much of it carried out in the early 1900's, we conclude that:

1. For electrons, the ratio $\dfrac{e}{m}$ is constant regardless of the nature of the gas in the Crookes tube that is the source of electrons. Intuitively, we would suspect this to be so, since we are dealing with a specific particle, the electron, having a fixed mass. As determined by Thomson, the value of this ratio is 1.77×10^8 coulombs/gram.

2. For positive ions, the ratio $\dfrac{e}{m}$ varies with the gas in the Crookes tube, since each gas forms a specific ion of fixed mass. For hydrogen, the element with the smallest mass, $\dfrac{e}{m}$ has the maximum value.

19.5 Determination of the charge on the electron (e)

In 1906, Robert Millikan, an American physicist, determined the absolute charge on the electron in the now famous oil-drop experiment. A laboratory apparatus similar to the one used by Millikan is shown in Figure 19-4 on the following page.

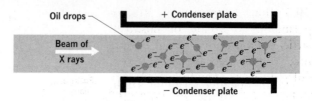

Fig. 19–4   Oil-drop experiment

Tiny drops of oil are sprayed by an atomizer into the upper chamber. These drops may become charged either by friction or by exposure to X rays. In both instances, a number of charged particles becomes attached to a single oil drop. The oil drop is first surrounded by the electric field of a condenser of known strength. The electric field is then adjusted to balance the gravitational force until the drop remains stationary.

Millikan made several thousand observations and found that the applied electric field was dependent on the number of charged particles attached to the oil drop. The values obtained were small whole-number multiples of 1.60×10^{-19} coulomb, the unit charge of the electron (e).

From the value of e, obtained by Millikan, and from the value of $\frac{e}{m}$, obtained by Thomson, the mass of the electron was found to be 9.11×10^{-28} g.

$$\frac{e}{m} = 1.77 \times 10^8 \text{ coulombs/g} \quad e = 1.60 \times 10^{-19} \text{ coulomb}$$

$$m = \frac{e}{e/m} = \frac{1.60 \times 10^{-19} \text{ coulomb}}{1.77 \times 10^8 \text{ coulombs/g}} = 9.11 \times 10^{-28} \text{ g}$$

19.6 Rutherford's experiment

In 1898, Thomson proposed that atoms consist of a sphere of positively charged electricity in which electrons are uniformly distributed. This "plum pudding" model was disproved by Rutherford's findings.

In Chapter 18, we learned that radioactive elements such as radium and polonium undergo changes causing them to emit alpha particles (helium nuclei). The English physicist Ernest Rutherford, in 1911, utilized these alpha particles to determine the structure of atoms.

Figure 19-5 shows a diagram of Rutherford's experiment. A stream of positively charged particles, emitted by a small amount of polonium, was allowed to strike a very thin piece of gold or copper foil. A fluorescent screen, placed behind the foil, registered flashes of light whenever an alpha particle struck the screen. Most of the alpha particles were able to pass through the metal foil with very little interference. However, a small but definite number of particles were deflected from their original paths. Although most of these deflections were at small angles, some appeared at relatively large angles.

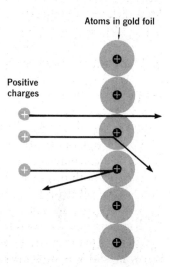

Fig. 19–5 Rutherford's experiment

Rutherford found that about one alpha particle in every 20,000 was deflected through an angle greater than 90°. In effect, some of these particles appeared to move back toward the polonium source from which they emanated. In the words of one of the investigators, "It was almost as incredible as if you fired a 15-inch shell at a piece of tissue paper and it came back and hit you."

To explain these observations, Rutherford formulated the nuclear model of the atom. He made the following assumptions:

1. The atoms of gold or copper in the foil consist almost completely of empty space. Therefore, most of the alpha particles succeed in passing through the metal foil without deflection.

2. Within the atoms in the foil, a small region called the *nucleus* is present. The nucleus possesses a relatively large amount of mass and a positive charge. The positively charged nucleus repels the positively charged alpha particles; this repulsion explains why some of the alpha particles are deflected.

3. Atoms are electrically neutral because they possess a sufficient number of electrons to balance the positive charge of the nucleus. These electrons are present in the otherwise empty space surrounding the nucleus.

19.7 Atomic numbers

Using different metals to deflect alpha particles, Rutherford and his co-workers concluded that each element possesses a characteristic number of positive charges in its nucleus. This was later confirmed by the English physicist Henry Moseley, who used the term *atomic number* to refer to the number of positive charges in the nucleus of an atom. Since each proton carries one positive charge, the atomic number represents the number of protons in the nucleus of an atom. The atomic number also equals the number of electrons outside the nucleus, which balances the positive charge of the nucleus.

19.8 The neutron

In 1932, the English physicist James Chadwick was studying the emanations produced by bombarding beryllium with alpha particles. At that time, scientists knew that the mass of the protons and the mass of the electrons accounted for about half of the atomic weight of an element. Chadwick was able to account for the other half of the atomic weight when he discovered that, under alpha bombardment, beryllium emits an uncharged particle with a mass slightly greater than the mass of a proton.

$$\ce{^{9}_{4}Be} + \ce{^{4}_{2}He} \rightarrow \ce{^{12}_{6}C} + \ce{^{1}_{0}n}$$

Because the particle is electrically neutral, it was named a *neutron*. The atomic weight (mass number), therefore, represents the number of protons and neutrons in the nucleus. (The weight of the electrons is negligible.)

19.9 Electrons and chemical reactivity

When atoms combine to form molecules, the atoms must first come together. As they approach one another, the outer portions of the atoms (but not the nuclei) interact. Thus the chemical properties of elements depend to a great extent on the arrangement and energy conditions of the electrons in the atoms. The *spectra* produced by elements, that is, the light emitted when atoms are excited by heat or by electricity, reveal a great deal about the electronic structure of atoms.

19.10 The spectra of atoms

White light produced by an ordinary incandescent bulb may be dispersed by a prism (see Figure 19–6 on the next page) to show all the colors or energies that make up the light. Since each color blends into the other, the spectrum is called a *continuous spectrum*.

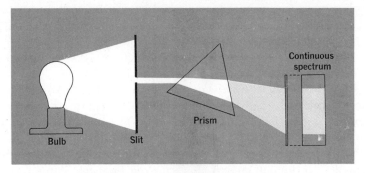

Fig. 19–6   Continuous spectrum

If the light source is a salt, such as NaCl or KCl in a hot flame, the spectrum produced is not continuous. Instead, a series of lines separated by dark spaces appears. In this *bright-line spectrum*, each line corresponds to light of a specific energy. Thus all sodium compounds produce the characteristic lines of the sodium spectrum, whereas all potassium compounds produce their own characteristic lines (see Figure 19-7).

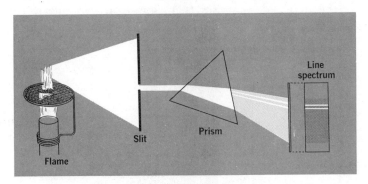

Fig. 19–7   Bright-line spectrum

Gaseous elements also produce characteristic bright-line spectra during electrical excitation in gas-discharge tubes. For example, a gas tube containing neon glows orange-red during discharge.

19.11 Emission and absorption spectra

To produce its characteristic spectrum, an element must first receive energy from a flame or from an electrical discharge. The energy is then emitted in the form of radiation, such as visible light or ultraviolet light. This type of spectrum is an *emission spectrum*. Thus a continuous spectrum and a bright-line spectrum are examples of emission spectra.

Another type of spectrum is produced when white light, containing all colors, is passed through the vapors of an element. A series of dark lines is observed, each line corresponding to a color absorbed by the gaseous element from the white light passing through it. This type of spectrum is called a *dark-line spectrum*, or *absorption spectrum*.

For a given element, the emission spectrum and the absorption spectrum are closely related. The dark lines in the absorption spectrum of the element represent the absence of the identical colors that are present in the emission spectrum of the element. The significance of these two types of spectra is that each atom can absorb only the definite amounts of energy (associated with definite colors) characterized by its absorption spectrum. Thus an atom can either emit or absorb the same amounts of energy that appear in its emission spectrum or its absorption spectrum.

19.12 The quantum theory

Radiant energy is energy that travels through space at the speed of light, which is 186,000 miles/second, or 3×10^{10} centimeters/second. Many characteristics of light may be explained by the wave model, which suggests that radiant energy consists of electromagnetic waves. These waves can be depicted as pulses that vibrate in a regularly repeating pattern (see Figure 19-8).

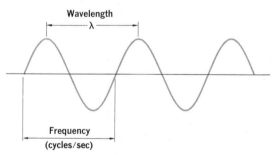

Fig. 19–8   An electromagnetic wave

The waves are characterized by frequency and wavelength (λ), the product of which is the speed of light.

$$\text{frequency} \times \text{wavelength} = 3 \times 10^{10} \text{ cm/sec}$$

$$\text{wavelength} = \frac{3 \times 10^{10} \text{ cm/sec}}{\text{frequency}}$$

Since the speed of light in a given medium is constant, wavelength and frequency are inversely related. The table that follows lists the different forms of radiant energy in order of decreasing wavelength and increasing frequency.

```
┌─────────────────────────────────────────────────────────────────┐
│        RADIANT ENERGY (ELECTROMAGNETIC WAVES)                     │
├─────────────────────────────────────────────────────────────────┤
```

decreasing wavelength	radio (including radar and television) infrared (heat) red ⎫ orange ⎪ yellow ⎪ green ⎬ visible light blue ⎪ indigo ⎪ violet ⎭ ultraviolet X rays gamma cosmic	increasing frequency

Cosmic rays and gamma rays have short wavelengths and high frequencies. Radio waves have long wavelengths and low frequencies. The wavelengths of visible light lie about midway between these two extremes.

The wave model explains many of the observed properties of radiant energy. At the beginning of the 20th century, however, scientists were forced to adopt another model to explain the nature of the radiations from heated solid bodies and the origin of the spectra obtained from the excitation of atoms.

The quantum theory, formulated in 1902 by Max Planck, a German scientist, provides a basis for relating the energy of an electromagnetic wave to its frequency. This theory describes radiant energy as follows:

1. An atom, when excited, can emit radiant energy only in the form of bursts or bundles, called *quanta*. (Prior to this assumption, it was thought that such energy was emitted continuously.)

2. When an atom absorbs radiant energy, it absorbs one or more complete quanta of energy.

3. The amount of energy in a quantum is proportional to the frequency of the radiant energy and can be expressed by the equation

$$E = h \times \nu$$

where E = energy, h = a universal constant called Planck's constant (6.63×10^{-34} joule-sec), and ν (the Greek letter *nu*) = frequency.

19.13 The Bohr Theory

In 1913, the Danish scientist Niels Bohr utilized the quantum theory to explain how the hydrogen atom produces its characteristic spectrum. This explanation included the following assumptions:

1. Electrons revolve around the nucleus in specific orbits, or energy levels, without radiating energy. This assumption is contrary to classical theory, which states that a charged body that is accelerating emits energy by radiation. The electron, moving in a circular orbit, is constantly changing direction and hence is accelerating. Therefore, according to classical theory, the electron should continue to lose energy by radiation. Eventually the electron should spiral into the nucleus.

2. Only certain energy levels are possible for the electrons in the atom. The electrons cannot exist at any other positions except those represented by the energy levels $E_1, E_2, \ldots, E_n$.

3. When an atom is in its ground (unexcited) state, its electrons are in orbits close to the nucleus at the lowest energy level, represented by E_1.

4. If an atom receives energy (is excited), an electron is displaced farther away from the nucleus to one of the higher energy levels, $E_2, E_3, E_4, \ldots, E_n$.

5. When an atom emits energy, an electron goes from a higher energy level to a lower energy level in one sudden transition, releasing one quantum of energy.

6. The frequency of the emitted radiation depends on the difference between the two energy levels in the transitions.

$$E_{\text{higher}} - E_{\text{lower}} = h \times \nu$$

These assumptions were used to explain the emission spectra of hydrogen (see Figure 19-9).

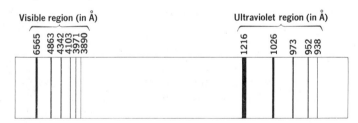

Fig. 19-9   Wave lengths in emission spectra of hydrogen

Let us assume that n represents the energy level of the electron close to the nucleus. For hydrogen in its unexcited state, n is assigned the value 1. When a hydrogen atom is excited by the input of energy, the electron is elevated to a higher energy level, where n may be 2, 3, or higher. The electron is unstable in the higher energy levels and must return to a lower level. In returning, the electron emits a quantum of energy.

Electron jumps may occur between several different energy levels. Such jumps result in the emission of numerous lines (see Figure 19-10).

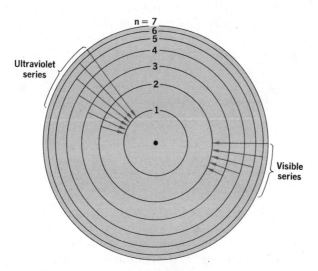

*Fig. 19-10   Some possible electron jumps in a
hydrogen atom*

Since the transitions that take place are always between very definite (and limited) energy levels, the quanta of energy that are emitted have definite energy values. These values correspond to the lines in the spectrum of the element.

From his observations of the spectrum of hydrogen, Bohr extended the nuclear model of the atom originally suggested by Rutherford. This is the model we have employed up to this point to explain the nature of chemical change. However, the nuclear model has many limitations which finally led to its abandonment and to the development of the wave mechanical model, discussed later.

19.14 The Uncertainty Principle

The Bohr Theory, assigning specific orbits to electrons, successfully explained the lines in the hydrogen spectrum. Attempts to extend the theory to atoms containing more than a single electron failed. The fundamental assumption that the orbiting electron does not approach the nucleus was not borne out by experimental measurement. It became apparent that other factors had to be considered for a more complete understanding of atomic structure.

Up to this point, we have been able to explain the structure of matter on the assumption that it contains tiny particles—electrons, protons, and neutrons. In 1924, the French physicist Louis De Broglie suggested that some of the properties of matter could be explained only by assuming that the electrons in matter had the properties of electromagnetic waves. For example, light waves are diffracted (scattered) on passing through a diffraction grating, a piece of glass on which thousands of closely spaced parallel lines have been ruled. In the same manner, a beam of electrons is diffracted on passing through a crystal. (The planes of atoms in the crystal behave as a grating.)

To understand the energy associated with electrons in an atom, it is necessary to consider how an electron can behave as a wave. Our modern concept of the atom discards the notion that electrons occupy definite orbits. Instead, the likelihood or probability of finding an electron in a certain position is stressed.

These ideas on probability were enunciated in the *Uncertainty Principle* in 1927 by Werner Heisenberg, a German scientist. Heisenberg stated that it is impossible to simultaneously know the energy and the position of any electron in an atom. The application of a measuring device changes either the energy or the location of the electron. Thus exact orbits, like those Bohr had suggested for hydrogen, cannot be assigned to the electrons in the atom. According to the Uncertainty Principle: The *probability* of finding an electron at a given distance from the nucleus can be determined. The position of the electron can then be described mathematically by a probability distribution.

19.15 Electron probability distributions

Figure 19-11 on the next page shows the probability distribution for finding the hydrogen electron, called a 1s electron, at different distances from the nucleus. Note that the probability increases and then decreases as the distance from the nucleus becomes greater.

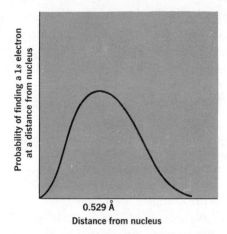

Fig. 19-11   *Probability distribution*
of a 1s electron

It is possible for the electron to be at any of these distances from the nucleus. However, the probability is greatest for the electron to be found at a fixed distance (0.529 Å). This distance corresponds to the most probable radius of the electron orbit, or energy level.

Thus the electron energy levels are not considered to be fixed orbits at specific distances from the nucleus. Instead, they are visualized as clouds of electrical charge surrounding the nucleus. The densest region of the cloud is at the radius of greatest probability, r, as shown in Figure 19-12 on page 388.

19.16 Principal quantum numbers and orbitals

Consider an atom with several electrons. Many of these electrons will occupy different energy levels; for each energy level, there is a different probability distribution. As in the Bohr model of the atom, electrons that are at higher energy levels possess a probability distribution which suggests that they are farther from the nucleus. These energy levels, called principal energy levels, are assigned numbers, called *principal quantum numbers*, $n = 1, 2, 3, 4, \ldots$.

Each of the principal energy levels has a maximum electron population — a condition verified by a study of ionization potentials (see section 20.8).

The electron probability distribution in a given energy level is called an *orbital*. An orbital therefore describes the most probable position an electron will occupy relative to the nucleus. The energy of an electron is determined chiefly by the orbital that it occupies.

19.17 The wave mechanical model of the atom

Utilizing the wave nature of the electron and the probability distribution of electrons in atoms, scientists have developed a model of the atom that is consistent with the observed properties of elements and compounds. This model, called the *wave mechanical model*, involves complex mathematics which need not concern us here. The essential ideas that we will utilize are:

1. An electron is characterized by four quantum numbers which describe its state in a given orbital. The first quantum number, called the principal quantum number, designated as n, describes the most probable distance of the electron from the nucleus. The second quantum number, designated as l, represents the sublevel the electron occupies and is described in the next section. The third quantum number, designated as m_l, indicates the orbital the electron occupies within a subshell.

2. The first three quantum numbers describe the energy of the electron. The fourth quantum number describes a characteristic called *electron spin* (an electron spinning about its axis and thus behaving like a tiny magnet). In our study, we shall be concerned chiefly with the principal quantum number.

3. According to the *Pauli Exclusion Principle*, developed by the Austrian-American physicist Wolfgang Pauli in 1925, no two electrons in an atom can have all four quantum numbers alike.

4. From a consideration of quantum numbers and the Pauli Exclusion Principle, it can be shown that the first principal energy level can contain no more than two electrons; the second energy level can contain no more than eight electrons; the third energy level can contain no more than 18 electrons; and the fourth energy level can contain no more than 32 electrons.

As scientists continued to study the spectra of atoms, they found that many of the single lines previously observed were actually composed of fine, closely spaced lines. It became clear that the origin of all of these lines could not be explained by electron transitions (jumps) between the principal energy levels. This led to the view that the principal energy levels are subdivided into sublevels the energy values of which differ only by small amounts.

19.18 Quantum sublevels

The number of sublevels in any principal energy level is equal to the principal quantum number, n. However, the K-level (or K-shell) contains only one energy level ($n = 1$). This is the same as saying the first principal energy level is not split into sublevels. The two electrons which may be contained in the first principal energy level are designated as $1s$ electrons.

The second principal energy level ($n = 2$) consists of two sublevels. The first sublevel is again designated as the s sublevel. The second sublevel is designated as the p sublevel. The electrons in the first sublevel are $2s$ electrons, and the electrons in the second sublevel are $2p$ electrons. Thus in the second principal energy level, there are two $2s$ electrons in the first sublevel, and there may be up to six $2p$ electrons in the second sublevel, or a total of eight electrons.

The third principal energy level ($n = 3$) is split into three sublevels: $3s$, $3p$, and $3d$, or a total of 18 electrons. The fourth principal energy level ($n = 4$) follows the pattern of energy-and-electron distribution that has been developing. There are four sublevels in the fourth principal energy level: $4s$, $4p$, $4d$, and $4f$, or a total of 32 electrons. The table that follows lists the different sublevels in each principal energy level and the number of electrons in each level.

PRINCIPAL ENERGY LEVEL OR SHELL	PRINCIPAL QUANTUM NUMBER (n)	MAXIMUM NUMBER OF ELECTRONS IN EACH SUBLEVEL				TOTAL NUMBER OF ELECTRONS
		s	p	d	f	
K	1	2				2
L	2	2	6			8
M	3	2	6	10		18
N	4	2	6	10	14	32
		number of orbitals in each sublevel				
		1	3	5	7	

19.19 Electron orbitals

Two important rules that the table in the previous section reveals are:

1. The maximum number of electrons in any principal energy level $= 2n^2$, where n is the principal quantum number.
2. The maximum number of orbitals in any principal energy level $= n^2$. Recall that an orbital describes the most probable position an electron will occupy relative to the nucleus.

Since the *s* sublevel can possess only two electrons, both of these electrons are represented by one orbital, called the *s* orbital. The *p* sublevel, with six electrons, has three orbitals, called *p* orbitals. The *d* sublevel, with ten electrons, has five orbitals, called *d* orbitals. The *f* sublevel, with 14 electrons, has seven orbitals, called *f* orbitals.

Although the two electrons in an orbital have the same energies, they differ in one respect: they have opposite spins. Therefore, two electrons in an orbital can have three quantum numbers that are the same, but they cannot have four quantum numbers that are the same (Pauli Exclusion Principle).

Keeping in mind the relationships we have just described for the number of orbitals in a sublevel, we can apply the rule for determining the maximum number of orbitals for the different principal energy levels.

For *K*, the first principal energy level, $n = 1$, and the number of orbitals $= n^2 = 1$. Thus as previously described, there is only a single *s* orbital in the first principal energy level. For *L*, the second principal energy level, $n = 2$, and there are n^2, or four, orbitals (one *s* and three *p*). The third energy level (*M*) contains 3^2, or nine, orbitals (one *s*, three *p*, and five *d*). The fourth energy level (*N*) contains 4^2, or 16, orbitals (one *s*, three *p*, five *d*, and seven *f*).

In section 19.21, we shall use the maximum number of electrons in a given quantum level and the corresponding orbital occupancy to further develop the Periodic Table.

19.20 Shapes of atomic orbitals

Orbitals describe the region of space occupied by the electrons in an atom. Quantum mechanics enables us to describe orbitals in terms of their geometric or spatial characteristics. The shape of an *s* orbital can best be depicted as a sphere with radius *r* (see Figure 19-12).

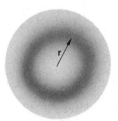

Fig. 19–12   The shape of an s orbital

The probability of locating the electron is greatest at this radius. Thus for hydrogen, the 1s orbital represents a symmetrical distribution of the single electron along the radius of the sphere.

All three p orbitals have similar energies, but the spatial distributions of the electrons are different. Since electrons tend to repel one another, the three p orbitals can be farthest apart when they extend into space at right angles to one another. The three p orbitals can be associated with x, y, and z axes which are at right angles to each other (see Figure 19-13).

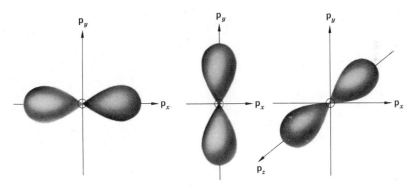

Fig. 19–13   The shape of p orbitals

The axes are designated as p_x, p_y, and p_z. The shape of the p orbital resembles a dumbbell. Similarly, the five d orbitals and the seven f orbitals have their characteristic shapes, which are considerably more complex than s or p orbitals.

The shapes of atomic orbitals are useful in predicting the angles formed by the bonds between atoms and the shapes of molecules when atoms combine. We shall return to this concept in the next chapter.

19.21 Electron configurations in atoms

To see how the electrons are arranged in atoms, let us proceed from one element to the next in order of increasing atomic number. As the atomic number increases by one, another electron is added to the atom. In all cases, the electrons are added to the lowest energy levels possible so that the atom achieves its most stable configuration.

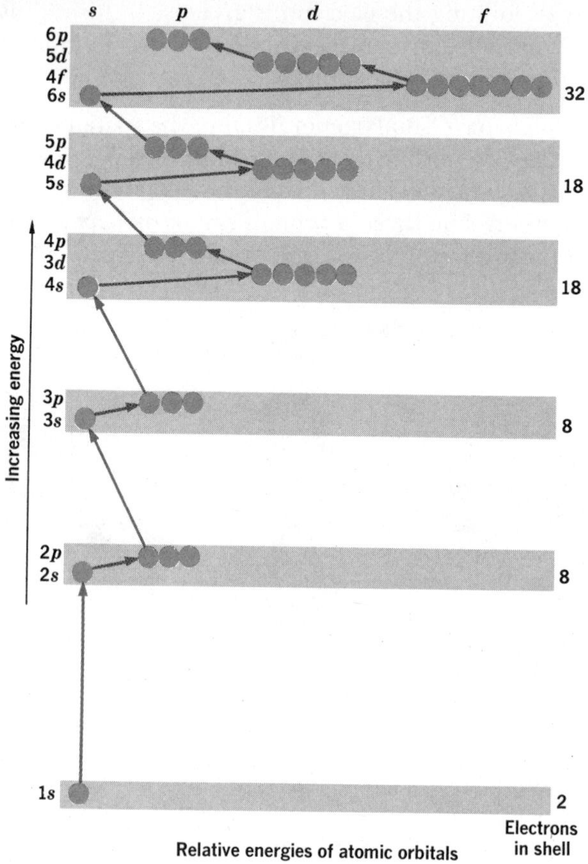

Fig. 19–14   Order of filling orbitals

Figure 19-14 shows the order in which the orbitals are filled. The *s* orbital is at the lowest energy level and can receive two electrons. The *p* orbitals have the next higher energy values; six electrons can be added to complete this energy level. Generally, the orbitals increase in energy value in the order *s*, *p*, *d*, and *f*. However, note in the preceding figure that the 4*s* orbital is at a lower energy level than the 3*d* orbital. Also note that the 5*s* orbital is lower than the 4*d* orbital. In other words, the *s* orbital of a higher principal energy level may be occupied before the *d* orbitals of a lower principal energy level.

This possible order of occupancy will be useful to recall a little later when we see how the electron configurations in the atoms are related to the positions of the atoms in the Periodic Table.

19.22 The modern Periodic Table

We can now arrange all the elements in order of increasing atomic number, following the rules we have set up for electron occupancy in specific energy levels, sublevels, and orbitals. Keep in mind that each successive electron enters the lowest energy level available.

The table on page 387 shows the maximum electron population and the number of sublevels in each principal energy level. Figure 19-14 on page 390 shows the order in which the orbitals in each sublevel are filled.

19.23 The first principal energy level

In hydrogen, the single electron enters the first principal energy level ($n = 1$) and the s sublevel. The s sublevel contains one orbital, which we will represent by a circle. A line drawn through the center of the circle represents the single electron. Diagrammatically, we may therefore represent the electron configuration of hydrogen as

$$1s$$

$$\text{H} \quad \oslash$$

Helium, atomic number 2, has two electrons in the $1s$ sublevel which complete the $1s$ orbital. The electron configuration is designated as

$$1s$$

$$\text{He} \quad \otimes$$

Since the maximum occupancy of any orbital is represented by two electrons, He has a completely filled $1s$ orbital. In addition, two electrons represent the maximum occupancy of the first principal energy level, and helium has also completed this level.

The horizontal arrangement of hydrogen and helium is called a *row*, or a *period*. The first row of the Periodic Table contains only H and He.

19.24 The second principal energy level

Lithium, atomic number 3, first fills the sublevel of lowest energy, the $1s$ sublevel, with two electrons. The third electron enters the next lowest energy level available—the $2s$ sublevel of the second principal energy level

($n = 2$). This energy level has two sublevels, s and p. Beryllium, atomic number 4, completes the $2s$ sublevel. In boron, atomic number 5, the fifth electron enters the p sublevel, which contains three p orbitals. We may represent the electron configurations of Li, Be, and B in the following diagrams:

	$1s$	$2s$	$2p$
Li	⊗	⊘	○○○
Be	⊗	⊗	○○○
B	⊗	⊗	⊘○○

In carbon, atomic number 6, the sixth electron enters the second p orbital rather than the first p orbital. This property may be ascribed to the tendency of similarly charged particles to repel one another and thus move as far apart as possible.

	$1s$	$2s$	$2p$
C	⊗	⊗	⊘⊘○

In the same manner, successive electrons are added to nitrogen, oxygen, fluorine, and neon until the second principal energy level is complete.

	$1s$	$2s$	$2p$
N	⊗	⊗	⊘⊘⊘
O	⊗	⊗	⊗⊘⊘
F	⊗	⊗	⊗⊗⊘
Ne	⊗	⊗	⊗⊗⊗

Note that Ne fills the second principal energy level. The second row of the Periodic Table contains eight elements.

19.25 The third principal energy level

The eleventh electron in Na must now enter the third principal energy level in the $3s$ subshell.

	$1s$	$2s$	$2p$	$3s$	$3p$
Na	⊗	⊗	⊗⊗⊗	⊘	○○○

We may complete the electron configurations of the next seven elements as we did in the previous principal energy level.

	$1s$	$2s$	$2p$	$3s$	$3p$
Mg	⊗	⊗	⊗ ⊗ ⊗	⊗	○ ○ ○
Al	⊗	⊗	⊗ ⊗ ⊗	⊗	⊘ ○ ○
Si	⊗	⊗	⊗ ⊗ ⊗	⊗	⊘ ⊘ ○
P	⊗	⊗	⊗ ⊗ ⊗	⊗	⊘ ⊘ ⊘
S	⊗	⊗	⊗ ⊗ ⊗	⊗	⊗ ⊘ ⊘
Cl	⊗	⊗	⊗ ⊗ ⊗	⊗	⊗ ⊗ ⊘
A	⊗	⊗	⊗ ⊗ ⊗	⊗	⊗ ⊗ ⊗

Comparison of the electron structures reveals the beginning of vertical similarities, called *columns, groups,* or *families.* Thus Li and Na mark the first two elements of the alkali metal family, followed later by K, Rb, and Cs.

19.26 Transition elements

Recall that the maximum number of electrons in the third principal energy level is 18. This level contains a d sublevel with five d orbitals having a total of ten electrons. When these ten electrons are added to the eight electrons in the $3s$ and $3p$ orbitals, the required total of 18 electrons ($n = 3$) is obtained.

The nineteenth electron of potassium might be expected to enter the $3d$ sublevel. However, from the order of filling orbitals, we note that the $4s$ orbital is lower in energy than the $3d$ orbital. The nineteenth electron of potassium enters the $4s$ orbital, and the twentieth electron of calcium completes this orbital. The next most energetic sublevel is the $3d$, followed by the $4p$.

	$1s$	$2s$	$2p$	$3s$	$3p$	$4s$
K	⊗	⊗	⊗ ⊗ ⊗	⊗	⊗ ⊗ ⊗	⊘
Ca	⊗	⊗	⊗ ⊗ ⊗	⊗	⊗ ⊗ ⊗	⊗

The twenty-first electron of scandium enters the $3d$ sublevel.

	1s	2s	2p	3s	3p	4s	3d
Sc	⊗	⊗	⊗ ⊗ ⊗	⊗	⊗ ⊗ ⊗	⊗	⊘ ○ ○ ○ ○

The next nine elements complete this sublevel, which is in the third principal energy level. Elements which complete inner (lower) energy levels before completing outer (higher) energy levels are called *transition elements.*

Note that the third row of the Periodic Table has eight elements. However, the third principal energy level has 18 elements. Ten of these elements are transition elements in the fourth row of the Periodic Table.

In the same manner, the thirty-seventh electron of rubidium enters the $5s$ sublevel rather than the $4d$. The thirty-eighth electron of strontium completes the $5s$ subshell. A new transition series from yttrium to cadmium now appears in which the $4d$ sublevel is filled. Krypton completes the fourth principal energy level.

The 18 elements from rubidium to xenon have electron structures similar to the electron structures of potassium to krypton, and they continue the vertical family relationships previously described.

The fifty-fifth electron of cesium enters the $6s$ sublevel in a similar manner, falling under Na, K, and Rb. The fifty-sixth electron of barium completes the $6s$ sublevel. At this point, another transition series — lanthanum to mercury — appears, consisting of 24 elements. This series results from the filling of seven $4f$ orbitals (14 electrons) and five $5d$ orbitals (ten electrons). Within this transition series, an inner transition series — lanthanum to lutetium — is also present. Sublevels beyond f are designated as $g, h, \ldots$, but electrons do not normally occupy these sublevels.

19.27 Filling *s* and *p* orbitals

It is interesting to observe that in any given energy level, s and p orbitals are always filled before the corresponding d and f orbitals. The d orbitals do not begin to fill until the s orbital of the following principal energy level is filled. Note that the maximum number of electrons in any outermost principal energy level (except for the first) will be eight electrons (two electrons in s orbitals and six electrons in p orbitals). To further illustrate these principles, we will examine the electron configurations of all the noble gases, shown in the table on the following page.

As we go from argon to krypton, the additional ten electrons enter $3d$ orbitals, all of which are filled before the $4p$ orbitals. Thus krypton has eight electrons in its outermost energy level. Xenon and radon (the remain-

ELEMENT	NUMBER OF ELECTRONS IN THE DIFFERENT SUBLEVELS *principal quantum number*					
	1	2	3	4	5	6
	s	*s p*	*s p d*	*s p d f*	*s p d f*	*s p*
helium	2					
neon	2	2 6				
argon	2	2 6	2 6			
krypton	2	2 6	2 6 10	2 6		
xenon	2	2 6	2 6 10	2 6 10	2 6	
radon	2	2 6	2 6 10	2 6 10 14	2 6 10	2 6

ing noble gases) complete inner orbitals in the same manner and have eight electrons in their outermost principal energy levels.

The table we have developed reveals both a horizontal arrangement called rows and a vertical arrangement called columns, or groups. We have already noted that all the noble gases are in the same column of the Periodic Table. The significance of each of the horizontal and vertical arrangements will be discussed later.

19.28 Periodicity in the properties of the elements

In the previous section, we developed the electron configurations of atoms according to the rules we set up. Afterward, we found that we had arranged the elements into columns and rows. Elements with similar properties fall into the same groups (vertical columns). All elements within a group have the same arrangement of orbitals in their outermost principal energy level, which accounts for the similar properties that these elements possess. In contrast, elements in a horizontal row show a variation in properties related to the changing number of electrons in their outermost principal energy levels.

Comparing the properties of lithium, sodium, and potassium, we note that each element has one *s* electron in its outermost principal energy level. As shown in the table on page 441, the properties of these three elements are very similar. Again, if we compare beryllium, magnesium, and calcium, each of which has two *s* electrons in its outermost principal energy level, we note that these elements, too, have similar properties. In the same manner, the properties of the members of the fluorine column can be ascribed to the presence of seven electrons (two *s* and five *p*) in the outermost energy level.

19.29 The first, second, and third rows

Let us review the arrangement of the Periodic Table shown on pages 620–621. The first row (from left to right) has only two elements, hydrogen and helium, because the K energy level can hold only two electrons in the $1s$ orbital. The second row contains elements with the L energy level gradually filling with electrons to a maximum of eight electrons in the $2s$ and $2p$ orbitals.

The same principle applies to the third row, where the M energy level gradually fills with electrons. One electron is present in the M energy level of sodium and eight electrons in the M energy level of argon. Even though the M energy level of argon is not complete, the next two electrons enter the N energy level (potassium and calcium) in the $4s$ orbital before the M energy level acquires the additional electrons needed to fill its $3d$ orbitals. This order of electron occupancy occurs because the $4s$ orbital is at a lower energy level than the $3d$ orbital.

19.30 The fourth row: the first transition series

The fourth row, containing the elements from atomic number 19 (potassium) through atomic number 36 (krypton), has ten more elements than the last two rows. The first two elements (potassium and calcium) and the last six elements (gallium through krypton) of the fourth period illustrate the addition of electrons to the outermost energy level (N).

The ten elements (scandium through zinc) between the first two and the last six have either one or two electrons in the outermost energy level. Note that, in these elements, electrons continue to be added to the M energy level to complete the $3d$ orbital. We have already referred to these ten elements, which comprise the first transition series. Remember that in transition elements, the energy level below the outermost principal energy level is only partially filled, and electrons enter d orbitals. Note that occasionally a $4s$ electron moves into a $3d$ orbital to make for an especially stable set of half-filled orbitals (Cr) or completely filled orbitals (Cu).

In the fourth row, there are three elements (potassium, chromium, and copper) each of which has one electron in its outermost energy level. Calcium, scandium, titanium, vanadium, manganese, iron, cobalt, nickel, and zinc each has two electrons in its outermost energy level. Potassium, chromium, and copper have many similar properties because each has the same number of electrons in its outermost energy level. However, potassium, chromium, and copper also show many differences in other properties.

It would appear, therefore, that the number of electrons in the next-to-the-outermost energy level also has an effect on the properties of an element. In the same way, calcium and scandium have two electrons in their outermost principal energy levels. However, calcium has eight electrons in the next-to-the-outermost principal energy level, whereas scandium has nine. This variation accounts for differences in their properties. In succeeding rows, the organization of the elements by their electron configurations follows the same pattern.

19.31 The fifth row: the second transition series

The fifth row also contains 18 elements and resembles the fourth row. Beginning with rubidium (atomic number 37) and terminating with xenon (atomic number 54), electrons should be added to the outermost (O) energy level. In yttrium (atomic number 39), however, and continuing through cadmium (atomic number 48), electrons are successively added to $4d$ orbitals. These ten elements comprise the second transition series. As in the first transition series, there are some exceptions to the order of filling orbitals (atomic numbers 41–47).

19.32 The sixth row: an inner transition series

The sixth row contains 32 elements, beginning with cesium (atomic number 55) and terminating with radon (atomic number 86). A third transition series begins with lanthanum and terminates with mercury. In this series, the elements are built up by the successive addition of electrons to inner N and O shells.

As indicated previously, the series from lanthanum to lutetium also constitutes a transition series, called the lanthanide elements. This is sometimes called a transition series within a transition series, or an *inner transition series*. The larger series first completes $4f$ orbitals (14 elements) and then $5d$ orbitals (ten elements) for a total of 24 elements. Note that variations and irregularities occur in the filling of these orbitals, but in general the same principles apply as in the filling of orbitals of lower energy. The lanthanides are all very similar in properties, which indicates that electron changes deep within an atom have little effect on the properties of the atom.

We have seen that the electron structure of an atom represents the key to its chemical properties. In later chapters, we will study in greater detail representative columns of elements and representative rows of elements. Electron configurations of all the elements are listed in the following table and apply to the lowest energy states (ground states) of the atoms.

ELECTRON STRUCTURES OF THE ELEMENTS

SHELL:		K	L	M	N	O	P	Q
SUBLEVEL:		$1s$	$2s\ 2p$	$3s\ 3p\ 3d$	$4s\ 4p\ 4d\ 4f$	$5s\ 5p\ 5d\ 5f$	$6s\ 6p\ 6d\ 6f$	$7s$
ATOM								
NO.	SYMBOL							
1	H	1						
2	He	2						
3	Li	2	1					
4	Be	2	2					
5	B	2	2 1					
6	C	2	2 2					
7	N	2	2 3					
8	O	2	2 4					
9	F	2	2 5					
10	Ne	2	2 6					
11	Na	2	2 6	1				
12	Mg	2	2 6	2				
13	Al	2	2 6	2 1				
14	Si	2	2 6	2 2				
15	P	2	2 6	2 3				
16	S	2	2 6	2 4				
17	Cl	2	2 6	2 5				
18	Ar	2	2 6	2 6				
19	K	2	2 6	2 6	1			
20	Ca	2	2 6	2 6	2			
21	Sc	2	2 6	2 6 1	2			
22	Ti	2	2 6	2 6 2	2			
23	V	2	2 6	2 6 3	2			
24	Cr	2	2 6	2 6 5	1			
25	Mn	2	2 6	2 6 5	2			
26	Fe	2	2 6	2 6 6	2			
27	Co	2	2 6	2 6 7	2			
28	Ni	2	2 6	2 6 8	2			
29	Cu	2	2 6	2 6 10	1			
30	Zn	2	2 6	2 6 10	2			
31	Ga	2	2 6	2 6 10	2 1			
32	Ge	2	2 6	2 6 10	2 2			
33	As	2	2 6	2 6 10	2 3			
34	Se	2	2 6	2 6 10	2 4			
35	Br	2	2 6	2 6 10	2 5			
36	Kr	2	2 6	2 6 10	2 6			

ELECTRON STRUCTURES OF THE ELEMENTS (Cont.)

		K	L		M			N				O				P				Q
SHELL:		1s	2s	2p	3s	3p	3d	4s	4p	4d	4f	5s	5p	5d	5f	6s	6p	6d	6f	7s
NO.	**SYMBOL**																			
37	Rb	2	2	6	2	6	10	2	6			1								
38	Sr	2	2	6	2	6	10	2	6			2								
39	Y	2	2	6	2	6	10	2	6	1		2								
40	Zr	2	2	6	2	6	10	2	6	2		2								
41	Nb	2	2	6	2	6	10	2	6	4		1								
42	Mo	2	2	6	2	6	10	2	6	5		1								
43	Tc	2	2	6	2	6	10	2	6	6		1								
44	Ru	2	2	6	2	6	10	2	6	7		1								
45	Rh	2	2	6	2	6	10	2	6	8		1								
46	Pd	2	2	6	2	6	10	2	6	10										
47	Ag	2	2	6	2	6	10	2	6	10		1								
48	Cd	2	2	6	2	6	10	2	6	10		2								
49	In	2	2	6	2	6	10	2	6	10		2	1							
50	Sn	2	2	6	2	6	10	2	6	10		2	2							
51	Sb	2	2	6	2	6	10	2	6	10		2	3							
52	Te	2	2	6	2	6	10	2	6	10		2	4							
53	I	2	2	6	2	6	10	2	6	10		2	5							
54	Xe	2	2	6	2	6	10	2	6	10		2	6							
55	Cs	2	2	6	2	6	10	2	6	10		2	6			1				
56	Ba	2	2	6	2	6	10	2	6	10		2	6			2				
57	La	2	2	6	2	6	10	2	6	10		2	6	1		2				
58	Ce	2	2	6	2	6	10	2	6	10	2	2	6			2				
59	Pr	2	2	6	2	6	10	2	6	10	3	2	6			2				
60	Nd	2	2	6	2	6	10	2	6	10	4	2	6			2				
61	Pm	2	2	6	2	6	10	2	6	10	5	2	6			2				
62	Sm	2	2	6	2	6	10	2	6	10	6	2	6			2				
63	Eu	2	2	6	2	6	10	2	6	10	7	2	6			2				
64	Gd	2	2	6	2	6	10	2	6	10	7	2	6	1		2				
65	Tb	2	2	6	2	6	10	2	6	10	9	2	6			2				
66	Dy	2	2	6	2	6	10	2	6	10	10	2	6			2				
67	Ho	2	2	6	2	6	10	2	6	10	11	2	6			2				
68	Er	2	2	6	2	6	10	2	6	10	12	2	6			2				
69	Tm	2	2	6	2	6	10	2	6	10	13	2	6			2				
70	Yb	2	2	6	2	6	10	2	6	10	14	2	6			2				
71	Lu	2	2	6	2	6	10	2	6	10	14	2	6	1		2				
72	Hf	2	2	6	2	6	10	2	6	10	14	2	6	2		2				
73	Ta	2	2	6	2	6	10	2	6	10	14	2	6	3		2				

ELECTRON STRUCTURES OF THE ELEMENTS (Cont.)

SHELL:		K	L		M			N				O				P				Q
SUBLEVEL:		$1s$	$2s$	$2p$	$3s$	$3p$	$3d$	$4s$	$4p$	$4d$	$4f$	$5s$	$5p$	$5d$	$5f$	$6s$	$6p$	$6d$	$6f$	$7s$
ATOM NO.	SYMBOL																			
74	W	2	2	6	2	6	10	2	6	10	14	2	6	4		2				
75	Re	2	2	6	2	6	10	2	6	10	14	2	6	5		2				
76	Os	2	2	6	2	6	10	2	6	10	14	2	6	6		2				
77	Ir	2	2	6	2	6	10	2	6	10	14	2	6	7		2				
78	Pt	2	2	6	2	6	10	2	6	10	14	2	6	9		1				
79	Au	2	2	6	2	6	10	2	6	10	14	2	6	10		1				
80	Hg	2	2	6	2	6	10	2	6	10	14	2	6	10		2				
81	Tl	2	2	6	2	6	10	2	6	10	14	2	6	10		2	1			
82	Pb	2	2	6	2	6	10	2	6	10	14	2	6	10		2	2			
83	Bi	2	2	6	2	6	10	2	6	10	14	2	6	10		2	3			
84	Po	2	2	6	2	6	10	2	6	10	14	2	6	10		2	4			
85	At	2	2	6	2	6	10	2	6	10	14	2	6	10		2	5			
86	Rn	2	2	6	2	6	10	2	6	10	14	2	6	10		2	6			
87	Fr	2	2	6	2	6	10	2	6	10	14	2	6	10		2	6			1
88	Ra	2	2	6	2	6	10	2	6	10	14	2	6	10		2	6			2
89	Ac	2	2	6	2	6	10	2	6	10	14	2	6	10		2	6	1		2
90	Th	2	2	6	2	6	10	2	6	10	14	2	6	10		2	6	2		2
91	Pa	2	2	6	2	6	10	2	6	10	14	2	6	10	2	2	6	1		2
92	U	2	2	6	2	6	10	2	6	10	14	2	6	10	3	2	6	1		2
93	Np	2	2	6	2	6	10	2	6	10	14	2	6	10	4	2	6	1		2
94	Pu	2	2	6	2	6	10	2	6	10	14	2	6	10	6	2	6			2
95	Am	2	2	6	2	6	10	2	6	10	14	2	6	10	7	2	6			2
96	Cm	2	2	6	2	6	10	2	6	10	14	2	6	10	7	2	6	1		2
97	Bk	2	2	6	2	6	10	2	6	10	14	2	6	10	8	2	6	1		2
98	Cf	2	2	6	2	6	10	2	6	10	14	2	6	10	10	2	6			2
99	Es	2	2	6	2	6	10	2	6	10	14	2	6	10	11	2	6			2
100	Fm	2	2	6	2	6	10	2	6	10	14	2	6	10	12	2	6			2
101	Md	2	2	6	2	6	10	2	6	10	14	2	6	10	13	2	6			2
102	No	2	2	6	2	6	10	2	6	10	14	2	6	10	14	2	6			2
103	Lw	2	2	6	2	6	10	2	6	10	14	2	6	10	14	2	6	1		2

Multiple-Choice Questions

1. When two neutral atoms approach each other, the particles that come closest to each other are the (1) protons (2) neutrons (3) mesons (4) electrons

2. When sodium is heated in a flame, energy is released. The energy is observed as (1) an absorption spectrum (2) white light (3) an emission spectrum (4) gamma rays

3. Different forms of radiation arranged in the order of decreasing wavelength are (1) radio waves, gamma rays, visible light, ultraviolet rays (2) gamma rays, radio waves, X rays, ultraviolet rays (3) radio waves, visible light, ultraviolet rays, X rays (4) X rays, visible light, ultraviolet rays, radio waves

4. The energy of a quantum of light emitted by a hydrogen atom depends on (1) the difference between two energy levels of the electron (2) the rate of reaction of hydrogen (3) the element bonded to the hydrogen (4) the number of protons in its nucleus

5. A difference between the characteristic emission spectrum and the absorption spectrum of an element is that (1) more lines are present in the absorption spectrum (2) the frequencies of the lines are greater in the absorption spectrum (3) the electron goes from a lower to a higher energy level in the absorption spectrum, and the reverse takes place in the emission spectrum (4) the absorption spectrum is formed by protons, the emission spectrum by electrons

6. According to the wave mechanical model, which of the following statements is *not* correct? (1) Four quantum numbers describe an electron in an atom. (2) Two electrons in an atom can have all four identical quantum numbers. (3) The energy of an electron increases with the principal quantum number. (4) An electron can have one of two kinds of spin.

7. The electrons in the s orbital (1) have two sublevels (2) have a probability distribution that may be represented by a sphere (3) are at the highest energy levels (4) are located in orbitals along perpendicular $X, Y,$ and Z axes

8. The electron configuration of scandium is $1s^2, 2s^2, 2p^6, 3s^2, 3p^6, 4s^2, 3d^1$. This shows that (1) the $4s$ electrons are at a lower energy level than the $3d$ electrons (2) the common oxidation number of scandium is $+1$ (3) three d orbitals are present (4) a new electron shell begins with the d orbital

9. The transition elements are those (1) that decay by radioactivity (2) with atomic numbers greater than 92 (3) that have incomplete inner electron shells (4) that have positive and negative oxidation numbers

10. The maximum number of f orbitals is (1) 1 (2) 3 (3) 5 (4) 7

Completion Questions

1. An absorption spectrum is formed when white light is passed through a gaseous substance which _____ definite colors from the white light.

2. An atom emits a quantum of energy when a (an) _____ goes from a higher to a lower energy level.

3. The modern view that it is impossible to be certain of the exact position of an electron in an atom is an outgrowth of the principle developed by _____.

4. Electrons in different orbitals in an atom possess different amounts of _____.

5. If n is used to designate the number of the principal quantum level, then n^2 gives the number of _____ for the electrons in that quantum level.

6. Three orbitals along perpendicular X, Y, and Z axes are designated by the letter _____.

7. An element that possesses two s and six p electrons in its outer shell is a member of the _____ family.

8. While the number of electrons in the p sublevel increases, the number of electrons in the _____ sublevel remains constant.

9. Planck developed our modern concept of radiant energy in which energy is emitted in small bursts or packets called _____.

10. The idea that electrons possess the characteristics of electromagnetic waves was suggested by _____.

True-False Questions

1. When a hydrogen atom is in the ground state, its electron is *farthest from* the nucleus.

2. In our modern view of atomic structure, the electron is represented as a cloud of electrical charge surrounding the nucleus. The probability of finding the electron is *least* where the cloud is most dense.

3. The *first* principal energy level of an atom contains eight electrons.

4. Two electrons in an orbital may have the same energy but different *spin*.

5. An orbital represents the shape of the *electron* cloud.
6. The atoms of the elements of the *halogen* family contain two *s* and five *p* electrons in their outer shells.
7. Elements in the same *row* of the periodic table possess the same number of valence electrons.
8. *Transition* elements can form positive ions with more than one oxidation number.
9. According to the quantum theory, the energy of a quantum is directly proportional to the *wavelength* of the radiation.
10. The energy required to remove the second electron from an atom is always *less than* the energy required to remove the first electron.

Decreases, Increases, Remains the Same

1. As the frequency of radiation increases, the wavelength _____.
2. As the frequency of a quantum of energy increases, the energy of the quantum _____.
3. As the energy of a quantum increases, the value for Planck's constant _____.
4. As an electron is displaced to higher energy levels, the force of attraction of the nucleus for that electron _____.
5. When an electron makes transitions between levels that come closer together, the energy emitted _____.
6. As the principal quantum number of an electron increases, the number of electrons in an *s* orbital _____.
7. On going from *s* to *p* to *d* sublevels, the orbitals _____ in number.
8. In a transition element, as an electron transfers from the next-to-the-outermost level to the outermost level, the oxidation number of the element _____.
9. As we go from top to bottom of a column of elements in the Periodic Table, the tendency to lose electrons _____.

Exercises for Review

1. Consider the Rutherford experiment that postulates the presence of a nucleus in the atom.
   a. Why was polonium used in the experiment?
   b. Why did the investigators conclude that the atom contains largely empty space?
   c. What evidence suggested that the positive charges in an atom are concentrated in one region?

2. List the numbers of protons and neutrons present in each of the following nuclei: (a) $^3_1$H (b) $^{31}_{15}$P (c) $^{79}_{34}$Se (d) $^{40}_{18}$Ar (e) $^{209}_{83}$Bi

3. Why do isotopes of the same element have the same electron structures?

4. Explain the difference between (a) an absorption spectrum and an emission spectrum (b) a bright-line spectrum and a continuous spectrum

5. Indicate the meanings of the following terms: (a) ground state of an atom (b) electron transition (c) excited state of an atom (d) quantum of energy

6. List the numbers of electrons in each principal energy level and in the s, p, and d sublevels for the following elements: (a) $_{20}$Ca (b) $_{13}$Al (c) $_{18}$Ar (d) $_{22}$Ti (e) $_{35}$Br

7. What is the number of s and p electrons in the valence shells of the following families of elements? (a) halogens (b) noble gases (c) carbon (Group IVA) (d) alkaline earth metals (Group IIA)

8. Distinguish between a row in the Periodic Table and a principal energy level.

Exercises for Further Study

1. Explain why s orbitals do not form bonds at definite angles.

2. Explain why lines with the same frequency appear in both the absorption and emission spectra of a given element.

3. *a.* Calculate the frequency of each of the following radiations:

ultraviolet light $\lambda = 3.5 \times 10^{-7}$ meter
yellow light $\lambda = 5.8 \times 10^{-7}$ meter
infrared light $\lambda = 9.0 \times 10^{-7}$ meter

b. Using Planck's constant, $h = 6.63 \times 10^{-34}$ joule-sec, calculate the energy in a quantum of each of the radiations given in part *a.*

4. *a.* According to the Bohr model, why was it necessary to discard an important concept of classical physics?

b. How did Bohr apply the quantum theory to his model?

5. *a.* Describe the important changes in the Bohr model of the atom necessitated by the adoption of the wave mechanical model.

b. Explain why these changes were made.

6. *a.* List the electron population of the element $_{24}$Cr, including the principal energy levels and sublevels.

b. Draw a diagram of a ladder. Label the different energy levels in the proper order, starting with the lowest energy level at the bottom of the ladder. Indicate the number of electrons at the proper levels for $_{24}$Cr.

7. Why are there only two elements in the first row of the Periodic Table and eight elements in the second row?

8. Explain why the properties of the elements of the lanthanide series are very much alike.

9. Describe an experiment that shows how electrons exhibit the properties of waves.

10. The following table lists the energy in electron volts for the hydrogen atom in the first three excited levels:

$$n = 1 \quad 0.0 \text{ ev (ground state)}$$
$$n = 2 \quad 10.2 \text{ ev}$$
$$n = 3 \quad 12.0 \text{ ev}$$
$$n = 4 \quad 12.7 \text{ ev}$$

Calculate all the possible energy values for electron transitions from these levels.

Chapter 20

CHEMICAL BONDING

20.1 Introduction

When two hydrogen atoms come sufficiently close together, they unite to form a molecule. However, when two helium atoms come close together, they do *not* unite to form a molecule but remain as separate atoms. Sodium atoms unite with chlorine atoms to form a stable species, whereas silver atoms and copper atoms do not unite. What are the factors that determine whether or not atoms will unite? What are the different ways in which atoms can unite? Some principles which govern the combining of atoms were given in Chapter 4. In this chapter we will extend these principles.

20.2 Chemical bonds

When atoms unite, attractive forces called *chemical bonds* tend to pull the atoms together. In Chapter 12, we saw that when a chemical bond forms, energy is released; to break a chemical bond, energy is consumed. Thus when two atoms are held together by a chemical bond, the atoms are at a lower energy condition than when they are separated. Throughout our work in science, the following principle recurs: Systems that are at low energy levels are more stable than systems at high energy levels. Chemical changes therefore tend to occur among atoms if the change leads to a lower energy condition and hence to a more stable structure.

20.3 Forces between atoms

The forces that tend to establish chemical bonds between two atoms result from the interactions between the protons and electrons present in the atoms. These forces include:

1. Repulsions between the electrons of the two atoms.
2. Repulsions between the nuclei of the two atoms.
3. Attractions between the nucleus of one atom and the electrons of the other atom.

A chemical bond results when the forces of attraction between the two nuclei and the electrons of the opposite atoms (force 3) are greater than the repulsions of the two electron systems and the repulsions of the two nuclei (force 1 plus force 2). Thus a chemical bond may be characterized as the force resulting from the simultaneous attraction of two nuclei for one or more pairs of electrons.

20.4 The sizes of atoms and ions

According to our wave mechanical model, an atom has no specific boundaries. It is more meaningful, therefore, to describe atomic size in terms of how closely atoms approach one another. Since the boundary designations are arbitrary, values representing sizes of atoms and ions are useful for purposes of comparison only.

We have already described what happens when one atom approaches another. If the net attraction forces overcome the net repulsive forces, bond formation occurs. In this situation, it is possible to measure the interatomic distances, frequently called *bond lengths*.

Consider the model of two gaseous iodine atoms shown in Figure 20-1B.

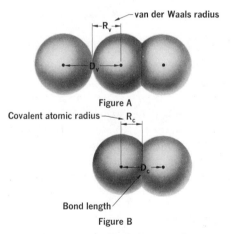

Fig. 20-1   Covalent and van der Waals radii

Distance D_c represents the internuclear distance between two *bonded* iodine atoms. This bond length is experimentally determined to be 2.67 Å. One half of the bond length (R_c), called the *covalent radius*, is 1.33 Å. Distance D_v in Figure 20-1A represents the internuclear distance between two *nonbonded* iodine atoms. It is the closest distance that the centers of two iodine atoms in adjoining molecules can approach each other, determined experimentally to be 4.30 Å. One half this distance (R_v) is called the van der Waals radius, which for iodine is 2.15 Å.

The values for covalent radii, also called atomic radii, shown in the Periodic Table on pages 620–621, are generally reliable since they are calculated from experimentally determined bond lengths taking polarity effects into consideration. On the other hand, van der Waals radii are subject to many variables that are difficult to measure. Hence, the values are somewhat unreliable. At best, both measures of the sizes of atoms retain considerable uncertainty.

The size of an atom in a covalent molecule differs from the size of the same atom in an ionic crystal. For example, the covalent radius for lithium is 1.33 Å, whereas the ionic radius for lithium is 0.60 Å. Since Li^+ has lost a $2s$ electron, its electron configuration is $1s^2$, which means the presence of a K-shell only. The loss of the L-shell causes a shrinkage in the ion. Conversely, the covalent radius of fluorine is 0.72 Å, whereas the ionic radius is 1.36 Å. Although the atom and the ion have the same number of electron shells, the additional electron in F^- causes stronger electron repulsion. This expands the $2p$ orbital and increases the size of F^-.

20.5 Bond formation by orbital overlap: an energy approach

Consider two hydrogen atoms approaching one another. Each atom possesses a single electron in its $1s$ orbital. We can consider the orbital of this electron as a sphere surrounding the nucleus. When two hydrogen atoms approach one another, the two spheres overlap, as shown in Figure 20-2. In this region of overlap (shaded area), both electrons "feel" the attraction of both nuclei. When an overlap between the two orbitals occurs, a decrease in energy occurs. The two combined atoms are at a lower energy condition than when they were apart, and a chemical bond has been formed.

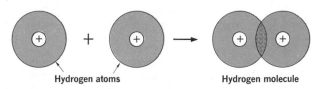

Hydrogen atoms   Hydrogen molecule

Fig. 20–2   Formation of a hydrogen molecule
by orbital overlap

20.6 Bond formation by orbital overlap: a structural approach

Since the maximum electron capacity of an orbital is two electrons, the $1s$ orbital in a hydrogen atom is half-filled. We have already represented the orbital of a hydrogen atom by a circle ○ and the electron by a line through the center ⊘. The orbital of the electron of a second hydrogen atom may be drawn the same, except that the line through the center of the circle is in the opposite direction ⊘. When the two atoms come close together and the two $1s$ orbitals overlap, a stable configuration of two electrons per orbital results. The overlap may be represented as ⊗. The overlap has produced a bond in which the nuclei of both hydrogen atoms simultaneously attract a pair of electrons (see Figure 20-3).

Hydrogen molecule

Fig. 20–3 Bond formation in a hydrogen molecule

In helium, the presence of two $1s$ electrons means that the $1s$ orbital is already filled, and no overlap is possible (see Figure 20-4). Hence, He atoms do not combine to form molecules.

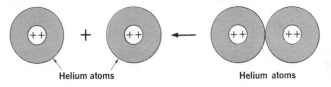

Helium atoms   Helium atoms

Fig. 20–4 Two helium atoms

Two different atoms, such as hydrogen and chlorine, may also combine by orbital overlap. This combination is represented schematically in the following diagram:

	$1s$	$2s$	$2p$	$3s$	$3p$	
Cl	⊗	⊗	⊗ ⊗ ⊗	⊗	⊗ ⊗ ⊘	
H					⊘	
					$1s$	

Note that hydrogen has one half-filled $1s$ orbital, and chlorine has one half-filled $3p$ orbital. These orbitals may overlap to form a bond. Unlike the two electrons in hydrogen, the two electrons completing this orbital are attracted more strongly by the nucleus of the chlorine atom than by the nucleus of the hydrogen atom. This is a significant difference to which we will return later.

20.7 Types of bonds

As we learned in Chapter 4, atoms may form two main types of bonds: ionic (electrovalent) bonds and covalent bonds. Ionic bonds are characterized by a transfer of one or more electrons from one atom (usually a metal) to a nonmetallic atom. Covalent bonds are characterized by a sharing of pairs of electrons between atoms. Sharing electrons occurs in different ways and creates different properties in the compounds that form. Whether atoms unite to form ionic or covalent bonds depends on their ionization potentials and their electronegativities.

20.8 Ionization potential (ionization energy)

When increasingly large amounts of energy are supplied to a gaseous atom, its most loosely held electron is elevated to higher energy levels that take it farther and farther away from the nucleus. The electron often travels sufficiently far from the nucleus so that the force of attraction holding the electron in the atom becomes very weak. The electron may escape completely from the atom, leaving behind a positively charged ion.

The energy that must be given to an isolated gaseous atom to enable its most loosely held electron to escape is called the *first ionization potential* of the atom. The additional energy that may cause the loss of the next most loosely held electron is called the *second ionization potential.*

The ionization potential of an atom is determined experimentally by gradually increasing the voltage between the two plates of a gas-discharge tube containing the atoms in question. Little or no current flows through the tube until the voltage becomes high enough for the atoms to be ionized, that is, to lose electrons. The ionization potential is then calculated from this voltage and is expressed in electron volts, ev. One electron volt is the amount of energy given to an electron when it is accelerated between two plates that have a difference in electric potential of one volt.

Ionization potentials are also expressed as ionization energies. To convert ionization potential in electron volts into ionization energy in kilocalories, we use the relationship

$$1 \text{ ev} = 3.8 \times 10^{-23} \text{ kcal}$$

All electrons are held in the atom by the attractive force exerted by the positively charged nucleus. As a result of this force, energy must be expended in removing an electron from the atom to form a positive ion.

20.9 What conditions determine the magnitude of ionization energy?

The amount of energy needed to remove the most loosely held electron from a gaseous atom depends on the following conditions:

1. The charge of the nucleus. As the nuclear charge (atomic number) increases, the force of attraction between the nucleus and the electrons increases.
2. The distance from the nucleus to the outermost electron shell, called the radius of the atom. As the number of electron shells increases, the radius of the atom increases. The electron is then held more loosely, and less energy is required to remove it from the atom.
3. The screening, or shielding, effect of the electrons of the inner shells. This tends to reduce the force exerted by the nucleus on the electrons in the outer shell.
4. The sublevel of the outer electrons. Generally, s electrons are more tightly held to the nucleus (they are at a lower energy level) than p electrons.

20.10 Ionization energies and the Periodic Table

It is also possible to remove more than one electron from a gaseous atom to produce ions with charges of $+2$ and $+3$. However, the second and third ionizations require greater amounts of energy than the first ionization because now the atom has a positive charge. For our purposes, we will study only the first ionization energies.

The following table lists the first ionization energies for a number of representative elements arranged in the order that they appear in the Periodic Table.

ATOMIC NUMBER	ELEMENT	IONIZATION ENERGY (kcal/mole)	ATOMIC NUMBER	ELEMENT	IONIZATION ENERGY (kcal/mole)
1	H	313.6	11	Na	118.4
2	He	566.7	12	Mg	175.2
3	Li	124.3	13	Al	137.9
4	Be	214.9	14	Si	187.9
5	B	191.2	15	P	241.7
6	C	259.5	16	S	238.8
7	N	335	17	Cl	300
8	O	313.8	18	Ar	363.2
9	F	401.5	19	K	100.0
10	Ne	497.0	20	Ca	141

The same ionization energies are shown in Figure 20-5 plotted in the form of a graph.

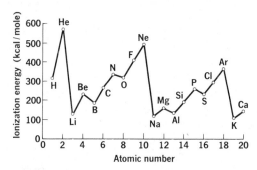

Fig. 20-5   Trends in ionization energies

The values for the ionization energies are given in kilocalories/mole. As we have seen, ionization energies reveal how firmly the outer (valence) electrons are held in atoms.

20.11 How do ionization energies relate to the behavior of atoms?

From a study of the values in the table on page 411, we can observe certain patterns of regular behavior:

1. The Group IA elements have the lowest ionization energies.

Within this group, called the *alkali metals*, the ionization energy decreases from 124.3 kcal for lithium to 90 kcal for cesium. The valence electrons of the alkali metals are held by weak forces; thus the alkali metals tend to form positive ions.

The alkali metals possess low ionization energies because their atomic radii are larger than the atomic radii of the other elements in a given row. From the smallest member of the alkali metal group to the largest (from the top to the bottom of column IA), the increase in the size of the atom produces a further decrease in the ionization energy.

2. The noble gases have the highest ionization energies.

These high values are associated with the presence of a very stable, low energy arrangement for all the electrons in the outer shells of these gases. The low energy condition exists when an atom has eight electrons in its outer shell: two electrons in the *s* orbital and six in the *p* orbitals (except for helium which possesses only *s* electrons).

3. The ionization energies increase from left to right across a row. Consider a row such as the row from lithium through neon. The increase is not uniform, as we can see from the irregularities between beryllium and boron, and between nitrogen and oxygen. The first irregularity arises because beryllium has only two electrons in its outer shell to complete its s orbital, a low energy orbital. Boron has a third electron in its outer shell, which is in a p orbital. This electron is at a higher energy level than the s electrons and requires less energy to remove it to form an ion.

The irregularity in the ionization energies for nitrogen and oxygen may be explained as follows: Nitrogen has five electrons in its outer shell. Two electrons complete the s orbital, and the remaining three electrons are in three different p orbitals (p_x, p_y, and p_z). This electron arrangement appears to provide an increase in stability. Oxygen possesses one additional electron, which is more loosely held in a completed p orbital than the three electrons in the half-filled p orbitals. This electron arrangement gives oxygen a lower ionization energy than nitrogen.

Despite these two irregularities, the ionization energies increase from the alkali metals in column IA to the halogen elements in column VIIA. This increase is caused by the increase in the positive charge of the nucleus and the decrease in the radius of the atoms. The result is to bring the outermost electrons closer to the nucleus.

The noble gases have large atomic radii. However, their extremely high ionization energies result from the special stability of the completed s and p orbitals that is associated with an outermost shell of eight electrons. Transition elements complete the orbitals in inner energy levels of atoms. Scandium, for example, begins a series of elements that complete the $3d$ orbital after the $4s$. This might suggest that during ionization $3d$ electrons are removed before $4s$ electrons. Experimentally, however, the reverse is observed. It must be remembered that during ionization the nuclear charge remains unchanged as the number of electrons decreases. But as we fill a given row of elements, the addition of an electron always increases the nuclear charge. Apparently, during ionization of transition elements, the repulsions between electrons force $4s$ electrons to leave before $3d$ electrons.

20.12 Stability based on electron structure

Our observations concerning the stability of electron structures can be summarized in a number of rules.

1. A filled orbital is more stable than a half-filled orbital.
2. Three half-filled p orbitals show an increase in stability over one half-filled or over two half-filled p orbitals.

3. Eight electrons in completed *s* and *p* orbitals provide an extremely stable structure.

Other rules will appear for special groups of elements, such as those in the different transition series, including the lanthanide and actinide series.

20.13 Electronegativity scale

We have described ionization energy as the amount of energy required to remove an electron from a gaseous atom. However, when an atom receives an electron and becomes a negative ion, the opposite process occurs —energy is released. The amount of energy that is released is called *electron affinity*.

Although electron affinities cannot be experimentally measured for most elements, it is useful to compare the ability of atoms in molecules to attract the electron pair that bonds the atoms. Chemists have therefore devised relative scales of electronegativity in which atoms with the strongest attraction for electrons have the highest electronegative values. The American chemist Linus Pauling (1901–   ), who brilliantly investigated the nature of the chemical bond, defined electronegativity as: "the power of an atom in a molecule to attract electrons to itself." A table of electronegativity values follows.

ELECTRONEGATIVITIES OF SOME ELEMENTS (ON THE ARBITRARY PAULING SCALE)

H 2.1						
Li 1.0	Be 1.5	B 2.0	C 2.5	N 3.0	O 3.5	F 4.0
Na 0.9	Mg 1.2	Al 1.5	Si 1.8	P 2.1	S 2.5	Cl 3.0
K 0.8	Ca 1.0	Ga 1.6	Ge 1.8	As 2.0	Se 2.4	Br 2.8
Rb 0.8	Sr 1.0					I 2.5
Cs 0.7	Ba 0.9					

The highest electronegativity value, 4.0, is assigned to fluorine because it possesses the greatest attraction for electrons. Further study of the electronegativity values in the table reveals:

1. In every horizontal row, the electronegativity value is lowest for the alkali metal (column IA).
2. The electronegativity values increase in a regular manner from the alkali metals to the halogen elements.
3. In every vertical column of the Periodic Table, the electronegativity values decrease from the top to the bottom of the column.
4. The most electronegative element is at the top of column VIIA. The least electronegative element (excluding the noble gases) is at the bottom of column IA.
5. Except for some irregularities that appear in the values for ionization energies, both the ionization energies and electronegativities follow similar trends. This is understandable because elements that have low ionization energies exert a weak attractive force on the outer electrons in their own atoms and also exert a weak attractive force on the outer electrons of other atoms. Therefore, we can predict that when an element with a high electronegativity reacts with an element of much lower electronegativity, there is a transfer of electrons, and ions are produced. When the difference in the electronegativity values for the two elements is about 1.7 or greater, the bond is principally ionic.

20.14 Energy changes during the formation of ionic bonds

What are the energy changes involved in the formation of a typical ionic bond, such as the bond between sodium and chlorine? Assume that we have vaporized the sodium, so that we have individual gaseous sodium atoms; assume that the molecules of chlorine gas are also split into atoms.

Sodium and other Group IA metals have low ionization energies (see the table on page 441). Therefore, a relatively small amount of energy is needed to remove the single s electron from the outer electron shell of a gaseous sodium atom. We can express this change as

$$\text{Na } (g) \rightarrow \text{Na}^+ (g) + e^- - E_1 \quad \text{(ionization energy)}$$

where E_1 is the energy that must be supplied to the sodium atom. A chlorine atom has seven electrons in its outer shell and one electron missing in a half-filled p orbital. The table on page 414 shows that the electronegativity value of chlorine is 3.0. This relatively high value indicates a strong attraction for electrons that will release energy, E_2, when an electron is acquired. The equation for this change is

$$Cl\ (g) + e^- \rightarrow Cl^-\ (g) + E_2 \qquad \text{(electron affinity)}$$

When sodium atoms and chlorine atoms meet, a transfer of an electron takes place, and oppositely charged ions form. The electrical attraction between the ions draws them together and, at room temperature, a solid ionic compound (a crystal) is formed. An additional release of energy, E_3, occurs.

$$Na^+\ (g) + Cl^-\ (g) \rightarrow Na^+Cl^-\ (s) + E_3 \qquad \text{(crystal energy)}$$

The chief reason that an ionic bond does form is that the combined energy released, E_2 and E_3, is greater than the energy consumed, E_1. Therefore, the net energy change is a release of energy.

$$E_{net} = \underset{\substack{\text{electron} \\ \text{affinity}}}{E_2} + \underset{\substack{\text{crystal} \\ \text{energy}}}{E_3} - \underset{\substack{\text{ionization} \\ \text{energy}}}{E_1}$$

This means that the Na^+ ions and the Cl^- ions in solid NaCl possess lower energy and greater stability than if they had remained as separated atoms. (To make our discussion more complete, it would be necessary to take into account the energy consumed in vaporizing sodium atoms and in dissociating chlorine molecules.)

20.15 Covalent bonds

The formation of covalent bonds was discussed in section 4.13. In our discussion, we pointed out that covalent bonds form when two atoms share one or more pairs of electrons. The chief difference between covalence and electrovalence is that in covalence no transfer of electrons from one atom to another occurs. No ions are produced; instead, electron pairs are shared by two atoms. The attractions for the electron pair need not be equal. As the difference between the attractive forces of two atoms for electrons becomes larger, the tendency to form an ionic (electrovalent) bond increases.

20.16 Nonpolar covalent bonds

Consider a hydrogen atom, with its one electron in an incomplete s orbital. This structure possesses a higher energy content than a helium atom, which has two electrons to complete the s orbital. However, two hydrogen atoms can combine to form a molecule by forming a covalent bond, whereas helium atoms remain uncombined. In the bond that links the hydrogen atoms, two electrons, one from each atom, complete the *s* orbital. The hydrogen molecule that forms has a lower energy content and a greater stability than the two separate hydrogen atoms.

The electron structure of an H_2 molecule may be represented by an electron-dot diagram as follows:

$$H \colon H$$

We must keep in mind, however, that such a diagram oversimplifies the true situation. The electrons are not in fixed positions as indicated by the dots. The electrons probably can be found, at any given time, in some position around or between the two atoms.

In section 20.5, we saw how the overlap of the electron orbitals may be employed to indicate how two atoms combine. One important observation we can make is that the two H atoms in the H_2 molecule are identical, each having an electronegativity value of 2.1. Consequently, both atoms exert equal attraction for the two electrons, which means that the electron pair is shared equally between them. This is the same as saying that the two electrons spend equal amounts of time around each atom.

The electron structure and the nuclei are the same for both atoms, so that the distribution of electrical charges is equal. The resulting H_2 molecule does not have any electrical polarity. This type of bond between two .identical atoms is called a *nonpolar covalent bond*.

The halogen elements also form diatomic molecules, which have a nonpolar covalent bond joining two atoms. The outer shells of all the halogen atoms contain seven electrons with one incomplete *p* orbital. On gaining one electron, an outer shell contains eight electrons and achieves the stable structure of the noble gases. In the electron-dot formula, two F atoms form a nonpolar covalent bond, uniting in a molecule of fluorine.

$$\colon \! \overset{\cdot\cdot}{F} \! \colon \! \overset{\cdot\cdot}{F} \! \colon$$

Again we see that the two atoms are identical, and the pair of electrons is shared equally by them.

20.17 Polar covalent bonds

When we investigate the union of an atom of hydrogen with an atom of chlorine, we find a somewhat different situation. The electronegativity value of hydrogen is 2.1; for chlorine it is 3.0. This large difference indicates that chlorine exerts a stronger attraction for electrons than hydrogen. The ionization energy for hydrogen is rather high, 13.5 ev, so that it is not easy to remove an electron from the hydrogen atom. Both of these factors—electronegativity and ionization energy—determine the type of bond that results. Since the electron is not removed from the hydrogen atom, a covalent bond is formed between hydrogen and chlorine atoms.

The electron-dot diagram for hydrogen chloride shows how the sharing of one pair of electrons produces a complete outer shell of two electrons for hydrogen and also a complete outer shell of eight electrons for chlorine.

$$H^{\times} + \cdot \overset{\cdot\cdot}{\underset{\cdot\cdot}{Cl}}\colon \longrightarrow H\overset{\cdot\cdot}{\underset{\cdot\cdot}{\overset{\times}{Cl}}}\colon$$

The greater electronegativity of chlorine, however, leads to an unequal sharing of the two electrons. Both electrons are pulled closer to the chlorine atom and away from the hydrogen atom. Another way of describing this situation is to say that there is a greater probability of finding both electrons close to the chlorine atom and a smaller probability of finding both electrons close to the hydrogen atom.

The effect of the unequal sharing of electrons is that the outer shell of the chlorine atom has six electrons entirely to itself plus more than half of the two shared electrons making up the covalent bond. This electron density gives chlorine a negative charge slightly greater than the positive charge of its nucleus. The chlorine region of the HCl molecule therefore obtains a negative charge. The magnitude of this charge is less than the charge of one electron.

In a converse manner, the hydrogen atom has less than half a share in the two electrons of the covalent bond. This negative charge does not equal the single positive charge of its nucleus. The hydrogen region of the HCl molecule obtains a positive charge equal in magnitude to the negative charge of the chlorine region. As a result of this unbalanced geometry of positive and negative charges, called *charge separation* or *charge displacement*, the HCl molecule is said to be polar. The bond between the hydrogen and chlorine atoms is a polar covalent bond. Thus a polar covalent bond always forms when electrons are shared by two atoms whose electronegativities are different.

20.18 Trends in the polarity of bonds

A wholly nonpolar covalent bond forms only between two atoms that are alike, for example, H_2, Cl_2, O_2, and N_2. When compounds are formed by the union of dissimilar atoms, differences in electronegativities become apparent. If only a small difference in the electron attractions of the two atoms exists, there will be a small displacement of the shared electrons toward whichever atom has the greater electronegativity. A bond with small polarity results. When the difference in the electronegativities of the two atoms becomes greater, the pair of shared electrons is pulled closer to the more negative of the two atoms. In this instance, the polarity of the bond is greater.

Elements belonging to the same group or neighboring groups in the Periodic Table have electronegativities which do not differ very much. These elements unite to form covalent bonds with a small polarity. When the atoms that unite come from groups which are farther apart in the Periodic Table, their electronegativities show greater differences. The resulting covalent bonds have a greater polarity.

What type of bond results when typical metal Z from Group IA or IIA unites with typical nonmetal X from Group VIIA? In such unions, the differences in electronegativities are large. The two electrons are pulled very far from Z, the atom with the small electronegativity. The pair of electrons is therefore completely removed from the influence of Z, and Z becomes a positive ion. X, the more electronegative atom, gains complete possession of both electrons of the orbital and becomes a negative ion. Thus the formation of an ionic or electrovalent bond represents the extreme example of increased polarity. The probability of finding the pair of electrons near the positive atom is now zero, but the probability is very high for finding the electrons near the negative atom.

20.19 Predicting bond type

Studying ionization energies and electronegativities enables us to predict the type of bond that forms between two atoms. Let us restrict our discussion to the fluorine compounds of the elements in the second row of the Periodic Table. These compounds are: lithium fluoride, LiF; beryllium difluoride, BeF_2; boron trifluoride, BF_3; carbon tetrafluoride, CF_4; nitrogen trifluoride, NF_3; oxygen difluoride, OF_2; and fluorine fluoride, F_2.

Keep in mind the approximation that an ionic bond may form when the electronegativity difference between two atoms is 1.7 or greater. From the table of electronegativities on page 414, we can see that LiF and BeF_2 are ionic. However, BF_3 shows only partial ionic character with considerable evidence pointing toward covalent bonding. The compounds from CF_4 to OF_2 show increasing covalence, and the electronegativity difference is less than 1.7. Finally, F_2 possesses a completely nonpolar covalent bond, and the electronegativity difference is zero. Note that as a row is crossed and fluorides are formed, the bonds change from ionic to covalent. Also note that some bonds possess both ionic and covalent character. The following table summarizes these bond types.

ATOMS	IONIZATION ENERGY (*electron volts*)	ELECTRONEGATIVITY VALUE	ELECTRON-DOT FORMULA OF GASEOUS COMPOUND	BOND TYPE
Li F	5.4 17.3	1.0 4.0	Li $\overset{\cdot\cdot}{\underset{\cdot\cdot}{:F:}}$	ionic
Be F	9.3 17.3	1.5 4.0	$\overset{\cdot\cdot}{\underset{\cdot\cdot}{:F:}}$ Be $\overset{\cdot\cdot}{\underset{\cdot\cdot}{:F:}}$	ionic
B F	8.3 17.3	2.0 4.0	$:F:B:F:$ with F above	partially ionic
C F	11.2 17.3	2.5 4.0	$:F:C:F:$ with F above and below	polar covalent
N F	14.5 17.3	3.0 4.0	N with three F	polar covalent
O F	13.6 17.3	3.5 4.0	O with two F	polar covalent
F F	17.3 17.3	4.0 4.0	$:F:F:$	nonpolar covalent

20.20 Coordinate covalent bonds

Let us consider another way by which covalent bonds form. When a particle (an atom or an ion) that can accept a pair of electrons unites with a particle that can donate a pair of electrons, a *coordinate covalent bond* forms between the two particles. Note that the pair of electrons shared by the two atoms is supplied by a single atom. In an ordinary covalent bond, each atom supplies one electron to form the shared pair.

The H^+ ion is an example of a particle that can accept a pair of electrons. The following electron-dot diagram shows how the H^+ ion can share electrons with oxygen that is part of a molecule of H_2O:

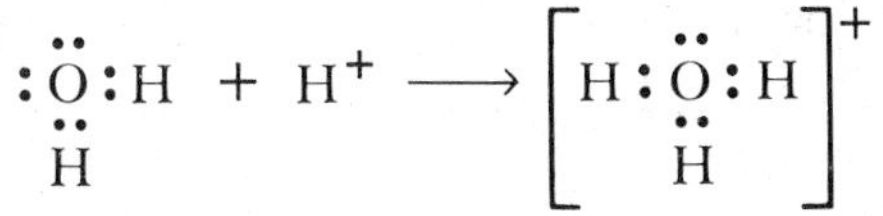

$$:\overset{..}{\underset{H}{O}}:H \ + \ H^+ \ \longrightarrow \ \left[H:\overset{..}{\underset{H}{O}}:H \right]^+$$

We can picture the formation of this bond in the following way. The O in H_2O possesses two pairs of electrons which are not shared with H atoms. An H^+ ion has a positive charge, and its outer electron level is completely unoccupied. When the H^+ ion approaches the O region of the H_2O molecule, the H^+ ion is attracted by the negative charges of the electrons of the O that are not bonded to H atoms. The H^+ ion then accepts two electrons into its outer shell. No transfer of electrons takes place, but a covalent bond forms between the H^+ and O. In this coordinate covalent bond, H^+ ion is the acceptor of a pair of electrons, and O is the donor.

Consider the following electron-dot diagram, which depicts the electron structure of an NH_4^+ (ammonium) ion:

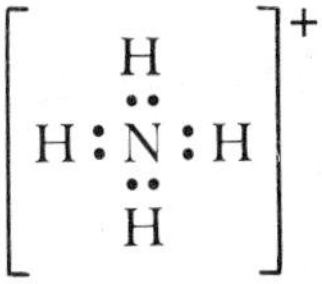

$$\left[H:\overset{\overset{\textstyle H}{..}}{\underset{\underset{\textstyle H}{..}}{N}}:H \right]^+$$

The N in the molecule of NH_3 (ammonia) is the donor of the pair of electrons. Here again, the H^+ ion acts as an acceptor of a pair of electrons. The four H atoms that are now united to the N atom are all identical. This means that NH_4^+ contains four covalent bonds which are all alike. The only difference is in the manner of formation of the last bond. Furthermore, the positive charge of NH_4^+ is not situated on one of the four H atoms but is spread out over the entire NH_4^+ ion.

Coordinate covalent bonds are also found in compounds such as hydrates. For example, in hydrated copper(II) sulfate, $CuSO_4 \cdot 5H_2O$, some H_2O molecules are bonded to a Cu^{+2} ion by coordinate covalent bonds. In the same manner, a Cu^{+2} ion may bond to NH_3 molecules. The combination of an ion and a molecule is called a *complex ion*, for example, $Cu(H_2O)_x^{+2}$, $Cu(NH_3)_y^{+2}$ (see sections 15.17 and 23.8).

20.21 Hydrogen bonds

Hydrogen and reactive electronegative nonmetals, such as fluorine and oxygen, form binary compounds with unusually high boiling points. Note, in Figure 20-6, the abnormally high boiling point of HF compared to the boiling points of the other hydrogen halides in Group VIIA (dashed line).

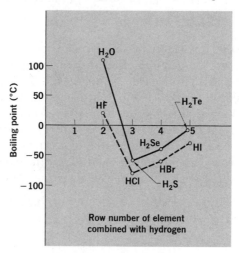

Fig. 20–6   Trends in boiling points
(Groups VIIA and VIA)

Also note the abnormally high boiling point of H_2O compared to the boiling points of the other binary hydrogen derivatives of elements in Group VIA (heavy line). Such behavior suggests that liquid HF and liquid H_2O are not composed of simple molecules. Instead, each liquid consists of molecules joined together in a chain by hydrogen atoms acting as bridges. We have already referred to this type of attractive force as a hydrogen bond. A *hydrogen bond* is formed by an atom of hydrogen which acts as a bridge between two highly electronegative atoms, such as oxygen or fluorine. The bond tends to create chains of weakly linked molecules.

Why does a hydrogen bond form in a molecule like liquid HF? Recall that HF has exceptionally strong polar bonds, which means that the H region of the molecule is positively charged, and the F region of the molecules is negatively charged. An attractive force exists between the H atom in one HF molecule and the F atom in another HF molecule, so that a chain of HF molecules is formed. This chain can be shown as

F—H · · · · F—H · · · · F—H

In this formula, the solid line is the bond in the parent HF molecule and the dotted line is the hydrogen bond. Similarly, H_2O, another polar covalent compound, is shown in Figure 20-7.

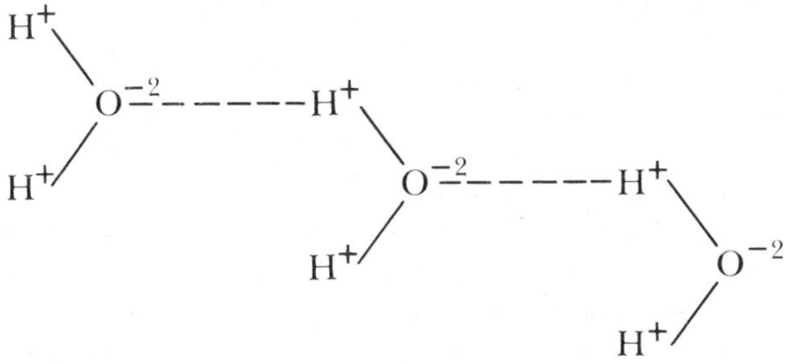

Fig. 20-7   Hydrogen bonding in water

If H_2O molecules were not hydrogen bonded, it is likely that H_2O would be a gas at room temperature. Hydrogen bonds unite H_2O molecules and hold them together in the liquid and solid states. Without hydrogen bonding, life as we recognize it probably could not exist.

20.22 Van der Waals forces

In section 9.3, we discussed attractive forces between gas molecules. When gases such as helium, hydrogen, oxygen, and nitrogen are cooled sufficiently, they liquefy. Continued cooling results in solidification. In the liquid state, the molecules of helium, hydrogen, oxygen, and nitrogen attract each other sufficiently to overcome the motion associated with the kinetic energies of the molecules of the gases. In the solid state, the molecules possess the least random motion. What is the nature of these attractive forces in gas molecules that have stable electron structures?

The melting points of elemental gases and many simple gaseous compounds (when solidified) are very low, generally below 0° C. The same is true of their boiling points. We can deduce that very weak forces act to hold these molecules in the solid state and in the liquid state. At slightly higher temperatures, the molecules separate from each other to form a gas. The attractive forces that hold together neutral molecules are called *van der Waals forces.* Melting and boiling points are a measure of the magnitude of these forces. Scientists believe that van der Waals forces result from the interaction of the electron clouds of neighboring molecules. These interactions may produce, by induction, oppositely charged regions in neighboring molecules, and in this manner account for the attractive forces.

Since van der Waals forces result from electron interactions, it follows that van der Waals forces become stronger as the number of electrons in a given species increases or as the size of the species increases. The table that follows lists the noble gases in order of increasing number of electrons. Note the increase in melting and boiling points.

GAS	ATOMIC RADIUS ($\overset{\circ}{A}$)	MELTING POINT (°C)	BOILING POINT (°C)
^{2}He	0.93	− 271.9 (26 atm)	− 268.9
^{10}Ne	1.12	− 248.7	− 245.9
^{18}Ar	1.54	− 189.3	− 185.7
^{36}Kr	1.69	− 157	− 152.9
^{54}Xe	1.90	− 111.5	− 107.1

Van der Waals forces are also related to the shapes of molecules. Thus symmetrical molecules pack more readily in crystals than do unsymmetrical molecules of the same composition. For example, the compound C_5H_{12} has several forms called isomers. In one form, called *n*-pentane (see below), the carbon atoms are arranged in a chain, and the compound melts at −130° C. In another form, called neopentane (see below), four carbon atoms are symmetrically arranged around the fifth carbon. This arrangement produces a form that packs more readily in the solid and melts at a higher temperature, −20° C.

n-pentane   neopentane

20.23 Bonding and the shapes of molecules

To understand the properties of substances more fully, we will investigate the shapes of their molecules. We will restrict our discussion to individual molecules, that is, to the gaseous state. Our interpretation of the architecture of molecules must conform first to the rules for the bonding of atoms and second to their observed properties.

We must first review the distinction between the polarity of the bonds possessed by the atoms and the polarity of the resulting molecule. The polarity of a diatomic molecule depends on the nature of the bond linking the atoms and the shape of the molecule. All molecules composed of the same two atoms or two different atoms have a straight-line shape, also called a linear shape.

Consider gaseous fluorine, F_2, which may be represented as F—F. The nucleus in each F atom attracts the electron pair equally, so that a pure nonpolar bond is formed. Gaseous hydrogen fluoride, HF, may be similarly represented as H—F. As before, the shape of the molecule is linear. However, note that F has a higher electronegativity (4.0) than H (2.1). The electron pair is displaced closer to the F nucleus, giving rise to a structure termed an *electrical dipole*. This is the same as saying that the F end of the molecule is negative and the H end is positive. Thus gaseous HF has polar bonds, and the molecule is polar.

Molecules consisting of more than two atoms may be polar or nonpolar, depending upon the shapes of the molecules.

20.24 Promotion and hybridization

Let us now consider a triatomic molecule, gaseous beryllium difluoride, BeF_2. The electron configuration of Be is $1s^2$, $2s^2$. The electron configuration of Be suggests that Be can form only a single bond by transfer of both $2s$ electrons to an atom with six valence electrons. However, the compound BeF_2 possesses two bonds.

How do we account for these bonds? Chemists postulate that one $2s$ electron is raised to the $2p$ orbital, a phenomenon called *promotion*. Although promotion requires the expenditure of some energy, the resulting structure acquires additional bonding capacity. The two bonds that form are neither true s nor true p bonds. Instead, the bonds are sp, called *hybrid bonds*, and may be represented by the following diagram:

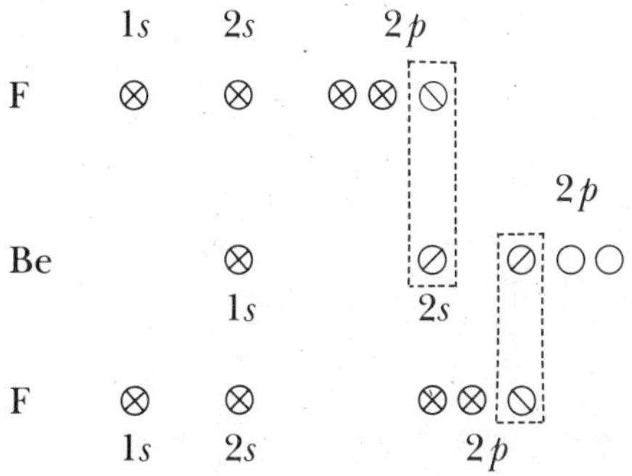

Hybrid bonds are sometimes referred to as mixed bonds. Further examples of hybrid bonds follow.

Note again that F has a higher electronegativity (4.0) than Be (1.5). As in HF, the electron pair is displaced closer to the F nucleus, which suggests that the Be—F bond is polar. However, we observe that the BeF_2 molecule is nonpolar. This seeming contradiction may be explained by assuming that the two F particles repel each other and are farthest apart when the three atoms lie in a straight line.

As shown in Figure 20-8, each bond in the BeF_2 molecule is polar.

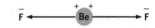

Fig. 20–8   Bonding in BeF₂

Since the bond directions are exactly opposite, the unbalanced charges cancel each other. The molecule as a whole is nonpolar chiefly because of its linear structure. Such molecules are said to have a *zero dipole moment*. Thus we see again that it is possible for a molecule to possess polar bonds, yet the overall molecule may be nonpolar. We may now proceed to a systematic study of the gaseous molecules of other members of the second row of the Periodic Table.

20.25 The planar triangular structure of BF₃

Let us consider the trifluoride of boron, BF_3. Measurements show that this compound is nonpolar despite the fact that the bond joining boron and fluorine, B—F, is somewhat polar in nature. The boron atom possesses the structure $(1s^2, 2s^2, 2p^1)$ depicted in the orbital diagram that follows. The notation $1s^2$ means two electrons in the $1s$ orbital. Similarly, $2s^2$ means two electrons in the $2s$ orbital and $2p^1$ means one electron $(2p_x)$ in the $2p$ orbital. This structure would seem to favor the $2p_x$ electron in the formation of a single bond with a fluorine atom.

$$1s \quad 2s \quad\quad 2p_x\ 2p_y\ 2p_z$$
$$\otimes \quad \otimes \quad\quad \oslash \quad \bigcirc \quad \bigcirc$$

However, the compound BF_3 possesses three bonds, which suggests the following structure:

$$1s \quad 2s \quad\quad 2p_x\ 2p_y\ 2p_z$$
$$\otimes \quad \oslash \quad\quad \oslash \quad \oslash \quad \bigcirc$$

The three resulting B—F bonds, all alike, are neither true *s* nor true *p* bonds. Instead, the bonds are sp^2 (a hybrid of *s* and *p* orbitals) and, as in the case of Be, are termed hybrid bonds. They are equally spaced at angles of 120° from each other, lying in a flat plane, as shown in Figure 20-9. The structure of the BF_3 molecule is called *planar triangular.* Although each B—F bond is polar, the molecule is nonpolar.

In the same figure, the heavy arrow represents a single bond dipole having the same magnitude and direction as two B—F bonds (dashed arrows). The third B—F bond (dashed arrow) is equal in magnitude and opposite in direction to the single bond dipole (heavy arrow). This causes a net cancellation of bond dipoles. We attribute the lack of polarity to the symmetry of the molecule, which causes a net cancellation of all the dipoles and produces a zero dipole moment.

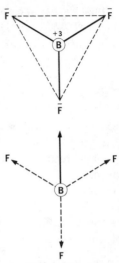

Fig. 20-9   The shape of the BF_3 molecule

20.26 The tetrahedral structure of CH₄

Proceeding to carbon, we will study one of its gaseous compounds with hydrogen, CH_4, which is more common than the corresponding fluorine compound, CF_4. The electron configuration (structure) of carbon is

$$1s \quad 2s \quad 2p_x \ 2p_y \ 2p_z$$
$$\otimes \quad \otimes \quad \oslash \ \ \oslash \ \ \bigcirc$$

This structure suggests that carbon atoms can form two bonds, in which the incomplete $2p_x$ and $2p_y$ orbitals are utilized. But carbon compounds generally show the presence of four bonds. Again, we can account for these bonds by postulating the promotion of a $2s$ electron to a $2p$ orbital.

$$1s \quad 2s \quad 2p_x \ 2p_y \ 2p_z$$
$$\otimes \quad \oslash \quad \oslash \ \ \oslash \ \ \oslash$$

This structure permits the formation of four sp^3 bonds. CH_4 illustrates another example of hybridization in which the *s* and *p* electrons form hybrid bonds which are alike, all having equal energies.

The four bonds, as shown in Figure 20-10, are directed outward from the carbon atom, forming equal angles of 109.5° with each other. The geometric form taken by the molecule of CH_4 is that of a regular four-sided pyramid, called a tetrahedron.

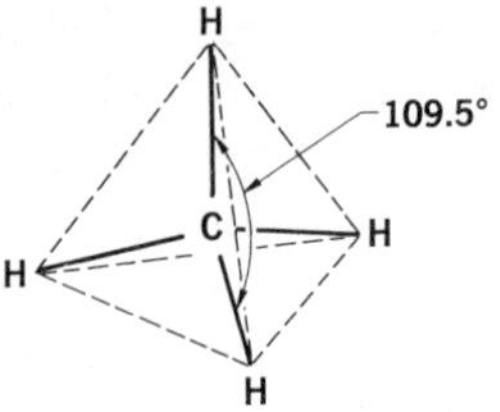

The C atom occupies the center of the tetrahedron, and an H atom is at each corner. This four-sided structure is consistent with the requirement of four equal bonds emanating from the C atom. Furthermore, the repulsions of the electron clouds of the four bonded atoms cause the atoms to take positions where they will be as far away from each other as possible. The student should make a careful note of this tetrahedral structure associated with carbon compounds. It will be of importance in our later study of these compounds in Chapter 28.

Fig. 20–10   The shape of the CH_4 molecule

20.27 The pyramidal structure of NH₃

As we proceed along the second row, we see that nitrogen possesses the electron configuration

$$1s \quad 2s \quad 2p_x \; 2p_y \; 2p_z$$

$$\otimes \quad \otimes \quad \oslash \; \oslash \; \oslash$$

Nitrogen utilizes the three p electrons in forming bonds with hydrogen, fluorine, and other elements.

The compound NH_3 gas deserves attention. As we learned earlier, the p orbitals are directed along the x, y or z axes at right angles to each other. We might therefore expect that the three N—H bonds would be at 90° to each other. However, it is thought that hybridization occurs with the formation of sp^3 bonds, so that the angles made with the N atom are almost tetrahedral. The shape of this molecule is a pyramid with the N atom at the apex and the three H atoms at the base (see Figure 20-11).

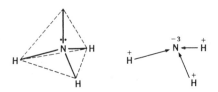

Fig. 20–11   The shape of the NH_3 molecule

Note in Figure 20-11 that the N atom possesses a pair of $2s$ electrons, which are not bonded to any atom. These electrons give the N region of the molecule a negative charge. The H atoms at the base of the pyramid acquire a positive charge because the bonding electrons are attracted away from the H atoms to the more negative N atom. Because the NH_3 molecule is not symmetrical, it has a net charge displacement and is polar. Furthermore, the molecule possesses a pair of electrons that are not bonded. These electrons may be donated to form a coordinate covalent bond with an atom that can accept an electron pair (see section 20.20).

20.28 The bond angle in H_2O

The last element we will discuss in this row is oxygen. Its electronic configuration is

$$1s \quad 2s \quad 2p_x \ 2p_y \ 2p_z$$

$$\otimes \quad \otimes \quad \otimes \ \oslash \ \oslash$$

The two p electrons that are available for bonding form bonds which, as we might expect, are at right angles. In H_2O, however, we find a bond angle of 104.5°. As in the case of NH_3, this discrepancy from the expected 90° angle is thought to result from the formation of sp^3 hybrid bonds, and consequently the bond angle is almost tetrahedral. The angular shape of a water molecule accounts for its polarity.

20.29 Second row halides

The following table summarizes the number and types of bonds and the shapes of gaseous halide compounds of elements in the second row.

ELEMENT	NUMBER OF BONDS	BOND TYPE	MOLECULAR SHAPE OF HALIDE
lithium	1	s	linear, diatomic molecule
beryllium	2	sp	linear
boron	3	sp^2	planar triangular
carbon	4	sp^3	tetrahedral
nitrogen	3	p^3	pyramidal
oxygen	2	p^2	bent
fluorine	1	p	linear, diatomic molecule

20.30 Double and triple (multiple covalent) bonds

Up to this point in our study of bonding, we have represented molecules showing the atoms bonded by single electron pairs or single bonds. Let us now consider what might happen if two oxygen atoms unite. From the electron configuration of each atom, note that the $2p_y$ and $2p_z$ orbitals are half-filled. An overlap of the $2p_y$ orbitals of two oxygen atoms would result in the formation of a single bond and a molecule that retains two half-filled $2p_z$ orbitals. This suggests an unstable situation. The formation of another bond by the overlapping of the two $2p_z$ orbitals completely fills the orbitals of both oxygen atoms.

Thus a molecule of oxygen should contain a double bond. Experimental evidence supports this conclusion—for example, more energy is required to break the double bond in an oxygen molecule than to break an O—O single bond in hydrogen peroxide.

In the same manner, two atoms of nitrogen are bonded to one another as follows:

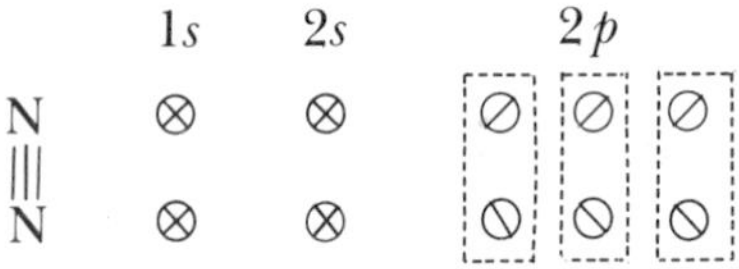

20.31 Structure and the properties of elements

In the previous sections, we saw how electronic structure determines both the number and type of atoms that unite and the geometry of the resulting gaseous molecule. In the sections that follow, we will see how this structure and the forces that act between particles influence the properties of elements in the solid state. We will again direct our attention to the elements of the second row of the Periodic Table, beginning with lithium. The principles that provide a basis for understanding the properties of these elements will hold for most of the elements in other rows as well.

20.32 Gases in the lithium row

The lithium row contains four elements—nitrogen, oxygen, fluorine, and neon—which are gaseous at normal conditions. The orbitals of the valence electrons in nitrogen, oxygen, and fluorine are completely occupied by the formation of the diatomic molecules, N_2, O_2, and F_2. The orbitals of the valence electrons in Ne, a noble gas, are already completely filled ($1s^2$, $2s^2$, $2p^6$). When these gases are cooled sufficiently to liquefy and finally solidify, they form molecular crystals. The molecules of the crystals are held together by weak bonds that we have termed van der Waals forces.

The weak bonds cause the liquids to boil at low temperatures (below $0°$ C) and the solids to melt at still lower temperatures. In contrast, strong covalent bonds bind the two atoms together in each of the molecules of N_2, O_2, and F_2.

20.33 Metals in the lithium row

At the beginning of the lithium row are two elements, lithium and beryllium, which have the typical properties of metals. Lithium has one valence electron, and beryllium has two valence electrons. This means that each metal has a number of unoccupied orbitals in the valence energy level.

	$1s$	$2s$	$2p$
Li	⊗	⊘	○○○
Be	⊗	⊘	⊘○○

It is impossible for atoms of lithium to combine with each other or for atoms of beryllium to combine with each other to form molecules by covalent bonding. There are insufficient valence electrons to permit the formation of covalent bonds. Therefore, the unoccupied orbitals remain unfilled.

Another characteristic of metallic elements is their low ionization energies. This suggests that the valence electrons can leave one atom and temporarily occupy a vacant orbital of a neighboring atom. Such electrons are called *nonlocalized*, or *mobile*. The freedom of motion possessed by nonlocalized electrons makes metals good conductors of electricity and heat.

Metals are also malleable; that is, they can be rolled or hammered into thin sheets. We may explain malleability by assuming that, in the crystalline form, the positively charged nuclei of different atoms in a layer are attracted to all the nearby mobile electrons that wander from one atom to another. The atoms are thus held together by this attractive force. However, the atoms may still slide past each other when a force is applied during rolling or hammering. The bond that results from the presence of nonlocalized electrons is called a *metallic bond.*

The two valence electrons attracted to many positively charged beryllium nuclei hold the beryllium atoms together strongly. This force is greater than the force exerted by the single valence electron in lithium, which holds the lithium atoms together. Thus the melting point of lithium is lower than that of beryllium. Lithium is also much softer than beryllium. These differences become apparent when we compare other metallic elements having one valence electron with neighboring atoms having two or three.

20.34 Nonmetals in the lithium row: boron and carbon

We have already seen that the elements in the third and fourth columns have high ionization energies and therefore form covalent bonds. The remaining elements in the lithium row, boron and carbon, exhibit properties based on the ability to form covalent bonds. Solid boron is nonmetallic, exhibiting a high melting point (2300° C) and a high boiling point (2550° C). It is as hard as diamond. The structure of the solid form of carbon is related to the bonds formed by carbon atoms.

Diamond and graphite are two common solid forms of carbon. In the diamond crystal, carbon forms four equally spaced covalent bonds with four neighboring carbon atoms, which are situated at the corners of a tetrahedron, shown in Figure 20-12. Let us direct our attention to any carbon atom in the diamond structure shown. We then see the four equally spaced carbon atoms surrounding it in a three-dimensional structure. Now if we select any one of these four atoms, we will see four other atoms surrounding it. The important observation to make is that there are

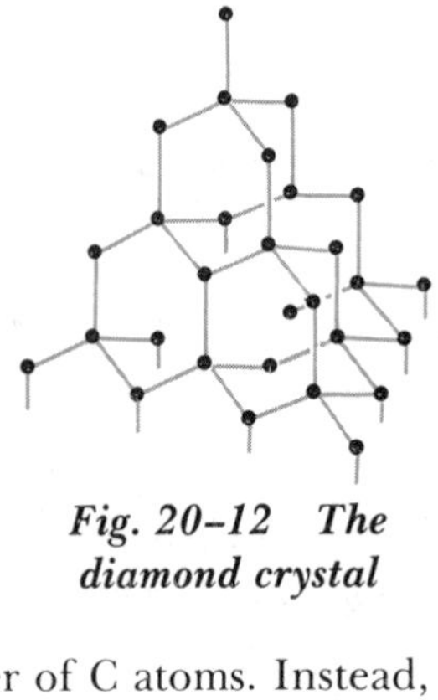

Fig. 20-12   The diamond crystal

no molecules of C_2, C_4, or any other small number of C atoms. Instead, all the atoms in the crystal are united together in one large network, which we have already termed a *network solid*, or a *macromolecule*. We can account for some of the properties of the hardest form of carbon, diamond, when we understand this type of structure.

Diamond is an extremely poor conductor of electricity because all electrons are firmly held in covalent bonds with no unoccupied orbitals. This means that electrons cannot move from one carbon atom to another because all the orbitals are filled. Such electrons are called *localized*. Diamond is very hard and has a high melting point (3500° C) because of the strong forces acting on the small atoms, which are held together by covalent bonds from all directions.

Graphite, another crystalline form of carbon, conducts electricity and is relatively soft. Like diamond, the carbon atoms in graphite form a network solid in which the atoms are covalently bonded. How do we account for the differences in the properties of diamond and graphite?

Both diamond and graphite have four valence electrons. In diamond, each carbon atom is tetrahedrally bonded to four neighboring carbon atoms in a three-dimensional structure. All the valence electrons in a carbon atom are therefore used up. This means that all the valence electrons are associated with a given carbon atom and result in the formation of localized bonds. In graphite (see Figure 20-13), each carbon atom is covalently bonded to three other carbon atoms in a flat or planar structure.

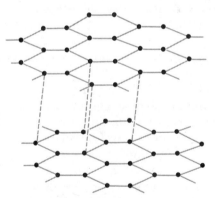

Fig. 20–13   The graphite crystal

As in diamond, the bonds in graphite are equally spaced. The fourth valence electron, however, is nonlocalized; that is, it does not belong to a specific bond. Instead, this electron spends an equal amount of time between the neighboring carbon atoms. The presence of mobile electrons permits graphite to conduct electricity.

The planar graphite molecules form giant layers of sheets which are bonded to one another by weak van der Waals forces. These sheets, because they are weakly bonded, can slide over one another and account for the softness and the lubricity of graphite.

Both diamond and graphite are unreactive at room temperature. The solid forms of carbon combine with other elements only when sufficient energy is supplied to rupture their covalent bonds and make electrons available for new bonds.

Other elements also form covalently bonded solids. These elements are located near the middle of the rows of the Periodic Table. We may predict that they are situated between the metallic elements which have free electrons and form metallic bonds and the nonmetals which have a few unoccupied orbitals to fill and form molecular solids.

20.35 Structure and the properties of compounds

The same attractive forces that influence the structures of elements in the solid state also influence the structures of compounds. The transfer of one or two electrons from a metallic element such as sodium (low electronegativity) to a nonmetal such as chlorine (high electronegativity) forms oppositely charged ions. The electrical attractions between these ions pull them together, so that ions of unlike sign become neighbors. The structure that forms is an ionic solid, such as crystalline NaCl, shown in Figure 9-8 on page 156. A crystal of NaCl is composed of ions situated at the corners of a cube, with equally constructed cubes extending in all directions. Notice that there are no molecules present; no specific Cl^- "belongs" to a specific Na^+.

Ionic solids are hard but brittle. When struck, they fracture, or cleave, along planes which are at definite angles to each other. The planes correspond to the arrangement of the ions in the crystal. Ionic solids have high melting points because of the strong forces holding the ions together. In the solid state, they do not conduct electricity, since there are no free electrons present. However, when melted, or fused, they are good conductors. Why? The added heat energy causes the ions to break away from each other. The molten salt now contains oppositely charged ions that are able to migrate to electrodes and serve as charge carriers.

20.36 Soft solids

What type of compounds form soft solids with low melting points? In compounds such as CH_4 or CCl_4, strong covalent bonds hold the atoms together in a symmetric arrangement and produce a nonpolar molecule.

Upon cooling, the solids form molecular crystals in which very weak forces act between the molecules of the solids. These are van der Waals forces similar to those in liquefied and solid oxygen and nitrogen.

As a rule, when a compound is composed of nonpolar molecules, the melting and boiling points are low. The compound is soft in the solid state, which means that the shape of the crystals can be easily distorted. The compound does not dissolve in water because there is little attraction between its nonpolar molecules and the highly polar water molecules. However, it does dissolve more readily in carbon tetrachloride, in carbon disulfide, and in benzene, which are all nonpolar solvents.

20.37 Solid network compounds

Silicon carbide (SiC) is an interesting compound. It is extremely hard, has a high melting point, and possesses a very regular crystalline structure. From the formula, we see that it is composed of equal numbers of silicon and carbon atoms. Both of these elements are in the fourth column of the Periodic Table and form four strong covalent bonds which are equally spaced. Silicon carbide exists as a network solid similar to diamond, except that half of its atoms are silicon. Sand, which is silica, SiO_2, is another example of a network solid. Many other natural compounds of silicon, such as clay or mica, are made up of network solids.

Multiple-Choice Questions

1. Which of the following statements is *false*? (1) In a family of elements, the largest atom has the lowest ionization energy. (2) In a row of elements, the noble gases have the highest ionization energies. (3) Three half-filled orbitals produce an increase in the ionization energy. (4) It is easier to form a +2 ion than a +1 ion.
2. The highest electronegativity value is shown by (1) fluorine (2) neon (3) lithium (4) cesium
3. The electronegativities of the elements in the Periodic Table show all the following variations *except* (1) Group IA elements have low electronegativities. (2) Noble gases have the highest electronegativities. (3) Largest atoms have the lowest electronegativities. (4) Isotopes have the same electronegativities.
4. When two atoms have equal electronegativities (1) they cannot unite (2) a polar bond forms (3) a pair of electrons is shared (4) a half-filled orbital results

5. When a chemical bond forms between two atoms (1) the forces of repulsion are greater than the forces of attraction (2) a pair of electrons is simultaneously attracted by two nuclei (3) an increase in potential energy results (4) the nuclei of the atoms become stable

6. Two helium atoms do not unite to form a bond because (1) helium is a gas (2) the orbitals are half-filled (3) the p orbitals are complete (4) each atom has two electrons in the $1s$ orbital

7. A factor that is *not* responsible for the low ionization energy of an atom is (1) the charge of the nucleus (2) the physical state of the element containing that atom (3) the number of electron shells (4) the sublevels of the electrons

8. A characteristic of all metals is that they (1) are solids (2) are silver-gray in color (3) have low ionization energies (4) cannot be vaporized

9. When the difference in electronegativity values of elements X and Y increases (1) the tendency to form an ionic bond increases (2) the bond becomes less polar (3) the shared electrons spend equal time between both atoms (4) the energy released during bond formation decreases

10. The electrons in the valence shell of a halogen element are s^2, p^5. When two halogen atoms unite (1) a transfer of an electron occurs (2) an s orbital is completed (3) a p orbital is completed (4) a polar molecule forms

11. In the NH_4^+ structure (1) nitrogen forms three covalent bonds and one ionic bond with hydrogen (2) nitrogen forms three covalent bonds and one coordinate covalent bond (3) nitrogen has lost one electron (4) hydrogen has donated electrons to nitrogen

12. The boiling point of water is higher than that of HCl (l) or H_2S (l) because molecules of water (1) are united by hydrogen bonds (2) contain heavy water (3) have strong ionic bonds (4) have high vapor pressure

Completion Questions

1. When two atoms having different electronegativities share a pair of electrons, the bond that forms is a (an) _____ covalent bond.

2. A bond formed when two atoms share a pair of electrons which were donated by a single atom is called a (an) _____ covalent bond.

3. The maximum number of electrons an orbital can hold is _____.

4. When two atoms approach each other and their orbitals overlap to form a stable configuration, a (an) _____ forms between the atoms.

5. The amount of energy required to remove an electron from a gaseous atom to form an ion is called the _____ of that atom.

6. When two like atoms unite to form a diatomic molecule, a (an) _____ bond is formed.
7. The halogen elements (Group VIIA) have high ionization energies and have _____ electronegativities.
8. The bonds in diamond are _____ (*localized, nonlocalized*).
9. The bonds in graphite are _____ (*localized, nonlocalized*).
10. A symmetrical molecule possessing polar bonds is _____ (*polar, nonpolar*).

True-False Questions

1. Ionization of a gaseous atom is an *exothermic* change.
2. The bond in a Cl_2 molecule is *a nonpolar covalent* bond.
3. In the formation of an ionic bond, the net energy released is *greater than* the energy needed to remove an electron from an atom.
4. When the electronegativity values of two elements differ greatly, the atoms of the elements unite to form *covalent* bonds.
5. A noble gas has a high ionization energy. This indicates that its valence electrons are at *low* energy levels.
6. Active metals have *high* ionization energies.
7. The transfer of electrons results in the formation of *covalent* bonds.
8. A molecule of CO_2 is *polar* because the atoms are arranged in a straight line with the carbon atom between two oxygen atoms.
9. When molecules of hydrogen gas condense to form liquid hydrogen, the molecules are held together by *van der Waals* forces.

Decreases, Increases, Remains the Same

1. For the noble gas family, as the atomic numbers decrease, the electronegativity values _____.
2. As the difference in the electronegativity values of two elements increases, the polarity of the bond formed between the elements _____.
3. In a family of elements, as the number of shells of electrons increases, the ionization energies of the elements _____.
4. When the distance between an electron and the nucleus increases, the energy of the system _____.
5. As two helium atoms approach each other, the force of repulsion between them _____.
6. As the positive charge of an ion increases, its covalent radius _____.
7. As the reactivities of metals increase, the ionization energies of the metals _____.

8. As the atomic numbers of elements increase, the maximum number of electrons that can exist in one orbital _____.

9. As the ionization energies of a family of elements decrease, the electronegativity values of the elements _____.

Exercises for Review

1. Using an electron-dot formula, show the arrangement of electrons in (a) an atom of magnesium (b) an atom of oxygen (c) a molecule of magnesium oxide, MgO

2. a. Why are the N—H bonds in the molecule of NH_3 directed along the three different axes?

   b. Is promotion of electrons required in this compound? Explain.

3. Why must electrons be promoted in order to form CH_4?

4. Explain why the formula H_2O properly represents the structure of gaseous water but is not entirely correct for liquid water.

5. The Ag^+ (aq) ion unites with NH_3 molecules to form a complex ion. Is the bond between Ag^+ and NH_3 ionic, covalent, or coordinate covalent? Explain.

6. Explain why the CO molecule is polar but the CO_2 molecule is non-polar.

7. From the values for electronegativities on page 414, select the ionic compounds from the following list. State the reason for each one selected. (a) CaF_2 (b) P_2S_5 (c) BCl_3 (d) CsI (e) $LaCl_3$

8. a. How do the electronegativity values of elements compare with their ionization energies.

   b. Explain why a relationship exists between these quantities.

9. Why does it require more energy to form a Ca^{+2} ion than to form a Ca^+ ion?

10. a. Why do Group IA elements have very low ionization energies?

    b. Why is the ionization energy of Rb lower than that for Li?

11. Using diagrams to show orbital overlap, diagram the formation of the following gaseous molecules: (a) H_2S (b) CaF_2 (c) BF_3 (d) CCl_4 (e) NF_3

Exercises for Further Study

1. a. In the solid state, molecules of NaCl and silicon carbide, SiC, do not exist. Why?

   b. Explain the differences in properties between these two solids on the basis of the types of bonds present.

2. *a.* How are the electron structures of H_2O and NH_3 similar?

   b. How do these similarities explain the action of H_2O and NH_3 in hydrogen bonding and in forming coordinate covalent bonds.

3. Explain why the compound KHF_2 exists but $KHCl_2$ does not exist.

4. The BF_3 molecule is not polar, but the NH_3 molecule is polar. Explain the reasons for this difference in terms of bonding and molecular geometry.

5. *a.* Why type of bonds are present in the SiF_4 molecule?

   b. What orbitals of the Si atom are involved? How do they originate?

   c. What is the shape of this molecule? Why?

6. Why is it necessary to employ the concepts of promotion and hybridization to explain the bonding in $BeCl_2$ but not in the bonding in BeO?

7. From these bonds — ionic, coordinate covalent, polar covalent, hydrogen, and van der Waals — select the bond most closely related to each of the following phenomena:

   a. liquefying O_2

   b. liquefying H_2S

   c. forming N_2 molecules

   d. $NH_3\ (g) + H^+\ (aq) \rightarrow NH_4^+\ (aq)$

   e. a molten solid that conducts electricity

8. Arrange the following molecules in the order of increasing bond polarity between the atoms. Begin with the least polar bond.

$$NO \quad MgS \quad H_2S \quad BaO \quad CO \quad F_2$$

9. The ionization potentials in electron-volts for the following five elements are: Mg, 7.6; Al, 6.0; Si, 8.1; P, 11.0; S, 10.4. The elements follow this order from left to right in the Periodic Table. Explain why the ionization potentials do not change in a regular manner.

10. The ionization potential of hydrogen is 13.6 electron-volts. Using the appropriate constants given on page 410, calculate the energy needed to form 1 mole of H^+ ions from H atoms.

11. Consider the change from liquid oxygen to atomic oxygen. Compare the two types of bonds that must be broken and the energy required for each type of bond.

12. A strip of magnesium burns vigorously in a bottle of oxygen. Using equations, show the changes that take place as the solid Mg and gaseous O_2 react to form the ionic solid MgO. Write $-\Delta H$ for the changes that release energy and $+\Delta H$ for those that require energy.

Chapter 21

THE ALKALI METALS

21.1 Introduction

The elements of the alkali metal family (Group IA) are lithium, sodium, potassium, rubidium, cesium, and francium. However, we will not discuss francium, the radioactive alkali metal, since it is comparatively rare and has a very short half-life. We have already described some of the properties of these elements in our introduction to chemical families in Chapter 7. Now we will extend our discussion.

The table on the facing page summarizes some important properties of the alkali metals.

21.2 Trends in the general properties

Note from the table that the outermost electron shell (valence shell) of each alkali metal has a single s electron. The next-to-the-outermost energy level has eight electrons (two s electrons and six p electrons), except for lithium, which has two electrons. This $s^2p^6s^1$ structure characterizes all these elements and serves to distinguish them from the copper family, which also has a single s electron in its outermost energy level. However, the copper family has 18 electrons in the next-to-the-outermost energy level (two s electrons, six p electrons, and ten d electrons).

As we proceed from lithium to cesium, the gradual increase in the number of energy levels—from one to six—accounts for the increase in atomic radius. In chemical reactions, the alkali metals tend to lose their outermost s electron to form a unipositive ion. The loss of this electron removes the outermost shell, which tends to shrink the atom. Thus the radius of each ion is smaller than the radius of the corresponding atom (as seen in the table).

21.3 Ionization potentials and spectra

We have defined the first ionization potential as the energy required to remove the most loosely held electron from the atom in the gaseous state. The nuclear charge increases from lithium to cesium, accompanied by an increase in atomic radius. Also, the outermost s electron is shielded from the nucleus (and its attraction) by increasing numbers of energy levels. As the atomic radii increase, we observe that it becomes less difficult to remove the outermost s electron, and the ionization potentials decrease.

THE ALKALI METALS

PROPERTY	LITHIUM	SODIUM	POTASSIUM	RUBIDIUM	CESIUM
atomic number	3	11	19	37	55
electron structure	$1s^2$ $2s^1$	$1s^2$ $2s^2, 2p^6$ $3s^1$	$1s^2$ $2s^2, 2p^6$ $3s^2, 3p^6$ $4s^1$	$1s^2$ $2s^2, 2p^6$ $3s^2, 3p^6, 3d^{10}$ $4s^2, 4p^6$ $5s^1$	$1s^2$ $2s^2, 2p^6$ $3s^2, 3p^6, 3d^{10}$ $4s^2, 4p^6, 4d^{10}$ $5s^2, 5p^6$ $6s^1$
atomic (covalent) radius (Å)	1.52	1.86	2.31	2.44	2.62
ionic radius, M^+ (A)	0.60	0.95	1.33	1.48	1.69
first ionization potential (ev)	5.39	5.14	4.34	4.18	3.89
electro-negativity	1.0	0.9	0.8	0.8	0.7
oxidation state	+1	+1	+1	+1	+1
E^0 (volts) $M\ (s) \rightarrow$ $M^+\ (aq)$ $+ e^-$	+3.05	+2.71	+2.93	+2.93	+2.92

The ionization potentials of the alkali metals are relatively low. Even the energy in a Bunsen flame is sufficient to excite the outermost s electron in alkali metal atoms to higher energy levels. Upon return to the lower energy level, the alkali metals emit characteristic spectra. For example, excited sodium atoms emit yellow light. We explain the yellow light by noting that the $3s$ electron, upon return to a lower energy level, emits energy equivalent to the frequency of yellow light, approximately 5890 Å. Upon resolution by a prism, the yellow light is composed of two very closely spaced lines. The yellow lines are useful in the identification of sodium atoms.

21.4 Electronegativity

Electronegativity values describe the attraction of an atom for the pair of electrons in a covalent bond. Generally, atoms of elements with marked tendencies to gain electrons have high electronegativity values. On the other hand, atoms that tend to lose electrons have low electronegativity values. Since the alkali metals have low ionization potentials (lose electrons readily), they also have low electronegativities. Furthermore, as the ionization potentials decrease with increasing nuclear charges, the electronegativity values decrease correspondingly.

21.5 What determines the magnitude of E^0?

The E^0 values represent the tendencies of atoms to lose electrons in aqueous medium. As has already been described for the formation of NaCl (s), the reaction can also be assumed to take place in several steps. The reaction changes the metal from a solid consisting of bonded atoms to separated aqueous ions. One of the steps, therefore, is the formation of individual atoms analogous to the vaporization of a solid. Assume that M represents an alkali metal.

$$(1) \quad M\ (s) \quad \rightarrow M\ (g) \qquad\qquad + \Delta H_{\text{vaporization}}$$

$$(2) \quad M\ (g) \quad \rightarrow M^+\ (g) + e^- \qquad + \Delta H_{\text{ionization}}$$

$$(3) \quad M^+\ (g) \rightarrow M^+\ (aq) \qquad\qquad - \Delta H_{\text{hydration}}$$

NET EQUATION $M\ (s) \rightarrow M^+\ (aq) + e^-$

Steps 1 and 2 involve changes that are endothermic, whereas step 3 is exothermic. The E^0 value represents the net energy for the three hypothetical steps. The energy required to evaporate each of the alkali metals (step 1) is about the same. The ionization energy (step 2) decreases somewhat with increased nuclear charge. It is the magnitude of the hydration energy term that largely determines the E^0 value.

Lithium (see the ionization potential) requires the highest energy of all the alkali metals to lose its outermost electron. Yet the E^0 value suggests that lithium atoms form aquated ions most easily. We attribute this apparent inconsistency to the large hydration energy value (-121 kcal/mole), which compensates for the difficulty lithium has in losing an electron (step 2). This phenomenon may also account for the sharp decrease in E^0 for sodium atoms ($\Delta H_{\text{hydration}} = -95$ kcal/mole).

21.6 Occurrence of the alkali metals

The marked tendency to lose electrons explains why none of the alkali metals occurs uncombined in nature. The following table summarizes the natural sources of common sodium and potassium compounds.

COMPOUND	OCCURRENCE	SOURCE
NaCl	brine, halite (rock salt)	seawater, salt wells, salt mines
$NaAlSi_3O_8$	feldspars	silicate rocks
$NaNO_3$	Chile saltpeter	naturally occurring deposits
KCl	mixture of KCl and $MgCl_2$	naturally occurring salt beds
$KAlSi_3O_8$	feldspars	silicate rocks

21.7 Preparation of the alkali metals

In the most common alkali metal compounds, the alkali metal has an oxidation number of $+1$. Therefore, the essential reaction that is involved in the extraction of the metal from its compound is

$$M^+ + e^- \rightarrow M \ (s)$$

Reduction may be carried out by using a metal that is a stronger reducing agent than the metal to be prepared. But since all the alkali metals are powerful reducing agents themselves (they lose electrons very readily), this method is impractical. Instead, the alkali metals are generally prepared by electrolysis of their molten (fused) compounds.

Sodium is prepared commercially by the electrolysis of fused NaCl in the Downs process. Figure 21-1 on the following page shows a Downs cell to which $CaCl_2$ has been added to lower the temperature at which melting occurs. Sodium is formed at the iron cathode and collects in the reservoir. Chlorine gas issues from the outlet around the carbon anode. To prevent these products from re-forming NaCl, the compartments at which oxidation and reduction occur are separated from one another. The essential reactions are

$$NaCl \ (l) \rightarrow Na^+ + Cl^-$$

ANODE $\quad 2 \ Cl^- \rightarrow Cl_2 \ (g) + 2 \ e^-$

CATHODE $\quad 2 \ Na^+ + 2 \ e^- \rightarrow 2 \ Na \ (l)$

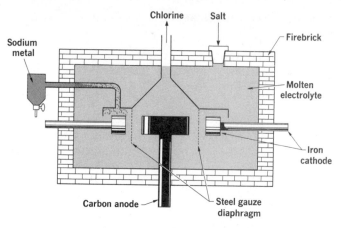

Fig. 21–1   The Downs cell

The alkali metals cannot be prepared by the electrolysis of aqueous solutions of their compounds. The E^0 table reveals that less energy is required to reduce H^+ *(aq)* ions or to reduce water molecules than to reduce the alkali metal ion. The electrolysis of aqueous solutions of alkali metal compounds therefore yields hydrogen gas rather than the alkali metal.

21.8 Properties of the alkali metals

The alkali metals are powerful reducing agents. This means that these metals readily give up their valence electrons to oxidizing agents. The reduction reactions of the alkali metals may be summarized as follows:

1. Reaction with hydrogen to form a hydride.

$$\overset{0}{2\ M} + \overset{0}{H_2} \rightarrow \overset{+1\ -1}{2\ MH}$$

2. Reaction with oxygen to form oxides.
   a. Lithium reacts with oxygen to form lithium monoxide:

$$\overset{0}{4\ Li} + \overset{0}{O_2} \rightarrow \overset{+1\ -2}{2\ Li_2O}$$

b. Sodium reacts with oxygen to form sodium peroxide:

$$2 \overset{0}{Na} + \overset{0}{O_2} \rightarrow \overset{+1}{Na_2}\overset{-1}{O_2}$$

with electron transfer: $-2\,e^-$ removed from Na and $+2\,e^-$ added to O_2.

3. Reaction with water to form a base and hydrogen.

$$2 \overset{0}{M} + 2 \overset{+1\ -2}{H_2O} \rightarrow 2 \overset{+1\ -2\ +1}{MOH} + \overset{0}{H_2}$$

with $-2\,e^-$ and $+2\,e^-$ transfer.

4. Reaction with ammonia to form an amide.

$$2 \overset{0}{M} + 2 \overset{-3\ +1}{NH_3} \rightarrow 2 \overset{+1\ -3\ +1}{MNH_2} + \overset{0}{H_2}$$

with $-2\,e^-$ and $+2\,e^-$ transfer.

Note how the reaction between an alkali metal and ammonia (reaction 4) resembles the reaction between an alkali metal and water. Thus MNH_2, the alkali metal amide, is the analog of MOH, the alkali metal hydroxide.

21.9 Uses of the alkali metals

The alkali metals are used in the manufacture of drugs, dyes, and other chemicals. Some have specialized uses, as shown by the following table.

ALKALI METAL	USE	PROPERTY
Na (*solid*)	as a reducing agent to extract those metals with lower E^0 values	very high E^0 (powerful reducing agent)
Na (*liquid*)	coolant in nuclear reactors	excellent heat conductor
Cs	photoelectric cells	because of very low ionization potential, outermost electron is emitted by action of visible light

21.10 Preparation of NaOH

The most common alkali metal compound, sodium chloride, occurs naturally in great abundance. It is an important ingredient of the human diet. Sodium chloride also is the industrial source of most sodium compounds and chlorine compounds.

We have already indicated that the electrolysis of aqueous NaCl (brine) does not yield metallic Na. Instead, NaOH, Cl_2, and H_2 are formed (see section 17.20). The complete reaction for the electrolysis of brine is shown in the following equation:

$$2 \text{ NaCl} + 2 \text{ H}_2\text{O} \rightarrow 2 \text{ NaOH} + \text{H}_2 \ (g) + \text{Cl}_2 \ (g)$$

Commercial electrolysis is carried out in electrochemical cells of the Nelson, Vorce, or Hooker type (see Figure 21-2).

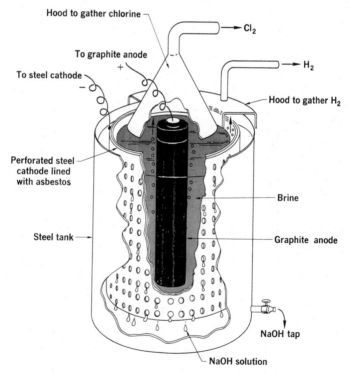

Fig. 21–2   The Nelson cell

Sodium hydroxide, commonly called lye or caustic soda, is also prepared by the Lye process.

$$Na_2CO_3 + Ca(OH)_2 \rightarrow 2\ NaOH + CaCO_3\ (s)$$

The reaction takes place in water solution, in which the difficultly soluble calcium carbonate precipitates out. Precipitation drives the reaction to the right to form a solution of NaOH. After the calcium carbonate precipitate has been filtered off, solid NaOH may be recovered from this solution by evaporating the water.

21.11 Preparation of Na₂CO₃ and NaHCO₃

Sodium carbonate, Na_2CO_3, and sodium bicarbonate, $NaHCO_3$, are prepared commercially by the Solvay process. In this process, ammonia gas, NH_3, and carbon dioxide gas, CO_2, are bubbled, under pressure, into brine until the solution is saturated. The reactions that occur are essentially ionic. The solution contains six ions as indicated in the following reactions:

$$NH_3\ (g) + H_2O \rightleftharpoons NH_4^+\ (aq) + OH^-\ (aq)$$

$$CO_2\ (g) + H_2O \rightleftharpoons H^+\ (aq) + HCO_3^-\ (aq)$$

$$NaCl\ (aq) \rightarrow Na^+\ (aq) + Cl^-\ (aq)$$

As the concentrations of $NH_3\ (g)$ and $CO_2\ (g)$ increase, solid $NaHCO_3$ separates out as shown in the reaction

$$Na^+\ (aq) + HCO_3^-\ (aq) \rightarrow NaHCO_3\ (s)$$

This reaction is an example of the *common ion effect*: The solubility of $NaHCO_3$ is decreased by the large excess of $Na^+\ (aq)$ in brine (see section 15.5). The net reaction is

$$Na^+\ (aq) + Cl^-\ (aq) + NH_3\ (g) + CO_2\ (g) + H_2O \rightarrow$$
$$NH_4^+\ (aq) + Cl^-\ (aq) + NaHCO_3\ (s)$$

$NaHCO_3$ may be converted to Na_2CO_3 by heating, which also regenerates some CO_2.

$$2\ NaHCO_3 \rightarrow Na_2CO_3 + CO_2\ (g)$$

Note that the Solvay process consumes NaCl and CO_2 only. The reactant NH_3 may be recovered by treating $NH_4^+\ (aq)$ with a proton acceptor (a base).

$$NH_4^+\ (aq) + OH^-\ (aq) \rightarrow NH_3\ (g) + H_2O$$

21.12 Preparation of other alkali compounds

The following table summarizes the preparation of common alkali metal compounds.

COMPOUND	COMMON NAME	PREPARATION
$NaNO_3$	Chile saltpeter	occurs in nature
$Na_2B_4O_7 \cdot 10H_2O$	borax	occurs in nature
NaBr	sodium bromide	action of bromine on hot NaOH $Br_2 + 6\ OH^- \rightarrow$ $5\ Br^- + BrO_3^- + 3\ H_2O$
NaI	sodium iodide	action of iodine on hot NaOH $I_2 + 6\ OH^- \rightarrow$ $5\ I^- + IO_3^- + 3\ H_2O$
KNO_3	saltpeter	action of nitric acid on KCl $4\ HNO_3 + 3\ KCl \rightarrow$ $3\ KNO_3 + Cl_2 + NOCl + 2\ H_2O$

Multiple-Choice Questions

1. A sodium ion, Na^+, has the same electron structure as all of the following particles *except* (1) Mg^{+2} (2) O^{-2} (3) Cl^- (4) Ne
2. In the reaction of Na (*s*) with Cl_2 (*g*), the step that releases energy is
   (1) Na (*s*) $\rightarrow$ Na (*g*)
   (2) Na (*g*) $\rightarrow$ Na^+ (*g*) $+ e^-$
   (3) Cl_2 (*g*) $\rightarrow$ 2 Cl (*g*)
   (4) Na^+ (*g*) $+ Cl^-$ (*g*) $\rightarrow$ Na^+Cl^- (*s*)
3. An important compound manufactured by the Solvay process is (1) sodium chloride (2) sodium hydroxide (3) calcium carbonate (4) sodium bicarbonate
4. In the reaction $2\ K + 2\ NH_3 \rightarrow 2\ KNH_2 + H_2$ (1) K replaces N (2) KNH_2 resembles an acid (3) the NH_2^- ion forms (4) K acts as an oxidizer

5. The alkali metals cannot be obtained by the electrolysis of aqueous solutions of their salts because (1) the freezing point of the solution is too low (2) the salts are insoluble (3) it is easier to reduce H^+ *(aq)* than to reduce the alkali metal ion (4) it is easier to oxidize H^+ *(aq)* than to oxidize the alkali metal ion

6. Lithium has a higher E^0 than any other alkali metal because lithium (1) has a higher ionization potential (2) has a higher energy of formation for its hydrated ion (3) is the least active alkali metal (4) has the largest radius of all the alkali metals

7. The alkali metals are able to emit their characteristic spectra at relatively low temperatures because (1) they have low ionization potentials (2) they have high ionization potentials (3) all their orbitals are complete (4) all the electrons in the alkali metal atoms are at the lowest energy level

8. The difference in the structures of Group IA and Group IB elements is that Group IB elements (1) do not form positive ions (2) receive electrons to complete their outermost shells (3) have more than eight electrons in the next-to-the-outermost electron shell (4) have more protons than electrons

9. Which of the following is *incorrect* as we go from the top to the bottom of Group IA? (1) Electronegativities decrease. (2) Ionization potentials increase. (3) Oxidation states are the same. (4) Ionic radii are less than their atomic radii.

10. Which of the following is a structural characteristic of the atoms of alkali metals? (1) They possess one *s* electron in the valence shell. (2) Their number of valence electrons can vary. (3) They possess half-filled *p* orbitals. (4) Their electron structures have maximum stability.

Completion Questions

1. Heating sodium bicarbonate forms sodium _____.
2. Potassium _____ can be produced by the electrolysis of a solution of potassium chloride.
3. In the electrolysis of fused sodium chloride, the product at the cathode is _____.
4. The compound $NaNH_2$ is formed by the reaction of Na with NH_3. In this reaction, _____ gas is also formed.
5. Na_2O_2 is the formula for sodium _____.
6. The alkali metals are produced commercially by the _____ of their molten salts.

7. The _____ of an element is a measure of the attraction of an atom for the electrons in a covalent bond.

8. _____ is a radioactive alkali metal.

9. In the electrolysis of a dilute solution of sodium chloride, _____ is formed at the anode.

10. The formula of the hydride of lithium is _____.

True-False Questions

1. The highest oxidation potential for the formation of a hydrated ion by an alkali metal is shown by the metal with the *largest* atomic radius.

2. Most sodium compounds are produced from naturally occurring sodium *sulfate*.

3. The formula of sodium *nitride* is $NaNH_2$.

4. When an atom of an alkali element reacts with water, hydrogen is *reduced*.

5. When an alkali metal unites with hydrogen to form a hydride, the hydrogen *donates* an electron.

6. When an alkali metal atom loses one electron, its electron structure resembles that of *a halogen*.

7. During the electrolysis of a salt of an alkali metal, the reaction at the cathode involves *reduction*.

8. Of all the alkali metals, *Cs* has the highest oxidation potential.

Decreases, Increases, Remains the Same

1. In the series LiCl, NaCl, KCl, RbCl, and CsCl, the distance between positive and negative ions _____.

2. With increasing atomic number, the volume of 1 mole of atoms of the alkali metals _____.

3. As the ionization potentials decrease in a column of elements, the electronegativity values generally _____.

4. With increasing radius of the atoms of the alkali metals, the number of electrons in the valence shell _____.

5. As the atomic numbers of Group IA elements increase, the ionization potentials _____.

6. As an alkali metal atom becomes an alkali metal ion, the radius of the atom _____.

Exercises for Review

1. *a.* Why does a solution of sodium hydroxide that has been exposed to the air contain sodium carbonate?

   b. Write an equation to show the change.

2. Why are deposits of sodium nitrate found only in desert regions on the earth?

3. Draw the electron-dot diagram for sodium hydride.

4. Explain why metallic copper can be obtained by electrolysis of an aqueous solution of copper(II) chloride, but sodium cannot be obtained by electrolysis of aqueous sodium chloride.

5. Which element in Group IA is the strongest reducing agent? Explain.

6. *a.* Name three important sodium compounds made commercially from sodium chloride.

   b. Describe briefly the steps in each process.

7. Write equations for the following reactions:

   a. $K\ (s) + H_2O \rightarrow$

   b. $Na\ (s) + H_2\ (g) \rightarrow$

   c. $Na\ (s) + N_2\ (g) \rightarrow$

   d. $Rb\ (s) + O_2\ (g) \rightarrow$

   e. $Li\ (s) + Cl_2\ (g) \rightarrow$

8. If francium could be obtained in sufficient quantities to study its properties, how would it compare with the other alkalis in (*a*) ionic radius (*b*) ionization potential (*c*) electrode potential (*d*) photoelectric effect (*e*) E^0

9. Why is it much more difficult to remove two electrons from a sodium atom than to remove a single electron?

Exercises for Further Study

1. Write equations for the reactions of (*a*) sodium peroxide with water to form oxygen (*b*) sodium hydride with water to form hydrogen

2. Write equations for the reaction at each electrode during the electrolysis of molten sodium hydride.

3. *a.* Sodium metal dissolves in mercury to form an amalgam. Is the sodium amalgam more or less reactive than sodium? Explain.

   b. How does the E^0 of the sodium amalgam compare with that of pure sodium? Explain.

4. How are the melting points of the alkali metals related to their ionic radii? Explain.

5. If hydrated sodium carbonate, $Na_2CO_3 \cdot 10H_2O$, sells for $0.50 per pound, at what price per pound would it be more economical to purchase anhydrous Na_2CO_3?

6. Draw the electron-dot diagram for sodium peroxide.

7. How do the electronegativities of the alkali metals compare with their ionization potentials? Explain.

8. How do we account for the fact that the E^0's for the alkali metals do not follow the same order as the ionization potentials of these metals?

9. Explain why sodium chloride is hard and brittle, while sodium is soft and malleable.

10. Using the model for the structure of metals, explain why the melting points and boiling points of the alkali metals decrease from Li to Cs.

11. Account for the following properties of the alkali metals:
    a. They are good conductors of electricity.
    b. They emit light on receiving energy.
    c. They are powerful reducing agents.

Chapter 22

THE ALKALINE EARTH METALS AND
THE ALUMINUM FAMILY

22.1 Introduction

In this chapter, we will discuss the alkaline earth metals (Group IIA) and the aluminum family (Group IIIA). This will give us an opportunity to compare both families and observe trends in their properties.

The elements of the alkaline earth metal family are beryllium, magnesium, calcium, strontium, barium, and radium. Beryllium and magnesium have properties that are somewhat different from the properties of the other alkaline earth metals; radium is radioactive.

The table on pages 454–455 summarizes some important properties of the alkaline earth metals.

22.2 Trends in the general properties

All the elements in the alkaline earth metal family possess a valence shell that has two s electrons. The members of this family have eight electrons in the shell below the valence shell, except beryllium, which has two electrons. This $s^2p^6s^2$ structure characterizes all these elements and serves to distinguish them from the zinc family, which also has two s electrons in its valence shell. However, the zinc family has 18 electrons in the shell next to the valence shell.

It is convenient to compare an alkaline earth metal with the element directly to its left in the Periodic Table, namely, the corresponding alkali metal. The alkaline earth metal always has an atomic number (nuclear charge) one unit greater than the alkali metal. The increase in positive charge produces a greater attractive force on the electron shells. In turn, this force tends to shrink the atom somewhat; therefore, the atomic radii of the alkaline earth metals are smaller than those of the corresponding alkali metals.

The alkaline earth metal ions have a charge of $+2$, and the alkali metal ions have a charge of $+1$. Consequently, the nuclei of the alkaline earth metal ions attract the remaining electron shells more strongly than the nuclei of the alkali metal ions. This means that the radii of the alkaline earth metal ions are smaller than the radii of the corresponding alkali metal ions.

THE ALKALINE EARTH METALS

PROPERTY	BERYLLIUM	MAGNESIUM	CALCIUM
atomic number	4	12	20
electron structure	$1s^2$ $2s^2$	$1s^2$ $2s^2, 2p^6$ $3s^2$	$1s^2$ $2s^2, 2p^6$ $3s^2, 3p^6$ $4s^2$
atomic (covalent) radius (Å)	1.12	1.60	1.97
ionic radius, M^{+2} (Å)	0.31	0.65	0.99
ionization potential (ev) first second third	9.32 18.2 153.9	7.64 15.0 80.1	6.11 11.9 51.2
electro-negativity	1.5	1.2	1.0
oxidation state	+2	+2	+2
E^0 (volts) $M(s) \rightarrow$ $M^{+2}(aq) + 2e^-$	+1.85	+2.37	+2.87

THE ALKALINE EARTH METALS (Cont.)

PROPERTY	STRONTIUM	BARIUM	RADIUM
atomic number	38	56	88
electron structure	$1s^2$ $2s^2, 2p^6$ $3s^2, 3p^6, 3d^{10}$ $4s^2, 4p^6$ $5s^2$	$1s^2$ $2s^2, 2p^6$ $3s^2, 3p^6, 3d^{10}$ $4s^2, 4p^6, 4d^{10}$ $5s^2, 5p^6$ $6s^2$	$1s^2$ $2s^2, 2p^6$ $3s^2, 3p^6, 3d^{10}$ $4s^2, 4p^6, 4d^{10}, 4f^{14}$ $5s^2, 5p^6, 5d^{10}$ $6s^2, 6p^6$ $7s^2$
atomic (covalent) radius (Å)	2.15	2.17	2.20
ionic radius, M^{+2} (Å)	1.13	1.35	1.52

ionization potential (ev)
  first
  second
  third
	5.69
	11.0
	43(?)
		5.21
		10.0
		36(?)
			5.28
			10.1
			—

electro-negativity	1.0	0.9	—
oxidation state	+2	+2	+2
E^0 (volts) M $(s) \rightarrow$ M^{+2} $(aq) + 2 e^-$	+2.89	+2.90	+2.92

22.3 Ionization potentials and E^0 values

The ionization potentials of the alkaline earth metals reveal a significantly large energy increase from the second to the third ionization potential. Therefore, the atoms can readily lose two electrons to form ions that have a +2 charge. But the removal of a third electron is much more difficult because this electron would have to come from a completed shell.

The larger nuclear charge on the alkaline earth metals and their higher ionization potentials indicate that the alkaline earth metals lose their valence electrons less readily than the corresponding alkali metals, which have a smaller nuclear charge and lower ionization potentials. The lower E^0 values for the formation of M^{+2} (*aq*) alkaline earth ions is further indication of the same trend in the two families of metals.

It is somewhat surprising that the E^0 values of the alkaline earth metals are still relatively high in view of their small atomic radii—a condition which should lower the E^0 values because of the stronger attractive forces between nuclei and valence electrons. In an aqueous medium, however, the alkaline earth metal ions react with water, liberating considerable hydration energy.

$$M^{+2} + H_2O \rightarrow M^{+2} \ (aq) + \text{energy}$$

This reaction tends to increase the net E^0 values; remember that Li (*s*) $\rightarrow$ Li^+ (*aq*) + e^-. (See section 21.5.)

In summary, the alkaline earth metals (except beryllium) are good reducing agents because of the low energy requirements for the removal of the valence electrons. In this respect, they are less powerful reducing agents than the corresponding alkali metals.

22.4 Occurrence of the alkaline earth metals

Like their column IA neighbors in the Periodic Table, the alkaline earth metals lose electrons too readily to be found uncombined in nature. The table on the next page summarizes the sources of some of the more common alkaline earth compounds.

22.5 Preparation of the alkaline earth metals

In all alkaline earth metal compounds, the metal has an oxidation number of +2. The essential reaction that occurs in the extraction of the metal from its compound is

$$M^{+2} + 2 \ e^- \rightarrow M \ (s)$$

The reaction indicates that the metal ion must be reduced. Another metal can serve as the reducing agent. If this method is not feasible, the metal

COMPOUND	OCCURRENCE	SOURCE
$Be_3Al_2(SiO_3)_6$	beryl	Brazilian and Argentine ores
$Mg_3H_2(SiO_3)_4$	talc	igneous silicate rocks
$MgCl_2$	magnesium chloride	seawater and salt wells
$MgBr_2$	magnesium bromide	seawater and salt wells
$CaMg_3(SiO_3)_4$	asbestos	igneous silicate rocks
$CaCO_3$	limestone	rocks
	marble	metamorphosed limestone
	coral	marine animals
$BaSO_4$	barite	rocks

ion can be reduced by electrolysis of a fused compound. Thus the alkaline earth metals may be prepared by reduction with aluminum or silicon under special conditions or by electrolysis of the molten halide, usually the chloride. The equations that follow summarize some important methods of preparing the more common alkaline earth metals:

MAGNESIUM $\quad MgCl_2\ (l) \xrightarrow[\text{fused}]{\text{electrolysis}} Cl_2\ (g) + Mg\ (l)$

$$2\ MgO\ (s) + Si\ (s) \xrightarrow{\text{above 2000°C}} SiO_2\ (s) + 2\ Mg\ (g)$$

Note that magnesium vaporizes at this temperature.

CALCIUM $\quad CaCl_2\ (l) \xrightarrow[\text{fused}]{\text{electrolysis}} Cl_2\ (g) + Ca\ (l)$

BARIUM $\quad 3\ BaO\ (s) + 2\ Al\ (s) \xrightarrow[\text{low pressure}]{\text{high temperature}} Al_2O_3\ (s) + 3\ Ba\ (g)$

22.6 Properties of the alkaline earth metals

With the exception of beryllium and radium, the alkaline earth metals generally behave as reducing agents. Like the alkali metals, the alkaline earth metals react with hydrogen, oxygen, and water – but not as vigorously. These reactions may be summarized as follows:

HYDRIDE FORMATION

Calcium, barium, and strontium, when heated with hydrogen, form white ionic solids called *hydrides* (MH_2).

$$\overset{\displaystyle \overset{-2\ e^-}{\lceil\qquad\qquad\rceil}}{\underset{\underset{+2\ e^-}{\lfloor\qquad\qquad\rfloor}}{\overset{0}{M} + \overset{0}{H_2} \rightarrow \overset{+2\ -1}{MH_2}}}$$

These hydrides react with water to form hydrogen.

$$CaH_2 \ (s) + 2 \ H_2O \rightarrow Ca(OH)_2 \ (s) + 2 \ H_2 \ (g)$$

OXIDE FORMATION

The oxides of magnesium, calcium, strontium, and barium (MO) may be formed by heating the metals in oxygen or by thermal decomposition of the carbonates.

$$\overset{0}{2 \ M} + \overset{0}{O_2} \rightarrow 2 \ \overset{+2 \ -2}{MO}$$

$$MCO_3 \ (s) \rightarrow MO \ (s) + CO_2 \ (g)$$

REACTION WITH WATER

Calcium, barium, and strontium react with cold water to form a base, $M(OH)_2$, and hydrogen. Magnesium reacts in the same manner, but only with boiling water.

$$\overset{0}{M} + 2 \ \overset{+1 \ -2}{H_2O} \rightarrow \overset{+2 \ -2+1}{M(OH)_2} + \overset{0}{H_2}$$

The hydroxides of these metals vary in solubility. Barium hydroxide, $Ba(OH)_2$, is sufficiently soluble to be used as a basic solution. Calcium hydroxide, $Ca(OH)_2$, is much less soluble; and magnesium hydroxide, $Mg(OH)_2$, is quite insoluble.

22.7 The ratio of charge to ionic radius

The atypical properties of beryllium result from its +2 charge and its small ionic radius. With small ions, the ratio of charge to size is considerable. Thus a relatively strong electrical field exists around the beryllium ion, which resists the removal of the two valence electrons. Beryllium, therefore, does not form ionic bonds. Instead, it tends to form strong covalently bonded compounds.

The other alkaline earth metals have the same +2 charge as beryllium but are larger in ionic size. The lower ratio of charge to size produces a weaker electrical field, which permits the removal of the valence electrons and leads to the formation of ionically bonded compounds.

The ratio of ionic charge to size for the alkaline earth metals is larger than the same ratio for the alkali metals. The larger ratio results from the double positive charges and the smaller ionic radii of the alkaline earth metals. Greater attractive forces bind the positive and negative ions in the alkaline earth compounds than in the related compounds of the alkali metals. Since solubility in water depends on the weakening of bonds, the compounds of the alkaline earth metals are generally less soluble than the corresponding alkali metal compounds. The halides and nitrates are exceptions to this rule.

22.8 Hard water and soap

Certain naturally occurring waters contain dissolved calcium, magnesium, and iron compounds, which means that Ca^{+2} (aq), Mg^{+2} (aq), and Fe^{+2} (aq) ions are present. What happens when soaps encounter these ions? Soaps are soluble metallic (usually sodium) compounds of a special group of acids called fatty acids (see section 29.7). For example, a water solution of $C_{17}H_{35}COONa$ (sodium stearate), a typical soap, furnishes aquated Na^+ ions and aquated $C_{17}H_{35}COO^-$ (stearate) ions. The metallic ions in hard water react with the stearate ions to form insoluble stearates.

$$Ca^{+2} (aq) + 2 \ C_{17}H_{35}COO^- (aq) \rightarrow (C_{17}H_{35}COO)_2Ca \ (s)$$

$$Mg^{+2} (aq) + 2 \ C_{17}H_{35}COO^- (aq) \rightarrow (C_{17}H_{35}COO)_2Mg \ (s)$$

This reaction changes a soluble soap to an insoluble curd, which renders the lathering action of the soap most ineffective. Curds may stain clothing. Certain hard waters decompose in boilers to form deposits that clog boiler pipes. Communities generally find it necessary to soften hard water.

22.9 Softening hard water

The principle involved in softening hard waters is to add a substance that lowers the concentration of the divalent metal ions so that the effect on soap is diminished. The specific softening methods, outlined below, depend on the nature of the hard water.

Hard water containing bicarbonates of magnesium and calcium is called temporary hard water because the compounds are unstable and may be softened by boiling.

$$Mg^{+2} (aq) + 2 \ HCO_3^- (aq) \rightarrow MgCO_3 (s) + H_2O + CO_2 (g)$$

Note that the concentration of Mg^{+2} (aq) ion is reduced by converting it into slightly soluble $MgCO_3$. Since boiling is expensive, especially for large-scale softening, inexpensive chemicals such as $Ca(OH)_2$ (slaked lime) are often used, as shown on the following page.

$$Mg^{+2} (aq) + 2\ HCO_3^- + 2\ Ca^{+2} (aq) + 4\ OH^- (aq) \rightarrow$$
$$2\ CaCO_3 (s) + 2\ H_2O + Mg(OH)_2 (s)$$

$Mg(OH)_2$ is more insoluble than $MgCO_3$, and $CaCO_3$ is more insoluble than $Ca(OH)_2$. Thus the formation of the precipitate removes both $Mg^{+2} (aq)$ and $Ca^{+2} (aq)$ from the solution.

Hard water containing sulfates of magnesium and calcium does not form insoluble magnesium and calcium compounds on boiling, and is called permanent hard water. It may be softened by using Na_2CO_3 (washing soda) or $Na_2B_4O_7$ (borax).

$$Mg^{+2} (aq) + CO_3^- (aq) \rightarrow MgCO_3 (s)$$
$$Mg^{+2} (aq) + B_4O_7^{-2} (aq) \rightarrow MgB_4O_7 (s)$$

All types of hard water may be softened on a large scale by treatment with *ion exchangers*. These ion exchangers may be either naturally occurring sodium aluminum silicates, called *zeolites*, or they may be synthetic organic resins.

The zeolites possess a porous, solid three-dimensional structure of strong covalently bonded negative ions made up of aluminum, silicon, and oxygen. Adjacent to the negative ions are positive ions, usually Na^+, which are loosely held by the attraction of opposite charges.

When hard waters are passed through the porous zeolites, Ca^{+2} and Mg^{+2} ions take the place of the Na^+ ions. The Ca^{+2} and Mg^{+2} ions bind to the zeolite molecule, lowering their concentration and softening the water. The ion exchange that occurs typifies an equilibrium system that shifts to the right by the addition of excess reactant.

$$Ca^{+2} (aq) + \underbrace{2\ Na^+ (aq) + 2\ Z^- (aq)}_{\text{zeolite}} \rightleftarrows 2\ Na^+ (aq) + CaZ_2 (s)$$

The zeolite may be regenerated; that is, the equilibrium may be shifted to the left by the addition of more $Na^+ (aq)$ in the form of salt. This is done by allowing a concentrated NaCl solution to pass through the ion exchange. The $Ca^{+2} (aq)$ ions and the $Mg^{+2} (aq)$ ions released in the reaction are discarded.

Ion-exchange resins are replacing zeolites in the softening of hard waters. These resins are organic polymers (see section 29.8) — three-dimensional, giant hydrocarbon molecules. By special chemical processes, ions (Re^-) are introduced at fixed sites in the molecule. The ions in the resin can now attract oppositely charged ions. An exchange occurs in which the oppositely charged ions become part of the resin, and metallic ions are freed. For example, consider a resin with the ionic site Re^- and the formula Re^-Na^+. The resin can react with hard water as follows (in the equation, all ions are aquated):

$$2\ Re^-Na^+ + Ca^{+2} \rightarrow (Re^-)_2Ca^{+2} + 2\ Na^+$$

In this manner, the Ca^{+2} ion, responsible for the hardness in water, is tied to the resin and removed. As in the zeolite softening method, for each Ca^{+2} ion two Na^+ ions have been exchanged.

22.10 Common alkaline earth metal compounds

The table on the following page summarizes the sources, properties, and uses of some common alkaline earth metal compounds.

22.11 The aluminum family

The elements in this family comprise Group IIIA of the Periodic Table and include boron, aluminum, gallium, indium, and thallium. The properties of these elements continue the trend in each of the rows of the Periodic Table following the alkali metals and the alkaline earth metals. Thus each element is characterized by two s electrons and one p electron, exhibiting an expected $+3$ oxidation state. The heavier elements may lose only the single p electron and thus show an oxidation state of $+1$, for example, thallium in $TlCl$.

Again continuing the trend, the elements in this family are less reactive than the elements in Group IA and Group IB, as shown by their lower E^0 values.

As expected, the ionization energies continue to increase and the tendency to form ions decreases. Thus boron, with the smallest atomic radius in Group IIIA, forms only covalent compounds such as boron trifluoride, BF_3.

$$\overset{\textstyle F}{\underset{\textstyle F}{\overset{\cdot\cdot}{\underset{\cdot\cdot}{B}}}}:F$$

As the atoms become larger, the tendency to lose electrons becomes more pronounced and the elements become more metallic. We will restrict the remainder of the discussion to aluminum, the most common member of Group IIIA.

ALKALINE EARTH METAL COMPOUNDS

FORMULA	NAME	SOURCE	PROPERTIES	USES
$MgSO_4 \cdot 7H_2O$	Epsom salts	epsomite (a mineral)	forms a variety of hydrates	1. medicinal purgative 2. weighting cotton and silk 3. fireproofing muslin
$CaCO_3$	limestone or marble	natural deposits formed by shells of sea animals	thermal decomposition yields lime $CaCO_3 (s) \rightarrow CaO (s) + CO_2 (g)$	1. source of many Ca compounds 2. building material 3. metallurgy of iron
CaO	lime or quicklime	decomposition of limestone in a kiln	reacts with water to produce slaked lime and considerable heat $CaO + H_2O \rightarrow Ca(OH)_2 + 16$ kcal	1. production of slaked lime, $Ca(OH)_2$ 2. smelting of metals 3. drying agent
$Ca(OH)_2$	slaked lime or limewater	slaking of lime	1. common base 2. reacts with halogens to form oxyhalogen compounds	1. preparation of mortar 2. manufacture of bleaching powder 3. purification of sugar
$CaSO_4 \cdot 2H_2O$	gypsum	natural deposits	partial dehydration yields plaster of Paris $2\ CaSO_4 \cdot 2H_2O \rightarrow (CaSO_4)_2 \cdot H_2O + 3\ H_2O$	1. source of plaster of Paris 2. building material
$CaCl_2$	calcium chloride	by-product in the Solvay process for making $NaHCO_3$	hygroscopic material	1. drying agent 2. freezing mixtures
$BaSO_4$	barite	natural deposits and by reaction $BaO_2 + H_2SO_4 \rightarrow H_2O_2 + BaSO_4 (s)$	1. stable against heat and atmosphere 2. absorbs X rays	1. paint pigment and filler 2. X-ray diagnosis
$Sr(NO_3)_2$	strontium nitrate	$SrCO_3 + 2\ HNO_3 \rightarrow Sr(NO_3)_2 + H_2O + CO_2 (g)$	produces characteristic red color in a flame	pyrotechnics and red flares

22.12 Preparation of aluminum

Aluminum is the most abundant metal in the crust of the earth, occurring widely in nature as clays and feldspars. It is difficult to extract aluminum from these minerals. Instead, aluminum is extracted from the mineral bauxite, a hydrated aluminum oxide. Continuing the trend in the third row of the Periodic Table, aluminum, like sodium and magnesium, is prepared by the electrolysis of its molten compound.

Commercially, this process is carried out in a furnace devised by Charles Hall in 1886. As shown in Figure 22-1, the furnace consists of a steel box lined with carbon, which acts as the cathode. Since aluminum oxide melts at a very high temperature, it is dissolved in molten cryolite (Na_3AlF_6), which melts at a much lower temperature. The anodes are a series of graphite electrodes.

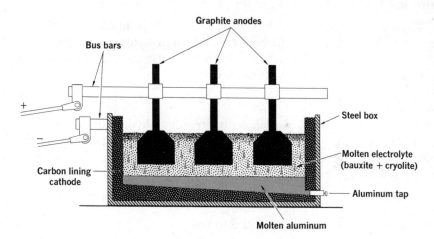

Fig. 22–1   The Hall process

The reactions are

$$Al_2O_3 \rightarrow 2\ Al^{+3} + 3\ O^{-2}$$

$$\text{CATHODE} \quad 4\ Al^{+3} + 12\ e^- \rightarrow 4\ Al\ (l)$$

$$\text{ANODE} \quad 6\ O^{-2} \rightarrow 3\ O_2\ (g) + 12\ e^-$$

At the temperature of the electrolytic cell, the aluminum is liquid and can be tapped off.

22.13 Properties of aluminum

Aluminum is a malleable and ductile metal about one-third as dense as iron. For its weight, it possesses high tensile strength. It is also an excellent conductor of heat and electricity.

Continuing the trend in the third row, aluminum is a reactive metal. It tarnishes readily in air to form a protective oxide coating. Aluminum reacts with acids; but unlike Na and Mg, aluminum also reacts with strong bases. (All ions are aquated.)

$$2 \text{ Al } (s) + 6 \text{ H}^+ \rightarrow 2 \text{ Al}^{+3} + 3 \text{ H}_2 (g)$$

$$2 \text{ Al } (s) + 2 \text{ OH}^- + 6 \text{ H}_2\text{O} \rightarrow 2 \text{ Al(OH)}_4^- + 3 \text{ H}_2 (g)$$

The tendency toward amphoterism as we proceed toward the center of a row is a characteristic trend in the rows of the Periodic Table.

Despite its high ionization energy, aluminum is an excellent reducing agent. This variance is attributed to the high hydration energy of the Al^{+3} ion, which is 1121 kcal/mole. Aluminum also reduces metallic oxides such as Fe_2O_3 in highly exothermic reactions.

$$2 \text{ Al } (s) + \text{Fe}_2\text{O}_3 (s) \rightarrow \text{Al}_2\text{O}_3 (s) + 2 \text{ Fe } (s) \qquad \Delta H = -203 \text{ kcal/mole}$$

In aqueous medium, aluminum is present as hydrated aluminum ion, $\text{Al(H}_2\text{O)}_6^{+3}$, a complex ion, the structure of which is discussed on page 480. $\text{Al(H}_2\text{O)}_6^{+3}$ can enter into acid-base reactions with water as shown in the following equation:

$$\text{Al(H}_2\text{O)}_6^{+3} + \text{H}_2\text{O} \rightarrow \text{H}_3\text{O}^+ + \text{Al(H}_2\text{O)}_5\text{OH}^{+2}$$

Additional protons can be donated to water.

$$\text{Al(H}_2\text{O)}_5\text{OH}^{+2} + \text{H}_2\text{O} \rightarrow \text{H}_3\text{O}^+ + \text{Al(H}_2\text{O)}_4(\text{OH})_2^+$$

$$\text{Al(H}_2\text{O)}_4(\text{OH})_2^+ + \text{H}_2\text{O} \rightarrow \text{H}_3\text{O}^+ + \text{Al(H}_2\text{O)}_3(\text{OH})_3 (s)$$

From these reactions, we conclude that a precipitate of hydrated aluminum hydroxide will be present in water solutions of aluminum salts. These reactions represent special cases of hydrolysis.

22.14 Uses of aluminum

Aluminum is used as a structural metal in aircraft, in automobiles, and in buildings. It is used in many household appliances and in alloys.

Multiple-Choice Questions

1. Which of the following is *not* correct in comparing Group IIA metals with the corresponding Group IA metals? (1) Group IA atoms have larger radii. (2) Group IIA ions have smaller radii. (3) Group IIA metals have higher first ionization potentials. (4) Group IIA metals have higher E^0 values.

2. Because the nuclear charge of an alkaline earth metal is one unit greater than it is for the corresponding alkali metal, the alkaline earth metals (1) have larger atoms (2) have smaller ionic radii (3) are more electronegative (4) are softer

3. A nonmetal that can be used to reduce Mg^{+2} is (1) oxygen (2) silicon (3) aluminum (4) phosphorus

4. Heating $MgCO_3$ forms (1) MgO (2) Mg_3N_2 (3) Mg (4) MgC_2

5. Beryllium is an *atypical* member of the Group IIA family because it (1) reacts with halogens (2) reacts with oxygen (3) forms covalent bonds (4) has two *s* electrons in the valence shell

6. Water containing Ca^{+2} (*aq*) or Mg^{+2} (*aq*) is hard water because it (1) has a high boiling point (2) forms insoluble compounds with soap (3) cannot be distilled (4) contains heavy hydrogen

7. The difference between temporary hard water and permanent hard water is that (1) only temporary hard water contains Ca^{+2} and Mg^{+2} (2) permanent hard water forms a lasting lather (3) temporary hard water contains bicarbonate ion (4) permanent hard water cannot be softened by distillation

8. Rocks can be tested for limestone by adding a few drops of hydrochloric acid because (1) bubbles show the release of CO_2 from the carbonate (2) the acid shows the hardness of $CaCO_3$ (3) calcium hydride forms (4) chlorine is released

9. Ion exchangers can be used for cleaning with hard water because they (1) form precipitates (2) do not form insoluble compounds with calcium (3) soften permanent hard water (4) form volatile compounds

10. The member of Group IIIA that forms a soluble base is (1) aluminum (2) gallium (3) indium (4) thallium

Completion Questions

1. The reaction of CaO with _____ produces calcium hydroxide.

2. When washing soda is added to hard water, calcium ions are removed by the formation of insoluble calcium _____.

3. Zeolites are used to soften hard water because they act as _____.
4. The formula for the compound present in seashells is _____.
5. The element in Group IIA that is radioactive is _____.
6. Hard water that can be softened by boiling is called _____ hard water.
7. The electrolysis of a molten alkaline earth metal hydride produces hydrogen at the _____ (*anode, cathode*).
8. All alkaline earth metal nitrates are _____ (*soluble, insoluble*) in water.
9. Elements in Group IIIA have _____ (*higher, lower*) E^0 values than the corresponding elements on their left in the Periodic Table.
10. The electrolyte in the Hall process is _____.

True-False Questions

1. To soften hard water, the concentration of dissolved *univalent* metal ions must be decreased.
2. *Sodium stearate* is an example of an ion-exchange resin.
3. Most of the calcium on the earth exists in the *uncombined* state.
4. The formula for plaster of Paris is *(CaSO₄)₂ · H₂O*.
5. When an ion-exchanger has been used to soften hard water, it can be regenerated by placing it in a solution of *calcium* chloride.
6. The presence of *sodium sulfate* in water will give it temporary hardness.
7. Calcium *hydroxide* dissolves in water, generating much heat.
8. Gypsum is a deposit of naturally occurring, hydrated *calcium carbonate*.
9. Aluminum hydroxide is a *strong* base.
10. When $Al(H_2O)_6^{+3}$ donates a proton, $Al(H_2O)_5^{+2}$ is formed.

Decreases, Increases, Remains the Same

1. In going from a Group IA element to the corresponding Group IIA element, we observe that the atomic radius _____.
2. As the temperature of hard water is increased, the concentration of dissolved bicarbonate ions _____.
3. When hard water is passed through an ion-exchange resin, the concentration of Ca^{+2} in the water _____.
4. As the alkaline earth metal ions (M^{+2}) become hydrated, the E^0 for the reaction $M\ (s) \rightarrow M^{+2}\ (aq) + 2\ e^-$ _____.
5. As the E^0 value for the electrode reaction of a metal increases, the ability of the metal to act as a reducing agent _____.

6. As the amount of Na^+ present in water increases, the hardness of the water _____.

7. When borax is added to water, the calcium ion concentration in the water _____.

8. As the atomic weights of the alkaline earth metals increase, the solubilities in water of the corresponding hydroxides _____.

9. As the ratio of charge to size for alkali metal ions decreases, the tendency to form ionic solids _____.

10. As the third ionization energies of the Group IIIA elements increase, the tendency to form ionic species _____.

Exercises for Review

1. Write equations for each of the following:
   a. the electrolysis of molten calcium chloride, $CaCl_2$
   b. the reaction of aluminum with NaOH
   c. the reaction of strontium metal, Sr, with water
   d. the boiling of water containing magnesium bicarbonate, $Mg(HCO_3)_2$

2. a. State the important similarities between the chemical properties of the alkaline earth metals and the alkali metals.
   b. State the important differences.

3. a. Explain why magnesium has a lower E^0 value than sodium.
   b. Explain why beryllium has a higher first ionization potential than lithium.

4. a. What is meant by hard water?
   b. What causes temporary hardness?

5. Complete and balance the following:
   a. $Ba(ClO_3)_2 \rightarrow$
   b. $CaSO_4 + Na_2CO_3 \rightarrow$
   c. $CaH_2 + H_2O \rightarrow$
   d. $MgSO_4 + Ca(OH)_2 \rightarrow$

6. Explain why the E^0 values of the alkaline earth metals are high despite their small atomic radii.

7. Explain why the oxides of Group IIA metals have high melting points.

8. a. Why is calcium chloride used in a freezing mixture?
   b. Is it more effective than sodium chloride in such a mixture? Explain.

9. In structural terms, explain why aluminum is amphoteric.

10. Why does boron form covalently bonded compounds only?

Exercises for Further Study

1. *a.* Why is the increase in the ionization potential for forming M^{+3} ion for Group IIA metals much greater than the increase in the ionization potential for forming M^{+2} ion?

   b. Explain why the ionization potential for forming M^{+2} is not very much greater than for forming M^+.

2. *a.* Draw a graph showing how the second ionization potential of the alkaline earth metals changes with increasing atomic number.

   b. On the same graph, use different lines to show the trends in the atomic radii and E^0 values.

   c. Which relationships vary directly with atomic number? Which ones vary inversely?

3. *a.* Barium ion, Ba^{+2}, is poisonous, yet $BaSO_4$ is given to patients prior to taking stomach X rays. Why is it safe to use $BaSO_4$ internally?

   b. Why is $BaCO_3$ unsafe to give a patient? (*Hint:* Recall the contents of stomach fluid.)

4. *a.* Explain why a precipitate of $Mg(OH)_2$ is not formed when aqueous ammonia, NH_4OH, is added to a solution of $MgCl_2$.

   b. Explain why a precipitate of $Mg(OH)_2$ forms when sodium hydroxide is used.

5. A sample of limestone contains 90% $CaCO_3$. Calculate the weights of CaO, $Ca(OH)_2$, and $Ca(HCO_3)_2$ that can be formed from one ton of this limestone.

6. Deposits of limestone are found in what are believed to have been coastal regions bordering bodies of water in prehistoric periods. Explain why this is probably true.

7. Aluminum fluoride is ionic, whereas aluminum chloride is covalent. Explain.

8. Explain why a molecule of aluminum chloride has the formula Al_2Cl_6 and *not* $AlCl_3$.

Chapter 23

THE TRANSITION ELEMENTS

23.1 Introduction

Across the first three rows of the Periodic Table, an increase in atomic number results in the addition of electrons to the incomplete outermost electron shell (discussed in section 19.29). But in the fourth row, following calcium, an increase in atomic number results in the addition of electrons to the incomplete next-to-the-outermost shell. A similar electron addition takes place as the atomic numbers increase in the fifth, sixth, and seventh rows. The elements that exhibit this atypical behavior are called the *transition elements*.

23.2 The transition series

Four transition series appear in the Periodic Table:

1. Scandium (21) through zinc (30). With increasing atomic number, electrons are added to the third electron shell; these elements complete $3d$ orbitals before $4p$ orbitals. Recall that the order of filling energy levels is $4s$, $3d$, and then $4p$.

2. Yttrium (39) through cadmium (48). These elements complete $4d$ orbitals before $5p$ orbitals. The order of filling energy levels is $5s$, $4d$, and then $5p$.

3. Lanthanum (57) through mercury (80). This transition series includes an inner transition series of 14 elements (the lanthanides) from lanthanum (57) through lutetium (71). In these 14 elements, a $4f$ orbital in the second-from-the-outermost electron shell is being completed. From hafnium (72) through mercury (80), a $5d$ orbital is being completed. The order of filling energy levels is $6s$, $4f$, and then $5d$.

4. The last transition series. This series is incomplete. It begins with actinium (89) and includes an inner transition series of 14 elements (the actinides), beginning with thorium (90) and ending with the last known element, lawrencium (103). In this series, $5f$ orbitals are being completed. If element 104 is discovered, it would continue the main transition series and appear under hafnium. The entire transition series would run through element 121.

Chemists do not agree as to the exact makeup of each of the transition series. On the basis of observed properties, the arrangement suggested on the preceding page appears reasonable.

23.3 Order of filling orbitals

Every transition series results from the tendency of the atoms of elements in the different series to complete orbitals in lower principal energy levels. Orbitals are filled in the order described in the previous section. Thus the 21st electron in scandium would normally tend to enter a $4p$ orbital since the $4s$ orbital (in calcium) is completely filled. However, the $3d$ orbital is of lower energy and is filled before the $4p$ orbital. Similarly, in the lanthanides, the $4f$ orbitals possess lower energy than the $5d$ orbitals and are filled in that order.

23.4 General properties of the transition elements

We may summarize the properties of the transition elements as follows:

The elements are metallic since they possess a small number of valence electrons, usually two, in the outermost shell of electrons.

Since electrons are completing inner shells while the number of electrons in the outermost shell remains virtually unchanged, the atomic radii of the elements in a given transition series exhibit only small changes. The first ionization potentials also do not vary greatly. Most elements exhibit related properties if they fall into vertical columns or families in the Periodic Table. The transition elements exhibit similarities in rows, or in horizontal arrangements, in the Periodic Table.

The most common property of transition elements is their multiple oxidation states or numbers. The energy content of the inner d electrons is almost the same as that of the outer s electrons. Both types of electrons may be utilized in bond formation. Thus in Cu(I) compounds, a $4s$ electron is used in bonding, whereas in Cu(II) compounds, one $4s$ electron and one $3d$ electron are used.

The usual oxidation numbers of the transition elements are $+2$ and $+3$. Exceptions are Cu, $+1$ and $+2$; Ag, $+1$ only; and Au, $+1$ and $+3$. Many transition elements, notably manganese and chromium, form polyatomic ions with oxygen, such as MnO_4^- and CrO_4^{-2}. The bonding in these ions is essentially covalent. Note that in MnO_4^- the oxidation state of Mn is $+7$, and in CrO_4^{-2} the oxidation state of Cr is $+6$.

Many compounds of the transition elements are colored. This property may be ascribed to the *d* electrons in incompleted energy levels which have energies that lie close to several energy levels. The difference between these levels is small and of the same order of magnitude as one of the frequencies present in visible light.

When electrons interact with visible light, one frequency (color) is selectively absorbed from the visible light. The resulting transmitted light is deficient in this frequency. Thus aqueous Fe^{+3} ion appears yellow because it has absorbed blue from visible light. Non-transition elements do not possess incomplete *d* sublevels. Thus electron interaction with visible light does not occur, and the compounds of non-transition elements are usually colorless. For example, contrast iron with six electrons in the incomplete $3d$ sublevel and rubidium with ten electrons in the completed $3d$ sublevel. Iron compounds are colored, whereas rubidium compounds are generally colorless.

Transition elements show a marked tendency to form complex ions. This property stems from the fact that these elements have vacant or incompletely filled orbitals, suggesting that atoms of these elements can combine with electron donors. Recall that NH_3 has one pair of unshared electrons used, for example, to bond to H^+ to form NH_4^+. In nickel ion, a typical transition element, we find one vacant $4s$ orbital and three vacant $4p$ orbitals. Thus Ni^{+2} can form four coordinate covalent bonds with

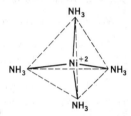

Fig. 23–1   The shape of the $Ni(NH_3)_4^{+2}$ ion

NH_3 molecules. Each of these four bonds involves one *s* and three *p* orbitals and is therefore an sp^3 hybrid bond. This means that the shape of the $Ni(NH_3)_4^{+2}$ ion conforms to the shape of its bonding orbitals and is therefore tetrahedral (see Figure 23-1). Similarly, copper forms complex ions, but the bonding orbitals involved result in a complex ion that is planar.

23.5 The copper family: copper, silver, and gold

Although Cu, Ag, and Au appear in different transition series, we may consider these elements as a family. The atoms of each element have a single *s* electron in the outermost electron shell and 18 electrons in the next-to-the-outermost shell. It is this characteristic which distinguishes these elements from the alkali metals, which also have a single *s* electron in the outermost electron shell but only eight electrons in the next-to-the-outermost shell.

The following table shows some of the important properties of the members of the copper family.

PROPERTY	COPPER	SILVER	GOLD
atomic number	29	47	79
electron structure	$1s^2$ $2s^2, 2p^6$ $3s^2, 3p^6, 3d^{10}$ $4s^1$	$1s^2$ $2s^2, 2p^6$ $3s^2, 3p^6, 3d^{10}$ $4s^2, 4p^6, 4d^{10}$ $5s^1$	$1s^2$ $2s^2, 2p^6$ $3s^2, 3p^{6,} 3d^{10}$ $4s^2, 4p^6, 4d^{10}, 4f^{14}$ $5s^2, 5p^6, 5d^{10}$ $6s^1$
atomic (covalent) radius (Å)	1.28	1.44	1.44
ionic radius, M^+ (Å)	0.96	1.13	1.37
first ionization potential (ev)	7.68	7.54	9.18
electronegativity	1.9	1.9	2.4
oxidation states	$+1, +2$	$+1$	$+1, +3$
E^0 (volts) $M (s) \rightarrow M^+ (aq) + e^-$	-0.52	-0.80	-1.68

23.6 The copper family and the alkali metal family

Let us compare the members of the copper family with the alkali metals having the same number of electron shells, for example: copper − potassium, silver − rubidium, and gold − cesium. We can see that the members of the copper family possess smaller atomic radii, which means smaller atomic volumes. This difference suggests that the densities of the members of the copper family are correspondingly higher. The metals of the copper family are also harder and have higher melting points, probably because these atoms tend to form covalent bonds.

The ionization potentials of the members of the copper family are higher than the corresponding values for the alkali metals. This is due, in part at least, to the higher nuclear charges and to the smaller atomic radii. The E^0 values for the copper family are considerably lower than the corresponding values for the alkali metals; in fact, the values are all negative. It is probable that the lower E^0 values are caused by the higher heats of vaporization ($+\Delta H_v$) and higher ionization potentials ($+\Delta H_i$). The copper family, having small atomic size, also possesses higher hydration energy values. The net effect of all these factors is to produce very low E^0 values. These values suggest that the metals in the copper family are not as reactive as the alkali metals. The members of the copper family, therefore, are found in nature both in the uncombined and in the combined states.

23.7 The metallurgy of copper, silver, and gold

The following table summarizes the occurrence and extraction of the members of the copper family.

METAL	OCCURRENCE	EXTRACTION
Cu	native (uncombined) and in ores such as cuprite, Cu_2O; chalcopyrite, $CuFeS_2$; and malachite, $CuCO_3 \cdot Cu(OH)_2$	ore is concentrated and impurities are oxidized in a series of complex reactions; impure copper formed is purified by electrolysis
Ag	native and in ores such as horn silver, $AgCl$, and argentite, Ag_2S	mercury is added to form an alloy with silver in the ore (amalgamation) which separates from the nonmetallic portion; silver amalgam is distilled to separate mercury from silver; silver is then purified
Au	largely native or as the tellurium compound, $AuTe_2$	by amalgamation and purification

Fundamental Concepts of Modern Chemistry

23.8 The chemistry of copper

The oxidation numbers exhibited by Cu in its compounds are $+1$ and $+2$. Thus copper forms two types of ions: Cu^+ or Cu(I), called *cuprous ion*; and Cu^{+2} or Cu(II), called *cupric ion*. In aqueous solution, Cu^+ (*aq*) is unstable, undergoing self-oxidation and reduction (disproportionation).

$$2\ CuCl\ (aq) \rightarrow CuCl_2\ (aq) + Cu\ (s)$$

or

$$2\ Cu^+\ (aq) \rightarrow Cu^{+2}\ (aq) + Cu\ (s)$$

The Cu^{+2} (*aq*) ion is more stable, but it can be reduced to Cu^+ (*aq*). The addition of glucose (or other reducing sugars) to alkaline $CuSO_4$ reduces Cu^{+2} (*aq*) to form a precipitate of brick-red Cu_2O. This reaction is used as a test to identify reducing sugars in blood or in urine.

REACTIONS WITH ACIDS

Copper reacts with nitric acid to form Cu^{+2} (*aq*) ion and a variety of oxides of nitrogen, depending on the concentration of the acid (see section 24.11).

$$3\ Cu\ (s) + 8\ \underset{\text{dilute}}{HNO_3}\ (aq) \rightarrow 3\ Cu(NO_3)_2\ (aq) + 2\ NO\ (g) + 4\ H_2O$$

$$Cu\ (s) + 4\ \underset{\text{conc.}}{HNO_3}\ (aq) \rightarrow Cu(NO_3)_2\ (aq) + 2\ NO_2\ (g) + 2\ H_2O$$

Although the E^0 value for Cu $\rightarrow$ $Cu^{+2} + 2\ e^-$ is negative, the E^0 value for the reduction of NO_3^- ion is positive. The net E^0 is therefore positive and supports the observation that the reactions are spontaneous. We can analyze this reaction, using the procedures described in section 17.13. First, we write the two half-reactions with their E^0 values.

OXIDATION $Cu\ (s) \rightarrow Cu^{+2}\ (aq) + 2\ e^-$ $E^0 = -0.34$ v

REDUCTION $NO_3^-\ (aq) + 4\ H^+\ (aq) + 3\ e^- \rightarrow$

               $NO\ (g) + 2\ H_2O$ $E^0 = +0.96$ v

To conserve electrons, the oxidation half-reaction is multiplied by 3, and the reduction half-reaction is multiplied by 2. The net reaction becomes

$$3 \; Cu \; (s) + 2 \; NO_3^- \; (aq) + 8 \; H^+ \; (aq) \rightarrow 3 \; Cu^{+2} \; (aq) + 2 \; NO + 4 \; H_2O$$

The net $E^0 = -0.34 \; v + 0.96 \; v = +0.62 \; v$.

On the other hand, copper will not react with dilute acids to form H_2 (g) since the net E^0 for this reaction is negative.

$$Cu \; (s) \rightarrow Cu^{+2} \; (aq) + 2 \; e^- \qquad E^0 = -0.34 \; v$$

$$2 \; H^+ \; (aq) + 2 \; e^- \rightarrow H_2 \; (g) \qquad E^0 = \quad 0.00 \; v$$

$$\text{net} \quad E^0 = -0.34 \; v$$

Copper reacts with sulfuric acid much the same as it does with nitric acid. The reduction products are usually SO_2 or S, depending on the temperature and the concentration of the acid.

$$Cu \; (s) + 2 \; \underset{\text{conc.}}{H_2SO_4} \; (aq) \rightarrow CuSO_4 \; (aq) + 2 \; H_2O + SO_2 \; (g)$$

COMPLEX ION FORMATION

Cu^{+2} (aq) ion reacts with OH^- (aq) ion to precipitate $Cu(OH)_2$.

$$Cu^{+2} \; (aq) + 2 \; OH^- \; (aq) \rightarrow Cu(OH)_2 \; (s)$$

When aqueous ammonia is used as the source of OH^- (aq) ion, the $Cu(OH)_2$ will first precipitate; then if excess NH_3 (aq) is used, the solid will dissolve to form soluble $Cu(NH_3)_4(OH)_2$, called copper ammonia hydroxide.

$$Cu(OH)_2 \; (s) + 4 \; NH_3 \; (aq) \rightarrow Cu(NH_3)_4^{+2} \; (aq) + 2 \; OH^- \; (aq)$$

In this compound, Cu^{+2} is united to four NH_3 molecules to form the stable complex ion $Cu(NH_3)_4^{+2}$, shown on page 305. This complex is another example of coordinate covalent bonding, discussed in section 20.20.

Copper has a coordination number of 4. The *coordination number* is the number of ions or molecules that are bonded to a central ion. This reaction, in which insoluble $Cu(OH)_2$ is changed to a soluble species, is another example of shifting an equilibrium system by utilizing Le Chatelier's Principle. The stress in this instance is the change from Cu^{+2} (aq) to

$Cu(NH_3)_4^{+2}$, which removes sufficient Cu^{+2} (*aq*) to prevent the formation of $Cu(OH)_2$. The solution has a deep blue color due to the presence of aqueous $Cu(NH_3)_4^{+2}$; the color serves as a test for Cu^{+2} (*aq*) ion.

Cu^{+2} (*aq*) ion also reacts with S^{-2} (*aq*) ion to form the very insoluble CuS ($K_{SP} = 3 \times 10^{-42}$).

$$Cu^{+2}\ (aq) + S^{-2}\ (aq) \rightarrow CuS\ (s)$$

The addition of HNO_3 to the precipitate converts the very low concentration of S^{-2} (*aq*) ion to free S, lowering the concentration of S^{-2} ion still further and below the value necessary to satisfy the K_{SP} value. Hence, CuS dissolves in HNO_3.

$$3\ CuS\ (s) + 8\ H^+\ (aq) + 2\ NO_3^-\ (aq) \rightarrow$$
$$3\ Cu^{+2}\ (aq) + 3\ S\ (s) + 4\ H_2O + 2\ NO\ (g)$$

23.9 The chemistry of silver and gold

The oxidation number exhibited by silver in its compounds is +1. Like copper, silver may also exhibit an oxidation number of +2, but such compounds are uncommon. Therefore, silver usually forms one ion, Ag^+.

Silver forms many compounds, among them soluble $AgNO_3$ and insoluble silver halides (except AgF). The low solubility of AgCl, AgBr, and AgI may be attributed to the very high values for the crystal energies (see section 20.14). These very high values are thought to arise from the large number of electrons in Ag^+ ion (46), which contributes to large van der Waals attractions between Ag^+ and halide ions (see section 20.22). These forces, added to the normal electrostatic ionic attractions, make for exceptionally stable crystal structures which resist deformation during dissolving.

The oxidation numbers exhibited by gold in its compounds are + 1 and +3. Unlike all metals except platinum, gold does not dissolve in nitric acid. This property of gold may be used to distinguish it from brass (an alloy of copper and zinc), which does dissolve in nitric acid. Gold is soluble in a mixture of nitric acid and hydrochloric acid, called aqua regia (see section 24.11).

Dissolving gold by adding HCl to HNO_3 has been erroneously ascribed to an increase in the oxidizing power of HNO_3. Instead, adding HCl to HNO_3 permits the dissolving of gold because the reducing power of gold has been increased. The increase stems from the presence of chloride ion in aqua regia, which forms very stable complex ions with gold.

$$Au\ (s) + 4\ H^+\ (aq) + NO_3^-\ (aq) + 4\ Cl^-\ (aq) \rightarrow$$
$$AuCl_4^-\ (aq) + NO\ (g) + 2\ H_2O$$

23.10 Uses of copper, silver, and gold

The following table summarizes some of the more important uses of Cu, Ag, and Au and the properties on which these uses depend.

METAL	USE	PROPERTY
Cu	manufacture of electrical wire manufacture of alloys such as brass (Cu, Zn) and bronze (Cu, Sn)	good conductor of electricity alloys of Cu, such as brass and bronze, are harder than Cu; bronze is more resistant to corrosion than Cu
Ag and Au	coinage metals when alloyed with Cu jewelry	hard and durable scarcity, appearance, resistance to tarnish

23.11 Chromium and manganese

Manganese follows chromium in the first transition series, which begins with scandium. The electron configurations of these elements are shown in the following table.

ELEMENT	COMPLETELY FILLED ORBITALS	HALF-FILLED ORBITALS
$_{21}$Sc	$1s^2, 2s^2, 2p^6, 3s^2, 3p^6, 4s^2$	$3d^1$
$_{24}$Cr	$1s^2, 2s^2, 2p^6, 3s^2, 3p^6$	$4s^1, 3d^5$
$_{25}$Mn	$1s^2, 2s^2, 2p^6, 3s^2, 3p^6, 4s^2$	$3d^5$

Vertically below chromium in the Periodic Table, we find molybdenum (42) and tungsten (74). Each of these elements, including chromium, has a total of 14 electrons in the outermost and next-to-the-outermost electron shells. Vertically below manganese in the Periodic Table, we find technetium (43) and rhenium (75). Each of these elements, including manganese, has a total of 15 electrons in the outermost and next-to-the-outermost electron shells.

In addition to resemblances between the elements in the chromium column and the elements in the manganese column, chromium and manganese, as members of the fourth row of the Periodic Table, also resemble each other. The discussion that follows will be restricted to chromium and to manganese. Although these elements are not very abundant, they are widely used.

23.12 The chemistry of chromium

Chromium forms a series of compounds, as shown in the following table.

OXIDATION NUMBER	COMPOUND	NAME	COLOR
$+2$	$CrCl_2$	chromous chloride chromium(II) chloride	blue
$+3$	$CrCl_3$	chromic chloride chromium(III) chloride	green
$+6$	Na_2CrO_4	sodium chromate	yellow
$+6$	$Na_2Cr_2O_7$	sodium dichromate	orange

Note that $CrCl_2$ and $CrCl_3$ are ionic compounds in which chromium forms positive ions. Na_2CrO_4 and $Na_2Cr_2O_7$ are also ionic compounds but of a different type. In these compounds, chromium is covalently bonded to oxygen to form a polyatomic ion, shown in the following electron-dot diagrams. As described previously, the specific colors of the ions are attributed to the interaction of visible light with electrons in incompleted d orbitals.

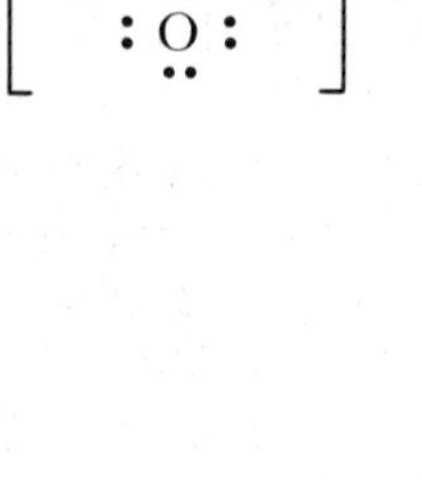

The chemistry of chromium may be summarized as follows:

OXIDES OF CHROMIUM

Chromium also forms a series of oxides with oxidation numbers of $+2$, $+3$, and $+6$. The oxides may be either basic, amphoteric, or acidic, as shown in the reactions that follow:

1. Basic reaction of Cr (oxidation state $+2$).

$$\underset{\substack{\text{chromous} \\ \text{oxide}}}{CrO} + H_2O \rightarrow \underset{\substack{\text{chromous} \\ \text{hydroxide}}}{Cr(OH)_2}$$

$$Cr(OH)_2 + 2\ HCl \rightarrow CrCl_2 + 2\ H_2O$$

2. Amphoteric reaction of Cr (oxidation state $+3$).

$$\underset{\substack{\text{chromic} \\ \text{oxide}}}{Cr_2O_3} + 3\ H_2O \rightarrow \underset{\substack{\text{chromic} \\ \text{hydroxide}}}{2\ Cr(OH)_3}$$

$$Cr(OH)_3 + 3\ HCl \rightarrow CrCl_3 + 3\ H_2O$$

$$Cr_2O_3 + H_2O \rightarrow 2\ HCrO_2$$

$$HCrO_2 + NaOH \rightarrow \underset{\substack{\text{sodium} \\ \text{chromite}}}{NaCrO_2} + H_2O$$

3. Acidic reaction of Cr (oxidation state $+6$).

$$\underset{\substack{\text{chromium} \\ \text{trioxide}}}{CrO_3} + H_2O \rightarrow H_2CrO_4$$

$$H_2CrO_4 + 2\ NaOH \rightarrow \underset{\substack{\text{sodium} \\ \text{chromate}}}{Na_2CrO_4} + 2\ H_2O$$

$$2\ CrO_3 + H_2O \rightarrow \underset{\substack{\text{sodium} \\ \text{dichromate}}}{H_2Cr_2O_7(Na_2Cr_2O_7)}$$

$$H_2Cr_2O_7 + 2\ NaOH \rightarrow Na_2Cr_2O_7 + 2\ H_2O$$

Thus the acidity of the oxides increases with increasing oxidation number, a principle that is characteristic of many elements.

CHROMATE – DICHROMATE EQUILIBRIUM

Another example of an equilibrium system that can be shifted by applying Le Chatelier's Principle is the change of CrO_4^{-2} to $Cr_2O_7^{-2}$ with increasing acidity (all ions are aquated in the reaction):

$$2 \ CrO_4^{-2} + 2 \ H^+ \leftrightharpoons Cr_2O_7^{-2} + H_2O$$

$$\underset{\text{yellow}}{\phantom{2 \ CrO_4^{-2}}} \qquad \underset{\text{orange}}{\phantom{Cr_2O_7^{-2}}}$$

The addition of H^+ shifts the equilibrium to the right to form the orange-colored dichromate ion. The removal of H^+ (the addition of OH^-) shifts the equilibrium to the left to form yellow-colored chromate ion.

OXIDIZING ACTION

In aqueous solution, Cr^{+2} and Cr^{+3} are typical metallic ions. CrO_4^{-2} and $Cr_2O_7^{-2}$ aqueous ions are strong oxidizing agents as shown below.

$$K_2Cr_2O_7 + 14 \ HCl \rightarrow 2 \ KCl + 2 \ CrCl_3 + 3 \ Cl_2 + 7 \ H_2O$$

OXIDATION $\quad 3 \ [2 \ Cl^- \rightarrow Cl_2 + 2 \ e^-]$

REDUCTION $\quad Cr_2O_7^{-2} + 14 \ H^+ + 6 \ e^- \rightarrow 2 \ Cr^{+3} + 7 \ H_2O$

COMPLEX ION FORMATION

Like copper, chromium forms complex ions with NH_3 and H_2O, for example, $Cr(NH_3)_6^{+3}$ and $Cr(H_2O)_6^{+3}$. In both of these ions, chromium has a coordination number of 6. Chromium forms four related compounds, the formulas of which may be written: $Cr(NH_3)_6Cl_3$, $Cr(NH_3)_5Cl_3$, $Cr(NH_3)_4Cl_3$, and $Cr(NH_3)_3Cl_3$. It might appear, at first glance, that Cr has a variable coordination number ranging from 6 to 3. However, the addition of excess $AgNO_3$ solution to 1 mole of each of these compounds precipitates different numbers of moles of Cl^- ions as AgCl (s). $Cr(NH_3)_6Cl_3$ precipitates 3 moles of Cl^- ion, $Cr(NH_3)_5Cl_3$ precipitates 2 moles of Cl^- ion, $Cr(NH_3)_4Cl_3$ precipitates 1 mole of Cl^- ion, and $Cr(NH_3)_3Cl_3$ forms no precipitate.

The results of this experiment offer proof that Cr has a coordination number of 6 because, in $Cr(NH_3)_6Cl_3$, 3 Cl^- ions are present and 6 NH_3 molecules are bonded to Cr. In $Cr(NH_3)_5Cl$, only 2 moles of Cl^- are present and 1 Cl atom and 5 NH_3 molecules are bonded to Cr. Similarly, in $Cr(NH_3)_4Cl_3$, 1 Cl^- ion is present and 2 Cl atoms and 4 NH_3 molecules are bonded to Cr. Finally, in $Cr(NH_3)_3Cl_3$, no Cl^- ions are present. Instead, 3 Cl atoms and 3 NH_3 molecules are covalently bonded to Cr. This compound does not conduct electricity and its molal boiling point elevation is $0.52°$ C, showing the presence of a single particle only, namely, $Cr(NH_3)_3Cl_3$. The structural formula of each of the compounds is

$$\left[\begin{array}{c} NH_3 \\ H_3N \diagdown \mid \diagup NH_3 \\ Cr \\ H_3N \diagup \mid \diagdown NH_3 \\ NH_3 \end{array}\right]^{+3} \quad 3\ Cl^-$$

$$\left[\begin{array}{c} NH_3 \\ H_3N \diagdown \mid \diagup NH_3 \\ Cr \\ H_3N \diagup \mid \diagdown Cl \\ NH_3 \end{array}\right]^{+2} \quad 2\ Cl^-$$

$$\left[\begin{array}{c} NH_3 \\ H_3N \diagdown \mid \diagup Cl \\ Cr \\ H_3N \diagup \mid \diagdown Cl \\ NH_3 \end{array}\right]^{+} \quad Cl^-$$

$$\left[\begin{array}{c} Cl \\ H_3N \diagdown \mid \diagup Cl \\ Cr \\ H_3N \diagup \mid \diagdown Cl \\ NH_3 \end{array}\right]^{0}$$

23.13 The chemistry of manganese

The chemistry of manganese is more complex than the chemistry of chromium because additional electrons from the incomplete $3d$ orbitals can enter into the formation of compounds. Manganese therefore exhibits many oxidation numbers. We will limit our discussion, however, to the compounds of manganese that parallel the compounds of chromium, as shown in the following table.

OXIDATION NUMBER	COMPOUND	NAME	COLOR
$+2$	$MnCl_2$	manganous chloride manganese(II) chloride	pink
$+4$	$MnCl_4$	manganic chloride manganese(IV) chloride	green
$+6$	Na_2MnO_4	sodium manganate	green
$+7$	$NaMnO_4$	sodium permanganate	purple

The oxides and hydroxides of manganese, like those of chromium, show a transition from basic to acidic properties as the oxidation numbers increase. $Mn(OH)_2$ is basic, MnO_2 is amphoteric, and $HMnO_4$ is acidic.

Manganese forms positive ions that have the typical properties of metallic ions. As with chromium, manganese forms polyatomic ions (manganate and permanganate) that are strong oxidizing agents (see section 17.7).

23.14 Iron, cobalt, and nickel

Iron, cobalt, and nickel follow chromium and manganese in the first transition series. In vertical sequence in the Periodic Table, we find: ruthenium (44) and osmium (76) below iron; rhodium (45) and iridium (77) below cobalt; and palladium (46) and platinum (78) below nickel. Ruthenium, rhodium, and palladium have densities of approximately 12 g/cm^3 and are called the light platinum metals. Osmium, iridium, and platinum have densities of approximately 22 g/cm^3 and are called the platinum metals. The platinum metals are relatively scarce and possess highly specialized uses.

The three vertical families of metals resemble one another, but the properties of iron, cobalt, and nickel (in the same row) are more closely related. The table on the facing page shows some important properties of this family.

The small atomic radii suggest a small atomic volume and consequently a high density. Thus Fe, Co, and Ni are hard and have relatively high melting points.

Fe, Co, and Ni each have completely filled 4s orbitals but incomplete d orbitals. The electrons in both orbitals possess about the same energy. The atoms may therefore lose two 4s electrons to form dipositively charged ions such as ferrous or Fe(II) ion, Fe^{+2}, cobaltous or Co(II) ion, Co^{+2}, and nickelous or Ni(II) ion, Ni^{+2}. Under certain conditions, the loss of a d electron may produce an ion with a charge of +3 such as ferric or Fe(III) ion, Fe^{+3}. Like the ions of other transition elements, these ions form colored compounds.

The E^0 values for Fe, Co, and Ni all lie above H, suggesting that they are moderately active metals. Note the E^0 values for the following half-reactions (all ions are aquated):

$$Fe^{+2} \rightarrow Fe^{+3} + e^- \qquad E^0 = -0.77 \text{ v}$$

$$Co^{+2} \rightarrow Co^{+3} + e^- \qquad E^0 = -1.84 \text{ v}$$

These values suggest that it is much easier to oxidize ferrous ion to ferric ion than to oxidize cobaltous ion to cobaltic ion. Indeed, only a few cobaltic compounds are known. However, Co^{+3} (aq) is a strong oxidizer.

$$4 \text{ Co}^{+3} (aq) + 2 \text{ H}_2\text{O} \rightarrow 4 \text{ Co}^{+2} (aq) + 4 \text{ H}^+ (aq) + \text{O}_2 (g)$$

PROPERTY	IRON	COBALT	NICKEL
atomic number	26	27	28
electron structure	$1s^2$ $2s^2, 2p^6$ $3s^2, 3p^6, 3d^6$ $4s^2$	$1s^2$ $2s^2, 2p^6$ $3s^2, 3p^6, 3d^7$ $4s^2$	$1s^2$ $2s^2, 2p^6$ $3s^2, 3p^6, 3d^8$ $4s^2$
atomic (covalent) radius (Å)	1.26	1.25	1.24
ionic radius, M^{+2} (Å)	0.75	0.72	0.69
ionization potential (ev) first second	7.9 16.1	7.9 17.3	7.6 18.2
electro- negativity	1.8	1.8	1.8
oxidation states	$+2, +3$	$+2, +3$	$+2, +4$
E^0 (volts) $M(s) \rightarrow M^{+2}(aq) + 2e^-$	$+0.44$	$+0.28$	$+0.25$

23.15 The metallurgy of iron, cobalt, and nickel

We may summarize the occurrence and extraction of iron, cobalt, and nickel as follows:

IRON

Iron occurs in the ores hematite, Fe_2O_3; taconite (iron oxide + silica); magnetite, Fe_3O_4; and siderite, $FeCO_3$. Most iron produced in the United States is extracted in the blast furnace (see Figure 23-2 on the following page).

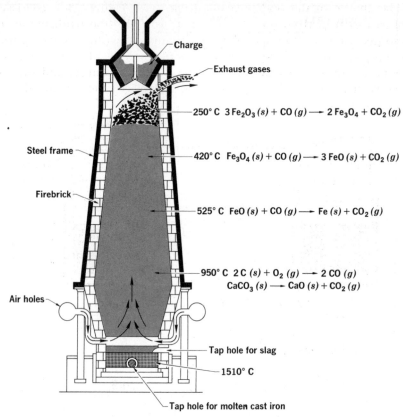

Fig. 23–2   The blast furnace

The charge that goes into the furnace consists of hematite, coke (reducing agent), and limestone (flux to remove impurities). The reactions that occur in the different temperature zones of the furnace are shown in the preceding figure. The product of the furnace is called pig iron, or cast iron; it contains C, S, Si, and P as impurities (less than 4%).

Pig iron is converted to steel in furnaces that remove these impurities by controlled oxidation and by slag formation. Examples of such furnaces are the open-hearth furnace, the electric furnace, and the oxygen top-blowing furnace.

The charge in the open-hearth furnace (see Figure 23-3) consists of molten cast iron from the blast furnace, iron ore (the oxidizing agent), scrap steel (source of additional iron), and limestone (flux). The impurities are removed by oxidation, forming both gaseous products and solid products. The gaseous products escape from the charge, and the solid products are converted to slag by a flux. The slag is then removed.

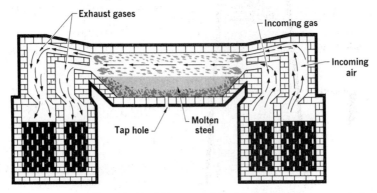

Fig. 23–3   *The open-hearth furnace*

The essential reactions are as follows:

$$C + O_2 \rightarrow CO_2 \ (g)$$

$$S + O_2 \rightarrow SO_2 \ (g)$$

$$Si + O_2 \rightarrow SiO_2 \ (s)$$

$$4 \ P + 5 \ O_2 \rightarrow P_4O_{10} \ (s)$$

$$\underset{\text{flux}}{CaCO_3} \dashrightarrow CaO + CO_2 \ (g)$$

$$CaO + SiO_2 \rightarrow \underset{\text{slag}}{CaSiO_3}$$

$$6 \ CaO + P_4O_{10} \rightarrow 2 \ \underset{\text{slag}}{Ca_3(PO_4)_2}$$

The furnace requires a high temperature obtained by a regenerative heating system in which the hot gaseous products are used to preheat the incoming gas and air. After the impurities are removed, specific amounts of carbon and other elements are added to give the steel desired properties.

The electric furnace process, shown in Figure 23-4, utilizes a high-temperature arc to supply the heat necessary to remove the impurities from cast iron. The charge in this furnace is essentially the same as in the open-hearth furnace, although the capacity of the electric furnace is smaller. More rigid control, however, can be exercised in the electric furnace, thus producing high-quality steel.

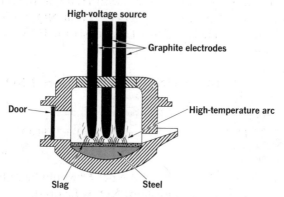

Fig. 23–4   The electric furnace

The charge in the oxygen top-blowing furnace resembles the charge in the open-hearth furnace. The impurities in the cast iron are very rapidly oxidized by blasts of air at tremendous speeds directed into the top of the molten metal. The desired elements are then added, the steel is removed, and the process is repeated. It is estimated that quantities of steel in excess of 200 tons can be produced in one hour.

COBALT

Cobalt occurs in the ores smaltite, $CoNiAs_2$, and carrolite, Co_2CuS_4. Ores are converted to cobalt salts by a series of complex reactions. The metal is extracted from the salt by electrolysis.

NICKEL

Nickel occurs in the mineral pentlandite, $NiS \cdot FeS$. Like cobalt, Ni is extracted by electrolysis. The ore is converted to the carbonyl compound $Ni(CO)_4$. When heated to 43° C, $Ni(CO)_4$ decomposes to yield Ni (Mond process).

23.16 The chemistry of iron

Iron forms Fe^{+2} and Fe^{+3} ions, each having characteristic properties. The E^0 value for the half-reaction Fe $(s) \rightarrow Fe^{+2} + 2\ e^-$ is 0.44 v. Thus iron reacts with dilute HCl or with dilute H_2SO_4 to form hydrogen gas.

$$Fe\ (s) + 2\ H^+\ (aq) \rightarrow Fe^{+2}\ (aq) + H_2\ (g)$$

On the other hand, iron does not react with HNO_3 to form hydrogen gas. Note from the table of E^0 values (page 329) that NO_3^- ion (in HNO_3) is more easily reduced than H^+. Thus Fe reacts with HNO_3 to produce an oxide of nitrogen. (All ions are aquated.)

$$3\ Fe\ (s) + 8\ HNO_3 \rightarrow 3\ Fe(NO_3)_2 + 2\ NO + 4\ H_2O$$

OXIDATION	$3\ [Fe\ (s) \rightarrow Fe^{+2} + 2\ e^-]$	$E^0 = 0.44$ v
REDUCTION	$2\ [NO_3^- + 4\ H^+ + 3\ e^- \rightarrow NO\ (g) + 2\ H_2O]$	$E^0 = 0.96$ v
		net $E^0 = 1.40$ v

If H_2 (g) were formed ($E^0 = 0.00$ v), the net E^0 would be only 0.44 v. Thus the formation of an oxide of nitrogen, NO, is favored.

Solutions containing Fe^{+2} (aq) ions tend to oxidize in air.

$$Fe^{+2}\ (aq) \rightarrow Fe^{+3}\ (aq) + e^- \quad E^0 = -0.77\ \text{v}$$

Such solutions are maintained in the form of Fe^{+2} by the addition of solid iron. If Fe^{+3} (aq) were to form, the Fe (s) would reduce it spontaneously to Fe^{+2} (aq).

$$Fe\ (s) + 2\ Fe^{+3}\ (aq) \rightarrow 3\ Fe^{+2}\ (aq)$$

OXIDATION	$Fe\ (s) \rightarrow Fe^{+2}\ (aq) + 2\ e^-$	$E^0 = 0.44$ v
REDUCTION	$2\ [Fe^{+3}\ (aq) + e^- \rightarrow Fe^{+2}\ (aq)]$	$E^0 = 0.77$ v
		net $E^0 = 1.21$ v

Iron forms complex ions in both oxidation states. For example, with the cyanide group (CN), Fe^{+2} forms the complex ion $Fe(CN)_6^{-4}$, as in potassium ferrocyanide, $K_4Fe(CN)_6$, also called potassium hexacyanoferrate(II). Similarly, Fe^{+3} forms $Fe(CN)_6^{-3}$, as in potassium ferricyanide, $K_3Fe(CN)_6$, also called potassium hexacyanoferrate(III).

Fe^{+2} (aq) ion reacts with aqueous $Fe(CN)_6^{-3}$ in a solution of $K_3Fe(CN)_6$ to form a dark blue precipitate (Turnbull's blue).

$$3\ Fe^{+2}\ (aq) + 2\ Fe(CN)_6^{-3}\ (aq) \rightarrow Fe_3[Fe(CN)_6]_2\ (s)$$
ferrous
ferricyanide

Fe^{+3} (aq) ion reacts with aqueous $Fe(CN)_6^{-4}$ in a solution of $K_4Fe(CN)_6$ to form a dark blue precipitate (Prussian blue).

$$4\ Fe^{+3}\ (aq) + 3\ Fe(CN)_6^{-4}\ (aq) \rightarrow Fe_4[Fe(CN)_6]_3\ (s)$$
ferric
ferrocyanide

Recent work seems to indicate that both dark-blue precipitates have the same composition, $KFe[Fe(CN)_6]$. However, it is not possible to indicate which Fe atom is in the +2 or +3 oxidation state since electrons can apparently move freely between the Fe atoms through the CN group acting as a bridge.

Fe^{+3} (aq) ion also reacts with aqueous SCN^- in a solution of KSCN (potassium thiocyanate) to form $[FeSCN]^{+2}$ (aq), a solution with a characteristic blood-red color. This reaction is used as a sensitive test for Fe^{+3} (aq) ion.

$$Fe^{+3}\ (aq) + SCN^-\ (aq) \rightarrow [FeSCN]^{+2}\ (aq)$$
thiocyano-iron(III)
(blood-red color)

23.17 The chemistry of cobalt and nickel

Cobalt, like iron, forms two types of ions, Co^{+2} and Co^{+3}. Unlike iron, only Co^{+2} is stable. Anhydrous (without water) Co^{+2} compounds are generally blue. In aqueous solution, the pink $Co(H_2O)_6^{+2}$ ion is formed. The change in color from blue to pink is utilized in the manufacture of certain inks and in predicting weather changes that are affected by varying humidity. Co^{+2} (aq) ion may be detected by adding potassium nitrite, KNO_2, dissolved in acetic acid, which forms a yellow, insoluble potassium salt of a complex ion, $Co(NO_2)_6^{-3}$. (All ions are aquated in the following reaction.)

$$Co^{+2} + 3\ K^+ + 7\ NO_2^- + 2\ CH_3COOH \rightarrow$$
$$K_3Co(NO_2)_6\ (s) + NO + 2\ CH_3COO^- + H_2O$$
yellow

Nickel resembles cobalt chemically. It readily forms Ni^{+2} ions, but rarely forms Ni^{+3} ions. Anhydrous Ni^{+2} compounds are generally yellow, whereas Ni^{+2} (aq) compounds are generally green. One test for Ni^{+2} (aq) ion is to add the organic reagent dimethylglyoxime to the unknown. The formation of a red solid indicates the presence of nickel.

Both cobalt and nickel, like typical transition elements, form complex ions with NH_3 and H_2O, for example, $Co(NH_3)_6^{+2}$, $Co(H_2O)_6^{+2}$, $Ni(NH_3)_6^{+2}$, and $Ni(H_2O)_6^{+2}$. Recall that NH_3 and H_2O each have one unshared pair of electrons. This permits the formation of coordinate covalent bonds in the complex ions.

23.18 Uses of iron, cobalt, and nickel

The uses of iron, cobalt, and nickel are summarized in the following table.

METAL	USE
iron	as pig iron from the blast furnace for castings; in the manufacture of steel and steel alloys
cobalt	high-speed tool steel alloys such as stellite; powerful permanent magnets such as alnico (Al, Ni, Fe, Co)
nickel	nonferrous metal alloys such as monel (Ni, Cu, Fe); coins and shock-resistant steel alloys

Multiple-Choice Questions

1. The transition elements (1) are nonmetallic (2) have incomplete valence shells (3) have half-filled orbitals (4) have incomplete shells next to the valence shells

2. The proper order of increasing energy levels is (1) $3d$, $4p$, $4s$ (2) $3d$, $4s$, $4p$ (3) $4s$, $3d$, $4p$ (4) $3d$, $3p$, $4s$

3. The lanthanide series is made up of elements that (1) are all man-made (2) do not form ions (3) have only complete electron shells (4) have an incomplete electron shell below the valence shell

4. All the following statements are true for the transition elements *except* that (1) they contain one or two valence electrons (2) the oxidation numbers are the same (3) the atomic radii of the elements in a given series are almost alike (4) they form complex ions

5. Group IB elements (copper family) differ from Group IA elements (sodium family) in that Group IB elements (1) have more than one oxidation number (2) are more active metals (3) have lower ionization potentials (4) are softer metals

6. Which of the following statements is *false*? (1) Ag has an oxidation number of +1. (2) Ag dissolves in HNO_3. (3) Au is not a transition element. (4) Ag dissolves in HI.

7. In the compound sodium dichromate, $Na_2Cr_2O_7$, the oxidation number of Cr is (1) +6 (2) +12 (3) +3 (4) +7

8. Cr_2O_3 reacts with a strong base, such as KOH, to form $KCrO_2$. With a strong acid, such as H_2SO_4, it forms $Cr_2(SO_4)_3$. This shows that Cr_2O_3 is (1) easily oxidized (2) easily reduced (3) amphoteric (4) a salt

9. One mole of which of the following compounds in 1000 g of water will have the lowest freezing point? (1) $Cr(NH_3)_6Cl_3$ (2) $Cr(NH_3)_5Cl_3$ (3) $Cr(NH_3)_4Cl_3$ (4) $Cr(NH_3)_3Cl_3$

10. The oxidation state of iron can be changed from $+2$ to $+3$ when (1) a $3d$ electron is removed (2) a $4s$ electron is removed (3) energy is released (4) covalent bonds are formed

Completion Questions

1. In the transition elements of the fifth row, added electrons go to complete the 4 _____ orbitals.

2. Ions of transition elements are _____ because they absorb energy from light.

3. Copper, _____, and _____ are metals that belong in the same vertical column of the Periodic Table.

4. In the reaction of copper with _____, one of the products is sulfur dioxide.

5. The number of ions or molecules united to a central atom is called the _____ number of the ion.

6. CrO behaves as a basic anhydride when it reacts with water to form _____.

7. The extraction of iron from iron ore takes place in a large structure called a (an) _____.

8. The bonding between cobalt and the water molecules in $Co(H_2O)_6^{+3}$ is _____.

9. A very rapid steelmaking process is called _____.

10. The major product of the blast furnace is _____.

True-False Questions

1. The first transition series of elements occurs in the *second* row of the Periodic Table.

2. The lanthanide series is an inner transition series containing *eight* elements.

3. One of the products of the reaction of copper with concentrated nitric acid is NO_2.

4. Mn has a half-filled $3d$ orbital.

5. The reaction of *chromous* oxide with water forms chromic acid, H_2CrO_4.

6. The coordination number of Cr in $Cr(NH_3)_6^{+3}$ is *3*.

7. The metals *nickel and cobalt* are used to make permanent magnets.

8. Addition of acid to K_2CrO_4 produces an excess of CrO_4^{-2} ions.
9. If element 104 is discovered, it would appear under *hafnium* in the Periodic Table.
10. In the reaction between Cu and different concentrations of HNO_3, Cu^{+2} and *NO* are always formed.

Decreases, Increases, Remains the Same

1. As the atomic numbers of the transition elements in a series increase, the number of electrons in the valence shell generally _____.
2. When increasing amounts of aqueous NH_3 are added to a $Cu(OH)_2$ precipitate, the amount of precipitate _____.
3. As the oxidation states of elements increase, the acidity of the corresponding oxides _____.
4. In the change from MnO_4^- to MnO_4^{-2}, the oxidation state of Mn _____.
5. Given: a series of elements with approximately equal atomic weights. As the atomic radii increase, the densities of the elements _____.
6. As the pH of the solution increases, the basic properties of CrO_3 _____.
7. As CrO_4^{-2} is changed to $Cr_2O_7^{-2}$, the oxidation state of Cr _____.
8. As we go from lanthanum to lutetium in the Periodic Table, the atomic radius generally _____.

Exercises for Review

1. Neighboring transition elements have similar properties, but neighboring elements that are not transition elements have different properties. Explain.
2. Why do no transition elements appear in the second series of the Periodic Table?
3. *a.* State the subshell designations for all the electrons in an atom of $_{26}Fe$.
   b. What properties may we predict from this structure?
4. Explain why the densities of the elements in Group IB (Cu group) are much greater than the densities of the elements in Group IA (Na group).
5. Write equations for the following reactions:
   a. $Ag + HNO_3 \xrightarrow{\text{conc.}}$
   b. $Cu + H_2SO_4 \xrightarrow{\text{conc.}}$
   c. $Cr(OH)_2 + HCl \rightarrow$

6. Why does Cu react with HNO_3 but not with HCl?
7. *a.* What is the chief product formed in the blast furnace?
   b. What is the composition of this product?
8. *a.* What is steel?
   b. What are the important elements present in steel?
9. *a.* Outline the principles involved in steel-making processes.
   b. Show how these principles are utilized in two specific processes.
   c. Describe the composition of three important steel alloys and indicate an important use for each alloy.
10. What property do transition elements possess that accounts for the formation of complex ions?

Exercises for Further Study

1. Explain why the actinide series is considered to be a transition series within a transition series.
2. Explain why the elements of Group IA and Group IIA have only one oxidation state and form colorless ions, whereas the metals in the transition series have more than one oxidation state and form colored ions.
3. Using a line for a single covalent bond and a double line for a double covalent bond, draw a diagram showing the structure of the $Cr_2O_7^{-2}$ ion.
4. Why do smaller ions, such as the Cu ion, tend to form more stable hydrates than larger ions, such as the K ion?
5. A jewelry manufacturer wants to recover silver and gold from metal scraps containing copper. How can he separate these metals chemically?
6. Write equations for the reactions of the following:
   a. Cu^{+2} *(aq)* with excess NaOH solution
   b. Cu^{+2} *(aq)* with excess NH_3 *(aq)*
   c. AgCl *(s)* with NH_3 *(aq)*
7. Balance the following, using the appropriate half-reactions:
   a. $K_2Cr_2O_7 + H_2S + H_2SO_4 \rightarrow S + Cr_2(SO_4)_3 + K_2SO_4 + H_2O$
   b. $KMnO_4 + KBr + H_2SO_4 \rightarrow Br_2 + MnSO_4 + H_2O + K_2SO_4$
   c. $FeSO_4 + H_2SO_4 + KMnO_4 \rightarrow K_2SO_4 + MnSO_4 + Fe_2(SO_4)_3 + H_2O$
8. The $Ag(NH_3)_2^+$ complex ion has a linear shape. Why?
9. Predict some properties for element 104.
10. Why does Cu form +1 and +2 ions, whereas Fe forms +2 and +3 ions?

Chapter 24

THE NITROGEN FAMILY

24.1 Introduction

The members of the nitrogen family (Group VA) are nitrogen, N, phosphorus, P, arsenic, As, antimony, Sb, and bismuth, Bi. The properties of N and P are closely related, and each of these elements is nonmetallic. Arsenic and antimony are slightly metallic; bismuth is essentially metallic. In the remainder of this chapter, we will discuss the reasons for these similarities and differences.

The following table summarizes some of the important properties of the members of the nitrogen family.

PROPERTY	NITROGEN	PHOSPHORUS	ARSENIC	ANTIMONY	BISMUTH
atomic number	7	15	33	51	83
electron structure	$1s^2$ $2s^2, 2p^3$	$1s^2$ $2s^2, 2p^6$ $3s^2, 3p^3$	$1s^2$ $2s^2, 2p^6$ $3s^2, 3p^6, 3d^{10}$ $4s^2, 4p^3$	$1s^2$ $2s^2, 2p^6$ $3s^2, 3p^6, 3d^{10}$ $4s^2, 4p^6, 4d^{10}$ $5s^2, 5p^3$	$1s^2$ $2s^2, 2p^6$ $3s^2, 3p^6, 3d^{10}$ $4s^2, 4p^6, 4d^{10}, 4f^{14}$ $5s^2, 5p^6, 5d^{10}$ $6s^2, 6p^3$
atomic (covalent) radius (Å)	0.70	1.10	1.21	1.41	1.46
first ionization potential (ev)	14.45	10.55	9.81	8.64	8.30
electro-negativity	3.0	2.1	2.0	1.9	1.9
oxidation states	all states from -3 to $+5$	$-3, -2,$ $+1, +3,$ $+4, +5$	$-3,$ $+3, +5$	$-3,$ $+3, +5$	$-3,$ $+3, +5$

24.2 Trends in the general properties

Each member of the nitrogen family possesses five valence electrons: two *s* electrons and three *p* electrons. Since the ionization potentials of nitrogen and phosphorus are relatively high, these elements do not form positively charged ions. Although the members of the nitrogen family do not normally lose their five valence electrons in chemical changes, antimony and bismuth can lose their three *p* valence electrons to form Sb^{+3} and Bi^{+3} ions. This illustrates the tendency of the Group VA elements to become more metallic with increasing atomic number. The shielding effect of the inner electron shells leads to an increasing tendency to lose electrons, as shown by decreasing ionization energy values. With the very reactive elements of the alkali metal family, nitrogen and phosphorus may form a triply charged negative ion: N^{-3} (nitride ion) and P^{-3} (phosphide ion).

The tendency of nitrogen and phosphorus to form -3 ions is considerably weaker than the tendency of the halogens to form -1 ions. The elements in a given row of the Periodic Table show different abilities to attract electrons and to form negative ions. This attraction depends on the nuclear charge of the atom. The members of the nitrogen family have lower nuclear charges than the corresponding members of the oxygen or the halogen families. The elements in the nitrogen family therefore do not attract electrons as readily as the corresponding oxygen or halogen families. This observation is borne out by a study of the electronegativity values.

With the exception of the nitrides (for example, AlN) and the phosphides (for example, K_3P), the members of the nitrogen family attain the noble gas structure by forming covalent bonds. The members of the nitrogen family form polyatomic oxygen ions, such as NO_3^- and PO_4^{-3} (phosphate ion). The bonding within the ions, however, is covalent. As described in section 24.9, one possible representation of nitrate ion is

$$\left[\ddot{\underset{\cdot\cdot}{O}} \!:\! \ddot{N} \begin{matrix} \ddot{\ddot{O}}: \\ \ddot{\underset{\cdot\cdot}{O}}: \end{matrix} \right]^{-}$$

Nitrogen and phosphorus, as typical nonmetals, form acidic oxides; arsenic and antimony form amphoteric oxides; and metallic bismuth forms a basic oxide.

ACIDIC OXIDES $N_2O_5 + H_2O \rightarrow 2\ HNO_3$

$P_2O_5 + 3\ H_2O \rightarrow 2\ H_3PO_4$

AMPHOTERIC OXIDES $Sb_4O_6 + 12\ HCl \rightarrow 4\ SbCl_3 + 6\ H_2O$

$Sb_4O_6 + 4\ NaOH \rightarrow 4\ NaSbO_2 + 2\ H_2O$

BASIC OXIDE $Bi_2O_3 + 3\ H_2O \rightarrow 2\ Bi(OH)_3$

24.3 The nitrogen molecule

The nitrogen molecule is diatomic and can be represented by an electron-dot formula as

$$: N ::: N :$$

Note the three pairs of shared electrons that constitute a triple bond. The other two pairs of electrons that do not contribute to the triple bond are called *nonbonding electrons*.

24.4 Preparation of nitrogen

Air contains about 78% by volume of nitrogen. The remainder is largely oxygen with small quantities of carbon dioxide, water vapor, and noble gases. Commercially, nitrogen is prepared from liquid air from which the components distill at different temperatures. Nitrogen has a lower boiling point ($-195.8°$ C) than oxygen ($-183°$ C) and distills off first.

In the laboratory, nitrogen is prepared by the decomposition of ammonium nitrite, NH_4NO_2.

$$NH_4NO_2\ (s) \rightarrow N_2\ (g) + 2\ H_2O\ (g)$$

Nitrogen prepared in this manner is always less dense than nitrogen prepared from the atmosphere. This observation, made by Sir William Ramsey and Lord Rayleigh in 1894, led to the suggestion that nitrogen prepared from the atmosphere contained some residual gas to account for its increased density. This residual gas was identified as argon and marked the beginning of the discovery of many other noble gases.

24.5 Properties and uses of nitrogen

Nitrogen is a colorless and odorless gas. The reaction $N_2 \rightarrow 2\ N$ requires 225.2 kcal/mole, which means that molecular nitrogen is very stable.

Thus molecular nitrogen, because of the stability of its bonds, is generally unreactive. With very reactive metals, such as lithium or aluminum, nitrogen forms nitrides that are ionic solids.

$$6 \text{ Li } (s) + N_2 \ (g) \rightarrow 2 \text{ Li}_3N \ (s)$$

$$2 \text{ Al } (s) + N_2 \ (g) \rightarrow 2 \text{ AlN } (s)$$

Nitrogen forms a series of oxides that have the characteristic oxidation numbers shown in the following table.

OXIDE OF N	NAME	OXIDATION NUMBER OF N
N_2O	nitrous oxide (dinitrogen monoxide)	$+1$
NO	nitric oxide	$+2$
N_2O_3	dinitrogen trioxide	$+3$
NO_2	nitrogen dioxide	$+4$
N_2O_4	dinitrogen tetroxide	$+4$
N_2O_5	dinitrogen pentoxide	$+5$

N_2O_3 dissolves in water to form HNO_2, nitrous acid; therefore, N_2O_3 is the anhydride of nitrous acid.

$$N_2O_3 + H_2O \rightarrow 2 \text{ HNO}_2$$

Similarly, N_2O_5 is the anhydride of nitric acid.

$$N_2O_5 + H_2O \rightarrow 2 \text{ HNO}_3$$

Nitrogen serves to dilute the oxygen of the atmosphere. Nitrogen is used in the manufacture of ammonia and in the case-hardening of steel. Nitrogen compounds are used in fertilizers to supply the nitrogen necessary for plant proteins. These nitrogen compounds are formed from the nitrogen of the air. The conversion of atmospheric nitrogen into useful compounds is called *nitrogen-fixation*.

24.6 Ammonia

Ammonia is a compound of nitrogen and hydrogen and can be represented by an electron-dot formula as

$$H \! : \! \overset{\displaystyle ..}{\underset{\displaystyle ..}{N}} \! : \! H$$
$$H$$

The bonding in NH_3 is p^3. The shape of the gaseous molecule is pyramidal (a pyramid with a three-sided base), shown in Figure 24-1.

Fig. 24-1 The shape of the gaseous NH₃ molecule

24.7 Preparation of ammonia

Ammonia, NH_3, is prepared commercially by several processes, including the Haber process, the heating of soft coal, and the Cyanamide process. A description of these processes follows:

1. The Haber process. Nitrogen gas and hydrogen gas react at approximately 500° C and 600 atmospheres pressure in the presence of a catalyst composed of oxides of iron and aluminum.

$$N_2 \ (g) + 3 \ H_2 \ (g) \rightleftarrows 2 \ NH_3 \ (g) + 22 \ \text{kcal}$$

   Under these conditions, the conversion of reactants to ammonia is about 50%. These conditions are obtained by applying Le Chatelier's Principle, described in section 14.12. The Haber process is an example of nitrogen-fixation.

2. Heating soft coal in the absence of air (destructive distillation). This process also produces coal gas, coke, and coal tar. The fractional distillation of coal tar yields phenol, benzene, and toluene — important raw materials used to prepare dyes and drugs. (*Fractional distillation* is the boiling off of the components of a mixture followed by condensation of the components at their individual boiling points.)

3. The Cyanamide process. In this process of nitrogen-fixation, gaseous nitrogen is passed over calcium carbide at a temperature of about 1000° C to form calcium cyanamide.

$$CaO + 3 \ C \rightarrow CaC_2 + CO$$
$$\text{calcium carbide}$$

$$CaC_2 + N_2 \rightarrow CaCN_2 + C$$
$$\text{calcium cyanamide}$$

$$CaCN_2 + 3 \ H_2O \rightarrow CaCO_3 + 2 \ NH_3 \ (g)$$

In the laboratory, ammonia is prepared by the reaction between NH_4^+ ions and OH^- ions. (In the reaction, all ions are aquated.)

$$NH_4^+ + OH^- \rightarrow NH_3 \ (g) + H_2O$$

$$2 \ NH_4Cl + Ca(OH)_2 \rightarrow CaCl_2 + 2 \ H_2O + 2 \ NH_3 \ (g)$$

Since ammonia is extremely soluble in water, it is collected by air displacement (see Figure 24-2).

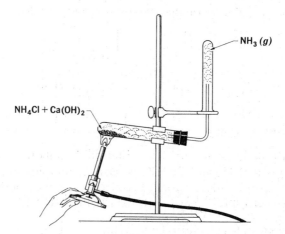

Fig. 24-2   The preparation and collection of ammonia

The reaction for the formation of ammonia is useful in detecting ammonium ion. The addition of base to an ammonium compound yields the characteristic odor of ammonia.

24.8 Properties and uses of ammonia

Ammonia is a gas that has an easily recognized, pungent odor. Ammonia and water are both polar molecules; hence, ammonia is extremely soluble in water. The solution of ammonia in water is called ammonia water. It is a weak base that furnishes aqueous NH_4^+ ions and aqueous OH^- ions.

$$NH_3 \ (g) + H_2O \rightarrow NH_4^+ \ (aq) + OH^- \ (aq)$$

Many of the properties of NH_3 can be better understood by emphasizing the similarities between the NH_3 molecule and the H_2O molecule, as shown by the electron-dot formulas on the following page:

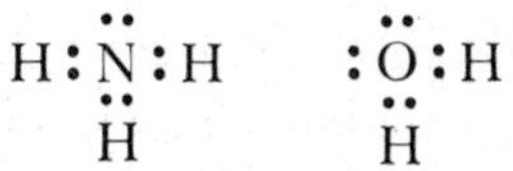

$$\overset{\cdot\cdot}{H:N:H} \qquad :\overset{\cdot\cdot}{O}:H$$
$$H \qquad H$$

Note the presence of at least one unbonded pair of electrons in each molecule, which creates a region in the molecule with a negative charge. The negative region allows additional bonding capacity with other particles such as protons.

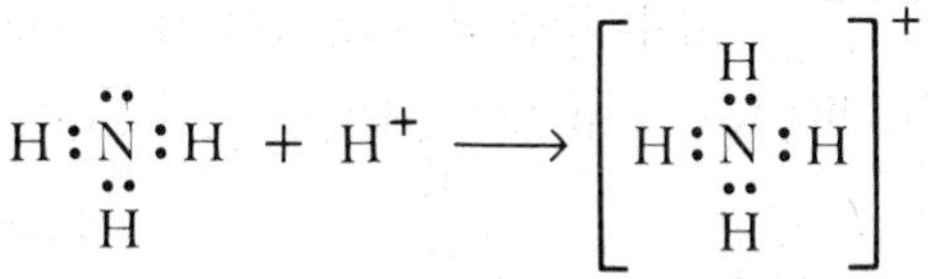

$$\overset{\cdot\cdot}{H:N:H} + H^+ \longrightarrow \left[\begin{array}{c} H \\ \overset{\cdot\cdot}{H:N:H} \\ H \end{array} \right]^+$$

ammonium ion

$$:\overset{\cdot\cdot}{O}:H + H^+ \longrightarrow \left[H:\overset{\cdot\cdot}{O}:H \right]^+$$

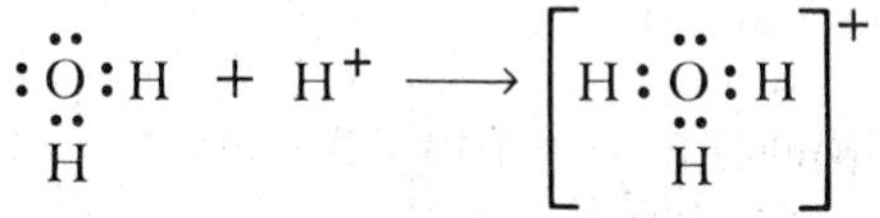

hydronium ion

We also indicated, in section 23.4, that this nonbonded (unshared) pair of electrons in NH_3 and in H_2O is used in complex ion formation.

In addition to accepting protons (behaving as bases), both NH_3 and H_2O can donate protons (behave as acids). Thus both NH_3 and H_2O are amphiprotic.

	AMMONIA	WATER
AS AN ACID	$NH_3 \rightarrow H^+ + NH_2^-$ amide	$H_2O \rightarrow H^+ + OH^-$
AS A BASE	$NH_3 + H^+ \rightarrow NH_4^+$	$H_2O + H^+ \rightarrow H_3O^+$

Just as water reacts with active metals at room temperature to form hydrogen and a base, liquid ammonia reacts with the same metals to form hydrogen and an amide. Thus amides are the nitrogen analogs of bases. If the formula of ammonia is written as HNH_2, the relationship to H_2O becomes even more apparent.

$$2\ H_2O + 2\ K\ (s) \rightarrow H_2\ (g) + 2\ KOH\ (aq)$$

$$2\ \underset{\text{ammonia}}{HNH_2}\ (l) + 2\ K\ (s) \rightarrow H_2\ (g) + 2\ \underset{\substack{\text{potassium} \\ \text{amide}}}{KNH_2}\ (NH_3)$$

At higher temperatures, both gaseous ammonia and water (steam) react with metals analogously.

$$3\ Mg + 2\ NH_3 \rightarrow Mg_3N_2 + 3\ H_2$$

$$3\ Fe + 4\ H_2O \rightarrow Fe_3O_4 + 4\ H_2$$

Ammonia may be catalytically oxidized by oxygen.

$$4\ NH_3 + 5\ O_2 \rightarrow 4\ NO + 6\ H_2O$$

We shall return to this reaction later because it is an important process for manufacturing nitric acid, HNO_3, from NH_3.

Most of the ammonia produced commercially is converted into useful ammonium compounds and into nitric acid. Ammonia liquefies easily and is used as a refrigerant. As a base, ammonia dissolves grease. Since ammonia also evaporates readily, ammonia water is a commonly used cleanser.

24.9 Nitric acid

The electron-dot formula for nitric acid, HNO_3, may be represented by two equivalent structures (resonance forms).

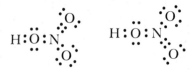

In each suggested structure, the bonding of one oxygen atom is different from the other two. However, all the properties of nitric acid indicate that the three oxygen atoms are bonded in a like manner. The actual electronic structure of nitric acid is some combination of the two structures depicted – a phenomenon called *resonance*. An extended discussion of resonance is beyond the scope of this book.

24.10 Preparation of nitric acid

Nitric acid is prepared commercially by the Ostwald process. Ammonia from the Haber process is catalytically oxidized to form an oxide of nitrogen which is, in turn, converted into nitric acid.

(1) $4\ NH_3\ (g) + 5\ O_2\ (g) \rightarrow 4\ NO\ (g) + 6\ H_2O$

(2) $2\ NO\ (g) + O_2\ (g) \rightarrow 2\ NO_2\ (g)$

(3) $3\ NO_2\ (g) + H_2O \rightarrow 2\ HNO_3 + NO\ (g)$

The NO is recycled and returned to step 2.

Nitric acid may also be prepared commercially and in the laboratory by the reaction between nitrate ion (from $NaNO_3$) and concentrated sulfuric acid, H_2SO_4. (See Figure 24-3.)

$$NaNO_3 + H_2SO_4 \rightarrow HNO_3 \ (g) + NaHSO_4$$

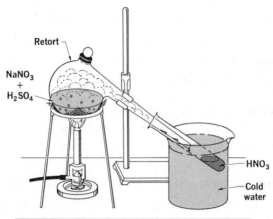

Fig. 24–3 *The preparation and collection of nitric acid*

Sodium nitrate (Chile saltpeter) represents the only important and abundant natural source of nitrates. H_2SO_4 is preferred over other acids to supply H_3O^+ ion because H_2SO_4 has a relatively high boiling point. The reactants must be heated to form HNO_3, which is more volatile than H_2SO_4 (boiling point of $HNO_3 = 83°$ C). The HNO_3 is separated from the other substances by distillation in a glass vessel called a *retort*.

24.11 Properties and uses of nitric acid

Pure nitric acid is a colorless liquid, soluble in water. It decomposes on heating or on exposure to light to form colored oxides of nitrogen. The decomposition reaction is

$$4 \ HNO_3 \rightarrow 4 \ NO_2 \ (g) + O_2 \ (g) + 2 \ H_2O$$

The properties of a nitric acid solution are based on H^+ (*aq*) ions and NO_3^- (*aq*) ions contained in the solution.

$$H^+ \ (aq) \ \text{IONS}$$

Nitric acid, a strong acid, turns litmus red and donates protons to bases.

$$H^+ \ (aq) + NO_3^- \ (aq) + K^+ \ (aq) + OH^- \ (aq) \rightarrow H_2O + NO_3^- \ (aq) + K^+ \ (aq)$$

In dilute solutions of HNO_3, the H^+ (aq) ions may be reduced by active metals to form hydrogen.

$$Mg + 2\ HNO_3 \rightarrow Mg(NO_3)_2 + H_2\ (g)$$
$$\text{dilute}$$

This reaction demonstrates that HNO_3 behaves as an oxidizing agent because of the presence of reducible H^+ (aq) ions.

NO_3^- (aq) IONS

The table of E^0 values (see page 329) reveals that 1 M NO_3^- (aq) ions are more easily reduced than 1 M H^+ (aq) ions. This means that HNO_3 can behave as an oxidizing agent because of the presence of reducible NO_3^- (aq) ions. In reacting with metals, NO_3^- (aq) ions are reduced to a variety of oxides of nitrogen. The extent of reduction of NO_3^- (aq) ions (oxidizing strength) depends largely on the concentration of the acid and the strength of the reducing agent. As the concentration of the acid decreases and as the strength of the reducing agent increases, the change in the oxidation state of N in HNO_3 becomes greater. In the following reactions of HNO_3 with metals, all ions are aquated.

$$4\ Zn\ (s) + 10\ \overset{+5}{HNO_3} \rightarrow 4\ Zn(NO_3)_2 + 3\ H_2O + \overset{-3}{NH_4NO_3}$$
$$\text{dilute}$$

OXIDATION $\qquad\qquad 4[Zn\ (s) \rightarrow Zn^{+2} + 2\ e^-]$

REDUCTION $\quad NO_3^-\ (aq) + 10\ H^+ + 8\ e^- \rightarrow NH_4^+ + 3\ H_2O$

$$3\ Cu\ (s) + 8\ \overset{+5}{HNO_3} \rightarrow 3\ Cu(NO_3)_2 + 4\ H_2O + 2\ \overset{+2}{NO}\ (g)$$
$$\text{dilute}$$

OXIDATION $\qquad\qquad 3[Cu\ (s) \rightarrow Cu^{+2} + 2\ e^-]$

REDUCTION $\quad 2[NO_3^-\ (aq) + 4\ H^+ + 3\ e^- \rightarrow NO + 2\ H_2O]$

$$Cu\ (s) + 4\ \overset{+5}{HNO_3} \rightarrow Cu(NO_3)_2 + 2\ H_2O + 2\ \overset{+4}{NO_2}\ (g)$$
$$\text{conc.}$$

OXIDATION $$Cu\ (s) \rightarrow Cu^{+2} + 2\ e^{-}$$

REDUCTION $$2[NO_3^-\ (aq) + 2\ H^+ + e^- \rightarrow NO_2 + H_2O]$$

The E^0 values of all the metals except gold and platinum are above the E^0 value for the reduction of NO_3^- (aq) ions. Nitric acid will therefore oxidize all metals except gold and platinum.

Nitric acid oxidizes concentrated hydrochloric acid to form nitrosyl chloride, which is an even more potent oxidizer than nitric acid.

$$3\ HCl + HNO_3 \rightarrow Cl_2 + 2\ H_2O + NOCl$$
nitrosyl
chloride

A mixture of three parts concentrated hydrochloric acid and one part concentrated nitric acid, called *aqua regia*, dissolves gold and platinum. In the presence of hydrochloric acid, the reducing power of gold and platinum is sufficiently increased (by forming complex ions with Cl^-) to reduce NO_3^- (aq) ions (see section 23.9).

Nitric acid engages in a series of reactions called *nitration reactions*. For example, glycerine, $C_3H_5(OH)_3$, reacts with HNO_3 to form glyceryl trinitrate (nitroglycerine), a highly explosive substance.

$$C_3H_5(OH)_3 + 3\ HNO_3 \rightarrow 3\ H_2O + C_3H_5(NO_3)_3$$

The addition of ferrous sulfate, $FeSO_4$, and concentrated H_2SO_4 to NO_3^- ion produces a brown ring. The brown color is due to the presence of nitrosyl iron(II) sulfate, $Fe(NO)SO_4$, and serves as a test for NO_3^- ion.

Nitric acid is used in the manufacture of explosives, fertilizers, and many metallic nitrates such as silver nitrate (an important photographic chemical). Nitric acid is also used in the preparation of countless dyes and drugs.

24.12 The phosphorus molecule

Molecular weight determinations indicate that below 800° C the phosphorus molecule has the formula P_4. Structurally, the phosphorus atoms are located at the corners of a regular tetrahedron and are bonded to one another by single covalent bonds. To account for all the valence electrons (20), each phosphorus atom has one pair of nonbonded (unshared) electrons. (See Figure 24-4 on the following page.)

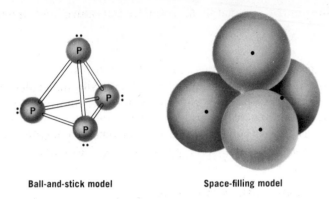

Ball-and-stick model   **Space-filling model**

Fig. 24–4   The P₄ molecule

24.13 Preparation of phosphorus

Phosphorus is prepared from rock phosphate, $Ca_3(PO_4)_2$, by reduction with coke (carbon) in the presence of sand, SiO_2, at high temperatures.

$$Ca_3(PO_4)_2 + 3\ SiO_2 + 5\ C \rightarrow 3\ CaSiO_3 + 5\ CO\ (g) + P_2\ (g)$$

At the high temperatures of the reaction, the phosphorus is vaporized and subsequently condensed.

24.14 Properties and uses of phosphorus

Gaseous phosphorus above 800° C, like gaseous nitrogen, forms a diatomic molecule in which the atoms are linked by a triple bond. As with nitrogen, note the presence of two pairs of unbonded electrons.

$$: P ::: P :$$

Like sulfur, solid phosphorus exists in several different forms. Chief among these are white phosphorus (also called yellow phosphorus) and red phosphorus. If white phosphorus is heated to about 250° C in the absence of air, red phosphorus is formed

white phosphorus → red phosphorus $\Delta H = -17$ kcal

Since the transformation is exothermic, red phosphorus is more stable than the white variety.

White phosphorus consists of individual P_4 molecules bonded by van der Waals forces. Red phosphorus consists of chains of linked P_4 molecules covalently bonded in a giant molecule. These structural differences account for the differences in the properties of the two varieties of phosphorus.

White phosphorus is volatile at room temperature and ignites spontaneously.

$$P_4 + 5\ O_2 \rightarrow P_4O_{10}$$

tetraphosphorus
decoxide

Because red phosphorus contains tightly bonded P_4 molecules, it is much less volatile and much less reactive than white phosphorus, which contains weakly bonded P_4 molecules.

Phosphorus is used largely in the manufacture of phosphate fertilizers, organic phosphates, and matches. It is also used to make special bronze alloys.

24.15 Phosphorus analogs of nitrogen

A complete discussion of the compounds of phosphorus lies beyond the scope of this book. For the most part, we will limit our study to the phosphorus analogs of nitrogen.

Phosphorus forms phosphine, PH_3, a hydrogen compound analogous to ammonia. PH_3 can accept a proton to form PH_4^+ (phosphonium ion). Like nitrogen, phosphorus also forms covalently bonded binary halogen compounds. Although nitrogen forms only NCl_3, phosphorus forms PCl_3 and PCl_5.

In PCl_5, phosphorus utilizes all of its five valence electrons, which means that ten electrons are involved in the five covalent bonds that are present. Although s and p orbitals are most frequently used in bonding, and account for a maximum of eight valence electrons, d orbitals in some cases may also be used. Thus in phosphorus, $3d$ orbitals are available for bonding to form PCl_5. The absence of d orbitals in nitrogen does not permit the formation of the analogous NCl_5.

24.16 Acids of phosphorus

Phosphorus forms a series of oxides that are acid anhydrides similar to the nitrogen oxide acid anhydrides. The most common oxide of phosphorus is tetraphosphorus decoxide, P_4O_{10}, the anhydride of phosphoric acid.

$$P_4O_{10} + 6\ H_2O \rightarrow 4\ H_3PO_4$$

Since phosphorus forms a number of phosphoric acids, H_3PO_4 is more properly called orthophosphoric acid. The removal of one molecule of water from H_3PO_4 forms HPO_3, metaphosphoric acid. The removal of one molecule of water from two molecules of H_3PO_4 forms $H_4P_2O_7$, pyrophosphoric acid.

506   *Fundamental Concepts of Modern Chemistry*

Orthophosphoric acid is a triprotic acid. It ionizes in three stages; the primary ionization is the strongest. (In the reactions that follow, all ions are aquated.)

$$H_3PO_4 \rightleftarrows H^+ + H_2PO_4^-$$

$$H_2PO_4^- \rightleftarrows H^+ + HPO_4^{-2}$$

$$HPO_4^{-2} \rightleftarrows H^+ + PO_4^{-3}$$

Thus, like sulfuric acid, which forms two types of salts, orthophosphoric acid forms three types of salts. Each of the three salts reacts (hydrolyzes) differently with water and thus has a different effect on indicators. Na_3PO_4 is strongly basic, Na_2HPO_4 is less basic, and NaH_2PO_4 is acid. This difference in behavior may be explained as follows:

1. PO_4^{-3} cannot donate protons but can only accept protons.

$$PO_4^{-3} + H^+ \rightarrow HPO_4^{-2}$$

   In an Na_3PO_4 solution, PO_4^{-3} ions accept protons from water and release OH^- ions.

2. HPO_4^{-2} can either donate protons or accept protons (amphiprotic). However, the reaction $HPO_4^{-2} + H^+ \rightarrow H_2PO_4^-$ has a greater tendency to proceed than the reaction $HPO_4^{-2} \rightarrow H^+ + PO_4^{-3}$. This means that HPO_4^{-2} is a stronger proton acceptor than donor. A solution of Na_2HPO_4 is therefore basic because HPO_4^{-2} accepts protons from water, releasing OH^- ions.

3. $H_2PO_4^-$ is also amphiprotic. The reaction $H_2PO_4^- \rightarrow H^+ + HPO_4^{-2}$ has a greater tendency to proceed than the reaction $H_2PO_4^- + H^+ \rightarrow H_3PO_4$. This means that $H_2PO_4^-$ is a stronger proton donor than acceptor. Thus a solution of NaH_2PO_4 is acidic.

24.17 Arsenic, antimony, and bismuth

Of this trio of elements, arsenic is the most nonmetallic, while bismuth is the most metallic. The term *metalloid* is used to characterize elements with properties that lie between the nonmetallic and the metallic. Thus arsenic, antimony, and bismuth are metalloids. Their analogous compounds often behave differently. For example, arsenic forms an acidic oxide, antimony forms an amphoteric oxide, and bismuth forms a basic oxide.

All three elements are poor conductors of electricity. They are also much less reactive than phosphorus. Since the E^0 values for the reaction X (s) $\rightarrow$ X^{+3} $(aq) + 3\ e^-$ are all negative for arsenic, antimony, and bismuth, these elements do not react with hydrochloric acid to form hydrogen. Instead, they may be oxidized to the $+3$ or $+5$ state, forming polyatomic oxygen ions, such as AsO_3^{-3} or AsO_4^{-3}.

24.18 Uses of arsenic, antimony, and bismuth

Arsenic is alloyed with lead in the manufacture of lead shot. Arsenates, AsO_4^{-3}, are used as insecticides. Since these compounds are poisonous, it is necessary to wash any food in contact with such an insecticide spray.

Antimony is alloyed with lead and tin to form type metal. This is an unusual solid which *expands* on solidifying, thus insuring sharp impressions. Antimony compounds are used on certain fabrics to permit them to be dyed.

Bismuth is used in the preparation of low-melting alloys in automatic fire extinguishers. Bismuth compounds are used as medicinals.

Multiple-Choice Questions

1. Which of the following is *not* correct? Nitrogen and bismuth (1) have the same number of electrons in their valence shells (2) are in the same column in the Periodic Table (3) have the same positive oxidation numbers (4) differ in their metallic properties

2. The Group V elements can form the following pairs of ions *except* (1) Sb^{-3}, Bi^{-3} (2) AsO_4^{-3}, PO_4^{-3} (3) N^{-3}, P^{-3} (4) AsO_3^{-3}, PO_3^{-3}

3. A nitrogen molecule (1) is polar (2) contains three pairs of shared electrons (3) is unstable (4) is very soluble in water

4. When nitrogen and lithium combine (1) a covalent bond is broken and an ionic bond forms (2) nitrogen is oxidized (3) a gaseous product forms (4) a covalent compound forms

5. Nitrogen fixation refers to the (1) decomposition of nitrogen compounds (2) formation of nitrogen atoms (3) liquefaction of nitrogen (4) conversion of atmospheric nitrogen to useful nitrogen compounds

6. In the reaction of ammonia with water (1) water acts as a base (2) both compounds remain nonpolar (3) ammonia is a proton acceptor (4) nitrogen is formed

7. When potassium reacts with liquid ammonia, one product is (1) N_2 (2) KNH_2 (3) KH (4) KOH

8. Chile saltpeter is a naturally occurring form of (1) NH_4NO_3 (2) $NaHSO_4$ (3) $NaNO_3$ (4) KCl

9. In the reaction of Zn with dilute HNO_3, which is the correct reduction half-reaction?
   (1) $NO_3^- + 2 H^+ + e^- \rightarrow NO_2 + H_2O$
   (2) $2 NO_3^- \rightarrow 2 NO_2 + O_2 + 2 e^-$
   (3) $NO_3^- + 10 H^+ + 8 e^- \rightarrow NH_4^+ + 3 H_2O$
   (4) $NO_3^- \rightarrow NO + O_2 + e^-$

10. The formula for the phosphorus molecule is P_4 because (1) all nonmetals have four atoms in the molecule (2) the molecular weight is found to be four times the atomic weight (3) phosphorus has four valence electrons (4) phosphorus has four allotropic forms

11. A particle that can act only as a base is (1) H_3PO_4 (2) HPO_4^{-2} (3) PO_4^{-3} (4) HPO_3

Completion Questions

1. H_3PO_4 is called a triprotic acid because each mole of H_3PO_4 can release _____ moles of protons.

2. The white and red forms of phosphorus are called the _____ forms of phosphorus.

3. Molecules of phosphorus have a tetrahedral shape in which each P atom is bonded to _____ neighboring atoms.

4. A commercial process for converting ammonia to nitric acid is called the _____ process.

5. In the reaction $NH_3 \rightarrow NH_2^- + H^+$, the ammonia acts as a (an) _____.

6. When a strong base is added to an unknown salt and the odor of ammonia is detected, the salt contains _____ ion.

7. Dinitrogen trioxide is the anhydride of _____ acid.

8. The compound of nitrogen with oxygen in which nitrogen has an oxidation state of $+1$ has the formula _____.

9. The phosphorus analog of HNO_3 is _____.

10. The antimony analog of NH_3 is _____.

True-False Questions

1. The change $P_4 \rightarrow 2 P_2$ probably takes place when the phosphorus changes from the *liquid to the solid* state.

2. In the reaction of magnesium with dilute nitric acid producing hydrogen, the oxidizer is *H_3O^+*.

3. Sulfuric acid is used in the preparation of nitric acid because the boiling point of sulfuric acid is *higher than* the boiling point of nitric acid.

4. *Water and ammonia* are both able to accept a proton because their molecules contain one or more pairs of nonbonded electrons.

5. The highest oxidation state for nitrogen is found in *dinitrogen trioxide*.

6. Large amounts of nitrogen are produced commercially by *decomposing ammonium nitrite*.

7. Group VA elements are *less* electronegative than the halogen element in the same row.

8. The oxidation states of nitrogen extend from −5 to +3.

9. A solution of Na_2HPO_4 is *more* alkaline than a solution of NaH_2PO_4.

10. The formula of the oxidation product in the reaction between gold and aqua regia is *NO*.

Decreases, Increases, Remains the Same

1. In the Group VA elements from nitrogen to bismuth, the acidic behavior of the oxides _____.

2. From H_3PO_4 to $H_2PO_4^-$ to HPO_4^{-2}, the ability to donate protons _____.

3. When PH_3 is changed to PH_4^+, the oxidation state of P _____.

4. As the atomic radii of the Group VA elements increase, the electronegativity values _____.

5. As more arsenic is added to lead to make lead shot, the hardness of the alloy _____.

6. As the temperature is increased in the reaction of nitrogen with hydrogen the percent of nitrogen that combines with hydrogen _____.

7. In the reaction of nitrogen with hydrogen to form ammonia, when a catalyst is added, the amount of ammonia in equilibrium with nitrogen and hydrogen _____.

8. As the concentration of nitric acid is increased in the reaction of zinc with nitric acid, the extent of reduction of nitrogen _____.

9. As the concentration of nitric acid is decreased in the reaction of zinc with nitric acid, the number of electrons released by zinc atoms _____.

10. As an ammonium compound is made more basic, the rate at which ammonia gas is released _____.

510 Fundamental Concepts of Modern Chemistry

Exercises for Review

1. *a.* How do the electronegativity values of the Group VA elements change with increasing atomic numbers?

    b. Explain why this change takes place.

2. *a.* List all the oxidation states shown by nitrogen in its compounds.

    b. Write the formula and name of a nitrogen compound for each oxidation state.

3. *a.* Write a formula for a binary compound of nitrogen and a formula for a binary compound of phosphorus where these elements exist as ions.

    b. Write a formula for a binary compound of antimony and a formula for a binary compound of bismuth where these elements exist as ions.

    c. State an important difference between these two groups of compounds.

4. *a.* List the oxides of nitrogen that are acid anhydrides.

    b. Write equations to show how each one reacts with water.

    c. Name the acid formed in each case.

5. Describe some similarities in the properties of NH_3 and H_2O.

6. Write equations for:

    a. the reaction of dinitrogen trioxide with water

    b. the formation of ammonia by the Haber process

    c. the reaction of sodium with nitrogen

    d. the reaction of ammonium chloride with sodium hydroxide

    e. the oxidation of ammonia by oxygen in the presence of a catalyst

7. Write equations for:

    a. the reaction of ammonia with water, forming ions

    b. the reaction of ammonia with hydrogen chloride, forming ions

    c. the reaction of the anhydride of nitric acid with water

    d. the reaction of the anhydride of phosphoric acid with water

8. *a.* What is the effect of increasing the temperature on the formation of ammonia produced by the reaction between nitrogen and hydrogen?

    b. What is the effect of increasing the pressure on this reaction?

9. Why is red phosphorus more stable and less reactive than white phosphorus?

10. Nitrogen can form a pentoxide but not a pentachloride. Explain.

Exercises for Further Study

1. Show how the oxides of nitrogen obey the Law of Multiple Proportions.
2. Explain, in terms of the electron structure of the atoms, why antimony and bismuth form ions with a +3 charge but do not form +5 ions.
3. Both oxygen and nitrogen are abundant elements in the atmosphere. How can we explain the fact that they do not combine to any great extent?
4. Describe all the bond-breaking and bond-making changes that take place in the Haber process.
5. How did the discovery that the density of nitrogen obtained by decomposing nitrogen compounds differs from the density of nitrogen obtained from air lead to the discovery of the noble gases?
6. Show how ammonium nitrate can be produced, starting with air and water.
7. Gaseous ammonia and gaseous hydrogen chloride are covalent compounds. Explain the changes that occur in the bonds when the two gases combine.
8. With the aid of equations, show the similarity in the reactions of metals with water and in the reaction of the same metals with liquid ammonia.
9. For each of the following, write the oxidation and the reduction half-reactions, showing the ions involved. Balance the complete reaction.
    a. $Ag + HNO_3 \rightarrow AgNO_3 + NO_2 + H_2O$
    b. $Mg + HNO_3 \rightarrow Mg(NO_3)_2 + NH_4NO_3 + H_2O$
    c. $H_2S + HNO_3 \rightarrow S + NO + H_2O$
    d. $FeSO_4 + HNO_3 \rightarrow Fe_2(SO_4)_3 + NO + H_2O$
10. Explain how ammonia can behave as an acid and also as a base. Use an equation to illustrate each reaction.
11. Draw electron-dot diagrams for (a) NH_3 (b) NH_4^+ (c) HNO_3 (d) $NaNO_3$
12. Explain why both nitrogen and phosphorus form trichlorides (NCl_3, PCl_3) but only phosphorus forms the pentachloride (PCl_5).
13. Write the electron-dot formulas for phosphor*ous* acid, metaphosphoric acid, pyrophosphoric acid, and orthophosphoric acid.

Chapter 25

THE OXYGEN FAMILY

25.1 Introduction

In Chapter 7, we described the members of the oxygen family. At that time, we developed qualitative relationships between this family and the halogens as an introduction to the Periodic Table. Now, having extended our atomic model, we return to the oxygen family to relate the properties of these elements to their electronic structures.

PROPERTY	OXYGEN	SULFUR	SELENIUM	TELLURIUM
atomic number	8	16	34	52
electron structure	$1s^2$ $2s^2, 2p^4$	$1s^2$ $2s^2, 2p^6$ $3s^2, 3p^4$	$1s^2$ $2s^2, 2p^6$ $3s^2, 3p^6, 3d^{10}$ $4s^2, 4p^4$	$1s^2$ $2s^2, 2p^6$ $3s^2, 3p^6, 3d^{10}$ $4s^2, 4p^6, 4d^{10}$ $5s^2, 5p^4$
atomic (covalent) radius (Å)	0.66	1.04	1.17	1.37
first ionization potential (ev)	13.61	10.36	9.75	9.01
electro-negativity	3.5	2.5	2.4	2.1
oxidation states	$-2, -1,$ $+1, +2$	$-2,$ $+4, +6$	$-2,$ $+4, +6$	$-2,$ $+4, +6$
E^0 (volts) $Z^{-2} (aq) \rightarrow$ $Z^0 + 2 \, e^-$	-1.23	-0.14	$+0.40$	$+0.72$

The table on the preceding page lists some of the important properties of the oxygen family: oxygen, sulfur, selenium, and tellurium. We will omit polonium, a radioactive element, from this discussion.

25.2 Trends in the general properties

All the elements in the oxygen family have six valence electrons. The size of each atom, expressed by its covalent radius, grows larger with increasing atomic number, indicating an increasing number of electron shells. As in the Group VA elements, the shielding effect of inner electron shells permits electrons to be lost more readily as the covalent radius increases. The ionization potentials therefore decrease with increasing atomic number. The ionization potentials are generally too high to permit the formation of a +6 ion (except polonium and tellurium). Consequently, with increasing atomic number, the nonmetallic properties of the oxygen elements decrease and the metallic properties increase. Again, we see the same trend as in Group VA.

The common oxidation states for the members of Group VIA, except oxygen, are -2, $+4$, and $+6$. For oxygen, the common oxidation state is -2. To attain the oxidation state of -2 and to complete their valence shells, the elements in Group VIA (indicated by Z_2 or Z) can react with hydrogen, carbon, phosphorus, other nonmetals, and metals.

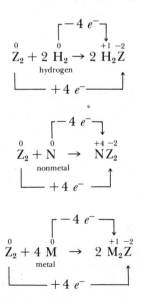

The compound H_2Z increases in reducing power from H_2O to H_2Te. Note that E^0 for $Te^{-2} \rightarrow Te^0 + 2\ e^-$ equals $+0.72$ volt, slightly less than E^0 for $Zn \rightarrow Zn^{+2} + 2\ e^-$, which is $+0.76$ volt. Thus Te^{-2} is almost as good a reducing agent as the common metal Zn in aqueous medium.

If metal M is sodium, potassium, or calcium, then M_2Z or MZ is an ionic compound containing positive M ions and negative Z^{-2} ions. The formation of a doubly charged negative ion, such as Z^{-2}, is an *endothermic* change. The formation of a singly charged negative ion, such as a halide ion, is an *exothermic* change. Apparently, the acquisition of the additional electron requires sufficient energy to overcome the repulsion between the two electrons. However, the reaction for the formation of Na_2O, for example, is spontaneous; the net ΔH is negative. As explained in section 20.13, the formation of a crystalline solid releases considerable energy favoring the stability of the crystal.

25.3 Electronegativity

The electronegativity values of the members of the family decrease with increasing nuclear charge. Sulfur, selenium, and tellurium exhibit positive oxidation states in forming covalently bonded, negatively charged, polyatomic ions, especially with oxygen. For example, in SO_3^{-2}, the oxidation number of S is $+4$, while in SO_4^{-2}, the oxidation number of S is $+6$. The oxidation states are positive because sulfur is less electronegative than oxygen. Only the members of the halogen family are more electronegative than the corresponding members of the oxygen family. Thus oxygen reacts with fluorine to form OF_2 ($O = +2$) and O_2F_2 ($O = +1$).

The chemistry of oxygen differs markedly from the chemistry of the other members of this family because oxygen has a much greater electronegativity (second only to fluorine). With the exception of fluorine, oxygen has greater electron-attracting power (a more negative oxidation state) than any element with which it is combined.

We have already noted the abnormal properties of H_2O, compared to H_2S, H_2Se, and H_2Te. These properties were ascribed to the presence of hydrogen bonding in water—a result of the high electronegativity value of oxygen (see section 20.21).

25.4 The chemistry of oxygen

We described the preparation of oxygen in section 6.14 and observed that the slight solubility of the gas in water permits its collection by water displacement (see Figure 25-1 on the following page).

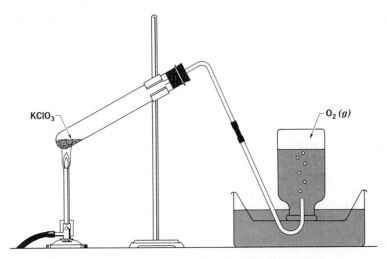

Fig. 25-1   The preparation and collection of oxygen

The electron-dot diagram for oxygen may be represented as

$$\ddot{\text{O}} \vdots \ddot{\text{O}} \vdots$$

Note the presence of two unpaired electrons, a structure associated with a type of magnetism called *paramagnetism*. For example, manganese has five unpaired d electrons which also make it paramagnetic. Unlike *ferromagnetism*, in which solids such as iron or nickel are strongly attracted to magnets, paramagnetism involves the *weak* attraction between magnets and substances such as oxygen or manganese.

25.5 The corrosion of metals

Exposure of metals to the atmosphere converts the metals into compounds. This process is called *corrosion*. When iron is involved, the process is called *rusting*. The chemistry of rusting is not completely understood. However, it appears that both water and oxygen are required for the formation of iron rust, a hydrated ferric oxide containing a variable amount of water. Because its water content varies, the formula assigned to rust is $Fe_2O_3 \cdot xH_2O$. A suggested equation to account for the formation of rust is

$$2\ \text{Fe}\ (s) + 1\frac{1}{2}\ \text{O}_2\ (g) + x\ \text{H}_2\text{O} \rightarrow \text{Fe}_2\text{O}_3 \cdot x\text{H}_2\text{O}\ (s)$$

It appears that the rusting process is accelerated by the presence of less reactive metals in contact with the iron. Electrochemical action may account for the increase in the rate of rusting.

Protective coatings, such as paints and greases, are generally utilized to retard corrosion. Metallic coatings are also employed. For example, zinc-plated iron (galvanized iron) corrodes very slowly because the zinc, being more reactive, forms a protective coating of zinc oxide on the iron.

25.6 Ozone

Oxygen exists in another gaseous molecular form, O_3, called *ozone*. Sulfur also exists in a number of different solid forms, discussed in section 25.8. Different physical forms of the same element in the same physical state are called *allotropes*.

Ozone is prepared by passing an electric discharge through oxygen.

$$3 \, O_2 \, (g) + 68.4 \text{ kcal} \rightarrow 2 \, O_3 \, (g)$$

Ozone has a higher energy content than oxygen and is a more powerful oxidizer. Mercury and silver are unaffected by oxygen but are oxidized by ozone.

Unlike oxygen, ozone is not paramagnetic. This suggests the absence of unpaired electrons. The structure of ozone may be represented by one resonance form as

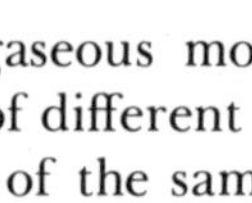

25.7 Peroxides

An important compound of oxygen is hydrogen peroxide, H_2O_2. The following diagram compares the structures of O_2 (oxygen molecule), O^{-2} (oxide ion), and O_2^{-2} (peroxide ion).

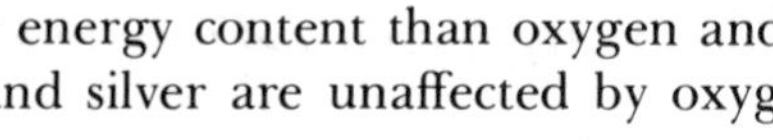

| O_2 | O^{-2} | O_2^{-2} |
| oxygen | oxide ion | peroxide ion |

Dilute hydrogen peroxide solutions are prepared by the action of sulfuric acid on a peroxide.

$$BaO_2 + H_2SO_4 \rightarrow BaSO_4 + H_2O_2$$

Barium peroxide is used in this preparation because the formation of insoluble $BaSO_4$ drives the reaction to the right.

More concentrated hydrogen peroxide solutions are prepared by the electrolysis of concentrated H_2SO_4. Solutions of 30% hydrogen peroxide are sold commercially. Care must be exercised in using such solutions because they can decompose explosively, liberating oxygen.

$$2\ H_2O_2 \rightarrow 2\ H_2O + O_2 + 47\ \text{kcal}$$

Concentrated H_2O_2 solutions also burn the skin. The concentration of H_2O_2 solutions used as antiseptics is about 3%.

The peroxide ion may be oxidized to oxygen gas or reduced to oxide ion, as in H_2O. Thus H_2O_2 can behave either as a reducing or oxidizing agent. (In the reactions that follow, all ions are aquated.)

1. Reducing agent.

$$2\ KMnO_4 + 5\ H_2O_2 + 3\ H_2SO_4 \rightarrow K_2SO_4 + 2\ MnSO_4 + 5\ O_2 + 8\ H_2O$$

REDUCTION $2\ [MnO_4^- + 8\ H^+ + 5\ e^- \rightarrow Mn^{+2} + 4\ H_2O]$

OXIDATION $5\ [O_2^{-2} \rightarrow O_2^{0} + 2\ e^-]$

2. Oxidizing agent.

$$\overset{\displaystyle \overbrace{\qquad -2\ e^- \qquad}}{\underset{\displaystyle \underbrace{\qquad +2\ e^- \qquad}}{\overset{+1\ +4\ -2 \quad\ +1\ -1 \qquad\quad +1\ +6\ -2 \quad +1\ -2}{Na_2SO_3 + H_2O_2 \rightarrow Na_2SO_4 + H_2O}}}$$

The decomposition of H_2O_2 into H_2O and O_2 involves the oxidation and reduction of peroxide ion. When the same particle undergoes both oxidation and reduction, the phenomenon is called self oxidation-reduction, or *disproportionation*.

$$\overset{\displaystyle \overbrace{\qquad -2\ e^- \qquad}}{\underset{\displaystyle \underbrace{\quad +2\ e^- \quad}}{\overset{+1\ -1 \qquad\quad +1\ -2 \qquad 0}{2\ H_2O_2 \rightarrow 2\ H_2O + O_2}}}$$

25.8 The allotropes of sulfur

Next to oxygen, sulfur is the most common member of the oxygen family. Sulfur is a yellow solid at room temperature and exists in several allotropic forms. If a solution of roll sulfur (a commercial variety of sulfur) in carbon disulfide, CS_2, is allowed to evaporate slowly, crystals of rhombic sulfur appear. Below 96°C, rhombic sulfur remains stable. If roll sulfur is melted and maintained between 96°C and 120°C, needle-shaped monoclinic sulfur is formed. At 96°C, both forms may be maintained in equilibrium.

Both rhombic and monoclinic sulfur consist of S_8 molecular units, each having its own geometric shape in its crystal. These units consist of eight-membered puckered rings, shown in Figure 25-2.

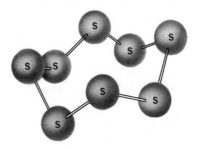

Fig. 25–2 The S_8 molecule

Each of the sulfur atoms is joined to another sulfur atom by a covalent bond. When sulfur is heated above its melting point, its viscosity increases. As the boiling point is reached, its viscosity decreases. These changes may be interpreted as follows: On heating, the S_8 rings rupture to form long chains of sulfur atoms. These long chains tend to become tangled and less mobile than the puckered rings; hence the increase in viscosity. Further heating breaks the long chains of atoms, resulting in decreased viscosity.

25.9 Occurrence of sulfur

Sulfur occurs naturally in the form of sulfide and sulfate mineral deposits, such as chalcocite, Cu_2S, and gypsum, $CaSO_4 \cdot 2H_2O$. Sulfur also occurs uncombined as the free element, thought to be a product of the bacterial decay of calcium sulfate. Sulfur is extracted from these beds by the Frasch process, shown in Figure 25-3 on the next page.

Three concentric pipes are sunk into the ground containing the sulfur beds. Superheated water (167°C) enters through the outermost pipe and melts the sulfur. Heated compressed air enters the innermost pipe, making the liquid sulfur light and frothy and forcing the sulfur to the surface through the middle pipe. The sulfur, thus mined, is almost 100% pure.

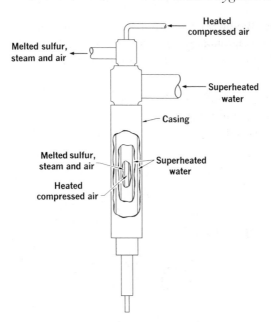

Fig. 25–3   The Frasch process

25.10 Properties, uses, and compounds of sulfur

Sulfur is less reactive than oxygen. Sulfur generally unites with metals to form ionic compounds and with nonmetals to form covalently bounded compounds. Examples of these reactions are

$$(1) \quad 2\ Na\ (s) + S\ (g) \rightarrow 2\ Na^+ + S^{-2}$$

$$(2) \quad S_8\ (s) + 8\ O_2\ (g) \rightarrow 8\ SO_2\ (g)$$

The oxidation number of sulfur changes from 0 to -2 in reaction 1. This change involves a gain of electrons and indicates that sulfur is an oxidizing agent. Similarly, in reaction 2, the oxidation number of sulfur changes from 0 to $+4$. A loss of electrons is involved, indicating that sulfur is also a reducing agent.

Most of the sulfur mined in the world is converted into sulfur compounds, principally H_2SO_4. Some sulfur is used to vulcanize rubber. Sulfur is also used as an ingredient in insecticides.

The most common sulfur compounds are hydrogen sulfide, H_2S; sulfur dioxide, SO_2; sulfuric acid, H_2SO_4; and a variety of ternary sulfur-oxygen compounds such as sodium sulfate, Na_2SO_4; magnesium sulfate, $MgSO_4$; and sodium thiosulfate, $Na_2S_2O_3$.

25.11 Hydrogen sulfide

Hydrogen sulfide, H_2S, is a gas that occurs naturally from the decay of organic matter. It is easily identified by its characteristic odor of rotten eggs. Volume for volume, hydrogen sulfide is more toxic than carbon monoxide, CO, one of the gases present in the exhaust of an automobile. Considerable care should be exercised in using H_2S in the laboratory.

H_2S may be prepared in the laboratory by the action of an acid on a sulfide.

$$H^+ \ (aq) + S^{-2} \ (aq) \rightarrow H_2S \ (g)$$

$$2 \ HCl \ (aq) + FeS \ (s) \rightarrow H_2S \ (g) + FeCl_2 \ (aq)$$

Because the gas is somewhat soluble in water, it is usually collected by air displacement (see Figure 25-4).

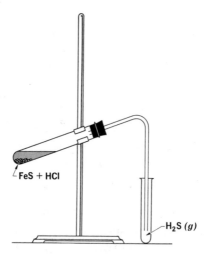

FeS + HCl

$H_2S \ (g)$

Fig. 25-4   The preparation and collection of hydrogen sulfide

Gaseous hydrogen sulfide is a covalently bonded molecule resembling water structurally.

$$H \overset{\cdot\cdot}{\underset{\cdot\ \ \cdot}{S}} H$$

The solution of H_2S in water forms a weak acid called hydrosulfuric acid. As a diprotic acid, it ionizes in two stages, as shown on the next page.

$$H_2S \ (g) + H_2O \rightarrow H_3O^+ + HS^- \ (aq) \qquad K_A = 1 \times 10^{-7}$$

$$HS^- \ (aq) + H_2O \rightarrow H_3O^+ + S^{-2} \ (aq) \qquad K_A = 1 \times 10^{-15}$$

The acid-base table (see page 291) confirms that HS^- (aq) is amphiprotic.

AS AN ACID $HS^- \ (aq) + OH^- \ (aq) \rightarrow S^{-2} \ (aq) + H_2O$

AS A BASE $HS^- \ (aq) + H^+ \ (aq) \rightarrow H_2S \ (g)$

NaHS reacts with bases and acids as follows:

$$NaHS + NaOH \rightarrow Na_2S + H_2O$$

$$NaHS + HCl \rightarrow NaCl + H_2S$$

Note that S in H_2S and in other sulfides has its maximum negative oxidation number, -2. This means that S^{-2} can only lose electrons; that is, sulfides can behave only as reducing agents.

25.12 Metallic sulfides

The sulfides of all the metals, except those of the alkali and alkaline earth metals, are only slightly soluble in water.

$$CoS \ (s) \rightleftarrows Co^{+2} \ (aq) + S^{-2} \ (aq) \qquad K_{SP} = 5 \times 10^{-22}$$

$$HgS \ (s) \rightleftarrows Hg^{+2} \ (aq) + S^{-2} \ (aq) \qquad K_{SP} = 1.6 \times 10^{-54}$$

The addition of acid to these sulfides increases their solubility because the H_3O^+ ions in the acid remove S^{-2} (aq) ions to form weakly ionized H_2S (or HS^-). The removal of S^{-2} (aq) ions shifts the equilibria to the right and favors the dissolving of the sulfides.

As the K_{SP} of the sulfide decreases for the more insoluble sulfides, the S^{-2} (aq) ion concentration necessary to saturate the solution also decreases. This means that HCl can reduce the S^{-2} (aq) ion concentration in CoS below that required to precipitate CoS, and the solid dissolves. HgS, however, does not dissolve in HCl. Despite the reduction of the S^{-2} (aq) ion concentration, enough S^{-2} (aq) ion still remains to satisfy the very low K_{SP} value of HgS.

Procedures involving the control of the acidity of H_2S solutions are utilized in qualitative analysis schemes to separate metal ions as insoluble sulfides. For example, adding concentrated HCl to a mixture of CoS and HgS permits the separation of Co^{+2} from Hg^{+2}. Following the separation, the metals are identified.

25.13 Sulfur dioxide

Sulfur dioxide, SO_2, is prepared commercially by burning elemental sulfur or by burning metal sulfides in an excess of air (roasting).

$$S + O_2 \rightarrow SO_2 \ (g)$$

$$2 \ ZnS + 3 \ O_2 \rightarrow 2 \ ZnO + 2 \ SO_2 \ (g)$$

In the laboratory, sulfur dioxide is prepared by the action of hydronium ion (acid) on sulfites or bisulfites.

$$2 \ H_3O^+ + SO_3^{-2} \ (aq) \rightarrow 3 \ H_2O + SO_2 \ (g)$$

$$H_3O^+ + HSO_3^- \ (aq) \rightarrow 2 \ H_2O + SO_2 \ (g)$$

$$2 \ HCl + Na_2SO_3 \rightarrow 2 \ NaCl + H_2O + SO_2 \ (g)$$

Sulfur dioxide may also be prepared by the reduction of concentrated H_2SO_4.

$$\overset{0}{Cu} + 2 \ \overset{+1 \ +6 \ -2}{H_2SO_4} \rightarrow \overset{+2 \ +6 \ -2}{CuSO_4} + 2 \ H_2O + \overset{+4 \ -2}{SO_2}$$

(with electron transfer: $-2 \ e^-$ from Cu; $+2 \ e^-$ to S)

SO_2 is a colorless gas with an irritating odor. It can be liquefied at 1 atmosphere pressure and below $10.1°$ C. SO_2 is soluble in water and is collected by air displacement (see Figure 25-5 on the facing page).

Like hydrogen sulfide, SO_2 reacts with H_2O to produce a weak diprotic acid, sulfurous acid, H_2SO_3.

$$SO_2 \ (g) + H_2O \rightarrow H_2SO_3$$

$$H_2SO_3 + H_2O \rightarrow H_3O^+ + HSO_3^- \ (aq)$$

$$HSO_3^- \ (aq) + H_2O \rightarrow H_3O^+ + SO_3^{-2} \ (aq)$$

Like HS^-, HSO_3^- is amphiprotic.

AS AN ACID $HSO_3^- \ (aq) + OH^- \ (aq) \rightarrow SO_3^{-2} \ (aq) + H_2O$

AS A BASE $HSO_3^- \ (aq) + H^+ \ (aq) \rightarrow SO_2 \ (g) + H_2O$

Thus $NaHSO_3$, which contains HSO_3^-, reacts with bases and acids.

$$NaHSO_3 + NaOH \rightarrow Na_2SO_3 + H_2O$$

$$NaHSO_3 + 2\ HCl \rightarrow NaCl + H_2O + SO_2\ (g)$$

The oxidation state of S in SO_2, as well as in HSO_3^- and SO_3^{-2}, is +4. Since sulfur exhibits oxidation states of −2, 0, and +6, SO_2 may behave as a reducing agent (be oxidized) or as an oxidizing agent (be reduced).

$$
\begin{array}{c}
\overbrace{\hspace{5cm}}^{-2\ e^-} \\
\text{OXIDATION} \quad \overset{+1\ +4\ -2}{Na_2SO_3} + H_2O + Cl_2 \rightarrow \overset{+1\ +6\ -2}{Na_2SO_4} + 2\ \overset{+1}{HCl} \\
\underbrace{\hspace{5cm}}_{+2\ e^-}
\end{array}
$$

$$
\begin{array}{c}
\overbrace{\hspace{4cm}}^{-4\ e^-} \\
\text{REDUCTION} \quad \overset{+4\ -2}{SO_2} + 2\ \overset{+1\ -2}{H_2S} \rightarrow 2\ H_2O + 3\ \overset{0}{S} \\
\underbrace{\hspace{4cm}}_{+4\ e^-}
\end{array}
$$

Sulfur dioxide and various sulfites are reducing agents and are used to bleach materials such as wool and silk, which would be destroyed by chlorine bleaches. In the manufacture of paper from wood pulp, calcium bisulfite, $Ca(HSO_3)_2$, dissolves the hard lignin in the wood and leaves behind the cellulose fibers.

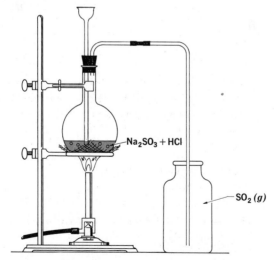

Fig. 25-5   The preparation and collection of sulfur dioxide

25.14 Preparation of sulfuric acid

Sulfuric acid, H_2SO_4, one of the world's most widely used industrial chemicals, is the most important sulfur compound. In sulfuric acid, sulfur has its maximum oxidation number, $+6$. The preparation of H_2SO_4 therefore involves the oxidation of sulfur to the $+6$ state. The burning of sulfur forms sulfur dioxide, SO_2, in which sulfur has a $+4$ oxidation state. The problem in manufacturing H_2SO_4 is to convert sulfur from $+4$ to $+6$.

In this country, H_2SO_4 is manufactured by the contact process, which may be summarized as follows:

1. SO_2 is produced from the burning of sulfur or metallic sulfides.

2. A mixture of SO_2 and excess air is passed over a catalyst, usually finely divided platinum or vanadium(V) oxide, V_2O_5. If platinum is used as the catalyst, impurities such as arsenic must be removed from the SO_2 in order not to "poison" the catalyst (reduce its effectiveness). The catalytic oxidation of SO_2 produces a satisfactory yield of SO_3 at a rapid rate at temperatures between $400°$ C and $500°$ C.

$$2 \ SO_2 \ (g) + O_2 \ (g) \rightleftarrows 2 \ SO_3 \ (g) + 46 \ \text{kcal}$$

3. The reaction between SO_3 and H_2O to form H_2SO_4 is very slow. This difficulty is bypassed by first reacting SO_3 with concentrated H_2SO_4 to form pyrosulfuric acid, $H_2S_2O_7$.

$$SO_3 + H_2SO_4 \rightarrow H_2S_2O_7$$

4. The pyrosulfuric acid is added to water to form H_2SO_4 of the desired concentration.

$$H_2S_2O_7 + H_2O \rightarrow 2 \ H_2SO_4$$

Sulfuric acid is also manufactured by the lead chamber process. In this process, SO_2, O_2, and H_2O react in the presence of oxides of nitrogen to form a complex compound, called nitrosyl sulfuric acid. The nitrosyl compound reacts with more water to form sulfuric acid, regenerating the oxides of nitrogen. The chemistry of these reactions is not completely understood. The lead chamber process produces dilute H_2SO_4, unlike the contact process, which can manufacture H_2SO_4 of any desired concentration.

25.15 Physical properties of H₂SO₄

Pure (100%) H_2SO_4 is a covalently bonded (molecular) liquid that can be represented as

$$\ddot{\underset{\cdots}{O}}$$

$$H\!:\!\ddot{\underset{\cdot\cdot}{O}}\!:\!\ddot{\underset{\cdot\cdot}{S}}\!:\!\ddot{\underset{\cdot\cdot}{O}}\!:\!H$$

$$\ddot{\underset{\cdot\cdot}{O}}$$

The liquid has a density of 1.85 g/cm³ and has an oily appearance, accounting for its older name, *oil of vitriol*. Sulfuric acid begins to boil at 290° C, decomposing into SO_3 and H_2O. In the laboratory, the concentrated acid is usually 18 M, which contains about 98% H_2SO_4.

25.16 Chemical properties of H₂SO₄

ACID-BASE REACTIONS

In aqueous solution, sulfuric acid, like hydrosulfuric acid and sulfurous acid, is diprotic.

$$H_2SO_4 + H_2O \rightarrow H_3O^+ + HSO_4^- \ (aq)$$

$$HSO_4^- \ (aq) + H_2O \rightarrow H_3O^+ + SO_4^{-2} \ (aq)$$

The reactions show that when H_2SO_4 reacts with bases, two types of salts are formed: bisulfates, or acid sulfates (HSO_4^-), and sulfates (SO_4^{-2}).

$$NaOH + H_2SO_4 \rightarrow NaHSO_4 + H_2O$$

$$2\ NaOH + H_2SO_4 \rightarrow Na_2SO_4 + 2\ H_2O$$

In dilute solution, the primary ionization of sulfuric acid is almost complete. Like HS^- and HSO_3^-, HSO_4^- is amphiprotic.

AS AN ACID $\quad HSO_4^- \ (aq) + OH^- \ (aq) \rightarrow SO_4^{-2} \ (aq) + H_2O$

AS A BASE $\quad HSO_4^- \ (aq) + H^+ \ (aq) \rightarrow H_2SO_4$

DEHYDRATING ACTION

Concentrated H_2SO_4 reacts with H_2O, forming hydrates and liberating considerable heat.

$$H_2SO_4 + H_2O \rightarrow H_2SO_4 \cdot H_2O + 288 \text{ kcal}$$

Thus extreme caution should be exercised in diluting concentrated H_2SO_4. The acid should always be slowly poured into a large volume of water with constant stirring. The tremendous affinity of sulfuric acid for water makes it an excellent drying agent for gases. A substance that has an affinity for water is called a *dehydrating agent*.

The dehydrating action of concentrated H_2SO_4 is demonstrated when the acid reacts with carbohydrates such as sugars (sucrose) or cellulose (wood, cotton).

$$\underset{\text{sucrose}}{C_{12}H_{22}O_{11}} + 11\ H_2SO_4 \rightarrow 12\ C + 11\ H_2SO_4 \cdot H_2O$$

This reaction also accounts for the charring action when concentrated H_2SO_4 comes in contact with carbohydrates.

OXIDIZING ACTION

Sulfuric acid contains two oxidizing particles, aqueous H^+ and SO_4^{-2}, each of which can undergo specific reduction reactions with metals.

When metals like zinc, which have E^0 values above hydrogen, react with dilute H_2SO_4, H^+ is reduced to H_2 (g).

REDUCTION $2\ H^+\ (aq) + 2\ e^- \rightarrow H_2\ (g)$

OXIDATION $Zn\ (s) \rightarrow Zn^{+2}\ (aq) + 2\ e^-$

$$Zn\ (s) + H_2SO_4\ (aq) \rightarrow ZnSO_4\ (aq) + H_2\ (g)$$

When metals like copper, which have E^0 values below hydrogen, react with concentrated H_2SO_4, SO_4^{-2} is reduced to SO_2 (g).

REDUCTION $SO_4^{-2}\ (aq) + 4\ H^+\ (aq) + 2\ e^- \rightarrow SO_2\ (g) + 2\ H_2O$

OXIDATION $Cu\ (s) \rightarrow Cu^{+2}\ (aq) + 2\ e^-$

$$Cu\ (s) + 2\ H_2SO_4 \rightarrow CuSO_4\ (aq) + SO_2\ (g) + 2\ H_2O$$

Metals that have E^0 values above hydrogen reduce the SO_4^{-2} in concentrated sulfuric acid even further to H_2S (g).

REDUCTION $SO_4^{-2}\ (aq) + 10\ H^+\ (aq) + 8\ e^- \rightarrow H_2S\ (g) + 4\ H_2O$

OXIDATION $4\ [Zn\ (s) \rightarrow Zn^{+2}\ (aq) + 2\ e^-]$

$$4\ Zn\ (s) + 5\ H_2SO_4 \rightarrow 4\ ZnSO_4\ (aq) + H_2S\ (g) + 4\ H_2O$$

25.17 Tests for sulfate and sulfite ions

Sulfate ions may be identified by the addition of aqueous barium chloride, $BaCl_2$. A white precipitate forms that does not dissolve in HCl.

$$SO_4^{-2} \ (aq) + Ba^{+2} \ (aq) \rightarrow BaSO_4 \ (s)$$
not soluble
in HCl

Sulfites also form a white precipitate with $BaCl_2$. The precipitate of $BaSO_3$, however, dissolves in HCl to form SO_2 (g).

$$SO_3^{-2} \ (aq) + Ba^{+2} \ (aq) \rightarrow BaSO_3 \ (s)$$

$$BaSO_3 \ (s) + 2 \ H^+ \ (aq) \rightarrow Ba^{+2} \ (aq) + H_2O + SO_2 \ (g)$$

25.18 Uses of sulfuric acid

Many chemical processes utilize sulfuric acid at one stage or another. The major uses include:

1. Production of fertilizers, such as ammonium sulfate and super-phosphate of lime.
2. Removal of rust and scale from steel (pickling) prior to plating steel with protective metal coatings.
3. Refining of petroleum to remove undesirable compounds from lubricating oils.

25.19 Thiosulfates

When aqueous metal sulfites are heated with solid sulfur, thiosulfates are formed.

$$Na_2SO_3 + S \rightarrow Na_2S_2O_3$$
sodium
thiosulfate

The electron-dot formula of a thiosulfate ion may be represented as

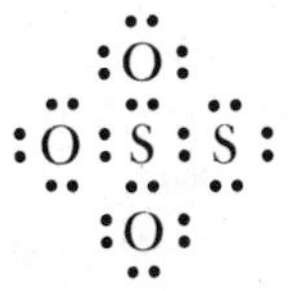

:Ö:
:Ö:S:S:
:Ö:

$S_2O_3^{-2}$ has a structure similar to SO_4^{-2}, except that an O atom has been replaced by an S atom. Thiosulfates are excellent reducing agents. Thus thiosulfates reduce colored iodine molecules to colorless iodide ions and tetrathionate ions.

$$2 \ Na_2S_2O_3 + I_2 \rightarrow 2 \ NaI + Na_2S_4O_6$$

sodium
tetrathionate

Silver halides dissolve in sodium thiosulfate to form stable complex ions.

$$AgBr \ (s) + 2 \ Na_2S_2O_3 \ (aq) \rightarrow NaBr \ (aq) + Na_3Ag(S_2O_3)_2^{-3} \ (aq)$$

This reaction is used in photography to remove from the film silver bromide, AgBr, which is unused, that is, which has not been acted on by the developer. The removal of AgBr is called "fixing" the film; sodium thiosulfate, commercially sold as hypo, is called a photographic fixer or fixing agent.

25.20 Selenium and tellurium

The remaining common elements of the oxygen family, selenium and tellurium, resemble sulfur chemically.

Selenium occurs naturally in sulfide ores and, like sulfur, has allotropic forms. Selenium forms a number of compounds analogous to sulfur, such as hydrogen selenide, H_2Se, and selenic acid, H_2SeO_4. When selenium is exposed to light, its conductivity increases considerably. This property is utilized in certain photoelectric cells. Selenium is also used to tint glass.

Tellurium occurs in nature as a telluride of lead, silver, and gold. Tellurium forms compounds analogous to sulfur and selenium, such as H_2Te and H_2TeO_4. Tellurium is used as an additive for steel and as a coloring agent for glass; but in general, tellurium has limited usefulness.

Multiple-Choice Questions

1. A comparison of the elements of the oxygen family reveals that (1) the largest atom has the highest ionization potential (2) the electronegativity values of the elements increase with the number of electron shells (3) all the elements contain four p electrons in the valence shell (4) all the elements have an oxidation state of +6

2. Which of the following is *not* a property of tellurium? (1) It combines with hydrogen. (2) It reacts with metals. (3) It forms Te^{-2} ion, which is a good oxidizing agent. (4) It has positive oxidation states.

3. The compound in which sulfur has the highest oxidation state is (1) H_2S (2) Na_2SO_3 (3) H_2SO_4 (4) $Na_2S_2O_3$

4. The two allotropes of oxygen differ in (1) the number of neutrons (2) the number of valence electrons (3) the number of atoms in the molecule (4) electronegativity

5. In the reaction $2 O_2^{-2} \rightarrow O_2 + 2 O^{-2}$ (1) oxygen is oxidized only (2) oxygen is reduced only (3) oxygen is oxidized and reduced (4) an allotrope forms

6. Hydrosulfide ion, HS^- (1) is a gas (2) is amphiprotic (3) donates protons to form H_2S (4) is a strong acid

7. Many insoluble metal sulfides dissolve in acid because (1) the H^+ ions of the acid decrease the S^{-2} ion concentration (2) the metals act as a base (3) the acid is oxidized (4) disproportionation takes place

8. The reaction that *cannot* form SO_2 is (1) $FeS + O_2$ (2) $HCl + NaHSO_4$ (3) $H_2S + O_2$ (4) Fe + hot concentrated H_2SO_4

9. Fuming sulfuric acid, $H_2S_2O_7$, is first formed in the manufacture of sulfuric acid because (1) fuming sulfuric acid is a product of the reaction $SO_2 + H_2O$ (2) SO_3 has limited solubility in water (3) fuming sulfuric acid is more stable than H_2SO_4 (4) sulfur has a higher oxidation state in fuming sulfuric acid than in sulfuric acid

10. Sodium thiosulfate is used in photography because it (1) darkens when exposed to light (2) oxidizes the film (3) dissolves unused silver halides (4) forms a black silver deposit

Completion Questions

1. In binary compounds with metals, the elements of Group VIA have an oxidation state of _____.

2. In the O_2^{-2} ion, the oxidation state of oxygen is _____.

3. In the crystalline forms of sulfur, the molecular units contain _____ atoms of sulfur in each unit.

4. The name of the stable form of sulfur at room temperature is _____.

5. A solution of hydrogen sulfide in water is called _____ acid.

6. SO_2 is the _____ of sulfurous acid.

7. The formula for sodium thiosulfate is _____.

8. The compound $Na_2S_2O_7$ is called _____.

9. Oxygen is paramagnetic because its molecule contains _____.

10. Less reactive metals in contact with iron accelerate the rusting of iron by _____ action.

True-False Questions

1. The highest oxidation state shown by oxygen in its compounds is +2.
2. *More* energy is released when an ion with a −2 charge is formed than when an ion with a −1 charge is formed.
3. The elements in Group VIA have *positive* E^0 values.
4. In the reaction $O_2^{-2} \rightarrow O_2 + 2 \ e^-$, oxygen acts as *a reducing* agent.
5. When HS⁻ reacts with OH⁻, HS⁻ acts as *an acid.*
6. When HCl is added to an aqueous solution of H_2S, the concentration of S^{-2} ions *decreases.*
7. The reaction of H_2S and SO_2 forms a sulfur compound that has an oxidation state of +6.
8. The reaction of concentrated sulfuric acid with sugar forms a black solid because sulfuric acid is *a coloring* agent.
9. *HgS* dissolves in HCl.
10. The boiling point of H_2Te is *above* the boiling point of H_2O.

Decreases, Increases, Remains the Same

1. As the ionization potentials of the Group VIA elements decrease, their electronegativity values _____.
2. From the top to the bottom of column VIA, the metallic properties of the elements _____.
3. As the electronegativity of element X increases, the extent of hydrogen bonding shown by the compound H_nX _____.
4. As a result of the reaction $3 \ O_2 + 68 \ kcal \rightarrow 2 \ O_3$, the energy of the product _____.
5. When molten sulfur is heated, the viscosity of the liquid _____.
6. In the series H_2S, HS⁻, S^{-2}, the acid strength _____.
7. When a strong acid is added to an insoluble sulfide, the solubility of the sulfide _____.
8. In the reaction $2 \ SO_2 \ (g) + O_2 \ (g) \rightleftarrows 2 \ SO_3 \ (g) + 46 \ kcal$, increasing the temperature _____ the concentration of SO_3 at equilibrium.
9. As a solution of sulfuric acid becomes more dilute, the density of the solution _____.
10. As more $Na_2S_2O_3$ is added to free iodine, the concentration of iodide ion _____.

Exercises for Review

1. *a.* Name two allotropic forms of oxygen and sulfur.
   b. What are the differences between these forms?
2. *a.* Devise an experiment to show that hydrogen peroxide can act as a reducing agent.
   b. What is the product formed when hydrogen peroxide acts as a reducing agent?
3. Name each of the following:
   a. O_2 *c.* O^{-2} *e.* OH^-
   b. O_2^{-2} *d.* H_2O_2 *f.* HO_2^-
4. Write chemical equations for the following reactions: (*a*) sulfurous acid + hydrogen peroxide (*b*) ozone + silver (*c*) forming hydrogen peroxide from barium peroxide
5. *a.* Name each of the following acids: H_2S (*aq*), H_2SO_3 (*aq*), H_2SO_4
   b. Name the sodium compound formed by each acid.
   c. Write the oxidation state of sulfur in each acid.
6. Write equations for the following reactions:
   a. $FeS + O_2 \rightarrow$
   b. $NaHSO_3 + HCl \rightarrow$
   c. $Ag + H_2SO_4 \underset{\text{conc.}}{\rightarrow}$
   d. $NH_3 + H_2SO_4 \rightarrow$
7. Explain why sulfuric acid is the most important manufactured chemical compound in our chemical industries.
8. Write equations to show how sulfuric acid acts as (*a*) an oxidizing agent (*b*) a dehydrating agent
9. Write four equations for the reactions that occur when sulfur is converted into sulfuric acid.
10. *a.* How can sulfate ion be distinguished from sulfite ion?
    b. How can sulfite ion be distinguished from bisulfite ion?

Exercises for Further Study

1. *a.* Compare the electronegativity values for the elements of Group VIA with the electronegativity values of their corresponding elements in Group VA.
   b. Account for any differences.

2. Explain why the ΔH value associated with each of the following changes is different:

    a. $F (g) + e^- \rightarrow F^- (g)$

    b. $O (g) + 2 e^- \rightarrow O^{-2} (g)$

3. a. What change in volume takes place as oxygen is converted to ozone?

    b. Why does the change take place?

4. Describe an experiment to show that ozone is more chemically active than oxygen.

5. Account for the changes in viscosity when molten sulfur is heated.

6. Using your knowledge of sulfur as a guide, give the names and formulas of the compounds of selenium with (a) hydrogen (b) oxygen (c) iron

7. Explain why insoluble FeS forms when H_2S is added to a solution of Fe^{+2} but does not form if the solution is first acidified with HCl.

8. By means of equations, show how (a) HSO_3^- can act as an acid or as a base (b) SO_2 can act as an oxidizer or as a reducer

9. In the reaction $2 SO_2 + O_2 \rightleftarrows 2 SO_3 + 46$ kcal, explain why the temperature used cannot be too high or too low. Base your explanation on the rates of reaction and on the equilibrium conditions for the reaction.

10. Suggest a reason to account for the fact that oxygen is the only element in Group VIA that is gaseous at room conditions.

Chapter 26

THE HALOGENS

26.1 Introduction

In Chapter 7, we introduced the halogens as an example of a chemical family of elements that reacts with metals to form ionic compounds. In this chapter, we will present a more detailed study of the halogens, relating their properties to electronic structure.

This family of elements—fluorine, chlorine, bromine, and iodine—forms a column (Group VIIA) in the Periodic Table directly to the left of the noble gases. We will omit astatine, a rare and radioactive halogen, from our discussion. The table on the following page lists some of the important properties of the members of this family.

26.2 Trends in the general properties

All halogens are characterized by the presence of two s electrons and five p electrons in the outermost valence shell. The stability of the corresponding (neighboring) noble gas may be attained by one of the following methods, in which X represents a halogen atom:

1. Formation of a covalent bond between halogen atoms.

$$:\overset{..}{\underset{..}{X}}:\overset{..}{\underset{..}{X}}:$$

2. Formation of a halide ion.

$$:\overset{..}{\underset{..}{X}}:$$

3. Formation of a covalent bond with hydrogen, carbon, or nonmetals.

$$H:\overset{..}{\underset{..}{X}}: \qquad :\overset{..}{\underset{..}{X}}:\overset{:\overset{..}{X}:}{\underset{:\overset{..}{X}:}{C}}:\overset{..}{\underset{..}{X}}: \qquad :\overset{..}{\underset{..}{X}}:\overset{:\overset{..}{X}:}{\underset{:\overset{..}{X}:}{N}}:\overset{..}{\underset{..}{X}}:$$

The electronegativity values reveal that fluorine has the greatest attraction for electrons and iodine has the least. This means that F^- is an extremely stable ion, whereas I^- is the least stable of the halide ions. Although fluorine has the smallest nuclear charge, it also possesses the smallest

PROPERTY	FLUORINE	CHLORINE	BROMINE	IODINE
atomic number	9	17	35	53
electron structure	$1s^2$ $2s^2, 2p^5$	$1s^2$ $2s^2, 2p^6$ $3s^2, 3p^5$	$1s^2$ $2s^2, 2p^6$ $3s^2, 3p^6, 3d^{10}$ $4s^2, 4p^5$	$1s^2$ $2s^2, 2p^6$ $3s^2, 3p^6, 3d^{10}$ $4s^2, 4p^6, 4d^{10}$ $5s^2, 5p^5$
atomic (covalent) radius (Å)	0.64	0.99	1.14	1.33
ionic radius Z^- (Å)	1.36	1.87	1.95	2.16
first ionization potential (ev)	17.42	13.01	11.84	10.44
electro-negativity	4.0	3.0	2.8	2.5
oxidation states	-1	$-1, +1, +3,$ $+5, +7$	$-1, +1,$ $+3, +5$	$-1, +1,$ $+5, +7$
E^0 (volts) $2 Z^- (aq) \rightarrow$ $Z_2 + 2 e^-$	-2.87	-1.36	-1.06	-0.53

atomic radius. As a consequence, electrons are attracted to its valence shell with great ease, accounting for the very high electronegativity value.

Fluorine is the most electronegative of all the known elements. Therefore, fluorine can only have a negative oxidation state (-1). The other halogens also possess an oxidation state of -1. However, in combination with elements that are more electronegative, chlorine, bromine, and iodine may attain positive oxidation states as well.

The values for the ionization potentials are high, revealing that it is extremely difficult to remove an electron from a halogen atom. In any given row of the Periodic Table, with the exception of the stable noble gas, the halogen possesses the highest ionization potential. As the atomic radius of a halogen atom increases, the distance from the nucleus increases. Thus the shielding effect of the layers of electron shells increases, and the ionization potentials therefore decrease.

26.3 The halogens as oxidizing agents

The preceding table reveals that, for the halogens, F_2 has the lowest E^0 value. Thus the half-reaction $2 \ F^- \ (aq) \rightarrow F_2 \ (g) + 2 \ e^-$ has the least tendency to proceed as written. Since I_2 has the highest E^0 value, the half-reaction $2 \ I^- \ (aq) \rightarrow I_2 \ (s) + 2 \ e^-$ has the greatest tendency to proceed. We may conclude that the reverse reaction for F_2 is the most pronounced. F_2 is therefore the most powerful oxidizing agent, and F^- is the least powerful reducing agent among the halogen elements. On the other hand, I_2 is the least powerful oxidizing agent, and I^- is the strongest reducing agent among the halogen elements.

Why is fluorine a better oxidizing agent than chlorine? The change from the free halogen to the corresponding aquated halide ion can be broken down into several hypothetical steps that show the energy change in each step. Remember that ΔH is positive for endothermic processes.

$$X_2 \ (g) \quad \rightarrow \quad 2 \ X \ (g) \qquad \Delta H_1 = +$$
halogen gas molecule   halogen gas atoms

$$2 \ X \ (g) \quad + 2 \ e^- \quad \rightarrow \quad 2 \ X^- \ (g) \qquad \Delta H_2 = -$$
halogen gas atoms   gaseous halide ions

$$2 \ X^- \ (g) \quad + H_2O \rightarrow \quad 2 \ X^- \ (aq) \qquad \Delta H_3 = -$$
gaseous halide ions   aquated halide ions

The $\triangle H$ values for fluorine correspond in sign to the $\triangle H$ values for chlorine. $\triangle H_1$ and $\triangle H_2$ have approximately the same magnitude. However, the fluoride ion has a much smaller atomic radius than the chloride ion. As in the reaction involving the hydration energy of the very small $Li^+ \ (g)$ ion, $\triangle H_3$ for fluoride ion is much higher (more negative) than $\triangle H_3$ for chloride ion. Thus in aqueous solution, the net $\triangle H$ value for

$$F_2 \ (g) + 2 \ e^- \rightarrow 2 \ F^- \ (aq)$$

is more negative than the net ΔH value for

$$Cl_2 \ (g) + 2 \ e^- \rightarrow 2 \ Cl^- \ (aq)$$

This is the same as saying that fluorine is a more powerful oxidizer than chlorine.

26.4 Nomenclature of the oxidation states of the halogens

Using chlorine as a typical example, the following table summarizes the oxidation states of the halogens in representative compounds.

OXIDATION STATE	H COMPOUND	K COMPOUND
-1	HCl, hydrochloric acid	KCl, potassium chloride
$+1$	HClO (HOCl), hypochlorous acid	KClO, potassium hypochlorite
$+3$	$HClO_2$ (HOClO), chlorous acid	$KClO_2$, potassium chlorite
$+5$	$HClO_3$ ($HOClO_2$), chloric acid	$KClO_3$, potassium chlorate
$+7$	$HClO_4$ ($HOClO_3$), perchloric acid	$KClO_4$, potassium perchlorate

26.5 The oxychlorine acids

The following electron-dot diagrams reveal the structures of the oxychlorine acids:

| hypochlorous acid | chlorous acid | chloric acid | perchloric acid |

In the halogen acids containing oxygen, H is bonded to an oxygen atom, not to a halogen atom. The strength of the bond between O and H determines the ease with which the acid may donate a proton (acid strength). The effect of adding O atoms to Cl is to weaken the OH bond: O is more electronegative than Cl and draws electrons away from the H in the OH bond. Thus acid strength increases as we go from oxidation state $+1$ to oxidation state $+7$.

The increase in oxidation state, however, decreases the oxidizing power of the oxychlorine ion. The ability to oxidize depends on the tendency to attract electrons. With additional O atoms, the tendency of Cl to attract electrons diminishes. Thus ClO^- is a stronger oxidizing agent than ClO_4^-.

26.6 The chemistry of fluorine

The extreme electronegativity of fluorine suggests unusual chemical reactivity, which explains why fluorine does not occur free in nature. The most common fluorine ores and minerals are fluorite (fluorspar), CaF_2, and cryolite, Na_3AlF_6.

Because fluorine is the most powerful oxidizing agent, no chemical can oxidize fluoride ion. E^0 for $2\ F^-\ (aq) \rightarrow F_2\ (g) + 2\ e^-$ has the highest negative value, -2.87 v. Any oxidizing particle used with F^- results in a net E^0 that is still negative. The reaction, therefore, will *not* proceed in the direction of oxidation of fluoride ion.

Fluorine is extracted from its compounds by electrolysis, a process initially developed in 1886 by Henri Moissan, a French chemist.

Fluorine is prepared commercially in an electrochemical cell, shown in Figure 26-1.

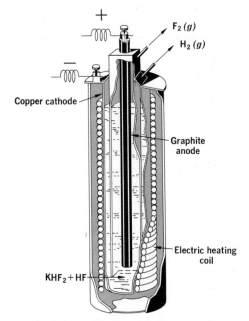

Fig. 26–1   Commercial preparation of fluorine

The electrolyte is a mixture of potassium hydrogen fluoride, KHF_2, and anhydrous hydrogen fluoride. The extreme reactivity of fluorine requires the electrolysis of the fused mixture. The container, which holds the electrolyte, is made of copper and also serves as the cathode. The anode is a graphite electrode. The fluorine that is liberated reacts with the copper to form a protective coating of copper fluoride. The reaction in the cell is

$$2 \text{ HF } (l) \rightarrow \text{H}_2 \ (g) + \text{F}_2 \ (g)$$

Fluorine reacts with metals to form metallic fluorides.

$$2 \text{ M} + \text{F}_2 \rightarrow \underset{\substack{\text{metallic} \\ \text{fluoride}}}{2 \text{ MF}}$$

Fluorine also forms compounds with nonmetals and with highly electronegative elements, such as oxygen and nitrogen. Note that in the compound oxygen difluoride, OF_2, fluorine, because of its extreme electronegativity, has an oxidation number of -1. This, in turn, gives oxygen an oxidation number of $+2$. (Oxygen usually has an oxidation number of -2.)

Fluorine forms a number of exceptionally stable compounds with carbon, called fluorocarbons. For example, $C_{12}F_{26}$ is a very stable liquid, impervious to the action of oxidizing agents and reducing agents even at temperatures near $1000°$ C.

Fluorine forms an analog of ethylene, C_2H_4, called tetrafluoroethylene, C_2F_4. Just as ethylene polymerizes (see section 29.8) to form polyethylene, tetrafluoroethylene polymerizes to form polytetrafluoroethylene, a plastic commercially known as Teflon. Like other fluorocarbons, Teflon is extremely stable and unreactive.

26.7 The chemistry of chlorine

Like fluorine, chlorine is a reactive element and thus does not occur uncombined in nature. We have already indicated that chlorine is extracted commercially from the chlorides obtained from salt deposits in mines, wells, and seawater. The process involves electrolysis of aqueous salt solutions (see section 17.20) in which chloride ions are oxidized at the anode.

1. Laboratory preparation. In the laboratory, chlorine may be prepared by the oxidation of Cl^- (aq) ion, usually in the presence of H^+ (aq), as shown in section 17.12. In the following reactions, showing the predominant species, potassium permanganate or manganese dioxide acts as an oxidizer (all ions are aquated):

$$2 \text{ MnO}_4^- + 16 \text{ H}^+ + 10 \text{ Cl}^- \rightarrow 2 \text{ Mn}^{+2} + 5 \text{ Cl}_2 \ (g) + 8 \text{ H}_2\text{O}$$

$$\text{MnO}_2 \ (s) + 4 \text{ H}^+ + 2 \text{ Cl}^- \rightarrow \text{Mn}^{+2} + \text{Cl}_2 \ (g) + 2 \text{ H}_2\text{O}$$

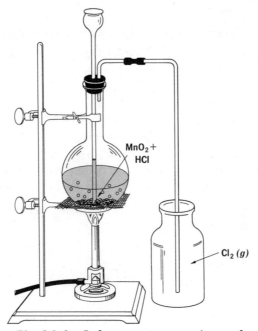

**Fig. 26–2   Laboratory preparation and
collection of chlorine**

The solubility of chlorine in water (0.99 g/100 g of H_2O at $10°$ C and 1 atm) makes it necessary to collect the gas in the laboratory by air displacement (see Figure 26-2). The gas has a green-yellow color and an irritating odor.

2. *Reactions with metals and nonmetals.* Like fluorine, chlorine combines with many metals and nonmetals. The metallic compounds are generally ionic, whereas the nonmetallic compounds are covalent.

$$Na\cdot \;+\; \cdot \ddot{\underset{\cdot\cdot}{Cl}}: \longrightarrow Na^+ \;+\; \left[:\ddot{\underset{\cdot\cdot}{Cl}}:\right]^-$$

$$\cdot \overset{\cdot}{\underset{\cdot}{P}}\cdot \;+\; 3\cdot\ddot{\underset{\cdot\cdot}{Cl}}: \longrightarrow :\ddot{\underset{\cdot\cdot}{Cl}}:\overset{\cdot\cdot}{\underset{}{P}}:\ddot{\underset{\cdot\cdot}{Cl}}:$$
$$:\ddot{\underset{\cdot\cdot}{Cl}}:$$

3. *Reaction with water and bleaching.* Chlorine reacts with water to form hypochlorous acid, a weakly ionized acid, and hydrochloric acid, a strongly ionized acid.

$$Cl_2 + H_2O \rightarrow HOCl + HCl$$

The E^0 for the reaction

$$Cl_2 \text{ (g)} + 2\ H_2O \rightarrow 2\ HOCl + 2\ H^+ + 2\ e^-$$

is -1.63 v and is more negative than the E^0 for permanganate ion (-1.51 v). Consequently, HOCl is a more powerful oxidizer than MnO_4^-. Because of its oxidizing power, hypochlorous acid is used commercially as a disinfectant and as a bleaching agent. Care must be taken that the HOCl does not weaken or destroy the fiber to be bleached. Such animal fibers as silk and wool are especially vulnerable, so that the use of HOCl as a bleaching agent is usually restricted to cotton or linen materials. In commercial bleaching, HOCl is obtained from the reaction between bleaching powder — a mixture of $Ca(OH)_2$, $Ca(OCl)_2$, and $CaCl_2$ — and an acid.

4. Oxyhalogen compounds. Hypochlorite ion decomposes on heating to yield chloride ion and chlorate ion.

$$3\ (OCl)^- \rightarrow 2\ Cl^- + (ClO_3)^-$$

Note that OCl^- is both oxidized and reduced, undergoing disproportionation (see section 25.7).

Potassium chlorate is produced by the action of chlorine on hot potassium hydroxide.

$$3\ Cl_2 + 6\ KOH \rightarrow KClO_3 + 5\ KCl + 3\ H_2O$$

This reaction is another example of disproportionation in which chlorine is oxidized to chlorate ion and is also reduced to chloride ion.

Potassium chlorate decomposes rapidly when heated in the presence of a catalyst to form oxygen.

$$2\ KClO_3 \rightarrow 2\ KCl + 3\ O_2 \text{ (g)}$$

This is a convenient method for preparing oxygen in the laboratory.

Potassium chlorate is a potent oxidizing agent, although not as strong as the corresponding hypochlorites. Oxidizable matter, such as phosphorus, sulfur, and sugar, reacts violently with chlorates and should never be mixed with chlorates.

26.8 The chemistry of bromine and iodine

Among nonmetals in a given column, as seen in Groups VA and VIA, the tendency to attract electrons diminishes with increasing atomic number. As the tendency to attract electrons diminishes, the tendency to lose electrons increases. Thus the elements exhibit increasing metallic properties as one goes down the column in the Periodic Table.

1. Commercial preparation. Bromine is prepared commercially from brine in salt wells and in seawater. After the brine in salt wells has been pumped to the surface, it is evaporated. The less soluble NaCl crystallizes out, while the more soluble NaBr remains in solution. Electrolysis is then utilized to oxidize bromine at the anode.

Seawater contains approximately 70 parts per million of bromine as dissolved bromides. To extract free bromine, the brine is acidified and chlorine is added. Since chlorine is a better oxidizer than bromine (see E^0 table, page 329), the reaction that occurs is

$$2\ Br^-\ (aq) + Cl_2\ (g) \rightarrow Br_2\ (l) + 2\ Cl^-\ (aq)$$

The bromine is vaporized by air that is bubbled through the water. The vapor is absorbed by a solution of Na_2CO_3, allowed to concentrate, and then re-formed by acidifying the solution.

$$3\ Br_2\ (l) + 3\ Na_2CO_3 \rightarrow 5\ NaBr + NaBrO_3 + 3\ CO_2\ (g)$$

$$5\ NaBr + NaBrO_3 + 3\ H_2SO_4 \rightarrow 3\ Na_2SO_4 + 3\ H_2O + 3\ Br_2\ (l)$$

Iodine is extracted from sodium iodate, $NaIO_3$, which occurs naturally with $NaNO_3$ in Chile saltpeter. As in the extraction of bromine from salt wells, the $NaNO_3$ is removed by evaporation and crystallization. The remaining liquid, containing IO_3^- ion, is reduced by sodium bisulfite, $NaHSO_3$, to form iodine.

$$2\ NaIO_3 + 5\ NaHSO_3 \rightarrow NaHSO_4 + 3\ Na_2SO_4 + H_2SO_4 + H_2O + I_2\ (s)$$

2. Laboratory preparation. Bromine is prepared in the laboratory by the oxidation of an acidified metallic bromide. Manganese dioxide is frequently used as the oxidizer.

$$2\ Br^-\ (aq) + 4\ H^+\ (aq) + MnO_2\ (s) \rightarrow Br_2\ (l) + 2\ H_2O + Mn^{+2}\ (aq)$$

Because bromine is a volatile liquid, it is collected by distillation (see Figure 26-3 on the next page).

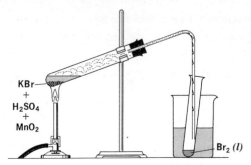

Fig. 26–3   Laboratory preparation and collection of bromine

Iodine is prepared in the laboratory by the oxidation of acid solutions of metallic iodides.

$$2\ I^- (aq) + 4\ H^+ (aq) + MnO_2 (s) \rightarrow I_2 (s) + 2\ H_2O + Mn^{+2} (aq)$$

Iodine is a volatile solid and is collected by evaporating the solid and condensing the vapors back to the solid state (see Figure 26-4). The transition of a solid directly to the gaseous state is called *sublimation*.

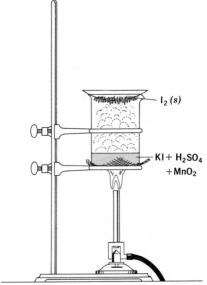

Fig. 26–4   Laboratory preparation and collection of iodine

3. Oxidizing power. The E^0 values (see the table on page 329) show that the order of oxidizing ability among the halogens is F, Cl, Br, and I. Thus Br_2 will oxidize I^- ion.

$$Br_2 \ (l) + 2 \ I^- \ (aq) \rightarrow I_2 \ (s) + 2 \ Br^- \ (aq)$$

Like chlorine, bromine and iodine react with metals to form ionic compounds and react with some nonmetals to form covalently bonded compounds.

Chlorine, bromine, and iodine exist as nonpolar diatomic molecules which are soluble in nonpolar solvents, such as carbon tetrachloride, CCl_4; carbon disulfide, CS_2; and benzene, C_6H_6. Since carbon tetrachloride vapors are toxic, another less toxic chlorinated hydrocarbon, perchlorethylene, C_2Cl_4, is often used in place of carbon tetrachloride. Solutions of bromine in nonpolar solvents are brown, and solutions of iodine in nonpolar solvents are violet.

26.9 Tests for halogens

The halogens may be identified by the tests indicated in the table that follows.

HALOGEN	TEST
fluorine	light-yellow gas that attacks glass
chlorine	green-yellow gas that displaces colorless Br^- (aq) ion to form dark-red Br_2: $Cl_2 \ (g) + 2 \ Br^- \ (aq) \rightarrow 2 \ Cl^- \ (aq) + Br_2 \ (l)$
bromine	dark-red liquid that displaces colorless I^- (aq) ion to form brown I_2: $Br_2 \ (l) + 2 \ I^- \ (aq) \rightarrow 2 \ Br^- \ (aq) + I_2 \ (s)$
iodine	purple-black solid that sublimes on heating to form dense violet vapors

26.10 Tests for halide ions

The aqueous halide ions may be identified by the tests indiciated in the table on the following page.

AQUEOUS HALIDE ION	TEST
F⁻	Addition of sulfuric acid and warming produce HF (g), which will etch glass.
Cl⁻	Addition of silver nitrate forms a white precipitate of AgCl, insoluble in HNO_3 and soluble in NH_3.
Br⁻	Addition of Cl_2 (g) liberates free bromine, which colors carbon tetrachloride or perchlorethylene orange.
I⁻	Addition of Cl_2 (g) or Br_2 (l) liberates free iodine, which colors carbon tetrachloride or perchlorethylene violet.

26.11 Uses of the halogens

The table that follows summarizes some of the important uses of the halogens.

HALOGEN	USE
fluorine	manufacture of important fluorine compounds: freon (dichlorodifluoromethane, CCl_2F_2), used as a refrigerant; Teflon, a plastic highly resistant to corrosion
chlorine	bleaching and disinfecting; manufacture of important chlorine compounds, dyes, and drugs
bromine	manufacture of ethylene dibromide, $C_2H_4Br_2$, used in antiknock additives for gasoline; manufacture of AgBr, used in photography; manufacture of KBr, used in sedatives
iodine	manufacture of tincture of iodine (I_2 dissolved in ethyl alcohol); manufacture of important iodine compounds, such as iodoform, CHI_3

26.12 The hydrogen halides

All the halogens form binary compounds with hydrogen that have the following general formula, where X represents a halogen atom.

$$H \!:\! \overset{\cdot\cdot}{\underset{\cdot\cdot}{X}} \!:$$

$$F_2\,(g) + H_2\,(g) \rightarrow 2\ HF\,(g) \qquad \Delta H = -64.2\ \text{kcal/mole}$$

$$Cl_2\,(g) + H_2\,(g) \rightarrow 2\ HCl\,(g) \qquad \Delta H = -22.1\ \text{kcal/mole}$$

$$Br_2\,(g) + H_2\,(g) \rightarrow 2\ HBr\,(g) \qquad \Delta H = -8.6\ \text{kcal/mole}$$

$$I_2\,(g) + H_2\,(g) \rightarrow 2\ HI\,(g) \qquad \Delta H = +6.2\ \text{kcal/mole}$$

From the table of electronegativities (see page 414), we note that fluorine has the highest value and iodine has the lowest. The polarity of the hydrogen halides therefore decreases with increasing nuclear charge.

26.13 The chemistry of the hydrogen halides

As we have indicated, the hydrogen halides may be prepared by direct combination of the elements. In every case, except in the preparation of HI, the reaction is exothermic and proceeds spontaneously. The reaction between H_2 and I_2 attains equilibrium as shown in the reaction

$$H_2\,(g) + I_2\,(g) \rightleftarrows 2\ HI\,(g)$$

The hydrogen halides may also be prepared by the action of sulfuric acid on a metallic halide, MX.

$$H_2SO_4 + MX \rightarrow MHSO_4 + HX\,(g)$$

The table of E^0 values (see page 329) reveals that the halide ions become more easily oxidized with increasing nuclear charge. Thus the reaction between H_2SO_4 and KBr generally results in the oxidation of Br^- ion to form Br_2. Similarly, the reaction between H_2SO_4 and KI produces I_2. To prepare pure HBr or pure HI, we react the phosphorus trihalide with water.

$$PBr_3 + 3\ H_2O \rightarrow H_3PO_3 + 3\ HBr$$

$$PI_3 + 3\ H_2O \rightarrow H_3PO_3 + 3\ HI$$

The hydrogen halides are all gases at room temperature. They dissolve in water to form acid solutions.

$$HX\,(g) + H_2O \rightarrow H_3O^+ + X^-\,(aq)$$

Consider the following table of melting points and boiling points of the hydrogen halides. If HF continues the trend in melting points illustrated by the other hydrogen halides, its melting point should be below the melting point of HCl. Instead, the melting point of HF is above the melting point of HCl. Similarly, the boiling point of HF does not follow the trend set by the other hydrogen halides.

HYDROGEN HALIDE	MELTING POINT (°C)	BOILING POINT (°C)
HF	−83	19.4
HCl	−112	−85
HBr	−86	−67
HI	−51	−36

The atypical properties of HF may be explained by the large difference in electronegativity between hydrogen and fluorine. This difference favors the formation of aggregates of HF through hydrogen bonds (see section 20.21). Melting and boiling first require energy to break these bonds, and then more energy is required to effect the change of state.

Hydrogen fluoride or its aqueous solution dissolves silica, a reaction utilized in etching glass.

$$4\ HF + SiO_2 \rightarrow 2\ H_2O + SiF_4\ (g)$$

Solutions of the hydrogen halides have typical acid properties. In addition, HI behaves as a reducing agent because of the ease in oxidizing I^- ion.

$$4\ \overset{+1-1}{HI} + \overset{0}{O_2} \rightarrow 2\ \overset{+1\ -2}{H_2O} + 2\ \overset{0}{I_2}$$

26.14 Uses of the hydrogen halides

Hydrogen fluoride is used to etch glass, as described above. In this process, the glass is covered with a thin layer of paraffin. The design or the figure to be etched is scratched through the paraffin, exposing the surface of the glass. The etching is carried out using vapors or a solution of HF. Care must be exercised in using HF in any form since it produces painful and slow-healing sores when in contact with the skin.

Hydrochloric acid is used in the manufacture of metallic chlorides, dyes, and drugs. It is used to pickle metals, that is, to dissolve metal oxide coatings before electroplating.

Hydrogen bromide and hydrogen iodide have limited use. Generally speaking, HCl, which is cheaper, may be used in place of HBr and HI.

Multiple-Choice Questions

1. Halogen elements attain a stable electron structure by (1) losing an *s* electron (2) completing an *s* orbital (3) losing a *p* electron (4) completing a *p* orbital

2. Which of the following statements describing fluorine is *not* correct? (1) It is the smallest halogen atom. (2) It has the highest ionization potential of the halogen elements. (3) It has a positive oxidation state when combined with oxygen. (4) Its ionic radius is larger than its covalent radius.

3. Of all the halogens, fluorine is the strongest oxidizing agent because it (1) is one element away from a noble gas (2) forms aqueous ions with the greatest release of energy (3) forms a diatomic molecule (4) has the lowest ionization potential

4. A salt of chlorous acid is potassium (1) chlorite (2) chlorate (3) hypochlorite (4) chloride

5. Perchloric acid, $HClO_4$, is a stronger acid than hypochlorous acid, $HOCl$, because (1) in $HClO_4$ the H atom is bonded to a Cl atom (2) the oxidation state of chlorine is lower in $HClO_4$ (3) HOCl forms OH ions (4) the oxygen atoms in $HClO_4$ weaken the O—H bond

6. Elemental fluorine is obtained by (1) oxidation of F^- with MnO_2 (2) replacement with chlorine (3) electrolysis of KHF_2 in liquid HF (4) electrolysis of a solution of CaF_2

7. To complete the equation

$$MnO_2 + 2\ Br^- + \underline{\hspace{2cm}} \rightarrow Mn^{+2} + Br_2 + 2\ H_2O$$

the necessary term in the blank space is (1) $4\ H_2O$ (2) $4\ H^+$ (3) $4\ OH^-$ (4) 4 HBr

8. In the reaction

$$3\ Cl_2 + 6\ KOH \rightarrow KClO_3 + 5\ KCl + 3\ H_2O$$

chlorine atoms are (1) oxidized (2) reduced (3) oxidized and reduced (4) neutralized by a base

9. The boiling point of HF is much higher than the boiling point of the other hydrogen halides. This is explained by the (1) hydrogen bonding in HF (2) greater ionization of HF (3) greater heat of formation of HF (4) decreased polarity of the H—F bond

10. Which of the following statements is *not* correct for the halogen elements? (1) Halogen elements form covalent bonds with nonmetals. (2) Halogen elements in oxyhalogen compounds have a positive oxidation number. (3) The electronegativities of the halogens increase with increasing atomic radius. (4) The halide ion has two s and six p electrons in its valence shell.

Completion Questions

1. One-half the distance between the nuclei of the atoms in a molecule of Cl_2 is called the _____ radius of chlorine.
2. The acid related to sodium hypochlorite is _____ acid.
3. In the oxyacids, the highest oxidation state for chlorine is _____.
4. Br_2 and I_2 are nonpolar molecules and are soluble in solvents such as CCl_4 or CS_2, which are _____ (*polar, nonpolar*).
5. Solutions of hydrogen halides act as typical acids because of the presence of _____ ions.
6. A radioactive element in Group VIIA is named _____.
7. The halogen element with the most negative E^0 value is _____.
8. The formula of a gaseous compound produced when glass is etched is _____.

True-False Questions

1. In combination with hydrogen, the halogens form *ionic* bonds.
2. The ionization potentials of the halogen elements are *less than* those of the neighboring noble gases.
3. $HClO_4$ is a stronger acid than $HOCl$ and a *stronger* oxidizer.
4. In the compound OF_2, the oxidation state of F is positive.
5. Compounds of chlorine with *nonmetals* contain a covalent bond.
6. The halide ion that has the highest oxidation potential is *fluoride* ion.
7. The halogen that has only one oxidation state in its compounds is *iodine*.

Decreases, Increases, Remains the Same

1. As the electronegativity values of the halogens increase, the corresponding ionization potentials _____.
2. When a halogen atom becomes an ion, the radius of the atom _____.
3. As the atomic numbers of the halogen elements increase, their oxidizing abilities _____.
4. From the lightest to the heaviest halogen element, the number of unfilled orbitals in the valence shell _____.
5. In the series chlorite, chlorate, perchlorate, the oxidation state of oxygen _____.
6. In the oxyhalogen acids, as the oxidation state of the halogen increases, the acid strength _____.
7. In the reaction of the halogens with hydrogen, $X_2 + H_2 \rightarrow 2\ HX$, as the atomic number of X increases, the energy released on forming a mole of HX _____.

Exercises for Review

1. Explain why all four common halogen elements cannot be obtained from their salts by oxidizers such as acidified MnO_2 or $KMnO_4$.
2. Does the size of an atom of a halogen element influence its electronegativity? Explain.
3. If the halogen X is a strong oxidizer, describe the oxidizing power of its ion X^-.
4. Write the chemical names of the following compounds:
    a. $NaOCl$ *d.* $NaIO_3$
    b. $Ca(ClO_2)_2$ *e.* $BaBr_2$
    c. $KClO_4$ *f.* $HOBr$
5. Write the formulas for the following compounds: (*a*) hypoiodous acid (*b*) barium perchlorate (*c*) calcium iodate (*d*) zinc hypobromite
6. Indicate the important naturally occurring source or compound containing (*a*) fluorine (*b*) chlorine (*c*) bromine (*d*) iodine
7. Complete and balance the following reactions:
    a. $MnO_2 + NaBr + H_2SO_4 \rightarrow$
    b. $Br_2 + H_2O \rightarrow$
    c. $Cl_2 + NaOH \xrightarrow{\text{warm}}$

8. *a.* When $KClO_3$ decomposes, which element is oxidized and which is reduced?

   b. Write redox equations for each change.

9. Predict some of the properties of astatine. Give reasons for your choices.

10. Is HF the correct formula for hydrogen fluoride or for hydrofluoric acid? Explain.

Exercises for Further Study

1. *a.* In the preparation of fluorine, both KHF_2 and HF are used. What is the function of each?

   b. Why is it not possible to electrolyze HF alone?

2. *a.* Why is the energy of hydration of the halide ion important in determining the activity of the halogen as an oxidizer?

   b. What effect does ionic size have on the energy of hydration?

3. Draw the electron-dot diagram for (*a*) NaOBr (*b*) $KClO_3$

4. *a.* Name the oxyacids of iodine arranged in the order of their increasing strengths as acids.

   b. Indicate the oxidation state of iodine in each acid.

   c. Indicate the strongest and the weakest oxidizer in the list.

5. The carbon compound $C_{12}H_{26}$ burns readily, but $C_{12}F_{26}$ is not combustible. Explain.

6. When bromine is extracted from seawater, bromine undergoes several changes in oxidation state. Write all the equations for these changes.

7. Iodine vapors have a violet color. A solution of iodine in a nonpolar solvent, such as CCl_4, is also violet. A solution of iodine in a polar solvent, such as water, is brown. Explain.

8. Account for the fact that hydrofluoric acid is a weak acid.

9. How would you separate a mixture containing F^- (*aq*), Cl^- (*aq*), Br^- (*aq*), and I^- (*aq*)?

10. Suggest a reason to account for the fact that Teflon is almost completely unreactive.

Chapter 27

THE NOBLE GASES

27.1 Introduction

The members of the family of noble gases (Group 0) are helium, neon, argon, krypton, xenon, and radon. These gases were discovered at the close of the 19th century, although their presence was suspected at least 100 years before. They were called the inert, or rare, gas family because they did not form compounds. Recently, compounds of the inert gases have been prepared, and this family has been renamed the noble gases. The table on the following page summarizes some of the important properties of the noble gases.

27.2 Trends in the general properties

With the exception of helium, in which the s subshell is complete, each noble gas has a complete s and p subshell in the outermost energy level. Atoms that possess eight electrons in this shell are extremely stable. Prior to 1962 there was no evidence of chemical reactivity for the noble gases. Recent work on compounds of the noble gases is discussed later in this chapter.

Molecules of noble gas elements are monatomic, revealing little or no tendency to engage in bond formation. The relatively high ionization potentials of the atoms of these elements seem to support this observation. The fact that the boiling points of these gases are all well below $0°$ C also illustrates the absence of strong attractive forces between the atoms. For example, of all the known elements, helium has the lowest boiling point, $4.1°$ K.

As added evidence of the presence of very weak interatomic forces, helium is the only element that cannot be solidified by cooling alone. Helium solidifies at $1.1°$ K at a pressure of 26 atmospheres. The melting points of the solidified inert gases are only a few degrees below the boiling points. Once again, very weak attractive forces between the atoms are in evidence.

PROPERTY	HELIUM	NEON	ARGON	KRYPTON	XENON	RADON
atomic number	2	10	18	36	54	86
electron structure	$1s^2$	$1s^2$ $2s^2, 2p^6$	$1s^2$ $2s^2, 2p^6$ $3s^2, 3p^6$	$1s^2$ $2s^2, 2p^6$ $3s^2, 3p^6, 3d^{10}$ $4s^2, 4p^6$	$1s^2$ $2s^2, 2p^6$ $3s^2, 3p^6, 3d^{10}$ $4s^2, 4p^6, 4d^{10}$ $5s^2, 5p^6$	$1s^2$ $2s^2, 2p^6$ $3s^2, 3p^6, 3d^{10}$ $4s^2, 4p^6, 4d^{10}, 4f^{14}$ $5s^2, 5p^6, 5d^{10}$ $6s^2, 6p^6$
melting point (°C)	-271.9 (at 26 atm)	-248.7	-189.3	-157	-111.5	-71
boiling point (°C)	-268.9	-245.9	-185.7	-152.9	-107.1	-62
atomic radius (Å)	0.93	1.12	1.54	1.69	1.90	2.2
first ionization potential (ev)	24.46	21.45	15.68	13.93	12.08	10.75
abundance in earth's atmosphere (parts per million by volume)	5.2	18.2	9430	1.1	0.09	6×10^{-14}

27.3 Occurrence

All the noble gases are found in the atmosphere, but radon is present only in trace amounts. In 1894, through the use of the spectroscope, helium, neon, and krypton were identified in the earth's atmosphere. In 1900, the gaseous radioactive disintegration product of radium was identified as radon.

27.4 Bond formation

The ionization potentials of helium, neon, krypton, and argon are relatively high, suggesting that the atoms of these elements show a very limited tendency to form bonds. The following table compares the ionization potentials of xenon with those of other common gaseous elements which also have high ionization potentials but which do form bonds.

GASEOUS ELEMENT	FIRST IONIZATION POTENTIAL (ev)
xenon	12.1
chlorine	13.0
hydrogen	13.6
oxygen	13.6
nitrogen	14.5
fluorine	17.4

27.5 Should the noble gases form compounds?

Of the gaseous elements listed in the preceding table, xenon has the lowest ionization potential. Since gaseous elements with higher ionization potentials (lesser tendency to lose electrons) form covalently bonded compounds, scientists wondered why xenon should not form such compounds. For example, oxygen and xenon have closely related ionization potentials. Molecular oxygen forms a covalent compound with platinum and fluorine, O_2PtF_6. Should not xenon form an analogous compound?

As we have already noted, all the noble gases have a stable structure which, in all cases except helium, includes two s electrons and six p electrons. This seems to indicate that xenon has no additional bonding capacity, since its s and p orbitals already have four electron pairs. Note, however, in the following electron-dot formula for the compound iodine pentafluoride, IF_5, that six bonding pairs of electrons (12 valence electrons) are available:

Is there a xenon compound like IF_5 that has six bonding pairs of electrons? The compound xenon tetrafluoride, XeF_4, if it could be prepared, would also have six bonding pairs of electrons. Furthermore, just as s, p, and d orbitals are utilized to give PCl_5 five bonding pairs of electrons (section 24.15) and to give Ni^{+2} ion four bonding pairs of electrons in the $Ni(NH_3)_4^{+2}$ complex ion (see section 23.4), perhaps these same orbitals could be used in the formation of XeF_4.

27.6 Electron configuration of noble gas halides

In 1962, Neil Bartlett, convinced that the oxygen-platinum fluoride compound suggested an analogous noble gas compound, succeeded in preparing $XePtF_6$. Shortly thereafter, other chemists synthesized xenon tetrafluoride by heating a mixture of one part xenon and excess fluorine at 400° C. White crystals of XeF_4 form when the reaction product is cooled suddenly.

$$Xe\ (g) + 2\ F_2\ (g) \rightarrow XeF_4\ (s)$$

To understand the bonding in XeF_4, let us first write the electron configuration for xenon, atomic number 54.

$1s$	$2s$	$2p$	$3s$	$3p$	$3d$	$4s$	$4p$	$4d$	$4f$	$5s$	$5p$	$5d$
2	2	6	2	6	10	2	6	10		2	6	

XeF_4 has a total of twelve valence electrons (eight from Xe and four from F), or six bonding pairs of electrons. The unoccupied $5d$ orbital in Xe is not much higher in energy than the completed $5s$ and $5p$ orbitals but much lower in energy than the $4f$ orbital. It has been suggested that hybridization of the $5d$ orbital with the $5s$ and the $5p$ orbitals may occur, especially in the presence of highly electronegative fluorine.

Thus hybrid orbitals are used in the formation of XeF_4. At present, it is thought that these orbitals have an sp^3d^2 orientation, and that there are six such orbitals for a total of 12 electrons. Figure 27-1 on the next page shows an arrangement of the 12 electrons.

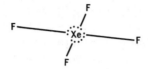

Fig. 27–1 Bonding arrangement in XeF₄

The shape of the XeF₄ molecule is determined by the shape of the sp^3d^2 hybrid orbital, which is described as square-planar and shown in Figure 27-2.

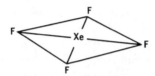

Fig. 27–2 The shape of the XeF₄ molecule

Studies of other species containing the same numbers of bonding electrons, such as BrF_3 and XeF_2 (ten bonding electrons) and IF_7 and XeF_6 (14 bonding electrons), suggest additional noble gas compounds. The following reactions summarize the preparation of such compounds:

$$Xe\ (g) + F_2\ (g) \rightarrow XeF_2\ (s)$$

$$Xe\ (g) + 3\ F_2\ (g) \rightarrow XeF_6\ (s)$$

The discovery of noble gas compounds teaches us that no single model of chemical behavior can remain unchanged. If extension of a model cannot account for additional observations, a new model must be sought.

Multiple-Choice Questions

1. Which of the following has a temperature closest to absolute zero? (1) ice water (2) liquid air (3) liquid helium (4) dry ice
2. The fact that the melting points of the noble gases are close to their boiling points indicates the presence of (1) strong forces between the molecules (2) weak forces between the atoms (3) ionic forces (4) polyatomic molecules
3. The most abundant noble gas in the atmosphere is (1) argon (2) neon (3) helium (4) radon

4. A comparison of the density of nitrogen obtained from compounds and the density of nitrogen obtained from air showed a difference because the (1) nitrogen from compounds was not pure (2) percent of nitrogen in the compounds was not the same as in air (3) composition of the compounds varied (4) nitrogen from air contained another gas

5. A glass vessel containing radium becomes radioactive because (1) the glass is changed to other elements (2) glass has a short half-life (3) the glass adsorbs a radioactive gas produced by radium (4) the glass acquires helium

6. All the noble gas atoms have (1) complete *s* orbitals (2) complete *p* orbitals (3) complete *s* and *p* orbitals (4) half-filled orbitals

7. A compound with the same number of valence electrons as XeF_2 is (1) N_2O_5 (2) PCl_5 (3) N_2O_3 (4) PCl_3

8. Noble gases differ from other gaseous elements because (1) only noble gases form monatomic molecules (2) molecules of the other gaseous elements cannot be decomposed (3) noble gases generally liquefy at higher temperatures (4) molecules of the other gaseous elements are generally polar

9. The formula of a noble gas compound is (1) XeF_3 (2) XeO_3 (3) $XeOF_2$ (4) $XeOF_3$

Completion Questions

1. The most abundant noble gas on the sun is _____.
2. A member of the noble gas family the atoms of which contain *f* electrons is _____.
3. If the maximum number of electrons in an orbital were one, the atomic number of neon would be _____.
4. In every row in the Periodic Table, the ionization energy of the noble gas element is the _____ (*highest, lowest*) in that row.
5. Among the molecules of the noble gases, the _____ (*largest, smallest*) molecules show the greatest tendency to form bonds.
6. The noble gas that has the lowest boiling point is _____.
7. The presence of the different noble gases can be detected by studying the light emitted by their excited atoms using an instrument called a (an) _____.
8. The formula of a noble gas compound containing xenon and oxygen is _____.

Exercises for Review

1. Explain how the boiling and freezing points of the noble gases indicate that only weak forces act between the atoms.
2. *a.* Describe a similarity that exists in the structures of liquid He and liquid H_2.
   b. How does this similarity explain the low boiling point of hydrogen?
3. Why does helium solidify only under increased pressure?
4. Some rocks and minerals contain small amounts of trapped helium. What is the possible origin of this helium?
5. *a.* Explain why it is possible for some of the noble gases to form compounds.
   b. Which noble gases show the greatest ability to form compounds?
   c. With which elements will the noble gases unite? Explain.
   d. Why are the bonding orbitals in noble gas compounds hybridized?

Exercises for Further Study

1. If noble gas compounds other than those containing xenon can be prepared, which of these compounds is most likely? Explain.
2. *a.* List the krypton analogs of three known xenon compounds.
   b. Which orbitals would be utilized in the formation of these compounds?
   c. Is it likely that these orbitals would be hybridized? Explain.

Chapter 28

ORGANIC CHEMISTRY

28.1 Introduction

Carbon forms an unusually large number of compounds, which are studied as a separate branch of chemistry, called *organic chemistry*. Carbon compounds are utilized in the manufacture of drugs, dyes, and plastics. The advances man has made in understanding the processes that occur in living organisms, including the conquest of disease, are based on progress in fundamental research in organic chemistry. The very large number of carbon compounds may be attributed to the unique bonding behavior of the carbon atom.

28.2 The bonding behavior of carbon

According to the rules for the arrangement of electrons in atoms, the configuration for a carbon atom may be represented as

$$1s \qquad 2s \qquad 2p$$

$$\otimes \qquad \otimes \qquad \oslash \oslash \bigcirc$$

In this state, carbon has two unpaired electrons — a bonding capacity of two. Experimentally, however, we find that carbon has a capacity for forming four bonds. In section 20.24, we have already explained this phenomenon in terms of promotion. If the $2s$ electrons are uncoupled and one electron is promoted to the $2p$ level, the following structure for a carbon atom is obtained:

$$1s \qquad 2s \qquad 2p$$

$$\otimes \qquad \oslash \qquad \oslash \oslash \oslash$$

The bonding capacity of carbon has now been increased to four. The energy required for the uncoupling and promoting of the $2s$ electron is far less than the energy that is gained by the increased bonding capacity. We therefore find four bonds in most carbon compounds.

The four unpaired electrons can be shared with the bonding electrons of other carbon atoms or with the bonding electrons of a variety of different atoms. The sharing of electrons between carbon atoms or between carbon atoms and other atoms, such as hydrogen, makes possible an almost unlimited number of compounds in which the atoms are arranged in chains and rings of varying complexity.

When carbon atoms share electrons with other carbon atoms, giant network structures of diamond or graphite result. However, the study of organic chemistry does not generally deal with these structures. Rather, organic chemistry is concerned with compounds containing C—H bonds as well as C—C bonds and with the derivatives of such compounds.

28.3 How atoms are bonded in carbon compounds

In carbon compounds, carbon atoms may be bonded to one another or to different atoms through single bonds (one pair of electrons), double bonds (two pairs of electrons), or triple bonds (three pairs of electrons). Compounds containing molecules in which carbon atoms are bonded by a single bond are called *saturated* compounds. When carbon atoms are bonded by double or triple bonds, the compounds are called *unsaturated.*

28.4 The carbon-to-carbon single bond

We have already seen that when a single carbon atom is bonded to four hydrogen atoms, the shape of the molecule is tetrahedral. (See Figure 28-1.)

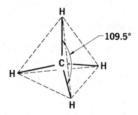

Fig. 28–1   The shape of the CH₄ molecule

This structure is more conveniently represented as

$$\begin{array}{c} H \\ | \\ H{-}C{-}H \\ | \\ H \end{array}$$

When two carbon atoms join through one pair of shared electrons, the bonds from each carbon atom point again toward the four corners of a regular tetrahedron, and the resulting bond angle is 109° 28′. For two carbon atoms and six hydrogen atoms, C_2H_6, the tetrahedral arrangement is shown in Figure 28-2.

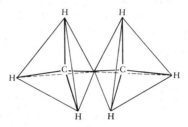

Fig. 28–2   The shape of the
C_2H_6 molecule

This structure is more conveniently represented as

$$\begin{array}{c} H \;\; H \\ | \;\;\; | \\ H{-}C{-}C{-}H \\ | \;\;\; | \\ H \;\; H \end{array}$$

Remember that these structures are represented in two dimensions only and are simplifications of the actual structures of the molecules.

28.5 The carbon-to-carbon double bond

When two pairs of electrons are shared between two carbon atoms (a double bond), the bond angle becomes 120°, and the molecule has a planar structure. The molecule C_2H_4 might thus be represented as

$$\begin{array}{cc} H & H \\ \ddot{C} :: \ddot{C} \\ H & H \end{array} \quad \text{or} \quad$$

$$\begin{array}{ccc} H & & 120° \;\; H \\ \diagdown & & \diagup \\ & C{=}C & \\ \diagup & & \diagdown \\ H & & H \end{array}$$

28.6 The carbon-to-carbon triple bond

When three pairs of electrons are shared between two carbon atoms (a triple bond), the bond angle becomes 180° and the molecule assumes a linear shape, as in the compound C_2H_2.

$$H : C ::: C : H \quad \text{or} \quad H{-}C{\equiv}C{-}H \;\; (180°)$$

28.7 The organization of organic compounds

To make possible the study of so large a number of organic compounds, a system of organization has been adopted. In this system, organic compounds are classified into large families. Each member of a family is structurally related to other members of the family. The simplest families are the compounds of carbon and hydrogen called *hydrocarbons*, which form the basis for understanding many other organic compounds.

28.8 Hydrocarbon families

Hydrogen and carbon form a variety of hydrocarbon families. The organization of these families is summarized in the following diagram:

HYDROCARBONS

ALIPHATIC   AROMATIC

ALKANES   ALKENES   ALKYNES   ARENES

(may be open-chain or cyclic)   (benzene and its derivatives)

28.9 The aliphatic hydrocarbons

The aliphatic hydrocarbons are subdivided into three groups, depending on the kind of carbon-to-carbon bond present.

THE ALKANES

The alkanes contain single bonds between carbon atoms. If the structure is an open chain, the general formula is C_nH_{2n+2}. The general formula states the fixed relationship between the number of carbon and hydrogen atoms. Typical alkanes are

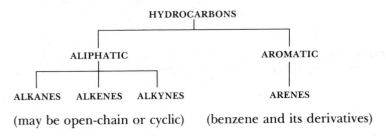

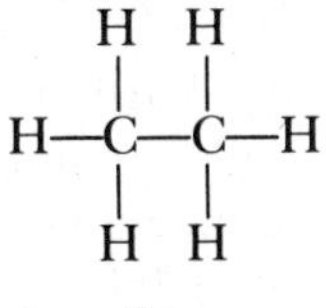

ethane 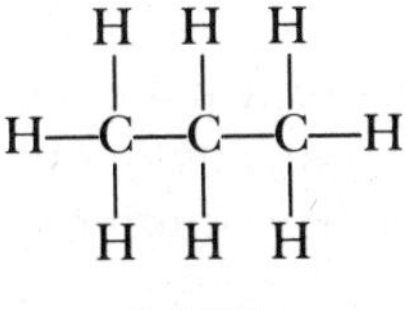   propane 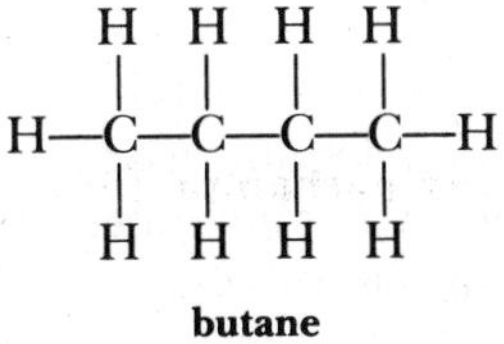   butane

Hydrocarbons that follow a general formula such as C_nH_{2n+2} are called a *homologous series*. Thus following butane are: pentane, C_5H_{12}; hexane, C_6H_{14}; heptane, C_7H_{16}; octane, C_8H_{18}; and so on. The suffix *-ane* distinguishes this family of hydrocarbons.

THE ALKENES

The alkenes contain one or more double bonds between carbon atoms. These compounds are also called *olefins*. When the molecule contains more than one double bond, it is termed a *polyolefin*. Alkenes containing one double bond per molecule constitute a homologous series: C_nH_{2n}. The simplest member of this series is ethene, or ethylene, written as shown in the three following formulas:

$$C_2H_4 \quad \text{or} \quad \begin{array}{c} H \\ \diagdown \\ C = C \\ \diagup \quad \diagdown \\ H \quad\quad H \end{array} \quad \text{or} \quad H - \underset{\underset{H}{|}}{\overset{\overset{H}{|}}{C}} = \underset{\underset{H}{|}}{\overset{\overset{H}{|}}{C}} - H$$

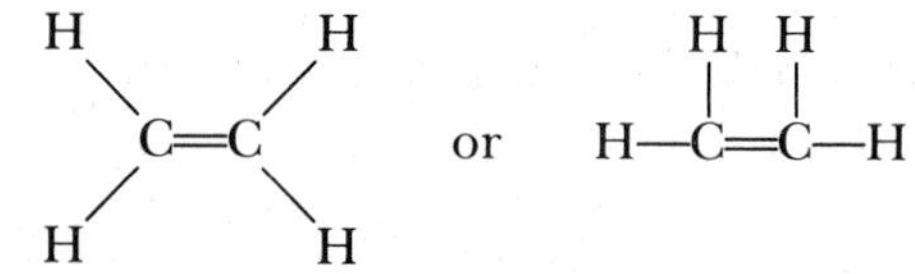

Other olefins are propylene, C_3H_6; butylene, C_4H_8; and so on. The suffix *-ene* distinguishes this family of hydrocarbons.

An example of a polyolefin is

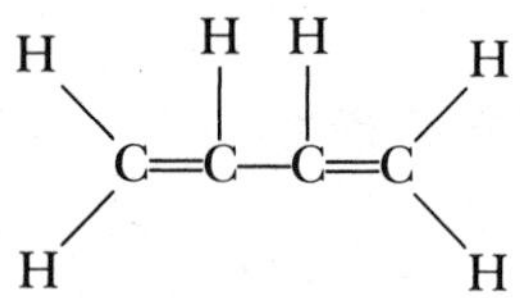

$$\begin{array}{c} H \quad\quad H \quad H \quad\quad H \\ \diagdown \quad\quad | \quad\ | \quad\quad \diagup \\ C = C - C = C \\ \diagup \quad\quad\quad\quad\quad \diagdown \\ H \quad\quad\quad\quad\quad\quad H \end{array}$$

butadiene

The suffix *-diene* distinguishes polyolefin hydrocarbons with two double bonds.

THE ALKYNES

The alkynes contain one or more triple bonds between carbon atoms. The homologous series C_nH_{2n-2} contains one triple bond per molecule. Alkynes are sometimes called *acetylenes*, after the common name of the simplest member.

$$C_2H_2 \quad \text{or} \quad H - C \equiv C - H$$

acetylene (ethyne)

Other alkynes are

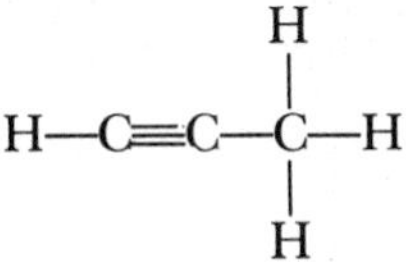

$$H-C\equiv C-\underset{\underset{\displaystyle H}{|}}{\overset{\overset{\displaystyle H}{|}}{C}}-H \quad \text{and} \quad H-C\equiv C-\underset{\underset{\displaystyle H}{|}}{\overset{\overset{\displaystyle H}{|}}{C}}-\underset{\underset{\displaystyle H}{|}}{\overset{\overset{\displaystyle H}{|}}{C}}-H$$

propyne, C_3H_4   **butyne, C_4H_6**

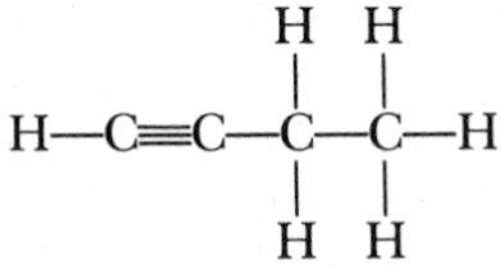

The suffix *-yne* distinguishes this family of hydrocarbons.

28.10 Open-chain and cyclic hydrocarbons

In the aliphatic hydrocarbons that we have discussed in the previous section, the carbon atoms are joined together like links in an open chain. Inherent in this structure is the possibility of adding more links (carbon atoms) to the chain. However, aliphatic hydrocarbons also form a group of compounds in which the carbon atoms form a closed ring rather than an open chain. Cyclobutane is an example of such a *cyclic* compound.

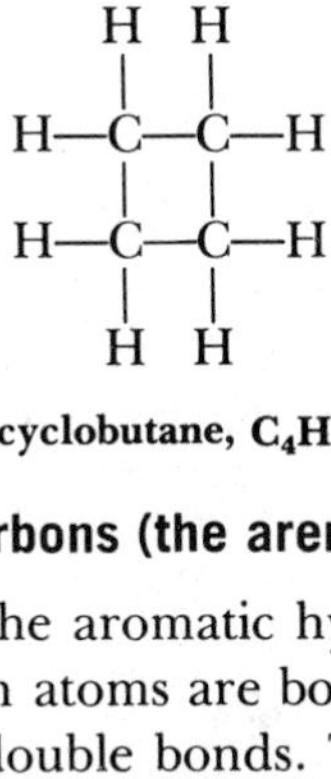

$$\begin{array}{c} H-\overset{\overset{\displaystyle H}{|}}{C}-\overset{\overset{\displaystyle H}{|}}{C}-H \\ |\quad\quad| \\ H-\underset{\underset{\displaystyle H}{|}}{C}-\underset{\underset{\displaystyle H}{|}}{C}-H \end{array}$$

cyclobutane, C_4H_8

28.11 The aromatic hydrocarbons (the arenes)

The simplest member of the aromatic hydrocarbon group is benzene, C_6H_6. In benzene, the carbon atoms are bonded in a six-membered ring, with alternating single and double bonds. The following model of alternating single and double bonds between carbon atoms in the ring was proposed by the German chemist Friedrich Kekulé in 1865:

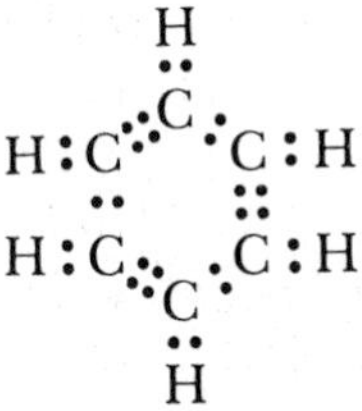

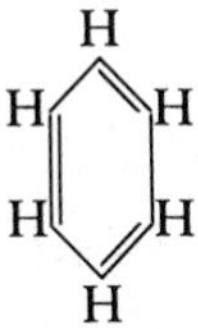

This model indicates that half the bonds (three) are single and the other half are double. However, all six bonds between carbon atoms in benzene are identical. (Experimentally, the bond lengths and bond strengths have been shown to be the same.) To make the model conform better with experimental evidence, it was proposed that benzene exists as a *resonance hybrid* of the following forms:

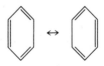

In the two formulas, the electrons bonding the carbon atoms are said to be delocalized; that is, they do not have a fixed position. This means that the structures in the two formulas are equivalent and that the electron bonding in the molecule is intermediate between the structures shown in the preceding figure. The resonating structure may be represented by a single figure.

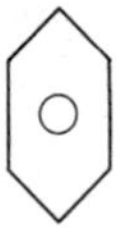

The circle in the ring represents carbon-to-carbon bonds that resonate between single and double-bond structures.

Many important aromatic compounds are derived from the benzene structure. For example, naphthalene, $C_{10}H_8$, has two benzene rings joined together.

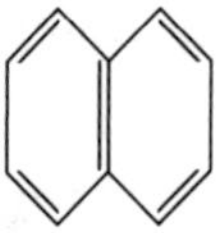

Similarly, anthracene, $C_{14}H_{10}$, has three benzene rings joined together.

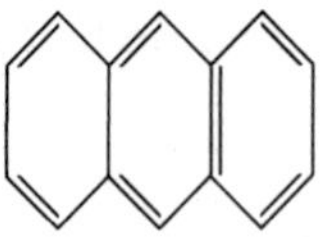

28.12 Uses of hydrocarbons

The following table summarizes the important uses of some typical hydrocarbons.

HYDROCARBON	USE
	Aliphatic Hydrocarbons
methane, CH_4 propane, C_3H_8 butane, C_4H_{10}	gaseous fuel
octane, C_8H_{10}	liquid fuel
ethylene, C_2H_4	starting material for the manufacture of the plastic polyethylene
acetylene, C_2H_2	gaseous fuel
	Aromatic Hydrocarbons
benzene, C_6H_6	solvent and starting material for the manufacture of many products, such as medicinal chemicals
naphthalene, $C_{10}H_8$ anthracene, $C_{14}H_{10}$	starting material for the manufacture of dyes

28.13 Functional groups

If a single hydrogen atom is removed from a hydrocarbon, the remaining structure is called a *hydrocarbon radical* and is designated as *R*. The radical can bond to an atom other than hydrogen. Radicals derived from alkanes or alkenes are called *alkyl* radicals. Radicals derived from benzene are called *aryl* radicals. Some common hydrocarbon radicals follow.

HYDROCARBON	HYDROCARBON RADICAL	NAME OF RADICAL
CH_4	CH_3	methyl
C_2H_6	C_2H_5	ethyl
C_3H_8	C_3H_7	propyl
C_4H_{10}	C_4H_9	butyl
C_5H_{12}	C_5H_{11}	pentyl (amyl)
C_6H_6	C_6H_5	phenyl

In many organic molecules derived from hydrocarbons, one or more hydrogen atoms in the hydrocarbon structure are replaced by another element or group of elements. The replacement element or group of elements is called a *functional group*. We will illustrate several functional groups in this section: halogens, alcohols, aldehydes, acids, ethers, ketones, esters, and amines.

HALOGENS – GENERAL TYPE RX

The following are examples of hydrocarbons in which a halogen has been substituted for a hydrogen.

NAME	FORMULA
monochloromethane (methyl chloride)	CH_3Cl or 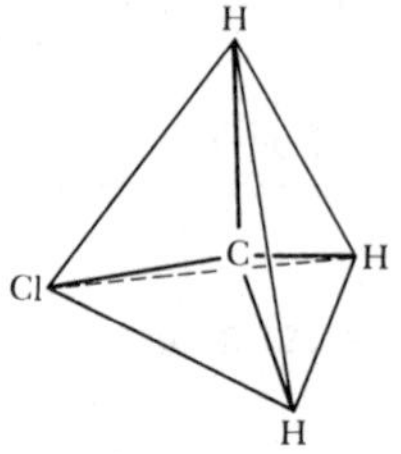
paradichlorobenzene	$C_6H_4Cl_2$ or 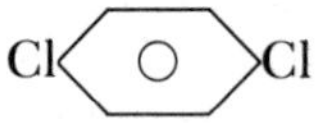
dichlorodiphenyl-trichloroethane (DDT)	$C_{14}H_9Cl_5$ or 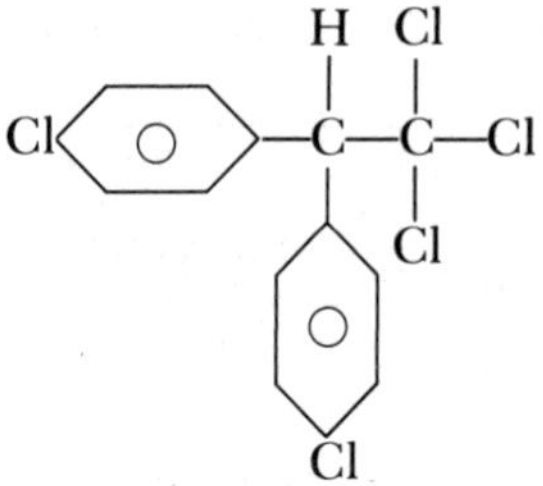

ALCOHOLS–GENERAL TYPE ROH

When the —OH group is combined with an organic radical, the molecule has certain specific properties and is classified as an *alcohol*. For example, alcohols, like other organic compounds but unlike inorganic bases, are generally nonionic. Alcohols, like water, react with certain metals to form hydrogen.

$$ROH + Na \rightarrow H_2 \ (g) + RONa$$

Examples of some common alcohols follow.

NAME	FORMULA
methyl alcohol (methanol)	CH_3OH or 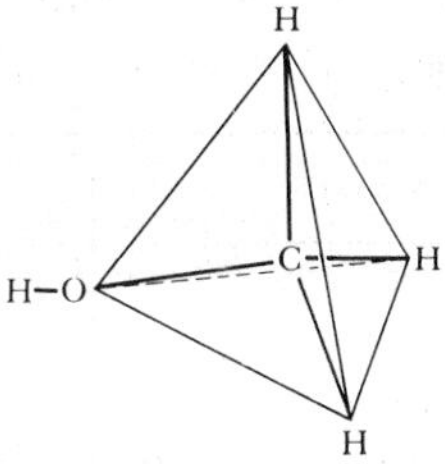
ethyl alcohol (ethanol)	CH_3CH_2OH or (C_2H_5OH) 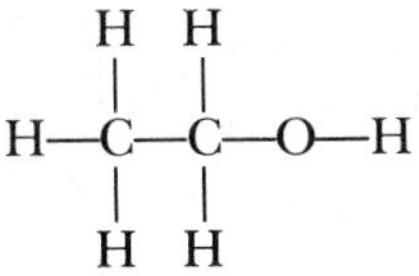
phenol	C_6H_5OH or 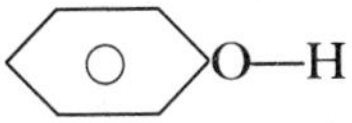
glycerol (glycerine)	$C_3H_5(OH)_3$ or 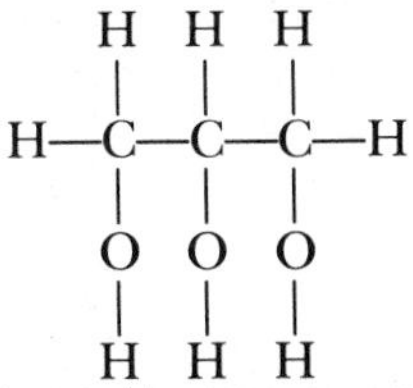

ALDEHYDES – GENERAL TYPE *R*CHO

A carbon atom with a double bond to an oxygen atom has the formula —C=O and is called a *carbonyl* group. The aldehyde functional group is a carbonyl derivative, with hydrogen on one side and an organic *R* group on the other side of the carbonyl.

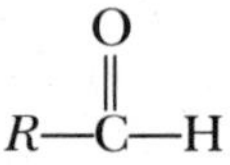

$$\underset{R-\overset{\displaystyle \overset{\textstyle O}{\|}}{C}-H}{}$$

Some aldehydes have distinctive odors and flavors, which are used in perfumes. The simplest possible aldehyde contains a —C=O group and two H atoms bonded to the C atom.

Some typical aldehydes follow.

NAME	FORMULA
methaldehyde, or methanal (formaldehyde)	HCHO or 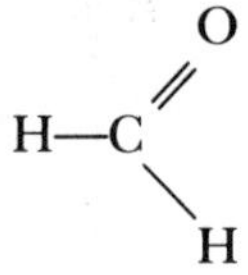
acetaldehyde (ethanal)	CH_3CHO or 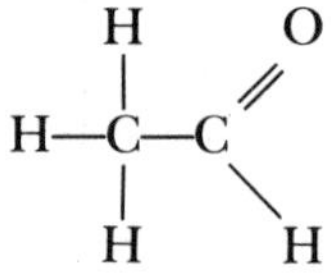
cinnamaldehyde	$C_6H_5(CH)_2CHO$ or 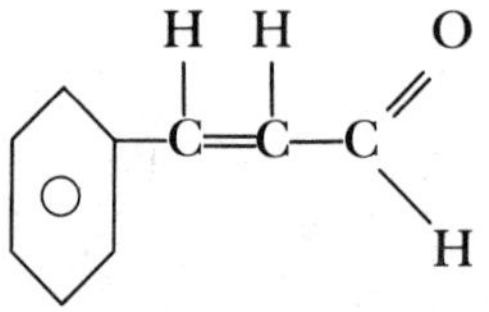

The cinnamaldehyde molecule is responsible for the flavor of cinnamon. In the table, note that the *R* is an aryl-alkyl combination.

ACIDS – GENERAL TYPE RCOOH

The functional group in organic acids is the carboxyl group.

Organic acids may contain one or more carboxyl groups, as shown by the following examples.

NAME	FORMULA
ethanoic acid (acetic acid)	CH_3COOH or
benzoic acid	C_6H_5COOH or
oxalic acid (a di-carboxylic acid containing two COOH groups)	$H_2C_2O_4$ or $(COOH)_2$ or
citric acid (a tri-carboxylic acid containing three COOH groups)	$COHCOOH(CH_2COOH)_2$ or

Note, in the preceding table, the alcohol group as well as three acid groups in citric acid. It is not unusual for a single organic molecule to contain more than one functional group.

Organic acids dissociate weakly to form hydronium ions.

$$RCOOH \rightarrow RCOO^- \,(aq) + H^+ \,(aq)$$

ETHERS – GENERAL TYPE *ROR'*

Ethers are analogous to inorganic oxides. The two R groups in ethers may be the same or different. Common hospital ether, called diethyl ether, has the formula

$$(CH_3CH_2)_2O \qquad \text{or}$$

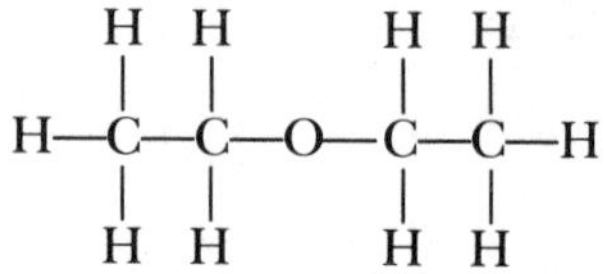

In the vanillin molecule, present in vanilla, there are three functional groups around the benzene ring: an aldehyde, an alcohol, and an ether.

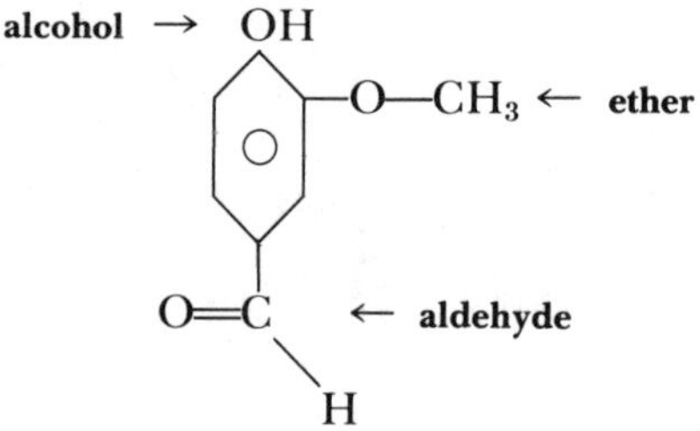

KETONES – GENERAL TYPE *RCOR'*

Ketones are also derivatives of the carbonyl group, with both sides of the

$$\overset{\text{O}}{\underset{}{\overset{\|}{-\text{C}-}}}$$

bonded to R groups. As with ethers, the R groups may or may not be the same. The common ketone dimethyl ketone (R groups are the same), called acetone, has the formula

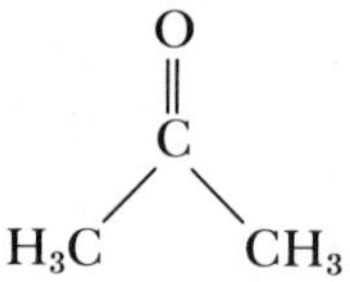

ESTERS – GENERAL TYPE $RCOOR'$

These compounds, which will be discussed more fully in section 29.6, can again be related to the carbonyl group.

$$R-\overset{\overset{\displaystyle O}{\|}}{C}-OR'$$

The molecules present in some fruit flavors are esters. The ester in which R is a four-carbon chain and R' is a five-carbon chain has the formula

$$CH_3(CH_2)_3-\overset{\overset{\displaystyle O}{\|}}{C}-O-(CH_2)_4CH_3$$

and is associated with the flavor of apple.

The molecule

is both an ester and an acid; it is named acetylsalicylic acid or, more commonly, aspirin.

AMINES – GENERAL TYPE RNH_2

These compounds can be pictured as derivatives of ammonia, in which one of the hydrogens in the NH_3 molecule has been replaced by an organic R group.

$$H-\overset{\overset{\displaystyle R}{|}}{N}-H$$

Examples of amines are methylamine, CH_3NH_2, and phenylamine, $C_6H_5NH_2$, also called aniline.

methylamine   **phenylamine**

Amines are used in the manufacture of dyes, medicinals, perfumes, and other useful products.

28.14 Naming organic compounds

Organic nomenclature is essentially based on the number of carbon atoms in the compound. As we shall discover in this section, the names of organic molecules are carefully constructed. Prefixes, suffixes, numbers, and root words serve as a blueprint for the structure of the molecule and the functional groups that it contains.

PREFIXES

Prefixes denote the number of carbon atoms in hydrocarbons.

PREFIX	NUMBER OF CARBON ATOMS
meth-	1
eth-	2
prop-	3
but-	4
pent-	5
hex-	6
hept-	7
oct-	8
non-	9
dec-	10

SUFFIXES

Suffixes indicate the presence of single, double, or triple bonds between the carbon atoms in hydrocarbons.

SUFFIX	BOND
-ane	single
-ene	double
-yne or -ine	triple

COMBINING PREFIXES AND SUFFIXES

By combining the rules for prefixes and suffixes, we can identify some hydrocarbons as follows.

FORMULA	NAME
$\begin{array}{cccc} & H & H & H \\ & \mid & \mid & \mid \\ H- & C- & C- & C-H \\ & \mid & \mid & \mid \\ & H & H & H \end{array}$	propane
$\begin{array}{cccc} & H & H & H \\ & \mid & \mid & \mid \\ H- & C= & C- & C-H \\ & & & \mid \\ & & & H \end{array}$	propene
$\begin{array}{ccc} & & H \\ & & \mid \\ H-C\equiv C- & & C-H \\ & & \mid \\ & & H \end{array}$	propyne

If the carbon atoms are arranged in a closed ring (other than benzene), the prefix *cyclo-* is added.

FORMULA	NAME
$\begin{array}{cc} H & H \\ \mid & \mid \\ H-C- & C-H \\ \mid & \mid \\ H-C- & C-H \\ \mid & \mid \\ H & H \end{array}$	cyclobutane
$\begin{array}{cc} & H \\ & \mid \\ H-C- & C-H \\ \parallel & \mid \\ H-C- & C-H \\ & \mid \\ & H \end{array}$	cyclobutene

Note that each carbon atom has a total of four bonds, representing four pairs of shared electrons. Also, each hydrogen atom has a single bond, representing one pair of shared electrons.

NUMBERING CARBON ATOMS

Often it is necessary to identify a specific carbon atom in a molecule. For example, in butene, different molecules result if the double bond is in the center of the molecule (as in formula *A*) or at the end (as in formula *B*).

A	*B*

H H H H
  | | | |
H—C—C=C—C—H
  | |
  H   H
 	
or
 	
CH_3—CH=CH—CH_3
	H H H H
	  | | | |
	H—C=C—C—C—H
	        | |
	        H H
	
	or
	
	CH_2=CH—CH_2—CH_3

	H H H H
	  | | | |
	H—C—C—C=C—H
	  | |
	  H H
	
	or
	
	CH_3—CH_2—CH=CH_2
	
	(Both *B* molecules are the same since the same groups surround the C=C structure.)

The specific molecules are identified by numbering the carbon atoms. Formula *A* thus becomes 2-butene (the number denotes the carbon atom just before the double bond), and formula *B* becomes *1*-butene.

To identify a double or triple bond in complex molecules, the longest continuous carbon chain is counted. The numbering is begun from that end of the molecule closest to the double or triple bond. The following examples will clarify this numbering scheme.

FORMULA	NAME
H H H H H H | | | | | | H—C—C—C—C=C—C—H | | | | H H H H or CH_3—CH_2—CH_2—CH=CH—CH_3	2-hexene
H H H H H | | | | | H—C—C—C—C≡C—C—C—H | | | | | H H H H H or CH_3—CH_2—CH_2—C≡C—CH_2—CH_3	3-heptyne

IDENTIFYING A FUNCTIONAL GROUP OR A RADICAL

Finally, the naming of organic molecules involves identifying any functional groups or radicals present and indicating the number of a specific carbon atom in the structure, if necessary. For example, to name members of the organic families discussed in the previous section, follow these conventions:

1. Hydrocarbon radicals and halogen compounds. Name the functional group and identify the carbon atom to which it is bonded.

```
  H H H            H   H           H H  H H H
  | | |            |   |           | |  | | |
H-C-C-C-H        H-C-C=C-H       H-C-C--C-C-C-H
  | | |            |   |           | |  | | |
  Cl H H           H   Br          H CH3 H H H
```

1-chloropropane   **2-bromopropene**   **2-methyl pentane**

2. Alcohols. Add *-ol* to the hydrocarbon name and identify the position of the OH group.

```
    H H H                H H  H
    | | |                | |  |
  H-C-C-C-OH           H-C-C--C-H
    | | |                | |  |
    H H H                H OH H
```

     1-propanol   *2*-propanol

In the preceding examples, note that these two propanols are not the same since different groups are attached to the —OH structure.

3. Aldehydes. Add the suffix *-al* to the root name.

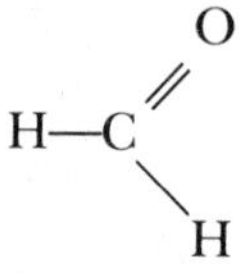

$$H-C\overset{\displaystyle O}{\underset{\displaystyle H}{\diagup}}\qquad H-\overset{\displaystyle H}{\underset{\displaystyle H}{C}}-C\overset{\displaystyle O}{\underset{\displaystyle H}{\diagup}}$$

methanal 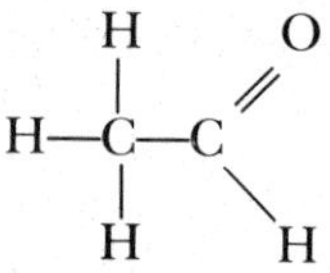   **ethanal**

4. Carboxylic acids. Add the suffix *-oic* and the word *acid* to the root. (Note that the prefix is obtained from the *total* number of carbons.)

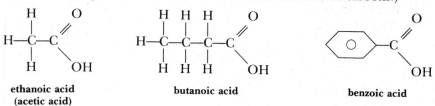

ethanoic acid   **butanoic acid**   **benzoic acid**
(acetic acid)

5. Ethers. In the general formula *R*—O—*R'*, name the two *R* groups and add the word *ether*.

$$CH_3CH_2\text{—}O\text{—}CH_2CH_3$$

diethyl ether

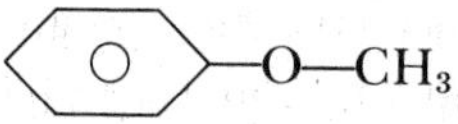

phenyl methyl ether: ⬡—O—CH₃

phenyl methyl ether

6. Ketones. In the general formula $R\text{—}\overset{\displaystyle O}{\underset{\displaystyle \|}{C}}\text{—}R'$, name the two *R* groups and add the word *ketone*.

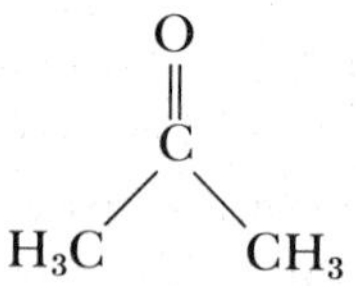

dimethyl ketone

7. Esters. The naming of esters depends on how they are formed.

$$C_2H_5O\,\boxed{H} + CH_3CO\,\boxed{OH} \rightarrow CH_3COOC_2H_5 + H_2O$$

ethyl   acetic   ethyl
alcohol   acid   acetate

8. **Amines.** In the general formula R—N—H, name the R group and

$$R-\underset{\underset{\displaystyle H}{|}}{N}-H$$

add the word *amine*.

$$H-\underset{\underset{\displaystyle H-N-H}{|}}{\overset{\overset{\displaystyle H}{|}}{C}}-H$$

methylamine

28.15 Common names of organic compounds

Some organic compounds are identified by their common names. Examples are listed in the table that follows.

TYPE	GENERIC NAME	COMMON NAME	FORMULA
alcohols	methanol	methyl alcohol or wood alcohol	CH_3OH
	ethanol	ethyl alcohol	CH_3CH_2OH
	pentanol	pentyl alcohol	$CH_3(CH_2)_3CH_2OH$
	benzol	phenol	⬡—OH
	1,2,3-propanetriol	glycerol or glycerine	$H-\underset{\underset{\displaystyle H}{|}}{\overset{\overset{\displaystyle OH}{|}}{C}}-\underset{\underset{\displaystyle H}{|}}{\overset{\overset{\displaystyle OH}{|}}{C}}-\underset{\underset{\displaystyle H}{|}}{\overset{\overset{\displaystyle OH}{|}}{C}}-H$
aldehydes	methanal	formaldehyde	$H-C{\overset{\displaystyle O}{\diagdown}}_{H}$
	ethanal	acetaldehyde	$CH_3C{\overset{\displaystyle O}{\diagdown}}_{H}$
ketone	dimethyl ketone	acetone	$\underset{H_3C \diagup \diagdown CH_3}{\overset{\displaystyle O \atop \displaystyle \| \atop \displaystyle C}{}}$

TYPE	GENERIC NAME	COMMON NAME	FORMULA
acids	methanoic acid	formic acid	$H-C\overset{\displaystyle O}{\underset{\displaystyle OH}{}}$
	ethanoic acid	acetic acid	$CH_3C\overset{\displaystyle O}{\underset{\displaystyle OH}{}}$
	octadecanoic acid	stearic acid	$CH_3(CH_2)_{16}C\overset{\displaystyle O}{\underset{\displaystyle OH}{}}$

28.16 Writing organic formulas

Three types of formulas for ethane are shown below.

FORMULA TYPE	FORMULA
1. molecular	C_2H_6
2a. condensed structural	CH_3CH_3
2b. extended structural	$\begin{array}{cc} H & H \\ | & | \\ H-C-C-H \\ | & | \\ H & H \end{array}$
3. three-dimensional structural	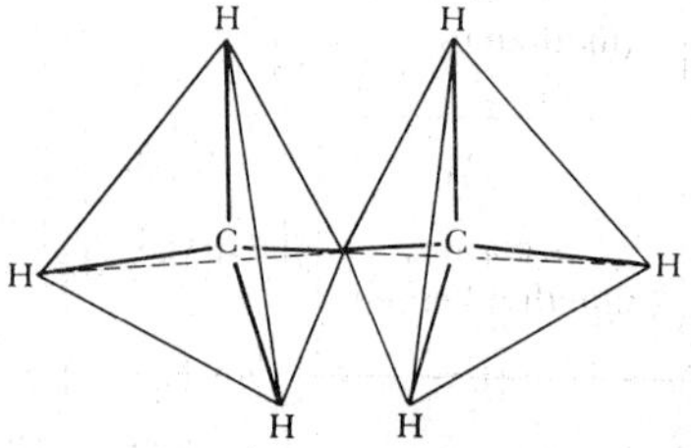

1. The *molecular formula* denotes the kind of atoms and the total number of moles of each atom present in one mole of the compound. The molecular weight fixes the molecular formula.

2. The *structural formula* shows the arrangement of the atoms in the molecule and may be shown in the condensed and extended forms.

3. The *three-dimensional structural formula* shows the arrangement of the atoms in the molecule and also shows shape and bond angles.

The following table reviews structural formulas for some common organic compounds. For simplicity, most of the hydrogen atoms have been omitted from the extended structural formulas.

TYPE	NAME	MOLECULAR FORMULA	CONDENSED STRUCTURAL FORMULA	EXTENDED STRUCTURAL FORMULA
alkane	butane	C_4H_{10}	$CH_3(CH_2)_2CH_3$	$-\overset{\mid}{\underset{\mid}{C}}-\overset{\mid}{\underset{\mid}{C}}-\overset{\mid}{\underset{\mid}{C}}-\overset{\mid}{\underset{\mid}{C}}-$
alkane	2-methyl propane	C_4H_{10}	$CH_3CH(CH_3)_2$	$-\overset{\mid}{\underset{\mid}{C}}-\overset{\mid}{\underset{\mid}{C}}-\overset{\mid}{\underset{\mid}{C}}-$, $-\overset{\mid}{\underset{\mid}{C}}-$
alkene	2-butene	C_4H_8	$CH_3CHCHCH_3$	$-\overset{\mid}{\underset{\mid}{C}}-\overset{\mid}{\underset{\mid}{C}}=\overset{\mid}{\underset{\mid}{C}}-\overset{\mid}{\underset{\mid}{C}}-$
alcohol	ethanol	C_2H_6O	CH_3CH_2OH	$-\overset{\mid}{\underset{\mid}{C}}-\overset{\mid}{\underset{\mid}{C}}-OH$
acid	acetic acid (ethanoic acid)	$C_2H_4O_2$	CH_3COOH	$-\overset{\mid}{\underset{\mid}{C}}-C\overset{O}{\diagdown OH}$
aldehyde	formaldehyde (methanal)	CH_2O	$HCHO$	$H-C\overset{O}{\diagdown H}$
ketone	acetone (dimethyl ketone)	C_3H_6O	CH_3COCH_3	$\underset{H_3C\quad CH_3}{\overset{O}{\|\|}C}$
ether	dimethyl ether	C_2H_6O	CH_3OCH_3	$-\overset{\mid}{\underset{\mid}{C}}-O-\overset{\mid}{\underset{\mid}{C}}-$
ester	ethyl acetate	$C_4H_8O_2$	$CH_3COOCH_2CH_3$	$-\overset{\mid}{\underset{\mid}{C}}-\overset{O}{\overset{\|\|}{C}}-O-\overset{\mid}{\underset{\mid}{C}}-\overset{\mid}{\underset{\mid}{C}}-$

28.17 Isomerism

We have indicated that the bonding behavior of carbon contributes to the large number of carbon compounds. The different ways in which the atoms in carbon compounds may be positioned also contributes to this large number. For example, when two carbon atoms, six hydrogen atoms, and one oxygen atom are arranged as

$$
\begin{array}{ccc}
& \text{H} & \text{H} \\
& | & | \\
\text{H} & \!\!-\text{C}-\text{C}-\text{OH} \\
& | & | \\
& \text{H} & \text{H}
\end{array}
$$

the molecule is an alcohol, C_2H_5OH, the familiar ethyl alcohol used in beverages. If the same kind and number of atoms are arranged as

$$
\begin{array}{ccc}
\text{H} & & \text{H} \\
| & & | \\
\text{H}-\text{C}-\text{O}-\text{C}-\text{H} \\
| & & | \\
\text{H} & & \text{H}
\end{array}
$$

the product is an ether, CH_3OCH_3, dimethyl ether, useful as a refrigerant. Both molecules have the molecular formula, C_2H_6O; but because their atoms are arranged differently, they represent different molecular species.

Isomers are molecules that have the same kind and number of atoms (same composition) but differ in the arrangement of the atoms.

The physical properties of isomers (melting point, boiling point) differ. Chemically, isomers may show marked differences in properties. The presence of isomers, as suggested previously, helps to account for the large number of organic compounds.

Isomers may be classified as structural isomers and stereoisomers, discussed in the sections that follow.

28.18 Structural isomers

Like all isomers, structural isomers have the same molecular formula but differ in the sequence of atoms in the molecule. In the example cited in the previous section, the sequence C—C—OH represents an alcohol, whereas the sequence C—O—C represents an ether. Such structural isomers are also called *functional isomers* because each isomer has a different functional group.

In hydrocarbons, different C—C sequences produce different isomeric forms. In ethane, C_2H_6, only one C—C arrangement is possible, and ethane has no isomers.

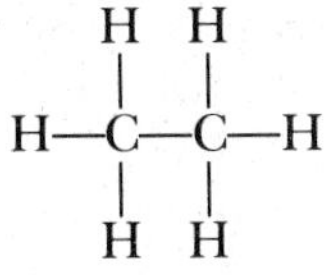

$$
\begin{array}{ccc}
 & H & H \\
 & | & | \\
H— & C— & C—H \\
 & | & | \\
 & H & H
\end{array}
$$

In propane, C_3H_8, only one C—C—C arrangement is possible, and propane also has no isomers.

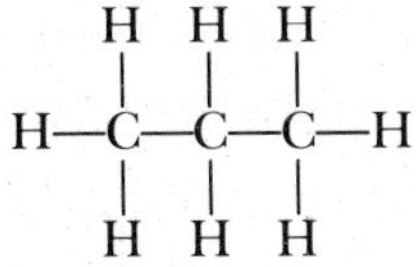

$$
\begin{array}{cccc}
 & H & H & H \\
 & | & | & | \\
H— & C— & C— & C—H \\
 & | & | & | \\
 & H & H & H
\end{array}
$$

Two sequences of carbon atoms are possible in butane: a *continuous* chain of carbon atoms, C—C—C—C, and a *branched* chain, C—C—C. The
$$| \atop C$$
continuous chain is called the *normal* (*n*-) compound, and the branched chain is called the *iso*-compound.

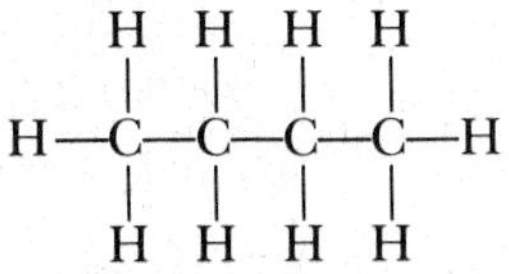

$$
\begin{array}{ccccc}
 & H & H & H & H \\
 & | & | & | & | \\
H— & C— & C— & C— & C—H \\
 & | & | & | & | \\
 & H & H & H & H
\end{array}
\qquad
\begin{array}{cccc}
 & H & H & H \\
 & | & | & | \\
H— & C— & C— & C—H \\
 & | & | & | \\
 & H & | & H \\
 & H— & C— & H \\
 & & | & \\
 & & H &
\end{array}
$$

n-butane 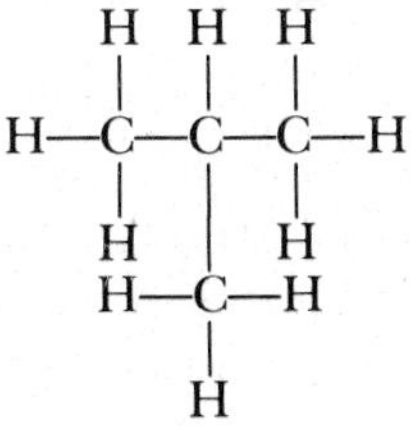   isobutane

The greater the number of carbon atoms, the larger the number of chain isomers. For example, the compound $C_{20}H_{42}$ has 366,319 possible isomers; the compound $C_{40}H_{82}$ has 62,491,178,805,831 possible isomers.

Other structural isomers involve the positioning of functional groups and the positioning of a double or triple bond.

EXAMPLE 1. Positioning of a functional group in an alkyl molecule. The molecular formula for both molecules is C_3H_7OH.

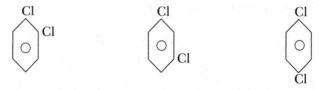

n-propyl alcohol
(1-propanol)   **isopropyl alcohol**
                          (2-propanol)

EXAMPLE 2. Positioning of a functional group in an aryl molecule. The molecular formula for the three molecules is $C_6H_4Cl_2$.

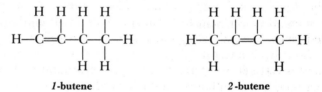

*ortho*dichlorobenzene   *meta*dichlorobenzene   *para*dichlorobenzene

EXAMPLE 3. Positioning of a double bond. The molecular formula for both molecules is C_4H_8.

$$
\begin{array}{cccc}
H & H & H & H \\
| & | & | & | \\
H-C{=}C-C-C-H \\
& & | & | \\
& & H & H
\end{array}
\qquad
\begin{array}{cccc}
H & H & H & H \\
| & | & | & | \\
H-C-C{=}C-C-H \\
& | & & | \\
& H & & H
\end{array}
$$

1-butene   **2-butene**

EXAMPLE 4. Positioning of a triple bond. The molecular formula for both molecules is C_4H_6.

$$
\begin{array}{cc}
H & H \\
| & | \\
H-C{\equiv}C-C-C-H \\
& | & | \\
& H & H
\end{array}
\qquad
\begin{array}{cc}
H & & H \\
| & & | \\
H-C-C{\equiv}C-C-H \\
| & & | \\
H & & H
\end{array}
$$

1-butyne   **2-butyne**

3. The alkanes are hydrocarbons which (1) have the same number of carbon atoms (2) fit the general formula C_nH_{2n+2} (3) have the same ratio of carbon atoms to hydrogen atoms (4) have double bonds
4. To explain the formula for benzene, C_6H_6, it is assumed that (1) the valence of carbon is 1 (2) alternate double and single bonds are present between carbon atoms (3) each hydrogen atom is bonded to two carbon atoms (4) the compound is saturated
5. Although both CH_3OH and $NaOH$ contain the OH group, the compounds differ in that (1) only NaOH is ionic (2) the O and H in NaOH are not bonded (3) CH_3OH is a strong acid, while NaOH is a strong base (4) the bonds in NaOH are all covalent
6. The formula C_6H_5COOH indicates that (1) the compound is derived from hexane (2) an acid group is present (3) seven carbon atoms are arranged in a chain (4) the compound is an alcohol
7. A difference between an aldehyde and a ketone is that (1) only the ketone contains $-C=O$ (2) only the aldehyde forms ions (3) in the ketone, the $C=O$ is bonded to two carbon atoms (4) a ketone can contain a minimum of two carbon atoms
8. The correct formula for *1*-butene is (1) $CH_2CHCH_2CH_3$ (2) $CH_2OHCH_2CH_2CH_3$ (3) $CHCCH_2CH_3$ (4) $CH_3CHCHCH_3$
9. The two isomers of propanol differ in (1) the number of carbon atoms (2) molecular weight (3) the type of functional group (4) the position of the functional group
0. Which of the following is *not* true for both CH_4 and NH_4^+? (1) Both are tetrahedral. (2) Both are covalently bonded. (3) Both are ionically bonded. (4) Both are symmetrical.
1. Carbon forms an unusually large number of compounds because carbon (1) is the second most abundant element on earth (2) combines with oxygen in many ways (3) unites with other atoms of carbon and hydrogen (4) forms both positive and negative ions
2. The carbonyl group, $-C=O$, is present in all of the following classes of compounds *except* (1) organic acids (2) alcohols (3) aldehydes (4) ketones

Completion Questions

1. Compounds that contain only carbon and hydrogen are classified as _____.

2. In the solid state, carbon atoms unite to form two types of network solids: diamond and _____.

. Benzene and compounds that contain a benzene ring are classified as _____ hydrocarbons.

28.19 Stereoisomerism

Recall that we have conveniently represented structural formulas as two-dimensional. Since the carbon atom is tetrahedral, the structures of molecules of carbon compounds are properly three-dimensional. It is therefore possible for two molecules to have the same sequence of carbon atoms and yet for the atoms in each molecule to have a different orientation in space. Such molecules are called *stereoisomers*. Two general types of stereoisomers are recognized: geometric and optical.

GEOMETRIC (CIS-TRANS) ISOMERS

Molecules *A* and *B* have different properties; for example, molecule *A* is polar, while molecule *B* is nonpolar.

When the two substituents (functional groups, such as Cl) are on the same side of the double bond, they are said to be in the *cis* position; when on opposite sides, they are said to be in the *trans* position. Thus molecule *A* is called cis-dichloroethylene and molecule *B* is called trans-dichloroethylene. Cis-trans isomerism occurs only when double or triple bonds are present and is caused by the restricted rotation around such bonds.

If the carbon-to-carbon bond is a single bond, as in *1*, *2*-dichloroethane, cis-trans isomerism cannot exist.

The molecule rotates freely around the single bond. This means that, according to the laws of probability, the two chlorine atoms spend an equal amount of time on the same side and on opposite sides of the molecule.

OPTICAL ISOMERS

If four *different* substituents (atoms or groups of atoms) appear on a single tetrahedral atom, such as carbon, the resulting molecule lacks symmetry. Two possible arrangements, or isomers, exist for such molecules. Each isomer is a mirror image of the other, as with left and right hands. This means that the molecule of one isomer *cannot* be superimposed on its mirror image (the other isomer). Each isomer also interacts differently with polarized light (light that vibrates in a single plane).

The different arrangements, or forms, are called *optical isomers*. An example of a molecule that has optical isomers is glyceraldehyde ($C_3H_6O_3$), shown as *A* and *B* in the structural formulas that follow:

The position of the OH group in molecule *A* (on the right side of the carbon atom) gives molecule *A* different properties from molecule *B*, in which the OH group is on the left side. Such spatial differences play an important role in the biological activity of molecules.

Glyceraldehyde is related to the common sugar glucose, $C_6H_{12}O_6$. Note the open-chain formulas of two optical isomers of glucose, called D-glucose and L-glucose. Just as in glyceraldehyde, each isomer is the mirror image of the other.

D-glucose   **L-glucose**

28.20 Recognizing isomers

Do two representations of a compound with the same molecular formula indeed represent isomers? If bonds must be broken and remade in order to go from one form to the other, then the forms *are* isomers. If the change can be made by merely rotating the molecule but without any bond breaking, then the molecules are *not* isomers. For example, consider the isomers of dichlorethylene, $C_2H_2Cl_2$.

If molecule *A* is rotated, structure is formed. These forms are identical; hence, they are *not* isomers. If the bonds in molecule are broken and remade, then molecule *B* or molecule *C* is formed. The forms (*A* and *B* or *A* and *C*) *are* structural isomers. If the C=C bond molecule *B* is twisted and partially broken, then molecule *C* is formed. These forms (*B* and *C*) are stereoisomers.

Note that rotation around the double bond in molecule *B* can form molecule *C*. This phenomenon requires only partial bond-breaking and involves the expenditure of minimum energy. On the other hand, changing molecule *A* to either molecule *B* or to molecule *C* requires complete rupture, which needs much greater energy. Thus it is more difficult to convert molecule *A* to either molecule *B* or to molecule *C* than to convert molecule *B* to molecule *C*.

Multiple-Choice Questions

1. Carbon forms four valence bonds because the carbon atom (1) has two electrons in the first shell and two in the second shell (2) has *p* orbitals (3) has equivalent *s* and *p* orbitals (4) utilizes *s* and *p* to form four equivalent bonds
2. An organic compound is classified as unsaturated if it (1) contain the maximum number of carbon atoms (2) is insoluble solvents (3) contains double or triple bonds (4) does not hydrogen

4. Organic compounds that contain one or more OH functional groups are called _____.

5. The $\overset{\overset{O}{\|}}{C}$—OH group, present in organic compounds, has the properties of _____.

6. Organic compounds with the general formula $R\text{NH}_2$ are classified as _____.

7. Two or more compounds that have the same molecular formula but different arrangements of atoms in the molecule are called _____.

8. The change of an electron from an s to a p orbital is called _____.

9. The general formula for organic (alkyl) chlorides is $R\text{Cl}$. When R is C_2H_5, the compound is named _____ chloride.

10. Isobutane contains a (an) _____ chain of carbon atoms.

True-False Questions

1. In saturated organic compounds, each carbon atom is united to four other atoms arranged at the corners of *a square.*

2. Cis-trans isomers are examples of *stereoisomers.*

3. Hydrocarbons of *low* molecular weight are used as gaseous fuels.

4. The compound $\text{CH}_3\text{OC}_2\text{H}_5$ is *a ketone.*

5. The name for the compound $\text{CH}_3\text{CH}_2\text{CHClCH}_3$ is *2-chlorobutane.*

6. Cis-trans isomers may exist when a *double* bond is present between carbon atoms separating two substituted groups.

7. The formula for octane is C_8H_{16}.

8. Hydrocarbons with a triple bond are *alkenes.*

9. Molecules that interact differently with polarized light are called *structural* isomers.

10. Butane forms *two* structural isomers.

Decreases, Increases, Remains the Same

1. As the bonds in hydrocarbon compounds change from single to double and triple bonds, the number of hydrogen atoms bonded to carbon atoms _____.

2. The bond angle between the hydrogen and carbon chain _____ as we go from ethane to ethene to ethyne.

3. In the compounds butane, butene, and butyne, the degree of unsaturation _____.

4. When ethylene is changed to polyethylene, the molecular weight of the compound _____.

5. In the series propane, propanol, propanal, the number of carbon atoms _____.

6. As the number of carbon atoms in hydrocarbons increases, the possible number of isomers _____.

7. In the three compounds orthodibromobenzene, metadibromobenzene, and paradibromobenzene, the number of carbon atoms separating the bromine atoms _____.

8. As their molecular weights increase, the boiling points of the aliphatic hydrocarbons _____.

9. When ethane is converted to ethyl chloride, the number of hydrogen atoms in the molecule _____.

10. As the number of bonds between two adjacent carbon atoms increases, the bond energy _____.

Exercises for Review

1. Geometrically, the atoms in a molecule of C_2H_2 are arranged in a straight line, but in C_2H_4 they are not in a straight line. Explain.

2. Why is it possible to have thousands of different compounds containing carbon?

3. What other elements can form bonds similar to the bonds formed by carbon? Why?

4. The two allotropes of carbon—diamond and graphite—have distinct crystalline structures. Account for the differences in properties on the basis of these structures.

5. *a.* Draw structural formulas for the isomers of hexane.
   b. Does dichloromethane form isomers? Explain.

6. Using the name of the parent hydrocarbon, name each of the following compounds: (*a*) CH_2Cl_2 (*b*) CHI_3 (*c*) CCl_2F_2 (*d*) C_2H_5Br

7. What similarities exist in the structure and properties of CH_3OH and HOH?

8. Write the name, molecular formula, and the structural formula for each of the following compounds containing three carbon atoms:
   a. the saturated hydrocarbon
   b. the hydrocarbon with one double bond
   c. the hydrocarbon with one triple bond
   d. two alcohols that are isomers
   e. an acid
   f. an aldehyde
   g. a ketone

9. *a.* Draw the structural formulas for all the isomers of pentane.
   b. How could you show that each structure is a different compound?
10. Explain why the formula C_3H_8O could represent more than one compound.
11. *a.* Describe and illustrate two general types of isomers.
    b. Briefly discuss the significance of each type.

Exercises for Further Study

1. Distinguish the meaning of the terms *saturated* and *unsaturated* when applied to organic compounds and when used to describe solutions.
2. Why are the principles of promotion and hybridization useful to explain the bonding characteristics of carbon?
3. *a.* Knowing that only one hydroxyl group can be bonded to a single carbon atom, draw structural formulas for all the alcohols possible with four carbon atoms in the molecule.
   b. Write the name of each compound.
4. If the generalized formula for the alkanes is C_nH_{2n+2}, write generalized formulas to fit each of the following types of compounds: (*a*) alkenes (*b*) alkynes (*c*) cycloalkanes (*d*) alkenes with two double bonds
5. Polyethylene forms when many ethylene molecules unite. Why does ethane not react in a similar way?
6. Compare the properties and structures of the following OH compounds: (*a*) CH_3OH (*b*) $NaOH$ (*c*) $ClOH$, or $HOCl$
7. *a.* How many isomers of $C_2H_4Cl_2$ exist?
   b. Draw the structural formulas.
   c. How many isomers of $C_2H_2Cl_2$ exist?
   d. Draw the structural formulas.
8. Explain the relationship between amines and ammonia, alcohols and water, ethers and water.
9. What compounds satisfy the formula C_nH_{2n} but do not contain a double bond?
10. Tartaric acid is a dihydroxy dicarboxylic acid the formula of which is $(COOH)_2(CHOH)_2$.
    a. Write a possible structural formula.
    b. Assuming that tartaric acid forms optical isomers, write the structural formulas of two such isomers.
11. *a.* Why are 16 stereoisomers with the formula $C_6H_{12}O_6$ possible?
    b. Write open-chain structural formulas for as many of these isomers as you can.

Chapter 29

THE REACTIONS OF ORGANIC COMPOUNDS

29.1 Introduction

The organization of organic compounds by functional groups forms a most useful basis for the study of organic reactions. In this chapter, we will discuss the chemistry of some typical functional groups, for example, hydrocarbons, alcohols, and acids. The reactions of these groups provide the key to understanding the synthesis of organic compounds.

29.2 Saturated and unsaturated compounds

The chemistry of the aliphatic hydrocarbons depends largely on the kind of bond that exists between the carbon atoms.

We have already described a molecule such as ethane as *saturated* because only one electron pair (a single bond) holds any two atoms together.

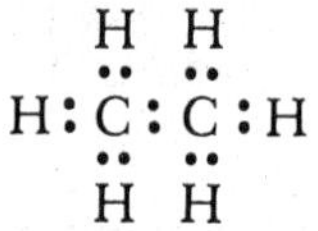

$$
\begin{array}{cc}
\text{H} & \text{H} \\
\overset{\bullet\bullet}{} & \overset{\bullet\bullet}{} \\
\text{H:C:C:H} \\
\underset{\bullet\bullet}{} & \underset{\bullet\bullet}{} \\
\text{H} & \text{H}
\end{array}
$$

By contrast, a molecule of ethene (ethylene) uses two pairs of electrons (a double bond) to bond the carbon atoms. Since one pair of electrons is sufficient to hold two carbon atoms together, two electrons are available for additional bonding, as indicated in the following figure:

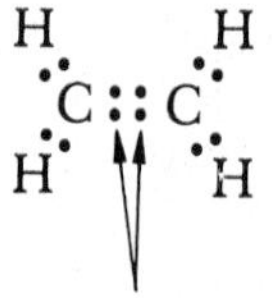

$$
\begin{array}{cc}
\text{H} & \text{H} \\
\text{C::C} \\
\text{H} & \text{H}
\end{array}
$$

The molecule can add two hydrogen atoms at the double bond, or one hydrogen atom and one chlorine atom, or many other combinations. Since additional bonding is possible in ethylene, this compound is said to be *unsaturated.*

29.3 Characteristic reactions of saturated hydrocarbons

At room conditions, saturated hydrocarbons are generally not very reactive. Oxidizing agents, such as MnO_4^- ion, and strong acids, such as H_2SO_4, cannot rupture the C—H or the C—C bonds in alkanes. At high temperatures, saturated hydrocarbons undergo the following reactions:

1. Combustion. In unlimited air supply, the reaction proceeds as follows:

$$CH_4 + 2\ O_2 \rightarrow CO_2 + 2\ H_2O + heat$$

In limited air supply, the reaction proceeds as follows:

$$2\ CH_4 + 3\ O_2 \rightarrow 2\ CO + 4\ H_2O + heat$$

$$CH_4 + O_2 \rightarrow C + 2\ H_2O + heat$$

Thus the combustion of a hydrocarbon always yields water. When the combustion is complete, CO_2 is also formed.

2. Substitution. Alkanes also undergo substitution reactions in which a halogen atom is substituted for a hydrogen atom.

$$CH_4 + Cl_2 \rightarrow CH_3Cl + HCl$$
methyl
chloride

This halogen substitution reaction takes place in the presence of light or at temperatures of 300° C or greater. A suggested mechanism for the reaction follows:

STEP 1. Light energy breaks the bond in Cl_2 to form two free chlorine atoms. These atoms are reactive, and each contains an unpaired electron.

$$Cl—Cl \rightarrow 2\ .\overset{..}{\underset{..}{Cl}}:$$

STEP 2. A chlorine atom reacts with methane to form hydrogen chloride and a methyl free radical (a reactive species containing an unpaired electron).

$$
\ddot{\underset{\cdot\cdot}{Cl}}\cdot \; + \; H\!:\!\overset{\displaystyle H}{\underset{\displaystyle H}{\overset{\cdot\cdot}{C}}}\!:\!H \;\longrightarrow\; H\!:\!\ddot{\underset{\cdot\cdot}{Cl}}\!:\; + \; \cdot\overset{\displaystyle H}{\underset{\displaystyle H}{\overset{\cdot\cdot}{C}}}\!:\!H
$$

methyl free radical

STEP 3. The methyl free radical reacts with a chlorine molecule to form methyl chloride and another free chlorine atom.

$$
H\!:\!\overset{\displaystyle H}{\underset{\displaystyle H}{\overset{\cdot\cdot}{C}}}\!\cdot \; + \; :\!\ddot{Cl}\!:\!\ddot{Cl}\!: \;\longrightarrow\; :\!\ddot{Cl}\!:\!\overset{\displaystyle H}{\underset{\displaystyle H}{\overset{\cdot\cdot}{C}}}\!:\!H \; + \; :\!\ddot{Cl}\!\cdot
$$

STEP 4. The free chlorine atom then reacts with methane as in step 2.

This reaction occurs in a chain-like fashion (see section 13.5). Step 2 cannot occur until step 1 has produced chlorine atoms. Step 3 cannot occur until step 2 produces the methyl free radical. Note that step 3 regenerates a chlorine atom to continue step 2. Since step 1 starts the chain, it is called the chain-initiating step. Steps 2 and 3 continue the chain and are called the chain-propagating steps. The chain is terminated when a chlorine atom combines with a methyl free radical.

Other reactions which alkanes may undergo are dehydrogenation and cracking.

3. Dehydrogenation. *Dehydrogenation* involves the removal of hydrogen atoms to produce an olefin (an unsaturated hydrocarbon having the general formula C_nH_{2n}). This reaction occurs only in the presence of a catalyst and at a high temperature.

$$
\underset{\text{propane}}{CH_3CH_2CH_3} \xrightarrow[\text{catalyst}]{\text{high temp.}} \underset{\text{propene}}{CH_3CH\!=\!CH_2} + H_2 \; (g)
$$

4. Cracking. *Cracking* involves a splitting of larger molecules into smaller fragments at high temperatures, often in the presence of a catalyst.

$$
\underset{\text{propane}}{CH_3CH_2CH_3} \xrightarrow[\text{catalyst}]{\text{high temp.}} \underset{\text{ethylene}}{CH_2\!=\!CH_2} + \underset{\text{methane}}{CH_4}
$$

Cracking is important in the production of motor fuels from petroleum fractions which have molecules that are too large (and thus not volatile enough) to make good fuels.

29.4 Characteristic reactions of unsaturated hydrocarbons

Note, from the table of bond energies in section 12.6, that more energy is released during the formation of a C=C or a C≡C bond than during the formation of a C—C bond. However, the alkenes (C=C) and alkynes (C≡C) are more reactive than alkanes (C—C). The alkenes and alkynes typically undergo *addition reactions* in contrast to the substitution reactions for the alkanes. Double or triple bonds open to make additional bonding electrons available. Four types of addition reactions follow:

1. Halogenation. The general reaction is

$$
R-\underset{\substack{|\\H}}{\overset{\substack{H\\|}}{C}}=\underset{\substack{|\\H}}{\overset{\substack{H\\|}}{C}}-R' + \underset{\text{halogen}}{X_2} \rightarrow R-\underset{\substack{|\\X}}{\overset{\substack{H\\|}}{C}}-\underset{\substack{|\\X}}{\overset{\substack{H\\|}}{C}}-R'
$$

An example of halogenation with bromine follows:

$$
H-\underset{\substack{|\\H}}{\overset{\substack{H\\|}}{\underset{\text{ethylene}}{C}}}=\underset{\substack{|\\H}}{\overset{\substack{H\\|}}{C}}-H + Br_2 \rightarrow H-\underset{\substack{|\\Br}}{\overset{\substack{H\\|}}{C}}-\underset{\substack{|\\Br}}{\overset{\substack{H\\|}}{C}}-H
$$
dibromoethane

2. Hydrogenation. In this reaction, the double or triple bond is saturated with hydrogen with the help of a palladium catalyst. Note that this reaction is the reverse of dehydrogenation. A typical hydrogenation reaction is

$$
\underset{\text{2-hexene}}{CH_3(CH_2)_2CH{=}CHCH_3} \xrightarrow[\text{Pd}]{H_2} \underset{n\text{-hexane}}{CH_3(CH_2)_4CH_3}
$$

A double or triple bond represents an especially reactive site in a molecule. Hydrogenation may use up this reactive site. Many foods contain unsaturated molecules the reactivity of which can be reduced by hydrogenation. This means that these foods will spoil less readily after hydrogenation.

Substances containing unsaturated molecules tend to be liquids which change to solids or semi-solids on hydrogenation. This change of state is utilized in the manufacture of margarine from a variety of natural oils containing unsaturated molecules.

3. Hydrohalogenation. The general reaction is

$$R-\underset{\underset{H}{|}}{C}=\underset{\underset{}{|}}{C}-R' + \underset{\substack{\text{hydrogen}\\\text{halide}}}{HX} \rightarrow R-\underset{\underset{H}{|}}{C}-\underset{\underset{X}{|}}{C}-R'$$

For example, if hydrogen chloride is added to ethylene, the product is monochloroethane.

$$H-\underset{\underset{H}{|}}{C}=\underset{\underset{}{|}}{C}-H + HCl \rightarrow H-\underset{\underset{H}{|}}{C}-\underset{\underset{Cl}{|}}{C}-H$$

monochloroethane

4. Hydration. This name is given to the general reaction

$$R-\underset{\underset{H}{|}}{C}=\underset{\underset{}{|}}{C}-R' \xrightarrow[\text{H}_2\text{O}]{\text{H}^+} R-\underset{\underset{H}{|}}{C}-\underset{\underset{OH}{|}}{C}-R'$$

in which an alcohol is produced from an alkene (olefin) with an acid as catalyst.

$$H-\underset{\underset{H}{|}}{\underset{\text{ethylene}}{C}}=\underset{\underset{}{|}}{C}-H \xrightarrow[\text{H}_2\text{O}]{\text{H}_3\text{O}^+} H-\underset{\underset{H}{|}}{C}-\underset{\underset{OH}{|}}{C}-H$$

ethanol

29.5 Characteristic reactions of the benzene ring

The bonds between carbon atoms in benzene have a partial double-bond nature (see section 28.11). However, benzene generally undergoes *substitution* rather than addition reactions that would tend to saturate the six-membered ring. A few of the more important substitution reactions which the benzene ring undergoes follow. (The substances that appear over the arrows in the equations are catalysts.)

1. Nitration. The net reaction, using nitric acid as the nitrating agent, is

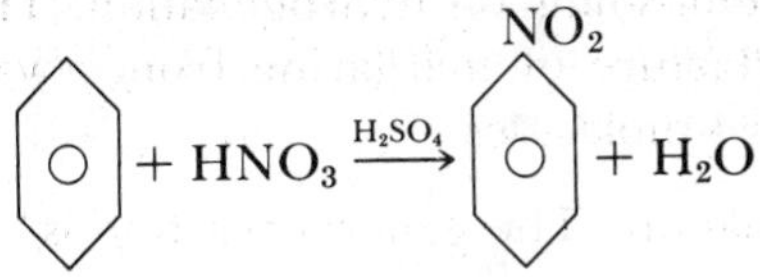

$$\text{C}_6\text{H}_6 + \text{HNO}_3 \xrightarrow{\text{H}_2\text{SO}_4} \text{C}_6\text{H}_5\text{NO}_2 + \text{H}_2\text{O}$$

nitrobenzene

2. Halogenation. The net reaction, using bromine as the halogen, is

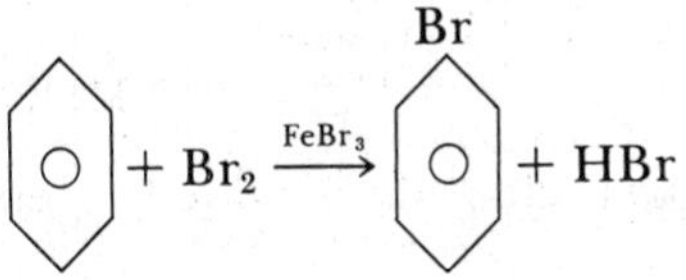

$$\text{C}_6\text{H}_6 + \text{Br}_2 \xrightarrow{\text{FeBr}_3} \text{C}_6\text{H}_5\text{Br} + \text{HBr}$$

bromobenzene

3. Alkylation. In this reaction, an alkyl group is substituted for a hydrogen on the ring. The ring is reacted with a halide of the R group to be substituted, so that the general reaction becomes

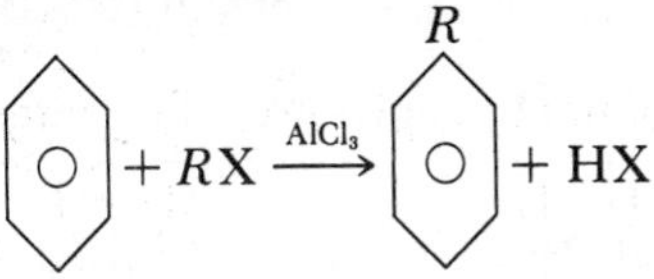

$$\text{C}_6\text{H}_6 + RX \xrightarrow{\text{AlCl}_3} \text{C}_6\text{H}_5 R + HX$$

For example, when a methyl group is to be placed onto the ring, the overall reaction is

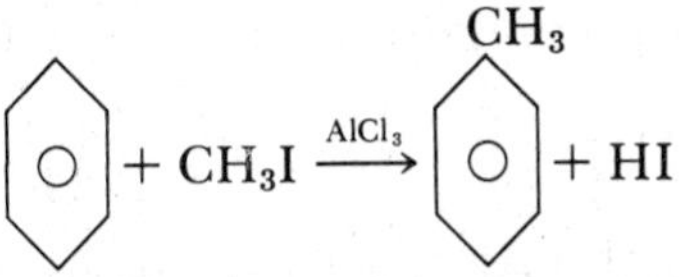

$$\text{C}_6\text{H}_6 + \text{CH}_3\text{I} \xrightarrow{\text{AlCl}_3} \text{C}_6\text{H}_5\text{CH}_3 + \text{HI}$$

4. Sulfonation. In this reaction, an SO_3H (sulfonate) group is substituted for an H on the ring.

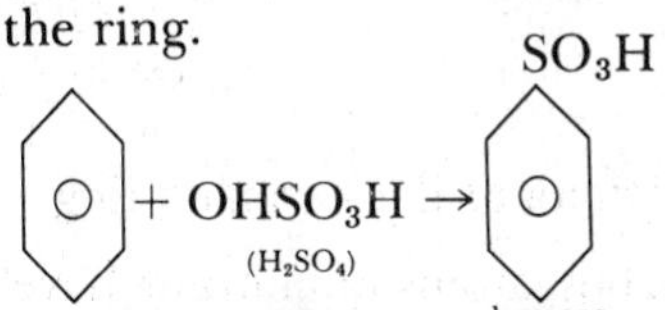

$$\text{C}_6\text{H}_6 + \text{OHSO}_3\text{H} \rightarrow \text{C}_6\text{H}_5\text{SO}_3\text{H}$$
$$(\text{H}_2\text{SO}_4)$$

benzene
sulfonic acid

An important addition reaction that benzene undergoes in the presence of sunlight at 50° C is the formation of benzene hexachloride, $C_6H_6Cl_6$ (an isomer of which is used to manufacture insecticides).

29.6 Characteristic reactions of alcohols

The —OH group in organic compounds does not possess the properties of a base which it has in inorganic bases such as $NaOH$ or $Ca(OH)_2$. Alcohols, as a matter of fact, are weakly acidic. Some of the key reactions of alcohols follow:

1. Reaction with sodium to liberate hydrogen gas. The reaction of sodium with ethyl alcohol is

$$CH_3CH_2OH + Na \rightarrow CH_3CH_2O^-Na^+ + \frac{1}{2} H_2 \ (g)$$

$$\underset{\substack{\text{replaceable} \\ \text{hydrogen}}}{\uparrow} \qquad \qquad \underset{\substack{\text{sodium} \\ \text{ethoxide}}}{}$$

(Recall that sodium reacts with water or with acids in the same manner.)

2. Reaction with hydrogen halides to produce an alkyl or an aryl halide. The general reaction is

$$ROH + HX \rightarrow RX + H_2O$$

The reaction of hydrogen bromide with ethyl alcohol is

$$CH_3CH_2OH + HBr \rightarrow CH_3CH_2Br + H_2O$$
$$\underset{\text{monobromoethane}}{}$$

3. Reaction with acids to form esters. In this reaction, water is split out between the alcohol molecule and the acid molecule. The general reaction is

$$R-O\boxed{H + HO}-\overset{\overset{\textstyle O}{\|}}{C}-R' \xrightarrow{H_2SO_4} R-O-\overset{\overset{\textstyle O}{\|}}{C}-R' + H_2O$$

If pentyl alcohol, $C_5H_{11}OH$, is allowed to react with acetic acid in the presence of concentrated H_2SO_4, the following reaction takes place:

$$CH_3(CH_2)_3CH_2O\boxed{H + HO}-\overset{\overset{\textstyle O}{\|}}{C}-CH_3 \xrightarrow{H_2SO_4} CH_3(CH_2)_3CH_2-O-\overset{\overset{\textstyle O}{\|}}{C}-CH_3 + H_2O$$

The product, called pentyl (amyl) acetate, is the ester which is responsible for the flavor of banana. Note that in naming the ester, the alcohol residue is named first, the acid residue second. Sulfuric acid catalyzes the reaction.

While some esters are responsible for fruit flavors, such as octyl acetate (orange) and amyl butyrate (apple), many esters have other valuable properties. For example, the molecule in which an alcohol and carboxyl group are in the ortho position on the benzene ring is called salicylic acid.

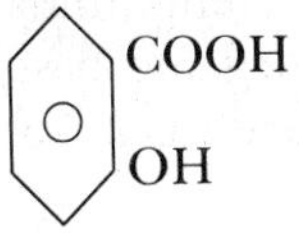

$$\text{C}_6\text{H}_4(\text{COOH})(\text{OH})$$

If the alcohol group is esterified with acetic acid,

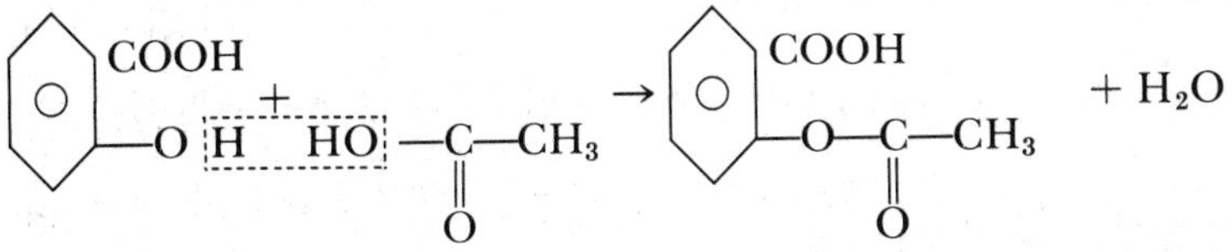

acetylsalicylic acid

the product is an ester (the acid group on the ring remains intact). The ester is acetylsalicylic acid, better known as aspirin.

The tri-ol (tri-alcohol) glycerine

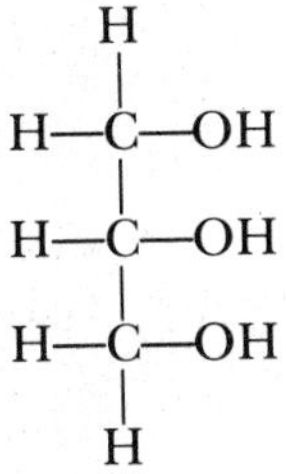

forms several important esters. When all three alcohol groups are esterified with nitric acid, the product is trinitroglycerine (nitroglycerine), a useful explosive and medicinal agent.

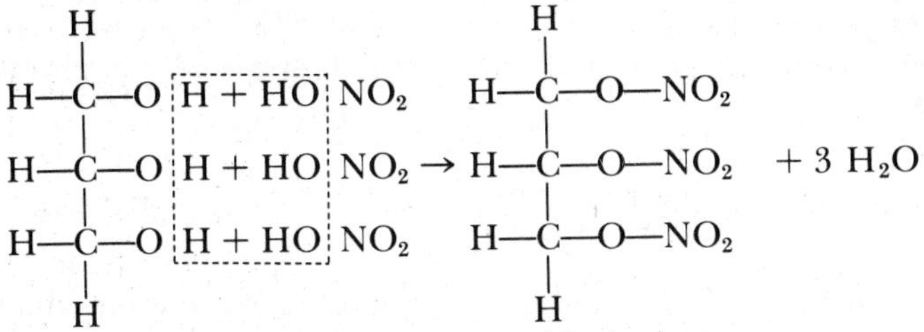

trinitroglycerine

A mixture of 75% nitroglycerine and 25% filler material constitutes dynamite. As a medicine, nitroglycerine serves to dilate the blood vessels and is used in such cardiac disorders as angina pectoris.

Many animal fats are tri-esters of glycerine. Their general structure is

The R groups belong to fatty acids such as stearic acid, $C_{17}H_{35}COOH$. Thus beef fat, glyceryl stearate, has the formula $(C_{17}H_{35}COO)_3C_3H_5$. (All the R groups are $C_{17}H_{35}$.)

29.7 Characteristic reactions of organic acids

The acidic, or replaceable, hydrogen (proton) in organic acids is the H of the carboxyl group.

As indicated earlier, organic acids may contain more than one carboxyl group, in which case they are termed dicarboxylic or polycarboxylic acids. In general, the carboxylic acids are relatively weak. Recall that K_A for $CH_3COOH = 1.8 \times 10^{-5}$. Following are some reactions of organic acids:

1. Salt formation. When acetic acid reacts with sodium hydroxide, the reaction that occurs is

For the reaction between benzoic acid and NaOH, the product is sodium benzoate, an important food preservative.

The two salts sodium acetate and sodium benzoate are ionic compounds and are water soluble. The cation is the alkali metal ion—sodium ion—and the anion is the organic portion—acetate ion and benzoate ion.

The sodium salt of stearic acid, $C_{17}H_{35}COOH$, is a soap (see section 22.8).

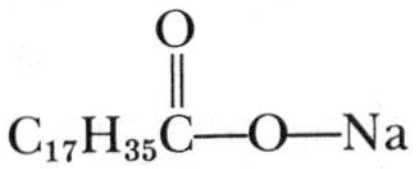

$$C_{17}H_{35}\overset{\overset{\displaystyle O}{\|}}{C}-O-Na$$

sodium stearate

2. Ester formation. This reaction typifies acids as well as alcohols (see section 29.6).

3. Amides as acid derivatives. The compound acetamide

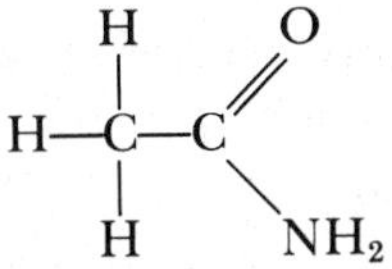

$$H-\underset{\underset{\displaystyle H}{|}}{\overset{\overset{\displaystyle H}{|}}{C}}-C\underset{\diagdown NH_2}{\overset{\diagup O}{}}$$

can be considered a derivative of acetic acid, with —OH in the carboxyl group replaced by —NH_2. Such molecules are known as *amides*. Another common amide is urea, the di-amide of carbonic acid.

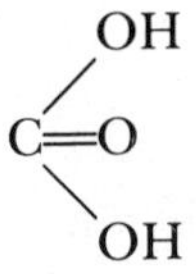

$$\underset{\diagdown OH}{\overset{\diagup OH}{C=O}} \qquad \underset{\diagdown NH_2}{\overset{\diagup NH_2}{C=O}}$$

carbonic acid   **urea**
(H_2CO_3)

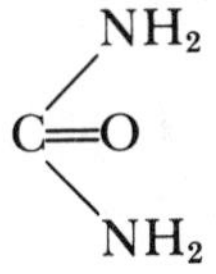

4. Organic acid anhydrides. Two acetic acid molecules may split out water between them to form acetic anhydride.

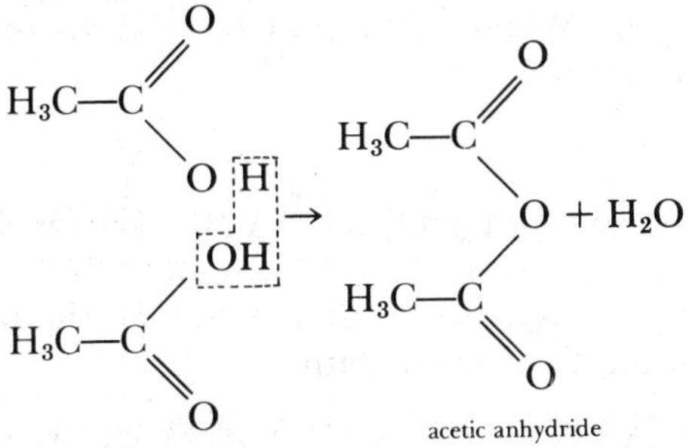

$$H_3C-C\overset{\diagup O}{\underset{\diagdown O\,H}{}} \quad H_3C-C\overset{\diagup O}{\underset{\diagdown}{}} \atop H_3C-C\overset{\diagup OH}{\underset{\diagdown O}{}} \rightarrow \quad {O + H_2O} \atop H_3C-C\overset{\diagup}{\underset{\diagdown O}{}}$$

acetic anhydride

Some of the less stable organic acids (such as maleic acid) are rendered more stable if kept in the anhydride form. When the acid is required, water is added to the anhydride.

5. Amino acids. These molecules have the general formula

$$R-\overset{\overset{\displaystyle H}{|}}{\underset{\underset{\displaystyle NH_2}{|}}{C}}-C\overset{\displaystyle O}{\underset{\displaystyle OH}{\diagup\diagdown}}$$

Frequently, the —NH_2 group is on the carbon adjacent to the carboxylic (acid) carbon. Amino acids will be discussed later in the chapter.

29.8 Polymerization

Consider the reaction between a two-carbon amino acid (molecule I) and a three-carbon amino acid (molecule II).

I   II

X   Z

At the site marked Y, water splits out between the two molecules, and a new bond is established between the carbon and nitrogen.

I   II

X   Y   Z

If this process is repeated, the H at site X may combine with the OH from another molecule II. Or the OH at site Z may combine with an H from another molecule I. By this process, a very long chain of alternating I and II units is formed. A molecule formed from simple repeating units, called *monomers*, is termed a *polymer*. The process by which a polymer is formed is termed *polymerization*.

Polymers are very large molecules with molecular weights in the thousands. The number of monomers that make up a polymer may go up to many thousands. The polymer just described is the molecule manufactured by the silkworm — natural silk. It is represented in the following structural formula, in which the letter n stands for the number of repeating units.

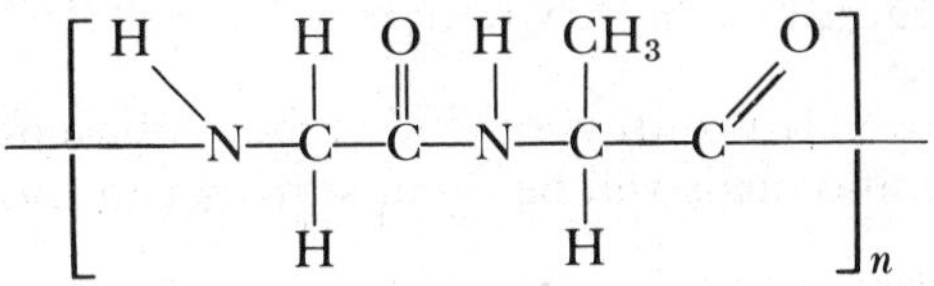

silk

In organic chemistry, the word *condensation* is sometimes used when water splits out between two molecules; thus the silk molecule above is called a *condensation polymer*. The process by which it is formed is called *condensation polymerization*. Many important synthetic products are condensation polymers, for example, dacron and nylon.

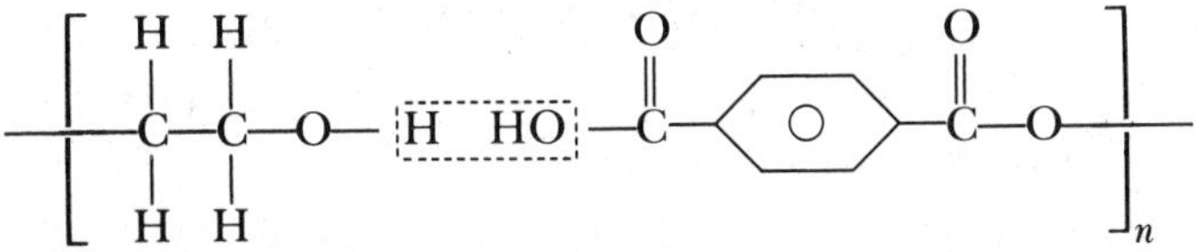

dacron

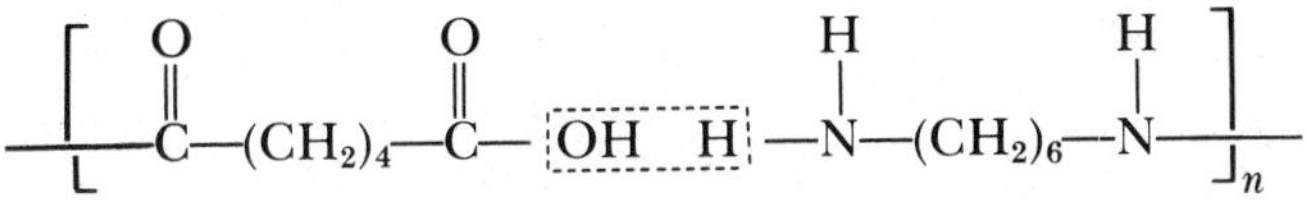

nylon

Different qualities of nylon and dacron are produced by varying the length of the chain and by various other processes which are beyond the scope of our study.

In another polymerization process, called *addition polymerization*, molecules of a monomer, such as ethylene, are polymerized to form polyethylene. Consider the structure of an ethylene molecule.

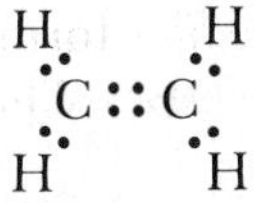

Two ethylene molecules may join as follows:

$$\begin{array}{cccc}
\text{H} & \text{H} & \text{H} & \text{H} \\
\text{H} \colon \ddot{\text{C}} \colon & \ddot{\text{C}} \colon & \ddot{\text{C}} \colon\colon & \ddot{\text{C}} \\
\text{H} & \text{H} & & \text{H}
\end{array}$$

If the process is repeated, polyethylene results.

$$\text{H} \colon \ddot{\text{C}} \!\!-\!\! \left[\begin{array}{c} \text{H} \\ | \\ \text{C} \\ | \\ \text{H} \end{array} \right]_n \!\!-\!\! \begin{array}{cc} \text{H} & \text{H} \\ \ddot{\text{C}} \colon\colon & \ddot{\text{C}} \\ & \text{H} \end{array}$$

Thus in addition polymerization, the monomer units contain double bonds to permit the molecules to link. If fluorine atoms are substituted in the repeating $\left[-\overset{\text{H}}{\underset{\text{H}}{\text{C}}}- \right]_n$ structure, $\left[-\overset{\text{F}}{\underset{\text{F}}{\text{C}}}- \right]_n$ or Teflon results. If chlorine atoms are substituted, Saran is formed.

29.9 Organic oxidation reactions

An acidified solution of potassium dichromate ($Cr_2O_7^{-2}$ ion) converts ethyl alcohol into acetaldehyde. The resulting solution has the green color of aqueous Cr^{+3} ion. In the following half-reactions, all ions are aquated:

OXIDATION $\qquad$ $3\,[CH_3CH_2OH \rightarrow CH_3CHO + 2\,H^+ + 2\,e^-]$

REDUCTION $\qquad$ $Cr_2O_7^{-2} + 14\,H^+ + 6\,e^- \rightarrow 2\,Cr^{+3} + 7\,H_2O$

NET REACTION $\quad$ $Cr_2O_7^{-2} + 3\,CH_3CH_2OH + 8\,H^+ \rightarrow 2\,Cr^{+3} + 3\,CH_3CHO + 7\,H_2O$

(We are assuming the absence of charged species in C_2H_5OH and CH_3CHO; consequently, the net oxidation numbers are zero.)

An acidified solution of potassium permanganate (MnO_4^- ion) converts acetaldehyde into acetic acid. The resulting solution has the colorless aqueous Mn^{+2} ion. In the following half-reactions, all ions are aquated:

OXIDATION $\qquad$ $5\,[CH_3CHO + H_2O \rightarrow CH_3COOH + 2\,H^+ + 2\,e^-]$

REDUCTION $\qquad$ $2\,[MnO_4^- + 8\,H^+ + 5\,e^- \rightarrow Mn^{+2} + 4\,H_2O]$

NET REACTION $\quad$ $2\,MnO_4^{-2} + 5\,CH_3CHO + 6\,H^+ \rightarrow 2\,Mn^{+2} + 5\,CH_3COOH + 3\,H_2O$

In both reactions, the molecules of the organic compounds have lost electrons; that is, they have been oxidized.

Alcohols may be conveniently classified into three groups that are useful in helping us predict the products of alcohol oxidation reactions.

GROUP	STRUCTURAL FORMULA	EXAMPLE
primary alcohols	R—CH_2OH	CH_3CH_2OH ethyl alcohol
secondary alcohols	$\begin{matrix} R_1 \\ \diagdown \\ \quad CHOH \\ \diagup \\ R_2 \end{matrix}$	$(CH_3)_2CHOH$ isopropyl alcohol
tertiary alcohols	$\begin{matrix} R_1 \\ \diagdown \\ R_2\text{—}C\text{—}OH \\ \diagup \\ R_3 \end{matrix}$	$(CH_3)_3COH$ tertiary butyl alcohol

Primary alcohols may be oxidized to the corresponding aldehydes (or acids).

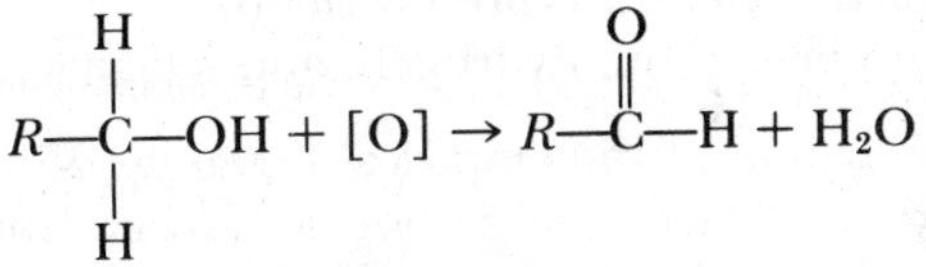

$$R\text{—}\overset{\overset{\displaystyle H}{|}}{\underset{\underset{\displaystyle H}{|}}{C}}\text{—}OH + [O] \rightarrow R\text{—}\overset{\overset{\displaystyle O}{\|}}{C}\text{—}H + H_2O$$

The symbol [O] represents the oxidizing agent.

Secondary alcohols may be oxidized to the corresponding ketones.

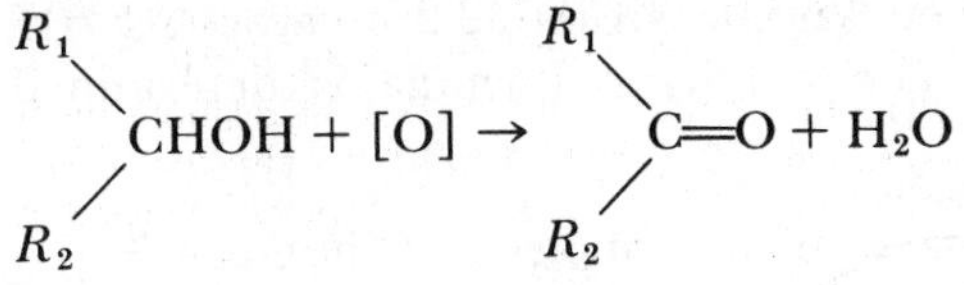

$$\begin{matrix} R_1 \\ \diagdown \\ \quad CHOH \\ \diagup \\ R_2 \end{matrix} + [O] \rightarrow \begin{matrix} R_1 \\ \diagdown \\ \quad C{=}O \\ \diagup \\ R_2 \end{matrix} + H_2O$$

Tertiary alcohols can only be oxidized to carbon dioxide and water.

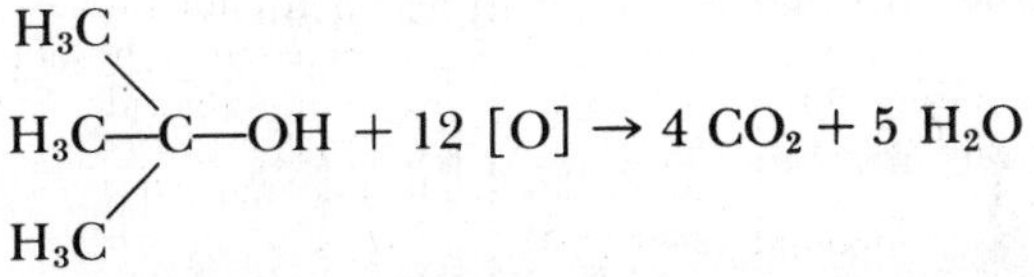

$$\begin{matrix} H_3C \\ \diagdown \\ H_3C\text{—}C\text{—}OH \\ \diagup \\ H_3C \end{matrix} + 12\,[O] \rightarrow 4\,CO_2 + 5\,H_2O$$

Alkanes may be distinguished from alkenes because the carbon-to-carbon double bond in an alkene is more reactive to oxidation than the single bond in an alkane. For example, alkenes can be oxidized to the corresponding glycol (double alcohol) using dilute potassium permanganate as the oxidizing agent.

$$H-\underset{\underset{\displaystyle |}{H}}{\overset{\overset{\displaystyle |}{H}}{C}}=\underset{\underset{\displaystyle |}{H}}{\overset{\overset{\displaystyle |}{H}}{C}}-H \xrightarrow{\text{MnO}_4^- \ (aq)} H-\underset{\underset{\displaystyle |}{\underset{\displaystyle OH}{H}}}{\overset{\overset{\displaystyle |}{H}}{C}}-\underset{\underset{\displaystyle |}{\underset{\displaystyle OH}{H}}}{\overset{\overset{\displaystyle |}{H}}{C}}-H$$

ethylene glycol
(automobile antifreeze)

29.10 The work of the organic chemist

Two important activities that concern the organic chemist are the determination of the structure of molecules and the synthesis of compounds.

DETERMINATION OF STRUCTURE

The basic steps in the determination of the structure of an organic molecule may be illustrated with a simple example.

STEP 1. Determination of the elements present. The organic compound is usually burned, and the products of the combustion are analyzed. This procedure reveals the elements present in the compound. Assume the elements present to be carbon, hydrogen, and oxygen.

STEP 2. Determination of the empirical formula. When a fixed weight of the compound is burned, the carbon is changed into CO_2, which is weighed. Hydrogen in the sample turns to H_2O, which is also weighed. The remainder of the compound is oxygen. The weight of each element in the compound is then converted to its percentage.

Suppose a given sample yields 52.2% carbon, 13.0% hydrogen, and 34.8% oxygen. The empirical formula is determined as follows (see section 11.5):

$$\text{relative number of moles of C atoms} = \frac{52.2}{12} = 4.35$$

$$\text{relative number of moles of H atoms} = \frac{13.0}{1} = 13.0$$

$$\text{relative number of moles of O atoms} = \frac{34.8}{16} = 2.18$$

$$4.35 : 13.0 : 2.18 = 2 : 6 : 1$$

The proportion of component atoms is $C_2H_6O_1$. Thus the empirical formula is C_2H_6O.

STEP 3. Determination of the molecular weight. Is the molecular formula identical with the empirical formula or some whole number multiple of it? The molecular weight of a compound fixes its molecular formula. Molecular weights may be determined from boiling or freezing point measurements (see section 15.2) or from instruments such as the mass spectrograph. Assume the molecular weight of our sample is 46 g/mole. This means that C_2H_6O is the correct molecular formula as well as the empirical formula. (If the molecular weight had been 92 g/mole, the molecular formula would be $C_4H_{12}O_2$.)

STEP 4. Determination of structural formula. Knowing the molecular weight does not yet tell us just how the carbon atoms, hydrogen atoms, and oxygen atoms are bonded. For example, a molecule of C_2H_6O might be

$$
\begin{array}{cc}
\underset{\text{ethanol}}{
\begin{array}{c}
\text{H} \quad \text{H} \\
| \quad\;\; | \\
\text{H—C—C—OH} \\
| \quad\;\; | \\
\text{H} \quad \text{H}
\end{array}
}
&
\underset{\text{dimethyl ether}}{
\begin{array}{c}
\text{H} \qquad \text{H} \\
| \qquad\;\; | \\
\text{H—C—O—C—H} \\
| \qquad\;\; | \\
\text{H} \qquad \text{H}
\end{array}
}
\end{array}
$$

or

Chemical methods may be used to distinguish between these structures. For example:

a. The C_2H_6O molecule reacts with sodium to yield hydrogen gas. The reaction is typical of an alcohol.

$$CH_3CH_2OH + Na \rightarrow CH_3CH_2O^-Na^+ + \frac{1}{2}H_2\ (g)$$

b. The C_2H_6O molecule reacts with hydrochloric acid to form ethyl chloride and water. This is another reaction that indicates an alcohol and not an ether.

$$C_2H_6O + HCl \rightarrow C_2H_5Cl + H_2O$$

c. Dimethyl ether is gaseous at room temperature and boils at $-34°\,C$. These properties distinguish it from ethanol, which is liquid at room temperature and boils at $78°\,C$.

SYNTHESIS OF COMPOUNDS

Once the structure of a given molecule is known, chemists attempt to prepare it first in the laboratory and then on an industrial scale. Countless important compounds have been produced by synthesis, such as pharmaceuticals, dyes, plastics, artificial fibers, artificial rubber, and insecticides.

For example, the drug aspirin is synthesized from salicylic acid as shown in section 29.6. Salicylic acid is derived from phenol, an important raw material obtained by the fractional distillation of coal tar.

Another example of a more complex synthesis involves the synthesis of alizarin, a red dye, from anthracene, one of the products obtained from the fractional distillation of coal tar. The steps in the synthesis of alizarin are shown in the following diagram:

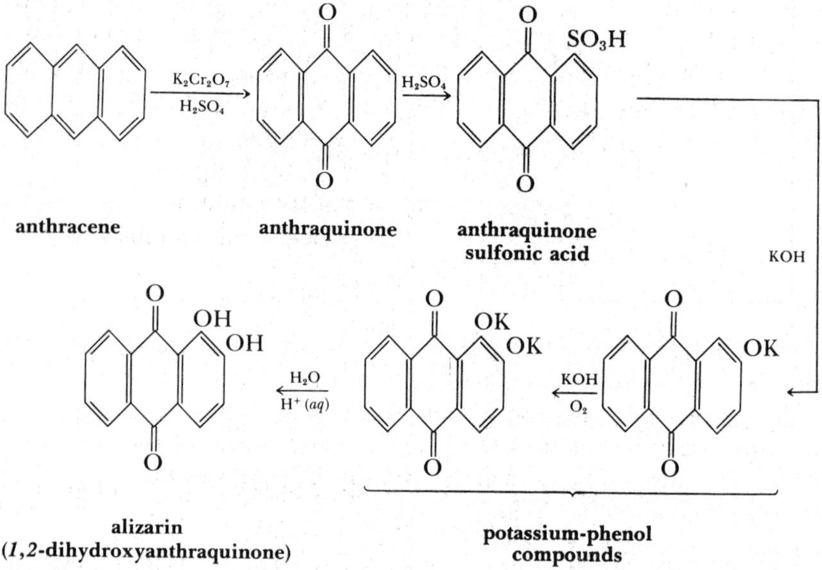

Note the similarity in the structures of anthracene and alizarin. Note also how each of the steps in the synthesis introduces the desired groups onto the rings. Finally, each of the products in the intermediate steps must be isolated and purified before the next step.

Synthesis also provides chemists with invaluable information about biochemical molecules and their reactions. For example, the synthesis of a very important hormone — insulin — is contributing to the study of pancreatic and intestinal diseases.

29.11 Petrochemicals

Petroleum is a naturally occurring mixture of hydrocarbons which may be separated by fractional distillation. A partial list of the hydrocarbon fractions obtained follows.

APPROXIMATE NUMBER OF CARBONS IN THE HYDROCARBON	FRACTION
C_1 to C_4	gases for fuels
C_5 to C_7	petroleum ether for solvents
C_5 to C_{12}	gasolines for fuels
C_{12} to C_{16}	kerosenes for fuels and for lighting
C_{16} to C_{20}	lubrication oils
C_{18} to C_{22}	greases and vaselines
C_{22} and up	paraffin waxes

As the number of carbon atoms in the molecule increases, the physical state of the compounds in the fractions changes from gas to liquid to solid. This change in state is in accord with the generalization that the van der Waals attractions between molecules increase as the sizes of the molecules increase. The increase in van der Waals attractions causes the gas to condense, first to a liquid and then to a solid.

29.12 Soaps and detergents

An example of a soap is the sodium salt of the C_{17} fatty acid (stearic acid), $C_{17}H_{35}COONa$. The sodium stearate soap molecule consists of a chain of carbon atoms. One end of the molecule, containing the hydrocarbon portion, is nonpolar; and the other end, containing COONa, is polar.

$$CH_3(CH_2)_{16}C \overset{\displaystyle O}{\underset{\displaystyle ONa}{\big\langle}}$$

sodium stearate

Sodium stearate can be produced from the natural fat glyceryl tri-stearate (beef fat) by a saponification reaction with sodium hydroxide.

$$(C_{17}H_{35}COO)_3C_3H_5 + 3\ NaOH \rightarrow 3\ C_{17}H_{35}COONa + C_3H_5(OH)_3$$

Saponification is the process of making soap by using a strong base to split a fatty ester into the metallic salt of the acid (soap) and an alcohol (glycerine).

The cleansing action of soap may be explained as follows: Normally greases and oils are immiscible with water because the oil-water interface has a high surface tension, which does not permit the oil and water to mix. As would be expected, the polar end of the soap molecule is water-soluble, while the nonpolar end is oil-soluble. When soap is added to an oil-water system, the polar end of the soap molecule is extended into the water and the nonpolar end dissolves the oil. The introduction of a soap molecule lowers the surface tension of the oil-water interface and permits penetration into the oil film.

Molecules that have both polar and nonpolar properties are classified as detergents. Soaps are detergents made up of a metal, such as sodium, linked to a fatty acid radical, such as a stearate. Synthetic detergents, called *syndets* or *soapless soaps*, are made without using fats. In place of the fat, a long-chain alkyl sulfate group is substituted.

<table>
<tr><td align="center">RCOONa</td><td align="center">R—O—SO$_2$—ONa</td></tr>
<tr><td align="center">**soap**</td><td align="center">**syndet**</td></tr>
<tr><td align="center">R is a long-chain alkyl radical</td><td align="center">R is an alkyl radical varying
from C_7H_{15} to $C_{18}H_{37}$</td></tr>
</table>

A common example of a synthetic detergent is sodium lauryl sulfate, sold commercially as Dreft. As in soaps, the presence of polar and nonpolar groups is responsible for the cleansing action of detergents. The chief advantage of detergents over soaps is that the calcium and magnesium salts are more water-soluble than the corresponding salts of fatty acids. This means that detergents will not precipitate scum when used in hard waters.

29.13 Sugars and carbohydrates

Carbohydrates are compounds of carbon, hydrogen, and oxygen in which the ratio of hydrogen atoms to oxygen atoms is 2 : 1 (as in water). Sugars and starches are examples of common carbohydrates.

Structurally, sugars are poly-alcohols. A molecule of glucose, for example, has the following cyclic structure, which is in equilibrium with the open-chain structure previously used:

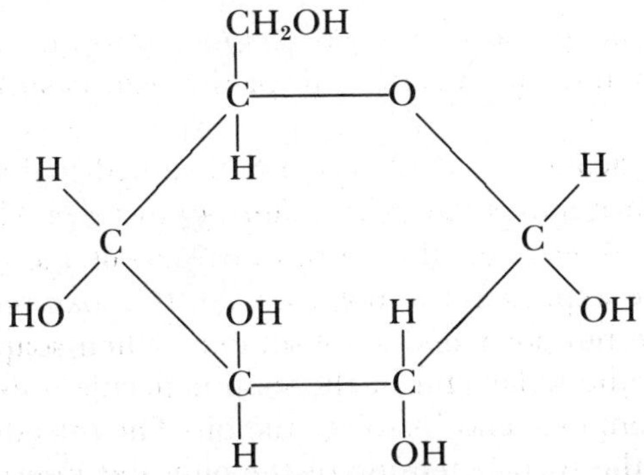

The formula may also be written in a shorter form in which the carbon atoms on the ring are omitted and a line indicates a bond in which a hydrogen atom is joined to a carbon atom.

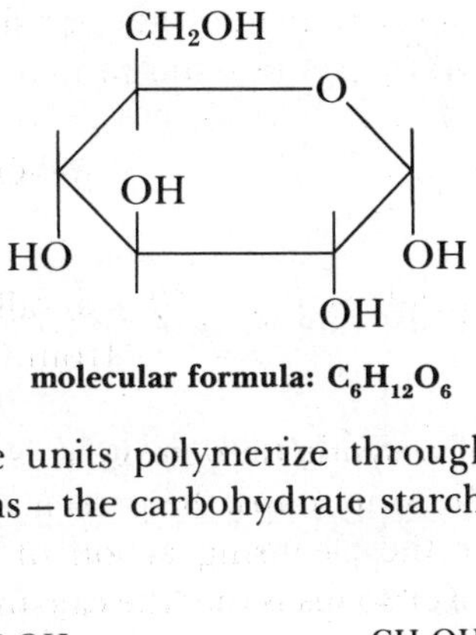

molecular formula: $C_6H_{12}O_6$

When many glucose units polymerize through a condensation mechanism, a polymer forms—the carbohydrate starch, which has the formula $(C_6H_{10}O_5)_n$.

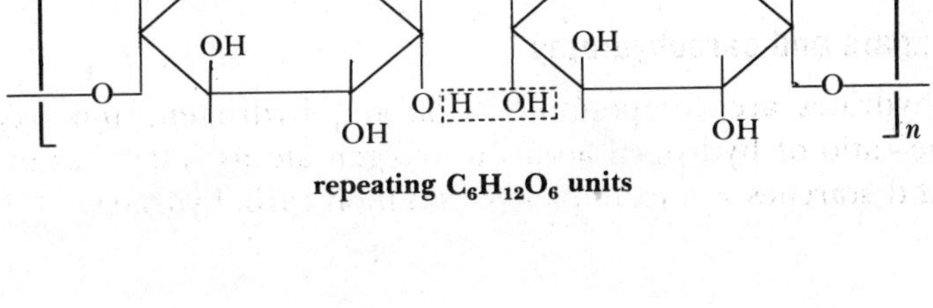

repeating $C_6H_{12}O_6$ units

Table sugar, or sucrose, is a molecule of two different C_6 units, one of glucose and one of fructose. It has the following structure:

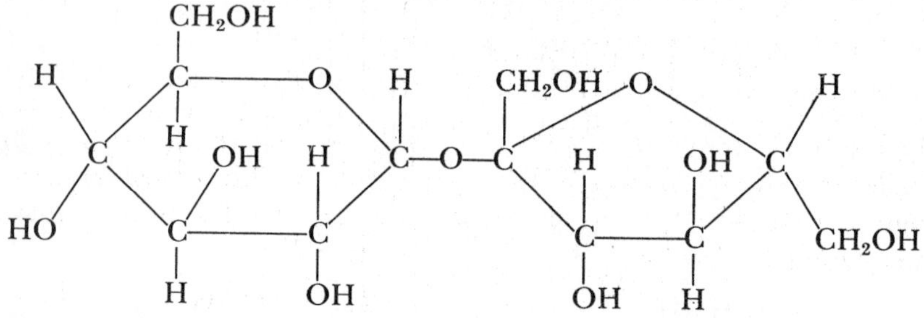

glucose unit   fructose unit

29.14 Proteins

Proteins are complex organic compounds containing carbon, oxygen, hydrogen, nitrogen, and frequently sulfur and phosphorus. Proteins are derived from amino acids in a type of reaction which may be illustrated as follows:

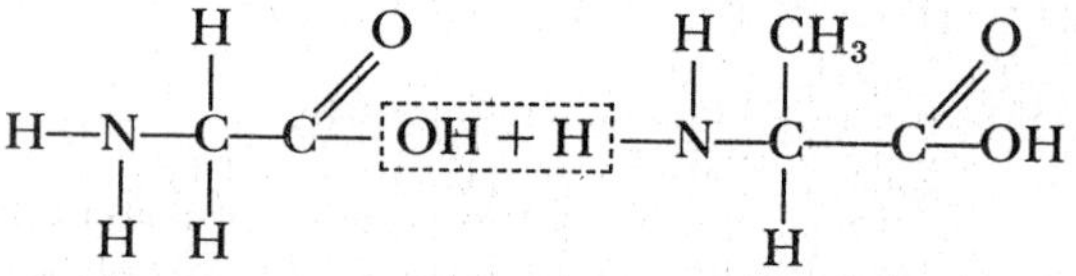

glycine
(aminoacetic acid)

alanine
(aminopropionic acid)

The resulting molecule, consisting of two joined amino acids, is called a *dipeptide*.

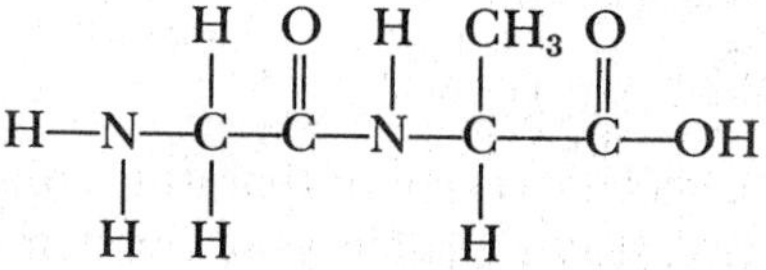

glycylalanine

The characteristic bond formed by the condensation reaction between amino acids is called a *peptide linkage*.

$$\left[\begin{array}{c} \quad O \quad H \\ \quad \| \quad | \\ -C-N- \end{array} \right]$$

When several amino acids join in this fashion, the resulting compound is called a *polypeptide*. Proteins are polypeptides with molecular weights ranging from 10,000 to many millions. A section of a protein may be generally represented as follows:

amino acid₁   amino acid₂   amino acid₃   amino acid₄

The R groups can represent different amino acid residues. Since about 20 amino acids are found in proteins, an almost endless variety of combinations is possible.

Proteins are divided into two general groups:

1. Fibrous proteins are made of long chains of polypeptides which are joined laterally by chemical cross-linkages. These proteins are stable, relatively insoluble molecules, such as keratin or collagen.

2. Globular proteins are made of a long chain of polypeptides folded into more or less elliptical shapes. Biologically active proteins, such as enzymes, belong to this group.

29.15 Nucleoproteins

Understanding the specific reactions that distinguish living material from nonliving material is a major problem in biochemistry. By investigating this problem, biochemists have learned that the transmission of hereditary characteristics and the synthesis of proteins can be attributed to the presence of *nucleoproteins.* These complex substances are found in the chromosomes of cell nuclei. They consist of nonprotein organic acids, called *nucleic acids,* and proteins. Nucleic acids, discussed in the following section, transmit genetic characteristics and control the synthesis of proteins in the cell.

29.16 Nucleic acids

The breakdown (by hydrolysis) of nucleic acids yields a mixture of the following substances: purines and pyrimidines (benzene-like nitrogen compounds), ribose or deoxyribose (five-carbon sugars), and phosphoric acid. Thus, unlike proteins, which are polypeptides, nucleic acids are complex esters of phosphoric acid, called *polyesters.*

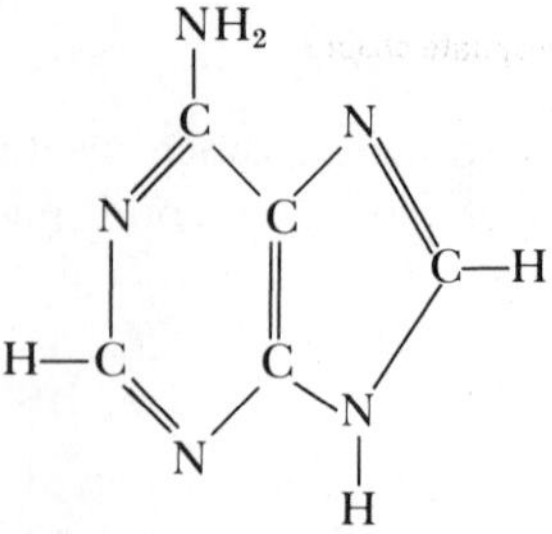

adenine (a purine)

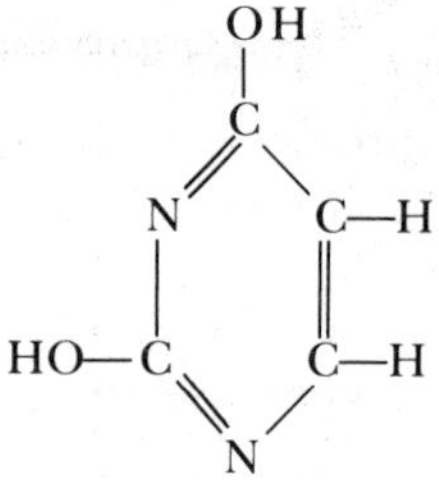

uracil
(a pyrimidine)

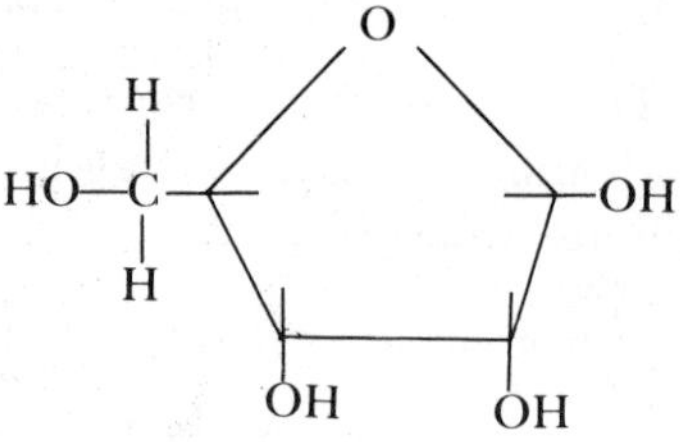

ribose

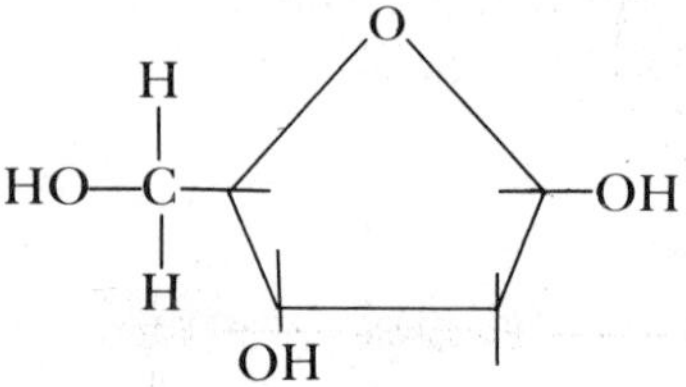

deoxyribose

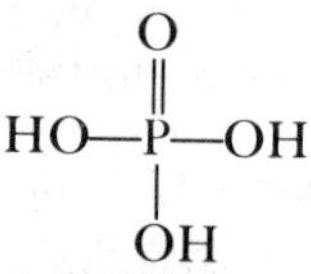

phosphoric acid

DNA (DEOXYRIBONUCLEIC ACID)

Deoxyribonucleic acid, called DNA, is an important nucleic acid present in the chromosomes of cell nuclei. DNA is classified as a *polynucleotide* and contains deoxyribose, purine and pyrimidine bases (adenine and thymine), and phosphoric acid. The exact number of constituents in DNA is unknown; however, it is thought to consist of *four* different nucleotide structures. Thus the nucleotides are the basic structural units from which DNA is made, just as amino acids are the building blocks of proteins.

By means of X-ray diffraction, the biochemists James Watson and Francis Crick developed a model of the DNA molecule. Pictured as a double-stranded helix about 20 Å in diameter, DNA is thought to be made up of two long-chain molecules twisted around each other. Each strand of the helix is a long-chain polymer consisting of a regular arrangement of alternating phosphate-deoxyribose chains with purines and pyrimidines attached to the sugar, as shown in Figure 29-1.

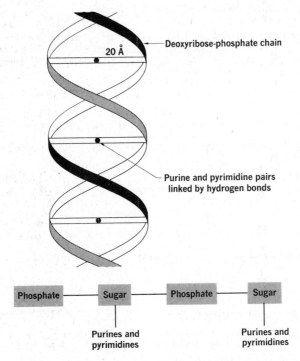

Fig. 29–1   The DNA molecule

The chemical structure of the DNA molecule can be pictured as follows (R = adenine or thymine):

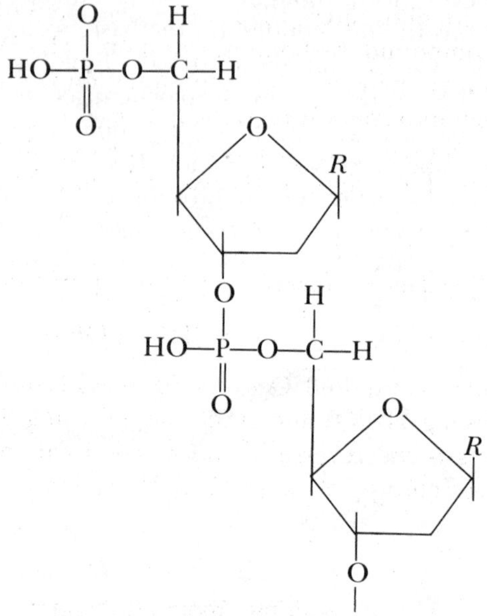

$$
HO-\overset{\overset{O}{\|}}{\underset{\underset{O}{\|}}{P}}-O-\overset{\overset{H}{|}}{\underset{}{C}}-H
$$

Estimates of the molecular weight of DNA vary from 1,000,000 to 4,000,000,000. The number of nucleotide units in a DNA chain varies from 3000 to 10,000,000. Despite this enormous structural complexity, the function of DNA in living cells is clear. DNA *replicates*; that is, it reproduces itself, permitting new cells to form and making growth possible. The chemistry of the replication process is very complex. It appears that the helix unwinds, forming two chains, each of which serves as a model for the formation of a new helix.

RNA (RIBONUCLEIC ACID)

Ribonucleic acid, called RNA, occurs mainly in the cytoplasm of the cell. Its function is to control the synthesis of protein. In structure, RNA usually consists of a single polynucleotide chain with an irregular arrangement of purines and pyrimidines in the phosphate-ribose link. X-ray studies indicate that the structures of the DNA and RNA molecules are closely related.

ATP (ADENOSINE TRIPHOSPHATE)

Another nucleotide, present in muscle tissue, is a purine-sugar derivative bonded to phosphoric acid and called adenosine monophosphate, AMP. This compound, by bonding additional H_3PO_4 molecules (an endothermic change), may be converted first into adenosine diphosphate, ADP, and then into adenosine triphosphate, ATP. ATP is used in the body as an energy source. The formula that follows shows the makeup of an ATP molecule. The symbol $\sim$ represents a high-energy bond.

$$\text{purine—sugar—O—}\underset{\underset{\text{OH}}{|}}{\overset{\overset{\text{O}}{\|}}{\text{P}}}\text{—O} \sim \underset{\underset{\text{OH}}{|}}{\overset{\overset{\text{O}}{\|}}{\text{P}}}\text{—O} \sim \underset{\underset{\text{OH}}{|}}{\overset{\overset{\text{O}}{\|}}{\text{P}}}\text{—OH}$$

The rupture of the end $O \sim P$ bond in ATP during hydrolysis is exothermic, forming H_3PO_4 and ADP and releasing 8 kcal of energy/mole. Note that this is the reverse of the reaction for the formation of ATP, which requires energy, obtained from the oxidation of glucose.

Multiple-Choice Questions

1. The burning of a hydrocarbon in air always forms (1) carbon (2) carbon dioxide (3) carbon monoxide (4) water
2. In the process of *cracking* (1) two alkane molecules always form (2) two alkene molecules always form (3) the number of carbon atoms in the molecules decreases (4) carbon atoms are split
3. Monochloroethane can be produced from ethene by (1) reaction with Cl_2 (2) reaction with HCl (3) hydrogenation (4) halogenation
4. A characteristic chemical property of benzene is that it (1) undergoes substitution reactions more readily than addition reactions (2) forms polymers (3) easily becomes saturated (4) acts as an oxidizing agent
5. The reaction of an alcohol and an acid forms (1) a salt (2) an unsaturated compound (3) a ring compound (4) a molecule of water
6. All natural fats are (1) acids (2) esters of glycerine (3) unsaturated (4) salts
7. Of the following, the compound that releases protons most readily is (1) *RCHO* (2) *RCOOH* (3) *ROH* (4) *RCOOR'*

8. A condensation polymer forms when (1) a gaseous monomer is changed to a liquid monomer (2) water is added to the molecules (3) H and OH are removed from two molecules of monomers (4) an acid reacts with a base

9. An example of oxidation is the conversion of (1) an aldehyde to acid (2) an acid to alcohol (3) an acid to ester (4) a monomer to a polymer

10. An organic compound reacts with sodium metal, forming hydrogen. The same compound will probably *not* (1) form an ester (2) be oxidized to form an alcohol (3) be oxidized to form an acid (4) react with HBr

11. The process of saponification results in the formation of (1) an ester (2) an alcohol (3) a molecule of water (4) a strong base

12. Starches and proteins are related because both (1) are carbohydrates (2) are condensation polymers (3) are produced by animals only (4) cannot be decomposed

Completion Questions

1. The reaction $C_{12}H_{26} \rightarrow C_6H_{14} + C_6H_{12}$ is an example of the process called _____.

2. In an addition reaction, Cl_2 combines with _____ to form dichloroethane.

3. The reaction of metallic sodium and propyl _____ forms hydrogen.

4. An organic acid that contains an NH_2 group is classed as a (an) _____ acid.

5. The dehydrogenation of a (an) _____ produces an alkene.

6. Different products can be obtained from petroleum by the process of _____.

7. Proteins are natural products formed by the condensation of molecules of _____ acids.

8. Detergents are organic compounds that can be used in place of _____.

9. The reaction of two amino acids produces a (an) _____ linkage.

10. A form of protein found in chromosomes is called _____.

11. A cyclic nitrogen compound produced by the hydrolysis of DNA is _____.

12. A five-carbon sugar contained in RNA is _____.

True-False Questions

1. The combination of ethene with hydrogen forms *ethyne*.
2. A difference between saturated and unsaturated compounds is that a *saturated* compound cannot undergo addition reactions.
3. Octyl butyrate is an ester formed from *butyl* alcohol.
4. In the formation of nitrate esters, *nitric* acid is used as a catalyst.
5. The joining together of many small molecules forms a large molecule called *a monomer*.
6. Glucose, fructose, and sucrose are examples of compounds classed as *hydrocarbons*.
7. Polypeptides form when molecules of *glucose* condense.
8. The reaction of potassium dichromate with an alcohol is *an oxidation* reaction.
9. The synthesis of protein is controlled partially by *RNA*.
10. An example of a phosphoric acid nucleotide is *AMP*.

Decreases, Increases, Remains the Same

1. As a result of the cracking process, the boiling points of hydrocarbons formed generally _____.
2. When an unsaturated hydrocarbon is saturated by hydrogenation, the melting point of the compound _____.
3. In the formation of a polymer by condensation, the percent of oxygen atoms in the product _____.
4. When an alcohol is oxidized to an aldehyde and then to an acid, the number of carbon atoms in the molecule _____.
5. From primary to secondary to tertiary alcohols, the number of carbon atoms adjacent to the C—OH group _____.
6. In the fractional distillation of petroleum, as the boiling point of the fraction increases, the number of carbon atoms in the molecules of the fraction _____.
7. When starch is digested to glucose, the molecular weight of the compound that is formed _____.
8. As the number of peptide linkages increases, the molecular weight of the protein _____.

Exercises for Review

1. Explain why some aliphatic hydrocarbons can react with halogens only by substitution, but other hydrocarbons can form addition compounds with halogens.

2. In the reaction of Cl_2 with CH_4, list the bonds that break and the bonds that form.

3. In the petroleum industry, cracking is sometimes carried out in the presence of hydrogen gas. Contrast the composition of the petroleum with the composition of the hydrocarbons obtained.

4. Rewrite the following equations showing the structural formulas for the compounds:

   a. $C_3H_8 + Cl_2 \rightarrow C_3H_7Cl + HCl$

   b. $C_2H_4 + HCl \rightarrow C_2H_5Cl$

   c. $C_3H_6 + Cl_2 \rightarrow C_3H_6Cl_2$

   d. $C_2H_4 + H_2O \rightarrow C_2H_5OH$

5. Why is concentrated sulfuric acid used in the formation of esters?

6. *a.* Describe two different polymers that occur in living matter.

   b. Give the monomers in each case, and show how the polymer forms.

7. Distinguish the following terms: (*a*) peptide, dipeptide, and polypeptide (*b*) ester and polyester

8. Distinguish between the following: (*a*) DNA and RNA (*b*) AMP and ATP

9. Briefly discuss the significance of the presence of nucleic acids in cellular material.

10. From the table of bond energies on page 212, show that unsaturated compounds are generally more reactive than saturated compounds.

Exercises for Further Study

1. The properties of benzene are not typical of the properties of an unsaturated hydrocarbon. Explain.

2. *a.* Show how monochloropropane can be prepared by three different reactions, starting with three different organic compounds.

   b. Use structural formulas in the equations to show these reactions.

3. Using radioactive oxygen in an alcohol, in an acid, or in both, describe an experiment to demonstrate if it is the OH in the alcohol or the OH in the acid that is used in esterification reactions.

4. Using structural formulas in the equations, show the reactions in which a water molecule is removed from (a) a single molecule of C_2H_5OH (b) two molecules of C_2H_5OH (c) a molecule of C_2H_5OH and a molecule of CH_3COOH

5. Explain why the reaction of ROH with HNO_3 forms an ester, but the reaction of ROH with HCl does not form an ester.

6. C_2H_5OH and $CH_3C\overset{\displaystyle O}{\overset{\|}{{}}}OH$ both have an OH group bonded to carbon.
   a. Contrast the properties of the O—H bond in the two molecules.
   b. What causes the difference?

7. Why is it more advantageous for living organisms to store carbohydrates as starch rather than as glucose?

8. a. How are the processes of digestion of starch and digestion of protein similar?
   b. What is formed in each case?

9. Why is dacron classed as a polyester synthetic fiber, while nylon is classed as a polyamide?

10. How can you use acidified potassium dichromate to determine whether an alcohol is 1-propanol or 2-propanol?

11. Explain how hydrogen bonding contributes to the replication of a DNA molecule.

12. Why does protein synthesis present so many difficulties to organic chemists?

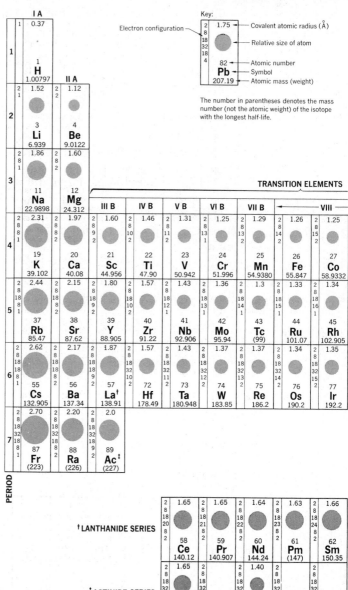

					0
					2 / 0.93
					2 — He — 4.0026

	III A	IV A	V A	VI A	VII A	0
	2,3 / 0.88	2,4 / 0.77	2,5 / 0.70	2,6 / 0.66	2,7 / 0.64	2,8 / 1.12
	5 — B — 10.811	6 — C — 12.01115	7 — N — 14.0067	8 — O — 15.9994	9 — F — 18.9984	10 — Ne — 20.183
	2,8,3 / 1.43	2,8,4 / 1.17	2,8,5 / 1.10	2,8,6 / 1.04	2,8,7 / 0.99	2,8,8 / 1.54
	13 — Al — 26.9815	14 — Si — 28.086	15 — P — 30.9738	16 — S — 32.064	17 — Cl — 35.453	18 — Ar — 39.948

I B	II B	III A	IV A	V A	VI A	VII A	0
2,8,16,2 / 1.24	2,8,18,1 / 1.28	2,8,18,2 / 1.33	2,8,18,3 / 1.22	2,8,18,4 / 1.22	2,8,18,5 / 1.21	2,8,18,6 / 1.17	2,8,18,7 / 1.14	2,8,18,8 / 1.69
28 — Ni — 58.71	29 — Cu — 63.54	30 — Zn — 65.37	31 — Ga — 69.72	32 — Ge — 72.59	33 — As — 74.9216	34 — Se — 78.96	35 — Br — 79.909	36 — Kr — 83.80
2,8,18,18 / 1.38	2,8,18,1 / 1.44	2,8,18,2 / 1.49	2,8,18,3 / 1.62	2,8,18,4 / 1.40	2,8,18,5 / 1.41	2,8,18,6 / 1.37	2,8,18,7 / 1.33	2,8,18,8 / 1.90
46 — Pd — 106.4	47 — Ag — 107.870	48 — Cd — 112.40	49 — In — 114.82	50 — Sn — 118.69	51 — Sb — 121.75	52 — Te — 127.60	53 — I — 126.9044	54 — Xe — 131.30
2,8,18,32,17,1 / 1.38	2,8,18,32,18,1 / 1.44	2,8,18,32,18,2 / 1.55	2,8,18,32,18,3 / 1.71	2,8,18,32,18,4 / 1.75	2,8,18,32,18,5 / 1.46	2,8,18,32,18,6 / 1.4	2,8,18,32,18,7 / 1.40	2,8,18,32,18,8 / 2.2
78 — Pt — 195.09	79 — Au — 196.967	80 — Hg — 200.59	81 — Tl — 204.37	82 — Pb — 207.19	83 — Bi — 208.980	84 — Po — (210)	85 — At — (210)	86 — Rn — (222)

Lanthanide series

2,8,18,25,8,2 / 1.65	2,8,18,25,9,2 / 1.61	2,8,18,27,8,2 / 1.59	2,8,18,28,8,2 / 1.59	2,8,18,29,8,2 / 1.58	2,8,18,30,8,2 / 1.57	2,8,18,31,8,2 / 1.56	2,8,18,32,9,2 / 1.70	2,8,18,32,9,2 / 1.56
63 — Eu — 151.96	64 — Gd — 157.25	65 — Tb — 158.924	66 — Dy — 162.50	67 — Ho — 164.930	68 — Er — 167.26	69 — Tm — 168.934	70 — Yb — 173.04	71 — Lu — 174.97

Actinide series

2,8,18,32,25,8,2	2,8,18,32,25,9,2	2,8,18,32,26,9,2	2,8,18,32,28,8,2	2,8,18,32,29,8,2	2,8,18,32,30,8,2	2,8,18,32,31,8,2	2,8,18,32,32,8,2	2,8,18,32,32,9,2
95 — Am — (243)	96 — Cm — (247)	97 — Bk — (247)	98 — Cf — (251)	99 — Es — (254)	100 — Fm — (253)	101 — Md — (256)	102 — No — (253)	103 — Lw — (257)

SOME SOLUBILITY RULES FOR WATER SOLUTIONS OF COMMON COMPOUNDS

(A substance is considered soluble if it can dissolve
to a concentration above 0.1 M at room temperature.)

Acetates.	All acetates are soluble.
Carbonates.	All carbonates have *limited* solubility except NH_4^+ and the alkali metal ions (Group IA).
Halides.	All chlorides, bromides, and iodides are soluble except Ag^+, Pb^{+2}, Hg_2^{+2}, and Cu^+.
Hydroxides.	All hydroxides have *limited* solubility except NH_4^+, the alkali metal ions (Group IA), and the alkaline earth metal ions (Group IIA).
Nitrates.	All nitrates are soluble.
Phosphates.	All phosphates have *limited* solubility except NH_4^+ and the alkali metal ions (Group IA).
Sulfates.	All sulfates are soluble except Sr^{+2}, Ba^{+2}, and Pb^{+2}.
Sulfides.	All sulfides have *limited* solubility except NH_4^+, the alkali metal ions (Group IA), and the alkaline earth metal ions (Group IIA).
Sulfites.	All sulfites have *limited* solubility except NH_4^+ and the alkali metal ions (Group IA).

INDEX